**DATE DUE**

# MONRO, HIS EXPEDITION WITH THE WORTHY SCOTS REGIMENT CALLED MAC-KEYS

# MONRO, HIS EXPEDITION WITH THE WORTHY SCOTS REGIMENT CALLED MAC-KEYS

*Edited by*
William S. Brockington, Jr.

Foreword by Geoffrey Parker

*Praeger Series in War Studies*

**Westport, Connecticut**
**London**

**Library of Congress Cataloging-in-Publication Data**

Monro, Robert.
    Monro, his expedition with the Worthy Scots Regiment called Mac-
Keys / edited by William S. Brockington, Jr. ; foreword by Geoffrey
Parker.
        p.  cm.—(Praeger series in war studies, ISSN 1083–8171)
    Originally published: Monro, his expedition with the Worthy Scots
Regiment (called Mac-Keys Regiment). . . . London : W. Jones, 1637.
    Includes bibliographical references (p.  ) and index.
    ISBN 0–275–96267–9 (alk. paper)
    1. Thirty Years' War, 1618–1648—Personal narratives, Scottish.
2. Monro, Robert.  3. Mackay's Regiment—History.  4. Thirty Years'
War, 1618–1648—Regimental histories.  I. Brockington, William S., Jr.
II. Title.  III. Title: Expedition with the Worthy Scots Regiment.
IV. Series.
D256.M63A3   1999
940.2′442′092
[B]—dc21        98–33578

British Library Cataloguing in Publication Data is available.

Library of Congress Catalog Card Number: 98–33578
ISBN: 0–275–96267–9
ISSN: 1083–8171

First published in 1999

Praeger Publishers, 88 Post Road West, Westport, CT 06881
An imprint of Greenwood Publishing Group, Inc.

Printed in the United States of America

The paper used in this book complies with the
Permanent Paper Standard issued by the National
Information Standards Organization (Z39.48–1984).

10 9 8 7 6 5 4 3 2 1

To Celeste

and my children,

Will and Robert

# Contents

# Foreword

Robert Monro (c. 1590–1680) may not be a household name even among military historians, and yet he invented a popular literary genre that has lasted down to the present day: the regimental history. *Monro his expedition, with the worthy Scots regiment called Mackay's,* first published in London in 1637, appears to be the first history of a regiment ever written, in any language.

The troops raised in the Scottish highlands by Sir Donald Mackay in 1626, to which Monro belonged, sailed to Denmark and eventually became part of a "Scots Brigade" comprising four regiments fighting for the "Protestant Cause" in the continental conflict known as the Thirty Years' War. Of these men, only one apart from Monro is known to have recorded and published his experiences: Sir James Turner, who enlisted at the age of eighteen as a lieutenant in one of the four regiments in 1632. Yet Turner's memoirs devoted scarcely four pages to the first two years of his military service, and dealt only with his own experiences. Monro, by contrast, published almost 100 pages on the same period and filled them with the deeds of his fellow-Scots. Admittedly, he normally mentioned only officers by name, but he included them frequently in his narrative and listed over one hundred of them in a five-page appendix.[1]

Most histories written by individual warriors in the seventeenth century (and subsequently) tend to concentrate on the exploits of their authors, and the personal narratives published by participants in the Thirty Years' War are no exception.[2] Most of them say relatively little about anything else. At one end of the scale, King Christian IV of Denmark's account of the most important day in his military career—26 August 1626, when he led his army into battle at Lutter-am-Barenberg in northern Germany—reads laconically "Fought with the enemy and lost. The same day I went to Wolfenbüttel."[3] At the other extreme, a recently published journal kept by an anonymous German soldier between 1625 and 1649 covers ninety printed pages, and yet most daily entries record only such mundane issues as where the author slept each night, what he ate and—

always—how many miles he marched. This Catholic soldier, who fought mostly for the Habsburgs, travelled all over Europe: to Modena in northern Italy (1625–26), almost to Paris in northern France (1636), and over most parts of Germany. He fought the Scots (including Monro) at Breitenfeld in 1631. In total he marched 14,000 miles during 25 years of service, ranging from just one year— 1648—in which he stayed put, to four in which he covered almost 1,000 miles.[4] Most military memoirs were preoccupied with marching and accommodation. Monro, although less obsessive (he did not always provide daily totals in his narrative), carefully logged the distances travelled by his regiment in both Danish and Swedish service between 1629 and 1633: perhaps 10,000 miles in all, including 20 miles in seven hours one night, "without halt or drawing of breath by the way," to launch a surprise attack. His English contemporary, Richard Symonds, entitled his detailed war journal between 1644 and 1646, filled with antiquarian as well as military detail, "A diary of the marches and moovings of His Majesty's Royall Army"—and during the first six months alone, that army travelled 1,000 miles.[5]

Most of these writers centered their narratives either on themselves (and wrote in the first person) or else on their cause (using "we" to refer to the entire army in which they served). Monro, by contrast, attempted a collective history of his particular unit. He claimed in his preface that he wrote "because I loved my Camerades," and intended his reminiscences "for my friends and not for the world," and both his examples and his *dramatis personae* came overwhelmingly from his own regiment (almost all the rest came from other formations of the Scots Brigade).

Only one parallel to Monro's work springs to mind—*The true history of the conquest of New Spain* by Bernal Díaz del Castillo, who had accompanied Hernán Cortés in the conquest of Mexico (1519–24). Díaz began to write his account in the 1550s, and worked on it until his death in 1584, but it appeared in print for the first time only in 1632. Although the author featured prominently throughout the work (its first word is "I"), he also went out of his way to pay tribute to the deeds of his fellow conquistadors; indeed, he devoted one long chapter specifically to recording the names and achievements of "the valiant captains and strong soldiers" with whom he had fought, and another to their "height, appearance and ages." In all, he managed to include details of perhaps 400 men.[6] It seems unlikely that Monro knew of this book, published (in Madrid) five years before his own; and, in any case, it concerned an army rather than a regiment.[7] And yet both works offer a gripping account of the great events in which their writers participated (the siege of Stralsund and the battle of Breitenfeld for Monro; the march to the valley of Mexico and the siege of Tenochtitlan for Díaz); both lionized their leaders (Gustavus Adolphus and Hernán Cortés); both were generous to their comrades and took the same pride in their achievements.

Three differences may be noted, however. First, Monro also showed generosity towards the unsuccessful and the incompetent—he praised Dodo von Knyphausen because although "unfortunate himself" (that is: he lost almost every action in which he commanded) he prepared well for war and managed to keep his army together in adversity. Díaz tended to laud only successful commanders. Second, Monro's story ended in disaster and stalemate: his hero, Gustavus, died in battle and his army remained thereafter leaderless and idle; while Monro returned to Britain where his own military career proved singularly unfortunate (see pages xvi–xviii below) and he ended his days in relative obscurity. Cortés and his small band of conquistadors by contrast, despite some near disasters, took over the entire Aztec empire; and Díaz lived in splendor on a vast estate until his death. Finally, Díaz's *True History,* extensively plagiarized for fifty years before publication, became an immediate best-seller in Spain and Spanish America. It immediately became one of the two or three standard accounts of the conquest of Mexico composed by a contemporary, cited with approval by all subsequent writers and revered since the eighteenth century as an "authority" on correct Castilian usage.[8] Monro's work, by contrast, was apparently only published with subsidies from Colonel Mackay and, since sales proved slow, in 1644 surviving copies received a new title page and re-appeared as *The Scotch military discipline learned from the valiant Swede.* Perhaps these three differences are related: most readers prefer stories that are complete, cathartic, and written by "winners" over those that are unfinished, evenly-paced and penned by "losers." That, no doubt, is why Robert Monro, far from becoming a household name, has been unjustly forgotten; and why his book, despite its fascination, has never been reprinted until Dr. Brockington's perseverance and erudition brought forth this splendid scholarly edition.

Geoffrey Parker

## NOTES

1. Sir James Turner, *Memoirs of his own life and times (1632–1670)* (Edinburgh, 1829: Bannatyne Club, vol. 28). Turner also served in the Swedish army in Germany between 1634 and 1639, and discussed his experience during that period in another work: *Pallas armata. Military essayes of the ancient Graecian, Roman and modern Art of War* (London, 1683). During the Civil Wars, Turner and Monro both fought in Scotland and Ireland, and both were captured by troops of the English Parliament and imprisoned. Monro's list of fellow-officers—six generals, thirty colonels, fifty-two lieutenant-colonels and fourteen majors—appears on pages 109–112 *infra.*

2. See the useful list of published accounts by German soldiers in Peter Burschel, "Krieg als Lebensform. Über ein Tagebuch," *Göttingischen Gelehrten Anzeiger,* 246 (1994): 263–72, at p. 264 n. 5; and by English participants in Paul Delany, *British autobiography in the seventeenth century* (London: Methuen, 1969), chap. 8.

3. Christian's diary quoted by E. Ladewig Petersen in Geoffrey Parker, *The Thirty Years' War* (second edition, London and New York: Routledge, 1997), 70.

4. Jan Peters, ed., *Ein Söldnerleben im Dreissigjährigen Krieg. Eine Quelle zur Sozialgeschichte* (Berlin: Akademie Verlag, 1993), see the maps and the total distance travelled provided by the editor for each campaign. Between 1632 (when his unit was surrounded and forced to surrender) and 1634 (when the Catholic victory of Nördlingen

allowed him to escape), the anonymous soldier served in the Swedish army, alongside the Scots Brigade!

5. For Monro, see *infra* pages 113–114 (898 "Dutch miles" in Danish service 1627–29) and 115–119 (779 "Dutch miles" in Swedish service 1629–33); for his forced march from Würzburg to Ochsenfurt and back, see *infra* pages 203–205. For Symonds, see Ian Roy, ed., *Richard Symonds's Diary of the marches of the Royal Army* (new edition, Cambridge: Cambridge University Press, 1997). For other examples of distances travelled, see Charles Carlton, *Going to the Wars. The Experience of the British Civil Wars, 1638–1651* (London: Routledge, 1992), 109.

6. Bernal Díaz del Castillo, *The true history of the conquest of New Spain,* edited and translated by A. P. Maudsley (5 vols., London, 1908–16: Hakluyt Society, 2nd series vols. 23, 24, 25, 30 and 40). See also the critical edition of Miguel León–Portilla, *Historia verdadera de la conquista de la Nueva España* (2 vols., Madrid: Historia–16, 1984: Crónicas de América, vol. 20.) The key chapters of collective biography are the last ones: 205–206; my thanks to Charlie Sharpe for estimating the total of names.

7. Moreover, several passages in the laudatory chapters about his colleagues remained unpublished in the longer and later manuscript version of Bernal Díaz's *True History,* available only in Guatemala: see the editorial notes in *Historia verdadera,* 1: 10–12 and 59–62, and the italicized passages (from the later manuscript version) in 2: 425–453 (chaps. 205–206).

8. For the first time in the *Diccionario de la lengua castellana* published in Madrid in 1726: see *Historia verdadera,* 1: 55.

# Preface and Acknowledgments

The most obvious acknowledgment is to Robert Monro. Without his memoir, there would be no book; and our understanding of the era of the Thirty Years' War would be greatly diminished. My first encounter with *Expedition* occurred when I utilized it for my master's thesis on Scottish mercenaries in the Thirty Years' War. For my further study of Scottish mercenaries in the early modern era, I obtained a microfilm copy of *Expedition*. Five years ago, in order to expedite my research, I began typing *Expedition* into computer files. As I approached the end of this task, I realized that my efforts should be offered to a much wider audience. The result is the volume you now have in your hand.

There are many thanks and acknowledgments that go with a project of this magnitude. First and foremost, my wife Celeste has been a tireless cheerleader throughout and my children have been patient with my absence. My parents and siblings have long been supportive and encouraging. In particular, my brother-in-law, Stephen B. Huttler, gave of his time and talent to make my work possible. I could not have purchased a copy of the original had not my great aunt, Charlotte Blake, provided for my post-graduate education. Professors John. P. Dolan and Peter Becker supervised my master's thesis, and their encouragement is greatly appreciated.

Many assisted in turning a microfilm copy into book form. Without the administrative support of the Department of History, Political Science and Philosophy at the University of South Carolina Aiken, the cost of producing this work might well have been prohibitive. Betty Reese did much of the original transferal from microfilm to photocopy; Gretchen Erb, Joan Stevens, Tanjia Ashley, and Lesley Young did yeoman's duty in the drudge of typing *Expedition* into computer files. My departmental colleagues, especially Professors Valdis O. Lumans and Robert E. Botsch, not only encouraged my efforts but also made useful suggestions. Professor Stanley F. Levine of the Department of Foreign

Languages translated Monro's Latin and provided insight into Monro's facility with languages. Joan Altman proofed the manuscript twice and read the Introduction for style and content. Heather Ruland Staines, History and Military Studies Editor at Praeger, made the process of publishing tolerable. Professor Derek Croxton of Ohio State University offered ideas concerning the Introduction and Glossaries. Finally, Professor Geoffrey Parker of Ohio State University, long been a source of inspiration for those in this field, offered important suggestions regarding the Introduction. His Foreword is also greatly appreciated.

Editing *Expedition* was neither easy nor quick, but it was a labor of love. While there are no copyright restrictions on the republication of the text of *Expedition*, this edition has been transcribed, annotated, and completely reset. All supplemental information—introduction, glossaries, bibliography, and index—was developed and added by the editor. Any errors of omission or commission are the sole responsibility of the editor.

# Introduction

*Monro, His Expedition with the Worthy Scots Regiment called Mac-Keys Regiment* [henceforth abbreviated as *Expedition*] was published in London in 1637.[1] It is a remarkable account of the military experiences of Colonel Robert Monro, commander of a Scottish mercenary regiment during the Thirty Years' War (1618–1648). It is also a military handbook, a narrative of travel experiences abroad, a statement of religious beliefs during an era of intense religious wars, and a compilation of intellectual musings by a highly literate mercenary officer. Its 367 pages are divided into two sections, with Part I chronicling the regiment's performance while in Danish service and Part II describing the activities while serving as part of the Scots Brigade in the Swedish army. Collectively, there are sixty-four "Duty" chapters that describe chronologically the military exploits of the regiment. Following each "Duty" chapter is an "Observation" chapter, wherein Monro offers his opinions, ideas, and advice regarding the "Duty" immediately preceding. Additionally, there is an Introduction of 16 pages, two Tables (indexes) totaling 26 pages, a two-part travelogue of 7 pages, a 5 page listing of Scottish regimental officers, and three chapters (41 pages) of distilled military wisdom by Monro for would-be officers.[2]

Historians generally consider *Expedition* to be an important primary source of the period, despite its never having been reprinted and its relative inaccessibility.[3] It is of particular value to those interested in the history of the Thirty Years' War, the nature of warfare during the early modern era in Europe, and Scottish military and emigration history.[4] However, only the military activities have been utilized to any extent; for various reasons, much of the rest of *Expedition* has been either overlooked or ignored.[5] Although Monro characterizes himself as "a rude, and ignorant Souldier,"[6] he clearly was a careful observer and a well read scholar of the military art.

Unfortunately, there are those who categorize *Expedition* as "far from being the production of an illiterate soldier who despises learning, it is saturated in a mass of irrelevant erudition."[7] This apparent prose barrier led another critic to complain that "with much painful care [Monro] has succeeded in rendering his book largely unreadable [because of] . . . a veil of heaviest baroque ornamentation."[8] Monro's acumen as a military historian has also been questioned. A contemporary, and competing, military author, James Turner, dismissed Monro, and hence *Expedition*, as "wanting military forethought."[9] Perhaps the most balanced description of Monro is that he "was a conscientious and thoughtful man, skilled in his trade but pedantic and over serious."[10] While some of these criticisms are certainly warranted, there is too much substance in *Expedition* for it to be dismissed as irrelevant, unreadable, or lacking in military insight. A product of the early modern era, its value must be assessed with its content in mind, not its style according to literary tastes.

The author of *Expedition*, Robert Monro, was of the Easter Ross Monros of Foulis Castle.[11] He was born about 1590, the younger son of a member of the Scottish upper class.[12] After attending "Colledge," young Robert traveled "in *France*, at *Paris*, and *Poictiers*, Anno 1615" with John Hepburn, who later also became a colonel in the Swedish army.[13] Following a "prentiship" with "the Kings Regiment of the Guards" in France,[14] he received in 1626 a commission as a lieutenant in a regiment being raised for Danish service by Sir Donald Mackay of Farr.[15] Along with his cousin Robert Monro, who was the Baron of Foulis and Head of the House of Monro, and his elder brother, John Monro of Obsdale, the regimental chronicler Monro served for seven years in the German wars, ultimately rising to the rank of colonel in the Swedish Army.[16]

Mackay's Regiment, which ultimately became Monro's Regiment, was often in the forefront of battle, causing Monro to note that it was "an ill custom too common to all Generals that they make most use in time of desperate service of those that do best serve them and when once they have experience of their valor they never omit to employ them on the most dangerous exploits and for reward they only do commend their valor when others are scarce remembered at all."[17] Monro himself was thrice wounded in combat and suffered numerous near misses. He was also burned in a powder explosion and survived a shipwreck, a fever, and his horse falling on him.[18] He was at home on a recruiting trip in 1634 when Habsburg forces virtually annihilated the Swedish army, including Monro's Regiment, at the Battle of Nördlingen on September 6, 1634.

Finding himself in Britain with no regiment to which to return, and hence no gainful employment, Monro sought to augment his income by appealing to his king. In 1634 Charles I authorized a patent for the construction of a hospital in Scotland for "suche officers and souldiours, lame and decayed in the warres, for the credite of our natioun." The hospital, to be administered by Monro, was to be built with contributions from "manie worthie cavalleirs of our nation serving the crowne of Sweden . . . whome God hes in a measure blessed." In addition, Monro received a three years' monopoly to manufacture weapons for the arming of soldiers going abroad, the profit from which would further support the institution.[19] This endeavor must not have been particularly successful for he applied to Charles I in 1637 for a warrant authorizing the recruiting of 800 men for the service of Sweden; Charles granted this as well.[20] Monro also hoped that *Expedition* might provide him with further funding for a return to the wars, and therefore dedicated the book to Prince Charles Louis, the nephew of Charles I. In the dedication, Monro noted that he was but "a poore Souldier" and that he would gladly return to the wars if only "such a leader as his Highnesse" would step forward with determination and with "gracious generosity."[21]

The "Trubles," by which was meant the religious disputation between Charles I and his Scottish subjects that began in 1637, abruptly terminated Monro's efforts at obtaining an income for himself in London.[22] These problems ultimately resulted in the Scottish Parliament's calling for the creation of a military force for defense, with levies to be raised and trained by "prime officers, [who] ought to be men of skill, and must be sent for out of Germany."[23] Monro's immediate availability resulted in his appointment as colonel of a regiment of 2,000 men, the first unit raised by Scottish Covenanters.[24] During the First Bishop's War (1639) Monro captured Edinburgh Castle, then advanced to Dumfries to protect the western frontier against an English invasion. The Pacification of Berwick in June 1639 ended the conflict, although without resolution; the Scottish army, including Monro's force, disbanded.

Unresolved issues led to the Second Bishop's War (1640), necessitating the reconstitution of the Scottish Covenanter army. The Scottish Parliament again appointed Monro as colonel and ordered his new regiment to Aberdeen to maintain order and to reduce royalist forces in the northeast. Monro successfully enforced Convenanter control, after which his regiment marched to the southeastern frontier, near Berwick, where it remained for the next eighteen months.[25] The Treaty of Ripon forced Charles to negotiate with the English Parliament, thereby allowing the Scots to reduce their forces.[26] The army of the Covenant disbanded in August 1641, although Monro's regiment was one of four to be retained.[27]

Following the outbreak of the Irish Rebellion of October 1641, with its stories of atrocities against Scots, the Scottish Parliament offered an army to Charles I for the suppression of the uprising in Ulster.[28] Named the army's major general, Monro was second-in-command to Alexander Leslie, Earl of Leven, another Scot who had served with distinction in the Swedish army.[29] The Scottish army arrived in Carrickfergus in March 1642, but the outbreak of the English Civil War in August turned the insurrection in Ulster into a sideshow. Still, King and Parliament viewed Ireland as an important source of soldiers and war matériel, and Monro was a significant player in the Irish Wars until his capture in 1648. Unfortunately for his legacy, however, he was never very successful. He found the Ulster Protestants uninterested in following Scottish dictates and the Ulster British adamantly opposed to Scottish proposals. There was little or no cooperation among the various commanders and very little financial support for the military forces being raised. "He was a military commander sent to Ulster in confusing circumstances . . . . The result was that he was . . . condemned from all sides and isolated and powerless in a situation he did not really understand."[30]

Monro's military predicament never improved in any substantive fashion. He swiftly learned that the Irish style of warfare was very different from the warfare that he had experienced. He sought to bring Irish rebels to a set-piece battle (the type he had been trained to fight), but the enemy vanished when closely pressed. He noted that "it will be a War in my judgement very strange, for in the whole march I had never any alarme given us being quartered in the fields untrenched."[31] When he finally achieved the battle he wanted, at Benburb, on June 5, 1646, he was decisively defeated, although this was probably as much due to his army having long suffered shortages of supplies and funding than to his generalship.[32]    Monro bemoaned the loss, stating, "for ought I can understand, the Lord of Hosts had a controversie with us to rub shame on our faces . . . for a greater confidence did I never see in any Army then was amougst[33] us."[34]

The withdrawal of 2,000 of his soldiers for service against a royalist army under Montrose in the Highlands (1644–1645), the continued friction between the Scottish army and their ostensible Ulster allies, and the changing nature of the English Civil War further weakened his efforts in Ireland.[35]    Then, on September 16, 1648, and with the assistance of some of his own soldiers, parliamentary forces surprised Monro "in bed with his ladye" and took his stronghold of Carrickfergus.[36] He was sent to the Tower of London, where he remained for five years. Upon his release, in August 1653, Monro, who was by then penniless, was given £10 to assist him in returning to Ulster,[37] where he found his estates, which had been acquired through marriage to Lady Montgomery, confiscated.[38] He appealed to Oliver Cromwell, who ordered the return of his lands, and thereupon lived out his life on the Montgomery estate near Comber, county Down.[39] His wife died in 1670, and the "honest, kind Major-general Munro," by then at least eighty years old and somewhat "melancholic,"[40] survived her by ten or more years.[41]

The life lived by Robert Monro was a mirror of the world in which he lived. Throughout the early modern era all western European states, great and small, were involved in war, either civil or international, and often both. By the late fifteenth century, despite inadequate bureaucracies and limited revenue from traditional sources, rulers developed standing armies to defend their realms or to expand them, wherever and whenever possible. In the sixteenth century, religious passions exacerbated political realities as the various reformation movements often required monarchs to defend the religious status within their realms as well as in adjoining areas. Additionally, over the course of the century, the influx of wealth from non-European areas allowed monarchs to expand and maintain ever larger armies, resulting in increasingly authoritative central governments. This situation—often described as the Military Revolution of early modern Europe—meant that successful wars, whether domestic or foreign, resulted in enhanced authority for monarchs.[42]

As conflicts widened in scope and intensity, military preparedness became one of the most profitable industries in Europe as entrepreneurs emerged to provide the states with the matériel of war.[43] Wastage—the loss of soldiers through battle, disease, and desertion—led to enormous demands for military manpower and was one of the most pressing military problems of the age. Military commanders decried the shortage of well-trained, reliable troops, rectifying the problem, in part, by the utilization of mercenaries. To meet the military requirements of the era, military entrepreneurs contracted to raise and maintain fully equipped military units for the use of their employers.[44] These contractors were usually individuals who had the proper connections—principally nobles, the younger sons of minor or impoverished nobles, and lesser gentry—as aristocratic or family ties meant acceptability and, hopefully, upward mobility. Officers, as well as the rank and file, often came from the poorest and least politically stable areas of Europe. With but few exceptions, European armies were either raised or supplemented in this fashion for almost three centuries.

While many areas of Europe provided large numbers of entrepreneur officers and their soldiers, Scotland possessed a variety of unenviable factors, which resulted in its becoming a veritable warehouse for mercenaries. In the three centuries prior to 1568, wars with England, which Scotland usually lost, resulted in a greatly weakened Scottish central authority.[45] Compounding the disorder caused by those wars was the political instability created by weak monarchs and warring noble factions.[46] With only intermittent interference from Edinburgh, Scottish nobles developed strong, personal armies based upon familial relationships or clans. Scotland thus evolved into a society designed for war within which those skilled in the military arts were recognized as essential and respected.

A further pressure on Scottish society was the lack of economic opportunity. Geography, climate, a paucity of arable land, and a feudal land-rent system combined to create a marginal economy in which recurrent mortality crises[47] continually threatened large segments of the population.[48] This, coupled with a population surge, resulted in famines occurring with alarming regularity by the late sixteenth century.[49] As war was an opportunity for social and economic advancement, it is small wonder that, with the dramatic increase in the number of dynastic and religious wars on the Continent, large numbers of Scots served Continental masters, either as the recruiters or as the recruited.[50]

Although Scots never constituted a high percentage of any army wherein they served, their value was recognized and their service was esteemed.[51] Over 1,100 Scottish officers served in various continental armies during the early modern era,[52] with at least 5 marshals, 18 generals, and 135 colonels appearing in that number.[53] While there were many military opportunities during the period, Scottish participation was particularly significant during the Thirty Years' War. Habsburg efforts at establishing its dynastic hegemony—as well as reestablishing Catholic conformity—throughout Europe led to this pivotal confrontation between Habsburgs and Bourbons. It erupted in 1618 as a political and religious confrontation between Bohemian nobles and their nominal overlords, the Habsburgs. Tragically, a localized conflict with specific local issues quickly expanded into an empire-wide war over religious and constitutional issues between Emperor and German princes.[54] This struggle, in turn, soon merged into a Continent-wide series of wars which not only resulted in a major alteration of the European balance of power but also consumed vast quantities of soldiers.[55]

During the era of the Thirty Years' War alone, levy authorizations for 55,720 Scots were issued by the Privy Council of Scotland to Scottish military entrepreneurs.[56] When these entrepreneurs left, they took with them a cross section of Scottish adult males, from clansmen to those who also hoped to be upwardly mobile or who had been affected by various population pressures. Recruiting officers appealed first to family or clan members to enlist for service abroad, a tactic most effective in Highland areas. For some enlistees, religious or political motives may have been a factor. For most, however, the primary reason for enlisting was always economic opportunity. It was deemed better to use learned fighting skills for opportunity than to subsist or starve[57] in an overcrowded Scotland.

The Thirty Years' War was the last, and certainly the most vicious, of the great religious wars of the era, and its totality resulted in many terrible consequences for the civilian population. Contemporary descriptions of the nature and impact of war during this period range from propagandistic hyperbole to brief descriptions of specific events and personages. These descriptions were, for the most part, provided by pamphleteers or diplomats with specific points of view and with the design of promoting their particular version of the truth.[58] Accounts by the combatants themselves are rare as rank-and-file soldiers were rarely literate and their officers only marginally more so.[59] *Expedition*, the only major work in English to deal with the conflict, is a public, yet introspective, view of the trials and tribulations of being a professional soldier in foreign service during that war. Monro's feelings and motives are clear reflections of the biases and prejudices of one who did not make policy, but only followed it.

*Expedition* was not meant to be a history of the Thirty Years' War; it was a regimental history—as well as a social history—told from the author's point of view. Monro was not an atypical mercenary officer of the period for he came from the upper stratum of Scottish society, which provided him with connections to those who offered contracts and those he would recruit.[60] That Monro attained the rank of colonel in the Swedish army is clear evidence of his talent; Gustavus Adolphus usually awarded rank through merit, and this was always the case if the candidate were foreign-born.[61] Although somewhat atypical in that he did advance to the rank of colonel, Monro's experiences and motivations were certainly typical. In an era of religious wars, he viewed his profession as one offering opportunity for service in a just cause. A Scots Calvinist, he began his autobiography by dedicating *Expedition* to "His Highnesse the Prince Elector Palatine of Rhine" and to "your Highnesse Royall Mother Elizabeth, Queene of Bohemia, Jewell of her sex, and the most resplendent in brightnesse of minde, for a woman, that the earth doth afford."[62] His undisguised antipathy for Roman Catholics, in general, and the papacy and the Habsburgs, in particular, clearly mark Monro's belief in the justness of the Protestant cause which he served.[63]

Monro noted other reasons for becoming a soldier-for-hire. He admitted that economic necessity and other, less worthy, reasons often forced men into service abroad. His cousin, the Baron of Foulis, for example, was "a little prodigall in his spending . . . [and was] advised by his friends . . . to look to the wounds of his house and family . . . [thus] he went beyond sea . . . well accompanyied with a part of his neerest friends." Monro cited this experience because he hoped to "animate other *Cavaliers* borne of lesse fortune to follow his vertues."[64] He stated that it was far better to "live honourably abroad, and with credit, then to encroach (as many do) on their friends at home, as we say in *Scotland*, leaping at the halfe loafe, while as others through vertue live nobly abroade, served with silver plate, and attendance."[65] He saw his profession as an opportunity to reach one's potential through hard work, diligence, and ability.

Monro wanted others to emulate him and his fellow officers, for he believed that a successful soldier was brave, courageous, honorable, loyal, and dutiful. The quest for *vertue*, as Monro termed it, was the highest calling for a soldier, much higher than personal reward or position.[66] Monro often reiterated his advice that "the world hath nothing so glorious as vertue"[67] for it ensured a good name and, perhaps, eternal fame. It was a dangerous life, but Monro hoped that *Expedition* would "allure you [the reader] to follow their vertues, that you may be partaker of their honour, for the further credit of our Nation."[68] *Expedition* was thus a positive statement regarding the opportunities offered by the mercenary profession. It was also a validation of the quality of Scottish soldiers and officers exported to the various continental wars.[69]

Monro believed that he, as well as most Scots, exemplified the characteristics of the successful soldier of *vertue*. Their Scottishness was, in part, the product of a kinship system in the early modern era which allowed Scots to maintain their identity in alien worlds.[70] It was also necessity which forced the military emigrants from Scotland, and war and shared danger which bound them together when abroad. Monro, himself a Highlander, included all Scots as a group and saw their underlying national characteristic as their love of war. He thrilled in combat and in the opportunity to overcome fear, and he considered most of his "Camerades" to be of like mind,[71] repeatedly praising his countrymen as being the best soldiers in either the Danish or Swedish armies.[72] He occasionally included other Britons in the upper tier, and he placed the Swedes close behind, but he asserted that no other ethnic group equaled the military prowess of Scots.[73]

Not surprisingly, Monro's perspective is that of an officer, and he reserved most of his accolades for his brother "Cavaliers." He rarely mentions anyone from the lower classes by name, finding the Scottish rank and file to be "resolute and stout" of heart but unworthy of being cited as individuals.[74] In Monro's opinion, the "Invincible Old Regiment" was critical to the successes of the Danish and Swedish armies.[75] Neither the Danish king, Christian IV, nor the

Swedish king, Gustavus Adolphus, could have achieved as much as they did without those "old expert officers and old beaten blades of soldiers."[76] Monro wrote *Expedition* "because I loved my Camerades"; it was intended for "my friends and not for the world."[77]

The production of a work of the length and complexity of *Expedition* was unquestionably laborious and time-consuming. While there are no records regarding Monro's creative processes, there are clues to the procedures and aids that he used. First, *Expedition* is too detailed to be the product of his memory or that of his fellow officers; and it is probable that Monro had compiled written records of his own, which served as memory prompts. He twice notes in *Expedition* that, during periods of inactivity, he "thought better to collect at this time somewhat of the actions of others, than to be altogether idle."[78] This strongly indicates that he kept a diary or a log of his activities while abroad. Such a log, or logs (which would have been, most likely, dictated to the regimental clerk) would have served the dual purpose of providing Monro with material for reports to his superiors and providing him with a record for later perusal to enhance his understanding of the military art.

Additionally, works such as *The Swedish Intelligencer*, which chronicled Swedish activities in central Europe between 1630 and 1634, were readily available to Monro at the time when he was writing *Expedition*. Details of treaties and accounts of military action elsewhere (to which Monro might not have had access while on service abroad) appear in his narrative of events.[79] For example, the Scots Brigade missed the Battle of Lützen (November 16, 1632), following its decimation at the battle for Alte Feste before Nuremberg on August 31, 1632,[80] yet Monro includes a lengthy description of the events which led up to and resulted in the death in battle of the Swedish king.[81] More than likely, *The Swedish Intelligencer*, as well as other accounts of the battle, provided the necessary details to flesh out Monro's account.[82]

There exists a substantive difference in content and style between the two parts of *Expedition*. Part I, containing only twenty-two "Duties" within its 89 pages, is focused almost entirely on the activities of Mackay's Regiment in Danish service between 1626 and 1629. Monro rarely describes events beyond his own narrow scope and shows little strategic vision or awareness of what was happening elsewhere. Much of the material contained within the "Observations" is heavily laced with examples from classical works, which Monro uses to validate his conclusions. Part II, with forty-two "Duties" in 181 pages, offers far more information and analysis regarding the course of the war during the Swedish phase. There are almost no classical references, but much data pertaining to the conduct of the war outside the parameters of Monro's ken is included.

There is no way of knowing precisely why the two parts are so dissimilar, but the most logical reasons are related to the events of the war and to Monro's role therein. Part I describes actions that took place following the Protestant debacle at Lutter, on August 24–27, 1626. When Mackay's Regiment arrived in north Germany in late fall 1626, it was divided and posted at several defensive positions along the Elbe River; but, like the rest of Christian IV's army, it was soon forced from the mainland. Except for three major actions by the regiment—Oldenburg, Breddenburg, and Stralsund—the regiment was either in garrison or participating in largely meaningless raids from late 1626 until May 1629, when it was dismissed from Danish service.[83] Monro's active military experiences in this period were infrequent and Danish successes, minimal. Many of his observations deal with banal details such as food and lodging, and his military observations deal primarily with matters of discipline and organization. It is likely that he read extensively during this period and noted similarities between the Danish situation and historical events. From 1630 until 1633, however, the Scots Brigade was continually involved in the campaigns of Gustavus Adolphus. Swedish successes meant less time for reading but provided a wealth of first-hand information for recording in a personal log and on which Monro could later reflect.[84]

Monro's rising status during service abroad was certainly a factor in content. As a junior officer between 1626 and 1629, Monro was not privy to tactical or strategic information at that time. Part I of *Expedition* is an excellent example of a "worm's eye view" of military writing, as Monro describes what happened in his immediate area but shows little awareness of events elsewhere.[85] His focus is the regiment, not the war; it is the perspective of a junior officer, not a commander. Only at Stralsund does Monro's narrative come into sharper focus, perhaps because the tactical and strategic success at Stralsund was achieved through Scottish efforts in conjunction with Swedish assistance. Almost one-fifth of Part I deals with the battle for Stralsund, and the themes that dominate the rest of *Expedition*—Protestantism, Scottishness, and *vertue*—are clearly delineated.[86] Monro emerges as a forceful, dynamic, and insightful mid-level officer, who would, within the year, initiate and engineer the transfer of Mackay's Regiment from Danish to Swedish service.

By the time he was hired by Gustavus Adolphus, Monro was a seasoned veteran with the rank of lieutenant colonel. Along with three other Scottish regiments in Swedish service, Mackay's Regiment was incorporated into the Scots Brigade, which played a significant role in the success of the Swedish army against the Imperial forces.[87] Monro, as a higher-ranking officer, was privy to more information, especially from Gustavus Adolphus who often spoke with his officers.[88] With experience, Monro had also become more aware of the nature of war and of the interrelationship between tactics and strategy as well as between the political arena and the military sphere. As such, he deemed it necessary to provide more information to his readers so that the Swedish successes could be better understood.

The actual task of creating *Expedition* was likely a joint effort between Monro and several amanuenses, which may, in part, explain some of the criticism of *Expedition* advanced by later readers. The strongest indication that *Expedition* was dictated to two or more scribes comes from spelling variations within the text. Spellings are consistently inconsistent, that is, a spelling will be relatively consistent for a number of pages, and a variation will suddenly occur for another block of material.  *Be* suddenly becomes *bee* and *we* becomes *wee*, and then they are switched back to the former.[89]   Spelling variations and inconsistencies do occur within *Expedition*, often on the same page and occasionally in the same paragraph.  Fortunately, the English spelling variations which appear in *Expedition* are only a nuisance, for they are generally close enough to current spelling practices to be easily recognizable.

A major problem with dictation occurs where things foreign and unfamiliar, especially place names and military terms, are transcribed.  Phonetic spelling results in variations and inconsistencies, a problem compounded when several scribes are utilized.  Capitalization follows only a moderately apparent pattern, but punctuation usage is confusing at best.  Sentence structure is occasionally nonexistent with thought followed by thought separated by commas, semi-colons, and periods, often at random.  Even though rules for English grammar were yet in the formative stage, and standardization of English was a thing of the future, *Expedition* still reads as if someone were thinking out loud—or dictating.  The biggest problem with dictation, however, is that, without extensive editing, the final product will ramble; this is patently clear in *Expedition*.

Yet another factor to be considered in accounting for the style and content of *Expedition* is Monro himself.  His memoirs are printed in standard English, not Scots-English.  All other written material attributed to Monro is printed in the same style.  When Monro's prose is compared with the style or spellings that appear in contemporary works written in Scots-English,[90] none of the writing attributed to Monro is similar.  His spoken English was probably excellent, but it surely betrayed his Scottish Highland origins.  The only quote attributed to Monro, a command ostensibly shouted by him to Scottish troops in 1643—"Fay Fay, ran awa frae awhenn rebels"[91]—shows that he spoke Highland Scots-English.

On the other hand, he was educated in college, which required Latin; he spent several years in France, necessitating French; and served seven years in the German wars, which called for a knowledge of Danish, Swedish, and German.  Using Scots in London would have limited his opportunities, and he surely avoided Scottish dialect as much as possible, especially in his written work.  Still, it cannot be presumed that he was able to purge his spoken word of his Scottish accent.  It can only be concluded, then, that the English amanuenses did their best to anglicize Monro's narrative for the intended audience.

One final reason for Monro's style may have been his own sense of possible social inferiority.  In wartime, successful players like Monro replaced "gentleman" warriors, who received positions through connections, and not necessarily talent.  The end of a war, however, left the successful, yet not socially acceptable, soldier in an insecure position.  Consequently, Monro used the style of prose popular at the time—baroque with frequent classical references—to validate his credentials as a gentleman, as well as to demonstrate his knowledge of the theory of war.  This tendency also lengthened the work with digressions and pontifications.[92]

Despite these problems, the final product transcends simple military history or the history of a specific body of troops during the time. While the content of *Expedition* provides an incredibly detailed narrative of military life in the seventeenth century, Monro's work personalizes the conflict as do few other works of the period. The accounts of battles in which he participated are, for the most part, clear word-pictures of the nature of war.[93] Monro leaves no doubt as to what combat was like for the soldier of the early modern era. The fury of the storming of a city,[94] the terror of an artillery bombardment,[95] and the exhilaration of victory[96] are graphic examples of military writing at its best.

Monro describes the lot of the Scottish mercenary in a detached (as if each were a report), yet personalized (told with feeling) manner. Little is omitted, including a humorous anecdote about a beer barrel being exploded by a cannon shot,[97] camp life,[98] grousing about pay being in arrears,[99] military-civilian relations,[100] back-stabbing officers,[101] fear,[102] and sickness and death.[103] His observations regarding commanders,[104] kings,[105] politicians,[106] and women[107] are diverse and insightful. Throughout, Monro manifests his Scottish pride in the military prowess of the Scottish soldiers by calling attention to their *vertue* and their skill. In sum, *Expedition* provides insight into the mind-set and behavior of a specific group of people at a particular place and time.

A more intriguing aspect of *Expedition* is its intended use as a military textbook. Monro's title states that his book was written "for the use of all worthie Cavaliers favouring the laudable profession of Armes."[108] Monro learned from experience that it took more than simple courage to become a successful soldier. It took preparation and foresight before an engagement, skill and leadership during the conflict, and proper management afterward if one were to be victorious. Monro's military perspicacity was simultaneously practical and theoretical. It is clear from *Expedition* that his extensive personal experience in the German wars gave him the opportunity to observe and experience the art of war with all its ramifications. Most important, he served under Gustavus Adolphus of Sweden, one of the great military innovators and captains of the age, whereby he could observe first-hand the intricacies of military genius. It was perhaps fortunate that he served Denmark first, for the juxtaposition of unsuccessful and successful gave him an opportunity to compare. As an older (and more mature) soldier, Monro's Swedish service taught him the practical lessons of battle tactics and strategy as well as the crucial interrelationship between diplomacy and warfare.

Monro's theoretical knowledge of the art of war was based on his extensive reading of classical military studies. He liberally sprinkled quotations and examples from the great military writers of earlier ages throughout *Expedition*, citing at least twenty-five classical and medieval works, as well as at least five contemporary works, as validation of his observations.[109] Monro urges those who would follow in his footsteps to read, for "A Souldier without letters is like a ship without a Rudder . . . ; but having letters, he findes wherewith he can be made wiser . . . . Therefore we see, that science to a man of warre is a brave Mistresse, teaching him to doe all things as they did on old times."[110] He emphasizes that a successful officer must read in order to add theoretical knowledge to practical experience. For this reason, Monro repeatedly connected his own wartime experiences with his extensive theoretical knowledge.

Monro was well aware of the changes in military matters, especially those related to the "new order of Discipline"[111] introduced by "the *Lyon* of the *North* the invincible King of *Sweden*."[112] He clearly states his precepts for military success in warfare in many of his "Observations," as well as in his "Abridgement of Exercises for Younger Soldiers,"[113] "Certain Observations Worthy of the Younger Officer,"[114] and "Christian Soldier Meditations."[115] Throughout the text he defines the basic military principles that he observed being utilized with success, exhorting his readers to learn and emulate what successful leaders did. Monro states that an able commander is an upholder of moral law, a skilled user of strategy and tactics, a self-disciplined person and disciplinarian, a builder of morale in the army, a ceaseless trainer of troops, and an even-handed rewarder and punisher.[116]

It is significant that Monro's observations and conclusions compare favorably with current military doctrine and that his understanding of the principles of war was sound.[117] Unfortunately, his advice is often intertwined with his moralizing and digressions, and much thus becomes lost in his prose. Only at the end of *Expedition*, where Monro presents in outline format his distilled understanding of the art of war, do his messages become precise. In conclusion, Monro's military observations had the potential for providing valuable advice to those who would *vertuous* Cavaliers, but the amount of verbiage utilized by Monro often makes his insights difficult to locate and utilize.

There are other possible, and less obvious, reasons for *Expedition*'s apparent lack of commercial success. Monro was a Scotsman, a factor of great significance in the British Isles. Scots were not well accepted in England prior to 1603, and the accession of James VI of Scotland as James I of England merely allowed Scots to intrude in English affairs. A book written by a Scot about a far-off war would therefore have had little impact in England in 1637. The timing of the publication is also a factor, for *Expedition* was published just prior to the wars between Charles I and the Scots. Although *Expedition* was dedicated to Prince Charles Louis, Monro was on the opposing side in the Bishops' Wars as well as during the English Civil War.

Monro's own lack of success in independent command during those wars, for whatever reasons, certainly prejudiced readers against the value of his commentary. These failures perhaps demonstrate Monro's lack of prescience as a "great captain," but they should not marginalize his accomplishments as a "fighting captain." After 1648, when Scotland was at war with Oliver Cromwell's England, Monro was again on the wrong side and was incarcerated in the Tower of London. The end of the civil wars found an aged Monro, living on his estates in Ulster, far from either his ancestral home or the seat of power. Interestingly, he had come full circle and was again a royalist.[118] Hence,

*Expedition*, essentially ignored before and during the wars and forgotten by the time of the Restoration, was simply not considered relevant.

In conclusion, for those reasons normally attributed to it, as well as for reasons beyond, Monro's *Expedition* should be considered invaluable. In an era dominated by warfare, Monro was an active participant in two significant conflicts of the seventeenth century. He was a seventeen year combat veteran in an era of brutal warfare and a military entrepreneur when mercenaries provided the bulk of soldiers for rulers. *Expedition* was written from the point of view of a junior officer who rose to a position of importance, and his interpretations of the nature of warfare and of military concepts are of value and merit. Monro's military accounts are, for the most part, precise, and the history of the "Duties" of Mackay's Regiment's is accurate, not "confused."[119] Yet his autobiography is more than a personal account by a military man in an era of total war. He was a Scottish Presbyterian fighting for Lutheran monarchs against a Roman Catholic emperor. *Expedition* is a fascinating chronicle of military life during wartime and of ethnicity in the early modern era. Monro took great pride in "the laudable profession of Armes" [120] as well as in his accomplishments, and those of the Scottish nation, in the German wars. Additionally, Monro's travelogue and narrative closely parallel other sources with regard to persons, places, and events. His "observations," while occasionally meandering and irrelevant, provide a window to a previous age, through which the early modern era can be better understood.

Still, the value of *Expedition* rests, not just on Monro's exactness as a chronicler, or even an interpreter of events, but upon his ability as a describer of events in which he himself took part. He presents the religious passions of the era, notes the difficulty of soldier-civilian relations, describes political machinations of princes, and offers opinions regarding people of all ranks and stations. *Expedition* is neither a simplistic regimental history written in baroque prose nor the turgid meandering of a pedant anxious to impress his audience with his erudition. Monro echoes, as well as adumbrates, military voices throughout the ages. Clearly seen is his pride in the Scottish national character, an awareness which is a vital component in the development of ethnicity. The shortcomings of *Expedition* are numerous, and Monro's microscope method certainly can be accused of limiting its value. However, the overall merit of Monro's work far outweighs its shortcomings. It is a volume that can, and should, be viewed as a lost treasure now available to be rediscovered. This being true, it is hoped that a new appreciation for Robert Monro and his *Expedition* will now emerge.

William S. Brockington, Jr.

## NOTES

1. Robert Monro, *Monro, His Expedition with the Worthy Scots Regiment (called Mac–Keys Regiment) levied in August 1626 by Sir Donald Mac–Key Lord Rhees,*

*Colonell for his Majesties service of Denmark, and reduced after the Battaile of Nerling, to one Company in September 1634 at Wormes in the Paltz. Discharged in severall Duties and Observations of service first under the magnanimous King of Denmark, during his warres against the Emperour; afterward, under the Invincible King of Sweden, during his Majesties life time; and since, under the Director Generall; the Rex–chancellor Oxensterne and his Generalls. Collected and gathered together at Spare–houres, by Colonell Robert Monro, at first Lievetenant under the said Regiment, to the Noble and worthy Captaine, Thomas Mac–Kenyee, of Kildon, Brother to the noble Lord, the Lord Earle of Seafort; for the use of all worthie Cavaliers favouring the laudable profession of Armes. To which is annexed the Abridgement of Exercise, and divers practicall Observations, for the younger Officer his Consideration; ending with Souldiers Meditations going on service* (London: W. Jones, 1637).

2. Citations from *Expedition* will utilize the pagination of the original and will cite the section of *Expedition* in which they are located. The following is a list of the sections, the order in which they occur in the original, and the abbreviations used for citations: Introduction (Intro 1–16); Part I, Danish Phase (I 1–89); Table of the First Part (Table I 1–8); List of Scottish Officers (List 1–5); Chronology and Miles: Part I, Danish Phase (Log I 1–2); Chronology and Miles: Part II, Swedish Phase (Log II 1–5); Part II, Swedish Phase (II 1–181); Abridgment of Exercises for Younger Soldiers (II 183–192); Certain Observations worthy of the Younger Officer (II 193–215); Christian Soldier Meditations (II 217–224); Table of the Second Part (Table II 1–18). For the location of each section within this edition of *Expedition*, see the "Table of Contents," vii.

3. Maurice J. D. Cockle, *A Bibliography of English Military Books to 1642 and of Contemporary Foreign Works* (London: Simpkin, Marshall, 1900), p. 111, commented that it was "printed at the sole expense of Lord Rhees, and most of the copies (which were but few) given to his friends." *Expedition* is considered "exceedingly scarce," according to a note appended to a copy in the Royal Artillery Institute, which also states that only two copies were located in Great Britain in 1900, one in the Royal Artillery Institute and the other in the British Museum. A more recent search (1998) uncovered six copies in the United States (Columbia University, Folger Library, Harvard University, Huntington Library, Library of Congress, and Newberry Library) and six in Great Britain (British Library, the Bodleian Library at Oxford University, Chetham's Library in Manchester, the University Library at Cambridge, the National Library of Scotland, and St. Andrews University Library) now available to researchers. Most assuredly, there are copies in private collections, but these are not readily available to scholars. According to David Stevenson, *Scottish Covenanters and Irish Confederates: Scottish–Irish Relations in the Mid–seventeenth Century* (Belfast: Ulster Historical Foundation, 1981), pp. 80–82, there were initially 1,500 copies printed, but sales "were evidently disappointing for in 1644 some were reissued with a new title page (may be seen in Stevenson, 81, or in Geoffrey Parker, *The Military Revolution: Military Innovation and the Rise of the West, 1500–1800*, 2nd ed. [Cambridge: Cambridge University Press, 1996], 25) as *The Scotch Military Discipline Learnd from the valiant Swede . . . collected . . . by Major Generall Monro . . . .* Copies of this rare second edition are to be found in the National Library of Scotland and in the J. T. Gilbert Collection in the Pearse Street Library, Dublin."

4. In the late nineteenth century, Scottish historical clubs and organizations sought to publish significant historical documents pertaining to Scottish history. *Expedition* was published in an accessible, albeit incomplete, version in John Mackay, *An Old Scots Brigade* (Edinburgh: W. Blackwood and Sons, 1885), which expanded his "Mackay's Regiment, 1626–1634" in *Transactions of the Gaelic Society of Inverness* 8 (1876/1879): 128–189. A comparison of the number of pages—367 in *Expedition* down to 62 in

"Mackay" and to 295 (including 100 pages of appendices, mostly documents) in *Scots Brigade*—indicates how much of Expedition was omitted.

5. Even the briefest perusal of literature dealing with any of the topics listed indicates the extent to which *Expedition* is cited. As an example, Michael Roberts, *Gustavus Adolphus, A History of Sweden: 1611–1632*, vol. 2 (London: Longmans, Green, 1958) cites Monro at least 51 times in his discussion of tactics (199–271) and in his account of the Swedish campaign in Germany prior to the Battle of Lützen (439–559 and 675–748).

6. *Expedition*, Intro–3. He also describes himself as a "poore Souldier" (Intro–4), who was also "shallow–brained" (Intro–7). He terms his writings as an account of "my tedious expedition, and shallow observations" (Intro–4) drawn "out of my little experience" (I–24). Such self deprecation should be dismissed either the style of writing popular at the time or as deference to social betters, to whom the book was dedicated and from whom Monro hoped to receive financial support.

7. J. H. Burton, *The Scot Abroad*, new edition (Edinburgh: W. Blackwood and Sons, 1898), 317. Burton states that *Expedition*'s title "is of itself a piece of tough and tedious reading. The confusion, ambiguity, and verbose prolixity of the narrative, involve the reader in immediate hopelessness, and keep him in perpetual doubt of the period, the persons, and the part of the world to which his attention is called." Burton grants that Monro's "unreadable book" "affords fine clear glimpses here and there of the character and habits of the Scottish cavalier of fortune."

8. Frans G. Bengtsson, "Robert Monro" in *Scots in Sweden*, ed. Jonas Berg and Bo Lagercrantz, trans. P. A. Hart (Stockholm: The Swedish Institute, 1962), 81–82. This is primarily based upon *Expedition*.

9. James Turner, *Memoirs of his own Life and Times 1632–1670*, ed. T. Thomson, Bannatyne Club, vol. 28 (London: for the Bannatyne Club, 1829), 23. Turner is here offering his opinion regarding Monro's qualities as leader of the Scottish army in Ireland, 1642–1649, but he also generally dismisses Monro's abilities. In *Pallas Armata, Military Essayes of the Ancient Grecian, Roman and Modern Art of War . . . Written in the Years 1670 and 1671* (London: Printed by M. W. for Richard Chiswell, 1683), Turner mentions neither Monro nor *Expedition* in the 372 pages. Turner cites both classical and medieval military authors (see pp. 33–156), as well as contemporaries such as Francesco Guicciardini and Niccolò Machiavelli. The only British authors mentioned by Turner are English (see pp. 160–163).

10. Stevenson, *Scottish Covenanters*, 82–83. Stevenson here states that "Monro showed a lack of ability to discriminate between the useful and the useless, the profound and the obvious."

11. Foulis Castle is on the northern shore of Cromarty Firth (north of Inverness) in the county of Ross and Cromarty. Easter Ross, that is eastern Ross, is the home of the clan of Monro.

12. Alexander Mackenzie, *History of the Monros of Fowlis* (Inverness: "Scottish Highlander" Press for A. and W. Mackenzie, 1898) is a history of Monro clan leaders and cadet (younger son) lines. Robert Monro was the second son of his father and was born no later than shortly after his father's death in 1589; but no specific birth date is listed (p. 169). Monro's father was the fifth son of the fifteenth Baron of Foulis, making Robert the younger son of a younger son. Both elements of kinship are important: the familial link provided status and connections, but the "younger son" standing provided little or no income. A chapter, "General Robert Munro—A Cadet of Obsdale," 210–264, in Mackenzie, *Monros of Fowlis*, is the best biographical source. Other, briefer biographies of Robert Monro include: Bengtsson, "Monro" and "Monro or Munro,

Robert" in *The Dictionary of National Biography* (*DNB*), edited by Leslie Stephen and Sidney Lee, vol. 13 (London: Oxford University Press, 1921), 635–636.

13. *Expedition*, II–75. While an absolute identification of Monro's "Colledge" of choice is not possible, it is likely that he attended St. Leonard's College of St. Andrews University. According to Dr. Norman H. Reid, Keeper of Manuscripts at St. Andrews University Library, two signatures of a Robert Monro appear on the list of January 19, 1609, for the academic session, 1609–10. The two Roberts were possibly the cousins who later served together: Robert, later the Black Laird, and Robert, the author. According to Arnott T. Wilson, University Archivist, a Robert Monro is listed in the Register of Laureations of the University of Edinburgh. As such a listing signifies graduation in Arts, this may also be Robert the author, for the date is July 27, 1609. Significantly, the words *tribunus militum* appear on the Register after the name, a phrase which also appears in the Introduction to *Expedition* (Intro-9) following the author's name [as well as following the names of John, his brother (Intro-15), and Robert, his cousin (Intro-14). See their biographical sketches on page 390 below.]. Robert Monro might well have attended both institutions. Poitiers was the site of a university popular with Celtic Britons from the fifteenth through the seventeenth centuries. A continental tours was considered to be an essential part of the education of a young man of birth, for refining social graces and establishing requisite connections.

14. *Expedition*, I–45. Because of the long-standing political and military alliance between Scotland and France (the Auld Alliance, 1295–1560s), the logical place for a young Scot of good birth to begin a military career was the French military. Scottish units served the French monarchy from the medieval period until the French Revolution. See Françisque Michel, *Les Ecossais en France, les Français en Ecosse*, 2 vols. (London: n.p., 1862).

15. According to Ian Grimble, *Chief of Mackay* (London: Routledge and Kegan Paul, 1965), 1, 14, 78–83, the Mackay clan and the Monros of Foulis had a long history of close working relationships. Exogenous marriages provided the Mackay clan with an expanded base of support in the western Highlands, with Macleod, Macdonald, Mackenzie, Sinclair, and Gordon providing significant alliances. Neil, a fifteenth-century Chief of Mackay, married Euphemia, daughter of George Munro of Foulis, in order to cement an alliance. Mackenzie, *Munros of Fowlis* (p. 84) cites another critical marriage alliance: Sir Hector Monro, nineteenth Baron and first Baronet of Foulis, was married, in July 1619, to "Mary, youngest daughter of Hugh Mackay of Farr and sister of Sir Donald Mackay, afterwards Lord Reay." This clearly aided the Monros in their quest for military service. While no muster rolls exist for the original regiment, which had an authorized strength of 3,000 men, Mackay, Monro, Sinclair, and other familial surnames predominate in the names appearing in *Expedition*.

16. Personal and place names are spelled in various ways in *Expedition*. Foulis appears as Fowles (I–1) and Foules (II–59); and Obsdale is rendered Obstell (I–19). Even modern spellings vary, for example Foulis is often written as Fowlis (Mackenzie, *Monros of Fowlis*).

17. *Expedition*, I–19.

18. This list of "favourable marke(s)," as Monro deemed battle wounds, is from *Expedition*, I–18, I–68, II–149 (wounds); I–51, II–149 (near misses); I–51 (burned); II–4 (nearly drowned); II–48 (fever); and II–173 (horse fell on him).

19. Charles I to Privy Council of Scotland, May 4, 1634, Fol. 15, b, *Register of the Privy Council of Scotland* (*RPCS*), ed. by David Masson, series 2, vol. 5, 1633–1635 (Edinburgh: H. M. General Register House, 1899), 333–334; Colonel Robert Monro to Privy Council of Scotland, June 1634, Fol.16a—Fol. 16b, *RPCS*, series 2, vol. 5, 334–336. All were probably to be part of a complex of buildings as Monro planned to store

the weapons at the hospital. Monro's bitterness at the failure of Sweden to pay its debts to its mercenaries, a fact he frequently complained about in *Expedition*, is also manifested in the patent. Charles bade the Privy Council of Scotland to request the crown of Sweden to fulfill its own terms of mercenary agreements, that is, to provide retired or incapacitated soldiers with their guaranteed pensions and to provide for the widows of soldiers.

20. Charles I to Privy Council of Scotland, May 13, 1637, Fol. 213b, *RPCS*, series 2, vol. 6, 458–459.

21. *Expedition*, Intro 2–5, II–109.

22. From John Spalding, *Memorialls of the Trubles in Scotland and in England, 1624–1645* (Aberdeen: Spalding Club, 1850). The Book of Canons was a revised liturgy which many Scots considered popish. The reading of the book at St. Giles Kirk in Edinburgh in July 1637 produced a riot and the beginning of an open break between Scotland and the King. In February of the following year, a "Covenant," signed by the nobles, was issued to the general public. As the positions of the Covenanters and the King hardened, it became clear that only a war could settle the issue. For a history of the period, see David Stevenson, *The Scottish Revolution, 1637–1644* (New York, St. Martin's, 1973).

23. Circular Letter, January 1639, Public Record Office MSS, Domestic Series, *Letters and Papers of Charles I*, vol. 410, no. 167.

24. Edward M. Furgol, *A Regimental History of the Covenanting Armies, 1639–1651* (Edinburgh: John Donald, 1990), 33–34.

25. Spalding, *Memorialls of the Trubles*, pp. 234–235, provides a contemporary view of the depredations of the Scottish levies on royalists during this period. He details at length the cruelty of Monro's troops; Spalding was, it should be noted, a royalist, and his criticism of Monro was predicated upon his personal allegiances. Furgol, *Regimental History*, 63–65, observes that Monro maintained strict discipline for his own forces and raised money by levying a contribution on Aberdeen. When some members of his force mutinied over lack of pay, Monro personally killed the leader of the mutineers, breaking the revolt. A statement of military rules for, and the oath taken by, Scottish soldiers of this time may be found in *Articles of Militarie Discipline* (Edinburgh 1639), reprinted as part of *The English Experience: Its Record in Early Printed Books*, vol. 77 (New York: Da Capo, 1969).

26. At Ripon (October 26, 1640) Charles agreed to pay the Scottish army £850 per day until a settlement could be reached. The Scots continued to occupy northern England until the money was paid. Lacking the funds to pay the Scots, Charles summoned the English Parliament.

27. Furgol, *Regimental History*, 63–65.

28. The Irish Rebellion, which took place throughout Ireland, resulted in the massacre of some 4,000 Ulster Protestants, and perhaps another 8,000 died from exposure after being expelled from their homesteads. There was no general and organized massacre of Protestants, but contemporary accounts of the atrocities were used to validate the repressive policies that followed. See Nicholas Canny, "What Really Happened in Ireland in 1641?" in *Ireland from Independence to Occupation, 1641–1660* ed. Jane H. Ohlmeyer (Cambridge: Cambridge University Press, 1995): 24–42, and P. J. Corish, "The Rising of 1641 and the Confederacy, 1641–45" in *A New History of Ireland*, vol. 3, *Early Modern Ireland, 1534–1691*, ed. T. W. Moody, F. X. Martin, and F. J. Byrne (Oxford: Clarendon, 1976): 289–316.

29. Leslie returned to Scotland in 1638, bringing two cannons, 2,000 muskets, and gunpowder, this according to the letters of demission from Queen Christina of Sweden and cited in Sir William Fraser, ed., *The Melvilles, Earls of Melville, and the Leslies,*

*Earls of Leven*, 2 vols. (Edinburgh: privately printed, 1890), 2, 391. Leslie commanded the Scottish forces during the First and Second Bishops' Wars, served briefly in Ireland, and commanded Scottish forces during the English Civil War. See C. S. Terry, *The Life and Campaigns of Alexander Leslie* (London: Longmans Green, 1899). See also Alexander Leslie, Earl of Leven, *Articles and Ordinances of Warre* (Edinburgh: n.p., 1640).

30.   Raymond Gillespie, "An Army Sent from God: Scots at War in Ireland, 1642–49" in *Scotland and War: AD 79–1918*, ed. Norman MacDougall (New York: Barnes and Noble, 1991), 129. For thorough accounts of the course of Irish history throughout the English Civil War, see Moody, *New History of Ireland*; Ohlmeyer, *Ireland, 1641–1660*; and Stevenson, *Scottish Covenanters*. For more information on the war in Ireland, see Jane H. Ohlmeyer, "The Wars of Religion, 1603–1660" in *A Military History of Ireland*, ed. Thomas Bartlett and Keith Jeffrey (Cambridge: Cambridge University Press, 1996): 160–187. Specifics regarding Scottish military efforts in Ireland, and especially Monro's role, may be found in Furgol, *Regimental History*; Gillespie, "Army Sent from God," 113–132; Hugh Hazlett, "The Recruitment and Organisation of the Scottish Army in Ulster, 1642–9) in *Essays in British and Irish History in Honour of James Eadie Todd*, ed. H. A. Cronne, T. W. Moody, and D. B. Quinn (London: Frederick Muller, 1949): 107–133; and Stuart Reid, *Scots Armies of the Civil War, 1639–1651* (Leigh-on-Sea: Partizan Press, 1982). Primary records regarding the war, which record correspondance to and from Monro, may be found in R. P. Mahaffy, ed., *Calendar of the State Papers Relating to Ireland, of the Reign of Charles I, 1633–1647* (London: H. M. Stationery Office, 1901) and C. S. Terry, ed., *Papers Relating to the Army of the Solemn League and Covenant, 1643–1647*, 2 vols., Scottish Historical Society, 2nd series, 16 and 17 (Edinburgh: T. and A. Constable, 1917).

31.   "Generall Major Monroe his Letter to Generall Lesley," May 13, 1642. *Published in A True Relation of the proceedings of the Scottish Armie now in Ireland by three Letters* (London: John Bartlet, 1642), 8. In *Expedition*, Monro explains the lessons he learned from Gustavus Adolphus, noting: "when he was weakest, he digged most in the ground . . . not onely to secure his Souldiers from the enemy, but also to keepe them from idlenesse" (*Expedition*, II–41). Reconnaissance for information and for keeping the enemy off guard was essential; a successful commander had to know "your Enemies Armie . . . you are to recognosce both his strength and order" (*Expedition*, II–204). That he did not have to encamp and that his sentries were never challenged was a mystery to Monro, at least at the time he wrote his letter, only a few weeks after he arrived in Ulster. In reality, what Monro experienced was a sample of guerrilla, rather than conventional, warfare.

32.   A recent interpretation—Ohlmeyer, "War of Religion," 180—notes that "the Confederate victory at Benburb can be attributed as much to the ability of the Catholic party to pay and supply the Army of Ulster with victuals, arms and munitions as to O'Neill's abilities as a military commander." The nature of warfare in Ireland during the period is analyzed by Rolf Loeber and Geoffrey Parker, "The Military Revolution in Seventeenth–Century Ireland" in Ohlmeyer, *Ireland, 1641–1660*, 66–88. Regarding Benburb, Loeber and Parker write (p. 73), "at the battle of Benburb in 1646 the confederate Army of Ulster, under Spanish–trained commanders, used the defensive techniques perfected by Habsburg troops to defeat a Scottish force, under Swedish–trained leaders, using the offensive tactics pioneered by Gustavus Adolphus." Tactics alone did not determine the outcome of Benburb; there were too many other factors involved. It is noteworthy that Robert Monro's name does not appear in the article. This may be due to the focus of the article (Irish Confederate efforts, not Covenanter or

parliamentary military efforts), but it is also indicative of the relatively low esteem assigned to Monro's military abilities.

33. Amougst is misspelled and no (sic) is inserted. The misspelled word is retained as it appears in the original, a practice utilized throughout this edition of *Expedition*. See the "Editor's Notes," xlv.

34. "Robert Monro to the Marquis of Argyll," June 11, 1646, in "The Lord Marques of Argyle's speech to a grand committee of both Houses of parliament the 25th of this instant June, 1646: together with some papers . . . and a letter from General Major Monro concerning the state of affairs in Ireland" (London: Printed for Lawrence Chapman, June 27, 1646). Monro's description of his army's "greater confidence" has been taken to mean that he was perhaps overconfident (Stevenson, *Scottish Covenanters*, 233), and hence incompetent (Turner, *Memoirs*, 23). He was probably making a statement regarding his faith in his soldiers at the time, a trust that was not rewarded with victory.

35. According to Stevenson, *Scottish Covenanters*, 310, Monro refused to involve himself in non-military matters. Although he often praised Gustavus Adolphus for his skill in melding military might with diplomacy ("covenants . . . cannot be made to keepe . . . but with stronger power, II–105), he himself acted in Ireland only as Scotland bade. The end of the first phase of the English Civil War in 1647, Scotland's support for Charles I, and the ensuing war between Parliament and Scotland left Monro in a precarious situation. His non-political stance left him vulnerable to intrigue, and the lack of pay for his troops further eroded his position as commander-in-chief of Scottish forces.

36. "A Letter concerning Colonel Monks surprising the Town and Castle of Carrickfergus and Belfast, in Ireland; and his taking General Major Monro prisoner" (London: n. p., 1648), states that Colonel George Monk convinced some in Monro's command to betray Carrickfergus by opening the town door to parliamentary forces. Stevenson, *Scottish Covenanters*, 263, cites other accounts which state that Monk's forces overpowered Monro's watch. In either case, the surprise and capture must have been particularly galling to Monro. He understood well that surprise was a necessary ally for victory, and he condemned in the strongest of terms those who allowed themselves to be surprised, particularly those caught sleeping. Monro describes three such incidents in *Expedition*: II–15, II–97, and II–178. Interestingly, Turner, a critic of Monro and of *Expedition* (see "Introduction," endnote 9), was himself captured by Scottish rebels in 1666. According to A. Crichton, ed., *Memoirs of Reverend John Blackadder* (Edinburgh: n.p., 1823), 136–138, Turner was taken in "his nightgown, nightcap, drawers and socks" hanging out of the window in a panic. Turner did admit to being surprised, but not to having panicked (Turner, *Memoirs*, 145–149).

37. Stevenson, *Scottish Covenanters*, 288. Monro warned of the dangers of being captured without funds in *Expedition*, I–24, when he instructs the officer "according to his station . . . to be well furnished of money . . . in a sure place, and in sure hands to maintaine him, being prisoner," else the time in prison would go badly.

38. Lady Montgomery was Monro's second wife. William Montgomery, comp., *The Montgomery Manuscripts (1603–1707)*, ed. George Hill (Belfast: Archer and Sons, 1869), 87–88, notes that Monro "had married Lady Jean Alexander, daughter of the first Earl of Stirling and widow of the second Viscount Montgomery of Ardes." His first wife, Jean, daughter of Walter Maver of Maverstone, Ireland, with whom he had a son and daughter (Mackenzie, *Monros of Fowlis*, 263–264), is referred to but once in *Expedition* (II–25), when Monro wrote that, in early 1630, "I went also to see my wife and Family; and having stayed but one night . . . I was not suffered in three yeares time to returne."

39. Montgomery, *Montgomery Manuscripts*, 169.

40. Montgomery, *Montgomery Manuscripts*, 168–169.

41. Montgomery, *Montgomery Manuscripts*, 213. Hill, annotator of the manuscripts, notes that, according to a will being probated in 1680, Monro was listed as owing £8.5s, which would probably not have been recorded were Monro deceased at the time. Mackenzie, *Monros of Fowlis*, 264, lists Monro's date of death as 1675.

42. Literature pertaining to the debate over a "Military Revolution" in early modern Europe is extensive. Michael Roberts, *The Military Revolution, 1560–1660* (Belfast: Marjory Boyd, 1956) and Parker, *Military Revolution*, are essential for understanding the thesis. For an overview of the debate, see Clifford J. Rogers, ed., *The Military Revolution Debate: Readings on the Military Transformation of Early Modern Europe* (Boulder, Colo.: Westview, 1995). See also Andre Corvisier, *Armies and Societies in Europe, 1494–1789*, trans. Abagail T. Siddall (Bloomington: Indiana University Press, 1978); Martin Van Creveld, *Supplying War* (London: Cambridge University Press, 1977); and Jack S. Levy, *War in the Modern Great Power System, 1495–1975* (Lexington: Kentucky University Press, 1983).

43. V. G. Kiernan, "Foreign Mercenaries and Absolute Monarchy," *Past and Present* 11 (1957): 66–86; reprinted in *Crisis in Europe, 1560–1660*, ed. Trevor Aston (London: Routledge and Kegan Paul, 1965), 139.

44. See Fritz Redlich, *De Praeda Militari: Looting and Booty 1500–1815*, Vierteljahrschrift für Sozial– und Wirtschaftsgeschichte, vol. 39 (Wiesbaden: Franz Steiner Verlag, 1956) and Fritz Redlich, *The German Military Enterpriser and His Work Force*, Vierteljahrschrift für Sozial– und Wirtschaftsgeschichte, vols. 47 and 48 (Wiesbaden: Franz Steiner Verlag, 1964 and 1965). See also William S. Brockington, Jr., "The Usage of Scottish Mercenaries by the Anti–Imperial Forces in the Thirty Years' War" (Master's thesis, University of South Carolina, 1968).

45. From earliest times Scotland and England were frequently at war, with the worst period being the three centuries after 1286. In that year the death without issue of Alexander III of Scotland led to a claim on the Scottish crown by the English king, Edward I. Scottish nobles swiftly sought an alliance with France which virtually assured hostility between Scotland and England for the next 275 years. Between 1286 and 1568, there were at least twenty–two major invasions of Scotland by England, with Scotland suffering disastrous defeats on at least nine occasions. Unfortunately for Scotland, victories over England were rare, with Bannockburn (1314) the only one of significance. For a general history of Scotland, see Gordon Donaldson, ed., *The Edinburgh History of Scotland*, 4 vols. (London: David and Charles, 1965–1977). For the chronology and brief descriptions of Scottish military history, as well as of general military history, see R. E. Dupuy and T. N. Dupuy, *The Encyclopedia of Military History from 3500 B.C. to the Present*, 2nd rev. ed. (New York: Harper and Row, 1986); MacDougall, *Scotland and War*; and John Sadler, *Scottish Battles from Mons Graupius to Culloden* (Edinburgh: Canongate, 1996).

46. Between 1406 and 1567 seven consecutive monarchs acceded to the throne at an average age of five. Even upon reaching their majority, monarchs were seldom provided the opportunity to extend their power. Two were murdered and two died while at war. A fifth died suddenly after a major military disaster, and a sixth abdicated. Only the last died peacefully, still a monarch. In the 176 years between the accession of James I and the attainment of his majority by James VI, a Scottish monarch actually ruled for only 99 of those years. It is reasonable to believe that a substantial proportion of the time a monarch actually ruled was spent trying to regain control of his kingdom. Noble factionalism, coupled with bloodfeuds and with a violence–prone honor code, frequently resulted in inter–clan warfare and feuds, which added to the anarchy that existed for long periods in Scottish history. R. A. Houston and I. D. Whyte, eds., *Scottish Society, 1500–*

*1800* (Cambridge: Cambridge University Press, 1989), includes several significant articles pertaining to various social developments of the period, including R. A. Dodgson, "'Pretense of Blude' and 'Place of Thair Dwelling': The Nature of the Highland Clans, 1500–1745," 169–198. See also K. M. Brown, *Bloodfeud in Scotland, 1573–1625: Violence Justice and Politics in an Early Modern Society* (Edinburgh: John Donald, 1986) for the changes in Scotland during the reign of James VI. Michael Lynch, in "National Identity in Ireland and Scotland, 1500–1640" in *Nations, Nationalism and Patriotism in the European Past*, ed. Claus Bjørn, Alexander Grant and Keith J. Stinger (Copenhagen: Academic Press, 1994), 116–117, succinctly comments that, "Scotland, still in the early seventeenth century a highly decentralised collection of pays largely held together by lordship and kindred . . . [was] a feudal realm undergoing rapid and bewildering change."

47. Mortality crises are historical events that endanger large segments of a specific population. War, famine, and plague are the most severe types of mortality crisis. The more severe the crisis, the greater the population pressure, that is, the greater the stress on the indigenous population and the more likely for there to be demographic movement.

48. Scotland, a small country of only 30,114 square miles, two-thirds of which is mountainous and incapable of supporting a large population, is about three-fifths the size of England (or about the size of the state of South Carolina). In the early modern era, most Scots survived through subsistence farming, for even with a temperate climate, a copious rainfall coupled with normally cloudy skies made farming difficult in most of Scotland even under the best of conditions. With inhospitable weather and terrain already working against them, the Scots compounded their difficulties through deforestation and poor farming techniques, which, in turn, led to extensive erosion. In years when there was drought, when it rained at the wrong time, or other climate changes resulted in a shortened growing season, crop failures resulted in widespread misery and suffering.

49. The early 1550s, 1560–1562, 1571–1573, and 1585–1587 were years of severe grain shortage, or dearth; while 1594–1598 was a period of severe famine in Scotland, as well as throughout Europe. There were also many other periods of localized dearth or famine. Only heavy grain imports from the Continent, when grain was available for sale, alleviated severe grain shortages. If the conditions that caused the famine in Scotland also caused crop failures throughout Europe, Scots had little choice but starvation or flight. Visitations of the plague usually accompanied famine, although the former occurred at other times as well. Severe outbreaks occurred in 1568–1569, 1574, 1584–1588, 1597–1599, and 1600–1609. Disease only added to the pressures on the population of Scotland. Mortality crisis information is from L. M. Cullen and T. C. Smout, *Comparative Aspects of Scottish and Irish Economic and Social History, 1600–1900* (Edinburgh: John Donald, 1976); T. M. Devine, "Social Responses to Agrarian 'Improvement': the Highland and Lowland Clearances in Scotland," in Houston and Whyte, *Scottish Society*, 169–198; Michael Flinn, *Scottish Population History from the 17th Century to the 1930s* (Cambridge: Cambridge University Press, 1977); T. B. Franklin, *A History of Scottish Farming* (London: Thomas Nelson and Sons, 1952); S. G. E. Lythe, *The Economy of Scotland in Its European Setting, 1550–1625* (London: Oliver and Boyd, 1969); *RPCS*, three series, 1569–1707, various editors, 37 vols.; T. C. Smout, "Famine and Famine-relief in Scotland," in L. M. Cullen and T. C. Smount, eds., *Comparative Aspects of Scottish and Irish Economic and Social History, 1600–1900* (Edinburgh: John Donald, 1976); T. C. Smout and Alexander Fenton, "Scottish Agriculture before the Improvers—An Exploration," *The Agricultural History Review*, vol. 13, part 2 (1965): 73–93; David Turnock, *The Historical Geography of Scotland since 1707* (Cambridge: Cambridge University Press, 1982); and G. Whittington and

I. D. Whyte, *An Historical Geography of Scotland* (New York: Academic Press, 1983). Agricultural changes and the price revolution left both Scottish nobles and their tenants financially hard–pressed in an era of inflation. T. M. Devine and S. G. E. Lythe, "The Economy of Scotland under James VI: A Revision Article" in *Scottish Historical Review*, vol. 50 (October 1971): 91–106, analyzes these trends. For an analysis of pressures to leave the land and demographic movement, see I. D. Whyte, "Population Mobility in Early Modern Scotland" in Houston and Whyte, *Scottish Society*, 37–58. In good times, Whyte concludes, betterment was the primary factor (pp. 43–54); but in hard times, subsistence was the motivation (pp. 54–57).

50.   The general pacification of the British Isles aided in the emigration to continental wars. James VI (1567–1625) finally controlled political violence in Scotland, and his accession to the throne of England in 1603 ended the dynastic wars with England. Ireland had once been a significant place for military opportunity; but the Elizabethan Wars for English control of Ireland, coupled with the efforts of James I to pacify Ireland, eliminated most opportunities. For information regarding Scots and the plantations of Ulster, see Michael Perceval–Maxwell, *The Scottish Migration to Ulster in the Reign of James I* (London: Routledge and Kegan Paul, 1973); Raymond Gillespie, *Colonial Ulster: The Settlement of East Ulster, 1600–1641* (Cork: Cork University Press, 1985); and P. S. Robinson, *The Plantation of Ulster: British Settlement in an Irish Landscape, 1600–1670* (New York: St. Martin's, 1984).

51.   Monro was quite proud that Gustavus Adolphus praised the Scots in front of the entire army after Leipzig (*Expedition*, II–66) and after the Battle of Alte Feste (*Expedition*, II–159).   Gustavus Adolphus also referred to them as his "Scottish Invincibles," this according to Mackay, *Scots Brigade*, 139.

52.   Information pertaining to Scottish officers who left the British Isles for the Baltic is from many sources, including: *Expedition*; A. Francis Steuart, ed., *Papers Relating to the Scots in Poland, 1576–1793* (Edinburgh: The Scottish Historical Society, 1915); *The Swedish Intelligencer* (London: Nathaniel Butter and Nicholas Bourne, 1633–34); and Turner, *Memoirs*.   Calendars, reference works, and registers that provide information include *Calendar of State Papers of England, 1611–1649* (*CSPD*), Domestic Series, 25 vols., various editors (London: H. M. Stationery Office, 1858–1898); *Calendar of State Papers Relating to Scotland* [*CSPS*]. 13 vols., various editors (Edinburgh: H. M. Stationery Office, 1881–1970); *DNB*; Sir Sydney Lee, ed., *The Concise Dictionary of National Biography*, Part 1, *From the Beginnings to 1900* (London: Oxford University Press, 1965); and the *RPCS*, all series.   Secondary sources of value were Alf Aberg, "Scottish Soldiers in the Swedish Armies in the Sixteenth and Seventeenth Centuries" in *Scotland and Scandinavia, 800–1800*, ed. by Grant G. Simpson (Edinburgh: John Donald, 1990); I. R. Bartlett, "Scottish Mercenaries in Europe, 1570–1640: A Study in Attitudes and Policies" in *Scottish Tradition*, 13 (1986): 15–24; Richard Brzezinski, "British Mercenaries in the Baltic, 1560–1683 (1)" in *Military Illustrated Past and Present*, vol. 4 (December 1986/January 1987): 7–23, and "British Mercenaries in the Baltic, 1560–1683 (2)" in *Military Illustrated Past and Present*, vol. 6 (April/May 1987): 29–35; Richard Brzezinski, *The Army of Gustavus Adolphus*, vol. 2, *Infantry*, vol. 262 of Osprey Military Men–at–Arms Series (London: Osprey, 1992); Richard Brzezinski and Richard Hook, *The Army of Gustavus Adolphus*, vol. 1, *Infantry*, vol. 35 of Osprey Military Men–at–Arms Series (London: Osprey, 1991); James Dow, *Ruthven's Army in Sweden and Esthonia* (Historiskt Archiv 13; Stockholm: Kungl. Vitterhets Historie Och Antikvitets Akedemien, 1965); Paul Dukes, "The Leslie Family in the Swedish Period (1630–35) of the Thirty Years' War," *European Studies Review*, 12 (1982): 401–24; James A. Fallon, "Scottish Mercenaries in the Service of Denmark and Sweden, 1626–1632" (Ph.D. dissertation, University of

Glasgow, 1972); Thomas A. Fischer, *The Scots in Prussia, The Scots in Germany*, and *The Scots in Sweden* (Edinburgh: Otto Schulze, 1903, 1902, and 1907, respectively); James Grant, *Cavaliers of Fortune* (London: Routledge, Warnes, and Routledge, 1859), *Memoirs and Adventures of Sir John Hepburn, Commander of the Scots Brigade under Gustavus Adolphus* (Edinburgh: William Blackwood and Sons, 1851), and *The Scottish Soldiers of Fortune* (London: George Routledge and Sons, 1889); G. G. Simpson, ed., *Scotland and Scandinavia, 800–1800* (Edinburgh: John Donald, 1990); Smout, T. C, ed., *Scotland and Europe, 1200–1850* (Edinburgh: John Donald, 1986); and Spalding, *Memorialls of the Trubles.*

53.   William S. Brockington, Jr., "Expanding Professions in the Seventeenth Century: Scottish Military Entrepreneurs in the Early Modern Era" (paper presented at the Carolinas Symposium on British Studies, Birmingham, Ala., October 1991).

54.   There were four major periods of war in the Empire: Bohemian Revolt, 1618–1620; Danish Intervention and Habsburg Victory, 1625–1629; Swedish Invasion, 1630–1634; and French Intervention, 1635–1648. Strategically, the Thirty Years' War was but one theater: the Austrian Habsburgs were seeking control of the Holy Roman Empire, and the Spanish Habsburgs were waging war in Flanders, Valtelline, and Franche–Comté, among other places. All the conflicts were related; Monro was acutely aware of the widespread nature of the war, for he continually referred to diplomatic and military activities, particularly during the Swedish phase (*Expedition*, II: 99–110).

55.   For an interpretative overview with extensive bibliography, see Geoffrey Parker, *The Thirty Years' War*, 2nd ed. (New York: Routledge, 1997). A sample of works pertaining to the Thirty Years' War in the European setting would include: Gunter Barudio, *Der Teutsche Krieg, 1618–1648* (Frankfurt a. Main: S. Fischer Verlag, 1985); Herbert Langer, *The Thirty Years' War* (Dorset, U.K.: Blandford, 1980); Stephen J. Lee, *The Thirty Years' War* (London: Routledge, 1992); Peter Limm, *The Thirty Years' War*, Seminar Studies in History (New York: Longman Group, 1984); David Maland, *Europe at War, 1600–1650* (London: Macmillan Press, 1980); Theodore K. Rabb, ed., *The Thirty Years' War*, 2nd ed. (New York: University Press of America, 1981); S. H. Steinberg, *The Thirty Years' War and the Conflict for European Hegemony, 1600–1660*, Foundations of Modern History, ed. A. Goodwin (New York: W. W. Norton, 1966); and C. V. Wedgewood, *The Thirty Years War* (London: Lowe and Brydone, 1938).

56.   Between 1624 and 1642, twenty-seven levies for over 38,500 men for the Baltic were authorized by Charles I and the Privy Council of Scotland. Various other levy authorizations included 3,800 for the Low Countries, 10,400 for France, and at least 2,900 in assorted other commissions (*RPCS*). Military entrepreneurs first received a license for a unit from a foreign king. This was followed by a request to the king; and then, in conjunction with the king's permission, the Privy Council of Scotland was petitioned. When a license was granted, recruiting then took place. The authorizations are truly astonishing figures, for if all levies were met and if the population were between 850,000 (W. Croft Dickinson, *Scotland from the Earliest Times to 1603*, 3rd ed. Archibald A. M. Duncan, ed. [Oxford: Clarendon, 1977], 374) to one million (Flinn, *Scottish Population*, 147), this would have been between 4 and 5 percent of the total population of Scotland. Calculating the adult male population at 150,000, the levied number for the Baltic alone would have equaled one-fourth of the adult male population of Scotland, a figure that doubtless was not reached.

57.   During the Thirty Years' War mortality crises aided the recruiters in their recruiting. The years 1621–1625, 1628–1630, and 1634–1636 were dearth or famine years in Scotland; and plague was especially bad between 1644 and 1648. The multitude of continental wars disrupted trade, and the civil wars which began in 1639 exacerbated the problems.

58.  See Elmer A. Beller, *Propaganda in Germany during the Thirty Years' War* (Princeton: Princeton University Press, 1940); William A. Coupe, *The German Illustrated Broadsheet in the Seventeenth Century*, 2 vols. (Baden–Baden: Verlag Librarie Heitz, 1967); and John Roger Paas, *The German Political Broadsheet, 1600– 1700*, vols. 4–5 (Wiesbaden: O. Harrassowitz, 1985).  A collection of *German Broadsheets* (1618–1648) may be viewed in the British Library.  Samples of contemporary printed materials include Hans Jakob Christoffel von Grimmelshausen, *Der Abenteuerliche Simplicius Simplicissimus*, 1669 edition (München: W. Goldman, 1961); *Swedish Intelligencer*; John Taylor, *Taylor, his travels, from the City of London in England to the City of Prague in Bohemia . . . with many relations worthy of note* (London: N. Okes, 1620); and Philip Vincent, *The Lamentations of Germany* (London: E. G for J. Rothwell, 1638).

59.  See Peter Burschel, "Krieg als Lebensform: Über ein Tagebuch" [review of *Ein Söldnerleben im Dreissigjährigen Krieg. Eine quelle zur Sozialgeschichte*, ed. Jan Peters (Berlin: Akademie–Verlag, 1993)] *Göttingschen Gelehrten Anzeiger* 246 (1994): 263–272.  Burschel references other contemporary accounts by military men, all of whom wrote in German.  The only other work in English with a significant amount of material regarding service in the Thirty Years' War is Turner, *Memoirs*, but only the first fifteen pages discuss his war experiences.  There are accounts in English of specific battles or experiences, but nothing like *Expedition*.

60.  Fallon, "Scottish Mercenaries," 92, lists nineteen Scottish nobles who served in the 1624–1635 era.  The Marquis of Hamilton; the Earls of Argyle, Nithsdale, Crawford, Lothian, Buccleuch, and Irvine; and the Baron of Foulis were but some of the Scottish nobles who became military entrepreneurs in hopes of achieving personal glory and economic advancement.  Sir Patrick Ruthven, Sir Robert Douglas, and Sir James King were younger sons of Scottish nobles who became generals for Sweden in the Thirty Years' War.  Family ties were very important for receiving contracts and for success in recruiting.  "In the wars of the seventeenth century, especially in Germany, under Gustavus Adolphus, there were engaged three generals, eight Colonels, five Lieutenant–colonels, eleven Majors, and above thirty captains, besides a great number of subalterns, of the name of Munro" (Mackenzie, *Munros of Fowlis*, 88).  Grimble, *Mackay*, 79, notes that Sir Donald had "3000 men whom it was apparently estimated that Mackay could still call to arms among his clansmen."  This figure is based upon a statement in a letter (included in the Reay family papers) from Sir Robert Gordon, who was at the court of James I, which stated that Mackay "assembled in a few months about the number of three thousand men," which was the number permitted by the royal warrant."

61.  Roberts, in *Gustavus Adolphus*, 2 vols. (London: Longmans, Green, 1953 and 1958, respectively); Roberts, *Military Revolution*; and Roberts, *The Swedish Imperial Experience, 1560–1718* (Cambridge: Cambridge University Press, 1979), emphasizes this aspect of the Swedish king as a critical element in his leadership and for his success on the battlefield.  Monro agreed absolutely with his principle of promotion (*Expedition*, II–13, II–35, II– 42, II–95, II–119).

62.  *Expedition*, Intro–2.

63.  Monro frequently expresses his own motives for becoming a soldier.  It was his duty to serve the grandson of his king.  *Expedition* was dedicated to Prince Charles Louis, son of Elizabeth of Bohemia (*Expedition*, I–3, I–21, and II–93), the daughter of James I; Charles Louis's father, Frederick V of the Palatinate and King of Bohemia had died in 1632.  Monro wished to return to the conflict in hopes of restoring his monarch's grandson to his rightful throne (*Expedition*, I–5, II–109).  He often expresses his pro– Calvinist/Protestant bias (*Expedition*, I–5, II–101); and his anti–Catholic and anti–

Habsburg bias was demonstrated almost as frequently, especially when discussing war atrocities (*Expedition*, I–39, II–124, II–156). He dismisses the latter group as "our adversaries and their damned crew of Jesuits and Monkes" (*Expedition*, II–167).

64. *Expedition*, I–3.

65. *Expedition*, I–36.

66. Virtù or vertù, in the medieval Christian sense, meant humility and chastity. Renaissance humanists redefined it more along classical lines, and virtù came to stand for manly valor in time of struggle. Machiavelli, for example, believed that "virtuous soldiers are strong and brave, virtuous generals intelligent and determined" (Niccolò Machiavelli, *The Prince*, ed. and trans. by David Wootton [Indianapolis: Hackett Publishing, 1995], xxix). "Virtue, to a Roman, was not humility or gentleness or peace, but virility, manliness, courage with energy and intelligence. This is what Machiavelli means by virtù," this according to Will Durant, *The Renaissance: A History of Civilization in Italy from 1304–1576 A.D.* Part V, *The Story of Civilization* (New York: Simon and Schuster, 1953) 556. Roberts, *Gustavus Adolphus*, vol. 2, 238, provides the Swedish king's own definition, which may also have influenced Monro's attitude regarding vertue: "Summa, I expect of him, under the article 'Virtue,' that he shall be of good life and conversation, diligent in ordering, laborious in performance, valourous in danger, various in his capacities, and swift in execution."

67. *Expedition*, I–3. His passion for vertue is a recurring theme throughout *Expedition*.

68. *Expedition*, Intro–7. Monro asserted that earning a reputation was worth far more than wealth or position, a message he espoused from beginning ("The world hath nothing so glorious as vertue," *Expedition*, I–13) to end ("For we are not worthy the name of Souldiers, if we glory [as many doe] more in gathering riches [that perish faster than they come] than we doe to get an immortall good name," *Expedition*, II–179). Perhaps this is the attitude of one who did not accumulate wealth abroad, and perhaps he truly believed this. Certainly the tone of the entire work lends credence to the latter.

69. Monro's opinion that Scottish mercenary captains in particular, and Scottish units in general, were capable and valued additions to the Protestant armies of the German wars is validated by the number of contracts issued to Scottish military entrepreneurs [see "Introduction," endnote 56]. However, in those continental armies in which mercenaries served, although upper class Europeans might accept upper class Scots, mercenaries were still viewed as foreigners. It required a longer period of time for the Scots to achieve rank, and promotion was often slow. In an era when knowledge of hygiene was nonexistent, and since Scots were often viewed merely as cannon fodder, many simply vanished from the records. In a survey of 1,106 Scottish officers who emigrated to the Baltic region between 1570 and 1660, 642 (58 per cent) were mentioned only once. Rarely was there any indication of their origins or of what happened to them. If they survived, served a successful monarch, and were talented in military matters, their chances of "making it" were good. Of course, most quit, died, or remained subordinate officers; but those who succeeded served to remind others that success could be achieved. From William S. Brockington, Jr., "Scottish Military Emigrants in the Early Modern Era: An Analysis of Demographic Movement in an Emergent Society, 1570–1660" (paper presented at the Southern Conference on British Studies, Fort Worth, Tex., November 1991). See also Mary Elizabeth Ailes, "From British Mercenaries to Swedish Nobles: the Immigration of British Soldiers to Sweden during the Seventeenth Century" (Ph.D. diss., University of Minnesota, 1997), and Fallon, "Scottish Mercenaries."

70. In cultural anthropology, a kinship system is the manner by which a society identifies relatives. A clan is a kinship system which traces its origin to a single ancestor; Scottish clans are patrilineal, although matrilineal lines can claim affiliated status with

the dominant clan. A kinship set is the interrelated group *in toto*; the alliance between the Mackay and Monro clans is an example of this. When Scots went abroad, their alien status often forced the extension of kinship sets to all Scots, point-of-origin notwithstanding. This primary group cohesion is a fundamental element of nationalism, and *Expedition* provides a clear example of this evolution.

71. Monro obviously enjoyed the adventure of soldiering, for he begins his narrative with "Who then would disdaine to follow warres, might be thought unwise" (*Expedition*, I–1). Soldiering was an integral part of vertue, Scottishness, and opportunity.

72. Monro praises the fighting prowess of Scots throughout *Expedition*, from, "I never did see more durable men against all Toyle, travell and tediousness, than they were" (*Expedition*, I:16) to "It was the custome observed ordinarily by his Majesty of Sweden, to make use of our countrimen on service, wherein he desired they should shew themselves examplary to others . . . in honour of the nation, that was ever glorious abroad" (*Expedition*, II–82). It pleased Monro that Gustavus Adolphus triumphed "with the helpe of the nation which was never conquered by any forraine enemy, the invincible Scots" (*Expedition*, II–68). He was particularly proud that few Scots served Catholic masters. Monro tells of one Scotsman who fought bravely for the other side but was killed in battle (*Expedition*, I–11). After the Battle of Leipzig/Breitenfeld (1631), Monro received permission to recruit Britons from those captured but found only three Irishmen, whom he declined to take (*Expedition*, II–73). Two Scots who served in the Imperial Army, and whom Monro found particularly praiseworthy, were Major Walter Leslie and Colonel John Gordon. Those two were captured at Nuremberg and spent five weeks with their follow Scots, "where we made merry as friends" (*Expedition*, II–145). It may also be that Monro's opinion of Leslie and Gordon was elevated by their participation in the assassination of Wallenstein on February 24, 1634, an account of which may be read in J. M. Bullock, *The Gay Gordons* (London: Chapman and Hall, 1908), 32–39.

73. Monro "expresse(s) my love, and thankfulnesse to my country, and to my deere Camerades, Britaines, Dutch and Swedens, (companions, not of wants, but of valour) eternizing their memory" in his dedication (*Expedition*, Intro–3). Monro's preference was that "his Armie should be all of Britaines, Dutch, and Irish" (*Expedition*, I–38), this before he served with the Swedes. Monro considered Germans to be good diggers (*Expedition*, II:39–41), but not particularly good soldiers, as they surrendered too quickly and changed sides too easily (*Expedition*, I:24–27). Monro never considered the Danes to be good soldiers (*Expedition*, I–61) and felt the Italians to be "silly simple . . . and without courage" (*Expedition*, II–15), this after their being surprised in garrison. Indeed, Monro never hesitated to comment on the soldierly qualities of any group. That this Scottish "national characteristic" identified by Monro is yet a popular topic for presentation may be seen in John Baynes with John Laffin, *Soldiers of Scotland* (London: Brassey's Defence Publishers, 1988) or Stephen Wood, *The Scottish Soldier* (Manchester: Archive Publications, 1987).

74. Monro almost never mentions the lower classes except as a group, a significant statement regarding class separation in the era. He refers to Scots rank and file as "resolute and stout soldiers" (*Expedition*, I–13), and notes that "Our Scottish High-land-men are prayse-worthy, who . . . made use of their vertue and courage in swimming the seas . . . they would not stay to be Prisoners" (*Expedition*, I–55). Interestingly, the term "Highland" is used just twice (*Expedition*, I–15 and I–55), despite the probability that most of the initial levy were Highlanders as well as a substantial number of later recruits. This omission may have been for several reasons: later Scottish levies came from throughout Scotland and he simply called all the recruits Scots; many in his reading audience would have recognized the differences between Highlanders and Lowlanders

and he did not need to make the distinction for them; and, for those who did not know the difference, a constant reminder of the distinctions would have been quite parochial, something Monro did not wish to be.

75. *Expedition*, I–37.

76. *Expedition*, II–164.

77. *Expedition*, Intro–7.

78. *Expedition*, II–136. Monro wrote earlier, "I remarked, so far as I could by report, the actions of others" (*Expedition*, II–99).

79. The most obvious reason for concluding that Monro used *The Swedish Intelligencer* is the amount of detail included in Part II vis-à-vis the lack of detail in Part I. Persons other than Scots and places beyond the environs of the regiment are much more in evidence in Part II. The presentation of material is quite similar, especially regarding matters such as treaty details and dates. On the other hand, specific information pertaining to the Scots in general and to Mackay's/Monro's Regiment in particular does not appear in *The Swedish Intelligencer*. This information, therefore, had to have come from Monro.

80. *Expedition*, II:147–152. When Gustavus Adolphus prepared to follow Wallenstein, he ordered the Scots Brigade to remain in "Schwabland" in order to build itself back up to strength, "considering the weakenesse of both our Regiments, that were weakned by the toyle of warre." "His Majesty then taking leave of our Briggad, in view of the whole Army thanked us for our former service, and in particular he expressed his affection unto me" (*Expedition*, II–159).

81. *Expedition*, II:162–170.

82. Two accounts which were circulating in London after 1633 may have been available to Monro and might well have provided him with some necessary information. "The Great and Famous Battle of Lützen . . . faithfully translated out of the French copy" (1633) and reprinted in *The Harleian Miscellany*, 3rd ed., vol. 4 (London 1809): 197–210, and George Fleetwood, "Letter to his Father, giving an account of the Battle of Lützen and the Death of Gustavus Adolphus" (1633) and reprinted in *Camden Miscellany*, ed. Sir P. G. Malpas–Egerton, vol. 1 (London: Camden Society, 1847. In addition, he might well have seen other letters or discussed the battle with some of the survivors.

83. Only the last was an important action strategically. Oldenburg (*Expedition*, I:17–21) was the first significant action by the regiment, which held a key position for a day before being evacuated (late September 1627). The loss of the castle of Breddenburg (*Expedition*, I:38–41) was a disaster for the regiment, with four companies of Scots massacred (September 1627). Monro was not present and his account is based upon the story of a survivor, lending credence to the probability that Monro took notes for later reflection.

84. It is also possible that the lack of a work for the Danish period comparable to *The Swedish Intelligencer* is a factor in the lack of detail. A less complex reason may be that the Danish war was further removed in time from his memory, and the more recent Swedish campaign was fresher in his mind. An even simpler explanation is that it was not as interesting to reflect upon the disastrous Danish actions as it was to analyze the successes of Gustavus Adolphus. The Swedish king validated everything Monro believed and was therefore worth preserving in greater detail.

85. Descriptions of his unit's action at Oldenburg (*Expedition*, I:17–19), the evacuation by sea after defeat at Oldenburg (*Expedition*, I:26–28), an attack on Aickilfourd (*Expedition*, I:50–51), or the failure of an attack on Kiel (*Expedition*, I:53–55) are excellent samples of "worm's eye view" writing and also superb battle descriptions. Monro's limited military experience coupled with his lack of access to

military information is reflected by his apparent reluctance to venture beyond the boundaries of his own, immediate knowledge. Nor does Monro offer insight regarding the interrelationships between various units during action. He rarely connects his tactical experience with a strategic vision and seldom digresses into political and military issues of which he had little knowledge or about which he had little understanding or concern. Even in hindsight, Monro did not broaden his perspective or provide more information, which could also indicate a lack of interest in the failures of the Danes.

86. Stralsund (*Expedition*, I:64–81) was seven weeks of virtually nonstop fighting, but the regiment's vertue sustained both the defenders and the town. Monro's account of the fighting at Straslund is probably the most often cited section of *Expedition*. This is due, in part, to the strategic significance of the battle, for Imperial general Albrecht von Wallenstein was defeated for the first time. It is also due to Monro's graphic descriptions in *Expedition* of the battle. Monro took justifiable pride in his regiment's success against Wallenstein.

87. The Scots Brigade, under overall command of Sir John Hepburn, comprised Mackay's, Colonel Lumsden's, Colonel Stargate's, and Hepburn's Regiments (*Expedition*, II–25). Its size ranged from several thousand (at incorporation in March 1631, with each regiment consisting of eight hundred to one thousand) to several hundred (after the attack on the Alte Feste).

88. It was an honor to have served under a great leader such as Gustavus Adolphus, to whom Monro referred as "the Invincible" or as "stout," meaning exceptionally brave (*Expedition*, II–6, 70). Gustavus Adolphus liked to converse with his officers and men: "We see . . . his Majesties disposition in entertaining his Officers kindly . . . esteeming them not as servants, but as companions" (*Expedition*, II–42). The Swedish king liked Monro, for, upon parting from the Scots Brigade, in September 1632, "in particular he expressed his affection unto me" (*Expedition*, II–159). That Monro idolized his former master may be seen in his assertion "O would to God I had once such a Leader againe to fight such an other day" (*Expedition*, II–70).

89. *Expedition*, II 1–2, is one of several places where this can be seen. However, wee can become we within the same paragraph or sentence, as may be seen at I–5.

90. A comparison of any document included in *RPCS* and documents from the *CSPD* makes the differences clear.

91. Stevenson, *Scottish Covenanters*, 131–2, provides the quote, noting that "Monro himself fought on foot with a pike, furiously shouting to his men as they gave ground."

92. Sir Thomas Kellie, *Pallas Armata or Militarie Instructions* (Edinburgh 1627), reprinted as part of *The English Experience: Its Record in Early Printed Books*, vol. 331 (New York: Da Capo, 1969), is an excellent example with which to compare *Expedition*. Published at about the same time, the 121 pages of Kellie's work are filled with Latin phrases, esoteric materials, and baroque prose. Monro probably had two purposes in mind as he dictated: to produce a work that met the standards of the day and to demonstrate his own erudition and learning to an audience that did not normally respect younger sons of Highland cadet lines, thereby elevating his own status. At the 1997 Carolinas Symposium on British Studies, Professor Charles Carleton of the Department of History at North Carolina State University provided this insight regarding social status and military success. Monro noted the distinction when he commented that "It should then be the duety of brave Generalls to make choice of brave and vertuous Commanders, not asking of whom they come, but where, and how long, have they practiced to be vertuous" (*Expedition*, I–20).

93. Examples include action at the Pass at Oldenburg, October 1627 (*Expedition*, I:20–27); the siege at Stralsund, June/July 1628 (*Expedition*, I:62–80), the assault on

Frankfurt on the Oder, April 1631 (II:32–35), the Battle of Breitenfeld, or Leipzig, September 1631 (*Expedition*, II:69–71), the attack on the castle at Würzburg, October 1631 (*Expedition*, II:78–81), and the attack on the Alte Feste, August/September 1632 (*Expedition*, II:147–150).

94. The storming of Frankfurt on the Oder, April 1631, is a sample of the horror of a city being sacked (*Expedition*, II:32–35).

95. At Ingolstadt, in April 1632, Monro's unit stood in battle order throughout the night. He wrote that it "was the longest night in the year . . . and he . . . who would sweare he was not afrighted . . . I would not trust him again" (*Expedition*, II–120).

96. The exhilaration of victory is described after Breitenfeld/Leipzig (*Expedition*, II:62–63).

97. *Expedition*, I–19.

98. A sample of garrison life may be found in *Expedition*, I:15–16. Monro compares the various beers of Germany, noting that his "choice of all beeres is Serbester beere, being the wholsomest for the body, and cleerest from all filth or barme, as their Religion (being good Calvinists) is best for the soule, and cleerest from the dregs of superstition" (*Expedition*, II–48).

99. Christian IV was a good paymaster, and Monro often complimented the Danish king on this score (*Expedition*, I–34, II–84). Pay that was slow in coming lowered morale and lessened loyalty. Gustavus Adolphus did not have the resources that Christian IV had, and his paymasters were often in arrears (*Expedition*, II:86–87, II–131).

100. Relations with farmers were dangerous, at best; and woe to the soldier caught alone by a group of farmers (*Expedition*, I:46–50, I–62, II–144). Townspeople liked the soldiers little more even if the soldiers were protecting them (*Expedition*, I:64–65).

101. "Fie then upon those judgements, that, for their owne aymes, hatch the Ruine of their Camerades, in fore-thinking, and pursuing evil . . . (to) plot the fall of their Camerades" (*Expedition*, I–13).

102. "Courage should grow by frequencie of danger . . . (although) when he comes abroade to the warres, at first, the thundering of the Cannon and Musket roaring in his eares makes him sicke, before he come neere danger" (*Expedition*, II–69).

103. Sickness was ever present (*Expedition*, II:10, 53), although Monro averred that "many died of pestilence and flux: but of our Nation fewest" (*Expedition*, I–16). The "accidents of war" meant that soldiers never knew when death would come (*Expedition*, II–155). For example, Monro describes how a single cannonball killed fourteen soldiers at Stralsund (*Expedition*, I–66). Even duels for honor killed men before their time (*Expedition*, I–82).

104. Monro clearly had standards by which he judged various commanders. See "Glossary of Persons," 387, for a listing of commanders and a brief biographical sketch.

105. Monro could not praise Gustavus Adolphus highly enough. Monro thought well of Christian IV's personal character (*Expedition*, I–35, I–54) but not of his military acumen. His greatest praise for Christian IV was reserved for the Danish king's ability to pay well and promptly (*Expedition*, I–34, I–84).

106. Monro was outraged by the disloyalty of the princes Gustavus Adolphus had come to save, calling them "cowards" who, "through their covetousnesse and niggardly sparing bin the cause and instruments of their owne overthrowes" (*Expedition*, II:196–197). He deemed Gustavus Adolphus a great negotiator and politician, capable of even-handed decisions, such as his Edict over all Franconia which provided for religious toleration (*Expedition*, II–85), or strong positions, such as his rebuke of the French ambassador who demanded that the Swedes leave the area of the Rhine (II–100). Carl von Clausewitz, *On War*, vol. 3, trans. by J. J. Graham and annotated by F. N. Maude. (London: Routledge and Kegan Paul, 1966), 106, notes that Gustavus Adolphus "had his

centre of gravity in his Army," which gave him great power as long as he was victorious. Monro was acutely aware that the Swedish king's power rested on his success on the battlefield.

107. His view of women may be seen in his description of Elizabeth of Bohemia, whom he described as "most resplendent in brightnesse of minde, *for a woman*" (emphasis added, *Expedition*, Intro–4)   Women were essential, but their role was prescribed as supportive of their men.   In a lengthy observation of soldier's wives (*Expedition*, II:26–30), he declares that "no women are more faithfull, more chast, more loving, more obedient nor more devout, then Souldiers wives" (*Expedition*, I–29).

108. *Expedition*, Intro–1.

109. *Expedition* cites classical and medieval writers from Arrian to Xenophon, showing that Monro read extensively in the classics as well as in medieval military literature. Cockle, *Bibliography*, lists English translations and dates of publication of the works available.   Of particular significance were the military histories of Aelian, Modestus, Frontinus and Vegetius, which had long been available in a single volume. Contemporary works such as Machiavelli's *On the Art of War* (1520, published in English in 1560) and discussions of the new ideas of Maurice of Nassau (Jacob de Gheyn, *The exercise of Armes For Calivres, Mvskettes, and Pikes After the ordre of his Excellence Maurits Prince of Orange* [1607] were also obtainable.

110. *Expedition*, II–196.

111. *Expedition*, II–3. Monro knew that Swedish service was of great merit to the Cavalier, for the Swedish king taught "his owne new discipline" (*Expedition*, II:2, 141), which Monro describes in "Abridgement of Exercises for Younger Soldiers" (*Expedition*, II:183–192). Monro also calls it simply the "new Discipline" (*Expedition*, II–141). Note that the title to the reissued *Expedition* reflected his appreciation of the new style of warfare: *The Scotch Military Discipline* (see "Introduction," endnote 3).

112. *Expedition*, I–6.

113. *Expedition*, II:183–192.

114. *Expedition*, II:193–215.

115. *Expedition*, II:217–224.

116. These concepts are described and discussed throughout *Expedition*. Comparing Monro with other military authors reveals his astuteness.   For example, Sun Tzu, in 500 b. c. e., wrote, "War is a matter of vital importance to the State . . . It is mandatory that it be thoroughly studied . . . Therefore appraise it in terms of the five fundamental factors . . . If a general who heeds my strategy is employed he is certain to win . . . When one who refuses to listen to my strategy is employed, he is certain to be defeated."   Sun Tzu, *The Art of War*, trans. Samuel B. Griffith (London: Oxford University Press, 1963), 63–71.   Sun Tzu's five fundamental factors are basically the same as Monro's. For an interesting comparison of western and oriental military thought during Monro's time, see William H. McNeill, "Keeping Together in Time," in *Military History Quarterly*, vol. 7, nr. 2 (1994): 100–109, for a look at Ch'i Chi-kuang and Maurice of Nassau, both sixteenth century military reformers.

117. Monro is occasionally categorized as a holdover from an earlier era because of the following statement regarding the pike. "The Pike, the most honourable of all weapons, and my choice in day of battell, and leaping a storme or entering a breach with a light brest-plate and a good head-piece, being seconded with good fellowes, I would choose a good half-Pike to enter with" (*Expedition*, II–192).   Such characterization ignores three points. First, the statement is usually taken out of context.   Just preceding the statement Monro observes that pikemen (with emphasis added) "being well led they *may* beate Musketiers *accidently* off the Feild, and *being well lined with shot* they are a safeguard against Horsemen."   This clearly states his awareness of the limitations of the

pike.    Second, the time-consuming process of reloading a musket left musketeers vulnerable and dependent upon pikemen for protection.   In hand-to-hand combat, the half-pike was indeed a good weapon to have.   Finally, the half-pike was a symbol of his rank, a point Monro would not have overlooked.   Furthermore, Monro was very clear about the value of training and exercise; the significance of muskets and artillery "without which no Armie can be gloriously led" (*Expedition*, II–211); and the need for intelligence, security, unity of command, discipline, logistics, clear communications and mobility (*Expedition*, II:197–215).   Monro's essential elements of success in warfare are currently characterized as the principles of war, a modern statement of which, as promulgated by the United States Army in the 1990s, is set forth and elucidated in *Field Manual 100–5, Operations* (Washington, D.C.: Department of the Army, 1993). Monro's principles for success are very similar to current military doctrine.

118. Montgomery, *Montgomery Manuscripts*, 213.

119.   Stevenson, *Scottish Covenanters*, 83.   "While many of the 'observations' which follow sections of confused narrative are sound enough, many are trite, sometimes to the point of absurdity."

120. *Expedition*, Intro–1, and throughout.

# Editor's Notes

When planning this edition of *Expedition*, it was determined that it should be as close to the original as possible. All punctuation, which is often bizarre at best, was retained, as was capitalization. As grammar usage, especially lengthy subordinate clauses and run-on sentences, are perhaps indications of dictation; it was important that the exact style used by Monro and his amanuenses be retained. Words italicized in the original were italicized; no attempt was made to maintain consistency in italicization.

As all references to Monro's account by later authors and historians use the pagination format that appears in *Expedition*, it was essential that the original pagination be retained. This was accomplished by incorporating *Expedition*'s page numbers, bracketed and in bold type, into the text at the precise point where each page changed. The following format was used to denote Monro's pagination: Introduction (Intro–1 through Intro–15); Part I, Danish Phase (I–1 to I–89); Table of the First Part (Table I–1 to Table I–8); List of Scottish Officers (List–1 to List–5); Chronology and Miles: Part I, Danish Phase (Log I–1 to Log I–2); Chronology and Miles: Part II, Swedish Phase (Log II–1 to Log–5); Part II, Swedish Phase (II–1 to II–182); Abridgment of Exercises for Younger Soldiers (II–183 to II–192); Certain Observations Worthy of the Younger Officer (II–193 to II–216); Christian Soldier Meditations (II–217 to II–224); Table of the Second Part (Table II–1 to Table II–18). These numbers are also noted in the Table of Contents.

There were, however, necessary changes and omissions. Hyphenation posed an interesting dilemma. It was often unclear whether a word followed by a hyphen appearing at the end of a line in the original was an actual hyphenation or simply a compound word divided at the end of a sentence. As these words rarely fell at the end of a line in this edition, the usage appearing most frequently in the original was applied. Therefore, words appearing with a hyphen appeared as such in *Expedition*, and no automatic hyphenation was used. The one exception to this general rule concerns instances where in the original, a word or part-word was hyphenated at the end of a page and the rest of the word was continued on the following page. For this edition, the hyphen was retained, pagination was inserted, and the word's continuation followed.

Some changes were unavoidable but not detrimental. The letters *s* and *f* which appeared in the original edition closely resembled an *f*. As these two letters are usually a problem for the reader of today, the modern *s* and *f* were used for this edition. Some dipthongs, such as a combined *oe* and the German letter *esszet*, appeared in the original; for clarity, these were changed to *oe* and *ss* respectively. Some omissions were made for editorial reasons. *Expedition* utilized the style of placing the first word of a following page as the last word on the preceding page; this extra word was eliminated as unnecessary. Monro's Tables, or Indexes, cite a page number and a letter for each reference. These letters appeared at the side of the original text, listed alphabetically beginning with A, and were used to help the reader locate more quickly on the page a specific reference. As there were never more than three letters per page, and as the placing of the letters would have been difficult at best, these extra letters were omitted, in both the Indexes and text.

The spacing between words and letters was very inconsistent in *Expedition*. Changes in font size, or the inclusion of extra spacing between letters of a word, were occasionally used by Monro for emphasis; this was not retained. The spacing between "Duties" and "Observations," between sections of text, and between parts varied greatly; this, too, was made consistent. Decorative letters at the beginning of each section could not be duplicated and were altered to standard font style and size. Decorative lines and other decorations within the text were omitted. The text usually included a decorative separating line between the end of a "Duty"–"Observation" block of material and the next block of material; a simple separating line was inserted herein. Where a specific section, such as Monro's "Introduction," had larger print for specific segments of text, standard font style and size were used. In general, then, the font size was made consistent.

Spelling and errata posed a particularly ticklish question. It was originally decided that [*sic*] would be used to denote obvious typographical errors,[1] that misspelled words with missing letters could be followed by corrections in brackets,[2] and that spaces where letters had obviously been omitted during the printing process could be added in brackets.[3] As the manuscript was proofed, however, spellings that at first had been viewed as inconsistent with all other spellings of the same word would be discovered several more times in disparate locations. Thus, determining whether the spelling as printed in the original was intentional or not was impossible. As nonstandard spellings may have been due more to differences between amanuenses than to misspelling or poor typesetting, it was decided to change nothing. Therefore, for the sake of maintaining the original, all words were spelled as in the original, including misspellings and typographical errors. Where gaps actually appeared in the original—that is, where there were actually missing letters—a tilde (~) was substituted. Some other examples of retained usage include the use of a *vv* instead of a *w* and *I* instead of *J* (e.g., Iohn  instead of John). Finally, neither this discussion nor the glossaries in which many spelling variations are listed should be construed as all-inclusive or as an index of all occurrences or (mis)spellings.

## NOTES

1. *The The* appears on *Expedition*, II-82, as does *was was* [*Expedition*, II–151]. Other probable typos include *baninished* [*Expedition*, I–29], *whhereof* [*Expedition*, I–60], *directious* (instead of directions) [*Expedition*, II–190], *feild* (instead of field) [*Expedition*, II–192], or *catttle* instead of *cattle* [*Expedition*, T–2–13]. These would have been followed by [*sic*] had the original plan been followed. Finally, misspellings for which the correct word was apparent would have been followed by the correction, enclosed in brackets, for example *firth*, and clearly meant to be *fifth* would have become *firth* [*fifth*] [*Expedition*, I–15] instead of [*sic*].

2. For example, *ILLUSTI* would have become *ILLUST*[*R*]*I* [Intro–12], *kils* would have become *kil*[*l*]*s* [I–22], *Segeant* would have become *Se*[*r*]*geant* [*Expedition*, I–34], *fro* would have become *fro*[*m*] [II–16], *Hepburs* would have appeared as *Hepbur*[*n*]*s* [*Expedition*, II–152], and Schwaland would have become Schwa[b]land [*Expedition*, II–204].

3. *Guids* would have become *guide*[*e*]*s* [*Expedition*, I–33], and *o* would have become [*t*]*o* [*Expedition*, I–33].

# MONRO
# HIS EXPEDITION
# VVITH THE VVORTHY
# *SCOTS* REGIMENT (CALLED
# *Mac-Keyes* Regiment)

levied in *August* 1626. by S*r*. *Donald Mac-Key* Lord *Rhees*, Colonell for
his Majesties service of *Denmark*, and reduced
after the Battaile of *Nerling*, to one Company in *September* 1634 at
*Wormes* in the *Paltz*.

Discharged in severall Duties and Observations of service
first under the magnanimous King of *Denmark*, during his warres
against the Emperour; afterward, under the Invincible King of
*Sweden*, during his Majesties life time; and since, under the
Directour Generall, the Rex-chancellor *Oxensterne*
and his Generalls.

*Collected and gathered together at spare-houres, by Colonell*
Robert Monro, at first Lievetenant under the
*said Regiment, to the Noble and worthy Captaine,*
Thomas Mac-Kenyee, of *Kildon*, Bro-
ther to the noble Lord, the Lord Earle of
Seafort; *for the use of all worthie*
Cavaliers *favouring the laudable*
*profession of* Armes.

To which is annexed the Abridgement of Exercise, and divers practicall Observations, for the younger Officer
*his Consideration; ending with the Souldiers*
Meditations going on service. [Intro-1]

## COLONELL
## MONRO TO
## HIS HIGHNESSE
## THE PRINCE ELECTOR
### *PALATINE OF RHINE,*
### *wisheth health, and happinesse.*

After seven yeares March in the warres of *Germany* with one Regiment, it being rent in the battell of *Nerlin*, at last I retired unto *Britaine*, to levie againe, for the further advancement of the good cause, and being at the Court of *England*, attending imployment, to expresse my love, and most humble respects unto your Highnesse, having bin an eye-witnesse [Intro-2] of the accidents most remarkable, which occurred in *Germany*, during those seven yeares warres, though a rude, and ignorant Souldier, I was bold to set pen to paper, to discharge a long seven yeares troublesome Expedition, in short Duties and Observations of service, cotaining a true & simple narration of the principall occurrences which happened in the course of this warre, without omitting one dayes March, in three yeares under the Magnanimous King of *Denmarke*, nor thereafter, in foure yeares March with the Royall Army, under the fortunate conduct of his Maiesty of *Sweden* of never dying memory.

Being induced thereto, chiefely, to testifie my humble respects unto your Highnesse, to whom I have ever vowed my best endeavours of service: next, to expresse my love, and thankfulnesse to my country, and to my deere Camerades, *Britaines*, *Dutch* and *Swedens*, (companions, not of wants, but of valour) eternizing their memory, who after death, like *Phoebean* Champions, ride triumphing in spite of envy, being praised by their enemies, for having valorously resisted their assaults, till they died standing, serving the publique, through their great love to your Highnesse Royall Mother, the Queene of *Bohemia*, your Highnesse selfe, and the remnant of the Royall Issue. Hoping therefore (for their sakes departed of worthy memory) my paines may be acceptable unto your Highnesse, for their sakes alive (that long for a new Leader) I have beene bold, to send unto your Highnesse at this time, worthy Counsellours, whose counsell your Highnesse may be bold to follow, and their vertues, being most Heroicke and examplary, may be imitated by your Highnesse, in going before us, as our [Intro-3] new Master, Captaine and Leader, being descended of the valiant *Bruce*, and of the first King of the *Stewarts*, through your Highnesse Royall Mother *Elizabeth*, Queene of *Bohemia*, Iewell of her sex, and the most resplendent in brightnesse of minde, for a woman, that the earth doth afford.

That great Monarch *Alexander* the great shewed his humanitie (in the wants of old age) to a poore and decrepite Souldier, being weary with great travell in the way, & lent him his own chaire, for to warme him by the fire: and being upon his death-bed (for all the pangs and paines of Death) he disdained not to shake hands with the meanest and poorest of all his Souldiers. So Mighty and Illustrious Prince, I, though a poore Souldier, doe Dedicate unto your Highnesse, these my dutifull Observations and Expeditions. Your Highnesse being eminent, as your dignity high, hath made me presume on your Highnesse goodnesse, which, I know, is full of pardons for those, that reverence your Highnesse person, as I doe. That I have prefixed your Highnesse name, was my duty, as to my Patron & Superiour, to whom I am ever most bound, especially in discharging of this my duty. Neither doe I pay this tribute unto your Highnesse, as to adde any thing unto your Highnesse knowledge, being already inriched with notable vertues, but rather to expresse my love and dearest respect, in all humility to him, whom I have vowed to follow (if my breath may last so long) till your Highnesse enemies be overcome.

Daigne therefore, Noble and Illustrious Sir, to let passe this my tedious expedition, and shallow observations, under the name of your Highnesse Patronage, to whom I wish the *Roman* Empire, for a possession, [Intro-4] as it was extended of old, from the River *Euphrates*, at the East, to the Ocean Sea, at the VVest, the fertillest part of *Africa*, at the South, and the *Rhine*, and the *Danube*, at the North; which to possesse, come, Noble Sir, unto the field, and fight before us, *Britaines*, *Irish* and *Dutch*, who long to see your Highnesse to fight with good lucke and victory, with strength and power, with wisdome and understanding, &c. against your Highnesse enemies, till your Highnesse Royall Mothers Throne be established, after her sacred Majesty, in your Highnesse Person.

Vouchsafe then, Noble Sir, of your gracious generosity, favourably to accept of my well wishing, and of these my Observations, and esteeme the Author thereof to be for ever

*Your Highnesse most humble
and obedient serviture,*

*ROBERT MONRO* [Intro-5]

## TO THE READER

*Noble, worthy, courteous, and loving* Reader, *if I could perswade thee to beleeve what profit the diligent and serious Souldier doth reape by reading, and what advantage he gaineth above him, who thinketh to become a perfect Souldier by a few yeares practise, without reading: Truely, thou wouldest use thy earnest diligence as well in the one as in the other; for I dare be bold to affirme, that reading and discourse doth as much or rather more, to the furtherance of a perfect Souldier, than a few yeares practise without reading.*

*For out of my owne experience, in my profession, having seene as many rare occurrences, and accidents of warre by practise (as hath not been seene the like in many yeares before) which shall appeare evidently by the subsequent Observations of one Regiments service: Neverthelesse; I must confesse, that reading and discourse of warres, inable the minde more with perfect knowledge, than the bare practise of a few yeares. Therefore, what these yeares past I have collected, by the one and the other, following the laudable profession of Armes, under the mightie and potent King of* Denmarke, *the space of three yeares, and since under his Majestie of worthy memory the Invincible King of* Sweden, *his Crowne,* [Intro-6] *and Confederats, in foure yeares; gathered together for the good, profit, and furtherance of thee and my Country: whereby I hope the noble and worthy minded* Reader, *shall be allured and animated to follow the Traces of those worthy* Cavaliers *mentioned in my Observations, of most worthy memories: Whereof some, from meane condition, have risen to supreme honour, wealth, and dignitie; though others perished in the way of preferment; for whose sakes, my Sword shall be ever ready against the common Enemy, that ruined the old and worthy Regiment; the memory whereof shall never be forgotten, but shall live in spite of time; and its vertues and fame be made knowne to all those interested in the quarrell. The example of those brave spirits (noble and worthy* Reader) *I hope, will allure you to follow their vertues, that you may be partaker of their honour, for the further credit of our Nation. Therefore, worthy* Reader, *what you find here, if you please, like; but howsoever, remember alwayes to censure sparingly the writings of the shallow-brained* Souldier, *not adorned with eloquent phrase; but with truth and simplicitie.* Plinius *saith, there was no book so little worth, but might be profitable in some things.* Cæsar *from his youth had his Observations: and the* Bee *out of the most poysonable herbs suckes the honey. Please to reade, and thou shalt finde something to delight thee; at least thou shalt see my thankfulnesse to my* Camerades *and* Country, *and examples of frequent mortality, to make thy use of. And as the starres take light from the Sunne; even so from* Histories, *men draw knowledge and wisdome. Let me intreate thee therefore, when thou wouldest avoide care, to looke on those observations, and by our examples amend thy life, and I shall be glad of thy profit, and not envy thy estate. If you ask; why I wrote these Observations? It was because I loved my* Camerades. *If why I published them, know it was for my friends, and not for the world, for which I care not, nor for any that is ungrate; but those which accept well of this, will encourage me betime, to take greater paines for their sakes, if they view them. Farewell.* [Intro-7]

EX NAVFRAGIO
VICTORIA
GENEROSI DOMINI
Dn. ROBERTI MVNRO
TRIBVNI MILITARIS,
EX PROSAPIA
BARONVM
DE FOVLES
ORIVNDI.

*Anno* M. D. C. XXX.

*Accipe, Posteritas, Scotici miranda Tribuni,*
*Quaeq; dedit virtus, mente sequace tene.*
*Vandalicas postquam* Gustavus *venit in oras,*
*Panus in Arctoum quàmare fundit aquas,*
*Prussiacis satagens Regi succurrere turmis*
Munrous *credit sèq; suòsq; salo.*
*Provehitur spatio haud longo. Mox turbine magno*
*Venti adversantes incubuere mari,*
*Fluctibus indomitis jactatur Martia pubes,*
*Ac perit hostili in littore quassaratis.*
*Attonitos Ductor verbis solatur amicis,*
*Et docet ut rupta puppe natare queant.*
*Subsidium lacerae monstrat fragmenta carinae,*
*Queis tandem in littus naufraga turba venit.*
*Postremos inter remoratur puppe Tribunus,*
*Dum salvos socios regiáq arma videt.*
*Praemia virtutis mox insperata sequuntur,*
*Vt, qua passa mari, jam meminisse juvet.*
*Ipsa sibi virtus pretium mercesq; laborum,*
*Viribus accrescens, quaeq; stupenda, patrans.*
*Magna peracturos terrâ quis crederet illos,*
*Queis vestes madidae ac languida membra vado?*
*Hostamen hostilem* Munrous *ductat ad urbem,*
*Et* Rugenvvaldo *sumere fraena jubet.*
*Infractos animis quum cernit; frangitur Hostis,*
*Ac properè victus Suedica jussa capit* [Intro-8]
*Navem unam perdens urbem lucratur & arcem*
*Mercator felix, corda movente* Deo.
*Hujus in auxilio sperans* Munroius *Heros*
*Ponere morigeros spemq; fidemq; docet.* [Intro-9]

SCHIFELBENVM
URBS ET ARX
MARCHIAE
*BRANDENBVRGICAE*
A GENEROSO
Dn. ROBERTO MVNRO
bene defensae.

ANNO
M. D. C. XXX.

*Vincere praeclarum est: sic & bene parta tueri.*
*Plurima* Munroi *laus ab utroq; venit.*
*Vt* Rugenvvaldum *rarà virtute subegit,*
*Sic* Schifelbenum *dexteritate tenet.*
*Vrbem ipsam linquit, nimiùm quia viribus impar,*
*Atq; Arcem firmat Martia gnava manus.*
*Figuntur muros circum justo ordine pali,*
*Et nova congeritur gleba ligonis ope.*
*Arcto sic spatio firmatur rara caterva,*
*Quae diffusa nimis debilitata foret.*
*Hostis adest. Vrbe ex media contendit ad Arcem.*
*(Nam pars exterior tuta palude manet)*
*Densis in tenebris satagit conscendere muros,*
*Ac ruptis portis mox aperire viam.*
*Fallitur ast multum, cauto stratagemate victus,*
*Artem cùm tenebras vincere posse videt.*
*Vicinis Arci tectis* Munroius *ignem*
*Subjicit, ac properè noctis opaca fugat.*
*Hosticus apparet passim per compita miles,*
*Ac denso plumbi tactus ab imbre cadit.* [Intro-10]
*Post alii abscedunt: Vrbemque Arcémque relinquunt,*
*Colbergam ut celeres obsidione levent.*
*Exstinguit flammas & jussa incendia victor,*
*Inque domos reliquas laetus ab Arce redit.*
*Solatur Cives: Mos hic est Martius, inquit,*
*Vrbs salva ut maneat, pars violanda fuit.*
*Discite Ductoris virtus quid provida possit,*
*Et grati Proceres pramia ferte Viro.*

Ioannes Narssius Anastasii F.
Dordraco. Batavus, Med. D. [Intro-11]

ILLVSTI AC GENEROSO DOMINO,
Dn. IOANNI
SINGELAIRE, COMITIS
CATHENESIAE FILIO, VICE-
TRIBVNO SCOTO,
*Prolibertate Germanica ad Neomarcam in superiore*
*Palatinatu fortiter vitâ defuncto.*

Anno M D C XXXII

EPITAPHIVM.

Qvi singulares, Lector, Heroes amas,
Specta *Johannis* busta *Singelairii.*
Prognatus ille Comite *Cathenesiae* (decus,
Cum foenore Patri reddidit magnum
Bellator ingens, providus, fortis, pius.
Batavo atque Regi militavit Cimbrico,
Servire dignus maximo tandem Gotho,
Ductor Tribuno proximus Munroio;
Vbique terror hostibus, carus suis.
Cum Francofurtum, quam Viadrus alluit, [Intro-12]
Peteretur armis, primus in muris fuit.
Post Lipsianâ clade vicit Tillium,
Pars magna Procerum, quos Polo virtus beat.
Talis frequenter visus, & regi intimus (perît,
Neomarcam ad urbem morte praecoci (heu!)
Et Dunawerdae membra deposuit sinu,
Duodetricenis haec ubi annis gesserat.
Triumphat astris victor hostis ac necis,
Orbemque memorem Scoticae gentis facit.

*Joannes Narssius* Anastasii F.
Dordraco-Batavus, Med. D. [Intro-13]

ILLVSTRI AC GENEROSO DOMINO,

Dn. ROBERTO
MVNRO,
TRIBVNO MILITARI,
Epitaphium.


*Ingenti clarus* Robertvs *robore* Mvnro,
*Qui* Baro de Foulles, *Munroidumq; caput,*
*Bina cui Legio peditúmque equitumque ministra,*
*Quam fociat Patriæ ac Relligionis amor,*
*Lipsiacis postquam certavit gnaviter oris,*
*Et passim Austriacis Martia damna dedit,*
*Hostili tandem prostratus vulnere multo,*
*Vlmiaco liquit membra caduca solo.*
*Spiritus ex superans ingenti robore  mortem*
*Heroum in Superis præmia digna capit.*
*Discite, Germani, grataque evolvite mente,*
*Pro vobis fortes quot cecidêre viri!*
*Pro vestrâ Heroes quot libertate necantur*
*Gente Caledoniâ Munroidúmque sati!*


Io. Narssivs, M.D.

Ann. 1633. [Intro-14]

ILLVSTRI AC GENEROSO DOMINO,

Dn. IOANNI
MVNRO,

TRIBVNO MILITARI,
Epitaphium.


*Hoc recubat tumulo Scoticâ de gente Tribunus,*
    Ianvs *qui* Mvnro *clarus in Orbe fuit.*
*Dicti de* Foules *illum genuere Barones,*
    *Queis Aquila & rugiens dat sua signa Leo.*
*Quorum nunc annis sexcentis bisque tricenis*
    *Nomine sub* Mvnro *stemma decusque vigent.*
*Hic pietate gravis, ac servantissimus aqui,*
    *Castus, & intrepido pectore bella gerens,*
*Militis effraenis rabiem dum voce coercet,*
    *Vnius ingrati fulmine tactus obît.*
*Lugent hunc Sueones: Luget Germanica tellus*
    *Herois fidi dedecorata nece.*
*Imprimis, unâ genuit quam matre, propago,*
    *(Nati nempe novem, nata quaterna) dolet.*
*Eum quadragenis quatuor bene vixerat annis,*
    *Vt vivat melius mors inopina dedit.*
*Vrbs Rheno incumbens,* Bacchi *que dicituæ* Ara,
    *Dat requiem membris, hoc decorata bono.*
*Spiritus aethereas Heroum scandit in oras,*
    *Ac desiderium linquit in orbe sui.*

Io. Narssivs, M.D.

Ann. 1633. [Intro-15]

# MONRO
# HIS EXPEDITION,
# AND OBSERVATIONS.

*The first Dutie discharged in* Holsten *at* Crempe.

The old Proverb is, *A good beginning makes a good ending,* and to lead a good life, is the way to a happie death. Immediatly after our landing at *Loughstad* on the *Elve,* by command of his Majestie of *Denmarke,* we were quartered in the fat and fertile soyle of *Holsten,* nothing inferiour in fertilitie to any part of *Dutchland,* except in Wines, having Corne in abundance, to the increase *Communibus Annis* of the twentie eight Corne, Wheat and Barly: in milke, nothing inferiour to *Holland,* and for the most part inhabited by *Hollanders,* especially the Cities. This Soyle hath also abundance of fresh and salt-water fishes; their Gentry live like Noble men; and their Communaltie live like Gentlemen. During our enquartring with them, our entertainment was answerable to our charges, where some Officers had allowance of a peece a day for keeping good Order. Lievtenant Colonell *Arthur Forbesse* had the Command over the Regiment in the absence of the *Colonell,* being hindred by sicknesse. Shortly after our going over, the Lievtenant Colonell departed this life, being a Gentleman of much true worth, and a valourous Commander, much regrated by the whole Regiment. Immediatly after his death, Captaine *Sanders Seaton* was by his Majesties Patent made Lievtenant Colonell to the Regiment, who did bring a strong Company of well exercised Souldiers, which were joyned to strengthen the Regiment. Captaine *Iames Dumbarre,* who did get Lievtenant Colonell *Forbesse* his Company, was placed *Sergeant Major,* Captaine *Sinclaire,* Captaine *Boswell,* and Captaine *Ennis* Companies were reduced to strengthen the other Companies of the Regiment, which being made complete, were mustred, cloathed, and payd of their muster-moneth. Who then would disdaine to follow warres, might be thought unwise. The Baron of *Fowles* comming over a voluntier, was allowed a free Table to entertaine an Earle, being ordinarily above sixteene persons at Table; his Visitors, horses and servants entertained accordingly. [1-1]

The Regiment mustered received colours, wherein his Majestie would have the Officers to carry the *Danes* crosse, which the Officers refusing they were summoned to compeare before his Majestie at *Raynesberge*, to know the reasons of their refusalls; at the meeting none would adventure, fearing his Majesties indignation, to gainestand openly his Majesties will, being then his Majesties sworne Servants: and for the eschewing of greater inconvenience, the Officers desired so much time of his maiestie, as to send Captaine *Robert Ennis* into *England*, to knowe his Majestie of *Great Britaines* will, whether or no, they might carrie without reproach the *Danes* Crosse, in *Scottish* colours: answere was returned, they should obey their will, under whose pay they were, in a matter so indifferent.

During the tedious winter, the Regiment was well exercised, and put under good discipline, as well the particular companies, as the whole Regiment, so that mine eyes did never see a more complete Regiment, for bodies of men, and valiant souldiers; as shall be seene in the discharge of their duties, begun with the sheding of *Duch-bloud*.

A *Duch* captaine, having out of a mad humour mutilated a souldier of my Captaines company of one finger. The souldier complaining to me, I made my Lievtenant-colonell acquainted with the manner, who sent to the Captaine to know his reason; The Captaine, not repenting of the wrong done, but rather bragging he would second the first, with a greater: he comming through my Quarters, I being exercising the company, the Sergeant overtakes him, and almost kill'd him, who made no defence, neither pressed ever to be repaired of his wrongs. This duty begun with the shedding of *Duch-bloud* by one of my name, and kindred. In the continuance of the storie, you shall heare much bloud shed, of all *Nations* in *Europe*, and of ours not the least. But of my freinds, and myne, too much.

### The first Observation.

The land of *Holsten* full of prosperitie at this time, having all things in a golden swimme, and waving carelesly in a swallowing plentie, having her heart full of pleasures, disdaining what was to come, ruine seazed vpon this land within six months, after our rising from quarters, to our first expedition, towards the *Waser* streame. At our comming into the land, the proudest sort of them, disdained souldiers, saying, they had no neede of strangers, they were sufficiently able themselves to hold out the Emperors forces, their passes were strong, their power in Armes were mightie of Horse and foote, as any *Province* in *Germanie*; notwithstanding whereof, in a short time, they felt the wrath of

*Heaven*, and were ruinated in the middest of their fortunes. I wish my Country, by a timely prevention to avoide the like, by suspecting the smooth streame, being ordinarily deepest; lest they should become subject unto their enemies, their land wasted with fire, and sword, their buildings, and plantings destroyed, their riches, and Iewels made spoyle of, their wives abused, and their daughters deflowred, themselves banished, and their Religion persecuted; in so much that their *Pastors* flying to the *Altar* for refuge, were cruelly put to death. Since therefore their enemies are our enemies, we ought to beware.

We ought also not to deny our betters in things indifferent, lest the askers love waxe drie, and his revenge grow great: for to a generous spirit, as it is [1-2] hard to begge, so it is harsh to be denyed. Our Officers refusing to carrie the *Danes Crosse* in their colours, disobliged his Majestie so farre, by their denialls of a thing indifferent, that after the death of our worthy Lievtenant Colonell *Arthur Forbesse*, Lievetennant-Colonell *Seaton* was preferred against the Officers wills, who once placed, would refuse nothing unto his Majestie he would command.

By his Majesties authoritie, against the Colonells will, Captaine *Duncan Forbesse*, and Captaine *Iohn Forbesse*, for alleaged insufficiencie, were put off their command, and their companies given to others, whom his Majestie favoured. But time that alters all things, having favoured them, they were restored to their companies againe.

When we have good dayes we slight them, when they are gone, we sinke under the wring of sorrow, for their losse; and want teacheth vs the worth of things more truely: and it is a true saying, *Blessings appeare not, till they bee vanished.* Our Officers that were discontented under the King of *Denmarke* without reason, having had both good quarters, and money, thereafter in other services would have been contented with lesse. We ought then, to make use of the present, preserving that we have, and if it goe, to grieve as little, as we may: yet we ought to owe a deare respect to the memorie of the good we lost.

Certainly, a good resolution is the most fortifying Armour a discreet man can weare; that can defend him against all the unwelcome frownes, that the poore world puts vpon him: with this, we can be servants as well as Lords, and have the same inward pleasantnesse in the checkes of fortune, that we carried in her softest smiles; It was *Zantippe's* observation, that she ever found *Socrates* returne with the same countenance, that he went abroad withall. I wish no man so spiritlesse, as to let all abuses presse the dulnesse of a willing shoulder: for resolution is always necessary in the waine of fortune, to save vs from discontentments, that usually deject us. A wise man makes the trouble lesse by fortitude, when a foole stoupes to it. The world hath nothing so glorious as vertue; which is like the passage of *Haniball* over the *Alpes*, a worke of trying toyle, of infinite danger, but once performed, it lets him in unto the worlds *Garden*, *Italy* leaving him a lasting fame.

My Chiefe and cosen, the Baron of *Fowles*, being in his travels in *France* a little prodigall is his spending, redacted his estate to a weake point, being advised by his friends timely to looke to the wounds of his house and family, and to foresee the best cure to keep burthen off his estate, having engaged his Revenewes, for teene yeares, to pay his Creditors, he went beyond sea a voluntier to *Germanie* with *Mac-Keyes* Regiment, well accompanyed with a part of his neerest friends: and having the patience to attend his fortune, his first employment was to be a Captaine of a company of *Scots* souldiers, leavied by himselfe, and there after advanced to be a Colonell of horse & foot of strangers, under the invincible King of *Sweden* of worthy memorie.

Thus farre of the Barron of *Fowles* in my first observation, to animate other *Cavaliers* borne of lesse fortunes to follow his vertues in being patient, though their preferments come not at first, loving vertue for her end.

Here also we see by the example of the *Dutch* Captaine formerly spoken of, that pride in a noble nature is as rare to be found, as humilitie in an unworthy minde; and arrogancie is a weede that ever growes in a dunghill, and no circumstance can make the expression of pride laudable: for the affronting [1-3] man by his owne follie, should be taught the way to his duetie, as the *Dutch* Captaine was, who, out of his pride and arrogancie, would second a first wrong with contempt, was taught humilitie, in so much, as he was made beholden to those for his life, whom out of his pride he had offended.

---

### The second dutie discharged, of the rising of the Regiment from Quarters going on their first March.

The Colonell recovered of his sicknesse tooke shipping from *Scotland* to *Holland*, and from thence over land to *Holsten*, accompanied with Captaine *Mac-Kenyee*, and Captaine *Pomfrey*, arrived in the latter end of *March Anno* 1627 in *Holsten*, where he was welcomed by his Regiment. At his comming, orders were given, his Regiment should be brought in Armes at *Eittho*, where his Majestie would take their Oathes of fidelitie. The Regiment being come together at the *Randezvouz*, was drawn vp in three divisions, artending his Majesties comming, in good order of battaile, all Officers being placed according to their stations orderly, Colours fleeing, Drummes beating, horses neying, his Majestie comes royally forward, Salutes the Regiment, and is saluted againe with all due respect, and reverence, used at such times; his Majestie having viewed Front, Flancks and Reare, the Regiment fronting allwayes toward his Ma^tie, who having made a stand ordained the Regiment to march by him in divisions, which orderly done, and with great respect, and reverence, as became; his Majestie being mightily well pleased, did prayse the Regiment, that ever therafter was most praise worthy. The Colonell, and the principall Officers having kissed his Majesties hand, retired to their former stations, till the Oath was publikely given, both by Officers, and souldiers being drawne in a Ring by conversion, as use is, at such times. The Oath finished, the Articles of warres reade, and published, by a Banke of the *Drummer* Major, and his associates, the Regiment remitted marches off orderly by companies, to their quarters, to remaine till orders were given, for their vp-breaking. The next day the Colonell, and Lievetenant colonell, were commanded to march over the *Elve* with seaven companyes, and to beset the Towne of *Stoade* with two companies, and then to march with the other five towards the *Waser* streame, to joyne with the *English* forces commanded by Generall *Morgan*, being foure Regiments of foote.

This Sergeant Major *Dumbarre*, with the remnant foure companies, was commanded towards *Lawenburg*, fearing the enemy was to crosse the *Elve*: our orders dulie followed, we are thus severed, marching to our severall Randezvouz, entring to take paines, for our former too much pleasure and riot, used in our winter quarters:

On this expedition towards the *Waser* streame, unfortunately Captaine *Boswell* comming after the Regiment was killed by a number of *villanous Boores*, ever enemies to souldiers: the *Cavaliers* death was much regrated of all that knew him, and no reparation had for his death. But the *Boores* being fled, the Dorpe was burnt off.

Being thus joyned to Generall *Morgan* his forces, where we remayned ten weekes, having had great dutie in watching, many alarummes, but lit- [I-4] tle service, so that our souldiers longing for service said, the *Emperialists* were no enemies; yet when the service was once offered, the smart came with it in great.

Our Lievetenant colonell and his company did march from vs towards *Lawenburg*, and joyned with the other foure companyes, and the Sergeant Major *Dumbarre* was sent to command the *Colonells* division on the *Waser*, the Colonell being gone to sollicite moneyes for the Regiment, seeing the *English* Regiment did get weekely meanes, whereas we were entertained on proviant bread, beere and bacon.

### The second Observation.

Nothing procures more faithfull service, then the Masters liberalitie. This magnanimous King his liberalitie we could not complaine of, having payd us in money, and with assignation of moneys, on our owne King; and good Quarters we had, which were not reckoned unto us; our true fidelitie his Majestie did oft-times commend, and our service both. Therefore in my opinion, that bloud is not be accounted lost, which is shed for a Noble Master. Diligent, and discreet servants, are the best friends a noble King, or Prince can be blest withall: And as our deserving in this service was good, our respect was more than answerable; having beene many times feasted, and Royally entertained, at his Majesties Table; being of servants, made companions to the King our Master. Let no man then thinke it bondage, to serve a noble Master, and a bountifull King, as this was; yet he that lackes this ambition, to be made companion to earthly Kings, following this worldly warfare, I would admonish him, to be thankfull to the King of Kings, for his peace, and quietnesse at home, and in his prosperitie, to make his acquaintance with God, that if adversitie come, he may be the bolder with his Maker, by prayer, which is the key to open heaven, and the meanes to remove our adversitie: for to reach unto God, wee must humble our selves by prayer, uniting us unto him, through the greatnesse of our love; for if we love God, we will be painfull to seeke him, and to find him, we must enter in the narrow way; and if wee will be partakers of his meate, we must first taste of his continencie; if we will follow him to the breaking of his Bread, like valiant Souldiers, wee must not faint, till wee drinke of his Cup; and to gaine him, wee must learne to lose our selves, for his sake. Let not then this saying be hard unto us, *Forsake your selves, take up your Crosse, and follow me*: if we faint at this, and not prove as resolute Souldiers, the next would be harder (the reward of *Poultrons*) *depart from me you cursed unto everlasting fire, I know you not.* While then we have peace, and quietnesse, I wish we may be familiar with this King of Kings, the Lord of Hosts, and say in particular, Thou art my King, O God; enter into his Tabernacle, and salute *Iesus Christ* thy Savior, and Redeemer, the head of all principalities, and powers, and let thy desire be, to be with him, in the land of the living. Then let the *Heavens* rejoyce, let *Sathan* flee, and *Hell* tremble, and let thy *Conscience* cry, *Christ* is my Savior; the world thou must despise, Heaven thou must desire, and in truth say, *Christ* is my Savior; without this assurance, all our knowledge, all our glory, all our honours, are imperfect, and of no effect: lest therefore, thou should'st check me, being but a vaine Souldier, saying, it is a good world, when the Fox begins to preach, leaving thee [1-5] to God, I will returne to my observation, on my Regiments March, the continuance of it, for nine yeares successive, in breadth, in length, in circle, in turning, in returning, in advancing to, and from our enemies, in weale, and woe, from the *Baltick* Sea, to the *Waser* streame, from the *Waser* streame, to *Rapine* in the *Marke*, from *Rapine* to *Wesmar* on the *Baltick* Coast, from *Wesmar* by water unto *Holsten* toward *Ouldenburg*, from thence by Sea, to *Hensberrie* in *Holsten*, from thence to *Denmark*, where in two yeares time, we did Circuit the Iland, with severall Marches, by land, and expeditions by water, being alike able for both, not like to the *High Dutch*, whose head nor stomack cannot endure the water. Being thanked of, by his Majestie of *Denmark*, having made peace with the *Emperour* in *May* 1629. from *Denmark* our expedition by water (having taken service anew, under the *Lyon* of the *North* the invincible King of *Sweden*) did continue towards *Spruce*, from thence to the *Baltick* Coast againe, and from thence to the River of *Danube*, that runs from the foot of the *Alpes* in *Swaubland* to the *Adriaticke* Sea, and, had out Master of worthy memory lived, we had crossed the *Alpes* into *Italie*, and saluted the *Pope* within *Rome*. But the losse of this *Lyon* to lead us, was the losse of many, and of this old Regiment, the remaines whereof are yet on the *Rhine*, where with twentie thousand *Scots* like them, I would wish to be, to doe service to the *Iewell* of *Europe*, the Daughter of our King the Queene of *Bohemia*, and to her Princely Issue.

My first advancement to preferment (through the love of my *Colonell*,) was on this first March, being without contradiction, though not without envie, placed to command, as Major over the Regiment, in the Major his absence.

So *Iacobs* blessing, bred *Esaus* hate, nature having made some as *Antipathits* to vertue, they were made sicke by my health. But for me, if another excell me in vertue, I will make him my example to imitate, not my block to stumble on: If in wealth, I'le with him blesse God, for his plentie, seeing God hath enough for me, and him both.

The killing of Captaine *Boswell* on this March, should be an advertisement to all *Cavaliers*, comming after a Regiment, or Army, upon March, to looke well unto themselves, not offering any occasion of offence, being weakest, for the Rascall sort of Communaltie, are ever soone stirred to mischiefe, especially an Army having past by, which, for the most part, never goes through Dorpe, or Village, but some notorious Villaine commits some insolency or other, for which oft times, the Innocent doth pay.

Having joyned after our March to Generall *Morgans* forces upon the *Waser*, being quartered in open Dorpes, the enemy not farre from us, it was my fortune to have the first nights watch, as Captaine of the watch to oversee all Guards, the *Avenue* to the Dorpe on all Quarters, being well beset, with convenient Guards, and Centries, under silence of night Generall *Morgan*, accompanied with foure Gentlemen with fire-locks to try us, being young Souldiers, gave fire on our outter Centry, our Centry having discharged, retired to the next Centry. I called the guard to their Armes, finding the *Alarum* continuing, caused the Sergeant of the Guard, with twelve Muskettiers, advance to Skirmish with them, to know what for *Alarum* it was, and to see what hinder hault they had: the Generall *Morgan* finding us discharging the dutie of understanding Souldiers, gave presently notice unto the Sergeant, what he was, and desired to speake with the Captaine of the [I-6] Watch, whereupon the Sergeant conveyed his Excellence unto me, to the place of my Guard, being the *Randezvouz* for the Regiment in case of *Alarum* to draw up unto, and finding the most part of the Regiment, on suddaine with their Colours in good order, praising them for their good watch-keeping, his Excellence asked for the *Colonell*, and went to see him.

It is the propertie of our Nation, an enemie being neere in time of an *Alarum* to be in readinesse before any other Nation, though at other times, on watches, or repairing to their Colours, on Marches or in Garrison, they are more carelesse than others. But once comming to earnest, or in great extreamitie of danger; to give them their due, they are not inferiour to any Nation, so farre, as I did ever see, or learne of others, older Commanders than my selfe. Yet many false *Alarums*, as we had on the *Waser* make Souldiers, and the most diligent, at last carelesse, till they feele the smart of some suddaine surprise, to rouse them, the better to goe readily to their duties.

The want of pay at the *Waser* made our souldiers a little discontent, seing the *English* get due weeekly pay; Neverthelesse, I did never heare of our Nations mutinie, nor of their refusall to fight, when they saw their enemies, though I have seene other Nations call for Guilt, being going before their enemie to fight, a thing very disallowable in either Officer, or Souldier, to preferre a little money to a world of credit.

It is a great part of a Colonels dutie, timely to foresee for all things necessary, that may give content to those under his command, lest being justly discontented, he might be greived, whiles it were not in his power to helpe himselfe, or others.

The liberality of a Colonell and his care in fore-seeing, for his Regiment, returnes to him oftimes with triple profit, being with moderation familiar with his Officers, making them, as humble friends, not as servant, under command, and he ought by all means eschewe to come in question, or publique hearing with his Officers: the onely means to make himselfe famous, and his Regiment of long continuance.

---

The third dutie discharged of our March from the Waser<br>towards Bysenbourg on the Elve.

Having thus remained the space of ten weekes under the command of Generall *Morgan* on the *Waser* side, we got orders to breake up, and to continue our march over the *Elve* under *Hamburgh*, and from thence, toward *Bysenbourg* Skonce, to joyne with the rest of our Regiment, the Colonell and Lievetenant Colonell being absent, Major *Iames Dumbar* commanded then in chiefe, receiving all necessaries fitting for our march, as ammunition; proviant, and waggons, for our baggage, our sicke souldiers being cared for, were left behinde, and we brake up from the *Waser* the tenth of Iuly 1627. a Regiment of Horse being commanded with us for our Convoy to the *Elve*, the first night we quartered at *Rottenburg* a strong passe, having a great Marrish on both sides, accessible onely by one narrow causey which leades through the marrish to the Castell, which is well fensed on both sides with Moates, Drawbridges, and slaught bomes, without all. [1-7]

The next day our march continuing, in the morning out fore-troopes having gotten Alarum retired on us, whereupon we drawing into Battaile, resolved to fight, and provided our selves accordingly for the enemies comming, which being found, but a false conception, nothing followed on it, but the continuance of our march, without further interruption.

The next night we lying in Quarters, our Guards orderly disposed; before day we had another Alarum, our duety duely discharged of all, both horse and foote, if the enemie had come we were provided; But the Alarmum proving false, we brake up, continuing our march toward *Buckstehood* appointed for our first Randez-vouz: where we were commanded to send to his Majestie at *Stoade*, for receiving of further Orders, and a company of Horse being directed with me, for my convoy, I was made choise of, to go to his Majesty for bringing Orders unto the Regiment. His Majesty being absent, Orders were given to me by a Generall Commissary to continue our march thorough *Buckstehood* and to quarter over night in the old land by the *Elve* side, till the next day we should crosse the River of the *Elve* at *Blanckeneas*, and from thence to march by *Hamburgh* through their Territories, and passe towards *Lovenburgh*, where we quartered a mile from it, continuing our march the next morning towards *Bysenburgh*, where we quartered in the fields, for five nights, till we knew of his Majesties further resolution.

### The third Observation.

All marches are occasioned by the accidents of the warfare. The reason of this march was the enemies Army drawing strong to a head in *Luniburgh* land, of intention to force a passage over the *Elve* to come the easier to *Holsten*, his Majestie being weake of foote in this quarter, having no great feare of his enemie on the *Waser*, where we lay before; we were therefore called to joyne with the rest of our Regiment at *Bysenburgh*. Another reason of this march was, the Kings forces in *Silesia* being also weake of Foote, standing in great neede of a timely supply, we being able to endure a long march, his Majesty resolved, after besetting well the passe on the *Elve*, to send us for a supplie unto the *Silesian* Armie: Neverthelesse many times we see in warres, though things be long advised on, and prosecuted after advise duely, yet the event doth not alwayes answer to mans conjectures: For it is a true old saying; Man proposeth, but God disposeth.

A Commander having the charge of a Regiment, or partie, on a march, ought in all respects to be as carefull and diligent as a Generall, that leads an Army, being subject to the like inconvenience of fortune. Wherefore he ought to be well provided of all things fitting for his march, that, in time of Rancounter with the enemy, he might the better discharge his duty, especially being provided with good store of Ammunition, both for the mouth and service, with sufficient fix Armes.

He ought also to keepe his Officers and Souldiers in continuall good order of discipline, without suffering the one, or the other to fall off from their Stations, without great and urgent occasions; and if any of them chance to fall off, he is obliged to foresee to their timely returnes. [1-8]

Likewise he ought not in any manner of way suffer violence to be used to *Boores*, or strangers in his march, and if such doth happen, he is obliged to do justice to all, and to see examplarie punishment done, to terrifie others from the like. He ought also, to be carefull to give none under his command just occasion of complaint, for want of their dues, either in quarters, or in distributing of their victualls, according to their strengths. He ought also on his march to be provident, in causing to bring their Proviant timely to their Randevouz, or Hawlts; seeing it to be rightly distributed, for avoiding of contentions happening most commonly at such times.

Also he must foresee before he makes a hawlt, that the ground be convenient where he drawes up, whether he be in feare of an enemie, or not; and at such times, he must be carefull, that centries be duly placed, at all parts needefull, and that no man be suffered to wander, or go astray, form the haulting part, for feare he be to seeke, when occasion should present either to breake up, to march, or otherwise, in case of Alarum, to have his Officers, or souldiers wandering, while as the enemie should charge, were a grosse error.

Likewise at his upbreaking from quarters, he should take notice of all complaints, and do justice accordingly: And he should have a speciall care of the sicke, either to transport them, or to foresee for their good usage, in case necessitie, or weakenesse force him to leave them behind. He ought also, to foresee before he march for his Guides and to give charge to keepe them from running away; and he ought to learne of the guide the inconveniences on the way that may be hindersome unto his march, that timely he might provide a remedie. His Guide should also know how far to go, that when he comes his length, he may timely provide for another. He ought also to learne the best way for his Baggage, and Ammunition to march on, and in case of suspected danger, he ought to ordaine a guard of Musketiers with a sufficient Officer to command for their convoy, and if it be such way, as that on occasion his Ammunition cannot be steadable unto him, in such a case he must not part from his Ammunition waggons; but rather to keepe one way, though it should be far about.

He ought never for pastime, or pleasure, on a suspected march neere an enemy, to go from the fight of his Troopes; for feare he should be absent in greatest neede, or that some misfortune might happen betweene those he commands himselfe, or against others incurring in their wayes. If occasion of service offer, he must never be dejected, but to encourage ever his owne most in the greatest extreamity, shewing testimonies of his inward valour and setlednesse of minde, by his by-past experience, testifying he is no Novice, not taking counsell of others, when he is with resolution to rancounter a brave enemy. [1-9]

He must be of judgment to consider on the sudden his enemies designe, and timely he ought to oppose his enemy, either with few, or with many, as he finds his best advantage, And if his enemy be too far stronger than he, he must timely resolve how to make a safe retreat, being forced thereto; Preserving his souldiers, to a fitter opportunitie: for once far ingaged, the retreat will be the more difficult to make without great losse; He ought alwayes to keepe a good reserve of fresh, brave, resolute fellowes to keepe faces on their enemies, while as others should be forced to turne backe on them: at such times, and in such occasions the resolution, the courage, and the judgment of a valourous Commander is best knowne; for many can advance rashly, that have never the wit, or judgment to retire bravely, as is ordinarily seene in many such Commanders, more stout, than wise. But lest I should enter too far to this purpose in this observation, for feare to be blamed my selfe for not retiring in time, it being a large field I entred in, let this suffice for this march of the Leaders duty.

Now to retire, being quartered a mile from *Lovenburgh* in a Dorpe, where the Boore for feare quit his lodging, so that for want of provision we were forced to send our Suttler called *Iohn Matheson*, towards *Lovenburgh*: in his absence our Boyes made use of his rugge to cover their faces; in drowning of Bee-hives, the rugge being rough did lodge a number of the Bees, which, when the Boyes had drowned the Bee-hives, they threw away: The Suttler comming late home we being a bed, went to rest; and putting off his cloathes, drew his rugge to cover him, but as soone as the Bees found the warmenesse of his skinne, they began to punish him for his long stay, That he was forced roaring like a madman, to rise, and throw off his rugge, not knowing (though well he felt) the smart of his sudden enemies; we called to him, asking, if he was mad: he made no answer, but still cried the Divell had bewitch'd him, in piercing him in a thousand parts, still rubbing and scratching, crying with paine, not knowing the reason, till a candle was lighted, and seeing the Bees, threw his rugge in a draw-well; The gentle reader may judge whether, or not, he was punished, for his long stay. Thus *Seria mista jocis.*

---

### *The fourth dutie discharged of our march from* Beysenburgh *to* Rapine *in the Marke, and of the storming of* Beysenburgh *Skonce.*

Having rested here three dayes on the fields, till our Colonell came from *Hamburgh* with a monethes meanes to the Regiment, our monies paid, we got orders for a new march towards *Rapine* in the Marke, where the old Markegrave *fon Turlaugh* lay at *Haggelberge* with a part of his Majesties Army, and the enemie lay against him on the other side of the *Haggell*, our orders were to divide our Regiment againe, and to leave Major *Dumbarre* with foure companies to beset *Bysenburgh* Skonce, the enemies army being then within five miles of it, ten thousand strong of foote besides Horse. The other seaven companies were ordained to march with the Colonell and Lievetenant colonell towards *Rapine*, as said, is; we severed not without teares, both of Officers and souldiers. But he that [I-10] serves a master, must obey. The first night our Camerades accompanied us to our quarters. The next morning our march continuing, newes overtakes us, the enemy is set downe before *Beysenburgh* Skonce. In the relation of the service I must be succinct; being loath, having not seene the service, to set any thing in Record, but what I know to be truth, neither can I be particular in the declaration of this service done by our countrimen, though it be generally well spoken of, overall Germany, yet I must say somewhat, and if my Report diminish from their credit, I protest it is not for lacke of love, but for want of information.

The enemy hearing we were marched, and having gotten true intelligence how strong they lay in the Skonce, he marched ten thousand strong, and lay downe within a cannon shot of the Skonce, and having begun his lines of approach, The first night, the Major made an out-fall, where having bravely showen their courage, and resolution, returned againe without great losse.

The enemy longing to be repared of this their bravade, resolved to storme the Skonce at all quarters, but finding resolution joyned with valour against him, after long fighting in vaine, he is beate off from the walles, and forced to retire at that time, with the losse of five hundred men at least. But having redoubled his forces the next time, sets on with greater fury than before, but is beate off the second time also, with losse; the third time he adventured, and, as was reported, the *Scots* defenders, as is well knowne, behaved themselves so well, that the enemy storming the walles, the defenders for want of powder threw sand in their enemies eyes, knocking them downe with the Butts of muskets, having beene divers times Pell, mel through others; at last the enemy is forced to retire without effectuating any thing.

Yet, gentle Reader, thinke that at such play, the losse was not onely of one side, but of both, for in defence of this Skonce being so oft stormed; that ever praise-worthy Captaine *Learmond*, Brother to my Lord *Balcomy*, being twice shot with a musket, received deaths wound, and after died at *Hamburgh*, in perfect memory, discharging his duety Christianly to God, as he did during his life time both to God and man.

For his sake, and in remembrance of his worth and valour, the whole Officers of the Regiment did weare a black mourning Ribben: in this conflict also was killed his Lievtenant, called *David Martin*, an old, stout and expert Officer: many other valourous fellows, that were there, carried the true markes of their valour imprinted in their bodies, for their Countries credit. There was also, a *Scottish* Gentleman under the enemy, who coming to scale the walls, said aloud, Have with you Gentlemen, thinke not now you are on the streets of *Edenburgh* bravading: One of his owne Country-men thrusting him through the body with a Pike, he ended there. This Skonce so well maintained by our Country-men, is to their prayse recorded at length in the *Dutch Story* of the *Danes* warres, where the curious Reader may learne more of it. The enemy finding this opportunitie to faile, at another passe above this on the *Elve* watched by *Dutch* surprising the watch, did come over the *Elve*: the newes comming to his Majestie, he presently sends Orders in the night to *Major Dumbarre*, who commanded the Skonce to retire, and to bring off his Cannon, and to cut off the bridge, and then to come by wa- [1-11] ter with his troups to *Lovenburgh*, and beset the Castle thereof with two Companies, and to retire with the rest to *Lukstad*, which accordingly was done, to their great credit.

*Major Wilson* being set with two Companies on the Castle of *Loven*, the enemy falling downe, *Generall Tillie* leading the Armie, comming before the Castle, doth summon it to render, the *Major* refusing, he is besieged, the enemies Batteries having playd a little on the Castle, the *Major* parlees for accord, before the parle, *Generall Tillie* is shot through the thigh, pledges delivered, the accord agreed on, he should march out with bag and baggage, Drummes beating, *Bale au Bouche*, with a Convoy granted to them to *Lukstad*, the Accord subscribed, but neither circumspectly nor wisely by the *Major*: at his out-comming his Colours are taken from him, having forgot to insert them in his Accord, he complaining of the breach is bidden reade it, and finding it was so, was forced to march without Coulors to *Lukstad*, where, for his over-sight, he was set from charge, with disgrace, and the Company restored againe to the right Owner, Captaine *Duncan Forbesse*, and incontinent *Major Dumbarre*, with foure Companies, was commanded to beset *Statholder Ransove* his Castle of *Bredenberg* in *Holsten*; the enemy having already falne into the Land. Which discourse I must now leave, and prosecute the continuance of our march towards *Rapine*.

After this service the renowne spread so abroad, where ever we came, that the Gentrie of the Country were ready meeting us, providing all necessaties for us. The Duke of *Wymar*, the Dukes of *Meclinburgh*, with a number of gallant Ladies, did visit us in our March, to congratulate with us the good fortune, and good service, done by our *Camerades*. But if we should looke to the outside of Souldiers, these foure Companies were the meanest of our Regiment to the outward appearance. Our March continues to *Rapine*, where we were to receive further orders of *Generall Major Slamersdorffe*: our orders were to draw up in Battaile before the Towne of *Rapine*, where the *Generall Major* would come, and see us, his intention being to bring the Towne under Contribution, otherwise to fright them with inquartring of the Regiment: his intention effectuated, we were led in quarters or Dorpes, for three dayes to rest us, seeing our intentions were to march unto *Silesia*.

### The fourth Observation.

In this observation, though the dutie be suddenly discharged, wee have much to amplifie the observation; first, by reason of the dispute that did arise betwixt his Majestie and the *Colonell*, for offering to Cashiere some of his Officers for alleaged insufficiency, by the information of some malignant Spirits amongst our selves, whose names I will suppresse, and the reasons also, letting some other tongue, not mine, divulge their shame. At this time also before our rising to this expedition we were discontented of the division made of our Regiment, being absolutely divided by his Majesties authoritie, without the consent of our *Colonell*, who would have been loath to have left Captaine *Learmond* behinde, that had done him so many notable good offices, and this noble Gentleman of famous memory, at his leave-taking of his *Colonell*, my brother and me, being then his intirest *Camerades*, with teares revealed unto us, whom he thought was the plotter of his stay, and withall did with griefe in a manner foretell his owne fall, alleaging we [1-12] should never meet againe. Therefore, for the love I bare to my deare *Cammerade*, I will point at the heart of those, who had a hand in the separation of the Regiment. I must therefore crave pardon a little, to expresse my dutie for the losse of this noble, and vertuous *Cavalier*, whose heart and eyes were ever fixed upon vertue, and upon his love to his deare friends. He hates not, but with cause, that is unwilling to hate at all. And it is the end that shewes the difference betwixt vertue and vice. Fie then upon those judgements, that, for their owne aymes, hatch the Ruine of their *Camerades*, in fore-thinking, and pursuing evill. And as the discharge of my last dutie was Tragicall, the reasons of it I will set downe obscurely, pointing at some, that every man may examine his own conscience, that had any hand in plotting, or hatching, (by villanous policie, bred of envie,) the ruine of their *Camerades*, the reward whereof doth still awaite them with shame in a killing ambush, *when the Lord of Hosts will bring to light the hidden plots of the malicious man.* Here I could make some to blush, that I know plotted the fall of their *Camerades*. But I will be dumbe, doing by them, as *Ioseph* thought to have done by *Mary*, in seeking to cover blemishes with secrecie, lest I should wound some so with my penne, as to make them by their *Camerades*, to be push't out of Company. But I will rather shew my charitie to the delinquent, by concealing of his fault, and tell him of it in secret, than openly to divulge his mischiefe, seeing I wish his amendment before the world should know his amisse: I will not therefore be too harsh, or virulent, hoping for his penitency, wishing God may enlighten his conscience, that while he hath time, he may crave pardon for his hatched evill. Being sorry for the losse of these two worthy *Cavaliers*, of famous memory, *Learmond* and *Dumbarre*, for whose sakes, with griefe I have pointed thus obscurely at the forger of these *Cavaliers* fall, whose name I will suppresse; though my heart knows him well; and hoping time may change him to another man, I will let him be his own *Beadle*, and for his punishment, I would not care, though he were made to sing an *Invective* against himselfe. But I pray God, we may be freed of the like our selves, and not to looke upon another; with a *Beam'd* eye, but rather to be our owne *Antidot's*, against all the poyson that another is able to spit upon us. Let us then have our eyes fixed upon vertue, and we shall finde a beautie, that will every day take us with some grace or other: For the world hath nothing so glorious in it as vertue, when shee rides *Triumphing*, as both these *Cavaliers* doe after death, in despight of their enemies, like *Phoebean Champions*, praysed by their enemies, for resisting their strongest assaults, are now renowned in despight of envie, and the abusive world. And the worthy Souldiers, their *Associats* in this memorable conflict, and hot storme, are not to be forgotten, but to be praysed for their valour. For though, as I said, by appearance to looke but on their outsides, they were the meanest in shew of our whole Regiment: yet *God that gives hearts, and courage unto men*, made them the instruments of our Regiments first credit in the warres of *Germany*. They were, I confesse, led by brave Officers, which were seconded and obeyed by resolute and stout Souldiers, that gained victory, and credit, over their enemies in extremitie, by casting sand in their eyes. This victory puts me in mind of a prettie Story, shewing that some times the meanest things, doe helpe us much against our enemies, especially, when the Lord will blesse our fighting, with meane Instruments, fighting for us for his owne glory. [1-13]

*Iovianus Pontanus* reports of *Alphons* being resolved by assault to take in *Vicaro*, his Souldiers having at the first past the countersharpe and fossie, scaling the walles, the Inhabitants not able to repulse them with stones, and the enemy unawares having surprised them, that they got not leasure to arme themselves, they threw Bee-hives amongst the enemy, which being dispersed, sticking under their Armes, and in their faces, forced the enemy to retire, uneffectuating his designe. Reade *Iovian* in his seventh Booke of *Alphons* his deed, *Cap.* 2.

*Ierome Osorius* reports the like Story, of one Captaine *Baregue*, a *Portugall*, in his eighth Booke of *Portugall*, who by throwing Bee-hives on his enemies, made them to retire. The like was done of late in *Hungaria*, on a Fort belonging to the Bishop of *Agria*, neere the *Turkes*, which with the like helpe was relieved of a sudden assault, the Souldiers not having time to goe to their

Armes, used this meane, and were saved thereby. We see then, that an immortall good name is attained unto by vertue and not by villany.

Here also in this conflict we see, notwithstanding of the enemies eager pursuit with fury, that resolution at last prevailes; for the defenders having at first resisted their fury, the enemy with losse being forced to retire, the assailers were discouraged, and the defenders incouraged. Therefore it is the dutie of a brave Captaine, that is to be assailed, to resist the beginnings well, and then the end must needs be glorious.

In such occasions, happie is that Commander, that, in extremitie of danger, is accompanied with a few trustie friends and Souldiers: He may be assured not to be forsaken, as I have beene some times by strangers. The valiant Souldier is ever best knowne in the greatest extremitie of danger, and a forebeaten enemy, once or twice repulsed, will be loath to continue his pursute: But he that would gaine honour, must resolve to contemne death, though ever before his eyes. Wherefore I would wish the brave Souldier to be ever well prepared to die, who should glory in nothing earthly more than in the tokens of his valour, being knowne they were got with credit, and not by infamie, as many unworthy Souldiers oft-times get wounds, but not with credit, while for their cowardise they are running away, yet they will vaunt amongst the unknowne, as if their wounds were credibly gotten. Here also we may see the resolution and courage of our Country-man to be prayse-worthy, though killed serving the Emperour; for though I loved him not, being mine enemy, yet I honour his memory, in serving them truely, whom he did serve, for his owne credit.

Of all professions men of our profession ought to looke neerest to their credits, being attained unto by much toyle, and travell; and is lost with little. Therefore it is said, that a valourous man his credit hangs, as it were, at one haire, and one little errour or oversight in command, can obnubilate all his former glory. Circumspect then had we need to be, to preserve this credit, so dearely bought, and easily lost.

We must not then looke to the outside of a man, but unto his vertues; for he that judgeth men of our profession by *Physiognomie*; shall oft-times be deceived; for he that is not stout by nature in our profession, having served out a seaven yeares prentiship under such a Leader, as the magnanimous King of *Denmarke*, such a one, though not stout by nature, by frequencie of danger is made stout, as a sword, fearing nothing, not death it selfe. And Souldiers thus used with danger, for the love of their Leaders, to gaine their [1-14] favours and good opinion, will undertake the hazard of the greatest dangers for their Commanders sake. Such then, that have travelled well, should by due have rest, since the Crowne is laid up and ordained for him that fights well. On the other part, to end this observation, as I did begin, there is no punishment more grievous, than the publique ill-will of all men; especially for just causes. And in my opinion, it is better to be buried in oblivion, than to be evill spoken of to posteritie.

---

### *The first Dutie discharged of our Retreat from* Rapine *to* Wismere *on the* Baltick Coast.

Having rested eight dayes at *Rapine*, of intention to have marched toward *Silesia*, to joyne with the Armie there, *God that disposes all things by his providence for our best*, provided that we went not; for the Armie there being beaten, and put to rout (whereof few escaped) The enemy after his Victory following downe to us-ward, and having crossed the *Elve* behinde us, our retreat towards the Kings Armie in *Holsten* was hindred, the passages being all beset by the enemies forces, so that there was no other passage free for our Armie to passe through, but onely to retire towards the *Baltick Sea*, to patronize the Isle of *Poule* for our safetie, till such time as shipping should be provided by his Majestie to transport us unto *Holsten*. Orders then were given to the whole Armie, to march with all celeritie from *Rapine* unto the Randezvouz, being appointed at *Perlesberg*, where having come together, we were neere ten thousand strong of horse and foot, being sufficiently provided of Artillery and Ammunition answerable to the strength of our Armie. Our march in great haste, night and day, continues towards *Wismere*, being afraid of our enemies, we feared we should not gaine so much time, as to put our Armie in assurance, within trenches, before the enemies comming: but being more affrighted, than we had reason, comming there betimes, we intrenched our selves within a Close Leager, before the Isle of *Poule*, a mile from *Wismere*: Where we made a draw-bridge over the passage to the Isle, and fortified it with Skonces and Redoubts on both sides; where we lay five weekes, till his Majestie provided shipping for our transportation unto *Holsten*, and fearing contrary winds might keepe us long on the Isle, it being in the Harvest time, we provided the Island with Corne and Cattle taken off the Country about, sufficiently to have entertained us the whole Winter in necessitie. In this Leager we had abundance of flesh, and of drinke, but we were slightly provided of bread and salt, where a Souldier had but one pound of bread allowed him in ten dayes, if that he tooke it not off the field. Our *Scottish* High-land men called this Leager the flesh Leager, and justly, for the Souldiers were so cloyed with flesh, that Oxen flesh was let lie on the ground, the Hides taken off by the Souldiers, and sold for a Can of Beere a Hide, the whole body left on the place untouched, and at last, the Souldiers weary of Mutton also, eating onely the heads and feet, being boyld with Wheat brought off the fields. In all this necessitie, the Towne of *Wismere* did prove very discourteous unto us, in not suffering to help us, with any thing they might spare for our money, but rather through their pride abused our Officers and servants, that entred their Towne to buy necessaries. [1-15]

### *The fift Observation.*

Here we have represented unto us, the mutability, of humane estates, and especially of warres, the wheele turning, we that looked to go forwards, were forced to retire, humane affaires being opposed as a marke to all the shots of discontentment; so that we ought not to rejoyce too much in a calme, or prove faint hearted in a storme. We reade of a Roman Captaine, who did tremble being victorious, as being uncertaine how long his good fortune might continue. And the Romans (as *Scipio* tould the Ambassadors of *Antiochus*) were not puft up by victory, nor cast downe by losse. And *Augustine* said, this life of ours, was doubtfull, blind, miserable, made of a floud of humors, ebbing, and flowing.

Notwithstanding whereof, it is the duety of a wise Commander to make use of the time, by diligent fore-sight, and wise deliberation, to save himselfe, and others so long as he may, and not to be dejected, at every buffet unconstant fortune doth give him.

As this old Generall his resolution at this time, having an enemy before him, was good, the enemy coming also behinde him, tooke his march betwixt both, and did come fortunately to his wished forecast, putting himselfe and his Army in assurance. This old Generall was of good experience, but not fortunate, neither were they fortunate whom he served, though of invincible courage, and of great understanding in warres: for, to give his Majesty of *Denmarke* his due, no man breathing, I thinke, carries a stouter heart then he doth: Yet I have seene his Majestie far dejected in spirit, through great losse, and no wonder, as you shall heare more particularly set downe in the seventh observation.

In this Retreat we were not voide of feare, but suspecting the worst, every man bethinking himselfe of his best safety, to eschew an apparet overthrow, a thing at all times most dangerous in an Army. Our Horsemen, being afraid of a retreat by water, and consequently the losse of their Horses, for want of shipping, and which was more, they feared the losse of their goods, and their owne imprisonment: but it was in vaine they should torment themselves before hand, for things without their powers to eschew. But they ought rather to have made use of the present, and to have foreseene the future so far as lay in them, resolving patiently against all crosses and to referre the event to God.

Here also I did observe the inconvenience that comes to souldiers, through eating much flesh without salt, or bread, which did bring diseases in the Leager, so that many died of pestilence and flux: but of our Nation fewest, for to speake truth, I never did see more durable men against all Toyle, travell and tediousnesse, than they were.

Likewise I did observe first here, that the Townes of Germanie are best friends ever to the masters of the field, in flattering the victorious, and in persecuting of the loser, which is ever well seene in all estates.

When we are happie in the spring-tide of abundance, and in the rising floud of plenty, then the world would be our servants: but when these pleasant waters fall to ebbing, then men looke upon us, at a distance. Wherefore adversity is like *Penelopes* night, which undoes all, that ever the day did weave. And our misery is so, that we can never trie a friend, but in the kicke [1-16] of malignant chance: so I confesse he is happy, that finds a true friend, but he is happier that findeth not extremitie to trie him.

### The sixt duety discharged of our expedition by Water from
Wismer *to* Heligenhoven, *and of our service at* Oldenburgh.

Having remained five weekes in this Leager, during which time,
preparation was making, for the transportation of the Army unto *Holsten*; seeing
the Emperors forces come from *Silesia*, and *Tillies* Army were joyned very
strong, which barr'd our passage from comming into *Holsten* by land, which
made us ship our Army for going unto *Heligenhoven*: and from thence to the
passe of *Oldenburgh* in *Holsten*, of intention to ly secured there, till the rest of
his Majesties forces might joyne with us. The Army then consisted of eight
thousand Foote, and Horse, besides those that were left behinde on the Iland
under the command of Generall Major *Slamersdorfe*.

Having all safely landed, at *Heligenhoven*: we marched towards the passe
of *Oldenburgh*, where arrived before night, our Leager was drawne out into the
most convenient part, for maintaining of the passe, where the first night we begin
to worke in the Trenches, and continue working the whole night, and the next
day, till noone, that the enemy was seene marching towards the passe, in full
Battalions of Horse, and foote, which before three of the clocke had planted
Batteries, to play with Cannon on our Leager and to force a passage over the
passe, which our Generall perceiving, gave orders, to double the Guards both of
Horse, and foote; As also strongly to *Barricade* the passe, and to cast up in the
night a redout before the passe: the night drawing on being darke, silence was
over all, on both sides of the passe.

But the day cleering, the Guardes on both sides begin the skirmish, the
Cannons on both sides begin to discharge, the Horse Guards charge one another,
till ours were forced to give ground; the foote Guards beginning to fight, the
reliefes were commanded on both sides to second their owne, the service
growing hot; and the passe in danger of losing.

My Colonell in all haste was commanded to march with the halfe of his
Regiment to maintaine the passe; The Colonell commanded me, to have the men
in readinesse, and to distribute Ammunition amongst the Souldiers; which done
the Colonell leading on marches towards the passe under mercy of Cannon, and
musket: the Generall meeting us bids aske the souldiers, if they went on with
courage; they shouting for joy, cast up their hats, rejoycing in their march,
seeming glad of the occasion. The Generall commending their courage, and
resolution, doth blesse them in passing. At our ongoing to the passe, the enemies
cannon played continually on the Colours, which were torne with the Cannon:
Also to my griefe, my Camerade Lievetenant *Hugh Rosse*, was the first that felt
the smart of the Cannon Bullet, being shot in the leg, who falling not fainting at
his losse, did call couragiously, go on bravely Camerades, and I wish I had a
Treene, or a woodden leg for your sakes; in this instant of time, and, as I
beleeve, with one bullet [1-17] the leg was also shot from *David Rosse* sonne to
*Rosse* of *Gannis*. The service thus hot, both of Canon and musket, many were
hurt at the ongoing, where I received a favourable marke, being hurt in the inner

side of my right knee, with the end of mine owne Partizan, being shot off, by the Cannon bullet. And we drawing neere to the passe, The *Dutch*, that were on service being all fled but the Captaine, the passe neere lost, my Colonell drawes off a plotton of Musketiers of the Right wing, being most of them brave young gentlemen of the Colonells owne companie, which in all haste with an Officer were directed to maintaine the passe, which being hardly pursued, sundry worthy young gentlemen did lie on the place in the defence of it, and sundry were hurt, as *Andrew Monro, Hector Monro, Alexander Tullough, Arthur Forbesse*, and divers more, of common souldiers. By this time, the rest of the Colonells division were not idle from service, the reliefes going often on, and the rest doing service along the passe, having a hedge for their shelter, The Body of the Pikes standing, for two howers in battell, under mercy of Cannon and musket, so that their suffrings and hurts were greater both amongst Officers and Souldiers, than the hurt done to the Musketiers, that were on service, for few of their Officers escaped unhurt, as Ensigne *Ennis*, Ensigne *Stewart*, Ensigne *Monro*, divers also were killed, as *Andrew Monro, Ferwhar Monro*, and *Murdo Powlson* was killed with a Cannon. In time of this hot service, powder being distributing amongst souldiers, a whole Barrell was blowne up, whereby the Colonell was burnt in the face, and many Souldiers spoiled: the enemy seeing our powder blowne up, presse to force the passage, and some comming over, Captaine *Iohn Monro* with a few Musketiers was commanded in a flat Champagne to encounter the enemy, who forced the enemy to retire, so that the passe was cleered againe by Captaine *Iohn* his valour, much to his credit.

The first division of our Regiment having thus maintained the passe for two howres hot service, then comes from the leager, for reliefe of the Colonells division, the Lievetenant Colonell, with the other division nothing inferiour to the first, who falling on fresh with man-like courage, the other division falls off, to refresh themselves: during their Camerades being on service, at the very entry the Lievetenant Colonell was hurt, Sr. *Patrick Mackey* and *Iohn Forbesse* of *Tullough*, both Captaines were hurt; Lievetenant *Andrew Stewart*, Ensigne *Seaton* and Ensigne *Gordon* were also hurt, and many gentlemen and common Souldiers were killed. This service continued in this manner from seaven a clocke in the morning, till it was past foure in the afternoone, first began, with the halfe of the Regiment, who were relieved by the other halfe, which continued till mid-day; after that the service not being so hot, as before, they went on to service by companies, one company relieveing another, till night that it grew darke, and then darkenesse, the enemy of valour, made the service to cease.

During all this time, our Horsemen stoode bravely in Battell under mercy of Cannon, and Musket, besides the foote, attending to second us, in case the enemy had set over, and forced the passe, which once he adventured to do, but was suddenly beaten backe: all this while, the Generall the Duke of *Weimar*, and both the Armies, were witnesses to the manly and brave cariage of this praise-worthy Regiment.

In the evening before night ammunition on both sides growing scarce, & darkenesse comming on, the service begins to beare up: by this time, there [I-18] is a Barrell of beere sent us, from the Leager, the Officers for haste caused to beate out the head of it, that every man might come unto it, with hat, or head-peece, they flocking about the waggon, whereon the Barrell lay, the enemies Cannonier gives a voley to their beere, which, by Gods providence, though shot amongst the mid'st of them, did no more harme, but blew Barrell and beere in the Ayre, the neerest misse that I did ever see; for many of them were downe to the grounde, whereof my brother, Captaine *Obstell* of worthy memory was one.

At night the service ceast, I was sent by the rest of the Officers to the Leager to my Colonell for Orders, to learne of the Generall, who should relieve us at night: My Colonell did go the Generalls Tent, and I with him, to have his Excellences resolution, who haveing Nobly accepted of the Colonell, did praise him and his Regiment, requesting him, that as the Regiment had done bravely all day, in being the instruments under God of his safety, and of the Armies, he would once more request him, that his Regiment might hold out the inch, as they had done the span, till it was darke, and then they should be relieved, as he was a Christian; And drinkeing to me, I returned with a Resolution to my Camerades, leaving my Colonell in the Leager: And as it grew darke, we were relieved by the Duke of *Weimar* his earnest and diligent intreaty, having proved our good friend, in urging to take us first off. The Generall having resolved to retire from the enemy, with the whole Army, by reason Ammunition grew scarce, and we having deserved best, were first brought off, getting orders to march in the night to ships.

### The sixt Observation.

The wise Ancients said, it was the principall thing in all things to looke unto the end: but it is the propertie of our Nation to be over wise behinde the hand; as we were after the service, having lost thereat a great many of our friends, we ought to have beene the more circumspect againe. But our condition is so, that no experience can make us wise, till we be soare beaten by others, and then we will grow kinde one to another.

Amongst the *Romans* none was admitted to the dignity of a Commander, till first he had past a prentiship under a brave Generall, where he was taught the use of Armes, and Novices durst not be so bould, as to intrude themselves in this honourable profession, in any degree, to take command on them, without long practise, and experience, as was requisite to undergo a charge in so high a calling, and of such importance, as to leade others: Neverthelesse, the ground worke or foundation of Military discipline once well laid, then they were suffered to advance by degrees unto high charges, proposing recompence, and reward unto those, that did merite, and to that effect, they invented severall sorts of Crownes, for the reward of their travells, and wisdome: Amongst others, the Crowne called *Obsidionall* was ordained, for those that entred first the besieged places, being of the most esteeme of all crownes, which was made of the Roote of the Herbes, or graine, that had taken Roote within the place besieged; also those that first scaled the walls, were wont to get a crowne of the Herbe

Woodbine, or *Parietaria*, Pellitory growing on the walls, and those that first entred the enemies Ports by [1-19] force, had also a crowne given unto them; And the crowne *Castean* was ordained, for him that first entred the enemies Trenches, and brake the *Palesades*, making way to enter unto the enemies Leager: Also a crowne was given unto those of the *Navall* Armie, that first entred the Enemies Gallies, or ships on Sea; this Crowne was made of gold, representing the Combat, and the Generall a foote, being victorious, had given him a crowne made of Hats, and Miters, and triumphing in a chariot, he carried a Hat made of Lawrell. At last, these crownes were made of Gold, laid over with pretious stones. They had also given them, for recompence of their travels, Chaines, and Bracelets, all to the end they might accustome themselves to vertue, and to the discipline and toyle of warres. Who then would not desire to be of this society, to get a crowne for well doing? On the contrary, Cowards, Poultrons, and Effeminate persons, were disdained, degraded and put off charge, while the valiant were honoured, advanced, and recompenced, as the Turke doth practice to this day; to the disgrace of Christians neglecting discipline, till they are overthrowne. It should then be the duety of brave Generalls to make choice of brave and vertuous Commanders, not asking of whom they come, but where, and how long, have they practiced to be vertuous. Then we see here, what was the custome of the Ancient *Romans*, in choosing the vertuous, that had past their prentiship, and not Novices to be Commanders: for we see, that the love of the Publique brings honour, pleasure and profit to the vertuous, who thinke on it sincerely; But those, that would raise their fortunes by the ruine of others, shall never prosper.

The reason of our coming to this passe of *Owldenburgh* was, to have stayed there in safety from our enemies, till we might joyne with our friends; but the Enemy prevented us, in coming betwixt us and our friends: then there was no remedy, but to hold him up at the passe, till our Army might joyne with us, and of this intention we resolved for best; to maintaine the passe, as we did, till Ammunition grew scant, and then we were forced to retire to our ships.

This King is powerfull by Sea, and is mightily well furnished of all things necessary for warres, of Armes, Artillery, Ammunition, victualls, money, and what else is requisit to set forwards a warre; and, which is more, a noble, and liberall Master, as ever I did serve.

Here also I observe the slownesse of our *Generall*, that did not patronize the passe some few dayes before the Enemies coming, that it might have beene fortified: for it was no time for us to fortifie the passe in the night, when the enemie came before us, and the next day, we were not suffered to worke, being otherwise imployed. Another oversight was, that our *Generall* did not know certainly, how we were provided of Ammunition, for though we had Lead in abundance, we wanted Bullets in time of need. Whereupon the *Generall* was accused, after our comming into *Denmarke*, and the blame was found in the Commissary, that had the charge of the Artillery, *Et jure*, for they were all Rogues, and deceived his Majestie, that trusted them too much. Neverthelesse, I cannot excuse the *Generall* of being ignorant of the provisions ordained for the

Armie; seeing he was certaine of the enemies comming: for it is most sure, if we
had been provided of Ball, we were sufficiently bastant to have kept the passe
against our Enemy, since it came not in the Enemies power, till we had left it
voluntarily in the night. The [1-20] enemy also retiring from us, hearing the
*Rhinegraves* forces were coming behinde him, of intention to joyne with us. I
observed also, that the *Generall* was too slow, in the encouragement of his
Officers and Souldiers, having delayed his exhortation to the very time of our
going on service. And it is easie, at such time, to *Prognosticate* by the
countenance going on service, how they are affected. But never men went on
service with more chearfull countenances, than this Regiment did, going as it
were, to welcome death, knowing it to be the passage unto life, especially
fighting in a good Cause, against the enemies of the Daughter of our King, the
Queene of *Bohemia*, for whose sake, our Magnificke and Royall Master did
undertake the warres, and for her sake, we resolved to have followed such a
couragious Leader, as the Earth this day affords none stouter, as mine eyes did
witnesse divers times: And for her sake, I perswade my selfe, our noble *Colonell*
did ingage his estate, and adventured his person, to have don her sacred Majesty
good service. I did also observe this day, that the best way to eschew danger, is
not ~o perceive it; for a man well resolved perceives no danger, neither doth any
thing seeme difficult unto him, that may import his credit. And the best
Commanders, in my opinion, as they are in measure remisse, not seeming
prodigall of their lives, though resolutely adventurous; and for me, I love a man
that is modestly valiant, that stirres not till he must needs: for he that is conscious
of his inward courage, is confident to shew it to the world, when he will; but a
man prodigall of life, oft-times indangers himselfe and others; for though he
have courage to lead them on, he lacks wit and discretion to bring them off, in
case of eminent danger. And at such times, as I condemne him that runnes away
first, I cannot allow of him, that, out of ostentation, will stay after all his
*Camerades* are gone, till he yeeld himselfe prisoner, or die unnecessarily there,
where he might have preserved himselfe with honour for a better occasion. I
have also observed, that a base fellow hath been killed running away, when a
valiant Souldier stood to it, and came off with credit.

I did also remarke the invincible courage and resolution of that worthy
Gentleman Lievtenant *Rosse*, who having lost his legge, wished for a wooden or
Treen legge, lying on the ground, as the example of pittie, that he, who was
indued with such courage, and Christian resolution, had not time in the warfare,
to have given the world greater proofe of his valour.

Here also I must condemne those arrogant Spirits, who contemne *God* and
Fate, that while as being on service, and being hurt, may retire with credit, and
on the contrary will be so foolishly valiant, as to stay on a second hurt, worse
than the first; as became that day of a young Gentleman of my name, and
kindred, who being shot in the Arme with a musket bullet, would not at my
desire retire, but slighting his wound stayed on service, till he was shot dead in
the head. *David Monro* Ensigne, being shot through the body above the left
pappe, went a little aside, till he was drest, and returned againe to his Station,

keeping his Colours in his hand, till night, before the enemy, never fainting with his wound, an example of rare courage, and of great strength of bodie, neither did he ever thereafter keepe bed or lodging one houre, more than ordinary, for all this hurt.

Here also I did observe, that the former distractions amongst the Officers of the Regiment were taken away, having been companions of equall danger against their enemies, made them love one another the better ever after: for Captaine *Iohn Monro*, helped Lievetenant colonell *Seaton*, being shot, [1-21] to his horse, having on the march two dayes before fallen horribly out, which verifies the *Scots Proverbe, Dogges will part Swine*, and make them agree amongst themselves. We see oft-times, that those that are feeblest themselves, are most ready to speake *Derogatively* of others. Here I might inferre divers instances, yet I will inferre, and onely point, for the present a little at those unluckie dispositions, that cannot endure any but themselves to be well thought of, for if one be justly praised, or advanced in recompence of his vertue, they will presently dismount his vertues, and stabbe him to the heart, *obnubilating* his brightest glory, with a *Butt* of *Detraction* bred of envie, nastie indeficient minds devising spots, where they find them not, a base office to make his tongue whip a worthy man. If I knew vice in another, I would nobly shew my charitie in concealing it, if he be absent; if present, I would not flatter: for the valiant man his tongue is ever the greatest coward in absence, for it is not good to deprave the fame of the absent, with a viperous Tongue: Therefore my advice were to thee, in such a case, to doe like the wise man, to learne somewhat by thine enemies outrage, as King *Philip* of *Macedon* learned well the lesson, who many times thanked his enemies for their outrage, which made him afterwards the more wise, more circumspect, and more setled: for nothing gives a man more good experience, than warres, lawes, love, and detraction: And for Detraction thou oughtest to be so wise, if thou be made the marke for *Calumniators* to shoot at, let them shoot, as they please, I would be hard, they should not pierce me. Being armed with a good Conscience, we should not care for their shooting, for though it sometime take root in the eares of some hearers, yet thy comfort should be, that one day, he shall kill himselfe, soone or late, as the poysonable birth kils the mother and such fellows should be punished, as theeves: seeing the one bereaves men but of their substance, but the other bereaves them of life, and death, and of their dearest friends also. And he should be holden as such a one himselfe till he brought his evidence; as the custome was of old: and for my selfe, I never found better remedie against them, than to disdaine them, as coming about the eares of a deafe man, that did not heare them, and this I found to be the best bridle, to curbe their tongues, for in the end he would hold his peace, and turne his tongue another way: but I must confesse, the tongue of a *Calumniatour* hath sometimes offended me, and grieved me much, but they profited me, in making me the more circumspect and diligent, in thinking on all circumstances, that might conserve my credit and reputation, to be avenged on them. And with the *Proverbe*, which I know to be true, I will conclude this point, things that grieve us, should lead us to repentance, seeing that which destroyes, instructs; and *God* oft-times, cleanses the inward man, by the outward, by the contrary course, leading us to our wished for Harbour: for there is no such great discommoditie, but brings commoditie with it; for those that are stinged by *Scorpions*, though at first it be very dangerous, yet at last, the hurt being cured by convenient remedies, it brings fruit with advantage, as experience hath taught, neither Flie, Bee, nor Wasp can harme those thus cured.

To conclude then this point of Detraction, men should be circumspect, what to determine of other mens actions, being on service: for I am of the opinion, that in time of hot service, no man doth remember the halfe of his owne actions, much lesse to remarke the actions of others, except some [1-22] circumstances, which he may remember. Thereafter we should be loath unnecessarily to bring our selves in question, in speaking evill of others: for commonly, at such times, cowards, or feeble men, that are not in action themselves, see more than others that are better employed: yet the feeble man is ever readiest to detract, for to prevent his owne insufficiency, too well knowne to others. But after this dayes service, our detractions, and distractions also, were almost taken away, being companions of the like danger, against our enemies: And I inferred this discourse of detraction, by reason, that at such service commonly men doe speake, as they doe favour, or rather, as their envie carries them; which fault as being too much in use in all estates, especially amongst Souldiers, I would wish from my heart that it might be eschewed.

Here also I observed, that want of circumspection in command, especially over young Souldiers, as we had to command, doe many times cause great inconveniences to follow, as was seen in the blowing up of our powder, whereby our *Colonell* was burnt in the face, and many more. Here I might speake somewhat of the hurt and inconveniency, that doth happen many times by Cannon, and powder, but I will referre it to a fitter place, to be spoken of.

Likewise I cannot here omit to speake somewhat of the resolution of some particular Souldiers, that were hurt on this service. *Hector Monro* of *Cool,* being shot through one of his feet, was desired to goe off, who answered, it was not time, till first he had emptied his Bandeliers against his enemies, before which time he was shot through the other foot also, and then was not able to come off alone, without helpe of others, and some of his *Camerades*, which helpt him off, going farther with him than he thought needfull for his safetie, or their credit, he wished them to retire, and discharge their duties against the enemy, as they had sufficiently done towards him. *Hugh Murrey* being desired in time of hot service, to goe and take off his brother being killed; he lacking powder said, going towards his dead brother, I will first emptie my brothers Bandeliers, as I have done mine owne, to be revenged on his enemies, before I take him off: in the meane time, he was shot in the eye himselfe, and that wondrous favourably, the Bullet some few dayes after having come forth at his nose, which is most true, though seeming incredible. This day also I observed an ill custome too common to all Generals, that they make most use, in time of desperate service, of those that doe best serve them, and when once they have experience of their valour, they never omit to employ them on the most dangerous exploits; and for reward, they onely doe commend their valour, when others are scarce remembred at all.

Here also I did see that on hot service, nothing can be more comfortable, than the getting of a timely reliefe, as we did get of the rest of our Regiment, for having long smarted under the mercy of Cannon and Musket, in hot service, so that a Souldier was not able to handle his Musket for feare of burning, having shot so oft, till his shoulder did ake; who can thinke, but to such a one a reliefe was welcome: truely I thinke no man that hath his foot in the fire, but would gladly take it out: yet I perswade my selfe, there were some here, who would suffer to burne before they retired with disgrace, or discredit, their honour being so deare unto them. The best proofes a Souldier can inferre of his valiant courage, are his wounds got [1-23] with credit, not running away, and the best exhortation a Leader can give common Souldiers is, to shew himselfe couragious, and then, without words, with a signe, some will follow him, in imitating his example.

Here also I did observe, that the *Dutch* are not the best Souldiers in extremitie of danger, though I confesse for the discharge of all dutie, otherwise very obedient, till it come to extremitie, and then commonly they make a Cloake of discontentment, and call for money, as they did this day. Likewise I cannot say, but Horse-men are usefull many times, as they were here; yet in my opinion, in their service, they are not to be paralleld to foot: For at the in-taking of Townes, and in hilly and mountainous Countries, that are straight by nature, they are not usefull, neither can they doe but little service, yet for their great charges, they are much harder to be entertained: Therefore my choice shall be ever, as most credible to command on foote, and if I were worthy to advise a King, or a Generall following warres, I would wish him to esteeme more of his foot Officers, than of his horse: then fewer should serve on horsebacke, and more on foote; and as his Charges should be lesse, his profit should be the more, his Armie the stronger, his Countrey lesse spoyl'd, his contribution to maintaine his Armie, the better payd, his treasure richer, his Victories more frequent, and more durable, his Conquest the better maintained.

This I dare presume to affirme to be all true, out of my little experience, and which is more, all the time I have served, where I have heard one fault imputed to a body of foote, I could instance ten defects in our Horsemens service: for the worst sort of them being too much given to plowndring, makes them neglect their duties, which fault also is too Common amongst many of their Leaders, though I have knowne some honest men amongst them free from this imputation: and for a King, or Prince, that must defend his Countrie, by sea (as our noble Mr: the King of *Denmarke* was) I would advise him, as unprofitable for his service and country, not to encertaine strangers in this kinde, so being their charges would far surmount the benefit that could redound by their service, yet I cannot say, but the *Rhinegrave* his Regiment was the only Regiment under the King at this time, that did best service, which was ever praise worthy.

Likewise, I have found by experience that those who fight best in occasions, have ever the best of it, though they chance to suffer losse, if it come to a retreat, commonly they are most respected and come first off, as we did at this time, and it is ever better to fight well, and to retire timely, then for a man to suffer himselfe to be taken prisoner, as many were that morning after our retreat: and in occasions, I rather choose to die honourably, then to live and to be prisoner to a churlish fellow, that perhaps would keepe me in perpetuall bondage, as many brave men are kept; or otherwise, at my taking, to be scurvely used, being stript naked by a Villaine, and then, if I lacked monies about me, to be cut and carved, and at last, poorely put to death, being naked without Armes to defend my selfe. My advise then is to him that cannot resolve to fight well, that he resolve according to his station, and charge, to be well furnished of money, not onely about him, but also, to have money to the best in a sure place, and in sure hands to maintaine him, being prisoner, and to pay his ransome; or otherwise, let him resolve to remaine in perpetuall bondage, except some noble friend or other have compassion on him. [I-24]

Likewise I would advise all worthy Souldiers, and Officers going on service, if they can, never to want some monies about them, that, if they chance to come as prisoners in undiscreete hands, they may cast a bone in the doggs teeth, to curry favour of the cruell curre.

I did also observe here, that continency is a vertue very necessary for a Souldier, for abstaining from many inordinate appetites, that followe his profession, that he may the better suffer hunger, cold, thirst, nakednesse, travell, toyle, heate, and what else patiently, never mutining for any defect: for it is the greatest victory we can attaine unto, to overcome our selves, and our appetites. Likewise I did observe, that Kings, and Generalls are very courteous to Cavaliers, while as they stand in neede of their service, in making their use of them, but the occasion once past, oft times they do looke on Cavaliers at a distance, as if they had not imployment for them; which should teach Cavaliers, to take their time with reason of their Masters also; and then they might care the lesse for them (being strangers or forraigne Kings) while as, they would disdaine them, having still a sure retreate to their owne King, and Master. Here also I found that a friend in neede was better then gold, for had not the Duke of *Wymar* beene our friend we had bin left behinde at the passe, and beene prisoners the next day with the rest of the Army. It is therefore ever best to do well, come after what may; for vertue in despight of envy, will not want a reward: And a stout Marriner that hath ridden out the storme with losse, as we did this day, rejoyces in the calme, when it comes, and he is said to merit the Crowne, that hath fought valiantly.

It is also very necessary, that at such service, as this was, if we have time; that we be carefull, to bring off our Camerades bodies killed on service, that died honourably before their enemies, to be laid in the bed of honour, in burying their bodies, as becomes Christians. We are also tied in duety to our Camerades, that were with us in danger, if either they be wounded, or mutilated, to care for their safeties, so far as lieth in our power: And we must not preferre the safety of our owne bodies, to the publique weale of our Camerades, and countrimen dead or living, but we ought, with the hazard of our owne lives, to bring off the dead and hurt.

An example of this duety, we have in the person of the President of *Chassangne* treating of the *Iewes* law, that did command, that the bodies of their dead enemies should not lie unburied. *Cæsar* caused to be buried the head of his enemy *Pompey* and wept at his death, as *Valerius Maximus* reports in his fift booke, and sixt Chapter. *Hercules* is thought to have bin the first that ordained to bury the bodies of those killed on service, and *David* calls them blessed, that were so thankefull, as to have buried *Saul*. *Iudas Macchabie* did cause to bury the bodies of the enemy killed in battaile, and *Alexander* restored unto the mother of *Darius* the dead bodie of her sonne, *Hanniball* did burie, the body of his enemy *Marcellus*, as *Valerius* affirmes. It is also expedient, for the common-weale, that the bodies of the dead be buried: and *Leonard Darez* reports that *Cyrus, Alexander*, and *Cæsar* did recommend their funeralls to their friends, as Lievetenant *Rosse* did his to his Captaine and me, which we performed in the best manner we could, for the time. If *Pagans* had such regard to their burialls, Christians should be more carefull, whose bodies sometimes were the receptacles of the holy Spirit, and of the immortall soule created to Gods owne Image. [1-25]

Here also I would report the commandement that we reade in the second chapter verse 23. of the fourth booke of *Esdras. Where thou findest the dead, put them in the grave* (with a certaine marke) *and I will give thee the first seate in my resurrection*: and the wise Ancients said, men should looke unto the end. My exhortation then is to all my worthy countrimen, and women, that were interessed in our losses in this dayes service, to consider, that when these gentlemen, and Cavaliers were borne, that they were marked and ordained to die honourably, fighting in the good cause; and for the liberty of our Kings daughter, the Queene of *Bohemia* and her distressed Royall Issue, under the magnanimous King of *Denmarke* our Master, who for her Majesties libertie, did hazard not onely his life, but his crowne; let them then that are interessed, as said is, in this our losse consider againe, that they died with great honour, and reputation, seeing they live eternally in their fame, having laid downe their lives, as servants of the publique, if not for their country, yet at least, as cannot be denied, for the liberty of their Kings Royall Issue: It then became them well, to have died standing. Therefore those mothers, friends, or Sisters, are to be condemned, that mourne for them that live (after their death) in their fame, and though their griefe be great, let them shed no teares, for feare it become of them, as became of that Ancient woman called *Vicia*, mother to *Futius Geminus*, who was killed at *Rome*, for having wept at the death of her sonne, that had lost his life in the publique service, as reporteth *Tacitus* in his 6 booke of his *Annals*, and our Saviour in the Evangelist Saint *Luke* doth forbid the widdow to weepe for her sonne that was dead, and St. *Paul* writing to the *Thessalonians* saith, *Brethren I would not have you ignorant of the estate of those that are asleepe*, to the end you do not over-mourne, as those do, that are without hope. Therefore, let us forbeare all teares for those departed, and if we should mourne, let us mourne with teares, even those most pretious teares for sinne, these are the Christian teares, that should be shed from our hearts, to reconcile us unto God, those teares are as the bloud of the soule, hurt and wounded with the sense, and feeling of our sinnes, before God these are the teares, that drawe Gods mercy upon us, as *David* cried unto God in the 56 *Psalme. Thou hast counted my wandering, and put my teares in thy bottle, are they not in thy Register?* Therefore though we be grieved at the losse of our friends, and at the losse of the day; Yet ô God, make us thankfull unto thee, for our deliverance, that we may rejoyce at our owne safety.

---

### The seventh Dutie discharged of our Retreat
### *from* Owldenburg *unto* Assens *in* Denmarke *by Sea.*

Having thus past the day at *Owldenburg*, the night (the friend of Cowards) coming on, what we durst not have done by day, being favoured by the mooneshine, when all were wearied with hot service and toyle in the day, begun to take rest, and refreshment by their fires, in the Leager all Guards relieved, and centries set out, being all of us, after a great storme in a quiet calme, we begin to take our retreat to the water: [I-26] our Generall being full of feare and suspition goes before, and our Colonell also; we follow, having the *avant-Guard* according to our Orders for going a ship-board, which orders were willingly obeyed, perceiving the danger was to follow, and in consideration that long before the Lievetenant Colonell Sr. *Patrick Mac-Gey* and Captaine *Forbesse* being hurt had retired for their safeties towards the Isle of *Feamor*, and from thence to *Denmark* to be cured. I supplying the place of the *Major*, our Regiment orderly retiring from the enemy, Captaine *Mac-Kenyee* and my brother *Obstell*, who before were companions in the day of danger, in the night did march together leading off the Regiment to be secured, and I bringing up the Reare, accompanied with some other Officers; we had no doubt of our safe retreate: the whole army being behind us made us halte the oftner, taking paines to bring up our hurt and sicke men; we marched but softly, *Py a Pyano*: at last by ten a clocke of the night we arrived on the shore, and drew up in battell attending the Colonells command for shipping, who had gone himselfe unto the Roade amongst the ships, to provide shipping, but could get no obedience, the feare was so great amongst the marriners; having heard the roaring and thundring of cannon and muskets in the day, feare so possest them all, that they lacked hands to worke and hearts to obey: and the Colonell coming a shore without bringing of ships to receive us, we made use of the time, our Camerades the horsemen having come before us, who ever begin confusion, were without orders, forcing ships to take in their horses, and had already possessed the whole Bulworke and shipping with their horse, I asking my Colonells leave, drew our whole Colours in front, and our Pikes charged after them; our musketiers drawne up in our reare by divisions, fortifying our reare in case the Enemy should assault us in our Reare, and then I advanced with our Colours alongst the peere, our Pikes charged we cleered the Peere of the Horsemen, suffring them to save themselves from drowning, where they found the Channell most shallow, and advancing thus to the end of the Peere, we seazed upon one ship with some horses in it, where we set our Colours, and making that ship launch off a little from the shore for feare of being aground, having mann'd the shipboat with an Officer, and some musketiers, we sent to force other ships out of the Roade to launch in and serve us, untill such time as the most part of our Regiment were shipped except some Villaines, who were gone a plundering in the Towne; but not knowing the danger they were in, they stayed all night from us and were taken by the enemy the next morning. Thus having shipped our men we were forced to quit our Horses and baggage: the Officers that were most diligent, as Captaine *Monro* and my brother *Obstell*, were busied the whole night ferrying souldiers from the shoare, especially the sicke and wounded, who were not able to helpe themselves: In the morning I shipped three boatefulls of wounded and sicke men, till at the last I was beaten from the shoare by the enemies horsemen. And my Colonells ship being under saile layd up to the winde, attending my comming with the last fraught, and then we followed the Route of the fleete, seeing the enemies Army drawne up in battell, horse, foote and Cannon, and our Army of Foote and horse opposite unto them; where I did see six and thirty Cornets of horse, being full troupes without loosing of one Pistoll give themselves prisoners in the enemies mercy, whereof the most part tooke service: As also I did see above five Regiments of foote, being forty Colours, follow [1-27] their examples, rendring themselves and their Colours without loosing of one musket. Iudge then, judicious reader, though we were sorrie for the losse of our Army, if we were glad of our owne safeties: I thinke we were, and praised be God with no discredit to us, or our Nation; for none can be blamed that doth what he is commanded: thus following our course the third morning we arrived before *Flinesborrie,* where our Randezvouz was appointed, and having sent a shoare for some victualls, whereof we stood in great neede, no man was blamed to provide for himselfe at such time, when the whole Country was to be left to our enemies mercy.

His Majesty being there, after hearing the certainty of his great losse, resolved to secure *Denmark*; having lost *Holsten* & *Yewtland* we got orders with expedition all of us to ship, and to hold forth our course unto *Assens* in *Denmark*, where his Majesty promised to meete us to dispose further of us, for his Majesties service, and we making saile follow our course and orders. At our parting the *Rhinegrave* with his Regiment did come thither the enemy at his heeles, and he at spurres following the King, till he had gotten the passe made good betwixt *Holsten*, and *Yewtland*, and his Majestie once safely arrived in *Denmark*, the *Rhinegrave* quitting *Yewtland* unto the enemy follows the King unto *Denmark*: We landed at *Assens* of our Regiment eight hundred Souldiers besides one hundred and fifty wounded and sicke men and being put in good quarters, we rest us, leaving the enemy to rest in the fat land of *Holsten*, and *Yewtland*, having a good broad and deepe fossey betwixt us, we were by Gods mercy secured.

*The seventh Observation.*

Here we see that the losse of a day, is the losse of a great part of his Majesties Kingdome: for the losse of his Armie was the losse of *Holsten* and *Yewtland*, so that here below we have no assured estate, from the King to the Clowne, whereof we have frequent examples in Histories, which should make none of all estates to glory too much, either in their peace, or prosperitie, as the *Holsteners* did: for though now thou be in peace and securitie, as they were before this day, thou oughtst to looke unto thy selfe, and to prevent the worst better than they did.

Therefore to discharge a part of my dutie to my Country-men and friends, I minde here somewhat to touch the misery of man through the inconstancy of humane affaires. *Isidore* writes, that it was the custome at *Constantinople* in the dayes of the Emperours Coronation, while as he sate in his Throne, a *Mason* came to him, presenting stones, that he might choose which he would to make his Tombe of, thereby putting him in minde of the inconstancy of humane fragilitie. We reade also of a simple Citizen in *Italy*, that became one of the most powerfull men in *Italy*, and coming to the dignitie of a Prince, being thirtie yeares, without interruption, in great prosperitie, tranquillitie, and peace, yea ever in the most dangerous time of warre, and his Children raised to high honours and dignities; this man thinking himselfe to be above the winde, a whirle-winde of warres, unlooked for, came on him and his from *Florence*, that he with his wife and children were taken prisoners, and sent to *Millane*, his goods confiscated, he was shut up in close prison, and died miserably: the *Venetians* appropriating unto themselves all his money he had in Bancke. [1-28]

We reade also of one *Francis Force*, that through his heaping up of wealth came to be made Duke of *Millane*, and after that intitled himselfe to be the Sonne of *Fortune*, and the Oracle of the Princes of *Italie*, being many yeares in prosperitie, was afterwards chased from his goods, as the *Holsteners* were then, but having recovered his lands and goods againe, he grew so insolent and proud of his prosperitie, that at last he was taken prisoner, and was kept till death in prison; mockt of the whole world, for his pride and greedinesse. The same Author *Guicchardine* in his seventh Booke in the I 57, doth record of *Bentioles* chased out of *Bullon*, where they long were in peace, the subjects of *Millane* being forbidden to receive them, the chiefest of them died of griefe, having never before tasted the Cup of adversitie: And so became of sundry in *Denmark*, that for feare did send away their goods by shipping unto the *Craggs* of *Norway*, to be kept there, whereof some were lost by Sea, and the owners afterward died of griefe, not having the courage to undergoe patiently their Crosse. *The Lord of his mercie preserve my Countrey and Friends from the like Visitation.* Let no man therefore flatter himselfe with prosperitie, riches, or honour, as *Agapetus* adviseth us in his *Politique Aphorismes.* All are borne alike, come of dust, our glory then should be of vertue, and not in riches, prosperitie, or honours; for we should esteeme of nothing so much, as of *Gods* judgements, praying his Majestie continually to divert them from us, esteeming more of our soules, than of deceivable riches, whereof the possession is uncertaine, as was seene at this time, both in *Holsten* and *Yewtland*, their riches went faster away than they came, and though they could have enjoyed them, yet at last they were forced to leave them to others. Since therefore we can carry nothing with us, but our good name, let us be ever carefull of that, discharging, so farre as we may, with a good Conscience our dutie to God and man, and this Heritage we cannot be robbed of, though the world should turne to nothing.

Here we see this *magnanimous* King his estate falling for his love to his Niece, the distressed Queene of *Bohemia*, and her Children, seeing her baninished from her Kingdome by the sword of her enemies, he hazards the losse of his Crowne and person, to get her restored, bringing the sword of his enemies within his owne Countrey, fortune having crossed him abroad: yet for all this, this *Magnanimous* King was not dejected, but with a couragious resolution makes use of the time, retiring to one corner of his Kingdome, to prevent the losse of the whole, being naturally fortified with a broad graffe, as the Isle of *Britaine*; being strong of shipping, having his Majestie of *Britaine* to friend, and the Estates of the united Provinces, he was carelesse of the Emperours forces by Sea or Land, not being able to harme his Majestie more than they did.

By this example we may see, what advantage our Soveraigne, the Kings Majestie of great *Britaine*, hath over all forraigne Kings in *Europe*, through the scituation of his Dominions, being mightie in power of men, shipping, and money, is able to make warre abroad, where he pleaseth, and to make a safe Retreat, when he pleaseth, being Master at Sea, as he can easily be, terrifying his enemies with one Armie abroad, and a strong Armie at Sea, he can offend whom he will, and retire when he list, forcing all *Europe* to be in feare of him, and his Majestie in feare of none, but of the King of Kings. The Lord therefore preserve his Majestie, his Children and Subjects, from the power of forraigne enemies; and I wish a great part of my [1-29] friends and Country-men were so farre addicted, to seeke the restitution of her Majestie of *Bohemia*, and her Royall Issue, as I am; the warres then should never end, till they were restored, and I avenged of my friends bloud, and mine owne, shed in the quarrell.

Here also I did observe his Majesties circumspection, in preventing the *Emperialists*, in coming by water unto his Kingdome, having beset all *Finland* with strong *Garrisons* of Horse and Foote, which kept strong guards, and good watch by night and by day, at such places on the Coast, as was most in danger of the enemies over-setting, till in the end, the enemy was forced to retire his Armie, leaving but a few men in Garrison in the Townes, which lay on the Coast, which Garrisons his Majestie with shipping did often visite, to their great hurt, with strong parties, retiring againe, having done his exployt, at his pleasure in safetie. This *Magnanimous* King, to my knowledge, deserved to have been worthily thought of, and well spoken of, for his noble enterprizing of the warre, being Leader and Generall in so good a cause. And though the successe was not answerable, I dare be bold to affirme, it was none of his Majesties fault, for his Majestie not onely bestowed much in advancing of it, but also did hazard himselfe and his Crowne in maintaining of it. Neverthelesse, there are always some Cynicks, that doe barke at his Majesties proceedings, without reason; where we may see, that no man, no nor Kings themselves can escape the lash of censure, and none can eschew to be traduced by the ignominious aspersions of the malevolent tongue. Therefore it is good to doe well, and then we need not care what is said; except the sayer put his name to his assertion, and then he may be made to foote his Boule, in maintaining of it, or unworthily to refuse it. Here also I did observe, that no Armour nor passe could remove the Generalls feare; for having once imagined the enemies over-coming, he was never fully setled, till he was safe a ship-board. And therefore I did see at this time that verified, that when man distrusteth God, it is then just with God to leave man to himselfe: for after our Retreat, being on the Roade, the Generall, being thronged in his owne Ship, could not command a Ship to transport his servants, till I forced a Ship for his Excellencies service; which should teach all men in Authoritie, while they have command, to command with discretion, lest the wheele should turne, and then they should be beholding to those, whom before they commanded.

Here also I did see mutinous Souldiers well rewarded, and it may be sooner than they thought; for the day before those that call'd for money when they were commanded to goe on service, the next day I being a Ship-board did see them turne slaves unto their enemies being taken prisoners, robbed both of Cloaths and money, and kept long in bondage, being forced to serve against their Conscience, such was their folly in calling for money when it was no time to tell it. Having at this time left our horses and baggage to our enemies, I observed somewhat on the love of men to those beasts, and the love of beasts to their Masters, as worth the noting, to confirme the kindnesse that should be entertained amongst Christians, and men of one profession; my brother *Obstell*, of worthy memory, had a Horse of our owne Country-breed, that was so familiarly acquainted with his Souldiers, and with the noise and touch of Drumme, that the whole day on our march, when his Master went a foote, he unled followed the Drumme a little aside from the Company, halting when they halted, and moving when [I-30] they moved fast or slow. Another Horse I left, that being in *Wismer Leager*, having rode out one day to a wood, halfe a mile from the Leager, to cause to cut timber, leaving my Horse standing alone, and my Cloake on my Saddle, a Rutter coming by, unknowne to me and my fellowes, steales my Horse away, who finding himselfe in strangers hands, skips loose, and runs to our Leager, being chas't and hunted at by more than a hundred Horsemen, out-runs them all unto the trenches, and running through the Leager, stands before my Tent, my Camerades wondering what became of mee, thinking I had been killed by the Horsemen, come and make search for me, and finding me, tell me of my Horse.

These beasts I have remembred for their love, for which I will set downe some particulars concerning the addresse, fidelitie, and bountie of some Horses; whereof I have formerly read. *Plinie* protests their prayses cannot be expressed. We reade of the *Numidians*, that were so much redoubted of the *Romanes*, that in their warres, they would at spurres, runne their Horses in middest of their enemies, without a bridle to governe them. In the Battaile of *Cannes*, *Hanniball* returning the next day on the place of Battaile, to looke more narrowly to the place, a *Romane* Knight halfe dead, hearing the noise of people, lifted up his head, of purpose to have spoke, but his voice failing, died: with the last gaspe, by *Hanniball* there roade a *Numidian* on that dead Knights Horse, who knowing his Master, begun to move his eares, to bray, and to leape, and rebound with such fury, till he casts the *Numidian* to ground, runnes through the dead bodies, and stands before his dead Master, and leaning downe his necke and shoulders, sheweth the desire he had that his Master should leape on him, to the great astonishment of *Hanniball*, and his followers. We reade also in the warres of *Germanie*, in the yeare 1176 the Dukes of *Saxon* forced by Armes to submit themselves to the Emperour *Henry* the fourth, giving the Emperour for pledges of their fidelitie, two yong Princes, Sonnes to a Marquesse, which were carefully kept in a Castle, that was very strong, the Captaine whereof moved by Compassion, and wonne by some presents, suffered them sometimes to goe abroad to take the ayre, and to ride their Horses thereabout: The Captaine going a hunting, takes these young youths with him, the prey found and hunted, shee is followed by all, not thinking of any other thing: The youths spurring hard out of sight, follow their course till they come to the River of the *Maine*, where they request a Fisherman to transport them in his little Cane or Boate to *Mentz*, offering him their little scarlet Cloakes for pay: The Fisherman helpes them from their Horses, and takes them in his Boate, and rowes downe the River, their Horses swimming after them to *Mentz*, where they and their Horses were graciously welcomed.

*Plinie* writes, that Horses wept at their Masters deaths, and it is recorded, that the Horse of *Cæsar* wept: foretelling his Masters death, and I perswade my selfe, the gentle Reader could adde somewhat to this purpose, if he listed, but thus farre to animate Christians to love, respect, and cherish their *Camerades*, and not to kill and backbite them, as too many are too ready to detract from others, to adde to themselves: a wrong way; for honour is compared well to a chaste Maide, that will never love them who would ravish her, but being courted shee may be moved.

Here I must not forget that dutie I owe to the remembrance of that worthy young Gentleman, *Arthur Forbesse*, Sonne to a worthy *Cavalier*, of fa- [1-31] mous memory, Lievetenant Colonell *Arthur Forbesse*, being a worthy valourous sonne, descended of a valiant Father. This young Gentleman being deadly wounded on service, and with hazard brought unto our Ship, within two dayes dyed. Likewise a Gentleman borne in the Isles of *Scotland*, called *Alexander Mac-Worche*; being wounded in the head, and shot in the arme, the enemies Horsemen shooting at him with Pistols, he leapes from the shoare, with his cloathes on, notwithstanding those wounds, and swimmes to my Cosen Captaine *Monro* his Boate, and being brought in died the next day, and was much lamented for of his *Camerades*, as a Gentleman of great hope.

I did also observe here, the inconvenience that happens to many brave Officers and Souldiers given to plundering, gathering together a little bootie for spending, which brings them commonly into their enemies hands, their punishment being farre more grievous, than their purchase was delightfull, and yet I thinke, the Guilt is worse than the punishment. To which purpose I will onely here inferre one Story. A *Pythagorian* bought a paire of shooes upon trust, the shooe-maker dyes, the Philosopher is glad, and thinks them gaine, but a while after his Conscience touches him, and becomes a perpetuall chider, he repaires to the house of the dead, casts in his money with these words; *There take thy due, thou livest to me, though dead to all besides.* Certainly, in my opinion, ill gotten gaines are farre worse that losses with preserved honestie. These grieve but once, the others are continually grating upon our quiet, and he diminishes his owne contentment, that would adde unto it by unlawfulnesse; for looking onely to the beginning, he thinkes not of the end. But in my opinion, if plundering, or making of bootie, at any time be excusable for a Souldier, it is onely in respect of the circumstances. Our friends being forced to quit their Countrey and their goods to their enemies, before it should inrich the enemy, it were not amisse to take it, or destroy it either with fire or water, before it were profitable to our enemies; and in this point onely I doe allow of this bootie making, providing it doe not hinder men from the discharge of their duties, in time and place: otherwise, our best goods, being impediments to the discharge of our honest dutie in our calling, are to be throwne away. And for mine owne part, a few bookes left by my friends, which mine enemy might have burnt, was all the bootie that I ever made: neither doe I repent me of my neglect in this point; having seene many make bootie, who had never the happinesse to enjoy it long. His Majesties care, in fore-seeing the safetie of *Denmarke*, merits praise: for by the preservation of *Denmarke*, his Majestie, like a skilfull Gamester, recovered againe all that he lost. Therefore we ought never to grieve for any thing past, but for sinne, and for that alwayes. And he spake well, that said, *He that hath himselfe hath lost nothing.* [I-32]

---

### The eight Dutie discharged of our Quartring and Mustring in Fune, and of the Colonels going for a Recreute unto Scotland.

Having happily arrived in *Denmarke*, at *Assens* in *Funland*, our Colonell goes a shoare to understand of his Majesties will and command, and being graciously welcomed, is made to dine at his Majesties Table: after dinner his Majestie discharging then the dutie of a Generall Quarter-Master, who wrote with his own hand the names of the dorpes ordained for our Quarters: as also did appoint a faire Hoffe, to receive all our wounded and sicke men, where they were to be entertained together, till they were cured, and to that effect, his Majestie graciously ordained skilfull Chirurgians, diligently to attend them, being an hundred and fiftie, besides Officers; then we got orders to land the

Regiment, and to draw up in a convenient part, till our sicke and wounded were first directed to quarters, and then to appoint our Watch (*viz.*) two Companies to watch at *Assens*, then having gotten Waggons, for transporting of our *Colonels* baggage and spare Armes, the severall Companies Quarters dealt out, the Furriers sent before, to divide the Quarters, every Company led by their owne guids, we marched off severally, by Companies, as our severall wayes did lie unto our Quarters, where we had rest for our former toyle, and good entertainment for our spare dyet, so that in a short time, we were all sufficiently refreshed, without feare of an enemy. Neverthelesse, our Watches were duely and orderly kept, and relieved by course, every second night: then Orders were given by the Commissaries to give in our Rolles, for mustering of us, that his Majestie might know, what losse we had sustainded on service, and that those that served well might be rewarded: we mustered sicke and whole neere nine hundred men under Armes, besides Officers, having lost on service, foure hundred men, that were killed in the place, and taken in our retreate. Before our coming to muster, Newes was come to his Majestie of the losse of the Castle of *Bredenberg* in *Holsten, Stathoulder, Ransowe* his chiefe residence, where Major *Dumbarre* did command, and was killed. The particulars of this service I referre to the next Dutie discharged.

The Major being killed, I having discharged the duty in his absence, by my Colonels respect to me and his Majesties favour, I had Patent given me, under his Majesties hand and Seale, as Major to the Regiment: as likewise Captaine *Lermond* his company then at *Luckstad*, being vacant, through the death of the Captaine at *Hamburgh*, was also disposed unto me; and orders were given unto the Commissary, that mustred us, according to my Patent to place me, as Sergeant-Major over the Regiment, which all duely obeyed by the Commissary, the Drummer Major, accompanied with the rest of the Drummers of the Regiment, being commanded, beate a bancke in head of the Regiment. The Commissary having his Majesties Patent in his hand, makes a speech, signifying his Majesties will unto all the Officers of the Regiment, and without any contradiction placed me Segeant Major, and delivering me my Patent takes me by the hand, as the Colonell did, Lievetenant-Colonell with the whole Officers of the Regiment, wishing me joy, with the generall applause of the whole *Soldateska*, which ceremony ended, [I-33] the Regiment marched off, by companies unto their severall quarters as before; The Colonell conveyed by his Officers unto his quarters, the Officers were appointed the next day, to meete at the Colonells quarter to receive money, and to understand further of the Colonells resolution, concerning the standing of the Regiment. At their returne the next day, they received two monthes pay for the Officers, and one moneths pay for the *Soldateska*, with promise of winter clothes. But the Souldiers coming into a good fat soyle, clad themselves honestly, which made them want commisse clothes; Yet none of us could say, but we served a liberall, and a bountifull Master: the money first payed by the Commissaries, they give orders in his Majesties name for keeping of good discipline over the Regiment, whereby the *Boores* should not complaine on the Souldiers Isolencie, which they needed not to use, getting willingly from the *Boores* both meate, and mony, with some clothes: Neverthelesse, there were alwayes amongst the one and the other, some churlish Rascalls, that caused complaints to be heard which made our proforce or Gavileger get company and money, for discharging his duety: for neither Officer, nor Souldier escaped due punishment, that was once complained on, untill such time, as his Majestie was satisfied with justice, and the party offended.  Thus continuing in our duety, the Colonell anew doth Capitulate with his Majesty, for bringing over from *Scotland* a thousand men to recreute the Regiment.  Officers were appointed of every company to go for *Scotland*, and for the most part the Captaines went themselves, leaving their Lievetenants in their absence to command their companies.  The Lievetenant Colonell taking a fore-loofe, did go unto *Holland*: I being left to command the Regiment, the Colonell and his Captaines Sr. *Patrick Mac-Gey*, Captaine *Annane*, Captaine *Monro* of *Obstell*, Captaine *Forbesse*, Captaine *Sinclare*, Captaine *Iohn Monro*, and Lievetenant *Robert Stewart*, the Barron of Fowles followed them in the spring, for leavying a company also.  They being gone, I was commanded by his Majesty to take orders from Generall Major *Slamersdorph* then resident at *Odensee* in *Funeland*, who immediatly after their going away, commanded me to take my quarters in *Assens*, where we kept our watch, seeing that part of the country was most in danger of the enemies pursute; where I had question with the Major of the *Rhinegraves* Regiment of horse, who should give out the orders in the Garrison, which did bring an emulation betwixt our Souldiers and the horsemen, so that in severall rancounters had in the Garrison, three or foure on each side were killed. To prevent this disorder, the Generall Major with some other associats came to *Assens* and held a Councell of warre, the businesse considered, the Major of Horse is removed to another Garrison, and Rut-master *Cratsten* is put with his Troupes in *Assens*, and the command of the Garrison was given unto me. Notwithstanding whereof our enmity with the horsemen did continue a long time, till the *Rhinegrave* himselfe had given orders to his whole Officers, examplarily to punish those insolent Rutters, who should be found to live otherwise then brethren with the whole *Scots* Regiment, so that by that time the coldnesse removed, we lived at more quiet during my being there, which was not long. [I-34]

## The eighth Observation.

First here we may see the wisdome and magnanimity of this King not cast downe with the losse of his Army, nor with the losse of the halfe of his country, but preventing his further losse for the safety of his country, and good of his Subjects, he with expedition, drawes himselfe and the remnant escaped of his Army within *Denmark*, to preserve them for a second fitter opportunity; As also to encourage his Subjects, that through feare, were on the flight by water unto other Nations, carrying their substance with them, feare comming unawares, having heard of their Kings losse and overthrow abroad, fame dispersing the rumours of the losse, much worse then it was, the people were so afraid, and so fearefull, that they enjoyed nothing without a frighted minde, no not their sleepe:

they trembled at the present miseries that might but come, they were anticipated in a more horrid habit, then any enemy could put them unto, meeting with evill before it came, making things but probable as certaine, as when one may fit even in a boate, he is in no danger, yet through feare stirring, he may drowne himselfe, and others, as we see often in battell that the valiant man constantly keeping his ranke, doth live, when as the feeble coward by stooping thinking to save his life, he loses it; when the brave soule knowes no trembling. *Cæsar* spake like *Cæsar*, when he bad the Marriners feare nothing. And this invincible and Magnanimous King, though ruffled by *Cæsar*, yet he encourages his subjects, by exhorting them to feare nothing, going at all times himselfe betwixt them and all dangers, he being the first many times ingaged, and the last coming off, casting as it were, through his valour, a kinde of honour upon God; believing in his goodnesse, casting himselfe in danger, trusting and confiding in his care onely. Not like an unworthy coward that eclipses his sufficiency, unworthily doubting that God will bring him off, unjustly accusing God, his power or his will, making himselfe his owne Saviour, he becomes his owne confounder.

But this magnanimous King setting his care upon God, and using the lawfull meanes, for his country, and kingdomes preservation, winning the love of God, and of his subjects, establisheth himselfe, and his Throne in despight of his enemies. Here also I have observed that good service done to a noble and liberall Master, as this King was, cannot be without reward: Therefore let the servant deserve, and the Master will recompence, if he be such a just Master as we served, where both loved each others, for their generous worthinesse. Who ever then is a servant, if he suppose his lot hard, let him thinke on the other part, that service is nothing els but a free mans calling, and comfort himselfe with the example of Kings, that are but servants (though more splendid) for the common-weale; and as this King our royall Master served for his country, let us that are servants serving strangers serve truely where we serve, for our countries credit, our owne weale, and our eternall fame which must live after us. This magnanimous King through the experience he had of our former true service, is desirous to have more of our countrimen to serve him, as we may see by the new employment laid on our Colonell and his Officers; Also on divers other Noblemen of our country, to bring unto him three other Regiments as [I-35] *Nidesdale*, *Spynie* and *Murkles* Regiments, we being the first that shewed them the way to be employed by his Majesty.

Here I will exhort all brave Cavaliers, of minde to follow the laudable profession of Armes, not to grudge, though their advancement or preferment come not at first, but with patience to awaite on Gods blessing, since preferment comes neither from the East, nor from the west. But it is the blessing of the Lord, given by man as the reward of vertue.

Who ever then would be famous by preferment, let him first study to be diligent and vertuous in his calling, and then doubtlesse God will dispose of him as he thinketh best for his owne Glory.

Here we see that the Barron of *Fowles*, of worthy memory, thought it no disparagement at first to follow my Lord of *Rhey* and his Regiment, as a voluntier, till he had seene some service, and attained unto some experience, and then beginning with a company, coming at last with credit to be Colonell over horse and foote, and that to animate others of his name, and kindred to follow his example, rather to live honourably abroad, and with credit, then to encroach (as many do) on their friends at home, as we say in *Scotland*, leaping at the halfe loafe, while as others through vertue live nobly abroad, served with silver plate, and attendance.

Officers of one Regiment ought to live as brethren together, not envying one anothers advancement, entertaining no other emulation, then the emulation of vertue, every one serving truely in their Stations, till such time occasion may be offered, for their advancement by degrees: for though their patience may be the longer, their credits will be the more, and their contentments at last will make them forgo and forget their former toyle, and disturbances having come to their proposed marke, though not altogether to their wished end. Here also we see that good discipline is requisite for keeping good order, that as vertue is rewarded; so vice may be punished: as we may see by the institution of the Emperiall lawes, whereof one we reade constitute by the Emperor *Frederick* the second in the code of *Iustinian*, bearing that the labourers of the ground might live peaceably with assurance over all, staying in their villages, labouring the ground, so that no man should be so bold, as to presume to take any such men prisoners, or to offer them any violence in destroying their Beastyall, or in takeing their goods from them, condemning them to death that did contemne, or violate his ordinance.

And *Cyrus* going to warre, commanded no man should trouble the labourers. *Xerxes* commanded the like, saying, the warres were against those that caried Armes, not against Shepheards.

*Bellisarius* that brave Commander under the Emperour *Iustinian*, was so strict against souldiers that troubled the *Boores*, that the souldiers going by the fruityards durst not throw downe one Apple, and for his good order kept, victualls were cheaper in the Campe then in Townes.

*Procopius* in his third booke of the *Gothes* warres in *Italy* reports, that *Totilas* King of the *Gothes* observed the same strict discipline in *Italy*, suffring the *Boores* untroubled, for paying the contribution.

*Nicephor Gregorius* affirmed, that while as in the front of an Army marched insolency and violence, orderly came in the reare defeate and ruine. And now a dayes the *Turkes* do observe stricter discipline in their Armies then Christians do; in so much that their Captaines must not suffer their [1-36] Souldiers to goe into Orchards or Vineyards, as they march by. And as order is necessary in an Army, so it is in a Regiment requisit to be kept, and punishment also to be used, for banishing all villany from a Regiment, as Gluttony, Drunkenesse, Whoredome, Opression, Playing, Diceing, Roaring, Swaggering: for it is not seemely that those, who should overcome others, should suffer themselves to be overcome with any such notorious vices; neither ought a brave fellow to vaunt of his valour, since it is not tolerable to kill men with words, without coming unto blowes; But he that comports himselfe modestly is to be commended.

Here also we see that the Emulation and strife begunne amongst Superiours and Officers of quality, brings at last the same amongst their inferiours and followers; as was seene in the disorders and quarrelling betwixt our Souldiers and the *Rhinegraves* horsemen, which was wisely prevented and taken away by the wisdome of their Commanders, that carried mutuall love and respect to each others: for the mutuall good deserving of both Officers, which was the chiefe instrument of their reconcilement, and taking away of their jarres, and idle quarrelling, arising of ostentation, an unworthy fruit growing out of Dunghills, withering faster then it groweth, their jarres thus once removed, thereafter our love waxed so great, that where we chanced both to be on one service, as at *Wolgast*, where we stood in neede of helpe, the *Rhinegraves* Regiment, especially Rutmaster *Hoomes* under God made our Retreate safe, as you shall heare in its owne place.

Here also I cannot passe over with silence the love that ordinarily is seene betwixt Officers, and their followers: being once put under good discipline they will undergo any thing for love of their Commanders and Leaders, who have taken paines and diligence in excercising them in the perfect use of their Armes, and in leading them bravely on occasions before their enemies, in making with exercise their bodies strong, and their heart valiant, then I say, what will they not undertake for the love of their Leaders? Truely, I must confesse, they will stand a thousand times more in awe to incurre their Officers wrath, whom once they loved through love, than in any wise, thorough feare of any punishment, that may be enjoyned unto them by Lawes: and if they love and respect their Officers, for feare to offend, even in their Marches, for their Officers credits they will march so orderly with Armes in their Rancks and Files, that you would thinke a whole Regiment well disciplined, as this was, were all but one body, and of one motion, their eares obeying the command all as one, their eyes turning all alike, at the first signe given, their hands going to execution as one hand, giving one stroake, yea many stroakes all alike, ever readie to strike, or hold up, as their Commander pleaseth; and thus exercised they were, that their enemies in all Rancounters could not but duely praise them, calling them the *Invincible old Regiment*: which alwayes rancountred with them on all occasions, so that *Mac-Keyes* name, was very frequent, through the glorious fame of this never-dying Regiment, never wrong'd by Fortune in their fame, though divers times, by their enemies valour, they sustained both losse and hurt: but would to God, we had alwayes met man to man, or that our Army had consisted all of such men, and such Officers, whereof, I was the unworthiest! If so had beene, our conquest had extended so farre, as the *Romanes* of old did extend the limits and borders of their Empire, which for my wish I would bestow on the Prince *Elector Palatine*, borne by the *Iewel* of *Europe*, [1-37] the Queene of *Bohemia* his Royall Mother; and if it were at my distribution, he should have all from the River *Euphrates* at the East, to the Ocean Sea at the West, the fertillest part of *Africke* at the South, and the *Rhine* and the *Danube* at the North; and yet I durst affirme, that his Grand-father King Iames of blessed and never-dying memory, might merit a farre greater possession for his Grand-childe, the Illustrious *Prince Elector Palatine* of the *Rhine*; and to have an Armie of such men, under his command, to be avenged on his enemies. I would wish their cloathes nor mine owne, came never off, till his enemies were made his footstoole to tread on, or to shew mercie, at his Highnesse pleasure: And for my wish, his Armie should be all of *Britaines*, *Dutch*, and *Irish*, such as *Vegetius* describeth the *Romane* Souldiers of old: and I, as one though unworthiest of a thousand *Britaine* Officers, would undertake to make such brave lads to dwell Summer and Winter in Tents, ever in readinesse to fight with our enemies, and to endure all incommodities, for the credit of such a Master, banishing far from him with valiant hands well armed, all the craft, power, and subtiltie that his enemies were able to devise against him: And we should, for his sake, be contented with such allowance as the *Emperiall* Lawes allow a Souldier, being onely so much as might maintaine life, or so much as Beasts get that are put to dyet, and we should be content to march with such expedition, without intermission, without quarter or Garrison, as neede requireth, never staying behinde, but always advancing, consenting willingly to undergoe correction, if we did to the contrary: but to march ever orderly in Rancks, as the way lay rough or even, foule or faire, as our Colours and Leaders went before us; Never quitting our Rancks, but with licence, till the cause were wonne, or that our Masters Throne were established. And if otherwise we went astray, we should be content to quit our allowance: and if this discipline were not strict enough, we should be content to have his Highnesse and *Royall Mother* restored, to doe as our Fathers did coming out of *Egypt*, marching alongst the spacious and wide Desert, that our Randezvouz might be appointed and set, till we arrived in *Cades*, that is to say, in the holy Land, where being victorious, we should bid our Master farewell, and rest with our Fathers.

---

### The ninth Dutie discharged of *Major Dumbarre* his Service at Bredenberg.

This noble Cavalier, of famous and worthy memory, having done notable good service at *Beysenburg* Skonce on the River of the *Elve*, as was formerly set downe, at his retiring to *Lugstad*, he was commanded with foure Companies of *Scots*, and certaine *Dutch*, the enemy having falne into *Holsten*, his order was to beset the Castle of *Bredenberg*, being a passe, but not strong, nor fortified *in Forma*. As I was informed by a valourous little Captaine, Captaine *William Lumsdell*, who was then *Ensigne* to the *Major*, who onely at that time escaped with his life, from the fury of the enemy, being within the house, while as the rest, in the fury, were put to the sword: This Gentleman who informed me, was with the Major walking abroad neare to the house at the enemies first appoaching, so that the [1-38] enemy unawares did come so neare, that they retiring to the Castle, had scarce time to draw up the draw-bridge, when the enemy with his forces, being, as was thought, ten thousand strong, led by *Tilley*, had the house environed on all quarters. The enemy sends a Trumpeter, summoning to render the place, which was refused. Whereupon they entred to approach, and the Defender resists. The service thus begun, *Comoedian*-like, ends very Tragically, the whole Court and lodgings running with bloud, with which the walles and pavement are sprinkled with our *Scottish* bloud, to be viewed and seene to this day. To be particular in the discharge of this dutie at large, not having seene the service, I will not, lest I should erre in giving notice unto the world, of things I did not know; but by report, which ordinarily holds not so true, as things we have both knowne and seene. In this house of *Bredenberg* there was a great number of men, women and children, besides the Souldiers, that had taken their flight thither as to a place of refuge, at the enemies first coming into the land. There was also in this house great store of riches, belonging to the Lord of the house, and to the Fugitives, that was brought from the Country. The Major valourously defended the place for six dayes, untill the time they had approached unto the moate, and shot two severall breaches in the wall, and being so neare, the enemy directed a *Drummer* unto the *Major*, to see if he would *Parle*; But the *Drummer* returned with an answer, that so long as there was bloud in *Dumbarre*s head, that house should never be given over: which answer so incensed the enemy against them, that they sware, if they got the upper hand over them, they should all die without quarters. Shortly after the answer was returned, the *Major* was shot dead in the head with a fire-lock; The rest of the Officers were ashamed to *Capitulate* for an Accord, the *Major* having refused: immediately after, Captaine *Duncan Forbesse* was killed, and after him, Lievetenant *Barbour*, and then Captaine *Carmichell*, who had no charge there, but came by accident to visit his *Camerades* before the Enemies coming, whose fortune was not to eschew the payment of that debt by longer continuation. The Enemy then passing the Moate or Fossey, with a generall storme, scorned all quarters, and being entred, cruelly put all to the sword making no difference of qualitie, age, nor sex, but all alike cruelly put to death: so that five or six at most escaped, whereof *Ensigne Lumsdell* miraculously was one.

The Enemy before this house was taken, as I was informed, lost above a thousand men, which made the Enemies crueltie the greater; and of our Regiment were killed above three hundred. And it is reported, that after the fury was past, they made inquisition for the *Majors* body, and having found it, they ript up his breast, tooke out his heart, sundered his gummes, and stucke his heart into his mouth; they also killed the Preacher, who being on his knees, begging life, was denied mercy.

### The ninth Observation.

Happie is he who opens the fruitfull earth, and croppes her plentie from her fertill bosome, tasting the harmony of peace, singing away his labours all day, having no note drowned with noise of Drumme nor Cannon, but sleepes with peace at night, not over-awde by the Tyrants of the earth, leading the Rancks of bloud and death, as these cruell murderers did at this time, by their monstrous and prodigious massa- [1-39] cre, breaking the peace of God, swimming in Christian bloud, without mercy to Officer, Souldier, or Preacher, heaping up

wrath on their own soules, against the day of their appearance before that great
*Iudge*, that shall judge both the quicke and the dead.

Out of our enemies crueltie used here, we ought to learne to forbeare the
like, lest one day we might be used as they used our friends and Countrymen: for
we may be revenged on our enemies crueltie, repaying them in a Christian
manner, without making Beasts of our selves; in not shewing mercy being sought
of us, which is to be more cruell than Lyons, who will not stirre those who
stoope unto them. And there is no greater token of injustice, than to doe that
unto another, that we would not have done unto our selves. And would'st thou
have mercy that refusest to shew mercy, being sought of thee? No truely; it is
just with God, that he misse mercy, that refuseth mercy unto others; and to have
courage without mercy, is to bragge of vertue, and lacke the right use of it.

Was there greater perfidie in the world than was used here at the in-taking
of this house, willingly to harme the dead, and the innocent? For to wrong an
innocent Preacher, was savage, beseeming a beast, not a man; and to give a
stabbe, as was done here, for the innocent smile of an Infant, was devillish
blacke at the heart. We reade in the *Turkish Story* of a childe, that strucke an
intending murtherer into a swound with offering to embrace him. Would to God,
all those that refuse mercy, were so stricken dead, to terrifie such tyrants as they
were! And I perswade my selfe, none but villanous persons, being Commanders
ever suffered the like to have beene done without moderation: but, I hope,
haughtie and violent minds will never blesse the owners; but that by
Domineering they shall fall like Dust.

This worthy *Cavalier*, of famous memory, after his death thus unchristianly
used, let no man judge by his end, that he in his life time used any man but
generously: for I dare affirme, though sometimes he was subject unto passion, it
continued not long, he being of a good, sweet, and milde nature, and very kinde
and constant, where he professed friendship, and as devout in the profession of
his Religion, professed in *Scotland*, as became a good Christian being sincere.
And commonly his custome was, leading Troopes on service, till he came in
Action, he went before them bare-headed, praying for a blessing to his actions,
as he hath told me himselfe, having asked a reason for this his manner of
carriage, he scorned in all his Onsets to have been any thing but a Leader,
alwayes teaching by the strongest authoritie, his owne forwardnesse by his owne
example: And as his humour scorned to be so base as to flatter, so he did hate to
be so currish as to bite. But he was ever indued with inviolable Amitie, joyned
with invaluable love; and as he was couragious, so he was constant; in the one,
withstanding his enemies, in the other, entertaining his friend. In a word, he was
a resolute Christian, and a man truely honest; and therefore I perswade my selfe,
his death was but the beginning of his joy, and the end of his misery: having
therefore written nothing amisse of him, I neede desire no pardon. But I know
some men will object, as a blame in him, that he refused a *Parlé*, while as there
was no appearance, either of reliefe, or holding out: to which, I cannot otherwise
answer, than he answered himselfe to some of the Officers that were most inward
with him, which was, that he was sorry the charge of the bloud of so many soules

did lie on his shoulders. But if he should give o- [I-40] ver that house, he was perswaded, the King his Master would cause to hang him, seeing he had enemies about his Majestie, who would make him die, though innocent. Therefore he resolved to die honourablie, rather than his name should be brought in question, and then to suffer at last. Here also we see a poore Minister in his last Act giving a good example, not terrified with the horror of death, nor crueltie of his enemies, but on his knees being denied of mercy from man, begs mercy of *God*, dying as a Martyr, persecuted unto Death.

A happie death to him, being resolved with God and his Conscience, to die innocently, like a valiant Souldier of Christ, incouraging others, even in the last Act of his Calling! A happie man, dying in sinceritie, time shall not out-live his worth; he lives truely after death, whose pious Actions are his pillars of remembrance; for though his flesh moulder to drosse in the grave, yet his happinesse is in a perpetuall growth, no day but addes some graines to his heape of glory.

---

### The tenth Duety discharged of our March unto Lowland, leaving three Companies in Fune.

My Colonell and his Officers being parted for *Scotland* to bring over a Recrew, I being left to command the Regiment: In November I received orders from his Majesty to leave three Companies in *Funland* and to march my selfe, with the other foure Companies, and the Regiment staffe unto *Lowland*: the reason of our march was: the Empirialists having by shipping crossed the Belt, and taken the Isle of *Feamor* under their contribution, *Lowland* the Queene Mothers dowry being next unto it, and without souldiers, his Majesty was afraid the enemy out of *Feamor* might set over with shipping, destroy the land, and retire againe, seeing there was no fortified City within *Lowland*, though it was the Fertilest soyle within *Denmark*: to prevent this inconvenience, I was ordained to march thither, and to quarter the Companies in the most convenient parts of the land, and to remaine there during his Majesties will, having onely charge to watch where our Garrisons lay, and the *Boores* were ordained to watch night and day alongst the coast, at such places where the enemy might land: This march though short was tedious, being in the middest of winter the wayes deepe and foule, being fat clay ground, the best and fertillest part in *Denmark*; and the march was the more troublesome, that we were forced in the winter time to crosse the Seas over the Belt twice.

Marching through *Langland*, having quartered there a night, there happened an odious complaint to be made on a souldier called *Mac-Myer* of *Monro* his Company, for forcing the *Boores* daughter, where he quartered. The *Boore* complaines to the Commissary, and the Commissary to me; to satisfie justice, we called a Councell of warres (having our Auditor with us) of the Regiment Officers; the businesse exactly examined, according to his Majesties

Articles, the souldier was condemned to die, and to be shot at a post, to terrifie others by his example from the like hainous sinne: The souldier getting time for that night to prepare himselfe for death, the minister [1-41] instructing him of his duety, the next morning the companies drawen to Armes, a Guard was directed to see the execution, the souldier couragiously and Christianly resolved, being tied to a post was shot dead by his camerades, who without any delay executed the command laid on them by the malefactor, whose Corpes was presently buried.   The next day having shipt, we crost over unto *Lowland*, where, according to his Majesties orders, we were well quartered and courteously received.   The Colonells company and Sr. *Patrick Mac-Geys* with the staffe, were quartered with me in *Marbo*, Captaine *Mac-kenyee* his company were quartered in *Rubee*, and Captaine *Monro* his company in *Necoppine*, where the Queene mother did remaine.

### The tenth Observtion.

Here I did observe that wisdome and vertue were the best Guards of safety, the one securing the soule, the other the estate and body: For this magnanimous and wise King, by his fore-sight and wisdome, did prevent the evill (by a timely fore-sight) which his enemies might have brought upon this Isle of *Lowland*, being the richest part within the Kingdome, for corne a Magazin, and a Garner for forraine countries: It abounds also in all sorts of fishes, the Ponds belong to the Gentry, making great commodity of their fish, being sold in the Cities and country, that are not Licentiat to have the like of their owne.   The Gentry of this land are much given to policy and oeconomy, following the example of their King, having great stalles and stables, containing above foure hundred Oxen, and their stables some threescore horses, being well fed and made lusty, they are sold to the *Germaines*, which yeerely brings unto the gentility great store of money: this Iland abounds in Deere and wilde foule.

This country is also plentifull of wood for building of ships, where his Majesty every yeare hath some builded by his owne master builder, a worthy gentlemen begotten of *Scots* Ancesters, called Mr. *Sinclaire*, who speakes the *Scottish* tongue, and is very courteous to all his countrimen which come thither. The Citizens also of this Iland, being very rich, build ships for their owne use, and some they sell unto strangers.

My hoste the *Burgomaster* of *Marbo*, sometime furnish'd his Majesty for building of his ships, to a reckoning of one hundred thousand *Rex Dolors*, so that in a word, in this little Ile of *Lowland* I did observe vertue to be habituall in it, and so was the peoples goodnesse distributive unto us and our souldiers, so that during our residence there, we were so welcome, that all things smil'd upon us, where it was my fortune one night to have gotten his Majesty to be my Ghuest, having then my quarter in the *Burgomasters* house, and though he was a King, I perswade my selfe he was contented with his entertainment, being both good and rare, whereof truly I had a good deale, but my Ghuest departed by three of the clocke in the morning without bidding me farewell; yet being his Majesties will,

I was well pleased, having sate up all night I was not for attendance in the morning, which his Majesty at his departure gratiously did excuse.

To returne then to my observation, I did see and learne here the truth of that proverbe in his Majesties person, that the wise man only is the cunningst fencer; no man can give a blow so soone, or ward and keepe himselfe so safely as the wise man, and nothing is to be placed above him, but God, [1-42] the King of Kings and giver of wisdome. To live is common, to be wise and good particular, and granted to a few: many I see wish for honour, for wealth, for friends, for fame, for pleasure; I desire but those two; vertue, and wisdome, which both I saw in this Magnanimous King, and in his country people following his Majesties example. We finde not a man that the world ever had so plentifull in all things, as was *Solomon*: yet his request was but one of these two, though indeed it includeth the other; for without vertue, wisdome is not; or if it be, it undoes us at last: and to returne to my observation, in my judgement it may be said of this Magnanimous King, as was said of *Cæsar*, *Semi-Deus est*: for as he is valiant, so he is learned, *Ex utroque Rex*, being valiant and wise, a Prince of an excellent spirit, capable of all good things, as I have seene, and observed in him: he is learned in the liberall sciences, and understands well the Mathematicks and the practise of fortifications, as a souldier studied in the Lawes, joyning Armes with Iustice, two great helpes for the governement of a Princely dignity: he handles well his Armes, and is expert in riding of horses, a strong man for wrestling, as all *Europe* affords, able for to give strokes, and the levellest shooter with a peece, that ever I did see; for with a pistoll he never misses a dogge in the head he shoots at; for experience in warfare, nothing inferiour to the greatest Captaines we reade of, easie to come to, and very affable, patient to beare with heate, cold, hunger, and most durable in travell; and if I were to wish for the personage of a man, mine eyes did never see his like, for a stately majesticke person, whom ever I will greatly respect and love for the good received, and shall be ever ready to serve him against all his enemies, my *Gracious Soveraigne* onely excepted, and his deerest Sisters Royall Issue, to whom I have vowed my best service.

Here also in this Kingdome I did observe, that there is nothing mooves subjects more to obedience, then the opinion they conceive of their Princes care and diligence, in the conservation of his Kingdome and subjects; and experience teacheth us, that the obedience due to Kings by their subjects is weake, if it be not grounded on feare and respective reverence. As authority is gotten by honourable and convenient carriage: so oftimes we see it is lost by evill carriage. So that all greatnesse destitute of vertue doth vanish in an instant; and therefore the Poets did say, that honour and reverence were the children begotten of Majestie and authority: the example wherof, we have in the person of *Charles* called the wise, who having seene *France* ruin'd by the former warres, under his predecessors *Philip* and *Iohn*, *Normandie* and *Piccardie* possessed by the *English*, and having *Edward* the third to deale with, the best and happiest King ever *England* had, who defeated the *French* in two Battells. This Prince resolved to keepe the rest, finding it to be as good to governe by counsell as by force of Armes, he did nothing rashly nor unfore-seene, but his designs were all well premeditated and digested, making choice of men wise, valiant, and knowing how to command in warres. *Edward* seeing his sword thus blunted, and the course of his victories by the wisdome of *Charles* interrupted, said, who did ever see one out of his chamber to give a man so much adoe without Armes? Thus *Charles* was so wise, that his enemies did make no difficulty to praise him, for he not onely freed his people from misery, but also gathered afterward a great treasure for his sonne, being called rich, as he was wise, and being [1-43] respected of his subjects, and of his enemies, as this *Magnanimous King of Denmark* is, for his prudence after his warres, is as much to be commended, as his valour was in preserving his subjects & *Throne* from his enemies, being redacted to a corner; and his counsell served also well, for the good of his subjects, the estate of his Throne, and for the recovery of his losses.   And therefore *Cicero* said, that counsell availed for the good of the State as well as Captaines, for it is oft seene in effect, that by the good advice of the one, the others have happily drawne, and governed their swords; And in another place he saith that *Agamemnon* Generall of *Greece*, did never wish for ten such great Captaines as *Ajax* was, but rather ten wise counsellours, as *Nestor* was, which made *Cicero* so often to proclaime the honour due to eloquence above valour, saying, *Cedant arma togæ, concedat laurea linguæ*: but joyned together, as in this Magnanimous King of *Denmark*, they worke one to anothers hands, for the establishment of his Throne, which I wish so long to continue as the world.   Here also we may learne to eschevv vice by the punishment inflicted upon this souldier for his exorbitancy, in having ravish'd a virgin of her honour, he was bereft himselfe of life, by Gods justice, punishing man for sinne examplary to others.

Against this sinne of ravishing Emperours ordained punishment, to wit, to lose their heads, and their goods also to be confiscate, but the law of the *Canonists* treates more meekely with ravishers, suffering them to marry those whom they ravished: But the Lord judgeing more severely, steeping his rods in viniger, ordaines stricter punishment for such malefactors.  To eschew therefore the committing of such villanies, I will here set downe some remedies to hinder man from such vices, that we may eschew the like punishment.  The first remedy then is to abstaine from the excesse of wine and meates, not to be drunke with wine, wherein there is dissolution.  The second remedy is to eschew idlenesse and too much sleeping, which is enemy to travell and diligence.  The third, to eschew the company of uncleane persons, whose delight is in filthy communications, for he that will touch pitch, must be defiled with it.  *Evill speeches corrupt good manners*; and with Wolves we learne to howle and cry. *Dina* the daughter of *Iacob* desiring to see what was not convenient, neither for her shamefac'tnesse, nor for the respect she ought to have carried to her fathers house, was ravished, violated, and was the cause of greater evill.  The fourth remedy is to keepe both women and maides in a convenient modesty of a chast behaviour, without which there is a doore opened to all villany and filthinesse, which is able of vertue to make vice.  The other remedies are, to live soberly and vertuously in our callings, eschewing evill company and filthy communications, loving rather to take paines in our callings, remembring our duty we owe to God, in not delighting in any uncleannesse, that we may eschew the malediction hanging over the heads of those, which continue in their filthinesse without repentance, abusing the long suffering and patience of the Lord our God and Father.

To conclude this observation, there are lawes and justice observed as well among souldiers, as in other governments, and the strictest justice that is, with least partiality: our lawes are the Kings Articles, we are sworne to obey our President or Iudge, he amongst us present having the command, to whom his Majesty joynes, as assessor to the Iudge, an Auditor for doing of justice, our Assisers or Iury we have not to seeke (*viz.*) a competent [1-44] number of thirteene of our owne Regiment, Officers, Captaines, Lievetenants, Antients, Sergeants, and Corporalls, till our number be full: our Proforce or Gavilliger brings in the complaints, and desires justice, in his Majesties name, to the party offended, and to his Master the Kings Majesty or Generall, that fuers or leades the warre; and every Regiment is bound to have an executioner of their owne, which if the Regiment wants, the Colonell is obliged to hire another to doe the execution for paiment, and sometimes as the crime and the person is respected, that is to suffer, he is honoured to be shot by his camerades, or beheaded, not suffering an executioner to come neare him. Other slight punishments we enjoyne for slight faults, put in execution by their Camerades; as the *Loupegarthe*, when a Souldier is stripped naked above the waste, and is made to runne a furlong betwixt two hundred Souldiers, ranged alike opposite to others, leaving a space in the midst for the Souldier to runne through, where his Camerades whip him with small rods, ordained and cut for the purpose by the *Gavilliger*, and all to keepe good order and discipline; for other lesser faults, there is ordained slighter punishments, as Irons, standing at a poast, his hands bound up above his head; likewise sitting on a Treen or woodden Mare, in some publicke place, to make him ashamed of his fault: As also sometimes to stand six or seaven houres longer than ordinary at the centrie posture; as I was once made to stand in my younger yeares at the *Louver gate* in *Paris*, being then in the Kings Regiment of the Guards, passing my prentiship, for sleeping in the morning, when I ought to have beene at my excercise, for punishment I was made stand from eleven before noone, to eight of the Clocke in the night Centry, Armed with Corslet, Head-piece, Bracelets, being Iron to the teeth, in a hot Summers day, till I was weary of my life, which ever after made me the more strict in punishing those under my Command.

---

*The eleventh Dutie discharged of our expedition by water*
*unto the Isle of* Feamer, *and of the in-taking of it.*

The twenty-second day of *March* 1627. his Majestie having come in person to *Lowland* with two thousand five hundred foote, having appointed Randezvouz at *Rubie*, I had orders to repaire with all diligence to the Randezvouz, with the foure Companies commanded by me of our Regiment: his Majesties intention being to ship at *Rubie*, to fall on the Enemy upon the Isle of *Feamer*, as being too neere in neighbourhood unto *Denmarke*: for preventing of their evill, his Majestie resolved to visit them before they should visit his Country, and in the extremitie of a bitter frost we were all shipped in open Skouts or Boats, where we lay three dayes with contrary winds in the Road very much perplext, and troubled with the extremitie of cold weather, being hard frost and snow: the storme continuing we were appointed to come ashoare, and to retire to our former quarters, till orders were sent us to rise againe, so that the sixt of *Aprill* we shipped againe. And on the eighth we anchored before the Island, where the enemy with diligence planted Ordnance for hindering of our landing. But was repayed againe by our Ordnance ten for one: During which service, we were [I-45] landing our Souldiers with small Boats by twenties and thirties. The enemy with Cannon and musket giving continuall fire on us, till at last seeing a strong body of Souldiers landed, and he having no horsemen to second his foote, he was compelled to retire his Cannon, making his Retreat to a strong Fort they had built of purpose on the Island, leaving the rest of the Island and the Cities at our mercy; the Townes being of no strength.

Before it was darke we were all landed, with our Cannon and Amunition, incamping for that night in the Fields, keeping strong Guards and diligent watch. The enemy being discouraged, we had not so much as one *Alarum*. The next morning his Majestie marched towards the Fort with his Forces and Artillery, and having himselfe recognosced or spied the Fort, retired, giving orders for our severall quarters: Our Souldiers were entred to worke the approaches, which were ordained and assigned to us to approach on. The enemy being scarce of victualls, and knowing of no reliefe, resolved as his best course to *Parlé*, and having sent forth a *Drummer*, which being received, and the *Parlé* granted, pledges being delivered *Hinc inde*, the accord goes on, and is presently agreed upon. The conditions granted to the enemy were somewhat hard, (*viz.*) that they should leave their Armes, Baggage, and Amunition within the Fort, and that they should come forth in his Majesties reverence, of mercy, or of none; which accordingly they did undergoe. But before their out-coming, there was a prohibition given to all our Souldiers, that no man should wrong or injure them: Neverthelesse, at their comming out, the Country Boores (ever cruell to Souldiers) remembring the hard usage of the Souldiers to them in the Winter time, seeing them come forth unarmed, ranne violently upon the Souldiers, knocking them pittifully downe, they caused great disorder, so that in the fury the Count of *Mongomrie*, Colonell to a French Regiment, was knockt to the ground, and left for dead, being taken for a *Walloone*, or one of the enemies Officers. This insolency of the Boores continued (in killing the poore Souldiers) till by his Majesties charge, I was commanded to put my Souldiers to Armes to suppresse the Boores, which was presently obeyed by my Souldiers, who againe robbed the Boores of that they had taken from the enemy, and withall were well knockt. The Tumult appeased, the enemies were sent away by Boats to *Holsten*, where they were put ashoare, and left; his Majestie then refreshed his Troopes for three dayes, during which time, the Island was brought under Contribution to his Majestie, and a Governour with a Garrison being left on the Island to keepe them in obedience, and to hinder the enemies returne, we were commanded to be in readinesse for a second Expedition.

### The eleventh Observation.

*Scipio* said, we were most in danger when we wanted businesse, for while we want businesse, and have no foe to awe us, we are readie to drowne in the mudde of vice and sloathfulnesse. So our Regiment having laine six moneths in idlenesse and sloath, eating and drinking, and sometimes doing worse, for lacke of employment in our Callings, falling out amongst our selves unnecessarily, and without reason abusing both Burgers and Boores, so that when we lacked employment, then was the *Gavilliger* and his Irons best employed, insolency domineering, so that when we came [1-46] to endure hunger, thirst, and cold on our shippes, we were growne so effeminate, that we could not sleepe without a good bed, our stomackes could not digest a Gammon of Bacon, or cold Beefe without mustard, so farre we were out of use, till this *Magnanimous* King came to lead us, who in a short time, without the helpe of Physicke, cured our cloyd stomackes, hardned our effeminate sides, instead of a warme Chamber, made us contented with a hole digged in the ground, to let the winde and Bullets flee over us, making hunger our best sauce, giving us employment, and to our *Gavilliger* rest and ease at home.

O how bright then doth the soule of man grow with use and Negotiation! Now could our Souldiers having made a little bootie on this Island, speake like *Cleanthes*, when he had laboured and gotten some Coyne, he shewes it his Companions, that he then could nourish another *Cleanthes*: even so our Souldiers shewing and telling their *Camerades* of their bootie, they rejoyced the hearts of their Leaders, whom before they had offended by their exorbitancy in their idlenesse, bringing joy with profit, when they were exercised in their Callings, banishing mischiefe from themselves by their diligence: for it is one of our greatest happinesse in our Calling, to have a minde and love to vertuous exercises, raising us daily to blessednesse and contentation; for every one shall smell of that he is busied in, and every noble Action addes sinewes to the vertuous minde: where on the contrary, surely he must be miserable, that loves not to be diligent in his Calling, when he ought to employ himselfe; for if he growes no better, yet sure it keeps him from doing worse, not having time by his idlenesse to entertaine the Devill. When our enemies least looked for us, then came we with *Bellona*, summoning him to the Combate, but he obeyes not, and for his cowardize we degrade him of his Armes, and banish him to some other corner to lurke in, seeing he lacked the courage to have made us sport at our landing, or to have given us an *Alarum* in our Quarters; to have once tryed what for Souldiers we were, or what resolution or conduct we had: for he ought to have busied us at our landing, as well with the spade and the shovell, as with the

Pike and the Musket, and so we could have said, we had an Enemy, as we had not, but a flying dastard or coward.

This Fort was scurvily given over, which any resolute Commander could well have kept for three dayes, during which time, he had added to his owne reputation, and subtracted doubtlesse from ours, by diminishing of our number, which at last would have made him get better Conditions of Quarters, and a more honourable Accord: for in such a case, I would choose before I came in my enemies Reverence without Armes, rather to fight to the last man, and if I chanced to be the last, I had rather die, being resolved, with resolution having Armes in my hands, than unawares, being unprepared, to be knockt downe miserably, when I looked not for Death.

Here I did see the *Ingenier* that built this Fort (who in time of working did oftentimes beate the Boores to make them worke) for his crueltie he was most cruelly beaten againe, and he running to his Majesties feete for refuge (thinking thereby to escape) was on his knees crying for mercy, so hard pursued by the multitude, that before his Majestie he was cruelly beaten dead, as the reward of his former tyranny, and so would God.

Here also we see, that oftentimes the Innocent doth suffer with the Guiltie, as hapned to that worthy *Cavalier* the Count of *Mongomrie*, being cru- [I-47] elly beaten by the rascall multitude: which should teach all Cavaliers bearing charge at such times, to looke unto themselves in attending their Master or Generall on horse backe, when an overcome enemy is marching out of strength or Towne, or otherwise they ought to be on the head of their charge attending their duety; or if for pleasure they would looke on, they ought to be on their Guard, lest being taken for private men, they might be disgraced receiving a Disaster, as this Cavalier did.

Happy therefore are those who can eschew evill by the example of others. Here also we see, that the best meanes to suppresse the insolency of the tumultuous multitude, is a band of well commanded souldiers with Armes, who are ever good servants, but more often cruell Masters. It is then the duety of a Generall in such cases, peremptorily to see that his accord be kept, which otherwise being broken causeth much evill and mischiefe to follow. His Majesty as he was diligent in the intaking of this Iland, so we see him carefull of the keeping of it, as his conquest, by leaving a Governor with a Garrison in it, to be his retreate, in case of neede, out of *Holsten*. We reade that *Guishcardin* in his history of the warres of *Italy* in his first booke, accuses under hand the *French*, that did enlarge their territories by Armes, and did not maintaine and keepe their conquests, but on the contrary did ruine themselves in the end.

The Emperour *Augustus*, having read the great conquest of *Alexander* in the East, he did wonder that *Alexander* did not take care to keepe them, as he travelled to winne them. It is said of *Pyrrhus* King of *Albany*, that where he once set his foote, he was conquerour there. But was ever unfortunate in keeping his conquest; and therefore the King *Antigonus* compared him to a gamester at dice, that lost his owne in hope of gaine. Examples we have of this at home without warres.

*Leonard Darrez* in his 3. booke of the warrs of *Italy* against the *Gothes*, *Totilas* King of the *Gothes* being made Conqueror of *Rome*, in his Harrangue made to his army concluded, that it was harder to keepe a country conquer'd, then to winne it: for in conquering oftimes (as here) the cowardize of the enemies helpes more then our owne valor, & to maintaine our conquest we had neede of valour and justice. That custome of the *Turkes* is commendable, that when he enters into his Chappell, the bed man of the Temple going before him, cries out aloud, that he remember, that the Empire attained unto by Armes and justice, is to be maintained with the like: so mutiny is and should be holden detestable amongst Souldiers, and in all well governed estates. For the use therefore of my fellow Camarades, and for the benefit of my country, I will speake somewhat at large of the fury, cruelty and barbarity of the multitude, mutinous and superstitious, that we may avoid the evill incident thereto, I will set downe here my collections on this point, which occurred in my observation. The Philosopher *Plato* called the wisest and most hounourable amongst the *Grecians*, sayes, the people are ungratefull, cruell, barbarous, envious, impudent, being composed of a Masse of fooles, naughty, deboist, and desperate: for all that is spoken by the wise, displeases the people that are incensed. And *Baleus* writing the lives of the Popes, writes of Pope *Iohn* the twenty third being asked what thing was farthest from truth, he answered, it was the vulgar opinion, for all things they praise merite blame, what they thinke is but vanity; what they say is but lies; they condemne the good, and approve the evill, and [I-48] magnifie but infamy: And *Nicholas Hanap* Patriarch of *Ierusalem*, in his booke of the unconstancy of the people, hath a whole chapter apart to this purpose, and *Arrianus* in his first booke praiseth much the wisdome of *Alexander* the great, in taking away from the people of *Ephesus* the meanes to mutine against the chiefe men of the Towne: for some of the mutiners being executed *Alexander* forbids to search, or punish the rest, knowing that if once the popular could loose the raine, there was nothing to follow but mischiefe, where the innocent might suffer as well as the guilty, as witnesse here the Count of *Mongomry*, that ranne the hazard of death, being long bedred after his beating, without sense or feeling. And *Thucydide* did in his third booke, speaking of those of the Isle of *Corfu*, did feele the evill of a sturdy popular having licence to doe evill, how much it was to be doubted, in so much that the Massacre being so cruell, that there was no villany left unpractised, and such strange things he writes of, that the Fathers did suffocate their owne children, and those that were runne to the Churches for refuge, were cruelly put to death; who pleases may reade the story, where it is set downe more at large. As also to reade the late Massacres in *France*, from the yeare 1560 to this present time, especially the Massacre of the twenty fourth of August 1572 in the chiefest Cities of the Kingdome, continuing without respect of age or of sex, as well against the dead as the quicke, as saith *Lactance* in his sixt booke and second chapter: humanity was so farre gone from men, that to take away the life of their neighbours was but sport, being become beasts drunke with custome of bloud, not sparing the innocent, but doing to all, what the hangman doth to malefactors. Therefore *Quintus Curtius* saith properly, that the deepe Sea in a tempest hath not more waves, then the tumultuous multitude hath changes; especially getting liberty by a new government: And *Titus Livius* in his fourth booke of the third Decad saith, so is the nature of the people to serve as slaves, or strike like Tyrants. Reade also *Thomas Fasell* in his tenth booke of the second Decad of the history of *Sicilie*, a memorable example of sedition, moved in *Palerne* of *Sicilie*, where *Iohn Squarelazop* was cheife leader, amply described in brave termes, he having seene the Tragedy himselfe, where he complaines of the ruine of the City, Iustice and Lawes being abolished, avarice rife, and pride did reigne and dominier (a pleasant story to reade and make use of) in the day robbing unpunished, spoyling the Church in all confusion. *Aristotle* says well, that such changes come by them that have eaten up their owne, and have no more.

There was also sedition moved at *Lisbone*, in the yeare 166 by the fantasies of the multitude, that was a flood that tooke away almost all the *Iewes*, that were turned Christians, whereof there were killed above a thousand, and the Massacre continuing three dayes was never appeased, till at night the third day *Arius Silvius* and *Alvare* of *Caster* gentlemen, and chiefe of the Iustices, came with men of warre in Armes to *Lisbone*, and appeased the tumult. The Kings Majesty hearing the newes of this horrible sedition, being much grieved did presently send unto *Lisbone* two of the chiefest of the Court, to wit; *Iackes Allmod* and *Iackes Lopes*, with full power to punish the Malefactors of such cruelty, where publiquely there was executed a great number of the seditious popular, and the Priests, that moved them to the sedition, were first put off their charge, then hanged, then burnt, the Iudges and Magistrates that were sloathfull to suppresse that popular rage [1-49] and fury, were some deprived of their estates, and condemned to great pennance, and the Towne itselfe was deprived of their priviledges and honours: I pray God to keepe my country from the like. Who pleaseth to reade the story, it is much worth, and of great observance for any good Christian.

Another notable story of the like we have in the beginning of the Reigne of *Charles* the fift successor to *Ferdinand* King of *Spain*: and *Sicil*, in whom did faile the race of the Kings of *Aragon*; the people being moved by a Monke continued long in seditions one after another, till God did remove it at last, and since they lived peaceable.

To conclude then this point, it is a vaine thing to be a follower of the popular sort: for none is the better for their praise, nor the worse for their blame. And therefore *Plutarch* said well, that one man could not be master and servant of the people, otherwise, perforce it behooveth him to fall into inconveniencie; as we reade in the fable written of the serpent, the taile whereof came one day to quarell the head, saying, he would goe his day about foremost, and not goe always behinde, which being granted unto him by the head, he found it worst himselfe, not knowing how or where to goe, and became the cause that the head was all spoyl'd and rent, being compelled against nature to follow a part without sight or hearing to leade it. The same we have seene happen unto those who in the Government of the publique would do all things to please the multitude, and being once tied to that yoake of slavery, in all things to will and agree with the common and lower sort, that oftimes are rashly moved and without reason, howsoever they cannot thereafter come off and retire, hinder or stay the fury and rashnesse of the people. And therefore the great servant of God *Moses* did properly comprehend in the blessings promised unto the *Israelites* their obedience to Gods lawes, that the Lord might establish them in the first ranke a head; in briefe that they should be as Masters, and should not be subject. Reade *Deut.* 28.

---

### *The twelfth Dutie discharged of our expedition by water to* Aickilfourd *in* Holsten*, and of the intaking of it.*

The eleaventh of Aprill 1628 we got orders to ship againe, and being shipped we sayl'd along the coast of *Holsten*, till we arrived before *Aickilfourd*, where lay a Garrison of the Emperialists, being five hundred strong, halfe Dragoniers and halfe foote souldiers, having anchored while we were providing for our landing, the Towne being no strength the *Dragoniers* marched away, leaving the Captaine of foote to defend the place, who had a Skonce without the Towne, with a running line from the Skonce to the Port of the Towne, and thinking us to be but a weake flying party, that durst not remaine long on the land, seeing the enemy lay strong of horse, and foote neereby, he resolved as his best, to defend the Skonce without, whereunto he drew his strength: his Majesty commanded us to land our forces, and to storme the Skonce, he staying a shipboard looking on [1-50] us, we land in all haste, being allmost two thousand foote of severall Nations, *English*, *Scots*, *Dutch*, and *French*: all about equall strength; we threw dice for the Avangard, who should fall on first, concluding those threw most should have the leading, and so successively to second one another, having throwne sixes, the honour of the Avangarde or leading fell on me and mine; the *English* falling next unto us, having put our selves in order, and dealt out Amunition, recommending the successe to the Lord, by our preacher Mr. *William Forbesse*, companion of our dangers, and having directed Ensigne *Allane* to recognosse or spie the best advantage, being retired, I commanded Captaine Lievetenant *Carre* with fifty musketiers to a broken house, that flancked on the Skonce, giving him orders to give fire from thence on their backs, as we marched to them in front, and in case of their retreate to the Towne, to cut off their passage, or at least to march in with them. Thus done, I gave charge to my musketiers that no man should give fire till I commanded, but to follow their Leaders still in good order. The ground we were to advance on to the Skonce, was plaine as pavement; the Skonce not being high, our resolution was to storme without giving fire and as we advanced those of the Skonce did give three severall salvees of musket thundring amongst us, whereof some felt the smart, and Captaine *Mac-kenyee* was favourably shot in the legge, and I more favourably in the hilt of my sword, which afterwards I gave to *Mac-kenyee*.

The most hurt was done to the *English* marching after us, led then by Captaine *Chamberlaine*, a worthy and a valorous gentlemen.   In this time we were advanceing, our musketiers commanded by *Carre*, giving fire on their flancks many were hurt, and the Captaine shot in the Arme seeing us give no fire, but marching hard to storme, he quit the Skonce and retired to the Towne, and enters the Port before us, shutting us out, and leaving a few hurt men behind him; we brake downe the Stacket, and the Towne not walled, we entred the broade side, and follow the enemy to the market-place, thinking he would fight up there.  But he retired into the Church, and shutting the doores defends the Church, shooting out he did us great hurt: our Souldiers not having forgotten their cruelty used at *Bredenberg*, resolved to give no quarters, and with a huge great ladder and the force of men we ran-forced the doore and entred.  I thinking to get the Officers prisoners, entred withall, but could not finde them: incontinent perceiving a great quantity of powder spread a thwart the Church, fearing the blowing up of the powder, I commanded every man upon paine of death to retire, the word not well spoken, the powder blew up, blowing the top of the Church, above a hundred were killed, and a number burnt pitifully, and I with Lievetenant *David Monro* standing behinde me, was also pittifully burnt: the blast past, Captaine *Chamberlaine* entring, findes the Officers, and gives them quarters as his prisoners: of the souldiers few or none of two hundred and fifty escaped.  The Towne was plundered, and his Majesty fearing the coming of the enemies Horsemen before our retyring, we got orders every man to shippe againe as we might best. [1-51]

## *The twelfth Observation.*

This service being but short, having had adoe (as formerly) with a slight Enemy, my observation must be the shorter: but to my great griefe, as we found afterwards the next day, this dayes service was but like a pleasant Weathergall, the fore-runner of a greater storme; for they made bootie this day, that had not the happinesse to enjoy it eight and fortie houres, as you shall heare in the next Observation.

Our hap here and good successe in making of bootie was soone restrained: no man, no beast, no creature, but hath some thing to ballast their lightnesse. One scale is not alwayes in depression, nor the other lifted ever high, but by the Beame is ever kept in motion; nothing but hath some thing to awe it: man with man is awed and defended, the world is but a perpetuall warre, and a wedding. When the *Assyrian* fell, the *Persian* rose, when the *Persian* fell, the *Grecian* rose; the losse of one man is the gaine of another.  It is *vicissitude* that maintaines the world.  Here (I say) our Souldiers made bootie by oppression, which brought a sudden consumption with it, *Hodie mihi, cras tibi*.  The dying Flie lectures out the worlds mortalitie, and though frequent, miserable man never thinkes of his end, till it be too late, ever epicuring our selves with this worlds joy, till at last we are seazed on unawares.

Here I must not forget the memory of our Preacher Master *William Forbesse*, a Preacher for Souldiers, yea and a Captaine in neede, to lead Souldiers on a good occasion, being full of courage, with discretion and good Conduct, beyond some Captaines I have knowne, that were not so capable as he: at this time he not onely prayed for us, but went on with us, to remarke, as I thinke, mens carriage, and having found a Sergeant neglecting his dutie, and his honour at such a time (whose name I will not expresse) having chidden him, did promise to reveale him unto me, as he did after their service, the Sergeant being called before me, and accused, did deny his accusation, alleaging if he were no Pastour that had alleaged it, he would not lie under the injury; the Preacher offered to fight with him, that it was truth he had spoken of him; whereupon I cashier'd the Sergeant, and gave his place to a worthier, called *Mongo Gray*, a Gentlemen of good worth, and of much courage. The Sergeant being cashier'd, never call'd Master *William* to account, for which he was evill thought of, so that he retired home and quit the warres.

Some men perhaps will blame our Conduct here, for pursuing men retired to a Church, being a place of refuge. First, I answer, our orders we had of our Master, were to beate our enemies, in taking them Prisoners, or by killing them, which we could not effect, neither the one nor the other, without entring the Church.

Secondly; They having banished the Gospell, and the Preachers of it out of the Church, we had good reason to banish them, who had made of the house of *God* a *Denne* of theeves and murtherers, as they were at *Bredenberg*, having killed our *Camerades*, and *massacred* our *Preacher*, being on his *knees* begging mercy, and could finde none.

Thirdly; They treacherously retired themselves to a Loft apart in the Church, for their owne safeties, and left traines of Powder to blow us up [I-52] at our entry, which made our Compassion towards them the colder; for when the subject of our hatred is sinne, it cannot be too deepe; and for my owne part, I refused not to shew compassion on those, who did beg it of me, and what others did in their fury, I did tolerate, not being powerfull to hinder them: yet truly my compassion was so much, that when I saw the house ordained for *Gods* service defiled with their bloud and ours, and the pavement of the Church covered over with the dead bodies of men, truely my heart was moved unto the milde streames of pittie, and wept, as is reported of *Cæsar*, when he heard how *Pompey* died. For in my opinion, pittie, though she be a downy vertue, yet she never shines more brightly, than when she is clad in steele, and it is thought that a martiall mans compassion shall conquer, both in peace and warre, and by a two-fold way get victory with honour. And generally we have found and observed, that the most famous men of the world, have had in them both courage and compasson, and oft-times wet eyes as well as wounding hands. *Fabius* did conquer, as well by delaying, as *Cæsar* by expedition. To end this observation, reason teacheth us to cast the bloud of the slaine upon the unjust Authors of it. That which gives the minde securitie, is just cause, and a just deputation; let me have these, and of all others, I shall thinke this one of the noblest and most manly wayes of dying.

*The thirteenth Dutie discharged upon our expedition by*
*water to* Kele, *and of our service there.*

Having retired all unto our shippes, his Majestie made saile againe alongst
the Coast of *Holsten,* till we entred before night, betwixt two lands that goe up
unto *Kele,* where by six a Clock at night we set saile, within musket shot of the
Towne: the Commander over the Garrison doth keepe himselfe and his people
very wisely silent and close, making his Majestie suspect there was no Souldiers
in the Towne, providing for the worst, he expected his advantage at our landing:
the whole night he was busied, and very provident, in working a running trench
alongst the Coast, neare the height of a man under ground, over against our
shippes, within the *Pallessads,* unseene or known of us, where in the dead of the
night he lodged, and placed a thousand Musketiers, giving them charge, never to
shoot, nor appeare, till first our Souldiers were almost landed: his Majestie not
expecting the like, by seaven of the Clocke in the morning, turnes the broad sides
of five great Shippes and two Gallies on the Towne, and shoots at once, for the
space of an houre, so fast as they could charge, seaventie halfe *Cartowes* at every
*Salve,* through and through the Towne houses, where many were lamed of legges
and armes, and freed of lives. Neverthelesse, the Souldiers within the Towne
never gave one shot of Musket during that time, but the Sling-pieces from the
Towne were spreading their Bullets thicke amongst our Fleete, which for the
most part, shot over, doing us no great hurt: in the end, our Cannon leaving
shooting, his Majestie sent orders to set a partie of two hundred Musketiers a-
shoare, we that were Officers met together in the Admirall shippe, and agreed to
command out the partie, and having cast Lots, it fell on the *Dutch:* they
suspecting the [I-53] danger, delayed, desiring the rest to command out alike,
which we refused; seeing the Lot had falne upon them, except his Majestie
would give a second command for it: thus contesting, we goe together towards
his Majestie, to know his Majesties further resolution, and we shew his Majestie
of the *Dutches* delay, on whom the Lot had falne; his Majestie considering better
resolved, the partie should be commanded proportionally of all Nations alike,
and to cast Lots who should send a Captaine to command them, the lot falling
upon the *English,* they command a Lievetenant that supplied the place of his
Captaine in his absence, the partie made ready, were sent from his Majesties
Ship ashoare, being twelve Musketiers in every Boate, with their Muskets in
readinesse; the enemy perceiving them coming, gives a *Salve* of a thousand shot
amongst them, twice before their landing, so that the halfe of them were killed:
yet the Lievetenant valourously led on the rest, and begins the fight ashoare, and
continues the skirmish hot on both sides for one halfe houre, till the most part of
our partie were killed, their powder spent, and perceiving no reliefe was to come,
his Majestie having considered the danger, the reliefe, though in readinesse, was
stayd. The Lievetenant being the last man, retired with credit, being thrice shot,
did come off, and died the next night. A Sergeant of Captaine *Mac-Kenyee* his

Company, called *Mac-Clawde*, an old expert Souldier, and a diligent, sonne to *Neale Mac-Clawde*, was killed, and twenty-two Souldiers of the thirtie that I commanded out of our Regiment, the rest being wounded, for fault of Boates, came swimming in their cloathes to his Majesties Ship, and were taken in.

The partie thus lost, the enemy begunne to thunder amongst our Fleete, with two halfe Cartowes and six Sling-pieces, where leaving our Anchors, he was thought the best Master that had his Ship first under saile: His Majesties Ship being the last, was twice shot through, and two Constables were shot in two in the waste. Thus forced to retire with great losse, we hold on our course towards the Isle of *Feamer* againe.

### The thirteenth Observation.

In time of this hot service, no man could perceive any alteration in the majestie of this King his Royall face, but rather seemed notwithstanding of his losse, as it were, triumphing over his enemies, and comforting others, most graciously said. We ought not to be astonished, when things happen unto us beyond our expectation: and that which was more esteemed as a *God* amongst the *Pagans*, was extraordinarily changeable, sometimes taking part with one, and sometimes with another. In a word, this *Magnanimous King* did abate nothing of his former courage, or of his gravitie: So that his very enemies, if they had seene him at so neere a distance as I did, they could not but have humbly reverenced his *Majestie* for his magnificke stature, higher than any ordinary man by the head: yet ashamed he was, to stoope for a Cannon Bullet, when they flew thickest.

And for the accomplishment of his vertues, Nature hath given him an extraordinary rich Presence, to wit, a face as manly as possible may be seene, worthy of a great King, well mixt in complexion, his eyes flaming and shining, full of courage, his beard browne, his nose Aquiline, or Emperiall, his voice manly, winning the hearts of those that see or heare him, in effect, [I-54] *A Royall King, full of assurance,* without any feare at all, in respect of man: yet full of Majestie, amiable to his friends, and terrible to his enemies.

Here then we may see, that it is the Lord that Guards and keepes *Kings* and *Princes* from imminent dangers that environ them, whereof Histories both ancient and moderne, are full of examples of the miraculous deliverance of great personages from dangers.

One notable Story I will bring to confirme this divine protection, in saving *Titus* sonne to *Vespasian*, appointed for the ruining of *Ierusalem*, to subdue and punish the *Iewes*. *Flavius Ioseph* in his sixt booke and second Chapter of the Warres of the *Iewes*, records of him, that before the siege was layd to the Towne, of minde to recognize, he fell unawares amongst an *Ambushcade* of his enemies, where then it was knowne, as much as ever, that it is the Lord who disposeth of the moments of warre, and of the life of *Kings*: for though *Titus* had no head-piece nor Corslet on his backe (having not gone to fight, but to recognize) of an infinite number of shot, shot at him, none touched him, though many were shot behind him, those darts shot aside at him, he rebated them with his sword, and those shot low, he made his horse skip to eschew them. The *Iewes* perceiving his resolution, made great noise, exhorting one another to runne at him, and to follow him where ever he went. A rare example of a rare deliverance, where we see that he is well guarded, whom the *Lord* keepes. Here also we may see, what difference there is betwixt Commanders, he in *Feamer* shewed himselfe no Souldier; neither yet the Captaine in *Aickleford*: but this brave fellow that commanded in *Keele*, preserved himselfe and others, and that with credit; where we see, that where wisedome and valour doe meet, oft-times the successe is answerable; and a mans discretion is seene when he abides a fit occasion, as this brave fellow did: where I finde alwayes, that those are the best Commanders, that are resolute and remisse, not hunting before he sees his prey, and then with advantage, if he would catch.

Here also, experience deare bought did teach us, that it is better in commanding men on exployts, to command them proportionally out of divers Regiments, than to command them all out of one, which were to undoe a Regiment: and we see often, that the examples of the noble carriage of Officers, doe much animate and encourage their followers to well-doing; and it is a comely thing for the servant of the publique, to teach by example, which makes his fame live after death, as this worthy *English Cavalier* did, especially being in the publique view of the King his Master, his Camerades, and his enemies, carrying their Characters from service, as the marks of his valour, without fainting, though wounded to death.

Here also our *Scottish* High-land-men are prayse-worthy, who for lacke of Boats, made use of their vertue and courage in swimming the Seas, not withstanding of their wounds, with their cloathes, shewing their Masters they were not the first came off, but with the last; following the example of their Leader, they would not stay to be Prisoners, as many doe at such times, and never returne.

I did also observe after this dayes service, an alteration in the common Souldiers behaviour, while as before we were to send out a partie of commanded men, we were troubled with the Souldiers, striving who should goe out on the partie, every one desiring it should be he, but after this dayes smart once felt by their Camerades, they learned to be more wise, and to [I-55] stay till they were commanded, and then they obeyed, though not so freely as before.

Here also I will entreat thee, Iudicious Reader, to give me leave to digresse somewhat, to discourse a little of Sea-fights, which occurred in the discharge of the last dutie, though not properly belonging to my scope. Yet in this retreat-making, as we were in danger of killing, so were we in danger of drowning, by the enemies Cannon piercing our shippes, repaying us for the hurt done by our Shippes and Cannon to their Towne and Souldiers, having in one houre discharged amongst them an infinite number of shot.

To give then notice to the Reader of his Majesties power by Sea, I will relate a Story of a Sea-fight, that happened betwixt the *Swedens* and the *Danes*, which was in the yeare 1564. the thirtieth of May: the Story is written by *Gasperence* in his Commentaries of the *Swedens* warres, as followeth.

Amongst other shippes, saith he, there was one which in greatnesse and excellent equipage, went beyond all humane apprehension, so that many affirmed, that since the memory of man, the like of her was not seene on the North Ocean, which by the *Swedens*, in their language, was called *Makelesse*, that is to say, *Matchlesse*, carrying two hundred pieces of Ordnance. The *Swedes* Admirall, trusting much in this shippe, did employ his whole force against the principall *Dane* shippe, called the *Fortune*, furiously cannonading her, till he had shot her fourteene times under water, and above one hundred times above water, on her Masts and Shrowdes: the Conflict of the first day being doubtfull, both the Armies being much indangered, the next day the *Danes* being sure of one side, next the land, and on the other side, having the *Swedens* Fleete, that pressed to make them ground, but the winde turned so, that the Danes having the winde at best, they chased the *Swedens* Fleete, scattering them so, that the Matchlesse being almost overthrowne by the strength of the *Danes* Fleete, was driven on a banke of sand, where she was burnt by the *Danes* with wilde fire, which the *Danes* launcht within her, the Admirall of the *Swedens*, called *Iacques Bagg*, and *Arrold Troll*, Councellour of the Kingdome, and a Lord called *Christopher Ander*, were taken prisoners. The *Swedens* finding their best strength lost flie, being followed of the *Danes*, whose ships being shrewdly battered by the Cannon of the *Swedens*, that it was impossible to fayle, or keepe the Sea longer, but were forced to harbour till they were helped. Where we see, by the ruine of this great Hulck, that GOD is not pleased when men make such Cities of Timber; but on the contrary, ruines them, not suffering any to grow proud of their might.

*Paul Iove* in his seaventy booke records a story of a Sea-fight, that happened betwixt the *French* and the *English*: Two *English* Ships having pursu'd one *French* Ship, of extraordinay greatnesse, called the *Cordeliere*, having fought long with Cannon, with fire staves, and with Artificiall fire pots, in one instant were miserabley consumed by fire, having lost above two thousand men, burnt, killed and drowned, and lost in ground thought incredible, neere two hundred peece of cannon, as reports *Hubbert Waleus*, who amply hath written this story; and of the losse of those ships, he writes in his addition to the History of *Gagwine*.

*Athene* makes mention of some worthy observation, in his fift booke, and [1-56] fift chapter. *Ptlomy Philadelph* King of *Ægypt*, had a great number of ships, amongst which were two, each one having thirty rankes of seates, call'd *Trigniti-remes*, so that they were marvelous great, and *Ptolomy Philopater* caused to build a ship, of two hundred and eighty cubits in length, and of forty eight cubits in hight from the Keele to the Poupe, with foure hundred Marriners, and foure thousand Rowers: and that ship of *Hieron* Prince of *Siracuse*, built by the skill of *Archimedes*, was yet greater then this other, according to the report of *Athene*, who reports things seeming incredible being a worthy Author, which according to his account did carry two thousand Tunnes, being a prodigious monster, so that there could not be found a sure harbour for that City built of timber; so that *Hieron* did send a present of all the wheate and provision within her to the King of *Ægypt*, for the reliefe of his country. *Plinius* writes of another ship in *Claudius Cæsar* his time, that carried six score thousand bushells of corne, whereof the mast was so great that foure men could not fathom it, where we may see, how these Princes of ould delighted in making of things out of measure.

More of this we may reade in our owne story, of the ships built by King *Iames* the fourth King of *Scotland*, whereof one was such a huge great ship as ever was seene on our seas: she was so great, that *Henry* the eight and *Francis* the first, Kings of *England* and *France* through jealousie caused to build every one of them a greater ship then the *Scottish* ship, which being made ready, and put to Sea, were improfitable for Navigation, and this *Scottish* ship also was improfitable, being lost by Admirall *Hamilton* on an exployt at *Bristoll*. Where she being robbed of her equipage, she rotted on that coast by succesion of time.

At *Venice* this day we heare of a faire ship, but not in comparison of these for quantity, of which *Iustinian* writes as followes, above water she is garnish'd with Columnes, many in number, guilded with fine gold. When any Prince or great man coms to *Venice*, the Duke & Senators to do him honour, leade him unto this ship, where before the mast on the highest stage or degree, is set the Duks chaire, where the Prince is set amongst the Ambassadors, and the Lords of the privy councell, and all men about, on bankes set lower, all the Senators with great silence and gravity, sitting on those bankes under them, are those that leade the ship, even by force against the streame, though the winde be contrary.

The territories of the Dutchie are seene, with the Dukes buckler, clad and covered with blacke, the ship is covered with Tapestry of velvet or scarlet, well bound that the winde may not discover those under it; at the Rudder there is to be seene, the Portrait of Iustice in cleane gold, having in the right hand a naked sword, and in the left a ballance: she is called *Bucentaure*, *bu* signifying great, and *centaure*, as the most ancient marke of ships built in the time of *Sebastian Siano* Duke of *Venice*; at the coming of the Emperour *Frederick Barbarossa*, for treating of the peace betwixt the Pope and the *Venetians*.

*Osorius* writes of the mighty ship of *Dian*, which alone fought against the whole fleete of King *Manuell*, and at last was taken: and in another place of the same story, he speaks of a great ship, called *Resse*, that fought valiantly against the *Portugalls*, and they being entred into her, there was made on the suddaine an artificiall fire, that so affrighted the pursuers, that they quit the *Resse*, retiring the farthest they could from her, which fire did not [1-57] burne, being artificially made, and the makers of it could extinguish it when they pleased.

To conclude then this observation and discourse of ships; I did observe here before Keele, fire being entred into one of our ships, and the souldiers throwing salt water on it, it still burnt the more, till I made them throw fresh water, and then it was quenched, having before read the like in *Plutarch* treating of the naturall causes. And *Venice* feared on the sea hath beene often in danger of burning, as *Sabellicus* writes in his sixt booke in the story of *Venice*, where he reports that the Temple St *Marke* was almost all burnt, and the Dukes Palace was preserved with great difficulty; which verifies, that fire and water are good servants but evill masters. God make us thankefull for this deliverance, and from many more since, having beene in danger of fire, water, sword, famine, pestilence, and from the cruelty of our enemies.

---

### The fourteenth Duty discharged at Grottenbrode in Holsten.

This Magnanimous King, yet still preferring the good of his country before his owne rest and quiet, with the hazard of his person, landed againe in *Holsten*, his forces not exceeding three thousand foote without horsemen: of intention, there to bring his Army together, he drew out himselfe a Royall Leager with a strong Forte in the middest of it, having the Isle of *Feamer* sufficiently provided of victualls and of Ammunition, to furnish his Army during that Summer, and leaving the most part of his strength a shipboard, he advanced himselfe with a thousand men, to a Dorpe called *Grottenbrode*, a mile from the shore, naturally well situated, which might be put in defence with little paines, to hold up an Army. His Majesty having drawne the draught of the Retrenchment, the *Boores* set to worke, I with the *English* and two *Dutch* companies, were made choise of, to Guard his Majestie and the workemen; the enemie lying strong with horse and foote, within two miles of us. The first nights watch was laid on me and my souldiers: by breake of day, a Corporall and twelve horsemen of the enemies were sent to try our watch, or rather, to betray us, which were holden up by our outer centry, who calling to the Guard, the Guard taking Armes: I directed a Sergeant, and a Corporall with twelve musketiers to advance, and to speake with those horsemen. The enemies Corporall finding himselfe wrong, pretended an excuse, alleaging he was come to offer his service to his Majestie, and then retired: whereof incontinent I did informe his Majesty, who presently considered he was a spie sent from the enemy: before midday he returned with fifteene hundred horse, and some Dragoniers; our intrenchment not ready, we draw to Armes, his Majesty directing the two *Dutch* companies to beset the passes, and finding his person in danger retired, with a few musketiers, and leaving me and the *English*, being of equall strength to defend the Dorpe, promising to provide me of amunition, and to send us reliefe: his Majesty thus retired, I caused a barricade of waggons to be made a hundred paces without the Dorpe, where I placed a Lievetenant and thirty musketiers, giving him charge, [I-58] if the enemy should advance to discover, or recognize, then to give fire on them, and not otherwise; This done, the rest of our Souldiers were placed for maintaining the entry of the Dorpe, and the *English* were appointed, as our reserve, to lye at Armes, to be in readinesse to second us; the enemy finding us provided, and their foote not being come up, they stand in Battell, and direct two Troupes of horse to try the passes, meaning to come betwixt us and our ships, to cut off our retreat, but finding we had the passe beset with musketiers, they were forced to retire backe, with the losse of three horsemen.

By this time, his Majesty did send Colonell *Holck* unto me (being come loose from the enemy on *Parole* to solicite his Ransome) to desire me, if the enemy forced entrance unto the Dorpe, that I should retire to the Church-yard, which was but cold comfort, so being his Majesty had no intention to relieve us, and consequently, at last we should be the enemies prisoners, after losing of our Colours, which grieved us most. But I desired the Colonell to shew his Majesty, that seeing I knew of no reliefe, if the enemy pursued us hard, I would choose rather to set the Dorpe on fire behinde us, and then commit my selfe, and the rest to the hazard of fortune in making our retreate, rather then to become prisoners to the enemy. The Colonell gone, we pressing to make a faire shew of a slight game, doubling our Guards before night, and making great Guard-fires in view of the enemy, his foote not come up, and seeing our resolution, he retired before night, where incontinent we imbraced the opportunity, and leaving some Dragoniers behinde us, we retired to our ships, giving orders to the Dragoniers to follow after us, so soone as they thought we were safely retired. Before midnight, the enemy having gotten his foot joyned with him, returned to the Dorpe, and the next morning advances towards us, till he was holden off by the fury of our Ordinance of the ships. In the meane time, his Majesty had above foure thousand *Boores* at worke, finishing the Leager, and royall Fort in the midest of it, whereon were placed eight pieces of Cannon, the Fort being higher then the Leager, did command the fields about, which being complete, the two *Dutch* companies were left to maintaine the Fort, and the rest had orders to ship their men and to retire to *Lowland*, his Majesty having understood, that the enemy had beleagerd *Trailesound*. The second night, after our going away, the enemy coming to pursue the Fort, the *Dutch* retire quitting the same, and their Cannon also, with the losse of fourescore men, so that his Majesties paines taken in *Holsten* was in vaine, the *Dutch* retiring from it unfoughten.

### The foureteenth Observation.

It is much to be lamented, when Kings, or great men preferre their owne ease and rest to the publique weale, suffering it to be overthrowne: on the contrary part, it is worth much commendation, when a King, or a Prince undertakes toyle and travell of his body, for the safety of his people, to keepe them in quiet from imminent ruine, with the hazard of his owne life preserving his subjects. Therefore men ought to call to minde often, the wise counsell of *Pericles*, who said that when the publique state was ruin'd, he that lived well at his ease, for his owne particular, should not escape [1-59] unruin'd, where on the contrary, the publique state being well, the poore feele the lesse discommodity and is comforted in some manner. *Cæsar* was of this opinion, when he said unto his Captaines and Lievetenants, no man could so well establish his condition, as that it could not perish, if the publique state were hurt: But if the publique state did florish, he might helpe and mitigate all the misery of all particular persons. And the Emperour *Antony* called the *Debonnaire*, was of that minde, when he tooke away the pensions of some pensioners of the publique, that did no service, saying, there was no people more cruell, or more villanous, then those that did eate up the publique. Would to God this magnanimous King had done so with a number of his Commissaries, that had misguided his rich Treasure, and were the undoing of his Army, where they should rather have died then wronged their King and country, and should rather have left by will and testament to their children, an example of their fidelity and honesty, then a rich Patrimony.

The Rogues, the Commissaries did much differ in their love to their King and Country, from that worthy gentleman of famous memory, we reade of in our owne Stories, called *William Seaton*, who is worthily recorded of, for his love to the publique, preferring it to his owne children, who being Govenour of *Barwicke*, he and his wife did choose rather to quit their owne lives, and the lives of their children, then to give over the place unto the *English*, choosing rather to keepe it, for the weale of the publique, and for the honour of their King and Country: preferring the publique-weale, to their owne particular: the story I neede not amplify, being well knowne. This Magnanimous King, scorning the attempts of his enemies, ceaseth not still to hazard his owne person and Crowne for the safety of his people: for he trusted and confided so much in God, that he knew well the Scepter was ordained for those that slighted it, and not for those did covet it greedily, as his enemies did.

Here also we see that the enemies forces being drawne towards *Trailesound*, minding that way to come unto *Denmark*, his Majesty was diverted from his resolution, and was forced to joyne with *Trailesound* to make a defensive warre, for the safety of his Country and people, for if the enemy had gotten *Trailesound*, he had an easie way to come into *Denmark*, wherein there were no great strengths, and getting shipping, Artillary and Amunition, (whhereof his Majesty was well provided) he had then the passe open unto *Britaine*, when he pleased. But he was wisely prevented by his Majesty and his Councell, God bringing things to passe according to his secret decree, and not according to the will of man.

Here also we see, that it is the duty of a Generall lying neere an enemy, to know all avenues well, and betimes to beset them well with diligence, and good watches; for if this passe at *Gottenbrode* had not beene timely well beset, his Majesty might have fallen into the enemies hands, the passage being cut off betwixt his Majesty and the ships.

Also in all extremities, it is the duty of Commanders to encourage their inferiours, otherwise the passengers may be affraid, if the Skipper or steersman gives over: as Commanders do looke to their owne credits, so they ought to be carefull of their followers safeties.

The *English* and our Nation are good seconds, one of another, being abroad, for commonly they take part one with another against any other [I-60] Nation; as happened here at *Grotenbrode*, where I did see fifty *English* and *Scots* chase above a hundred *Danes*, with swords into the sea, deeper that their waste, running into the Sea for their safeties, whereupon there was a complaint made unto his Majesty by the Commissary on my *Camerade* Captaine *Chamberlaine* and me, for not suppressing our Souldiers insolency, from abusing of the *Danes*

Souldiers. The occasion of their quarrelling was, the *Danes* Boores being commanded out for the Kings service, and for the defence of their Countrey, they had fortie dayes provision with them, and being well furnished with dry Beefe and Bacon, while as our Souldiers did get nothing but hard Bisket and Beere, they devised that one coming behinde the *Danes* Souldiers for taking up his knapsacke, while as another should cut the strings before, and then to runne away with it; this Stratagem being oft practised by the *English* and *Scots* against the *Danes*; at last, the *Danes* resolved being stronger in the fields than they both were, to fight for their Knapsackes: the occasion being offered, they yoake or joyne with swords, and fight in the Leager, and the *Danes* were forced to give ground, and to retire within the Sea for their safeties, sundry on both sides being hurt, their Officers appeased the Tumult, and after Captaine *Chamberlaine* and I, though innocent of the fault, were mightily chidden by his Majestie: his Majestie assuring us, if the like happened againe, he would punish us, and not our Souldiers, which made us afterwards looke more narrowly to their behaviour and carriage, making them live more peaceable with their *Camerades*, in not oppressing them; for it is a hard time when one Wolfe eats up another.

---

### The fifteenth Dutie discharged of our March from Lowland to Alzenheure, and from thence to Trailesound by water.

The eight of May 1628. I being at *Copemanhagen*, soliciting for our Regiment, orders were given unto me, to be sent to *Lowland* and to *Fune*, to make our Regiment march in all haste to *Alzenheure*, and there to attend for their orders: the orders I did direct to Captaine *Mac-Kenyee*, commanding him to keepe good discipline in his March, and strict, being in his Majesties owne Land; he receiving the orders breakes up the twelfth of *May* from *Lowland*, and continues his March to the Randezvouz. The Garrisons also in *Funeland* breake up the said day, and continued their March towards their Randezvouz. On the March through *Zeland*, Captaine *Mac-Kenyee* his Souldiers being quartered in a Dorpe, the Boores goe to Armes to hinder their inquartering, the Souldiers seeing the Boores take Armes, stayd not to be led by their Officers, but entered the skirmish with the Boores, where at first *Salve*, foure of the Boores were killed dead, and sundry hurt, the rest flie away, leaving the Dorpe to the Souldiers to be quartered in; the blame of this accident was laid on the Commissary appointed for the Convoy, who being absent was to answer for the wrong; but the Commissary caused for revenge, a Boores daughter to complaine on three Souldiers of Captaine *Mac-Kenyee* his Company, alleaging they had all three forced her; so that the Souldiers were apprehended, conveyed in [1-61] Irons to *Copemanhagen*, to be examined there before the Generall Commissary, the State-holder and me: who being examined, no proofe was found against them but accusations, whereupon they were remitted to prison till further triall, where there was an act made, they should suffer no tryall, except I were present.

Neverthelesse, in my absence, they were all three executed, (*viz.*) *Donald Rosse*, *Iames Dumbarre*, and *Alexander Caddell*, who went to death without acknowledging the fact, still pleading their innocency. The Lievetenant Colonell *Alexander Seaton*, being then come from *Holland*, was ordained by his Majestie in all haste to ship three Companies, and to goe with them for the reliefe of *Trailesound*, I being appointed to stay for the other Companies comming; they being come to *Alshenure*, were shipped also, and arriving at *Copemanhagen*, it behoved me in all haste to ship, and follow the Lievetenant Colonell, for reliefe of *Trailesound* being hard beleager'd, where I entred the twenty-eight of *May*, and was no sooner drawne up in the Market place, but presently we were sent to watch at *Franckendore*, to relieve the other Division, that had watched three dayes and three nights together uncome off, that being the weakest part of the whole Towne, and the onely poste pursued by the enemy, which our Lievetenant Colonell made choice of, being the most dangerous, for his Countries credit; where we watched fortie eight houres together, till we were relieved againe by the other Division, and so *Singulis noctibus per vices*, during six weekes time, that my cloathes came never off, except it had beene to change a suite or linnings.

### The fifteenth Observation.

This Towne of *Trailesound* being hard beleager'd by the *Emperialists*, they desired humbly the protection and assistance of his Majestie of *Denmarke*, which was willingly granted unto them: having accorded on their Conditions, his Majestie made choice of our Regiment to be sent thither, having had sufficient proofe of our former service, in his Majesties presence, and under command of others his Majesties Generalls; So that before others we were trusted on this occasion, where we did come with a timely reliefe to those Burgers, that were wearied and toyled with watching, and also hurt by their enemies, whom they had beaten from their walles twice before our coming.

In this accident, which hapned in *Zeland* betwixt the Boores and our Souldiers, we may see the Antipathy that is betwixt Souldiers and Boores, where the one cannot with patience indure the sight of the other, without some present jarre, so that it were impossible to make them agree together, if *Military Discipline* were not strictly observed, and the transgressours exemplarily punished.

Here also I cannot omit the over-sight committed by those Belly-gods the Comissaries, that serve the publique State worst, yet are oft-times best recompenced; whose neglect on this March, was the cause of shedding the innocent bloud of the poore Labourers, and of the Souldiers also: and it was pittie, such a King should entertaine so many of this sort of belly-gods, that studied nothing so much, as to fill their own Coffers, and to raise their houses, without any care had of the Publique Weale.

Here also I cannot allow of that vaine custome amongst the Officers, that [I.62] will make a bad choice for a little ostentive credit, having the good in their election, to make choice of the worst; for in occasions against our enemies, we should rather take all advantages, as of strength, of ground, of Sunne and winde: and shall he not be thought yet unwiser, who may be the Instrument to save his people on service, that willingly will make choice of a place to lose them.

No menagrie in my opinion comparable to that which spares the lives of men from losing, and I perswade my selfe, I need not insist in this reprehension, seeing the actor, though out of time, was sorrowfull enough for his evill choice.

Here also I did observe, that frequent danger doth encourage the feeblest Souldier, who by daily dangers, and the familiaritie made with death, in stepping every day over the bodies of dead men, who perhaps never before had seene one die naturally, much lesse to see daily and hourely examples of violent death, learning wit, by by-past losses, and experience had in the exercise of our Calling, being hardned with toyle and travell. Therefore, in my judgement, no man is more worthy of the name of a Souldier, than he that indures best wearisome toyle and travell in this honourable Calling, not withdrawing the shoulder, but by pushing it forwards couragiously, having once begun: for though in all affaires of this kinde, the beginnings seeme hard and difficult, yet soone after we finde it lighter, according to the measure of our advancement, and reward in the end, we enjoy still the greater contentment, as became of me the first time my friends led me up a steepe hill, when my breath begun to faile me, looking behinde, and seeing what way I had put by, the rest to the top of the hill seemed nothing unto me, being so neare the end of my travell, but was plesant rather than tedious. And therefore we use to say, He that beginneth well hath halfe ended.

At our entry in this Towne, our travell and toyle once begun, continued night and day for six weekes, till we grew hard with travell, yet not hard, as many of the *Dutch*, that are hard against the Musket Bullet, this proofe we lacked. He that shews himselfe honest in his calling and Travells, the Travell passeth, the honestie remaineth: But on the contrary, when we have taken delight in evill, the delight passeth, and the evill remaineth. Happie therefore are those who travell in well-doing; for when the paines are gone, then doe they enjoy the pleasure.

We reade of *Cincinnatus* brought from the plough to the *Senate*, to be made *Consull* for his Travell: the like we reade of *Quintus* taken form his plough to be a *Consull* also; a great change. No wonder then to take a man from the plough to be a Souldier; as the Porter of *Fowles*, called *Mac-Weattiche*, who, in this Towne of *Trailesound* did prove as valiant as a sword, fearing nothing but discredit, and the down-looke or frowne of his Officers, lest he should offend them. [I-63]

### The sixteenth Dutie discharged of our Watches and Accidents, that occurred in this Towne, before the Enemy did storme our Workes.

The twenty-eight of *May* 1628, not without danger both by water and from land, we entred the Towne of *Trailesound*, the Emperiall Armie lying before it, having their batteries neere the water; at our in-coming they shot our Mast, having grounded before our in-coming, we ranne the hazard both of drowning and killing; but being againe without hurt come off, our Camerades wearied of watching, immediatly after our entry we relieved the watch at *Franckendor*, being the onely Poast in the Towne most pursued by the enemy.

The order of our watch was after this manner: of the seaven Companies one Company watched still on the Island before the Towne, called the *Hollomne*; the other three Companies were ordained by foure a clocke afternoone, to parade in the Market place, and afterwards to march to their Poast at *Franckendor*, without the walles on scurvie outworkes, which were but slightly fortified with a dry Moate, the enemy lying strong before us, and approaching neare, we fearing a sudden on-fall, those that were relieved of the watch by five of the clocke, were ordained againe to meet by nine of the clocke at night, and to watch againe on the by-watch, till foure of the clocke in the morning, whereof the one halfe were appointed to lie in readinesse at their Armes without the Port neere the workes, while as the other halfe were appointed also to lie in readinesse at their Armes on the Market place, to attend all occasions of Alarums, either within or without the Towne: and thus we watched nightly, relieving one another, for the space of six weeks.

The rest of the Postes, above the walles, were also beset by the *Dutch*, but none had the halfe of our duties to discharge, by reason the whole approaches were made by the Enemy to us, as being the weakest part. Notwithstanding of this our great nightly watch and dutie kept, the Burgers of the Citie did prove very ungratefull and unthankfull to us, in not quartring our Souldiers, as they ought to doe: for Captaine *Monro* his Company did lie on the streets foure nights unquartred, till the fortnight that they came off the watch, unknowne to their Officers, they went to the Burgo-Master his owne house, and said, they would quarter with him, if there were not orders taken for their quartring, but receiving a soft answer, they retired for that night: in the meane time, the Burgo-master did complaine to Colonell *Holke*, then Governour, who did cause to assemble a Councell of warre, where the Lievetenant and Company were both accused, as mutiners; the Lievetenant proving he knew nothing of it, and that the Souldiers had done it without his knowledge, he was assoyled and made free by the sentence of the Councell of warre: But the Company were ordained, being divided in three Corporalships, that out of every Corporalship one should be hang'd, who were to draw Billets out of a Hatt, which were all blankes, till one had the Gallowes on it.

The order and sentence of the Councell of warre being duly obeyed, three were led aside, and committed to prison, to be resolved against the exe- [I-64] cution, and the rest were remitted to their Quarters, of the three ordained to be executed, it was concluded againe, by the intercession of the Officers made to the Govenour, that one might suffer, who againe being two *Scots* and a *Dane*, having drawne lots, it fell to the *Dane* to be hang'd, the Governour himselfe being a *Dane* also, he could not of his credit frustrate justice, seeing before he was so earnest to see our Nation punished for a fault, whereof he was rather guilty himselfe, not having appointed them quarters as he ought, so that the *Dane* suffred justly for a *Danes* fault.

The Captaines of some Companies being absent in *Scotland*, having gone for recruets, the duety being great, Lievetenant *Saunders Hay* was made Captaine to *Annan* his company, being informed the Captaine was to remaine in *Scotland*: Ensigne *Gordon* being made Lievetenant to Sr. *Patrick Mac-Gey*, being long sicke in *Lowland*, and having a little recovered, on his journey to *Trailesound*, at *Copmanhaggen* in *Denmark*, died suddainely being a resolute brave young Cavalier, and of good parts, was much lamented.

He being dead Ensigne *Gawin Allen* was made Lievetenant, and *Patrick Dumbarre*, a young gentleman, of worth and merit, was advanced to be Ensigne.

During our residence here, our orders were so strict, that neither Officer, nor souldier was suffered to come off his watch, neither to dine or suppe, but their meate was carried unto them, to their poste. The enemy approaching hard, and we working fast, for our owne safeties, where sometimes, we salyed out, and did visit the enemy, in his Trenches, but little to their contentment; till at last, the enemy did approach right under our worke, where sometimes, being so neere, we begun to jeere one another, so that the *Dutch* one morning taunting us, said, they did heare, there was a ship come from *Denmarke* to us, laden with Tobacco and Pipes, one of our souldiers shewing them over the worke, a Morgan sterne, made of a large stocke banded with Iron like that shaft of a halbert, with a round Globe at the end with crosse Iron pikes, saith, here is one of the Tobacco pipes, wherewith we will beate out your braines, when ye intend to storme us.

We did also nightly take some prisoners of them, sometimes stealing off their centeries, which made many Alarums in the night, and in the day time. Here a man might soone learne to exercise his Armes, and put his courage in practise: and to give our Lievetenant Colonell his due, he had good orders, and he did keepe both Officers and souldiers under good discipline, and he knew well how to make others understand themselves, from the highest to the lowest.

### The sixteenth Observation.

When Cannons are roaring, and bullets flying, he that would have honour must not feare dying: many rose here in the morning, went not to bed at night, and many supped here at night, sought no breakefast in the morning: many a Burger in this City, coming forth in his holy-dayes-clothes, to take the ayre, went never home againe, till he was carried quicke or dead, where some had their heads seperated from their bodies, by the Cannon; as happened to one Lievetenant and thirteene Souldiers, that had their foureteene heads shot from them [I-65] by one Cannon bullet at once: who doubts of this, he may go and see the reliques of their braines to this day, sticking on the walles, under the Port of *Franckendore* in *Trailesound*.

It is said, that valour is then best temper'd, when it can turne out of sterne fortitude, unto the mild streames of pitty: who could behold these accidents, and not be moved with pitty and compassion: and who will not weepe at the casuall miseries our calling is subject unto, in following oft-times the leading of an ambitious Generall, yea and of an ambitious Captaine, yea the following of an ambitious Souldier, delighting sometimes to treade over his enemies, as happened many times unto us during this siege?

Who then is more compassionate, in peace or warre, then the martiall man? Observe generally, and you shall finde, that the most famous men have both courage and compassion; of which in this City we had neede; of courage against our enemies, and of compassion to our friends, Camerades, and sometimes to our enemies.

You see here we were made to keepe double watch, as wise men ought to do: for when we kept steddy watches, the enemy could not harme us much, being wary of our selves, and he that can do this, he surely merits the name of a good Souldier, but oftimes, we are our owne worst enemies, and killing our selves we neede no other enemy against us. Therefore at such a Siege as this was, sobriety and temperance were requisite to a Souldier, as well as valour to defend him from his enemies.

Here our enemies were our pedagogues teaching us verture, every moment minding us of our duety to God and man: yea minding us both of Death, and of Iudgement: here we needed no dead mans pawe before us, to minde us of Death, when Death it selfe never went night or day with his horror from our eyes, sparing none, making no difference of persons, or quality, but *æquo pede*, treading alike on all came in his way, whose houre was come.

Here I wish not the gentle reader to mistake this insurrection of *Monro* his company for a mutiny. It was not; neither against their Officers, nor yet in prejudice of their Masters service. Therefore I would rather terme it, a rude ignorance in seeking their due, though unformally, whereof their Officers had no part, and therefore were made free by a Councell of warres, but the unthankefulnesse of the Citizens (in sparing their meanes from feeding of those that kept them, their wives and children, from the furious rage of their enemies, at such time as they themselves did looke for no safety, till they came for to relieve them) cannot be well excused, but their unthankefulnesse was so much the greater, that they err'd against the very lawes of hospitality, being in their unthankefulnesse farre inferiour to Beasts. For we reade, that the *Athenians* did bring those guilty of unthankefulnesse before the Iustice, to be punished, and that justly; because he that forgets a benefit received, without making any satisfaction, doth take away humane society, without which the world could not subsist: and therefore such Citizens, as would not acknowledge the good received, ought to be banished the City, as unthankefull, for a man evill in particular, cannot be a good member of the publique, as many villanous traitors were in this Towne of *Trailesound* during the Siege, that for their particulars would have sold the Towne, and the common good to their enemies; [I-66] such fellowes some of them were made slaves, being not worthy the name of free Citizens: and the Canon lawe makes the ungratefull the most detestable of all men; And therefore they were cruelly punished.

To make then the ingratitude of the Citizens of *Trailesound* towards Souldiers the more odious, I will inferre the Stories of Beasts here to accuse them; *Elian* writes of a *Dragon* mindfull of the good done to him (as these Rogues were not) in these termes, in his thirteenth booke. In *Achaia* there was a Towne called *Petra*, where a young boy did buy a *Dragon* very little, feeding it diligently, making of it, playing with it, and making it ly in his Bed, till it became great, and a *Dragon* in effect: those of the place fearing some evill by it, did cause it to be carried unto a desert: the boy becoming a man also, and certaine yeares after, returning from a feast, with some of his Camerads, they met with Robbers, and crying out for helpe, there comes the *Dragon* running on the Robbers, killing some, putting the rest to flight, saves the life of him that had done him good.   A memorable acknowledgment to convince those of *Trailesound*.

We may joyne to this story, the memory of the *Lion* healed by *Androt* the *Roman* slave, whose life afterwards the *Lyon* saved.   The story is written by *Gellius* and *Elian*, and also now set out in verse by *Dubartas*, in the sixt day of the first weeke.

Here also we may see the profit and benifit good order doth bring uno the observers of it: though we thought hard, not to be suffered to come off our Postes for our ordinary recreation, nor yet to sleepe from our Postes, we found at last the benefit redounded unto our selves: for while as the enemy pursued us hard, we were at hand to defend our selves, and to maintaine our credits; otherwise, it had become of us, as it became in the *Swedens* wars in *Germany* of *Magdeburg* on the *Elve*, and of *Franckeford* on the *Oder*, being both lost through negligence and carelesse watch, which made much innocent bloud to have bin shed in both.   And therefore I cannot but praise the worth of my Lievetenant Colonell, for his good order and strict discipline kept in *Holke* his absence, being in *Denmark* at his wedding, we being then in greatest danger of our enemies.

---

## The seventeenth Dutie discharged of the storming of our Poast, and of our losses and the enemies.

The twenty sixth of Iune 1628, the Duke of *Fridland Walenstine* Generall to the Emperiall Army, having come to visit the beleaguering, and finding *Felt* Marshall *Arnehem* had line six weekes, and not gotten it in, the Generall being offended, at his coming he did Recognosse the whole Towne, and finding our Poast to be the weakest part thereof, by reason of the situation and of the insufficiency of the workes, the wall not exceeding the hight of a man, he resolved to pursue it by storme, swearing out of a passion he would take it in, in three nights, though it were hanging with Iron chaines, betwixt the earth and the heavens. But forgetting to take God on his side, he was disappointed by him, who disposeth of all [1-67] things at his pleasure, being the Supreme watch-man himselfe, that neither slumbers nor sleepes.

We having then gotten intelligence of *Walenstine* his coming, we look't the better unto our selves, and having in the evening or twilight set out our Perdues, we strengthened all our Poasts, and we placed our by-watch in the *Ravelin*, to be in readinesse, as also I commanded foure score musketiers, under the command of Captaine *Hay*, to sit by their Armes and to be in readinesse, to supply all defects might happen by a timely succours, as they should be commanded; likewise I caused to double all centries, and so sitting downe to rest us, we were passing the time by discourse, betwixt ten and eleven a clocke at night, when as our centry gives fire and calls us to our Armes: at our rising we finde the enemy approaching above a thousand strong, with a shoute, *Sa, Sa, Sa, Sa, Sa, Sa*, thus it went on cheerefully, and every man to his Station. The worst was, we had without a halfe moone unfinished, where Ensigne *Iohnston* was with fifty musketiers, that were forced to retire under ground one after another at a sorting Port, where some were lost before their entry: they being entred, then begun our souldiers to make service, and I give charge to Quarter Mr. *Bruntfeild*, a valorous gentleman, with a guard to keepe the enemy from entring at the sorting Port: thus the service being hot on all quarters, especially *Mac-kenyees* quarter, being next the enemy, was hardest prest, where I having visited him, did send him fifty musketiers of supply, and then I did visite Lievetenant *Beaton* his Poast, whom I found both carefull and vigilant in resisting the Enemies entry valiantly, with his associats, who were two capable Segeants called *Embrey* and *Simpson*, who were both killed this night.

Then I did visit the *Dutch* quarters, being betwixt me and the Ravelin: which I thought to be in least danger. The Cavalier their Captaine being a *Beamish* gentlemen, both stout and diligent, the most part of his Souldiers, the *Dutch* having left him, he was much over-prest with the enemies, them also I was forced to supply with fifty musketiers of our Nation, under the command of Captaine *Hay*, otherwise the enemy had fallen in betwixt us and the Raveline. But this valorous gentleman the *Beamish* Captaine being killed; Captaine *Hay* by his valour maintained the Poast, till the fury of the enemy begun a little to settle. In this time, for one houre and a halfe, the service being hot, sundry were killed of us, but three for one of the enemy, which finding himselfe resisted with valour, being relieved by a fresh supply of another thousand men, set on more furiously then before, where sundry of our Officers were shot, as Lievetenant *Beaton*, Ensigne *Dumbarre*, Lievetenant *Arburthnot*, quarter Mr. *Bruntfield*, & my selfe; divers others were killed, as Sergeant *Mac-kenyee*, Sergeant *Young*, *Mosieur Gordon*, *Monsieur Stewart*, *Monsieur Tullough*, all gentlemen of my Colonells company, with divers more, and Captaine *Mac-kenyee* was also shot favourably athwart the Belly, and I being wearied and growne stiffe with my wounds, being helpt off, did meete a fresh reliefe coming to us, led by

Lievetenant *Andrew Stewart*, a valorous gentleman, and of good conduct, Brother to the noble Earle of *Traquare*: I did exhort them *en passant*, to carry themselves well, they answered me cheerefully, as became resolute Souldiers, who were desirous to vindicate their camerades bloud against their enemies: the reliefe being come, the service went on afresh on both sides, the enemy storming againe with the third reliefe, which continued so long, till a number of our Officers more [I-68] were killed and hurt, as Lievetenant *Stewart*, Ensigne *Seaton*, Ensigne *Ennis*, Captaine *Armes*, *Andrew Monro*, and divers more were hurt. Druing this time, our Lievetenant Colonell was busied within the Towne, in commanding the reliefes, and in sending orders to the other Poasts to looke unto themselves, who would not misse one man to succour or helpe us in our greatest neede. Notwithstanding, that the whole force of the enemies was imployed against us alone.

The second reliefe that came to our Poast, was led by Colonell *Frettz*, newly come to Towne, with some *Swedens*, who, though not admitted to Command, out of his generositie, being accompanied with his Lievetenant Colonell *Mac-Dougall*, and his Major, called *Semple*, with fourescore Musketiers, voluntarily did come to succour and helpe our Nation; who at his first coming, received deaths wounds, whereof he died shortly after. His Lievetenant Colonell also was taken prisoner, and was missing for six moneths, we not knowing whither he was dead or alive. The Major also was killed instantly at his first coming to service; so that the last time, and on the last storme, by the breake of day the enemy was once entred our workes, and was beate backe againe with great losse, with swords and pikes and butts of Muskets, so that the day cleering the enemy was forced to retire, having lost above a thousand men, and we neare two hundred, besides those who were hurt. He that was on this nights service from the beginning to the ending, being in action, might avouch he did escape danger. The enemy forsaking our workers unconquered, the graffe filled with their dead bodies, equall to the bancks, the workes ruin'd in the day time could not be repair'd, which caused the next nights watch to be the more dangerous.

### The seventeenth Observation.

The Emperour *Alexander Severe* had reason to say, that Military Discipline did conserve and maintaine the Estate: And so might the magnanimous King of *Denmarke* say of this service, and the Towne of *Trailsound*, the Citizens of it, before this time being sluggish, dissolute, cowards, spend-thrifts and voluptuous, are now by this Discipline made active, menagers, valiant, sparing and honest: the thankes whereof they owe unto our Nation, whose bones lie in their ground, and to our Country-man, who since hath beene their Governour, for the reward of his verture, was appointed by his Majestie of *Sweden*, of worthy memory, and set to Command over them and their Citie. And it is most sure, that the observance of good discipline is the maintaining of Kingdomes, Cities, and Common-wealths, making them to flourish; where discipline is well kept, as it was here during our beleagering, for then we had no thought of gathering of money, but of gaining of credit; here were no Novices, but expert Souldiers to resist both the craft and valour of their enemies, who did feele the smart of their valourous resistance, in heaping their dead bodies one upon another in the graffe.

During the time of this hot conflict, none that was whole went off at the coming of the reliefe, but continued in the fight assisting their Camerades, so long as their strength served, ever esteeming more of their credit than of their safetie, through the desire they had to be revenged of the losses sustained by their Camerades. On the other part, it was reported of *Walestine*, [I-69] that he was so eager to get in the Towne, that his Officers retiring off servce being hurt, he caused to shoot them dead, calling them Cowards for retiring with so small hurt. Here also I purpose to speake somewhat of the *Emperialists* custome, entring on service, shouting like *Turkes*, as if crying would terrifie resolute Souldiers: No truely; we were more encouraged, having long expected for their coming, being all of us well resolved for the Combat, we were greedie of honour, and therefore we longed to try our enemies valour: Seeing we were more overjoyed of their coming, than any wise terrified; and we received them with Volees of Cannon and Musket in their teeth, which faire and well come was hard of digestion unto some of them: and it might be well said of them, as the *Proverbe* is amongst the *Bactrians*, that the dogges did barke more than they did bite, especially the Fleete Curres; for true courage consists not in words, neither ought we to looke for much courage, where we heare many boysterous words. But on the contrary, true valour doth consist in the greatnesse of courage, and in the strength of the valiant Arme, and not in the Tongue: and the first people, that did practice this lowde crying of martiall resolution, and of rejoycing in battell, were the *Israelites*, who in the most part of their fighting used those cryes, as testimonies of their faith, and of their earnest calling for the helpe of the Almightie. And a Lord of *Africke* being to fight against the *Portugalls*, his Troopes ready to fight, he said unto them, they should not cry but strike hard, for saith he, those men whom you see, are not accustomed to be afraide with words nor voyce; for it is not in cryes, but in valour, that men should establish the hope of Victory. Neverthelesse, we reade in Histories, that the *Romanes*, and other warlike Nations, were wont in Battells, as to this day in approaches, even as in fields, to cry alowd: and therefore we say among our selves at home, that he is to be pittied, that is surprized with the cry of his Enemies. We reade also of the *Savages*, whom the *French* doe call *Tokniambous*, that before they come within halfe a mile, they cry like Devills at the first sight of their enemies, redoubling their cryes coming neare hand, sounding their hornes, lifting their Armes here and there in a boasting manner, fighting so long as they are able to move hand or foote, never giving ground or turning backe till they die.

*Tacitus* reports, that the *Germanes* of old, did sing going to fight: and wee reade of *Cato* the *Censor*, that he taught young men to fight standing in one place, and he used to say often, that words were more powerfull to terrifie, and to chase an enemy, than the stroaks of the hand. And the same *Cato* said, he loved not the Souldier that did shake his hands marching, that staggred with his feet in fighting, & snorted lowder in sleeping, than he did cry coming to fight. And *Cæsar* said, that in every man was seene a certaine moving and naturall readinesse and promptitude, that kindled them with a desire to fight: which Generalls and Commanders of Armies ought diligently to intertaine, and not extinguish. Wherefore it was, that the Ancients before they fought, caused to sound their Trumpets, beate their Drummes, and made their Souldiers cry hard, esteeming that did encourage their Troopes, and affright their enemies. The *Macedon*s also began their fighting with crying and shouting; and *Curtius* reports, that as soone as the Armies saw one another within shot of Musket, the *Persians* began to cry furiously, and the *Macedon*s, though fewer in number, did so answer them, that the tops of the Mountaines and Woods resounded againe to the Echo of their Cryes. The like we reade in [1-70] our owne Story, where the Author in his ninth Booke makes mention of *Henry Piercie* Earle of *Northumberland*, and Regent of *England* at the East, being come unawares into *Scotland* with seven thousand men, was driven away by the Boores and Herds, by the helpe of Stone-Bagges, as they are called to this day in our High Lands of *Scotland*, being used by the Inhabitants to fright Wolves, and to chase Deere and other Beasts from their grasings: the Instrument is made of dry skinnes made round like a Globe, with small stones in it that make a noise, as they did neere the *English* Campe, that their Horses brake loose through the fields, where after long flying they were taken by the Boores of the Country. If then we should cry at all, let it be such a noise as may terrifie our enemies, being strong, couragious, and brave.

*Plutarch* reports, that the cry of Souldiers made a Raven flying in the ayre to fall downe being astonished: and *Titus Livius* saith, that when the multitude of people did imbarke, that few or none were left in *Italie* and *Sicile*, coming together, and crying, the Birds astonished fell out of the ayre: and *Paulus Æmilius* reports the like, that when the *Christians* besieged *Tyre*, a Pigeon was seene in the Ayre, which made the *Christians* raise such a noise, that the Pigeon fell downe, as if it had been stricken with thunder, and that they found a Letter about the necke of the Pigeon, that the *Sarazens* had sent to the besieged, shewing they should be soone relieved, if they would take good courage, and maintaine the Towne for certaine dayes: and the *Christians* having men with them, who understood the same language, did write another Letter, which they tyed to the necke of the said Pigeon, and let him goe; which Letter carried, that the beseiged had neede to looke to themselves, that they had given good proofe of their valour and fidelitie, and that their Fortune was, not to give them hope of reliefe; the passages being closed up by their enemies, and the *Tyrians* thus deceived, give over the Towne unto the *Christians*.

The like we reade practized at the siege of *Harlam*, which made the Towne hold out long: and it is certaine, such Poasts are made fall downe with the noise of crying, and of Cannon and Musket, so that their packetts are taken from them. Here also was wonderfull, the losse and dammage done by Cannon, especially the Morters of the enemy, carrying Bullets of Stone within the Towne of three hundreth pound weight, and some that carried Bullets of one hundreth and sixtie pound, and in one day there were shot on the Port of *Franckendore*, where we went out to our watch, above seven hundreth and sixtie shot of Cannon, the noise whereof was heard above thirtie *English* miles. Also we reade, that at the Battell of *Lepanto*, in the yeare 1572. where the *Turkes* were defeated with great losse, that the noise of the Cannon was heard from the place, above sixtie *Scottish* miles. But on the Sea they are heard a great deale farther, as having neither hill nor wood to hinder the sound in the Ayre.

Here also I did observe, how happie it is when Officers and Souldiers love one another, refusing to undertake no danger to supply their *Camerades*, their lives being dearer unto them than their owne: which was evident by the timely reliefe, which discouraged the Enemy, and made them at last perceiving their owne losse to be great, having effectuated little, in the end to settle. To speake in particular of any mans valour, at this time, seeing to my knowledge, I perceived no defect neither in Officer nor Souldier; but so [1-71] farre as to my griefe, I did speake of the *Dutch* that left their Captaine, which since I confesse to be a warlike Nation, being now long hardned by the custome of warres, but on desperate service, as this was, I would wish, if I had libertie to choose, other seconds: neither can I commend those *Dutch* that would not send us reliefe in our great danger; for though we ought to looke to our owne houses, when our neighbours are on fire, yet Christian compassion ought to move us to supply the defects of our brethren; but when Souldiers and Officers preferre their ease, with whole skinnes, to the safetie of their *Camerades* in danger, then such may be justly called simple, without moderation, abandoning their *Camerades*, they lose their good name, and bring their reputation and valour in question. Who will not then blame such, and who will not praise those, th~t in extremitie, contemned life and their ease, to relieve their *Camerades*: as Colonell *Fretts* his Lievetenant Colonell and Major did, fighting against our enemies? Him then I esteeme as a valiant Souldier, that fights against the enemy, embracing wounds for his Mistresse, and that is contented to lie on the ground, being weary, and that makes no difference of food to serve his appetite, without sawce; being contented with a nod for a sleepe; to such a Souldier nothing is impossible or hard to attempt; and such Souldiers to command were my choice, that cared not for gold nor money, but for credit: and Souldiers have most feare when they are best fed, best clad, best armed, and when their purses are best furnished; but when the Souldier glorieth in his povertie, then doth the Armie flourish, then doe they overthrow their enemies. And therefore it was the saying of *Demetrius* to *Xerxes* King of *Persia*, going to make warre in *Greece*, that *Greece* did ever entertaine povertie, and lodged vertue brought in by wisedome and severe discipline: by which meanes their dominion remaineth unconquered, so long as they were enemies to vice, and were glad in their povertie, as may be well spoken of our owne Nation at home, that hath suffered and done so much and more for our freedomes, than any Kingdome in *Europe*, which this day makes our Soveraigne to say, *Nobis haec invicta miserunt centum & septem proavi*, being left unconquered in his succession of one hundred and seven Kings: for what have we to doe with gold or great riches, so long as we can command our owne appetites and desires?  And if we thirst after gold, let us valiantly bring it from a farre with credit, to inrich our Countrey with, and to supply the necessities of our poore at home; and then having served long credibly abroad, his Majestie our Soveraigne may grant unto us after our dismission from other service, the liberties and priviledges which were granted by *Charlemaine* unto his Souldiers, after he had subdued the *Saxons* and *Lumbards*, which I will wish his Majestie to grant unto us, saying, Goe your wayes my Souldiers, you shall be called valiant, companions of Kings, and Iudges of the wicked, live henceforth free of Travell, give good advice to Princes for the Common-weale, be protectors of widdowes, helps to the fatherlesse, waite on great men, with your wisdome, and desire of them life, cloathes, and entertainement, and he that refuseth you, let him be detested and infamous, and those that wrong you, let them be accused, as of treason.  But take heede yee spoyle not through drunkennesse, pleasure, or other vices, the great honour and priviledge you have attained unto, through your just travell in warres, for feare, that, that which we grant unto you for honour, may not redound to your dishonour and punishment; which we reserve to our selves, and to our Successors Ro- [1-72] mane Kings, if by chance you commit any excesse.  It is a good thing and worth commendations, to have defeated Kings, assaulted Townes and Provinces, Strengths and Castles. But it is a thing much more worth commendations, to overcome your own passions, a marvaile surpassing all marvailes, that he who did overcome so many, at last overcomes himselfe.  The first and best of all Victories, which cannot be attained unto without contemning of riches.

To conclude then this observation, happie are those Cavaliers that ended their lives in the defence of their Countries credit, a brave interchange, where worthy Cavaliers, in undergoing a temporall death for eternall fame and glory, gaine life after death.  Miserable is the brevite, and more miserable the uncertaintie of life.  Since then, we are sure we cannot live long, and uncertaine if we live at all, being like leaves on trees, we are the sport of every puffe that bloweth, and with the least guste, may be shaken from our life and nutriment: we travell, we study, we fight, that labour may pay us the losse of our ill expended time, while death whiskes about us with a *Pegasean* speede, flies unawares upon us, and with the kicke of his heele, or the dash of his foot, we are driven downe to dust, and lie there.  Many a stout fellow this night at *Trailesound*, and five weekes before, did expire in their oppugnations, leaving their breath in the places where they laid their Siege.  Certainly, if we could thinke of lifes casualties, we would neither be carelesse nor covetous.  What availes then a man, to exhaust his very vitals, for the hoording up of fatall gold, not thinking how a haire or a flie may snatch him in a moment from it?  Why should we then straine our selves for more than is convenient?  We should never care too much for that we are not sure to keepe; yet we should respect somewhat more than for our owne time, that we may be beneficiall to posteritie; but for mine owne part, I will cast this, as my life on Gods providence, and live here as a *Pilgrime* of one night, not being sure to see the morrow.

*The eighteenth Duty discharged of the second*
*nights storme at* Trailesound *and of the successe thereof.*

The Lievetenant Colonell having visited me the next day at my lodging, being not able to stirre out of my bed, he declared unto me the losse sustained by the Regiment, both of Officers and Souldiers, and he suspecting the enemy would storme againe at night, being battering the walles furiously the whole day, having shot at *Frankendore* neere eight hundred shot, he desired to heare my opinion, how I would have the Poast beset at night with the Regiment; my advise was, to cause beate a bancke by the Drummer Major; and the whole Drummers of the Regiment athwart the City, commanding upon paine of death, that all Officers, and Souldiers able to carry Armes under the Regiment should repaire at parad time, to the market place, there to receive further orders, and that at their coming, to appoint all the Officers, that were not hurt, to command the whole Souldiers, to be all put under the Colonells company, till such [1-73] time, as the Recreuts should come from *Scotland*, and then every man should be suffered to serve againe under their owne companies, as before, and this order being followed, they would be well commanded having sufficient Officers to leade them, giving them orders how to behave themselves, in case the enemy should storme their workes, seeing they were not able to defend them long, being weake of forces, and the workes almost ruin'd the night before.

This determined, the watch being drawne up, they march to the former Poast, getting orders from the Lievetenant Colonell, if the enemy should presse them hard, they should retire themselves orderly to the Ravelin, and quit the outer workes, seeing that from the Towne wall, and Ravelin, they were able with Cannon and musket to cleanse out the enemy againe.

So entring on their watch, and the night being come on, the enemy furiously did invade them, and they defended the workes a long time, till in the end being prest hard, they retired according to their orders, to the Ravelin, whereupon the enemy followed them with a shout and a cry, as if the Towne had beene wonne, which did put the Burgars, and the rest of the Souldiers that were on other Poasts, in great feare, thinking all was past recovery.

Notwithstanding of this sudden feare, our Souldiers valiantly and bravely defended the Ravelin with Pikes and fire-workes, the enemy having advanced bravely to the cutting of the *Pallessades*, pressing also to undermine the Ravelin by working under it, which our folkes did hinder, by countermineing.

The enemy also, had another forrell, or advantage by reason of a new worke, which was uncomplete, betwixt the Ravelin and the outward workes, where he did lodge himselfe, having the new workes as a Breastworke, to defend him from our shot.

The night thus past furiously on both sides, not without great losse, being well fought, both of the pursuer and defender, in the morning our Souldiers some of them being Armed with Corslets, head-peeces, with halfe pikes, Morgan

sternes and swords, being led with resolute Officers they fall out, Pell mell
amongst the enemies, and chase them quite out of the workes againe, and retiring
with credit, maintained still the Triangle or Ravelin; The enemy considering his
losse, and how little he had gained, the Towne also being not void of feare,
thinking the third night, the enemy might enter the walles, being thus doubtfull
on both sides, the enemy sends a Trumpeter, to know if they will treate for
conditions; our Lievetenant Colonell having the command, for the time (in
Colonell *Holke* his absence) I thinke was glad of the offer, to prolong time, till
his Majesty of *Denmark* might send a fresh supply. Pledges delivered *hinc inde*,
a still-stand or cessation of Armes was concluded on by both parties, for a
fortnights time, then Articles were drawne up, to be advised on, which continued
in advising certaine dayes, in the end the treaty being almost agreed on, to the
subscription, orders come to our Lievetenant Colonell to dissolve the treaty,
seeing his Majesty of *Denmark* had folke in readinesse to come in all haste with
Colonell *Holke*, for their reliefe. Whereupon my Lord *Spynie*, a *Scots* Noble
man, with his Regiment, with sufficient provision of money and Amunition, were
sent unto the Towne, and being entred, the treaty was rejected and made voide.

[I-74]

At this time also Sr. *Alexander Lesly*, (an expert and a valorous *Scots*
Commander) with some *Sweden*s forces, was sent to governe the Towne, his
Majesty of *Sweden* having condescended with his Majesty of *Denmark*, that his
Majesty of *Denmark* should dismisse the protection of *Trailesound* in favour of
his Majesty of *Sweden*, and to that effect the *Danes* forces should be drawne out
of the Garrison, for to give place to the *Swedens*; in the meane time, the
command was turned over upon Sr. *Alexander Lesly*, whom Colonell *Holke* did
assist with the *Danes* forces, till they were removed, the absolute command
being given to Sr. *Alexander Lesly*, as Governour for his Majesty of *Sweden*.

In time of the still-stand, I tooke a soare losse under my Lievetenant
Colonell his hand, & seale, to goe by Sea to *Copmanhagen*, to be cured there,
seeing no Chirurgian in *Trailesound* would undertake to cut the bullet out of my
knee, without hazarding me to be lame, which to prevent, I choosed rather,
though with infinite paine, to keepe the bullet a fortnight, till I came to
*Copmanhagen*, where happily I found better cure.

### The eighteenth Observation.

Two things we must respect, so long as we live, our inward integrity, and
our outward uprightnesse, our piety towards God, and our reputation amongst
men, the one makes our life famous, the other our death happy, so both together
bring credit to the name, and felicity to the soule, Then whensoever our breath is
made but aire, we shall be blessed, leaving a sweete odour behinde us, and men
will regrate our losse, as at this time they did our hurt.

He whom before I was wont to obey and visite, came now, and visited me, I
not being able to stirre, my Lievetenant Colonell came to comfort me, having
neede to be comforted himselfe by good advise, how to defend the workes the

second night, a generall feare having possessed the hearts both of Burgers and Souldiers, and I, to encourage him, did tell him a story of *Augustus* the Emperour, who being neere death commanded, that after his decease, all his friends should clap their hands, and laugh unfainedly, as the custome was when a Comedy was well acted: even so said I, though I was sorry at our losse; yet I was glad for being hurt, when I looked to be kill'd, and having acted my part of the play, for that time, and retired off the Stage, all I could doe was but to minde my Camerads of their duties. In the meane time, the Enemies cannon having shot foure great bullets of a hundred and sixty pound weight, out of morters, through the top of my lodging even to the bottome, where I did lie, affrighting me still, when my feete were not able to shift away my body; yet recommending my soule to God, I resolved, he was well guarded, whom the Lord had a care of, and having delivered me from many dangers, I still confided he would not suffer me to be smother'd under walles: For which and all his blessings I doe infinitly thanke his Majesty, in giveing me time to doe any thing, that may please his Majesty, for my deliverance.

To make my Lievetenant Colonell laugh, I did tell him a story of a vision, that was seene by a Souldier of the Colonells company, that morning before the enemy did storme, being a predictive dreame, and a true. One *Murdo Macclaude* borne in *Assen*, a Souldier of a tall stature, and valiant [1-75] courage, being sleeping on his watch, awakened by the breake of day, and jogges two of his Camerades lying by him, who did finde much fault with him for sturring of them, he replied, before long you shall be otherwise sturred, a Souldier called *Allen Tough* a *Loghaber-man*, recommending his soule to God, asked him what he had seene, who answered him, you shall never see your country againe, the other replyed, the losse was but small if the rest of the company were well, he answered no, for there was great hurt and death of many very neere, the other asked againe, whom had he seene more, that would dye besides him, sundry of his Camerades he tould by name, that should be killed: the other asked what would become of himselfe, he answered, he would be killed with the rest: in effect, he describeth the whole Officers by their cloathes that should be hurt: a pretty quicke boy neere by asked him, what would become of the Major, meaning me, he answered, he would be shot, but not deadly, and that the boy should be next unto me, when I were hurt, as he was.

This discourse ended, I wished my Lievetenant Colonell to set all care aside and to looke to himselfe, and to the credit of his Nation, in maintaining of the place, till the reliefe should come, and so we parted.

Here I did observe, that no city, be it never so strong, or so well beset, nor no Armour, be it of what proofe it will, is able to encourage a fearefull heart, as in this City, and at this time, were many of the Burgars, Souldiers, strangers, Officers, of women and children, who were tormented by the feare of death, and of their meanes, whose feare was generally so great, that they were bereft both of wisdome, and courage, as people given over, so that their feare in some sort did frustrate their lawfull defences: the like I did never see, neither wish to see againe, for the enemy could not, though victorious, put them in a worse habit, nor make them seeme more miserable, than I did see them at this time, making themselves unfit to resist their enemies, and they were all of them in mine eyes, like to the swordfish, having weapons, but they wanted hearts; they had quaking hands without use: and in a word, if the enemy had seene them, as I did, he would rather pitty them as cowards, then kill them like gallants.

Notwithstanding of this feare, which possessed the burgars, and those Souldiers that had not beene on occasion, yet our Nation, that are ever most couragious in greatest extremity, failed nothing of their wonted valour, but having once retired to the Ravelin, maintained it couragiously, repelling the enemies valour, with resolution built on vertue, and love of credit, so that they made their enemie with great losse, to be frustrate of his hoped for victory, finding the valour of the *Scots* tempered with constant resolution and vigorous spirits, his fury was made to setle by little and little, till at last, resolution, the strong Armour of the descreete Souldier prevailed against all the shuffles and cries of the enemy, and the defender, seeing the storme past, and the tempest cease, he laughes and smiles with as much honour, quiet and safety, as before he suffered toyle, griefe, or injury.

Here we see the use of treaty, and still-stand (or truce) ordained of Policy, that every man may presse to winne his owne aymes. The Souldiers that in six weekes before, were wounding, and killing one another, are now coming and discoursing together as friends, where I did remarke and observe, that it is much easier to be reconciled with an enemy, then to conquer him. [I-76]

Now in time of these still-stands, by discourse they presse to finde out one anothers actions, and to observe one anothers faults and excursions, treasuring up against the day of advantage, for the confounding of one another, at their first out-falling, and like the *Crocodile*, they slime one anothers way, to make one another fall, coming in occasions againe: and therefore it was the answere that *Seneca* gave unto himselfe, when he asked *Quid est homini inimicissimum*? he answered, *Alter homo*. Our enemies studies are the plots of our ruine, leaving nothing unattempted, which may induce our dammage, and the danger is ever most, when we see it not. Yet I thinke, he that can be a worthy enemy, can, reconciled, be a worthy friend; and he that, in a just cause, can fight against us, can likewise in the like cause, being reconciled, fight with us, and if he be unworthy reconcile him too, if it were but to be freed of his scandalous tongue, and that also will be worth thy labour, and he that upon good termes refuseth reconcilement, may be stubborne, but not valiant nor wise: for he that wilfully continues an enemy, teacheth his enemy to do him a mischiefe if he can: and that endeavour is well spent, that unmaskes an enemy, or makes a friend: for as the one begets a treasure; the other, it may be, raiseth a siege; and that man is wise, that is kinde to his friends and sharpe to his enemies: but he is wiser, that can entertaine his friends in love, and make his enemies like them, as our Nation did here at *Trailesound*, in keeping their Masters love to the best, for their loyalty, and in maki~g their enemies thinke well of them; and love them for their brave carriage and valour.

Likewise I did observe here the benefit that ariseth to a Kingdome, City or State through a good Government; and what a blessing it was to a Towne perplexed, as this was, to get a good, wise, vertuous and valiant Governour, in time of their greatest trouble, which shewes that we are govern'd by a power above us: for oftimes, that, which we desire or feare, doth seldome happen. This City having feared the Emperours tyranny to come over them, desired the King of *Denmark* as their protector, yet God, by his providence, gave them another, to wit, the invincible King of *Sweden*, who provided them an able Governour in their greatest neede, to wit, Sr. *Alexander Lesly*, who immediatly after his entry tooke the command upon him, keeping both the *Dane*, their Souldiers, and the Burgars under his command, and direction, as worthy of his authority, flowing from the King his Master of most famous and of never dying memory, it faring then with *Trailesound*, as with *Sara*; she became fruitfull when she could not believe it, and they became flourishing having gotten a *Scots* Governour to protect them, whom they looked not for, which was a good *Omen* unto them, to get a Governour of the Nation, that was never conquered, which made them the onely Towne in *Germany* free, as yet, from the Emperiall yoake, by the valour of our Nation, that defended their City in their greatest danger.

To conclude then, for the love I beare to the Crowne, that doth protect them, knowing their dispositions by experience to be froward, factious, and proud, having as yet some Wolves amongst them, that the folde may be quiet, let the factious heads be made higher by a pole than their bodies, cutting off the tumultuous; whereby their Governour, by a majesticke awe, may keepe the rest in a strict subjection, lest slacknesse and connivence may undermine an unsetled Government; for it is no crueltie to denie false men [1-77] libertie, that are so infected, though there be some honest men amongst them; let them serve their Governour, and let him beare the sway, as becomes the dignitie of the place, that having once wonne the field, he may be sure to keepe it: for though I hate the evill people, for their former unthankfulnesse to our Souldiers and Nation, yet the love I beare to their Protector and Governour, makes me thus plaine; whose happinesse I wish to endure while there remaineth a stone in the Citie, and his fame eternally.

---

### The nineteenth Dutie discharged of the out-fall made by Spynies *Regiment, and of their Retreate made good by Captaine* Mac-Kenyee.

The treatie dissolved, the new supply being come out of *Denmarke*, Sir *Alexander Leslie* being made Governour, he resolved for the credit of his Country-men, to make an out-fall upon the Enemy, and desirous to conferre the credit on his owne Nation alone, being his first Essay in that Citie. And therefore made choice of *Spynies* Regiment, being their first service, to make the out-fall, ordaining Captaine *Mac-Kenyee*, with the remainder of our Regiment, in the Lievetenant Colonell his absence, to second them, for making good of their retreate.

My Lord *Spynie* being present with his Regiment, consisting of brave and valourous Officers, being all worthy Cavaliers of noble descent, and of good families, having action, valour, and breeding answerable to their charges, they were desirous to gaine honour and credit against a powerfull enemy, with whom they were to be ingaged; they went on with boldnesse and confident resolution, and falling into the enemies workes, they forced the enemy to retire, and to give ground, even to the body of their Armie: And delighting in the shedding of their enemies bloud, who had shed so much of their Country bloud before, they pursued them hard, following them unto their maine reserve or battell, where they seazed on their Cannon: but the enemy being too strong, and his forces still augmenting, they were made to retire with the losse of some brave Cavaliers, especially the losse of Sir *Iohn Hume* of *Aiton*, the first Captaine of the Regiment, who, after many bloudy wounds received, was taken prisoner, being a brave resolute Cavalier, of good carriage and moderation in all his actions, who after died of his wounds with the enemy, being a prisoner long, and was much lamented of all that knew him.

Here also was killed the valourous Captaine *Mac-Donald*, who in valour succeeded his worthy predecessors; for with his owne hands, as is credibly reported, he killed with his sword five of his enemies, before he was kill'd himselfe. Divers also of these Officers were hurt, as Capt: *Lundesey* of *Bainsho*, who received three dangerous wounds, Lievetenant *Pringle*, who was hurt also, and divers more, they being made to retire, their powder being spent, to make their retreate good, falls up Captaine *Mac-Kenyee* with the old *Scottish* blades of our Regiment, to suppresse the enemies fury, they keeping faces to their enemies, while their Camerades were retiring, the service went on afresh, where Lievetenant *Seaton* his Company alone led by Lievetenant *Lums-* [I-78] *dell* (in absence of their owne Officers, being then all under cure) there was lost of *Seatons* Company above thirtie valourous Souldiers, and the Lievetenant seeing Colonell *Holke* retiring, desired him to stay a little, and to see if the *Scots* could stand and fight or not. The Colonell perceiving him to jeere, shooke his head, and went away: in the end Captaine *Mac-Kenyee* retired softly from his enemy, keeping faces towards them with credit, till he was safe within workes. And then made ready for his march towards *Wolgast*, to finde his Majestie of *Denmarke*.

### The nineteenth Observation.

Here we see, that when his Majestie of *Denmarke* did quit the protection of *Trailesound* unto his Majestie of *Sweden*, Sir *Alexander Lesly* being made Governour, following the example of *Iustinian* the Emperour, to put his authoritie in practize, He commanded out a partie, and was obeyed by those he commanded: which should incourage all brave Cavaliers to serve well and faithfully, where they serve, without spot or blemish, that in the end they may expect so great a reward, from so great a Master, as we see here bestowed for valour and fidelitie upon our Country-man, being trusted with such a charge on a frontier Garrison, though a stranger, before his Majesties owne Country-men; where he againe following the example of *Alexander* the Great, who caused a Combat to be fought with one of *Darius* Captaines, before the Armie should fight, and his Captaine returning victorious, he (I say) tooke that as a good presage of his future fortune, in beating of *Darius* his Armie. *Tacitus* saith also, that the *Germanes* were wont to fight, and try their valour, first after this manner, by parties, for presages of greater service to follow. And we finde, that the valourous Generall *Scanderbegge*, King of *Epirus*, did fight many Combats himselfe, for to give good presages of future victories, whose fortune was till his death to be ever victorious. The like fortune I heartily wish to this noble and worthy Cavalier, happie alreadie and blest in bringing honour to his Country, being in all his time, beyond apprehension, happily excellent.

To conclude then this observation, here we may see the benefit of good order, where those that were in great danger, are happily preserved by the goodnesse of good order and discipline, and by the timely succours of their valourous Camerades, taking the enemies blowes and shots in their owne bosomes, to rescue their friends from danger, to the great prayse of that noble Sparke, Captaine *Mac-Kenyee,* being full of worth, as the purest *orientall Diamond*, shining amongst the greatest Stones, who did scorne to turne face from his enemies, but retired orderly, offending his enemy in defending his friends, till both he and they were returned with credit, though with losse: for where order is kept, as in this retreate was done by that noble Sparke, all things flourish and thrive, and I wish from my heart, he had followed his profession; for though he be honourable enough, as he is, none can blame me for wishing him better, he having once commanded me, and shall still while I live. [1-79]

---

### The twentieth Dutie discharged of the Regiments March to Wolgast, *and of their Retreate unto* Denmarke.

His Majestie of *Denmarke* having given over the protection of *Trailsound* unto the King of *Sweden*, immediatly after he did ship some forces of foote and horse in *Denmarke*, which he did land at *Wolgast* in *Pomeren*, of intention to patronize the Dukedome of *Pomeren* against the Emperour: And being come to *Wolgast*, his Majestie did recall the remainder of our Regiment from *Trailesound*, who were not then foure hundred strong at their out-coming, having lost in six weekes neare five hundred good men, besides Officers; the Regiment led then by Captaine *Mac-Kenyee*, in the absence of his Superiours, he continued his March towards *Wolgast*, where they joyned with his Majesties Armie: being no sooner arrived, they were instantly commanded on service. The enemy having falne strong against his Majestie, he did plant fourteen pieces of Ordnance, and playd on the Kings battell, till his Majestie perceiving the danger, not being bastant to resist the enemy, retired confusedly in great haste to

*Wolgast*; and having lost without fighting the greatest part of his Armie, our Regiment and the remnant of *Spynies* Regiment had beene cut off, had not Rutmaster *Hoome* and some of his Camerades, of the *Rhinegraves* Regiment of horse charged the Enemy thrice, keeping them up till the most part of his Country-men were retired in safetie, and then were made by their enemies to retire at the spurres themselves, having endangered their owne safeties for the good of their Camerades. His Majestie finding the enemy pressing hard, fearing much to be surprized or taken, he did give Captaine *Mac-Kenyee* charge to comand the whole *Scots* that were there, and divers others, and to skirmish with the enemy before the Ports, till his Majestie were retired, and then to make his retreate over the Bridge, and to set it on fire, which the Captaine did orderly obey, doing his Majestie the best service was done him in the whole time of his warres, not without great danger of the Captaine and his followers, where the Bridge once burning, he was then the happiest man that could first be shipped; Ensigne *Lindesey* brother to *Bainsho* was shot with a Cannon-Bullet in his shoulder, and notwithstanding was brought off, and miraculously cured.

The Regiment thus shipped, they met with their Colonell, being come from *Scotland* with the *Recreut*, who retired with his Majestie unto *Denmarke*, and were mustered.

### The twentieth Observation.

In defense of this Towne of *Trailesound*, our Regiment did lose neare five hundred men, and of the remnant escaped, both of Officers and Souldiers, I doe not thinke one hundred were free of wounds received honourably, in defence of the good cause. Who will then say, but that bloud was better lost than kept, when it returnes with advantage, having brought credit to themselves and Countrey? Let none then mourne for the losse gotten so honourablie. Let none then, I say, bedew their eyes for them we [I-80] left behinde us, seeing the gaine is equall to the losse, if not more; for them we had, we knew were not alwayes to stay; yet what we have gained, is permanent and eternall; those we lost, I confesse, we loved, yet that love ought not to be so violent as to undoe our selves with wanting of it. Neither can we so slenderly forget their memory, being our noble friends, and who were ornaments to our Regiment and Country, and helpers of our credits. Shall we not then be sorrowfull for their losses, that lost themselves to make us renowned in their deaths, and, while they lived, were our most faithfull and loving Camerades, even unto their last breath: But since they are gone before us, to take in quarters in heaven, following their great Captaine, who hath made the way open for them, being stricken, as *Iob* saith, by the hand of the Lord, and yet placed at his right hand, shall we be sorry for them? No; we will rather rejoyce, and thinke we must follow them, when we have fought that good fight against our enemies, we shall be crowned with them in glory, and rejoyce following the *Lambe* where ever he goeth, and till then his right hand will sustaine us, as before; for he is our helper, and hath sworne by his right hand, and the Arme of his strength, that he will not forsake us, till we rest with him in glory.

Here also we see, that his Majestie having trusted our Nation more than his owne, or the *Dutch*, he doth leave them ingaged with the enemy, till his Majesties retreate were made sure, both first and last. Where we see, that friendship and true service is best tryed in extremitie; for no greater testimony can be given of true sevice, than when the servant doth endanger his own life and hononr for the reliefe of his Master; as that young Cavalier, Captaine *Mac-Kenyee* did here, being a generous act, for the safetie of a King, which ought to be recorded; to vindicate his honour from oblivion, whose memory merits to be rewarded, that others might imitate his noble example.

Here also we see, that sufferance in a noble manner causeth love, for that young Cavalier *Henry Lindesey*, then an Ensigne, not able to helpe himselfe, his Camerades loving him dearely, and the more for his noble sufferance, they helpt him off from the crueltie of his enemies, to preserve his life for a better occasion, who by Gods providence was miraculously healed, having lost a great part of his shoulder, a wonder in an age, such wounds to be cured.

---

*The twenty-one Dutie discharged at* Copemanhagen, *where the Regiment was completed againe with the Recreut.*

As all things are preserved by a glorious order; so his Majestie after his retreate, beginneth againe to make up the body of an Armie, to be setled all Winter in quarters within *Denmark*, that against the Spring he might either beate the enemy out of *Holsten*, or otherwise with his sword in his hand, make an honourable peace: after which resolution taken, there was order sent to my Colonell, to bring his Regiment to the fields, and to reforme the weake Companies, that have no Recreut brought over, and to [I-81] strengthen the rest of the Companies, till the Regiment was made complete.

Sir *Patrick Mac-Gey* having stayd in *Scotland*, his Company was cashier'd, and Captaine *Annans* also, in place whereof the Colonell did get from his Majestie two Companies, that were sent over by Colonell *Sinclaire*, (*viz.*) Captaine *George Stewart*, and Captaine *Francis Trafford*, which were both joyned to the Regiment. The Lord of *Fowles* having leavied a Company in *Scotland*, joyned also to the Regiment, & *Iohn Sinclaire* was made Captaine Lievetenant to the Colonels Company, Lievetenant *Stewart* being married, having stayd in *Scotland* with his wife, his place was given to *Eye Mac-Key*, and *William Brumfield* was made Ensigne to Captaine *Mac-Kenyee*. The Lievetenant Colonell having quit the Regiment, I succeeded to his place, and his Lievetenant *Andrew Stewart*, the Earle of *Traquairs* brother, succeeded Captaine to the Company, Ensigne *Seaton* being made Lievetenant, the Captaines brother *William Stewart* was made Ensigne, *Tullough* his Company was recreuted, and was full by his old Officers *Beaton* and *Iohnson*: *Iohn Monro* his Company being recreuted, long *David Monro* was made Lievetenant, and long *William Stewart* Ensigne; Captaine *Monro* of *Obstell* his Company being complete, *William Carre* was made Lievetenant, and *Hector Monro* Ensigne.   The Regiment thus complete was mustred, and received a moneths meanes, together with a reckoning of their by-past rests, with an assignation on his Majestie of great *Britaine*, for the payment of the moneys.

The Regiment thus contented, the Colonell, Captaine *Monro* of *Obstell*, and Captaine *Mac-Key* returning for *Britaine*, the Regiment being left under my command, was directed to winter Garrisons as followeth.

The Colonels Company commanded by *Iohn Sinclaire* as Captaine, *Iohn Ennis* Lievetenant, and *William Mac-Kenyee* Ensigne, were quartered in *Langland*, Captaine *Monro* of *Fowles* his company was sent to lie in *Feamer*, *Andrew Monro* being his Lievetenant, and *Iohn Rhode* Ensigne.

Captaine *Monro* of *Obstell* his company was quartered there also, and the foresaid Officers.

Captaine *Iohn Monro* his company and his Officers were also quartered there.

Captaine *Forbesse* of *Tullough* his company and Officers were quartered in *Malline* in *Skoneland*.   Captaine *Mac-Kenyee* his company and Officers foresaid, were quartered with me in *Malline* in *Skoneland*.   Captaine *George Stewart*, *Robert Hume* Lievetenant, and *Iohn Sanders* Ensigne, were quartered in *Alzenburgh*.

Captaine *Francis Trafford* his company, being *Welsh*, with his Officers were quartered in a Dorpe in *Skoneland*.

Captaine *Andrew Stewart* his company and Officers were quartered in *London* in *Skoneland*.

My company which was *Lermonds*, with the Officers did lie in Garrison in *Luckstad* in *Holsten*.

The Officers that were reformed went to seeke their employments (*viz.*) Captaine *Sanders Hay* went to *Sweden*, and was made Major to Sir *Patricke Ruthven* in *Spruce*.

*Patricke Dumbarre* was made Captaine to a Company of *Danes* Souldiers. There happened also a mis-fortune this Winter in *Feamer*, where Lievetenant *Andrew Monro*, a valourous young Gentleman, was killed in Combate by a [I-82] *Dutch*, called *Ranso*, and Lievetenant *William Mac-Key* succeeded in his place, being made Lievetenant to *Fowles* when *William Gunne* was preferred by me, as Ensigne to the Colonells Company: the rest of the Garrisons lay in quiet all Winter, during which time his Majesties Commissioners lay at *Lubeck*, treating for a peace with the Emperour.

## The twenty-one Observation.

In the Firmament we see all things are preserved by a glorious order; the Sunne hath his appointed circuite, the Moone her constant change, and every planet and Starre their proper course and place, the Earth also hath he unstirred stations, the Sea is confined in limits, and in his ebbing and flowing dances, as it were, after the influence and aspect of the Moone, wherby it is kept from putrefaction, and by strugling with it selfe, from over flowing the land. So that in this world, order is the life of Kingdoms, Honours, Artes: for by the excellency of it, all things florish and thrive; and therefore we see, that this order is requisite to be observed in nothing more than in military discipline, being the life of it. Regiments then maintained in good order, the Army can be but well ordered, and the Army well ordered, the King and country cannot but stand, both in peace and warre, for seldome we see any goodnesse in the refusing to obey good orders. And we heare ordinarily, that one bad voice puts twenty out of tune, and that it is the chiefe property of a good Souldier, first to learne to obey well, in keeping of good order, and then doubtlesse, in time being advanced, he cannot but command well, so that here in ordering of this, as in all things, we see vicissitudes and alterations, some Regiments made up and continue in florishing order, other Regiments reduced taking an end, as occasion and accidents of warre doe happen, *Spynie*s Regiment was reduced, and my Lord of *Rhees* Regiment is made up againe. Where we see, that as vicissitude maintaines the world; even so concord is a great meanes of continuance, as discord is too often of discontinuance, and ruine. Likewise we see, that no estate is free from mutability, and change, which is the great Lord of the World, who will be adored and followed as soone as order doth faile: but where order is kept, and concord (as in this Regiment) change hath no place to ruine, though well to alter; for order was so kept by this Regiment, like to brave Souldiers, who in a running skirmish come up, discharge, fall off, flie, and yet reinforce themselves againe, having kept order in their proceedings, which though now she admits of some change, being reinforced againe and joyned together with the chaine of love and respect, she admits of no confusion or ruine; but is ready againe with her brave Souldiers being reinforced in a strong body to make head unto their enemies, one day to be revenged of their former losses, as, God willing, shall be cleered in the sequell of my discharge of dueties and observations, of this new reformed body of the old Regiment.

My cozen Lievetenant *Andrew Monro* being killed in combat, I have more then reason to condemne and disallow of that miserable sort of fight, where oftimes the victorious puts himselfe in a worse case, both of soule and body, than he that is killed. Yet this kinde of fighting hand to hand, called *Monomachia*, hath bin much practised, both amongst *Pagans* and *Christians*, even amongst all Nations, as it is yet. Of old it did serve for [I-83] proofe of things hidden, being in one rancke with the burning iron, and scalding water, to the end men might discerne the innocent from the guilty: this kinde of violence of proofe was so common, that *Fronton* King of *Denmark* made a law, as reports the *Saxon* history, that all differences whatsoever should be decided by the combat, and *Leoden* reports, that yet to this day they observe the same in *Muscove*. But wise men finding this custome deceivable, in deciding the truth, and so uncertaine, that many times the innocent doth succumbe; and therefore it was forbidden by the civill, and canon law, as is evident by severall ancient constitutions, inserted in the Decretalls.

Nothwithstanding whereof, amongst the *Romans* it became so common, as to be thought but a sport, which made the name of fighters esteemed of amongst the *Romans*, as we reade in the *Cod. Titulo de gladiatoribus*, and therefore this custome being displeasing unto the Emperour *Iustinian*, he commanded all should be subject unto the Iudge, and said, that valour without justice, was not to be allowed of. This combat betwixt those two was well fought of both, in presence of many witnesses; where it was thought, that the *Dutch-man* was hard, so that a sword could neither pierce him, nor cut him. This fashion of fighting is so common, that we neede not illustrate it by examples of Histories, either ancient or moderne; but who so would satisfie their curiosity in this point, let them but reade *Preasack* his *Cleander*, a story well worth the reading. And truely dayly experience teacheth us (as in this accident) that the end of combats doth shew often that he, who appeales, often times doth receive the reward of his temerite, which might be cleered by many examples, amongst the ancients. We have one very notable, written by *Quintus Curtius*, where *Dioxippus* the *Athenian*, that brave fighter being all naked, and smered over with oyle, as the fashion was then, with a hat of flowers on his head, carrying about his left Arme a red sleeve, and in the right hand a great batton of hard greene timber, durst enter in combat against *Horrat Macedonian* carrying on his left Arme a bucler of brasse, and a short pike in the right hand, a jacdart-staffe as we terme it, or something like it, and a sword by his side: at their approaching, *Dioxippus* with a nimble flight, and a pretty cunning shift of his body, eschewed the stabbe or thrust of the staffe, and before the *Macedonian* could have wielded the Pike, the other doth breake it in two with his cudgell, and quickly closing with his adversary gives him such a knocke on the shinnes, that he fell to the ground, his heeles above his head, tooke his sword from him, and would have kill'd him with his batton, had not the King saved him. Thus much of combats, which for my part, though I cannot allow of, neverthelesse I should be loath to refuse to fight in a just quarrell, but would rather referre the successe to God, to determine of, then to let that be called in question, which is dearest unto me. [I-84]

---

*The twenty-second Dutie discharged being the last under his Maiesties service of* Denmarke, *of our expedition by water unto* Holsten.

His Majesty being resolved in Aprill 1629, with his sword in his hand to conclude a settled and a sure peace with the Emperour; or otherwise to free *Holsten* and *Yewtland* from the tyranny of the Emperiall Army, and to that effect his Majesty did gather his forces together to a head in *Denmark*, where they were to be shipp't for landing at *Angle* in *Holsten*: so that orders were given to me, his Majesty having provided shipping, to transport our Regiment from all quarters, and to meete at *Angle*. Before our parting, Captaine *Forbesse* of *Tullough*, and

Captaine *Andrew Stewarts* Companies were put on warre ships to lie before *Wismar*, I having shipped with the rest of the Regiment, we sailed unto *Holsten*, and landed at *Angle*: where the Regiment being come together, we were one thousand foure hundred strong besides Officers, and having lyen at *Angle* till the peace was concluded, his Majesty did thanke off, or dismisse his Army, save a few number that was kept a moneth longer, till the enemy had marched out of the country: we being discharged of service, and having gotten our honourable passes we were directed, by his Majesty to the *Rex-marshall* toward *Funeland*, with orders from his Majesty, that he should reckon with us, and give us contentment accordingly. The reckoning made, we were forced to accept of two parts, and to discharge the whole, having made no reckoning but for us who were present, leaving our Colonell being absent, to make his owne reckoning thereafter with his Majesty.

Likewise his Majesty did give orders to the *Rex-marshall* to provide shipping and victuall for our Officers and Souldiers, to transport them for their country, which accordingly was obeyed. As also his Majesty did give orders to ordaine us, both Officers and Souldiers free quarters in *Alzenheur*, till the shipps were ready to saile. So that we being free from our honourable Master his service, we were ready to imbrace new conditions from a new Master.

### *The twenty-second and last Observation on our* Danes *service.*

Here concluding our *Danes* service, we see that the end of warres is peace, and that the end of this peace was the beginning of greater warre, under a new Master. Happy therefore is that man, or that Regiment that can say, while as they are thanked off, we have served truely and with credit our last Master; and then they may be assured of a second Master, having wonne a good name, as this Regiment did, under his Majesty of *Denmarke*, in whom the least omission could never be found, much lesse to have committed any grosse errour worthy imputation: And therefore we were Graciously dismissed, and honestly rewarded according to the time. [I-85]

Captaine *Andrew Stewart* (brother to the noble and worthy Earle of *Traquaire*) being soliciting businesse at *Copmanhagen* contracted a feaver and died there, being in his Camerades absence honourably buried by the Stathoulders direction; whose death, as untimely, was much regrated by all his Camerades, he being a valorous and expert Commander.

Likewise *Iohn Hampeseede*, an old true servant to my cozen the Barron of *Fowles*, he dying of a feaver at *Angle* leager, was honourably buried there.

This *Danes* warre thus ended, was the beginning of a greater warre, as is said: for the Emperour (in Summer 1629. The *Danes* peace being made in August 1629) did send assistance of men unto the *Pole*, against his Majesty of *Sweden*, under the command of the Felt-marshall *Arnhem*, which the next summer did bring the sword of the *Sweden* against himselfe. So that we see there is nothing here on earth to be expected by us, more then a continuall warfare. Lord therefore make us dayly to warre in that spirituall warfare, serving truely the King of Kings and Lord of hosts, fighting that good fight against our spirituall enemies, where he that overcomes, receives for a reward (instead of worldly glory) an immortall Crowne of Glory in the Heavens.

## The Colonells Observation of the Kingdome of Denmarke.

Having had the honour to have dined with his Majesty at his Table, then in the gorgeous, & pleasant Palace of *Freddesborree*, taking leave of his Majesty, having kissed his hand, I retired to *Alzenheur*; where I began to thinke, that this King could have said of his whole Kingdome, as *Scipio* said, you see not a man amongst all those, but if I command him, he will from a Turret throw himselfe into the Sea: even so this Magnanimous King, to my knowledge, was of absolute authority in his Kingdome, as all Christian Kings ought to be in theirs ever obeyed in the Lord, without asking the head a reason; Why doe you command us thus? For we reade that the favour of the Lord was in *Iuda*, in giving them one heart in doing, and obeying the commandements of the King, and of their Magistrates and Principalls, as I did cleerely observe in this Kingdome of *Denmarke* the goodnesse of government, for the florishing of the Kingdome; where *Totus orbis componebatur ad exemplum Regis.* He commanding, they obeyed; both lived in prosperity, the Ruler or King Heroick, wise, noble, magnanimous and worthy.

The Gentry, Citizens and Communalty obedient, which made their joy and felicity to continue, in despite of their mighty foes, and that by reason of his Majesties Government in military discipline, who doth entertaine a great number of Officers yeerely, having good allowance for commanding of Souldiers trained up in peace, against warre, such as Colonells, Lievetenant-Colonells, Majors, Captaines and other inferiour Officers, which are still entertained at the countries charge, in exercising of Souldiers for his Majesties emploiment, being alike ever ready in all Provinces for peace or warre. Would to God we were so well provided in our owne country at home, and then we needed not to feare any forraine enemy, that are enemies to God, to our King, and to our Religion. [1-86]

And for the better maintaining of warre, no Kingdome or King I know, is better provided of a *Magazin*, then this magnanimous King, for Armes, brasse ordnance (whereof every yeere his Majesty doth cast above a hundred peeces) being sufficiently provided of Amunition and of all sorts of fiery *Engines*, to be used by Sea or Land, together with Armour sufficient for to arme a great Armie of Horse. His Majestie is also sufficiently well provided of shipping, and yearely doth adde to the number, which ships are built by two worthy Scottish-men, called Mr. *Balfoure*, and Mr. *Sinclaire*, being both well accounted off by his Majestie, who in like manner hath a Reprobane at *Copmanhagen*, for making of Cords and Cables for his shipping and Kingdome, where I was informed, that in twenty foure houres time, they were able to furnish the greatest ship the King had, of Cables and of all other tackling and cordage, necessary to set out the Ship.

Likewise by his Majesties Artizens within the Kingdome, all sort of stuffes and silkes are woven, sufficient to serve the Kingdome, and his neighbours that please to buy.

Moreover this Kingdome is worthy commendation, for the order of Iustice and Lawes, having their Law-books deciding all controversies amongst them, and if it come to any great difference, the Kings Majestie, as being above the Law, sits in judgement as the Interpreter and Director of Iustice, and according to his Princely dignity, mitigates as pleaseth his Majestie the law, and decides the controversie.

This Kingdome also is praise-worthy, for the purity of their Gentry, being as ancient and noble, as any other Kingdome, and can bragge of a purer and cleerer bloud of Gentility, then many Nations can: for they never ally or enter into marriage with any inferiour to themselves, be they never so rich, if they be Burgars or Plebeians, they never marry with them; and if one of their daughters will, through love, miscarry in her affection, to marry a Citizen, they will not thereafter doe so much as to honour her with their company, but on the contrary, shee loseth both her portion and honour, not suffering her to carry the armes of her familie.

Moreover, this Nation is praise-worthy for their entertaining of learning, and of the liberall Sciences professed in their owne Vniversities, where their children are well taught and trained up, after a noble and heroick manner, within their owne Kingdome, not onely in their Studies of the liberall Sciences, but also in their exercise of body, as fencing, dancing, singing, playing of Instruments, and riding of horses, and what else are noble Recreations, as learning of forraine languages, *Spanish, Italian, French, Dutch*, and such like, and afterwards their youth being well travell'd, returning from their Travells, they attend on the Chancellarie, as under-Secretaries to States-men, to enable them to be profitable members in the Commonweale. And being *foris familiat*, according to their gifts and qualities, they are preferred to Government and charges under his Majestie, in all Provinces of the Kingdome of *Denmarke, Yewtland, Holsten*, and *Norway*.

His Majestie also is praise worthy for his *Oeconomie* in keeping of Store-houses to feed Oxen, and stalles for keeping of milch Cowes, whereof is received yearely great income of moneys, for Butter and Cheese made in great quantitie by *Hollanders* in *Denmarke, Holsten*, and *Yewtland*: which parts abound also with all sorts of Fish, which inricheth his Majesties treasure infinitely, together with their trading by Sea to the fishing in *Greeneland*, [1-87] bringing great commoditie to the Subjects, in serving themselves, as also in bringing of money into the Kingdome, by furnishing of others. Also this Land abounds in Corne, which makes great cheapnesse in this Kingdome, where I have lived nobly entertained with two servants for twelve shillings sterling a weeke, being a whole winter in Garrison at *Malemce* in *Skoneland*. Where I did see and observe the custome used by the *Danes* Gentrie in their house-keeping, wherein they are not prodigall, but yet very noble, not differing much from our owne customes at home, entertaining many persons attendant, but not with costly or daintie fare, but aboundant in meate and drinke; obliging also they are in entertaining strangers of fashion; they keepe long Tables, at which there sit sometimes above thirtie persons: ordinary Tables they use besides, ordained for the attendants of the familie, who sit not till their Masters have halfe din'd or sup't: they keepe also many horses, hounds and hawkes, with attendance answerable, which makes their families great.

Here I did observe, that the Subjects doe follow the example of their King, in their apparrell, in their vertues, and Oeconomie, where I did see vertue to have beene alike habituall in King, Gentry, Citizens, and Country, being all in their degrees extraordinary rich, not onely in money, but also in Iewells and plate; nothing inferiour, in my judgement, to any neighbour Country. It was observed in the Court of the Emperour *Maximilian* the second, a good Prince and a vertuous, that many Lords and great Seignieurs not onely clad themselves according to the colour he wore, but also had the same vessells and moveables: the greatest Ladies also followed the Empresse; so that those kinds of cloathing that before were disdained and out of request, were then followed, all being clad with skinnes and leather. The Emperour and the Empresse not disdaining to carry and weare them, the rest followed: the pearles and precious stones did rise to the great price, that they are now at by the rich, that made the price so high, that the poore could not attaine unto them. To shew this by example, we reade of *Sabina Poppæa*, to whom nothing was wanting, but shame and honestie, being extremely beloved of *Nero*, had the colour of her haire yellow, like Amber, which *Nero* esteemed much of, in singing Verses made on her on the Cittern: and from this came that the whole Damsels of *Rome* and *Italie* did like best to have that colour of haire in their Buskins, Bracelets and cloathing, and the Amber, which before was in no esteeme, became very deare, seeing *Nero* esteemed of it; which makes *Plinie* report, speaking of the Comoedians apparell, that they carried so much Amber, that it was admirable to behold; which shewes, that the examples of great personages have great power, in matters of moment and consequence, as it hath in things of lesse importance.

For as *Villeius Paterculus* spake of the Emperour *Augustus*, a good Prince teacheth his Subjects to doe well, and as he is the greatest in estate, even so he is the greatest in example, the people casting their eyes on their Prince, sitting high, in sight of all, they delight narrowly to consider all he doth and saith, and they looke unto the most hidden things of his actions, as through little holes: and therefore before all places, the Kings Court ought to be holiest, and cleerest of all vices, and endued with most honestie, which betimes will make the whole Kingdome conforme. To confirme this, we reade in our owne story a memorable example; how the King *Iosina* tooke [1-88] pleasure and delight to discourse much with Physicians and Chirurgians; in a short time the Lords and Gentrie did accommodate themselves to the Princes humour, that many ages after, there was no noble familie in *Scotland*, that was not expert and well taught in dressing and healing the wounds of the body. A knowledge very necessary for men of our profession, that oft-times are lost for want of good cure. And we reade, that King IAMES the fourth, following the laudable custome of his Ancestors, was very expert in this kinde, in healing of wounds. A noble knowledge of so noble a Prince, and so great a Captaine, as he was!  And the common Proverbe is, that the little prettie dogges or puppies doe any thing to please their Mistresses; and we say, he smells of the pot he hath licked.  Here then you see the power of good and bad examples.

　　To conclude then.  Let us learne by the good examples aforesaid, to follow the vertuous examples of our noble Master the King, not neglecting the service and dutie we owe to the King of Kings, since our lives here are but like bubbles of the water, now seene, now vanisht. [I-89]

# THE
# TABLE OF THE
# FIRST PART.

### A.

### B.

### C.

Captaine Mackey *and* Captaine Forbesse *of* Tullough *shot*
      *at* Oldenburg.                                                                    *18*
Captaine Mack-donald *having valorously behaved himselfe, was*
      *slaine at* Trailsound.                                                        *78*
Captaine Mackenyee *as a pure sparke amongst Diamonds did*
      *shine amongst Officers for his valour at* Trailesound.        *79*

                                                                **[Table I-1]**
Captaine Boswell *killed by Boores.*                                          *4*
Captaine Mackenyee *under God, was the instrument of his*
      *Majestie of* Denmarks *safety at* Wolgast.                            *81*
Change *hath no place to ruine, though well to alter where order*
      *and concord is kept, as was in our Regiment.*                    *83*
Captaine Andrew Stewart, *brother to the Earle of* Traquare, *died*
      *at* Copmanhagen, *and was buried there.*                          *86*
Captaine Monro *his valour in clearing the passage.*                *18*
Citizens *of* Trailsound *compared to the Swordfish, having weapons*
      *but wanting hearts, and had quaking hands without use.*      *76*
Colonell Mackey *with his owne division defends the Passe at*
      Oldenburg.                                                                    *17*
Colonell Mackey *had his face spoyled with Gunpowder.*        *18*
Colonell Frets *a Leeflander was slaine on our post at* Trailsound.   *69*
Count *of* Mongomery, *cruelly beaten by the Rascall Boores, being*
      *mistaken.*                                                                    *47*
*The nature of the* Common *people, is to serve as slaves, or to strike*
      *like Tyrants.*                                                                *40*
A Caveat *for making Booty.*                                                    *32*
Citizens *of* Trailsound *forgetting benefit, were more unthankefull*
      *then beasts.*                                                                *66*
Charlemaine *his priviledge granted to those had served well.*    *72*
A Cavalier *ought patiently to attend his preferment.*              *3*
Continency *in all things is most necessary for a Souldier.*        *25*
*Men ought patiently to undergoe their* Crosses, *and not to despaire*
      *as some did in* Denmarke.                                              *86*
*He that thinkes on deaths* Casuality, *ought neither to be carelesse*
      *nor covetous.*                                                              *86*
Cowards *may be compared to dogs, that doe barke more then bite.*   *70*
*The* Cruelty *was great the enemy used in harming the dead and*
      *innocent.*                                                                    *40*

D.

*It is a worthy and brave enterchange when men attaine unto*
      *eternall fame and glory after* Death *for a temporall* Death.    *41*
*The strictnesse of* Discipline *is the conservation of an Army.*    *36*

*It were impossible to make Boores and Souldiers agree together*
        *without the strictnesse of Military* Discipline.     62

*It is never good in plenty, to* Disdaine *Souldiers, left in adversity*
        *they may prove unusefull.*     2

*The observance of* Discipline *is the maintaining of Kingdomes,*
        *Cities and Common-wealths.*     69

Dumbarre *renowned in despite of envy.*     13

*It is the* Duty *of valorous Commanders, to care for the buriall*
        *of the slaine though their enemies.*     25

*We are* Drowned *in the mud of vice and slothfulnesse, while*
        *we want businesse, and have no foe to awe us.*     46

[Table I-2]

## E.

*An* English *Cavalier being deadly wounded, retired bravely*
        *at* Keel.     55

Ensignes *six of* Scots *shot at* Ouldenburg.     18

*A rare* Example *of strength and courage in Ensigne* David Monro.     21

Emulation *of Superiours by example groweth amongst inferiours.*     37

*The whole Officers were hurt except one* Ensigne Ihonston.     68

*He that wilfully continues an* Enemy *teacheth his enemy to doe*
        *him mischiefe if he can.*     77

*Though the* Enemy *be unworthy, reconcile with him to be freed*
        *of his scandalous tongue.*     77

*The* Enemy *studies all the plots of our ruine, and the danger is*
        *ever most that is least seene.*     77

*Experience teacheth that neither Fly, Bee, nor Waspe can harme*
        *those that are healed of the sting of Scorpions.*     22

*The best* Exhortation *a Leader can give Souldiers, is to shew*
        *himselfe valorous.*     23

Enemies *prove oftimes good pedagogues, setting both death*
        *and judgment before us.*     66

## F.

Feare *doth put us in a more horrid habit then any enemy can doe.*     22

*It is not good to* Feele *the ill of the sturdy popular having once*
        *loosed the reine.*     48

Friends *that are trusty, the best companions of danger.*     14

*To be a* Follower *of the popular sort is a vaine thing.*     50

*The* Foote *is alwayes more usefull in warres and lesse chargable*
        *then Horse.*     23

Fortune *having crossed his Majesty of* Denmarke *in his warres*
        *abroad brought the sword of his enemies within his*
        *owne Kingdome.*     29

## G.

| | |
|---|---|
| *The* Germans *are commonly friends to the victorious* et e contra. | *16* |
| Germans *of old did sing, going on service.* | *70* |
| *Those that thirst after* Gold, *let them bring it valiantly from afarre,* *to supply the poore at home, or to decore and enrich their* Country. | *72* |
| *A man is glad to come off with credit being hurt, as I was at* Trailsound, *where I thought to be slaine.* | *75* |
| *Ill* Gotten *gaines is farre worse then losses with preserved honesty.* | *31* |
| Gentlemen, *three of my Colonells Company slaine at* Trailsound, Gordon, Stewart, *and* Tullough. | *68* |

[Table I-3]

## H.

| | |
|---|---|
| Honour *compared to a chaste made.* | *31* |
| Happie *are those that travell in well-doing, for when the paines are gone then doe they enjoy the pleasure.* | *63* |
| Hugh Murray, *his brother being slaine, would not carry him off till he had beene revenged, and then himselfe shot in the Eye, the Bullet came out at his Nose.* | *23* |
| Hector Monro *being shot in one foot, would not retire till first he emptied his Bandeliers, and being shot then through the other foote, was carried off by others.* | *23* |
| *We ought never to glory too much in peace or prosperitie, as the* Holsteners *did, but rather to prevent the worst.* | *28* |
| *The* Highland *Souldier his predictive Dreame seene at* Trailsound. | *75* |

## I.

| | |
|---|---|
| *A* just *cause and a* just *deputation, is that which gives the minde securitie. And he dyeth well that dyeth fighting for a* just cause. | *53* |
| Iustice *the strictest that is observed amongst Souldiers.* | *44* |
| *An* Isles *Gentleman being deadly wounded, did swimme with his Cloaths and wounds to escape the fury of his Enemies.* | *32* |

## K.

| | |
|---|---|
| *As forraine* Kings *make use of Cavaliers in their need, so they ought with reason if not rewarded, make their retreat to their King and Master, being disdained without respect.* | *25* |
| *Our* Knowledge *is of none effect without assurance in God through* Christ. | *5* |

## L.

## M.

S.

T.

Trailsound *became flourishing by their hopes, having got Sir*
    Alexander Lesly *for their Governour.*                                77

## V.

Vertue *and wisedome are the best guards of safetie.*                 42

## VV.

The Watch *on the Elve surprised.*                                          24
Wounds *gotten with credit are the best tokens of courage in*
    *a Souldier.*                                                          23
Women *are forbidden to shed teares for their children that dyed*
    *standing serving the Publique.*                                26
The wise *man is onely the cunningest Fencer.*                           42
Watch *in beleaguered places is the maine pointe to be looked unto.*     64
In Warres Summum Ins *is found to be* Summa Injuria.                     64
Walestein *his pride was great when he caused to kill the hurt*
    Officers *retired with slight wounds.*                          69
A worthy *Enemy reconciled can be a worthy Friend.*                     77

                                                 **[Table I-7]**

That man is *wise that is kinde to his Friend and sharpe to his*
    Enemy, *but he is wiser that can entertaine his Friend*
    *in love and make his Enemy like him.*                           77

                                                 **[Table I-8]**

# THE
# LIST OF THE
# SCOTTISH OFFICERS
# IN CHIEFE (CALLED
### the Officers of the Field) that
### served his Majesty of *Sweden*,
### *Anno*, 1632.

The Marquesse of *Hamilton* Generall of the *Brittish* Army.

Sir *Iames Spence* Generall over *Scots*.

Sir *Patrike Ruthven*, Governour of *Vlme*, and since Generall.

Sir *Alexander Lesly* Governour over the Cities along the *Baltique* Coast, and since Felt-marshall over the Army in *Westphalia*.

Generall Major *Iames King*, since Lievetenant Generall.

Sir *David Drummond* Generall Major and Governour of *Statin* in *Pomeren*.

Sir *Iames Ramsey* Generall Major had a Regiment of *Scots*, and since was Governour of *Hanaw*.

#### *Colonells that served then of* Scots.

My Lord of *Rhees Mackey* Colonell to a Briggad of *Scots*.

Sir *Iohn Hepburne* Colonell succeeded to command the *Scottish* Briggad, and since was slaine in *France*.

Sir *Iohn Ruthven* Colonell to a Briggad of *Dutch*, and since Generall Major.

Sir *Iames Lumsdell* Colonell to a Regiment of *Scots*.

*Alexander Ramsey* Colonell and Governour of *Creutzenach*.

[List-1]

*Robert Lesly* Colonell to a Regiment of *Scots*.

*Robert Monro* Baron of *Fowles* Colonell of Horse and Foote over *Dutch*, and since died of his wounds at *Vlme*.

*Iohn Monro* of *Obstell* Colonell to a Regiment of *Scots*, and since slaine on the *Rhine* in the *Weteraw*.

*Lodovicke Lesly* Colonell to a Regiment of *Scots*, which was Sir *Iohn Hamiltons*.

*Robert Monro* Colonell to a Regiment of *Scots*, which was my Lord of *Rhees*.

*Iames Carre* Colonell to a Regiment of *Scots*, and since Generall Major.

Sir *Fredricke Hamilton* Colonell to a Regiment of *Scots* and *Irish*.

The Master of *Forbesse* Colonell to a Regiment of *Scots*.

*Alexander Hamilton* Colonell to a Regiment of *Scots*.

The Earle of *Crawford Lindesey* Colonell to a Foote Regiment of *Dutch*, and since slaine.

*William Baily* Colonell to a Regiment of foote of *Dutch*.

Sir *Iames Hamilton* Colonell to a foote Regiment of *Scots*.

*Iohn Forbesse* Colonell to a foote Regiment of *Dutch*, slaine in *France*.

*Hugh Hamilton* Colonell to a foote Regiment of *Dutch*.

Sir *William Ballentine* Colonell to a fote Regiment of *English*.

Sir *Iames Ramsey* Colonell to a foote Regiment of *English*, and since died at *London*.

*Alexander Forbesse* called *Finnesse Forbesse* Colonell to a Regiment of *Finnes*.

*Walter Leckey* Colonell to foote.

### *The* English *Colonells served then.*

Colonell *Austin* Colonell to an *English* Regiment served in *Germany*.

Sir *Iohn Cassells* Colonell to a foote Regiment of *English*, which was levied

by Sir *Thomas Conway*; who was cast away on the coast of *Denmarke* with his Lievetenant Colonell *George Stewart*.

Sir *George Fleetwood* Colonell to a foote Regiment of *English* that served at this time in *Spruce*.

### Scots *Colonells that served at this time in* Sweden, Leefland *and* Spruce.

*Iames Seaton* Colonell to foote of *Swedes*.                    [List-2]

Colonell *Kinninmond* Colonell to foote of *Swedes*, since dead.

Colonell *Thomson* Colonell to foote of *Swedes*, since dead.

Colonell *Scot* Cloonell to foote of *Finnes*, since dead.

*William Cunninghame* Colonell to foote of *Scots, in Spruce*.

*Francis Ruthven* Colonell to foote of *Dutch*, in *Spruce*.

Sir *Iohn Meldrum* Colonell in *Spruce* to foote.

### *Lievetenant Colonells who served then, whereof since some have beene advanced.*

*Thomas Hume* of *Carolside* Lievetenant Colonell of Horse; since a Colonell in *France.*

Lievetenant Colonell *Dowglas* since a Colonell of Horse in *Germany* under the *Swede.*

*Henry Muschamp* Lievetenant Colonell, since was a Colonell and was slaine at *Nerling.*

*Alexander Lesly* Lievetenant Colonell, since a Colonell to foote.

*Alexander Cunninghame* Lievetenant Colonell, since a Colonell to foote.

Lievetenant Colonell *Vavazer*, since a Colonell to foote.

*William Gunne* Lievetenant Colonell, since a Colonell to foote of *Dutch.*

*Iohn Lesly* Lievetenant Colonell, since a Colonell to foote of *Scots.*

Lievetenant Colonell *Finnesse Forbesse*, since a Colonell.

*Alexander Forbesse* called the *Bald*, Lievetenant Colonell, since a Colonell.

*Robert Stewart* Lievetenant Colonell, since a Colonell.

*Hector Monro* Lievetenant Colonell, since a Colonell, and being made Knight Baronet died at *Hamburg*, and was buried at *Buckstehood* in the *Oldland* on the *Elve.*

Sir *George Dowglas* Lievetenant Colonell, since Ambassadour for his Majesty of Great *Britaine*, in *Spruce*, died in *Germany*, and was transported and buried in *Scotland.*

*George Lesly* Lievetenant Colonell, since Colonell.

*Iohn Lindesey* of *Bainshow* Lievetenant Colonell, since slaine at *Newbrandenburg.*

Lievetenant Colonell *Monypenny*, Lievtenant Colonell to horse.

*Alexander Lindesey* Lievetenant Colonell, since slaine in *Bavier.*

*Iohn Sinclaire* Lievetenant Colonell, was slaine at *Newmarke.*

*William Stewart* Lievetenant Colonell, succeeded to *Sinclaire.*

*Henry Lindesey* Lievetenant Colonell to *Lesly* the younger.

*William Lindesey* Lievetenant Colonell to Horse.

*Iames Henderson* Lievetenant Colonell to Foote.

Sir *Arthur Forbesse* Lievetenant Colonell to foote, was slaine in combat neere *Hamburg.*

*Robert Weere* Lievetenant Colonell, since slaine in *Saxony.*    [List-3]

*Iohn Lyell* Lievetenant Colonell to foote.

*Iames Dickson* Lievetenant Colonell, since slaine in the *Paltz.*

*Sandelens* Lievetenant Colonell, since slaine in the *Paltz.*

*William Borthwicke* Lievetenant Colonell to foote.

*Macdowgall* Lievetenant Colonell, since slaine in *Schwabland.*

*Iames Hepburne* Lievetenant Colonell, since slaine in *France.*

*Robert Hannan* Lievetenant Colonell to foote, died in *Alsas*.
*Iohn Monro* Lievetenant Colonell to foote.
*Robert Lumsdell* Lievetenant Colonell to foote.
*William Herring* Lievetenant Colonell to foote.
Sir *Iames Cunninghame* Lievetenant Colonell to foote.
*William Spence* Lievetenant Colonell to foote.
*Iohn Ennis* Lievetenant Colonell to foote.
*Poytaghee Forbesse* Lievetenant Colonell to foote.
*Iohn Forbesse* of *Tullough* Lievetenant Colonell, was slaine at *Nerling*.
*George Forbesse* Lievetenant Colonell to foote.
*Alexander Hay* Lievetenant Colonell of Dragoniers.
*David Leslie* Lievetenant Colonell to Horse.
*Iames Drummond* Lievetenant Colonell to horse.
*Kinninmond* the elder Lievetenant Colonell to foote.
*Kinninmond* the younger Lievetenant Colonell to foote.
*Francis Sinclaire* Lievetenant Colonell to foote.
*Gordon* Lievetenant Colonell, since a Colonell to foote of *Dutch* under the
Crowne of *Sweden*.
   *Iohn Henderson* Lievetenant Colonell, since a Colonell under the
Emperour.
*William Troope* Lievetenant Colonell slaine in the *Paltz*.
*Potley* Lievetenant Colonell to foote, under Sir *George Fleetwood*.
*Arthur Mon-gorge* Lievetenant Colonell to foote.
*Iames Mongomry* Lievetenant Colonell slaine in combat.

Scots *Majors*.

Major *Ruthven* slaine at *Nerling*.
Major *Mill*.
Major *Cunninghame*.
Major *Iohn Forbesse*.
Major *David King*, slaine at *Nerling*.
Major *Bodwell* slaine at *Wertzburg*.
Major *Mackenyee*, since Generall adjutant under the Felt-marshall *Lesly*.
Major *Sidserfe* slaine at *Nerling*.
Major *David Monro*.
Major *William Falconer*.
Major *Francis Sinclaire*.                                         [List-4]
Major *William Keith*.
Major *Sanderson*.
   Major *William Bruntfield* died of his wounds at *Buckstehoode* in the
*Oldland*.

*Diverse Captaines and inferiour Officers of the Nation followed the Army being
in charge, whom I omit out of this List.*                        [List-5]

# MONRO
# HIS EXPEDITION
# *IN*
# GERMANY.

| The first Part | Moneths<br>Weekes.<br>Dayes. | Dutch<br>Miles |
|---|---|---|

| | Moneths Weekes. Dayes. | Dutch Miles |
|---|---|---|
| *Tvesday the tenth of* October 1626. *from* Cromartie *in* Scotland *to* Lugstad *on the* Elve *by Sea, Dayes* | 5 | 300 |
| W*ee wintered in* Holstein *in good Quarters, Moneths* | 6 | |
| *From* Lugstad *on the* Elve *we marched to the*Weser streame *above* Bremen, *Dayes* | 4 | 12 |
| *On the* Weser streame *we remained weekes Ten,* | | 10 |
| *The tenth of* Iuly 1627. *we  marched from the* Weser *to* Bucstihoode, *Dayes* | 3 | 12 |
| *From the* Oldland *we crossed the* Elve *at* Blanckenesse *and continued our Expedition to* Beysenburg *on the* Elve *in* Mechlenburg, *Dayes* | 3 | 10 |
| *At* Beysenburg *we rested Dayes five.* | 5 | |
| *From* Beysenburg *to* Rapin *in the* Marke *of* Brandenburg *we marched, Dayes* | 6 | 18 |
| *At* Rapin *we rested dayes Eight.* | 8 | |
| *From* Rapin *we retired to the Isle of* Poole *on the* Baltique Coast, *having marched Dayes* | 6 | 28 |
| *At* Poole *Leaguer we rested five weekes.* | | |
| *From* Poole *by water to* Heligenhoven, *Dayes* | 2 | 40 |
| *From* Heligenhoven *we marched to* Oldenburg, *Day* | 1 | 3 |
| *At* Oldenburg *we were dayes three.* | 3 | |
| *From* Oldenburg *we retired in a night.* | 1 | 3 |
| *From* Heligenhoven *on the Coast of* Holsten *to* Flensborre *by water, Dayes* | 2 | 40 |
| *From* Flensborre *to* Assens *in* Denmarke *by water,Dayes* | 5 | 50 |
| *Having arrived in* Funeland *in* Denmarke *we were quartered in* [Log I-1] Denmarke *till we went to* Trailsound, *being Eight Moneths.* | 8 | |
| *From* Assens *in* Funeland *we marched unto* Lowland *and crossed the* Palt *twice being on the* March, *Dayes* | 5 | 14 |

|  | Time | Miles |
|---|---|---|

*Having arrived at* Marbo *in* Lowland, *we quartered our*
*Companies in* Marbo, Rubie *and in* Nicoppen, *where we*
*lay in good Quarters foure Moneths.*

| *From* Marbo *we marched to* Rubie *in a Day.* | 1 | 4 |

*We lay three dayes and nights in extremity of cold weather*
*in open Boats before* Rubie, *attending a faire winde, and in*
*the end were forced to land and march a Day backe.* ... 1 ... 4

*The sixt of* Aprill *we marched to* Rubie *againe in one Day.* 1 ... 4

*From* Rubie *we sayled to* Feamer, *and landed in a Day.* 1 ... 16

*From* Feamer *to* Aikel-ford *by water alongst the Coast*
*of* Holsten *in one Day.* ... 1 ... 16

*From* Aikel-ford *againe being shipped we sayled alongst*
*the coast before* Kyel *in one Day.* ... 1 ... 18

*From* Kyel *we returned by water unto* Grottenbrodde *in*
Holsten, *Dayes* ... 2 ... 34

*At* Grottenbrodde *in* Holsten *we lay weekes three, where*
*we did worke and complete a Royall Leaguer and a Fort*
*within it.*

*From* Feamer *to* Rubie *by water we sayled backe unto*
Lowland. ... 1 ... 16

*From* Rubie *to our Quarters in* Marbo *and* Nicoppen,
*where we lay weekes six in good Quarters.* ... 1 ... 4

*From* Lowland *to* Alzenheur *in* Denmark *we marched*
*through* Fuister *and* Zealand, *Dayes* ... 4 ... 18

*From* Alzenheur *we sayled unto* Trailsound *in* Pomeren. 2 ... 60

*At* Trailsound *being beleaguered we lay seven weekes,*
*where we had great paines and sustained great losse.*

*From* Trailsound *we marched unto* Wolgast, *Dayes* ... 2 ... 6

*At* Wolgast *wee remained dayes Ten.*

*From* Wolgast *we sayled to* Copmanhagen, *Dayes* ... 2 ... 60

*At* Copmanhagen *in* Denmark *the Regiment was made*
*complete againe, and wee were quartered in good Quarters*
*during Eight Moneths without any hostile imployment,*
*being treating for a peace.*

*In* Aprill 22. *wee sh~pped at* Malmee *in* Skonland *in*
Denmarke, *and sayled unto* Holsten *towards the Isle of*
Angle, *in dayes* ... 3 ... 60

*We lay at* Angle *in* Holsten *till the Peace was concluded*
*in the latter end of* May 1629. *that we were thanked of or*
*dismissed by his Majestie of* Denmark, *and were shipped*
*againe from* Holsten *to* Alzenheur, *being by water Dayes* 3 ... 60

*Summa* Miles by water and land travelled under
his Majestie of *Denmark* in three yeares. ... 898

[Log I-2]

# MONRO
# HIS EXPEDITION
# IN GERMANY
# VNDER HIS MAIESTY
# OF *SWEDEN*
of blessed memory.

*The Second Part.*

|  | Time. | Dutch Miles. |
|---|---|---|
| *In* Iune 1629. *sent from* Alzenheur *to the* Pillo *into* Spruce *first three Companies, and then three by water, Dayes* | 4 | 100 |
| *These six Companies did lie a whole yeare in Garrison in* Brounesberry *in* Spruce *without hostile Imployment.* |  |  |
| *The thirteenth of* August 1630. *shipped at the* Pillo *in* Spruce, *and landed the eighteenth at* Rougenvald *in hinder* Pomeren, *being at Sea, Dayes* | 5 | 80 |
| *At* Rougenvald *we lay nine weekes in good quarters.* |  |  |
| *From* Rougenvald *to* Colberg *we marched, Dayes* | 2 | 7 |
| *From* Colberg *we marched to* Shevelbeane *in the* Marck. | 1 | 5 |
| *From* Shevelbeane *to* Griffenberg *in* Pomeren, *Dayes* | 1 | 5 |
| *From* Griffenberg *to* Primhausen *we marched, Dayes* | 2 | 7 |
| *At* Primhausen *in extreame cold weather we lay in the Fields three weekes.* |  |  |
| *From* Primhausen *we marched to* Statin, *Dayes* | 2 | 9 |
| *At* Statin *we lay Moneths two, getting weekly pay.* |  |  |
| *From* Statin *we marched to new* Brandenburg, *Dayes* | 3 | 10 |
| *At* Brandenburg *we rested after in-taking of the Towne Dayes three.* |  |  |
| *From* Brandenburg *we marched to* Trepto *and from thence to* Letz *in Dayes* | 2 | 7 |
| *At* Letz *we rested three dayes, and then marched to* Damaine. | 1 | 1 |
| *At* Damaine *we lay dayes three before the Towne was taken in, and marched to* Trepto, *Dayes* | 2 | 5 |

[Log II-1]

| | Time | Miles |
|---|---|---|
| *At* Trepto *we lay three dayes, and from thence marched to* Malchen *in* Macklenburg, *in Dayes* | 2 | 6 |
| *At* Malchen *wee remained dayes eight, and marched to* Fridland *in dayes* | 2 | 6 |
| *At* Fridland *wee remained dayes eight, and marched to* Anclam *in Dayes* | 2 | 6 |
| *From* Anclam *having layn there dayes foure wee marched backe to* Fridland *in Dayes* | 2 | 6 |
| *At* Fridland *wee lay dayes six at our back-comming, and then marched unto* Swede, *in Dayes* | 3 | 12 |
| *At* Swede *we rested dayes eight, and then marched to* Francfurt *on the* Oder, *in Dayes* | 5 | 15 |
| *After the in-taking of* Francfurt *we marched to* Lantsberg *on the* Wart, *and lay before it dayes eight ere it was taken, in dayes* | 2 | 9 |
| *From* Lantsberg *we retired to* Francfurt *backe in Dayes* | 2 | 9 |
| *At* Frankfurt *we rested weekes five and then marched to* Berlein *in the* Marke Brandenburg *in Dayes* | 3 | 11 |
| *From* Berlein *we marched to* Spando, *day* | 1 | 4 |
| *At* Spando *wee rested dayes foure, and marched then to* Spotsdam. | 1 | 4 |
| *At* Spotsdam *wee lay dayes tenne, and retired to* Spando *backe.* | 1 | 4 |
| *At* Spando *againe we lay dayes ten, and then marched backe to* Berlein. | 1 | 4 |
| *At* Berlein *wee lay Dayes foure, and then marched to* Barno *in Dayes* | 2 | 9 |
| *At* Barno *we lay Dayes twelve, and then marched to old* Brandenburg *in Dayes* | 4 | 15 |
| *At old* Brandenburg *we rested Dayes ten, and then marched to* Rawtenaw *in Dayes* | 2 | 5 |
| *From* Rawtenaw *we marched to* Tangermond *on the* Elve *in Dayes* | 2 | 6 |
| *From* Tangermond *we marched to* Verben *downe the* Elves *side in Dayes* | 2 | 5 |
| *At* Verben *we lay in Leaguer Weekes five, and then marched to* Vyttenberg *on the* Elve *in Dayes* | 6 | 22 |
| *At* Vittenberg *in* Saxon *we lay dayes eight, and then crossing the* Elve, *marched to* Dieben *in Dayes* | 2 | 5 |
| *At* Dieben *we lay Dayes three, and then marched to the place of Battaile called* Gods-acre *neare* Leipsigh, *in dayes* | 2 | 5 |
| *From the place of Battaile, we marched to* Leipsigh | 1 | 2 |
| *At* Leipsigh *we lay Dayes three, and then marched backe to* Hall *in Dayes* | 2 | 5 |

|  | Time | Miles |
|---|---|---|
| At Hall *we rested Dayes nine, and then we marched* to Ertfurt *in* Duringland *Dayes* | 3 | 9 |
| At Ertfurt *we lay dayes eight, and then marched to* Smalka *over the* Walt *in dayes* | 2 | 6 |
| *From* Smalka *to* Mainigane *in* Franconia, *Day* | 1 | 3 |
| *From* Mainigane *to* Millarstot *Day* | 1 | 3 |

|  | | **[Log II-2]** |
|---|---|---|
| *From* Millarstot *to* Nistot *on the* Sale *in* Franconia, *Day* | 1 | 3. |
| *From* Nistot *to* Hammelburg *Day* | 1 | 3. |
| *From* Hammelburg *to* Gemund *on the* Maine *Day*. | 1 | 3. |
| *From* Gemund *to* Carlstot *on the* Maine *Day* | 1 | 2. |
| *From* Carlstot *to* Vertzburg *Day* | 1 | 2. |
| *From* Vertzburg *to* Oxenford *on the* Maine *in a night* | 1 | 4. |
| *From* Oxenford *backe to* Vertzburg *Day* | 1 | 4. |
| At Vertzburg *we lay neare five Weekes, and then marched downe the* Maine *to* Procelden *in Dayes* | 2 | 6. |
| *From* Procelden *we marched to* Vertzhem *Dayes* | 2 | 6. |
| *From* Vertzhem *to* Miltenburg *Dayes* | 2 | 6. |
| *From* Miltenburg *to* Sultzbach *Day* | 1 | 4. |
| *From* Sultzbach *to* Steinhem *Day* | 1 | 1. |
| *From* Steinhem *to* Offenbach, *before the Ports of* Frankfurt | 1 | 1. |
| *From* Offenbach *the seventeenth of* November *we marched through* Francfurt *unto* Heghst *Day* | 1 | 2. |
| At Heghst *we rested foure dayes, and then crossed the* Maine *and marched by* Darmestot *unto the* Bergstros *towards* Oppenhem Sconce *Dayes* | 2 | 6. |
| At Oppenhem *before the Sconce was gotten in, we lay in the open fields in extremity of cold, and then crossed the* Rhine *and tooke in* Oppenhem Towne *and* Castle, *where we rested three Dayes.* | | |
| *From* Oppenhem *we marched to* Mentz *on the* Rhine *in dayes* | 2 | 5. |
| *Before* Mentz *we lay in extreme cold weather foure dayes in open fields, before we got it in, and then rested the Army there for ten Weekes.* | | |
| *From* Mentz *we marched neare* Frankfurt *in day* | 1 | 4. |
| *From* Francfurt *we marched to* Asschaiffenbourg *on the* Maine *in day* | 1 | 5. |
| *From* Asschaiffenbourg *we marched unto* Franconia *towards* Estenfeld *in Day* | 1 | 4. |
| *From* Estenfeld *we marched to* Lor *in Day* | 1 | 4. |
| *From* Lor *we marched to* Gamund *in Day* | 1 | 4. |
| *From* Gamund *we marched to* Carlstot *in day* | 1 | 2. |

|                                                                                      | Time | Miles |
|--------------------------------------------------------------------------------------|------|-------|
| *From* Carlstot *we marched to* Tettelbach *in* Franconia *in day*                   | 1    | 4.    |
| *From* Tettelbach *we marched to* Oxenford *in day*                                  | 1    | 4.    |
| *From* Oxenford *we marched to* Vintzin *in day*                                     | 1    | 4.    |
| *At* Vintzin *we rested three dayes and then we marched to* Volmarsdorffe *in day*   | 1    | 4.    |
| *From* Volmarsdorffe *to* Furt *on the* Pegnets *in day*                             | 1    | 4.    |
| *From* Furt *to* Schwabach *Day*                                                     | 1    | 3.    |
| *At* Schwabach *we rested two dayes, and marched to* Weysenburg *dayes*              | 2    | 6.    |
| *From* Weysenburg *to* Nerling *Dayes*                                               | 2    | 6.    |
| *From* Nerling *to* Donavert *Day*                                                   | 1    | 3.    |

**[Log II-3]**

|                                                                                                                        | Time | Miles |
|------------------------------------------------------------------------------------------------------------------------|------|-------|
| *At* Donavert *we lay before it was taken dayes two, and rested thereafter dayes three, and then crossed the* Leacke *at* Rhine *in Day* | 1    | 2.    |
| *From* Rhine *to* Ausburg *Day*                                                                                        | 1    | 5.    |
| *From* Ausburg *to* Aichstad *in Baviere Day*                                                                          | 1    | 4.    |
| *From* Aichstad *towards* Engolstat *Dayes*                                                                            | 2    | 7.    |
| *From* Engolstat *to* Gaisenfels *Day*                                                                                 | 1    | 2.    |
| *From* Gaisenfels *in Baviere to* Morsburg *Day.*                                                                      | 1    | 4.    |
| *At* Morsburg *we rested foure dayes, and from thence to* Landshude *Day*                                              | 1    | 3.    |
| *From* Landshude *to* Freisin *Day*                                                                                    | 1    | 4.    |
| *From* Freisin *to* Munchen *Day*                                                                                      | 1    | 4.    |
| *At* Munchen *we lay three weekes, and then marched backe to* Donavert *in dayes*                                      | 4    | 15.   |
| *From* Donavert *backe to* Veysenburg *Dayes*                                                                          | 3    | 9.    |
| *From* Veysenburg *to* Furt *on the* Pegnets *Dayes*                                                                   | 3    | 9.    |
| *At* Furt *we lay dayes eight, and marched then to* Lauffe                                                             | 1    | 4.    |
| *From* Lauffe *to* Harsburg *in Day*                                                                                   | 1    | 4.    |
| *From* Harsburg *in the upper* Palatinate *to* Amberg *Dayes*                                                          | 2    | 7.    |
| *From* Amberg *backe to* Harsburg *dayes*                                                                              | 2    | 7.    |
| *At* Harsburg *we lay weekes three, and then retired to* Nurenburg *in dayes.*                                         | 2    | 6.    |

*At* Nurenburg *we lay in Leaguer three Moneths till the succours was come, and then we braveerd the* Emperiall *Leaguer.*

|                                                      | Time | Miles |
|------------------------------------------------------|------|-------|
| *From* Nurenburg *to* Newstad *dayes*                | 2    | 5.    |
| *From* Newstad *to* Vintzen *dayes*                  | 2    | 6.    |
| *From* Vintzen *to* Dunkelspeill *daies*             | 2    | 6.    |
| *From* Dunkelspeill *to* Donavert *daies*            | 3    | 9.    |
| *From* Donavert *to* Rhine *on the* Leake *day*      | 1    | 2.    |
| *From* Rhine *to* Newburg *on the* Danube *day*      | 1    | 3.    |

|  | Time | Miles |
|---|---|---|
| *From* Newburg *to* Rhine *backe day* | 1 | 3. |
| *From* Rhine *to* Ausburg *day* | 1 | 5. |
| *From* Ausburg *to* Aichstat *daies* | 2 | 6. |
| *From* Aichstat *to* Lantsberg *daies* | 2 | 7. |
| *From* Lantsbers *to* Ausburg *daies* | 2 | 5. |
| *From* Ausburg *to* Rhine *backe againe daies* | 2 | 5. |
| *From* Rhine *againe to* Ausburg *day* | 1 | 5. |

*At* Ausburg *the Armie did lie after his Majesties death, neare three Moneths without any hostile imploiment.*

| | | |
|---|---|---|
| *From* Ausburg *to* Vlme *in February* 1633 *we marched daies* | 3 | 9. |
| *From* Vlme *to* Memming *we marched daies* | 2 | 6. |
| *From* Memming *to the* Passe *at* Kempten *dayes* | 2 | 7. |
| *From the* Passe *we marched backe to* Middelhem *in* Schwabland *daies* | 2 | 7. |
| *From* Middelhem *to* Kauffebeyren *we marched daies* | 2 | 7. |
| *From* Kauffbeyren *to* Kempten *we marched day* | 1 | 4. |
| *From* Kempten *backe to* Pibrach *daies* | 2 | 7. |
| *From* Pibrach *to* Munderkin *on the* Danube *daies* | 2 | 6. |

[Log II-4]

| | | |
|---|---|---|
| *From* Munderkin *to* Retlingam *in* Vertenbergland *in a night* | 1 | 5. |
| *From* Retlingam *to* Eslengan *day* | 1 | 4. |
| *From* Eslengan *to* Munderkin *backe dayes* | 2 | 6. |
| *From* Munderkin *to* Pibrach *backe dayes* | 2 | 6. |
| *From* Pibrach *to* Vlme *on the* Danube *dayes* | 2 | 6. |
| *From* Vlme *to* Donavert *being the end of the second part of the Expedition, which we marched in dayes* | 3 | 9 |

Summa Dutch *Miles of the March made under his Maiesty of* Sweden *and the Crowne in* Germany *in foure yeares, extends to*     779.

[Log II-5]

# Part, II.

## THE MANNER OF OVR

## INGAGEMENT WITH HIS MAIESTIE

*of* Svveden, *in Anno, 1629. And of the Colonels*

*Iourney and mine unto* Sweden *in*

*Februarie, 1630.*

Ovr Regiment thanked of by his Majesty of *Denmarke* in *May,*1629. my Colonell being in *England*, I hearing his Majesty of *Sweden* (much ingaged against the *Pole* in *Spruce*) did stand in great need of a supply of Foot, thought then, it was a fit time for me being out of service, to offer my service unto his Majesty of *Sweden*; whereupon I did direct *David Martins* Auditor with my letters, and warrant to his Majesty, to treate with his Majesty for a Commission, and money for bringing unto his Ma^tie a Regiment of Foot, over which my old Colonell should command. His Majesty condescending to my desire, dispatcheth my Commissioner backe againe with a Commission, and monies to me in the Colonels name; and in his absence I did direct as a beginning of the Regiment, *Fowles*, Captaine *Monro*, and my owne Captaine, being three Companies of the Regiment unto *Spruce*, before the Colonels comming from *England*, and after there were sent unto *Spruce* three Companies, (*viz.*) Major *Synnots*, Captaine *Bullions*, and Captaine *Lermond's* Companies, which sixe for that yeare, remayned in Garrison in *Brownesbery* in *Spruce*; other sixe Companies of the old Regiment, the Colonell directed from *Holland* to *Sweden*, in *November 1629.* where they remained in Garrison till *May,*1630. when they were sent into *Dutchland*, commanded by the Colonell, whose Company was led by Captaine Lieutenant *Gunne*, Lieutenant Colonell *Lindesey* his Company was led by Lieutenant *Pringle*, Captaine *Sinclaire*, Captaine *Moncreife*, Captaine *Ennis*, and Captaine *Beaton*, made out the other sixe Companies of the Regiment: Captaine *George Stewart*, and Captaine *Francis Trafford*, having quit their Companies for their better preferment: Captaine *Monro* of *Fowles* being advanced to be a Colonell of Foot, his brother *Hector Monro* succeeded as Captaine to his brothers Company, which was under me in *Spruce*: thus farre then may suffice, for the manner of our Ingagements.

My Colonell and I, having wintered both in *Denmarke*, in *February* 1630. wee crost the *Sound* and tooke our Iourney unto *Sweden* through *Skonland*. In our way, wee were nobly and courteously entertained by the Governour of *Warden* Castle, and from thence were mounted with the Governours best Horses, being convoyed by his servants, till wee entred in *Gottenberge*, where we rested two dayes, till the Governour did provide us of Passes, guides and horses, towards his Majesty, then at *Stockholme* in *Sweden*; where on our journey we did visit that worthy *Cavaliere*, Colonell *Alexander Hamilton*, at his Worke-houses in *Vrbowe*, being then imployed in making of Cannon and fire-workes, for his Majesty of *Sweden*; from whence the Colonell did con- [II-1] vey us to his Quarter, where we were kindly entertained and welcommed by him, and his Officers: From thence we continued our Iourney, and did visit Captaine *Sinclaire* at his Quarter, where wee were also well entertained, having stayed with him on *Easter* Sunday, and from thence wee travailed to *Stockholme*, where wee had first the honour of his Majesties presence and conference; after kissing of his Majesties hand, we tooke our lodgings where we stayed certaine dayes, his Majesty being making preparation for the transporting of his Majesties Army unto *Dutchland*.

The first Sunday after our comming, his Majesty did invite the principall *Cavaliers* that were in Towne of our Nation, for to accompany his Majesty at a Feast appointed in honour of the Order of the *Garter*, where Thirteene *Cavaliers* of our Nation did sit at his Majesties table, and were Royally entertained; This Feast past, his Majesty having ordered his Foot Army in the Fields, after his new order of Discipline of *Briggades*, then first brought in use, at which time his Majesty having showen unto my Colonell and his Officers, the Order of his Majesties discipline, in which Order, his Majestie commanded to put my Colonels Regiment, which was presently obeyed, insomuch, that his Majesty was so well pleased with the capacity of my Colonels Souldiers going so orderly and readily to their Duties, that his Majestie did wish in open presence of the Army, that all his Foot were so well disciplined as my Colonels Regiment: for which, his Majesty would bee content to be indebted of a huge great summe of money, and having caused the Regiment march by towards their Quarters, his Maiesty did mightily and much praise the Regiment for their good Order; saying, hee hoped one day, to get good service of those men for his monies; shortly after this, his Maiesty did Ship his Army for *Germanie*, with which, my Colonell and his Regiment went also: I having gotten his Majesties Patent over a free Squadron, of the Companies that were in *Spruce*, I was directed to the *Rex Chancellor* there, with Orders from his Maiesty to his Excellence, to direct me and my Squadron with all diligence, after his Majesty unto *Dutchland*; according to which, having arrived in *Spruce*, and delivered my Commission to his Excellence; I was immediatly directed to my Garrison to order the Companies for a Muster, and being mustered, and payed of two moneths meanes, there was Shipping provided for mee and my Companies at the *Pillo*, in *August* 1630. for transporting of us into *Dutchland*, according to his Maiesties will and Orders given unto me to follow his Majestie, and our Ships being victualed, wee attended the winde. [II-2]

THE SECOND

PART, OF MONRO

HIS EXPEDITION VNDER HIS

Majesty of Svveden, discharged in

severall Duties and Observations.

*The first Dutie discharged in the* Swedens *service of our Expedition by Water from* Pillo *in* Spruce *unto the Coast of* Pomerne *at* Rougenvalde.

The twelfth of *August,* 1630. having received his Excellence Orders the *Rex Chancellor,* for to Ship my Souldiers at the *Pillo,* and from thence to transport them unto *Dutchland,* towards *Wolgast* in *Pomerne,* in obedience to the orders, having divided the Companies at the *Pillo,* my owne Company, Captaine *Hector Monro's,* and Captaine *Bullions* Company, were put with my selfe in a Ship of his Majesties called the *Lilly-Nichol;* The other three Companies, (*viz.*) Major *Senotts,* Captaine *Iohn Monro's* and *Lermonds,* were put on another Ship of his Majesties, called the *Hound,* our Horses and Baggage being put on a small Skoote or Boat, the winde favouring us, we being victualed for a weeke, we make sayle from the *Pillo* towards *Pomerne,* having calme weather for two dayes: The third day with a strong winde, and a great tempest from the West, wee were severed from the Fleet, and our Ship striking a leake, we were driven unto *Burnehollem* Roade in *Denmarke,* where the tempest being past, wee goe a shore, to victuall our ship anew: the winde favouring us, we weigh Anchor againe, and setting sayle, we take our course towards *Wolgast,* being neere the Coast, the winde contrary, wee were not able to double our Course, and our ship being leake, we durst not adventure farre from land, and putting forty eight Souldiers to pumpe continually by turnes, they were not able to keepe her dry, and being overcharged with much water, though there blew a great winde after us wee made but a slow Course, our resolution was, being tur- [II-3] ned backe, and before the winde, to make for *Dantsick,* as our best refuge: But keeping so neere the land, under night, wee bayed within lands, the winde blowing hard with a great tempest on the shore, being a shallow sandy Coast, all sayles being up, by Eleven a clocke at night, we struck on ground, our Ship old and weake breakes in the middest below, but kept fast above, our Souldiers comming all above hatches, they were pittifully drenched and wet with the waves, and being in danger of out-washing, they tye themselves with Ropes to the ship sides, yet two that tooke a pride in their swimming, (a *Dane,* and a *Scot,* called *Murdo Piper*) thinking by swimming to gaine the shore, were both drowned, the Mariners setting out one Boate after another, were both broken, and they being feeble fellowes they lost courage; thus under the mercy of the raging Seas and waves, going higher then the mastes over the ship sides; wee patiently attended the Lords mercy with prayers, till One of the clocke the next day, during which time,

I forced the Mariners and Souldiers, that could best worke, having cut the Masts, and the ends of the Crosse yards, with Deales and the Deckes of the ship to make a floate; being made, it was tyed to the ship within with Towes, hanging at it, which the waves could carry ashoare, the floate thus ready, with strength of men was let downe by the Ships side, whereon foure of the most couragious Souldiers did adventure to goe, some Boores a shoare having got hold of the Towes, that were bound to the Floate, with the helpe of the waves, drawe the Float ashoare, and being drawne backe to the ship, wee did continue in this manner ferrying out our souldiers, till at last the most part were landed, who being landed sought along the Coast, and finding a Boate, did bring it with Horses on a Waggon, whereof wee made use in landing the rest of our souldiers, whereof I remayned the last; till I saw our Armes landed. But our Amunition and Baggage being lost, we were in a pitifull feare, being neere unto our Enemies, and above Twenty *Dutch* miles from his Majesties Army, being without fixe Armes, and lacking Amunition, wee had nothing to defend us, but Swords, and Pikes, and some wet Muskets, the enemy being neere, our resolution behoved to be short, where having learned of the Boores, how neere the Enemy was unto us, I suffered none to goe from us, lest we might be discovered to our enemies.

After advisement I sent Captaine *Bullion* with a Guide, to the Captaine of the Castle of *Rougenvalde*, belonging to the Duke of *Pomerne*, offering if hee would furnish us some fixe Muskets, with some dry Amunition and Bullets, wee would cut off the Enemy that lay in the Town, and defend Town and Castle from the enemy for his Majesty, till such time as his majesty might relieve us, the proposition so pleased the Captaine; that hee gave way to my suite, and withall, hee, for feare of such suspition, goes unto the Countrey, having sent a Gentleman with Amunition to me, to convey me a secret way unto the Castle, where I should receive Fifty muskets, my Captaine retiring to me, with the Gentleman and Amunition, I marched till I came safe to the Castle, and then from the Castle falling on the Towne, with commanded Musketiers, under the command of Captaine *Bullion*, I stayed my selfe with the reserve, my folkes entering the Towne, the Enemy a loft drew to Armes: thus service begun; my partie being strongest, some of the enemy shot, the rest got quarters and mercy, our Watch duely set, the Keyes of the Towne and Castle being delivered unto me, my greatest care was then, how to put our selves in safety against our Enemies, being [II-4] at *Colberge* within seven miles of us, I begun to learne from those on the Castle, what passes did lye betwixt us and *Colberge*, I was told of a little River did lye two miles from us, which was not passable but at one Bridge, where I went to Recognosce, and finding it was so, I caused them to breake off the Bridge, where I did appoint a company of Boores, with Armes, and Horses by them to watch the passe, and if in case the enemy should pursue them, they had Orders from me to defend the passe so long as they could, commanding them also at the first sight of the Enemy to advertise me, whereby they might be supplyed, and I put on my Guard.

Being retyred from the passe, immediately I did send a Boore on Horsebacke, in the night, to acquaint his Majesty of *Sweden* (the Army then lying at

*Statine* twenty *Dutch* miles from us) with the manner of our hard landing, and of our happy successe after landing; as likewise, disiring to know his Majesties will, how I should behave my selfe in the those Quarters, the Enemy being strong, and I very weake, his Majesty returned for resolution unto me, that I should doe my best to fortifie, and beset the passes, that were betwixt me and the Enemy, and to keepe good watch, and good order over the Soldiers, and not to suffer them to wrong the Country people, whom I should presse to keepe for my Friends.

This Order being come, I begun with the Country Boores, first, to fortifie the Passages without me, and next to make Skonces and Redoubts without the Towne, as also to repaire the Fortifications about the Castle, and in cleansing of the Mote, that it might be deeper of water, the other parts also without me, I brought under Contribution to his Majestie, by sending parties of *Dragoniers* athwart the Country, in *Hinder Pomerne*, betwixt me and *Dantsicke,* being twenty *Dutch* mile in length, which all in short time I did bring under contribution to his Majesty. As also the Enemy having had a *Magazin* of Corne, at *Rougenvalde*, and *Stolpe*, by our landing here; was made good for his Majesties use and his Army.

Being thus busied for a few dayes, another ship of the same Fleet, being long beaten with the tempest at Sea, at last was forced for scarcety of victuals, to Anker on the same Coast, being foure hundred men, of *Colonel Fretz Rosse* his Regiment of *Dutch*, his Lieutenant Colonell called *Tisme Howsue* did come ashore, intreating me to supply him with victuals, which I did. In the meane time he asked my advice, if he might land his Soldiers there, I told him I had no counsell to give him, seeing there was no necessity of his landing, and which was more, his Orders were to land at another part, so that he had to advise whether he should follow his Orders, or for second respects if hee might neglect his Orders, so that on all hasards he landed his people also, which were quartered with me in the Towne: Shortly after, he would contest with me for command, which bred a coldness betwixt us. *Whereupon* I again advertised his Majestie of our difference, desiring his Majesty might dispose of the Command; his Majesty offended with the other, did send an absolute warrant unto me, to command him, and the whole *Garrison* at my pleasure, for the well of his Majesties service, during our being there, where we remained nine weekes, fighting and skirmishing with the enemie, till Sir *Iohn Hepburne* with his Regiment was sent by his Excellence the *Rex Chancellor* from *Spruce* to relieve us. [II-5]

### *The First Observation.*

Having thus by the providence of God happily landed againe on the faire, fertill, and spacious Continent of *Dutchland*, with a handfull of old experimented Soldiers, able to endure all misery, toile, or travell, being valourous to undertake any perill or danger, they were to be commanded upon, being led by such a Generall as Gustavus the *Invincible*, their new Master was: (under whose command and conduct, as their supreame Leader, and me, as his Majesties and my Colonels inferiour Officer, they marched from the Coast of *Pomerne*, out of *Rougenvalde*, through *Dutchland*, unto the foot of the Alpes in *Schwabland.*)

This city of *Rougenvalde* in *Pomerne*, lyes midway betwixt *Dantsicke,* and *Statine,* being alike distant, twenty Dutch mile from both, and is a pleasant seate, being one of the Duke of *Pomerne* his chiefe Residence, not distant above one English mile from the Sea, it doth abound in Corne, Fruit, and store, Cattell, Horses of good breed, Fishponds, and Parkes for Deere, and pastorage, whereof it hath enough, where we were nobly entertained, and kindly welcommed of the inhabitants, especially of the Captaine and his civill Bed-fellow, to whom, under God, we were beholden for our safeties, the Remembrance whereof we are bound never to forget.

Here, I did remarke as wonderfull, that in the very moment when our ship did breake on ground, there was a *Sergeants* Wife a shipboard, who without the helpe of any women was delivered of a Boy, which all the time of the tempest she carefully did preserve, and being come ashore, the next day, she marched neere foure English mile, with that in her Armes, which was in her Belly the night before, and was Christened the next *Sunday* after Sermon, being the day of our thankesgiving for our Deliverance, our Preacher Mr. *Murdow Mac-kenyee* a worthy and Religious yong man, having discharged his part that day, after with much regrate did sever from us, and followed my Lord of *Rhee* our Colonell unto *Britaine*.

Being thus escaped from danger of sea, and from our enemies, I did keepe the Soldiers ever exercised in watching, in working, in parties against our enemies, lest that resting from the *Hostile* employment, they should become seditious, immodest, and turbulent; and to this effect, when they were not employed in parties against the enemies, I sent them by parties in the Country, on *Militarie* execution, to bring the possessors under Contribution to his Majesty, making them hate and renounce the Emperialists, whom formerly they were forced to obey; so that by this meanes, the Country was brought into subjection to the King, and my Soldiers were put under as good discipline and command, as any served his Majesty; which discipline made their continuance the longer in the service: where it was rare to finde one Regiment in an Armie, that did change so many Officers as they did in foure yeares, as the Observations on their duties will cleare to the world, in despight of their *Enviers* whatsoever. But I hope no worthy spirit of *Heroicke* minde will thinke an evill thought of the vertuous.

We may see here, that in the greatest extremities, both Officers and Soldiers have greatest need of Courage, and Resolution: For nothing should seeme hard to daring men, that are of courage, which never doth beget, but the opinion and censure of vertue. For we see at this time, that to dare was [II-6] the beginning of victory, being better to hazard to save our selves and others; then to be the instrument to lose us all by flying, as some of our Officers advised me at our landing, to marche backe to *Dantsicke*, which if we had, the enemy getting intelligence, he could with ease overtake us, and cut us all off, as he did, some yeeres before, cut off in the same Country three Regiments of *Dutch* who were going to serve his Majesty against the *Pole*.

Here also, I found by experience, that the stedfast, and invincible vigour of the minde rising against crosses, doth helpe much, especially where necessity requireth such resolution.    For being in the greatest extremity of danger, resolving with God, I thought as my safest course to bide Gods leysure, I sate on the *Gallerie* of the ship, being assured it would be the last part, that would remaine together of the whole, and being so neere land, I was never dejected and cast downe, nor did I doubt of our safe landing, seeing we had victuals and were in hope, the storme would not continue, being in the middest of *August.*

Here we may see by this Christian advertisement, that no part of our life is exempted or freed from griefe or sorrow. But on the contrary, we are exposed to all kinde of miseries and troubles, so that we see, that children doe sucke with the milke of their *Nurses*, certaine beginnings of the evill to come, our misery growing as doth our age and we see it true: for the godly; they sigh and groane under the burthen of their adversities, having no comfort they can enjoy, but out of the written word of *God*, a fruit whereof the wicked hath no part. *Therefore* they sayd well, who said, that *Philosophicall* precepts were not so powerfull to heale the wounds of the soule, as are those of the word of *God*.

Men of our profession ought ever to be well prepared, having death ever before their Eyes, they ought to be the more familiar with *God*, that they might be ever ready to embrace it, not caring a rush for it when it came, doing good while they may.  For now we flourish, in an instant we wither like *Grasse*; now we stand, presently we fall, our life carrying with it when we received it, the seed of death, and that which did begin our life, doth open the doore to it, to goe away: For in our birth, our end did hang at our beginning; and, according to the custome of that worthy *Emperour*, our actions should be ever before our eyes, as if presently we were to appeare in Iudgment, before the Eternall *our God*, and that cry should never depart out of our eares, cryed unto *Philip* King of *Macedon, Philippe, memento mori, Philip remember, thou must die:* For man shall never behave himselfe as he ought in this World, except at all times he have death before his eyes, thinking on the houre and moment of his departure alwayes, contemning the *Exteriour* things of this World, giving himselfe unto the inward cogitations, that doe profit the soule and the life thereof, rejoycing beyond all things in the Testimony of good Conscience.

---

*The second Dutie, discharged of our march from* Rougenvalde
*to* Colberg, *and thence to* Shivel-beane, *and of our service there.*

Sir *Iohn Hepburne* being sent with his Regiment (from *Spruce)* to relieve us, I was ordained with my Folks to march before *Colberge*, where Generall Major *Kniphowsen* did command in the *Blackering* thereof [11-7] (which I did) and being come there, a Poaste was assigned for us to watch at.  In the meane time, the Generall Major getting intelligence, that the enemies Army (lying at *Gartts* and *Griffinhawgen*, on the Oder) had intention to relieve *Colberge*, and so being in his march, he must needs passe by the Towne and Castle, of *Shevelbeane* in the *Marke,* being a passe distant but five miles from *Colberge,* he thought expedient, to *Recognosce* the place, by sending of *Colonell Hepburne* thither, with a Troope of Horsemen for his *guard,* and convoy; who having seene the place, advised *Kniphowsen* to beset it with a Garrison, being of consequence to hold up the Enemy, if he should march thereon with the Army, whereupon I was made choise of, with my Folks to beset it, being sent for in the night to breake up, and to march thither in all haste; I had command to speake with *Kniphowsen* in my going, for receiving further Orders.

The Companies marched by; I following my Orders desired to know what the Generall Major had to command me, who gave me Orders in writing, I should march thither, and in case the enemy should pursue me, I should fight to the last man, and not to give over the Castle, though I should be forced to quit the Towne: Receiving Orders for some Ammunition, I tooke leave of *Kniphowsen,* and continued my march to *Shevelbean,* then layd almost waste with Pestilence, the Inhabitants being fled away, I had slight quarters for my Soldiers, which being quartered, having visited the Towne and Castle, I appointed the manner of our Watch, and did beset the Poastes, from our *Guards,* which were kept both in the Towne and on the Castle, and then I sent Orders to the Boores of the *Graveshaft,* to come in the next day, with Spades, Shovels and Axes, for to repaire the workes, that were almost ruined, being a scurvie hole, for any honest *Cavalier* to maintaine his credit by.

Before my comming, two Troopes of *Bawtees* Horsemen (*viz.*) Major *Roustene,* and *Long-fretts,* were quartered there, who getting intelligence the Army was to march upon me, being Horsemen, quit the Garrison to our selves, and took them to the Fields, to joyne with their *Colonels* Regiment, being neere hand, so that our Quarters thus enlarged, we were glad to be rid of their trouble, as they were to eschew the Enemies comming, serving better in the Fields, then they could doe within Walles; The Horsemen gone, I was evill sped, for being put on such a place with such orders, appointed to fight to the last man, where no *Cavalier* with credit could hold out twenty foure houres, being pursued by an Army, except the Lord extraordinarily would shew mercy: *Neverthelesse,* getting three dayes longer continuation before the enemies comming, we did worke all of us night and day, till we had *Stacketed* the Wall about, the height of a man above the *Parapet,* having made a breast-worke of earth within the Walles round about, with Traverses within, for cleering out the Enemy, if he had entered at a breach; our Work ended, and our Ports Ranforced with Earth to resist the force of the *Pittards*; we see in the afternoone the Enemies squadrons of Foot and Horse, about eight thousand strong, marching unto us, having Artillery conforme, we finding them marching within reach, I caused to salute them with two small shot, wherewith a Rut-master, and a Lievtenant of horse were killed, which made the rest march out of distance: The Army drawne up in Battell without reach of our Canon, they sent a Trumpeter summoning us to a treatie, he was answered; we had no such Orders, but we had Powder, and Ball at their ser-
[II-8] vice. Whereupon they commanded a Captaine with a hundred and fiftie

musketiers towards the Porte, directing proportionally to the rest of the Portes: our souldiers in the beginning before the Portes killed of them above thirtie souldiers, and two Livetenants, I not being able to maintaine the Towne, retired with my folke on the Castle: I being retired, the Burgers made up, set open the Portes to the enemie, giving him entrance, who did bring in his whole Artillerie, and Amunition to the market place, and then sent to mee a Drummer to see, if I would render up the Castle upon good conditions, then they were in my power, but if not, I should have no quarters afterwards.

They got their first Answer againe, and then the service beginnes anew on both sides, and they begunne before night to plant their Batteries, within fourtie pace of our walles, which I thought too neere, but the night drawing on, wee resolved with fire workes, to cause them remove their quarters, and their Artillerie.

*Having* throwne some fiery *Granades* on the houses, and seeing they wrought no effect, I hired a stout souldier with a Pike to reach a firye Ball I had made (upon the top of the next house that lay to the Castle) which in the end was fired, so that the whole street did burne right alongst betwixt us, and the enemy, who was then forced to retire, both his Cannon, and souldiers, and not without great losse done unto him by our souldiers, by meanes of the firelight; where other two Officers, and eighteene of their souldiers were killed.

The day cleering up, I fell out after with fourescore Musketiers, and tooke thirteene Crabbats prisoners. The Army leaving us for that time they marched forwards for the releefe of *Colberg*, and I retired to the towne to comfort the Burgers, for their losse sustained by the fire, caused through necessitie, having no other meanes to escape our enemies fury.

I being retired to the Castle, and the enemy marching to *Colberg*, having made up eighteene Dragoniers to march after the enemy for bringing me intelligence, if his Majesties forces from *Statin* were come betwixt the enemie and *Colberg*, my party retiring shewes, that the field Marshall *Gustave Horne,* and Colonell *Mackey,* that comanded the comanded musketiers, were joyned with *Kniphowsen, Bawtish,* and Sir *Iohn Hepburne*; and were lying over-night, before a passage betwixt the enemy, and *Colberg.*

The next morning being darke till nine a clock with a thick mist, the horsemen charging one another, they came in confusion on both sides, being affrighted alike, retired from each others with the losse of fourescore men on both sides: The particulars whereof I will not set downe, having not seene the service, though I was within hearing of their Cannon and Muskets both.

Two horsemen of *Bawtish* Regiment, that had charged through the enemy came, and reported to me openly, in presence of many souldiers, that the *Swedens* were all beaten, I being offended at the manner of their report, I caused to imprison both of the horsemen, till I knew greater certainty, and calling my souldiers together, I was prepared for the enemies returne. But he passing by a mile from us, I sent Dragoniers to cut off his passage, giving them charge to cut off the Bridges, but his Dragoniers being there before mine, to be quit of their ill, my Dragoniers returned againe in safetie, allowing passage to their enemies:

within few days after, having escaped this inconvenience, I was recalled from thence, by his Majesties order, to joyne with the Felt-marshall *Horne*, then at *Griffinberg*, with a party of the Armie, where before my [II-9] departing, I tooke an Attestation, from the Amptman of the Castle, of the good order and Discipline, that was kept by vs there; And being glad I was rid with credit of such a place, I marched to *Griffenberg* to finde the Felt-Marshall.

## The second Observation.

The fore-sight of a wise Commander availes much, in preventing the intentions of our Enemies; First, in besetting the passages, through which he might come upon us, which doth hinder his march in giving us the longer time to bee prepared for his comming: Next, the farther our wings are spred without us, our Body is the better guarded by good intelligence: Thirdly, by this meanes, wee can better provide our Army with thinges necessary: Fourthly, the passages without being kept, they being next the Enemy, wee can have the more timely advertisement of our enemies designes, so soone as they are hatched.

This Cavaliere *Kniphowsen*, though hee was unfortunate, he had both the Theorie and Practick befitting a Commander; whom once I did heare say, that one Ounce of good Fortune was to be preferred before a Pound weight of Wit; which hee knew well by his owne experience; and to my knowledge, though hee was unfortunate himselfe, yet *Cavalieres* under his command, could learne by him much good order and discipline.

And though in his life-time, hee loved not our Country-men; Neverthelesse, for the love I carried to his vertues, I would not omit to make mention of his worth. No feare of danger, or death can be an excuse to a man, to serve the Publique in his calling.

Before I was commanded to enter this Towne, the Infection was great; yet none of us did forbeare to converse with the Sicke, though daily examples of mortality were frequent amongst us; for on our Watches, we knew not the cleane from the foule; Neverthelesse, it behoved us all to passe on our duties as wee were commanded; and though I know no reason for it, fewer Souldiers dyed of the infection than Burgers.

Yet one rare Sparke, being a resolute fix Souldier with a Musket, as ever I commanded, dyed here of the Pest, called *Andrew Monro*, who being but Eighteene yeares of age, though little of stature, no toyle nor travell could overset him; and as hee was stoute, so he was merry, and sociable without offence, such another was his Cozen *Iohn Munro*, *Kilternies* grand-child, who dyed of burning Feaver, being alive without feare before his Enemy, and of a merry and quicke disposition: I made onely mention of their names, because they lived vertuously, and dyed with farre more credit, then if they had dyed at home, where their names had never bin recorded for their worth and vertues.

It is the duty of a Commander, to whom a Frontier Garrison is put in trust, timely to fore-see all wants, and defects about the place hee is trusted with, as to repaire the workes, to provide it with victuals, with powder, with Ball, Match and Armes; for it were not good hee had his materials to seeke, when he is resolved to begin his worke.

Likewise his workmen, if they bee not sufficiently furnished before-hand, he will be forced to dismisse them, before his worke be credibly ended: his over-seers must be also good and diligent, otherwise, there may bee too many crevices in their building, and he himselfe must give good example in over-seeing all, and in fore-seeing of all inconveniences, not trusting unto others, to [II-10] discharge those duties; hee is bound to discharge himselfe; and in case of extremity of danger, hee must ever bee the first himselfe to looke unto it, and the last in comming from it; otherwise hee can neither maintaine the place, nor his credit.

Hee must also be very modest, and secret, in not revealing the dangers hee fore-sees, but be amending of them, for feare to discourage others.

Likewise wee see here, that it is alike with a Commander keeping a strength sometimes, as it is with a body, whereof some members are infected with a Canker, that to preserve the body they must resolve to lose a member, as it was with us at this time, being forced to burne a part of the Towne, to preserve the rest and our selves; otherwise, all must have beene lost.

But God favouring us by the winde, that obeyeth when hee commandeth, and the Element of the Fire also, supplying the defect wee had of Water in our Graffe (being but dry on that side) wee were guarded with fire in stead of water, and that bravely.

The Enemy being gone, wee preserved the rest of the Towne in quenshing the fire.

Here also, wee may see the benefit we reape, when Frontier Garrisons are well beset, if the Enemy fall into our Land, as wee are able to affront him in his comming, so in his going, taking alwayes Prisoners of him; and this is the right use of Strengths; that when wee suffer losses in the Fields, wee have time to draw breath againe, our Garrisons being well beset, as was seene in the Peace made betweene the King of *Denmarke* and the Emperour. For if his Majesty of *Denmarke*, had not built *Luckstad* on the *Elve*, hee had hardly recovered *Holsten* againe; even so this Garrison being set here, gave time (by the holding up of the Enemy) to his Majesties forces, that were come from *Statin*, to bee before the enemy at *Colberg*; for if they had fought better, I had observed the more:

---

*The third Dutie discharged of our March to Prymhaussen*
*neere* Stargard, *and from thence to* Statin.

Being recalled from *Shevelben* wee joyned with the Felt-Marshall *Horne*, at *Griffinberg;* taking our march towards *Prymhaussen*, a great Dorpe neere *Stargard;* his Majesty being then at *Colnoe*, drawing his Forces together, hee intended to try the Enemy before Winter, having met with the most part of his Forces at *Prymhaussen*, the word was spred, his Majesty had dealt out winter Quarters, to move the enemie to doe the like, that they drawing to Quarters, his

Majesties Armie being together, they might take advantage of the Enemy being setled in their Quarters.

Wee having stayed with the Felt-Marshall, till the Colonell went for *Scotland*, accompanied with Major *Monro*, Captaine *Francis Sinclaire*, Master *Hugh Mowat*, and Lieutenant *Barrie*; they being gone, his Majesty commanded I should march to *Statin*, and joyne with the Regiment, and to receive Orders from Generall Major *Lesley*, beeing Commandant for the time; where, by the way at *Colnoe*, I did speake with his Majesty, [II-11] who told mee, hee was to preferre Captaine *Bullion*, (being one of my Captaines then) to be Generall quarter Master to Horse; As also shewed to me, that hee had imployed Colonell for new leavies, and therefore he had recalled mee to remaine with the Regiment in his absence, recommending unto me diligence, in keeping good Discipline, and in defending of the Postes, which should bee intrusted to our watching, seeing wee were to watch on *Here Tyvell* his Post: Thus his Majesties admonitions received, I was dismissed, to continue our march to *Statin*, where wee being no sooner arrived, but Generall Major *Lesly* appointed me my Quarters and Poste to watch at.

The next day his Majesty directed Captaine *Dumaine* to mee, with an Order under his Majesties Hand and Seale to place him Captaine over *Bullion's* Company. The Order I reverently received, and appointed the *Cavaliere* the next day in the afternoone to come to mee, seeing the next morning I was to ride to his Majesty, being loath his Majesty should diminish my priviledge, having the freedome by his Majesties capitulation to place the Officers of the Regiment, as they were vacant, and not his Majesty, having once disposed of that priviledge.

Being come to *Colnoe*, I moved Sir *Iohn Hepburne* to accompany me towards his Majesty to assist me; his Majesty asked whether I had placed the Captaine, or not; I answered, that finding it prejudiciall to his Majesties service, I had resolved to acquaint his Majesty first therewith, seeing the Cavaliere, though otherwise sufficient, hee lacked Language, to command the Company being *Dutch*, his Majesty replyed, hee would soone learne so much *Dutch*, as to comand a Company; and thus sayd, his Majesty asked, on whom would I bestow the Company; I answered, to a Cavaliere that deserved well of his Majesty, called *David Monro*, then my Lieutenant: his Majesty turning to Generall *Banniere*, replyed disdainfully, what shall I thinke? Hee would place his own Cozen, and not obey my Orders: whereupon I returned to place Captaine *Dumaine* in obedience to his Majesties will, for that time.

Major *Iohn Monro* gone for *Britaine* with his Colonell, disposed his Company to his Lieutenant *William Stewart*, who was younger Lieutenant, then *David Monro*, yet once comming before him, hee was still elder Captaine, and consequently neerest preferment, under that Regiment, through this change onely.

Likewise, by the death of Major *Synnot* at *Statin*, Captaine *Iohn Sinclaire*, being a worthy Cavaliere, was preferred to bee Sergeant Major, and *Synnots* Company was put by the Lieutenant, and disposed to Captaine *Semple*: In like manner Lieutenant *Pringle* dying at *Statin*, *Henry Lindesey* was advanced to be his brothers Lieutenant.

During this Harvest, 1630. the Pest raged so at *Statin*, that divers brave Souldiers of the Regiment, were buried there; Neverthelesse, a great deale fewer dyed of them, then either of *Dutch*, or *Swedens*, which was seene on our march towards *Brandenburg*, being stronger then other Regiments, that at their landing were twice stronger then wee; for no extremity of Hunger, Pestilence, or Sword could ever make one of them runne away from their Colours.

The Colonell being gone for Leavies, ingaged my brother *Obstell* to bring over a Regiment of Foot for his Majesties service, Major *Iohn Monro* being preferred to bee his Lieutenant-Colonell, and Captaine *Ennis* his Major, [II-12] being gone for *Scotland* after the in-taking of *Brandenburg*.

The Colonell gave another Commission for a Regiment of *English* to Sir *Thomas Conoway*, to whom Captaine *George Stewart* (a brave and a valorous Gentleman) was preferred to bee Lieutenant-Colonell, and Captaine *Mongorge* Major; but the misfortune happened, that in their over-going, both the Colonell and Lieutenant-Colonell were cast away, being drowned on the Coast of *Denmark,* and afterwards, the Regiment having lost three Companies by Sea, the overplus were commanded for a time, by the Major, which afterwards were disposed by his Majesty to Sir *Iohn Cassels* to bee made up againe to a Regiment.

At this time, Colonell *Lumsdell* having brought over also a Regiment of *Scots*, Captaine *Robert Stewart* came over his Lieutenant Colonell, having served at first as Ensigne and Lieutenant to Captaine *Mackenyee* under this Regiment, and there after came againe unto *Spruce*, Captaine under Sir *Iohn Hamiltons* Regiment, in *May* 1629. And was preferred after the In-taking of *Virtzberg*, having beene before at the Battaile of *Lipsigh*: during this time wee lay at *Statin*, his Majesty did take in both *Garts*, and *Griffen-hagan*, and after retyring to *Statin*, did prepare for his march towards new *Brandenburg*.

### The third Observation.

As Vicissitude maintaines the world, so all temporall things here below are subject to Changes and alterations: for the world it selfe was never wholly under one long; and in Commandment changes are most frequent, being caused through the manifold accidents occuring in Warres, as by the frequency of our mortalities, in the profession of Armes; And also by the severall intentions of men, according to their capacities and severall wits, which tend some times to good, sometimes to evill, and oft to nothing, or to worse.

Likewise by example, here wee see inferiours must yeeld to their betters in some things, though without reason, giving way to Princes that are absolute. Yet it is the duty of the inferiour to maintaine his Right, lest he should be thought too simple, in over-passing it; For though perhaps at first wee bee not heard; yet it may happen, that afterwards we be not incroached upon, more in that kinde; For as a Generall commands his Armie; so should a Colonell command his

Regiment, that hee may advance the vertuous according to merit, and good deserving, more then by favour; If hee would be well esteemed of, hee ought to have the understanding to preferre (for reward) the respective and the obedient, and to holde backe onely those, who do not well understand either themselves or others.

Here also we see, that sometimes it is easier speaking with Kings by their inferiours, then to proud Generals, that although they beare the title, lacke the discretion, that should season their Commands. For wee find oft times many of them doe command more through absolute authority, then through either love, respect or reason to their Inferiours: and for my part, I had rather follow with little meanes a Commander, who would respect me in reason for his love, then to follow a proud Generall, for greedinesse of meanes, that taking the snuffe in his nose would affront me without reason; such Generals I did never follow, neither will follow (though I should quit the wars) for my owne contentment. [II-13]

Wee see oft times, that the faults of the Inferiours are laid on the shoulders of their Colonels, which should make Superiours to make the better choice of their Officers, especially in eschewing those, as pestiferous, who are inclined to factions, or given to sow sedition amongst Camerades, such are circumspectly to be avoided by the sound judgement of the *Colonell*, desirous to live in peace, with those who ought to be his friends, that hee may be the more able to offend his Enemies. When both love and feare are in the hearts of the inferiours, then the Command is not burthensome, nor the obedience slavish; for sometimes, as good obeyeth, as hee that commandeth, the Title onely with the authority being laid aside.

Sundry *Cavalieres,* that carried charge under this Regiment in *Denmarke,* wee see in the beginning of this new Warre; for having attained to a little experience under this Regiment, they are now like the Eagles birds, that how soone they can but flee, they take Command on themselves, and that most worthily, knowing, that it is ambition grounded upon vertue, makes the meanest Souldier mount from the lowest centrie, to the top of honour to bee a Generall; as some of our worthy Countrimen have done under the Crowne of *Sweden*, to their eternall glory.

To conclude this Observation as I begun, seeing all things here are but humaine, unstable, and but waves, and tossing, wherein there is nothing sure, but that, which is tyed to the Anchor of true Pietie: for our very life, brings many things with it contrary to our expectation. Therefore, wee ought not to aske when, or where, but we should be ever mindfull how wee are prepared; for they live ill, that thinke they shall live ever. Men will command, and bee commanded so that they may live, but not live so, as they are commanded to live well.

### The fourth Duty discharged of our March to New-Brandenburg, *and of the In-taking of it.*

His Majesty after overcomming his Enemies at *Garts*, and *Griffen-Hagan,* having retired to *Statin,* and made preparation for a happie new-yeares march in the beginning of *Ianuary,* 1631. Wee brake up from *Statin,* taking our march towards the *New-Brandenburg,* the earth clad over with a great storme of Snow, being hard frost, wee carried along great Canons of Batterie, and a number of small Canon, being well provided for all thinges belonging to Artillery; our little Army consisting then of eight Thousand Horse, and Foot, having left the rest of the Army under Command of the Felt-Marshall *Horne,* before *Landsberg* in the Marke: our march the first Night went no further, then beyond the passe at *Lasknets,* where wee quartered over night: breaking up the next morning, wee continue our march for three dayes towards *Brandenburg,* where there lay in Garrison as Commandant, Colonell *Marizane* with Five hundred Horse, and twelve hundred Foot: being as complete to looke on, as you could wish.

His Majesty, being come by Three a clocke in the after-noone, within shot [II-14] of Canon to the Towne, drew us in Battaile, and then divided out the Poasts, where the Briggads should lye; commanded out the Horse watches, to lye without the Foot, other Troupes were also commanded forth for battering the Streets, and the rest of the Horsemen, being directed to Quarters, The Foot battaile ordered, Drums beating, Colours advanced, and flying, every Briggad by divisions marched to their Poastes, where being arrived, their Watches duely set, the rest were setled in their Quarters, being Commanded, both Officers and Souldiers, not to stirre out of Quarters from their Armes, but to attend on Orders.

In our by-going, being within distance of Cannon to the Towne, we were saluted with Cannon, Hagbuts of Crocke, and with Musket; where, within a short time, wee rendered unto them their exchange with the interest; the service continuing so long, as they did (the night bringing silence over all, till day begun to breake againe) and then at our Poast there lay before the Port, a little Tri-Angle, with a Water-graffe about it, and a Draw bridge, wee passing through the Graffe, that was not deepe, stormed the Tri-Angle, and made the Enemy retire within the Towne walles, who fearing a generall storme, did presently cause to beate a Drum, desiring a Parlee, which was granted; pledges delivered *hinc inde,* the Treatie went on, and the Accord was made, and subscribed; they should march on with bagge and baggage, Horse and Foot, with full Armes, which should have a Convoy to *Hagelberg,* and so accordingly they marched out; and then his Majestie to refresh the Armie, caused to make Quarters for the whole Foot within the Towne, where wee lay two nights well entertayned.

His Majesty having a greater enterprise in hand, hee commanded out a Thousand choise Musketiers towards *Trepto,* two miles from *Brandenburg,* and the enemy being acquainted with their comming, hee did retyre to *Dameine,* the Leader of the party leaving two Companies in *Trepto,* marched forwards with the partie to take in a Castle on a passe lying in his way, betwixt *Trepto,* and *Dameine*; whereon were fifty commanded musketiers; who after a little defence made for their credit, did capitulate for quarters, being afraid of the Armies comming, they gave over both Castle and passe. His Majesty (leaving a few number of commanded men in *Brandenburg*, with a Commissary, for ingathering of Contribution, and Proviant for the Armie) he did breake up, and marched towards a little Towne, lying on the passe below *Dameine*, called *Letts*: where in the Castle there lay above sixe hundred men of the *Imperialists*, that might have foughten for good quarters; but being carelesse of their Watch, our commanded Musketiers, having past the Bridge, were suffered to enter within the Castle, before the *Garrison* could get to their Armes, and being thus surprized, they got worse quarters, then if they had fought.

The Soldiers and Officers that first entred, made good booty; and having got gold chaines and money in aboundance, by reason the *Emperialists* had lyen long there, who though they gathered the whole money of the Country, yet they had not the wit to transport it away, being silly simple *Italians*, and without courage, the poorest Officers that ever I looked on, and unworthy the name of Souldiers, for though they knew of our march, they suffered themselves pittifully to be surprized. [II-15]

### The Fourth Observation.

Notwithstanding of the extremitie of cold, we see his Majesties diligence, neglecting no time, making use of Winter, as of Summer, being an expert Generall, who in his judgement was nothing inferiour to the greatest Generall we read of, as doe witnesse his valorous actions. He seeing at our comming to *Brandenburge*, what advantage the ground yeelded to the enemy, to have hindered our comming unto it, As also perceiving what hurt the enemy was able to have done us, before our down-lying (having known their strength, that were within, both of horse and foot) if hee had beene a resolute, and a couragious Commander, as hee was not, hee had tried our fore-troopes, before our comming so neere, which made his Majesty judge they would not hold out long.

Here at this time, a young Cavaliere desirous of honour, and greedy of good instruction, could have learned fro this King the way to command well; as likewise with order to direct all things fitting, how to pursue any place or strength he came before, as his Majestie did there, being the first part, wherein I did observe his Majesties dexteritie in Command, discharging the dueties of severall Officers, being but one man, he never doubted to put in execution what he once commanded, and it was well done; and no alteration was to be found in his Orders; neither did he like well of an Officer, that was not as capable to understand his directions, as he was ready, in giving them: Neverthelesse, hee would not suffer an Officer to part from him, till hee found he was understood, by the receiver of the Order.

Such a Generall would I gladly serve; but such a Generall I shall hardly see: whose custome was; to bee the first and last in danger himselfe, gayning his Officers love, in being the companion both their labours and dangers; for hee knew well how his souldiers should bee taught to behave themselves, according to the circumstances both of time and place, before they were led to fight, and being carefull to their credits, hee would not suffer their weakenesse, or defects to be discerned, being ready to foresee all things, which did belong to the health of his souldiers, and his owne credit. Hee knew also, the devices and Engines of his enemie, their Counsell, their Armies, their art, their discipline: As also the nature and situation of the places they commanded; so that he could not bee neglective in any thing belonging to his charge; and he understood well, that an Army being brickle like glasse, that sometimes a vaine and idle brute was enough to ruine them; and to breake them, like the bricklest glasse that is.

His Majesties further diligence, after the intaking of *Brandenburg* we see, he giving neither time, nor leasure to the neerest Garrisons that were at hand, to resolve, what they had to doe; for one strength was no sooner taken, but incontinent, the commanded Musketiers, and horsemen, were presently closing up the passages of the rest, before they could either retire, or send for supply; And so being long, sleeping in a carelesse securitie, some of them were taken, before they could bee prepared for to fight, or to take about their ports or bridges; so farre were they out of use with hunting, and making good cheere, that they were surprized, *inter pocula*: having regarded their bellies, more then their credits. [II-16]

Where I did see, the saying of the Prophet cleered, that faith, *Men doe annoy themselves, in gathering goods, and cannot tell who shall enjoy them*; For I thinke the *Italians* never minded, that the riches which they gathered in *Pomeren*, should be suddenly transported from the *Sunne* unto the *Northerne* cragges and cliffes of *Sweden*; being led by the *Lyon of the North*, the Invincible King of *Sweden*, of never dying memory.

---

### The fifth Dutie discharged of the Intaking of Dameine *by Accord.*

Generall Major *Kniphowsen*, being come with a supply of horse and foote to our Army at *Letts,* and being joyned with us, his Majestie did give him orders to desire from the Colonells of all Regiments of foote and horse (according to a *Swedens* custome used at such times) the List of their marching men, and of their sicke, the Lists being severally given; our Army did *effective* consist of fifteene thousand men, of foote and horse, able to fight.

The next morning every Regiment of foote, according to custome, was commanded to have a competent number of Cannon baskets ready made, to be transported the next day on Waggons before *Dameine*, which we were to beleaguer; Therefore this preparation was made before hand for the Batteries, the wood being scarce and farre thence.

The fourteenth of *Februarie*, we did breake up, horse and foote, and marched towards *Dameine* from *Letts*, our horsemen were directed to lie without us, on both sides of the Towne alike, so that the Towne could get no supply, without they would first beate our horsemen, and next our foote; His Majestie remaining with the Infantry, as his choice, we incamped on a hill, and about it within Cannon shot of the Towne, being our best Quarters in the extremitie of the cold, without house or shelter to defend us from the winde.

At our first drawing up in battell, a worthy Gentleman called *Robert Rosse*, one of our Regiment, was kill'd with the Cannon, being blowing of *Tobacco* before the Regiment; died instantly, and was transported to *Letts*, where he was honourably buried in the Church, whose last words were worth the noteing, saying, *Lord receive my Soule*.

His Majestie having first disposed of the Horsemen, in giving them their directions, the foote was standing in battell, under the mercy of the Cannon, behinde this hill for two houres, while his Majestie was in viewing and recognoscing both Towne and Castle: which done, the Guards were commanded forth to their severall Posts, to the Artillerie, and to his Majesties baggage, then his Majestie directed Generall Major *Kniphowsen*, and his Forces, with the thousand commanded Musketiers, to take in the passage that went to the Castle, on which service was commanded *Here Tivell* his Lievetenant Colonell, called ~~~~~~~~~~~ who commanded the partie; under whom was, with the commanded men of our Regiment, Lievetenant *George Heatly*, the service beginning hot on both sides, striving for the passe, the Lievtenant Colonell was killed. At which time Lievetenant *Heatly* be- [II-17] ing shot, notwithstanding, behaved himselfe valourously, being the first with his Musketiers that cleered the passe from the enemy, in making them give ground, he possessed the mill on the other side of the passe, till the rest of the commanded Musketiers did follow the enemy to the Castle; where *Kniphowsen* with his Forces did advance, the passe being free.

His Majestie having given Orders where the Batteries should be made, giving Generall *Banier* charge to attend the Armie, as it begunne to grow darke, his Majestie accompanied by Colonell *Tivell*, went to appoint the place where the approaches should beginne, where the Guards should be kept that were to guard the workmen, in case of an out-fall: where presently both the Guards, and the men that should worke, were commanded forth, with sufficient Officers to oversee them. Likewise there were men commanded from every Regiment proportionably, for making the Batteries, and a strong Guard was appointed to guard the Cannon against an out-fall; others were commanded from every Regiment, to make more Cannon Baskets, and the Furiers, with Convoyes, were ordained to returne to *Letts*, for bringing of Proviant to every Regiment.

This all orderly done, he that had meate in his Knapsacke, being free of dutie, could invite his Camerade to supper, and make merry till he were commanded on dutie himselfe, where divers did eate that were not sicke on the morrow.

The enemy perceiving the next morning the Guards by the approaches, saluted them with Cannon and Musket, and were saluted againe, though not so kindly as friends doe one another. The service continued the whole day, his Majestie oft visiting the Castle, being hardest prest, as of most consequence; for the Castle once wonne, the Towne could not hold out.

Vpon the Castle were seaven Companies of Colonell *Holks* Regiment, who fearing to be blowne up by a Mine, entred in treatie, and were content to take service under his Majestie, and to render their Colours, which immediatly was agreed upon, and their Colours brought to be planted and spred on our Batteries, as tokens of his Majesties victory. The Cannon in the meane time from our Batteries, thundring till night on their workes, they begunne to be discouraged, finding the Castle was given over, they were out of hopes to maintaine the Towne longer.

The next morning Captaine *Beaton* of our Regiment, having the guard in the Trenches, the enemy falling out strong, the *Dutch* retired and gave ground, while our folke maintained their Poasts valiantly in sight of his Majesty, who commanded Generall *Bannier* with some Musketiers of *Here Tyvells* Regiment and ours (led on by Major *Potley* an *English* Cavalier of good worth) to second the Guards, and to beate backe the enemy in plaine champagne, Generall *Bannier* advanced, the enemy playing hard with cannon on them, Notwithstanding whereof, entering the skirmish, the enemy was beate backe not without great losse on both sides, where I cannot but commend *Bannier* his carriage, being in sight of his King, as his Majesty did commend our Nation for their good behaviour and charity: for a Captaine of *Banniers* Regiment being left for dead on the field, his countrimen for feare, refusing to bring him off, he was voluntarily brought off by our countrimen, to their great praise, who after disdaining his Camerades and thanking our countrimen, he died of paine and agony before night. [II-18]

After this show made of courage, by the besieged, they being discouraged, desired a Parle, where Major *Greeneland* an *English* Cavalier then serving the Emperour, was sent out to make the accord with his Majesty, pledges delivered by both, the accord agreed on was subscribed; where it was concluded, the Governour should march out with flying Colours, and Armes, and with two peeces of Ordinance, with bag and baggage, and a convoy to the next Emperiall Garrison, providing the Governour should leave behinde him all cannon, being threescore peeces of Brasse, all store of Amunition and victuall, and all spare Armes, and to march forth precisely the next day by twelve of the clocke.

But had the Governour the Duke of *Savellie* bin so valorous, as those he commanded, he might, in respect of the season & situation of the Towne, have kept the City a moneth longer, so that to our Iudgments he was no good Souldier, knowing his Generall was able to relieve him.

The enemy thus march't away, and his Majesty having beset the Garrison, heareing Generall *Tylly* with a strong Army had taken resolution to visit his Majesty in *Maclenburgh*, he stood not long on advisement, but out of hand disposed of his Army couragiously, wisely, and circumspectly, as the event did witnesse his Majesties good command an resolution: *Damaine*, beset with *Swedens*, Generall *Bannier* was ordained to stay there, for to command the Garrison, and to keepe correspondence with his Majesties, and with others in case of *Tyllies* coming: Generall Major *Kniphowsen* was sent with his owne Regiment, and six companies of my Lord of *Rhees* commanded by his

Lievetenant Colonell *Bainshow* to lie at new *Brandenburg*, Major *Sinclair* with two companies was ordained to lie at *Triptowe*, the *Grave Fonottenburg* with his Majesties Regiment of horse, and my squadron of Foote was appointed to lie at *Malchene*, his Majesty himselfe with the rest of the Army were to lie at *Pooswell*, being the passe unto *Pomeren*, and to the Oder, Felt-marshall *Horne* being recall'd with his forces from *Landsberg*, was ordained to lie at *Freedland*: all having their instructions and orders in writ, which they durst not passe one jot; to th'end, that where ever *Tyllies* Army would settle, the rest of our Army from the severall Garrisons, should come together to relieve the party besieged, if his Majesty thought fitting. So leaving *Damaine*, having lost three hundred men before it, our march houlds out, according to our severall orders and instructions.

### The fifth Observation.

All things were atchieved unto here, by the goodnesse of a glorious order, being seconded with skilfull and valorous Officers and Souldiers, obedient even unto death, every one by revolution keeping his certaine time and turne, and that with strictnesse, each being greedy of their owne honour and advancement, under this noble King and Generall who liked of no wicked Souldier, living out of compasse and rule; such as were birds of the Divells hatching, all such were banished from this Army, that was led by Pious and religious *Gustavus* of never dying memory; who could not abide any that would profaine Gods ordinance, or that refused to give obedience to good orders.

Here at *Letts*, before our rising to *Dameine*, I would not but pitty, though an enemy, the *Italian* Governour, that commanded in *Letts*, who suffered [II-19] himselfe, the place, and his followers to be surprised, knowing of the Armies approach: for we see by his example, that goods evill conquest with great paines, are soone lost, going away with wings swifter then the winde; whereof Histories are full of examples, to which purpose I will inferre one story, I have reade of *Hugolene Gerrardesque Depise*, as records, *Paulus Æmilius* in the eighth booke of the *French* story. This *Hugolene* being a Commander for the *Pope* over the *Guelfes*, having chased a part of the *Gibelins* that were with the Emperour, terrifying the rest, he became so greatly renowned amongst his owne folke, that he commanded what he pleased, and was made Lord and Governour of a City (as this *Italian* was here) being accounted noble, rich, magnificent, and learned, he was married, having good issue, he abounded in all riches, more then he could desire or wish, being counted happy, and at his ease according to his owne minde, and the opinion of his friends; he made a feast on his birth day, and having assembled his friends; being merry he fell into commendation of his owne worth and honour, extolling himselfe above the Clouds so farre, that he begun to aske of one of his neerest friends, if he thought he lacked any thing to make him happy: the other considering the uncertainty of worldly affaires, and the deceitfull vanities thereof that perish in a moment, when the Lord pleaseth but to breath, said; certainely the wrath of God cannot be farre from this thy great prosperity. Incontinent the Forces of the *Gibelins* begining to stirre, unexpected come about the lodging, breake in through the Ports kill his children, and take himselfe, who begging life being refused,was miserably murthered, and all his goods taken by the enemy in *Italy,* in the yeare 1288. to teach all mortall men not to glory too much in uncertaine riches, that come but slowly and goe way swiftly.

Those men that are meanely risen, may justly be checked here, that when they have attained unto wealth, riches and honour, presently they will begin to counterfeit the Nobility, pressing to tread in their foote-steps, though not belonging unto them: for wealth attained unto, it may be by unlawfull meanes, should not make the owners too proud of it, lest suddenly it may be lost, as chanced to *Hugolene.* Neverthelesse some fantastick Officers, that cannot governe themselves nor their wealth, they will hunt and hawke, with traines on Princes bounds (as I have knowne some doe being abroad) thinking themselves equall to Princes, whereof they were farre short, and they will have their silver plate, their gold, their silver, their Iewells, their Coaches, their horses, their traines, and Officers of houshold counterfeiting greatnesse and great men, having, it may be, but little worth besides, suffering themselves in their Pompe to be surprized, their goods taken from them, and then to be cast in a close dungeon or prison, till they die for want, the reward of their pride; whereas it had beene better, they had lived with greater sobriety and modesty, and then if misfortune should happen unto them, they would be the more respected, and consequently the sooner set at liberty.

I have read of Cavaliers that served long and truely with credit, whose mindes were not set on outward things perishable; but rather their hunting was after a good name, renowne and credit to leave behinde them, when all other things might be stripped from them; which in my opinion were more to be commended then those that would counterfeit worth being without it. But on the contrary, I have knowne some Cavaliers, that hunted af- [II-20] ter credit, did gaine much renowne, and were riche in credit, though poore otherwise, leaving no more houshold stuffe behinde them, but a spit and a pot, being so given to sobriety in their life times, that sometimes they were contented with a morsell of dry bread from a Souldier. Not that I would have any Cavalier, that hath merited well, to be carelesse to maintaine himselfe in credit, according to his charge, if by lawfull meanes he can doe it, and if plenty increaseth, I would wish him timely to dispose of it, for his neerest friends or succession in a part, and the overplus I would wish him to bestow for the weale of the publique, and the adorning of his country, that after his death, the monuments of his vertue, and the Trophees of his victories might live, and speake to succeeding ages, that such a one hunted well in attaining unto honour, and perpetuall renowne and credit.

Here also by the example of a worthy Master and Leader, being the Phoenix of his time, for a Generall, that he who hath seene his variable essaies, and learned to lay up the same in store, if he follow but his Masters precepts, and observe his orders, he cannot but in time merit the title of a judicious Commander; and doubtlesse one day having past his prentiship well under such a

Master, he cannot but merit honour and reward, and then may be made choise of for the service of his King and country, before those who had not such experience under such a Leader. In remembrance of whom, I will inferre an accident happened his Majesty of famous memory, the time of his beleaguering.

His Majesty walking alone on a marrish that was frozen, of intention with a prospective glasse, to spie into the enemies workes, the Ice breaking his Majesty falls up to the middle in water, being neere my Guarde, where captaine *Dumaine* did command, who seeing his Majesty fall in, went towards him, of intention to helpe him out, which his Majesty perceiving, lest the enemy might take notice of them both, his Majesty wagged his hand that the Captaine might retire, which the enemy perceiving, shot above a thousand shot of Musket at his Majesty, who at last wrought himselfe loose, coming off without hurt, and sat a while by our guarde-fire.

The Captaine being a boldspoken gentleman, well bred, and of good language, began very familiarly to finde fault with his Majesty, for his forwardnesse in hazarding his Majesties person in such unnecessary dangers; on whom, at that time, the eyes of all *Europe* were fixed, expecting their freedome and reliefes (from the tyranny of their enemies) to come from his Majesty, and in case any misfortune or sinister accident (as God forbid) should happen unto his Majesty, what then would become of his Majesties confederates, and which was worst, what would become of many brave Cavaliers of fortune, who had no further hopes then to live, and to be maintained under his Majesty their Leader?

His Majesty having heard the Captaine, patiently thanked him for good counsell, and he could not but confesse his owne fault, which he could not well helpe, seeing his minde was so, that he thought nothing well done which he did not himselfe, and so went to dinner, where before he changed his wet clothes, in a could Tent, he called for meate, and dined grossely, and taking a great draught of wine went and changed his clothes, and immediatly coming forth againe, while as the enemy had fallen out, as was said before in the discharge. [II-21]

The time of this out-fall, our Souldiers being commanded under Major *Potley* to beate backe the enemy, going on service, there happened a merry Accident to one of our Country-men (then Ensigne to my Colonells Company) called *Iames Lyle*, being in sight of his Majestie, going downe a steepe hill, the enemy playing hard with cannon, the Ensigne happened to fall forwards, the winde blowing off his Periwigge, which tumbled downe the hill, the Major sware a great oath, the poore *Cavaliers* head was shot from him and seeing him rise againe without his halfe head, sware the Cannon had shot away the skinne, with the haire of his head being bald.

His Majestie at this time also seeing a *Dutch* Captaines cloake about him going on service, commanded to recall him, and to command out another, which was a disgrace to the Captaine, whom his Majestie openly reproved, saying, If he had intention to have fought well, he would have felt no cold, and consequently the carrying of his Cloake was needlesse.

In this meane time his Majestie looking on, from the enemies Battery a Cannon Bullet came so neare his Majestie, though he was really stout, he was made to stoope, and behinde his Majestie, the thigh was shot from a *Swedens* Captaine, belonging to the Artillery, who died the same night.

Here I cannot let passe an oversight unworthily committed by Generall Major *Kniphowsen*, while as the enemy was marching out, the Guard of the Posts being committed to the *Swedens*, having got command from his Majestie to let no Officer nor Souldier come within the Towne, till the enemy was marched out, *Kniphowsen* pressing in was put backe by the Captaine that commanded: Whereupon *Kniphowsen* not knowing what direction the Captaine had, or from whom, he lifting a Battoun, brake it on the Captaines head, which was evill thought of by his Majestie and the whole Officers of the Armie. Neverthelesse, we never heard of the Reparation: so that I would never wish my noble friend to lie under an affront, though done by any forraigne King, for if I could not be revenged, I would serve against him to be revenged, if not of him, yet at lest of his, for which I crave pardon, having spoken rather like a Souldier than a Divine, for nothing should divert my heart sooner from my Superiour, than disdaine or contempt.

---

### *The sixth Dutie discharged of the Intaking of* Brandenburg, *and of Maior* Iohn Sinclaire *his escape out of* Trepto.

Generall Major *Kniphowsen* with his Regiment and six Companies of my Lord of *Rhees* Regiment, commanded then by Lievetenant Colonell *Lindesey,* were appointed to lie in new *Brandenburg:* when as the enemy lay downe before *Brandenburg,* I was recalled from *Malchene* with my squadron to joyne with Feltmarshall *Horne* at *Freedland,* being commanded to leave a Captaine with a hundred Musketiers behinde me of commanded men to beset *Malchene:* at this time also Major *Sinclaire* with his own Company, and Captaine *Semples,* were commanded to beset *Trepto,* which lay but two miles from *Brandenburg;* his Majestie with the rest of the Ar- [II-22] my, being at *Posewall, Tilly* with his Army being ingaged in the beleaguering of *Brandenburg,* consisting then of twenty-two thousand foote and horse, having twenty-six pieces of Ordnance, with all furniture answerable, he beleaguered *Brandenburg,* thinking his Majestie being so neare, might be moved to ingage his Army with disadvantage to relieve it: But his Majestie being more wise, and having had a greater designe in his head, he suffered *Tilly* to try his Forturne against a place of no such importance, as to ingage a King and a Crowne, a Countrey and an Army, in relieving of it; and his Majestie relying much on the wisedome, discretion, and valour of Generall Major *Kniphowsen,* as that of himselfe he was sufficiently able to make an honourable Accord, when better could not be. And in the meane time, to divert the enemy from him, his Majestie did make a Carracole with the halfe of his Army towards *Swede* on the River of the *Oder,* where he built a ship-bridge over the River and caused to fortifie it with Skonces, that in his option he might come and goe on both sides of the River, till Feltmarshall *Horne* might joyne with him.

Generall *Tilly* hearing the King was marched, and fearing some great designe, he pressed *Brandenburg* so much the harder, with continuall shooting of Cannon till a Breach was made, and then out of time *Kniphowsen* did send his Lievetenant Colonell with a Drummer to the breach, to desire a Parle, but being neglected by the enemy, as too late. The Parle refused, Lievetenant Colonell was killed, the enemy having given Orders for a generall storme, which going on, Lievetenant Colonell *Lindesey* and Captaine *Moncreiffe* were both killed, and Lievetenant *Keith* and Ensigne *Haddon*, were also cut downe in the fury, with many a brave Souldier besides, who being denied Quarters, fought valiantly to the last man.

The other *Scots* Officers of the Regiment, being within the Towne, as Captaine *Ennis*, Captaine *Gunne*, Captaine *Beaton*, and Captaine *Lermond*, with their Officers and Souldiers, were for the most part, taken prisoners, with Lievetenant *Lyell*, and some other inferiour Officers, Captaine *Ennis* being on another Poast without the Port, which was not stormed at all, the enemy having entred on the other side of the Towne, where in the fury they did put the most part to the sword, and coming through the Towne Port, upon *Ennis* his Poast behinde him, he and Lievetenant *Lumsdell* did leape into the Graffe, and saved themselves through a marrish from the fury of their enemies, and came to us to *Freedland*. *Brandenburg* thus taken in, a partie was sent towards *Trepto*, where *Sinclaire* did command, getting orders to take it in also. But *Sinclaire* did behave himselfe valiantly in falling out upon the enemy, who retired againe without great hurt, and maintained the Towne for two nights, till he had received Orders from the Feltmarshall to quit it in the night. And after that he did joyne with us at *Freedland*.

The Feltmarshall knowing that *Brandenburg* being taken, the enemies Forces would march upon him, and he having Orders and instructions in writing from his Majestie, he retired with his Army over the passe towards *Ancklam*, the enemy advanced to *Freedland*, finding us to be gone, they retired in haste backe to *Brandenburg*, and from thence they march backe againe to *Rapine*, suspecting his Majestie had marched before them towards *Magdeburg*: *Tillies* Army being marched, we retired to *Freedland*, from whence Ensigne *Greame*, with some Dragoniers, was sent to *Brandenburg* to take Order for the hurt and sicke, whom Generall *Tilly* had left behinde him, which were plon- [II-23] dered, and some others killed by the Ensigne and his Souldiers, who had also runne the same hazard by the enemy his Crabatts, had they not retired in time; after whose returne, my Musketiers being come from *Malchene*, we were readie to march.

## The sixth Observation.

The crueltie and inhumanitie used here by *Tillies* Armie, giving so ill quarters to our Nation, to Burgers, and to those that served at the Altar, was not long unpunished, at such places, as they least expected.

And Generall Major *Kniphowsen* was not voide of blame, for refusing a Treatie in due time, seeing he had no certaintie of reliefe, and being left to capitulate with the enemy, at his owne discretion (by his instructions he had from his Majestie) he ought to have embraced the opportunitie of time (which once past is not to be recovered) in capitulating with the enemy for honourable Quarters, rather than to have brought himselfe and others to the slaughter, for he who delayes to embrace time when it is offered, must not presse to recover it, and oft-times good occasions in warfare are lost when Commanders are ignorant of their enemies doings. Therefore while time is, we ought to be diligent and carefull; for it is better to be in safety through preventing, than basely to suffer under our enemies, occasion being past, which oft-times in warres helpes more than vertue it selfe: for if *Kniphowsen* had embraced *Tillies* offer when he might, our worthy Camerades had not suffered as they did, which sufferance after that made Cavaliers being freed out of prison, to seeke Conditions else-where for their advancements such as Captaine *Ennis*, being first made Major to Colonell *Monro* of *Obstell*, was afterward Lievetenant Colonell to the Master of *Forbesse*, after the death of that worthy Cavalier Sir *Arthur Forbesse*. Likewise Captaine *William Gunne*, being come out of prison, was after advanced by Sir *Patrick Ruthven*, Generall Major and Governour of *Olme*, to be his Lievetenant Colonell over the *Dutch* in *Schwabeland*.

Captaine *Beaton* was made Major, and afterward Lievetenant Colonell to young Colonell *Skeutte*.

Captaine *Lermond* also was advanced to be Captaine of Dragoniers, and *Iames Lyel*, having served long under Sir *Iohn Ruthven* his Regiment, the Regiment reduced, and the Captaine leavying againe for the *French* service was pittifully murthered by knaves in *Westphalia*.

*Henry Lindesey* advanced to be Captaine of his Majesties Leeffe Regiment under Grave *Neles*, after for reward of his vertue and valour, was preferred to be Lievetenant Colonell to Colonell *Alexander Lesly* the younger: Captaine *Brumfield* was made Major to Colonell *Gunne*, and after that Regiment was reduced, being under Sir *Iohn Ruthven*, was pittifully hurt in Combate, and then resolutely died of his wounds at *Bucksteehood*, being much lamented by all that knew him, for as valourous and expert an Officer, as any of his qualitie was under our Armie: so that we see here, that though the Regiment suffered great losse at *Brandenburg*, neverthelesse the valiant Officers were advanced according to their former good carriage.

Likewise I cannot with silence here passe by the valourous carriage of Major *Iohn Sinclaire* at *Trepto*, in making a faire shew of a bad game, while as the [II-24] enemy came before *Trepto* with a partie of a thousand Musketiers, he not having a hundred Musketiers within the Towne in all, neverthelesse fell out with fiftie amongst a thousand, and skirmished bravely and orderly with the enemy, and retired againe with credit, making the enemy thinke that he was a great deale stronger within walles. I confesse as it was well ventured, so the Cavalier was beholden to Fortune, in coming so safely backe. But I will not advise my friend to make use of the like; for if the enemy had haply got a prisoner of his, who could have shewed his true strength, that might have caused the losse of all. But the Cavalier, did hazard faire to gaine credit: for as he was valourous in Conduct, and amongst others, even so being singled out, he feared no man, as you shall see in the subsequent observations before we end our march.

Here also I did observe the difference betwixt the King our Master and old *Tilly*; where I did see his Majesty, though younger, out-shoote the elder in experience, who by winning of a Dorpe (which was afterwards slighted) with the losse of two thousand men, over and above the toyle sustained by his Army, and the losse of some cannon, he lost *Francford* on the *Oder*, where three thousand were put to the sword, in requitall of his cruelty used at *Brandenburg*.

---

### The seventh Dutie discharged of our march to Swede, and our reformation there, being made into Briggades.

*Tillies* Army being marched backe to *Rapine*, the Felt-marshall with his Army did breake up from *Freedland* with Horse, Foote, and Artillery towards *Swede* to joyne with his Majesty, continuing our march for three dayes to the passe at *Lecknetts*, where we rested two dayes, sundry Officers having taken Forloffes of his Excellence to goe unto *Statine*, to provide themselves of cloaths and necessaries, expecting for a long march, where I went also to see my wife and Family; and having stayed but one night, our march continued so farre in prosecuting our victories, that the enemy coming betwixt me and home. I was not suffered in three yeares time to returne, so long as his Majesty lived, which was much to my prejudice.

Being arrived at *Swede* on the *Oder*, and joyned with his Majesties Army, after our coming being drawne out to the fields, we were made into *Briggades* both horse and foote, where Sr. *Iohn Hepburne* being made Colonell of the *Briggad*, his Regiment, Colonell *Lumsdells*, *Stargates* and ours, made up the *Briggad*, where *Lumsdell* & I had the Battaile, Colonell *Hepburne* his Regiment made up the right wing, and Colonell *Stargates* the left, which on our march was changed by turnes, and thereafter was still called the *Scots Briggad* commanded by *Hepburne*. Sundry other *Briggads* were made up, as the yellow or leeffe *Briggad*, commanded by the Baron *Tyvell*, the blew *Briggad*, commanded by Colonell *Winckle*, and the white *Briggad* [II-25] called *Dametts*, where having lien some few dayes, we were preparing for our march towards *Francford* on the *Oder*.

### The seventh Observation.

Generall *Tilly* was no sooner marched with his Army, but incontinent, the Felt-marshall did follow his example, to joyne with his Majesty. Where we may see, that these two wise Generalls did soare in the skies with their Armies, casting boards like warre ships, to get advantage one of another.

We see here that Cavaliers, though tied by Gods ordinance to live with their wives, being once severed and tied to serve, they cannot with credit quit their charge to come to their wives. The King himselfe being once engaged in the *Dutch* warres, was deprived for two years, from the sweete society of his Queene, which should teach women, and men of meaner quality, after their examples, to be patient in absence; for more love was never betwixt two, then was betwixt his Majesty and his Queene, no love could goe beyond their love each to others, except the love of Christ, God and man, towards man. For the love of this Queene, to her husband the King, did equall the love of the wife of *Hieron*, whom we read of in *Plutarch* his *Apophthegmes* for her rare continence and respect carried to her husband, shee never felt the breath of anothers kisse, but her husbands. Which in my opinon, this Queene of *Sweden* could well for her love to her husband have done, if it were possible, as is reported by *Plinius* of *Arria*, wife to *Cecinna Pætus*, who being condemned to die, with liberty to choose the forme of his death, his wife going to visit him, did exhort him to die valiantly with great courage, and taking good night of her husband, she strucke herselfe with a knife in the body, and drawing out the knife againe presented it to *Pætus* her husband, with these words, *Vulnus quod feci Pæte, non dolet, sed quod in facies*: as one would say, the wound I gave my selfe hurts me not, but the wound which you shall give grieves me.  We read also of *Portia, Cato* his daughter, and wife to *Brutus*, who hearing of her husbands death, in despight of all that were about her, filled her mouth with hot burning coales, and was suffocated for griefe.  We reade also a memorable story of the wives of the *Menyans*, recorded by *Plutarch* in his fourth booke of Illustrious women, their husbands being in prison and condemned to death, for having enterprized against the King of *Sparta* the *Laecedemonian* custome being to execute their malefactors in the night, these noble women, under pretence to speake with their husbands, being appointed to die, got license of the Guards to goe within the prison, and having put themselves in place of their husbands, whom they made to put on their Gownes, taught them to cover their faces with vailes, as being extreamely sorry, carrying their heads downward, they escaped out of their hands.

Having inferred this discourse on a Queene, yet wife to the best Souldier in our dayes, lest Souldiers wives should be worse thought of than others, having seene more love, more indulgence, better obedience, and by appearance more chastity in them to their husbands, than ever I did see in any other profession, I will here yet inferre a rare example of a Souldiers wife, to encourage others to follow and imitate her vertues. The story [II-26] we reade written by *Barnard Scardeon* in his third booke of *Padua*, that *Blanch Rubea* of *Padua*, being retired with her *Baptist de la Porte*, within the fortresse of *Bassean*, pertaining to the *Venetians*: *Acciolen* banished out of *Padua* with all his forces, assailed the said place, being valorously defended, it was impossible to get it, but by Treason; *Baptist* not losing courage, though surprised, running unto the Port with his Armes in his hand, but suppressed by the multitude of his enemies having gotten entry, he was killed by the hand of *Acciolen*; his wife *Blanch* did fight valiantly in the conflict, being armed with steele and with courage, farre beyond her sex. The enemy being victorious, she was taken perforce, and brought before the Tyrant, who being ravished with her beauty, at first making much of her, then desireth to ravish and bereave her of her honour, shee defending her selfe by words and prayers of entreaty escaped his hands, and finding the window open skips downe, where she was found sore hurt, and halfe dead, but by the diligence of good Chirurgians, she was made whole as before, and was solicited by the Tyrant againe, which she refusing to yeeld unto, being bound was forced by the Tyrant, shee keeping her griefe within herselfe, gets liberty to goe see the dead body of her husband *Baptist*; and pretending to doe some ceremonies about his Corps, and having opened the Grave, she crying, streached herself in the Grave, and violently with her hands pulls the stone that covered the grave over her, and her head being bruised, she died presently above her husband: in the yeare 1253.

The Ancient *Germans* did marry their wives on the condition they should be their companions in travells and dangers; and as *Cornelius Tacitus* reports, one husband married but one wife, being but one body and one life. And *Theogene* the wise of *Agathocles* said, she was companion of his troubles and adversity, as she was of his prosperity: and being in love my selfe with the verture of such women, rare to be found, I will yet enrich this observation with a notable example that happened in the yeare 1466. betwixt *Bonne, Lumbard* or *Greeson*, and *Peter Brunore* of *Parme*, as the *Italian* story records, which I here represent in favour of vertuous women, to incourage that sex more and more to the like vertue, being so pleasant where ever it is found to be seene. *Bonne* borne in the *Wealkie* of *Talhine*, in the country of *Greeson*, in which place *Peter Brunore Parmesan* one day walking alone, a brave Cavalier, and a Knight well experimented in warres, leading his Army, in passing by he sees this young Damsell feeding her sheepe in the fields, being little of stature, of browne colour, not pleasant, or faire to see to, but very merry, playing then with her fellowes; wherein she shewed a certaine quicknesse of spirit that the Knight *Brunore* looking on her attentively, observing all her gestures, and hoping of some great good of her, caused to take her, and leade her away with him against her will; that in time being accustomed with him, he made her divers times change clothes, and clad her at last like a boy, by way of pleasure and recreation of spirit, leading her oft a hunting, and using her to ride, and spurre horses, and other exercises, wherein shee shewed her quicknesse and dexterity; and though the Cavalier did keepe her but for pleasure, recreation, and pastime; neverthelesse, she did set her selfe to serve him with a love and diligence incredible, in such sort, that willingly she could endure all manner of labour, trouble or toyle of body or of minde, that *Brunore* could not under- [II-27] goe, and went ever with him, as with her Master, in all his journies, assisting him in all dangers, following him on foote, and on horsebacke, through dales and mountains, by water and by land, with an intire and faithfull obedience, without over-leaving of him, or without grudging in any sort: she went also with him towards *Alphonse* King of *Naples*, for at that time this Cavalier and Knight *Peter*

*Brunore*, did serve under *Francis Sforce* which party he after quit; but having afterwards changed his minde, he resolved to quit *Alphonse* King of *Naples*, and to retire to serve his former Master, the Count of *Sforce*, and while as he was making preparation for his flight, the businesse not being so privily carried, but that the King perceiving it, secretly caused to apprehend *Brunore*, and cast him into prison, where he was kept long without hope of reliefe; Wherefore *Bonne* being restlesse, till she should see the day when the Knight *Brunore* were at liberty, she went to all the Princes and Potentates of *Italy,* and to the King of *France*, to *Philip* Duke of *Burgoigne*, to the *Venetians*, and to many more, of whom she attained letters in favour of her deare and wellbeloved master, so that *Alphonse* wonne by such requests and the intreaty of so great men, was as it were constrained to set *Brunore* at liberty, and gave him unto that valorous warrier that did for him; who having gotten him loose, to doe yet greater service to her Master, did obtaine so much by her meanes at the *Venetians* hands, that they accepted of *Brunore* unto their service, and was made Leader to the Army of so great a Republique, and there was a great pension ordained for his entertainment; by which deeds of friendship, the Knight did know the faith, the vertue, and the valour of his *Bonne*: he esteemed it not honest to keepe her longer as a servant, as he had done till then, but married her, keeping her as his lawfull wife, making still great esteeme and account of her, following her counsell in all his affaires of weight, and importance, during which time, he attained unto great reputation under the *Venetians*, his enterprizes still coming fortunatly and happily to passe. This valiant Dame of his was still seene in Armes, when occasion was offered to fight, and when it was needefull to leade the Infantry, going before, she appeared like a Magnanimous Leader and warriour, being very capable in warlike matters, whereof she gave divers times good proofe, especially with the *Venetians* against *Francis Sforce* at that time Duke of *Millaine*, where she made her selfe knowne, while as the Castle of *Panon* besides *Bresse* was lost, her courage did appeare so great, that every one did wonder at it, for being armed from head to foote, shewing her selfe more couragiously then any other at the storme, the Targe on her arme, and the Cutlesse in her hand, she was the meanes the place was recovered. At last the *Venetians* having great confidence in *Brunore*, and in the counsell and valour of *Bonne* his Lady, he was sent for the defence, and keeping of *Negrepont* against the *Turkes*, where by the Fortifications, they two made while they remained there, the *Turkes* had never the courage to hurt or impeach them, in end, *Brunore* dying, and buried with great respect and honour, *Bonne* his Lady returning towards the *Venetians*, for to get her husbands pension confirmed to two of her sonnes, and falling sicke, caused to make a Tombe of great charges, which she desired to be perfected before her death, and being dead, she was buried there, in the yeare 1468. Therefore it was well said, that there were three things seemed pleasant in Gods sight, the love betwixt brethren, the friendship betwixt neighbours, and man and wife continuing in uni- [II-28] on and mutuall loyalty. Who likes to reade a pleasant story to this purpose, let him read *Nauclerus* treaty of the Emperour *Conrade* the third, in his warres against *Guelly* Duke of *Baviere*, who was forced for his safety, to retire within

*Rhinesberg*, where the Towne being taken by accord, by the perswasion of Ladies, he would grant no other condition, but that the women should transport themselves out of the Towne in safety, with so much as they could carry, and no more, where one taking the Duke on her backe, the rest of the wives their husbands, the accord thus kept, and the Emperour *Conrade* moved to compassion, beholding their love and vertue, pardoned the Duke, and restored the Towne to their former liberties. And *Bodin* in the preface of his history reports that *Laurence de Medices* was healed of a grievous disease, by reading of this story without any other helpe; I wish it may worke the same effect upon all those that reade it, especially the Female sex, in making them follow the vertuous examples of these noble Ladies, in loving their husbands beyond all other things whatsoever, and those that will not be moved thereto, I wish them the death of that *Roman* Lady, reported of by *Quintus Curtius* and *Titus Livius*; called *Publia Cornelia Annea*, who lived twenty yeares without once offending of her husband, and seeing him die, contracted such griefe for his death, that she threw herselfe into the grave with her husband, where she died, and lay with him. This wish I hope cannot be taken in ill part by the vertuous Ladies; that are like *Cornelia*, but I feare there is none such at all. To conclude then this point of my observation; in my judgment no women are more faithfull, more chast, more loving, more obedient nor more devout, then Souldiers wives, as daily experience doth witnesse, and none have more reason to be so, then some of them, whose husbands doe daily undergoe all dangers of body for their sakes, not fearing death it selfe, to relieve and keepe them from dangers. To th'end you may see, that the noble parts and vertues before mentioned, are not proper alone unto the Feminine sex, I will here inferre some notable examples of the good will, love and faithfullnesse of husbands to their wives, especially Souldiers, whereof amongst many, for the present, I will, to content the Reader, mention two or three, that are notable, whereof one happened at this time in our warfare, worthy to be recorded, of that noble, valorous, pious and worthy Cavalier, the Felt-marshall *Gustave Horne*; the Peste having entred his lodging, and taken away two of his Children, seazed on his vertuous Lady, daughter to the Chancellor of *Sweden*; the Cavaliers love was so great, that in the extremity of her sicknesse, he never suffered her to be out of his armes till she died, and then caused her to be put in a Silver Coffin, that she might be transported for her country, to be buried amongst her friends; and his love was so great unto her that after her death, though a young man, he could never be moved to leade his life with any other woman. Another example we reade in the story written by *Plinie & Valerius Maximus*, that is very notable to this purpose. *Sempronicus Gracchus*, finding two serpents coming out of his bed, enquired of *Theologues* what might that accident presage? they answered, that if he killed the she serpent, his wife should die, and if he killed the he serpent, he should die himselfe; he loved his wife *Cornelia* so dearely that he commanded to kill the he serpent, and shortly after he himselfe died.  Also that which we reade of *Meleager* sonne to *Danneus* is notable, who would not rise out of his chaire, for the reliefe of the [II-29] Towne he was in, for his father, mother, brethren, or sisters, all crying and calling for his helpe, who nothing cared for their ruine: but how soone *Cleopatra* his wife came to him, desiring his helpe, and telling him, the enemy was alreadie entred the Towne, and was setting the houses on fire; this stony-hearted man, who before could be moved by nothing, at the desire of his wife, went to Armes against the enemy, and repulsing them backe, saved the Towne from wracke and ruine, and the Citizens from death: for this *Meleager* (as all honest men ought to doe) esteemed his wife and himselfe but one; so that he could deny her nothing.   Here it may be, some will alleage, he was *Iohn Thomsons* man.  I answer, it was all one, if shee was good: for all stories esteeme them happie, that can live together man and wife without contention, strife, or jarres, and so doe I.  And, in my opinion, no wife can be ill, that wants the gall; for the gall in the body is the feare of choler, from which the love of man and wife should be free, and as of gall, so of despite, of anger and of bitternesse.

---

### The eight Dutie discharged of our March to Francford
### on the Oder, *and the intaking of it, the third of* Aprill 1631.

The twenty-fourth of *March* 1631. his Majestie having disposed of his Armie, in putting them in good Order in Briggaddes, horse and foote, through the severall occasions and accidents happening in warre, his Majestie before his march, finding the enemy lay strong in the Silesian and at *Lansberg*, lest he might fall downe unto *Pomeren* and *Marke*, to disturbe the new forces that were expected to come from *Spruce*, and from *Scotland*, his Majestie directed Feltmarshall *Horne*, with a part of his Horse that crost the bridge at *Swede* unto *Pomeren*, and the *Wart*, to collect the forces there, for to be fured and led towards the *Wart* and *Lansberg*, to give the enemy somewhat to thinke on, while as his Majestie might march with the rest of the Armie (consisting then of ten thousand foote and horse) towards *Francford*, where under the command of the Feltmarshall *Tuffenback*, and the Grave *Fon-Schonberg* Governour of *Francford* on the *Oder*, there were drawne together of the *Emperialists* neere nine thousand foote and horse. General *Tilly*, with this maine Armie then lying at *Rapin*, after his returne, from *Brandenburg* with two and twentie thousand foote and horse, his Majestie then not being sure, neither of his brother in law the Duke of *Brandenburg*, nor yet of the Duke of *Saxon*, though the League was ended with the King of *France*, his Majesties affaires thus standing doubtfull, we marched towards *Francford*, with a resolution to prie into the enemies designes, more than any wayes resolved for a beleaguering, having such strong enemies and Armies about us, without assurance of our pretended friends and confederates: yet having continued our march till within a mile of *Francford*, our enemies retiring out of all quarters were come into one body at *Francford*, who having joyned, we did heare the enemy was almost as strong within, as we were without, and he having of us the advantage of the Towne behinde him for his retreate, we expected no other thing, than that [II-30] the enemy should come out, and offer us

Battell. Wherefore his Majestie himselfe discharging the dutie of a Generall Major (as became him well) having sought the ayd and assistance of Sir *Iohn Hepburne*, beginneth to put the Armie, horse, foote, and Artillery in order of Battell, the commanded Musketiers, as his forlorne hope, advanced before the Army, having placed plottons of them by fifties, to march with his squadrons of horse, all being in even front, the signe given for advancing, Trumpets sounding, Drummes beating, Colours displayed, advanced and flying, every Commander directed and appointed on his Command and Station; the magnifick and royall King leads on; this Royall Army marching in battell order for halfe a mile, as comely as one body could doe, with one pace, and one measure, advancing, stopping, moving, and standing alike, till at last coming neere the Towne, and finding no Hostile Ranconter made by the enemy, we hault standing a while in Battell, and then resolved, being the enemy durst not meet as in the fields, we would presse on the sudden to be Masters of *Francford*, or not at all; knowing of the neerenesse of our enemies, and of the great strength they had together: and seeing we were not sure of the Princes, we resolved the taking of time was the best for us; and incontinent, his Majestie commanded out the most part of his *Cavalerie*, to make a Carracolle behinde us, betwixt us and *Berleine*, fearing Generall *Tillie* with his Armie might come behinde us, whiles we were ingaged with the Towne, keeping onely of all the *Cavalerie* the Rhinegrave and his Regiment, besides the *Infanterie*, in case of our falling, to second us against the horsemen, that were within the Towne.

The *Cavalerie* thus directed, his Majestie then perceiving the feare of his enemies, having voluntarily fiered their fore-Towne (tooke their feare as a presage of his future victory) commanded a part of the commanded Musketiers to goe in, through the fore-Towne being on fire, and to lodge themselves, being advanced to the very port, till such time as his Majestie should dispose of the rest of the Armie, in directing every Briggade apart to their severall poasts. The yellow and the blew Briggade were directed to lodge in the Vineyards on the side of the Towne next *Castrene*, being commanded to advance their guards before them, while as the rest of the Briggade should lodge and lie in one body at their Armes, to be still in readinesse in case of an out-fall; the white Briggade, called *Damits* Briggade, was appointed to lodge in the fore-Towne, to guard the commanded Musketiers that lay betwixt them and the danger, at the Port right under the walles. *Hepburne* his Briggade was commanded to lie neare unto the other Port, and to advance their guards also; the rest of the commanded men to lie neare vnto the other Port, and to advance their Guards also; the rest of the commanded Musketiers being commanded by Major *Iohn Sinclaire*, were commanded to lye on a hight neere a Church-yard, that was direct before the enemies workes, besides which, there was a Battery made, and the Artillery and Amunition of the Armie (as commonly as usuall) was placed behinde our Briggade, and the *Rhinegraves* horsemen behinde us; all things thus ordered and placed, commanded folkes out of all Briggads were commanded out proportionally for making of Cannon Baskets, and for casting of Trenches.

Then, according to custome, his Majestie himselfe and Colonell *Tyvell* went to Recognosce neare the wall, where Colonell *Tyvell* was shot in the left arme, his Majestie then making openly great moane for him, alleaging he [II-31] had no helpe then, but of *Hepburne*; in the same instant my Lievetenant *David Munro* was shot in the legge with a Musket Bullet, and my Major *Iohn Sinclaire*, commanding the commanded Musketiers neere to his Majestie, where the Battery was making, the enemy hanging out a Goose in derision, they presently fell out above two hundred of them upon our Guard, who received them with volees of Musket, and they being too strong for the guard, his Majestie commanded the Major to send an Officer and fiftie Musketiers more to second the Guard. Neverthelesse, the enemy still pushing our guard backwards, making them give ground, incontinent his Majestie commanded the Major with a hundred Musketiers more to fall on, and to resist the enemy in relieving the Guard, which the Major suddenly obeyed, making the enemy retire with greater haste than he advanced, where their Lievetenant Colonell and a Captaine were taken prisoners, and after the Major taking in a Church-yard, that lay right before the enemyes workes, and keeping his Guarde there, he did keepe the enemy under awe, so that we were no more troubled with their out-falling, though diverse of our Officers and souldiers were hurt by them from their workes, the Church-yard being no shelter for our Guard, that lay just under their workes. On Sunday in the morning, being *Palme*-sunday, his Maiestie with his whole Armie in their best apparell served God; his Maiestie after Sermon, encouraging our souldiers, wished them to take their evill dayes they had then in patience, and that he hoped before long, to give them better dayes, in making them drinke wine insteade of water they were then drinking, and immediately his Maiestie gave orders unto Generall *Bannier*, to command all the *Briggads* to be in readinesse, with their Armes, against the next orders: this command given, some of the commanded men, that were under *Sinclaire* suspecting a storme, provided themselves of some ladders.

By five of the clocke in the afternoone, his Majestie comming towards our Briggade, called for a *Dutch* Captaine under *Hepburnes* Regiment named *Guntier,* and desired him to put on a light corselet, with his sword drawne in his hand, and to take a Sergeant and twelve other good fellowes with him, and to wade through the graffe, and then to ascend to the top of the wall, and to see if men could be commodiously lodged, betwixt the mud wall of the towne, and the stone-wall, and then to retire so suddenly as they might, which being done, his Majestie getting resolution, that there was roome betwixt the two walles to lodge men, the *Briggade* being alreadie in battaile, they fall on at a call, the Captaine being got back without hurt, whervpon his Majestie directed *Bannier* and *Hepburne* with our *Briggad* to passe the graffe, and to storme, And if they repused the enemy from the outward wall, to lodge under the stone-wall, betwixt both the walles, and if the enemy fortuned to retire to presse in with him, the like orders given to the rest of the *Briggads*, all being in readinesse, his Majestie having a number of Cannon great and small charged on the batteries, caused to give notice at all postes, that when the Cannon had discharged, the first *Salve* in the midst of the smoake, they should advance to the storme, as they did, where in passing the graffe, we were over the middle in water and mud, and ascending to storme the walles, there were strong pallessades, so well fastened and fixt in the wall, that if the enemy had not retired from the walles in great feare, we could not, but with great hazard, have entred.

The enemy feebely retiring, our Commanders and Leaders following [II-32] their orders received from his Majestie, we presse to follow in after the enemy, at a great sallying port, that was betwixt both the walles, that opened with two great leaves, where they entred: after their Retreate, they planted a flake of small shot, that shot a dozen of shot at once; besides which there were set two peeces of small Ordinance, that guarded also the entrie, and musketiers besides, which made cruell, and pittifull execution on our musketiers, and pikemen, the valorous *Hepburne*, leading on the battaile of pikes, of his owne *Briggad*, being advanced within halfe a pikes length to the doore, at the entry he was shot above the knee, that he was lame of before, which dazling his senses with great paine forced him to retire, who said to me, bully *Munro*, I am shot, whereat I was wondrous sorry, his Major then, a resolute Cavalier, advancing to enter was shot dead before the doore, whereupon the Pikes falling backe and standing still, Generall *Banier* being by, and exhorting all Cavaliers to enter, Colonell *Lumsdell* and I, being both alike on the head of our owne Colours, he having a Partizan in his hand, and I a halfe Pike, with a head-piece, that covered my head, commanding our Pikes to advance we lead on shoulder to shoulder, Colonell *Lumsdell* and I fortunately without hurt, enter the Port, where at our entry some I know received their rest, and the enemy forced to retire in confusion, being astonished at our entry, they had neither wit nor courage, as to let downe the Portcullis of the great Port behinde them, so that we entering the streets at their heeles, we made a stand till the body of our Pikes were drawne up orderly, and flancked with Musketiers, and then we advanced our Pikes charged, and our Musketiers giving fire on the flancks, till the enemy was put in disorder.

After us entred Generall *Banier*, with a fresh body of Musketiers, he following the enemy in one street, and *Lumsdell* and I in another, having rancountred the enemy againe, they being well beaten, our Officers tooke nine Colours of theirs, which were to be presented to his Majestie, and the most part of the Souldiers were cut off, in revenge of their crueltie used at *New Brandenburg*, but some of their Officers got quarters, such as they had given to ours.

The Regiment defeated, wee directed an Officer with a strong partie to possesse the bridge, and that to hinder their escape: their passage being cut off, they were also cut downe themselves, till the streets were full of dead bodies, and that the most part of our Souldiers and Officers disbanded to make bootie, leaving me and a few number of honest Souldiers to guard my Colours, which disorder, I confesse, stood not in my power to remedie. Thus farre for *Lumsdells* part and mine, which I dare to maintaine to be truth.

And as I have spoken truth of our owne Actions, without ostentation, which no man can controlle that is friend to vertue: I will now relate other mens Actions, so farre as I know to be truth by relation of my honest Camerades.

Lievetenant Colonell *Musten*, being appointed to command the Musketiers of *Lumsdells* Regiment, and of my Colonells, then under my command he seeing us entred did follow after us, and commanded those he led on execution apart, giving no better Quarters than we did. The *Dutch* also remembring the enemies crueltie used at *Brandenburg*, they gave but slight Quarters. [II-33]

Major *Iohn Sinclaire*, as I was credibly informed, being accompanied with Lievenant *George Heatly*, being both resolute and stout, were the first that came over the walles with ladders, who at their first entry having but a few Musketiers with them, they were charged on the streets by the enemies Curassiers, or best horsemen, where they were force to stand close, their backs to the wall where they entred, and to give severall Salves of Muskets upon the enemy, till they were made to retire.

Likewise after we were entred, the yellow and the blew Briggads, being esteemed of all the Army both resolute and couragious in all their exploits; they were to enter on the *Irish* quarter, where they were twice with great losse furiously beaten off, and were cruelly spoyled with fire-workes throwne by the *Irish* amongst them. But at last they having entred, notwithstanding the inequality of their strength, the *Irish* though weake stood to it, and fought with sword, and pikes within workes a long time, till the most part of the Souldiers fell to ground, where they stoode fighting, so that in the end, Lievetenant Colonell *Walter Butler*, who commanded the *Irish*, being shot in the arme, and pierced with a pike through the thigh, was taken prisoner, so that the next day, it was to be seene on the poast where the best service was done: and truely had all the rest stood so well to it, as the *Irish* did, we had returned with great losse, and without victory.

The fury past, the whole streete being full of Coaches and rusty waggons richly furnished withall sorts of riches, as Plate, Iewells, Gold, Money, Clothes, Mulets and horses for saddle, coach and waggons, whereof all men that were carelesse of their dueties, were too carefull in making of booty, that I did never see Officers lesse obeyed, and respected than here for a time, till the hight of the market was past: and well I know, some Regiments had not one man with their Colours, till the fury was past, amd some Colours were lost the whole night, till they were restored the next day, such disorder was amongst us, all occasioned through covetousnesse, the roote of all evill and dishonesty.

At last the execution past, his Majesty entred himselfe, being guarded with the *Rhine-Grave*, and his horsemen, who immediatly were commanded to crosse the bridge, and to follow the enemy at their heeles, being on flight towards *Glogoe*, where the Felt-marshall *Tuffenbacke*, the Count of *Schonberg*, and Mounte *DeCucule* had retired with such as escaped.

His Majesty having but scarce quartered in the Towne, the fire beginning to burne the City accidentally; Orders were given with the stroake of Drume with a Bancke beaten in all streetes, that all Officers and Souldiers, under paine of death, should repaire presently to their Colours, on the other side of the Oder, in the outer workes, where Sr. *Iohn Hepburne* was ordained to command within the workes, except such as were appointed to guard the Portes of the Towne, his Majesties quarter and the Generalls lodging on the market place, where a strong guard was kept to supresse plundering, and the insolency of Souldiers. Neverthelesse these orders proclaimed and published, many disobeyed remaining in the Towne for plundering.

In this conflict, the enemy lost neere three thousand men, besides the Officers that were killed (*viz.*) foure Colonells, *Herbenstine*, *Heydo*, *Walestine*, and *Ioure*, and above thirty six Officers were killed.

Likewise there were taken prisoners, Colonell *Sparre* with five Lievete-[II-34] nant Colonell of *Dutch* amd one *Irish* Cavalier, that behaved himselfe both honourably and well; Colours also they did lose, as I did see the next day made Counte of before Generall *Bannier*, forty one, and Cornets of horse nine.

On our side were lost also at least eight hundred men, whereof the blew and yellow, for their parts, lost five hundred.

His Majesty also did get here a great deale of provision for the Army, as Corne, Amunition, and eighteene peeces of Ordinance.

The next day his Majesty appointed Generall Major *Lesly* as Governor over the Towne, giving him orders to repaire the ruinous workes, and walles, as also orders were given for burying of the dead, which were not buried fully in six dayes, in th'end they were cast by heapes in great ditches, above a hundred in every Grave.

The next day we were ordained to assemble our Regiments, and to bring them together in Armes, that they might be provided of what they wanted of Armes, having lost many in their disorder.

### The eighth Observation.

His Majesty going to rancounter his enemy, before his rising from his Royall Leager at *Swede*, did wisely dispose of his Army, in making it into Briggads, that coming unto the action, he should not neede to thinke on the *Theorie*, when it were time to practise, as many young Commanders are forced to doe, beginning to learne of others, that which is defective in themselves, who are to be pittied, that undertake to leade others being ignorant themselves: but this wise Generall, at this time, did not only order his Army, as he would have them to stand in Battaile, but also knowing the gifts, and severall parts, his chiefe Officers of the field were indued with, he disposeth of them, in appointing such places for them, in fighting against their enemies, as did best befit their vertues, which all he knew before hand, partly by his owne experience, and partly, by enquiring of others, their qualities and vertues.

*Secundo*, his Majesty doth forecast with himselfe, what the enemy, being strong might intend against him, and accordingly, fore-saw wisely how to prevent him, in dividing his Army, by sending the Felt-marshall on the one side of the *Oder* with a part of his Army, going himselfe on the other, leaving the bridge and passage at *Swede* well fortified and beset with Souldiers, to the end, that which of both Armies might be constrained to retire over the bridge, being safe might then conveniently joyne with the other.

As his Majesty was wise in fore-seeing what might happen, he was also diligent, in taking time of his enemies on the sudden, before they could come together; so that after this victory obtained, his Majesty did not only get elbow roome by the enemies removing over the *Elve* and the *Oder*; but also he did gaine time to settle his affaires with the Princes; for those who would not before his victory, scarce keepe correspondence with his Majesty, afterwards his Majesty having freed their country from their enemies, they were then content to intreate for his friendship, by their Ambassadours, and he like to a cunning gamster, taking the Ball at the right rebound, embraced their friendship, and confederacy, having bound them [II-35] up, in a more strict manner then before, till in th'end, they were forced to dance after his pipe.

Here likewise I did observe, that it is never good, to trust too much unto our owne strength, as our enemies did, who at their banqueting, and *inter pocula*, before that the storme went on, though hearing the noyse of our Cannon, they fell a laughing, as wondring what the *Swedens* meant, thought they to fly over the walles, and granting he could enter, were they not so strong as he? Many more idle discourses they had, extolling themselves in their pride, boasting of their strength and courage, not setting God before them, they disdained and contemned their enemies, but suddenly in an instant they found their owne follies, being brought unto feare and astonishment, so that at last, their wits confounded, and consequently their actions confused, and their enemies, though weake instruments, by the power of the God of Armies were made strong and couragious, for punishing them in repaying of their former Barbarity, and cruelty used by them at new *Brandenburg*, where we see, the lord repayeth their wickednesse, when they least expected.

*Tiffenbacke,* the Felt-marshall was much to blame for his command, being so strong within the Towne as we were without, that he did not adventure to fight us in the fields, or at least, to have tried our conduct and valour, with a strong party; his not daring to adventure with us made is the more couragious and resolute to seeke him, though with disadvantage, having once found him to be a timorous enemy, keeping himselfe close within walles, for we know well, the greater his strength was within, if once we entred, his confusion would be the greater: for a multitude within a strength especially horsemen, many servants and baggage breede ever confusion, for avoiding whereof, the Governour had the more reason to have tried us in the fields, whereby he had encouraged his Garrison, who seeing he durst adventure to meete us without, being retired, they would not be afraid within walles.

So it is never good to resolve to be alwayes the defender, but rather according to the time, and circumstances, sometimes to try Fortune, as well by pursuing as by defending, that our credit may not be called in question, neither for too much slownesse, nor too much forwardnesse, but still to presse for the Mediocrity, being the true vertue of Fortitude, without which no Souldier can attaine commendation, if he doe participate of either extreames, as this Felt-marshall did, staying within walles. Yet some, I know will object, that I ought rather to praise the actions of the enemy, to make ours the more glorious, to which I answer, ours at all times, as here, were so splendid, that no Lustre could be added unto them, our Leader *Gustavus* being *Illustrissimus* himselfe, and the favourite of Fortune, to whom all things succeeded fortunatly by taking of time, the most pretious of all things, especially in warres, which sometimes helpes as much as vertue it selfe.

The forwardnesse and courage of Major *Iohn Sinclaire*, and of his Colleague, Lievetenant *Heatlie*, is not to be over-past, they being the first gave good example to enter this Towne, in going over the walles with ladders, with a weake party of fifty musketiers, that ventured to follow them, which were hardly received by the enemies horsemen, neverthelesse they valorously defended themselves, and made their enemies to retire with losse, so [II-36] that, as my intention here, is not to over-praise my friends vertue, I would not on the other part be silent in giving them their due, answerable to their merits, and no more.

We see also by experience dayly, that at all times, as here, no man ever served God for nought, who rewardeth men, though not through merit in respect of his God-head, of whom we can merit nothing, yet of his infinit bounty is ever ready to reward them truely that doe serve him: his Majesty with his Army having served God in the morning, at night he was made victorious over his enemies.

And that his Majesty in the afternoone on the Sabboth pursued his enemies, there was a necessity in it: Generall *Tillies* Army being on their march for the reliefe of the Towne, his Majesty was forced to take the opportunity of time, which once being past doth never returne.

Here we may see the evill, that feare bringeth within a City or Strength causing disorder and confusion, but if all those within this Towne had stood to their defence, as Lievetenant Colonell *Butler* did and the *Irish, Francford* had not bin taken.

Therefore, when resistance is not made, as it ought to be, the victory is easily attained: for nothing encourageth more, then good example, *Et contra*. And I did observe here, that no nation esteemed good Souldiers, are inferiour to the *Dutch* in maintaining a storme, or in extremity of danger, they being otherwise good Souldiers for obedience to command, in watches, marches, working about workes, and in doing all other dueties befitting their profession, being in company of others.

Pike-men being resolute men, shall be ever my choyce in going on execution, as also in retiring honourably with disadvantage from an enemy, especially against horsemen: and we see oftimes, as we found here, that when musketiers doe disbandon, of greedinesse to make booty, the worthy pike-men remaine standing firme with their Officers, guarding them and their Colours, as being worthy the glorious name of brave Souldiers, preferring vertue before the love of gold, that vanisheth while vertue remaineth.

This vice of avarice is alike common to the superiour Officer, and to the inferiour Souldier, which oftimes makes the superiour to be despised as well by the common Souldier, as by his betters: And therefore publique imployments of command should never be given to such greedy persons; for as sparing in a private person is commendable, being done without hurt to another; even so the vertue of liberality is due to him that is publiquely imployed: as also he ought to have splendor in his carriage, and not to give evill example to others his inferiours, if once he be honoured with command in leading of others. I must then againe condemne this kinde of avarice, that makes men for booty abandon their Colours and their duety, they being the cause oftimes of the overthrow of their worthy Camerades standing to fight, when they were employed in making of booty, for which many time, they are contemned, and their money taken from them by the multitude, with disgrace and danger of their lives: for though sometimes they make booty, they have not the fortune to enjoy it one quarter of an houre, thanking God to be rid of it with their lives, though not with their credits.

It is the duety of valiant Commanders, and of brave Souldiers, when- [II-37] ever fire entreth into a City, strength or Leager, suddenly with their Armes to repaire to their Colours, lest at such times, the enemy being neere hand should be ready to take advantage: but here the baser sort of Souldiers, neither for obedience to his Majesties command, nor for love of their Officers, nor of their owne credits, would stirre to attend their Colours, though the enemy had shewed himselfe to pursue the City.

Here also, the enemy was to blame, for leaving provision and Amunition behinde them, whose duety it was rather to destroy it by fire or water, then to leave it to their enemies. But we see, there is no counsell against the Lord invented by man, able to worke, blessed be his name for ever.

---

*The ninth Dutie discharged of the intaking of* Laudsberg *on the* Wert *by accord.*

The fifth of Aprill 1631. his Majesty having left *Francford* on the *Oder* well beset, under the command of Generall Major *Lesly*, who had direction to see the fortifications repaired, as likewise, Generall *Bannier* was left to command over the Army, his Majesty having taken two and twenty hundred commanded musketiers, eight hundred horsemen, twelve peece of Cannon great and small, with Amunition answerable, with spades, shovels, and axes, where the Colonell of the Artillery called *Leonard Richardson*, was commanded to goe with them for to attend his charge: As also Colonell *Hepburne* was commanded to leade the party, and I was sent as Lievetenant Colonell, to second him in this employment. Colonell *Hepburne* having viewed the party, and taken notice that all things were in good order, commanded the party to march, having had a blacke-smith, that dwelt at *Landsberg*, for our guide, we continued our march, the first day, being come within foure miles of the Towne, we quartered at a passe on the high way, and the next morning breaking up, we marched forwards, till on the way, our fore troopes did meete with a Regiment of *Crabbats*, where, after long skirmish and losse sustained by both the parties, in th'end, the Colonell that led the *Crabbats* being deadly wounded, retired to the Towne, casting off all bridges behinde them, which hindered us for a day.

The eight of Aprill, we lay downe before a skonce royall, built on a strong passe, betwixt us and the Towne. This skonce well fortified was well provided of Cannon; It had also a wide Graffe of running water, and a draw-bridge, which was taken up at our coming, and then they discharged their Cannon on us; where at first there were killed some six Souldiers: the night drawing on, our watches set forth, I was appointed by his Majesty to be Captaine of the watch, being ordained to oversee the making of the Batteries: As also I was commanded to set forwards our workes, both for intrenching, and for running our lines of approach to the skonce, wherein I was so busied, that the whole night I went never off my feete, but [II-38] from one part to another, having had sundry Alarums, though not of continuance.

His Majestie having taken quarters in the neerest Dorpe, he left two Rutters to attend on me, that if the enemy should fall out against us, incontinent one of them might be sent to acquaint his Majestie, who having rested for that night, coming before day to visit the workes, and finding them not so farre advanced as he did expect, he falls a chiding of me, notwithstanding of my diligence used the whole night, in keeping the Souldiers still at worke, with the small number of materialls we had to worke with. But no excuse, though true, would mitigate his passion, till he had first considered on the circumstances, and then he was sorry he had offended me without reason. But his custome was so, that he was worse to be pleased in this kinde, than in any other his Commands; being ever impatient, when workes were not advanced to his minde, and the truth is, our Country Souldiers cannot endure to worke like the *Dutch*, neither when they have taken paines, can they worke so formally as others.

Our batteries being readie against the morning, the whole day our Cannon played on the Skonce so fast, as they could be charged, but to no purpose, the earthen wall being so thicke and so well set together, that they scorned us and our Cannon both.

His Majestie seeing nothing to be effectuated this way, resolved to try a second way, by the advise of the Black-smith, that knew all the passages towards the Towne, notwithstanding that the whole land on that side was covered over with water: This Black-smith advised his Majestie, to cause a Float-bridge to be made, and then setting over the water, he would lead us through shallow passes, where we might come behinde the Skonce, cutting off their passage from the Towne, and then the Skonce wanting reliefe might be ours.

According to this plot, his Majestie commanded Lievetenant Colonell *Dowbatle*, with two hundred and fiftie Dragoniers for foote, and me with two hundred and fiftie Musketiers to follow the Black-smith, and to surprize the enemies Guard, which being done by us, we were commanded to make the place good, till Colonell *Hepburne* with a thousand Musketiers should be sent after to second us, *Dowbatle* and I having fortunately surprized the Guard, making them retire to the Towne, leaving the Skonce in our power; Colonell *Hepburne* being advanced towards the Skonce, tooke it in on accord, and the Souldiers were made to take service, and their Officers made prisoners.

In this time *Dowbatle* his Dragoniers having followed the enemy with hot skirmish within shot of their walles, his powder being spent, desired I should fall on and relieve him and his, as I did, continuing the service till we made the enemy retire over a bridge that was hard by the Towne, so that I was forced, for our owne safeties, having lost divers Souldiers, that were killed with the Cannon, to divide my Souldiers, making the halfe of them to cast up a running Trench, while as the rest were hot skirmishing with the enemy, being in danger of both Cannon and Musket, but my Souldiers once getting in the ground, we fortified our selves against their Cannon, and resolved in case of their outfalling, to maintaine the ground we had formerly wonne, with the losse of our bloud, having lost in one halfe houre above thirtie Souldiers, whereof six were killed with the Cannon. [II-39]

The enemy finding the Skonce was lost, and us so farre advanced on the strongest side: Feltmarshall *Horne* with his Forces marching on the other side that was weakest, they presently did send a Drummer on our side to parlé for quarters, whom I received, and being hood-wink't, he was sent with a Convoy to his Majestie, who condescended to the Treatie, and pledges being delivered, the Treatie went on; the Accord subscribed, his Majestie came and thanked *Dowbatle* and us, for our good service, where large promises were made unto us of reward, and to Colonell *Hepburne* also, for taking in of the Skonce.

The enemy being strong in the Towne, and above twice our strength, his Majestie resolved to send to *Francford* for more Forces, both of horse and foote, to come to him before the enemy was suffered to march out of the Towne, to whom conditions were granted to transport foure pieces of Ordnance, and the Souldiers to march out with full Armes, bagge and baggage, with Drummes beating, and flying Colours, and a Convoy of Horsemen towards *Glogoe*.

His Majestie having beset the Garrison, as soone as they marched out, having seene their strength, we were ashamed of their carriage, being the eldest Troopes, and the choice, by report, of the whole Imperiall Armie, who cowardly did give over such a strong Towne, being without necessitie, and in hope of reliefe.

One of my Captaines called *Dumaine*, having contracted a feaver here before *Lansberg*, being removed to *Francford* died there, and being buried, my Lievetenant *David Monro* was preferred to be Captaine of his Company, and Ensigne *Burton* was made Lievetenant, and *Bullion* his brother having taken his passe, my Sergeant *Andrew Rosse* was made Ensigne to Captaine *David*, and *William Bruntfield* was preferred to be my Lievetenant, and *Mongo Gray* Ensigne.

This Towne being taken, both *Pomeren* and the Markes of *Brandenburg* were cleered of the *Emperialists*, being sent up unto *Silesia*.

The next Sabbath, his Majestie, that was ever ready to reward good servants for vertue, he caused to make our guide the Black-smith (being a stout fellow and a craftie) Burgo-master of the Towne, who did get from his Majestie two hundred Duckets besides.

His Majestie on the Sabbath day in the afternoone suffered the principall Officers of his Armie (such as Generall *Banier*, and Lievetenant Generall *Bawtis*, and divers others) to make merry, though his Majestie did drinke none himselfe; for his custome was never to drinke much, but very seldome, and upon very rare considerations, where sure he had some other plot to effectuate, that concerned his advancement, and the weale of his State.

### The ninth Observation.

This Towne of *Lansberg* being a Frontier Garrison lying neare the borders of *Pole* on the *Wert*, the having of it made *Pomeren* sure, and the *Marke*, giving unto his Majestie the freer passage unto *Silesia*; and therefore it was that his Majestie did use the greater diligence and celeritie in obtaining of it, with as great honour and reputation, as could be imagined, in respect of the inequalitie of strength betwixt us and our enemies: As also in consideration of the situation of the place, being on the one side fortified [II-40] by nature, yet beyond nature and probabilitie of reason. This strong Garrison was forced to yeeld to *Gustavus*, who was *Mars* his Minion, and Fortunes Favourite, or rather their Master, as we see by his frequent Victories obtained against his enemies, who, though strongest, are made to submit to the weakest partie, where we may see, that as industry is fruitfull, so there is a kinde of a good Angell, as it were waiting ever upon diligence, carrying a Lawrell in his hand, to crowne her. And therefore it was, that they said of old, that Fortune should not be prayd unto, but with hands in motion, which made this valiant King love ever to be busied in vertues exercise, befitting a Generall, that carried a minde as this Invincible King did, while he lived, still rising to blessednesse and contentation.

It is commonly seene, that those who feare least are commonly overcome, as became of *Francford* on the *Oder*, and this Towne also: and though victory we see be from God, yet to overcome an enemy, the courage and skill of Commanders is very requisit and necessary. And where good military discipline is observed, as was done here; there confidence doth arise, perswading us, we can doe what we please. Of this opinion was our Leader, and our Armie never doubted of their owne valour, nor of their Leaders good Conduct, which made our Victories the easier to be gotten.

Here also we see the goodnesse of intelligence, for had his Majestie not gotten the Black-smith, or some other like unto him, to have beene intelligencer and guide to winne through the shallow Trinkets he led us, to the Damme upon the head of their Watch, who were surprized; hardly could we have overcome this Towne, on such a sudden, for without this good of intelligence, which is so necessary, and of so great a moment in warres, nothing, or very little can be effectuated in unknowne places. For good Intelligencers are so requisit in an

Armie, that no meanes ought to be spared on them, providing they be trustie: for one designe or secret of our enemies well knowne, may bring all the rest we desire to a wished end, or at least, preserve us and ours from danger. This Black-smith, that was our guide in leading us towards our enemy, at our first on-going on service, the enemy playing hard with Muskets, neverthelesse he went on without feare, under-taking alike danger with our selves, but finding in time of hot service some falling besides him, our powder being a little wet, and not giving so good report as the enemies did, he then said, he would returne to his Majestie, and send us better powder, yet I thinke, though here there did appeare some lacke of constant resolution in him, that time, exercise, and frequency of danger would make him a brave fellow, being of a strong and a good able body, but in my opinion, the stoutest of men, till they be a little acquainted with the furious noise of the Cannon, will naturally feare and stoope at the first.

Likewise his Majestie was to be commended for his diligence by night and by day, in setting forwards his workes; for he was ever out of patience, till once they were done, that he might see his Souldiers secured and guarded from their enemies; for when he was weakest, he digged most in the ground; for in one yeare what at *Swede, Francford, Landsberg, Brandenburg, Verbum, Tannermonde, Wittenberg*, and *Wirtzburg*, he caused his Souldiers to worke more for nothing, than the States of *Holland* could get wrought in three yeares, though they should bestow every yeare a Tunne of gold: and this he did, not onely to secure his Souldiers from the enemy, but also to keepe them from idlenesse. When they were not employed on service, they were [II-41] kept by good discipline in awe and obedience, and that with as great moderation, love and discretion as could be.

And his Majestie knew well, that our Nation was of that nature, that they could take to heart the austere carriage of their Commanders, were they never so good. For while as sometimes, through his Majesties impatience, he would cause to imprison some of our Country-men, without solicitation, his Majestie was ever the first did minde their liberties; for he knew their stomacks were so great, that they would burst or starve in prison, before they would acknowledge an errour committed against their Master, except it were of negligence.

Moreover, nothing can more discourage a Citie, Fort, or Strength, that is beleaguered, than when they see their secrets discovered, and their passages from reliefe cut off; as it was seene of those that yeelded up the Skonce to Sir *Iohn Hepburne*, being contented to come in the Colonells mercy, seeing themselves barred from all reliefe.

Likewise the dutie of Leaders, that lead men on service, ought to be limited with discretion, and not to advance further than with conveniency they may retire againe, if need be, lest by too farre advancing, they not onely indanger themselves, but also ingage others, for their reliefes, to indanger all: and a fault committed in this kinde, through too much forwardnesse, merits a harder censure, than remissenesse with discretion, seeing in the latter, a man is but censured alone, but committing the former errour, he loseth himselfe and others.

Here also we found by experience, that the spade and the shovell are ever good companions in danger, without which, we had lost the greatest part of our followers. Therefore in all occasions of service, a little advantage of ground is ever profitable against horse, foote, or Cannon. And for this it was, that the best Commanders made ever most use of the spade and the shovell, and that in such ground as was found most commodious for their safeties.

We see also here his Majesties disposition in entertaining his Officers kindly after victory, esteeming them not as servants, but as companions in his mirth, as a wise Master ought and should doe to those he findes obedient to his Commandements, incouraging them another time to undergoe any service or danger for his sake, that was so kinde and familiar with them, joyning their hearts as well with his love, as with his bountie; for he knew well nothing was more able to bring victory next under God, than good Commanders: As also his Majestie knew, that to be courteous unto his Officers was the way to triumph over his enemies.

---

*The tenth Dutie discharged of our March to* Berlin, *and from thence to* Spandaw, *and backe to* Botsaw.

The eighteenth of *Aprill* 1631. the enemy being marched out of *Landsburg* towards *Glogo*, his Majestie having beset *Landsburg* with a Garrison, we marched backe to *Francford* on the *Oder*, where we [II-42] did rest us with the Armie till the twenty-ninth of *Aprill*, during which time, there were Ambassadours going mutually betwixt his Majestie and the Duke of *Brandenburg*: at last having condescended on some points, his Majestie brake up with the Armie, and marched towards *Berlin*, and were quartered by the way at a passe called *Panco*, being one of the Duke of *Brandenburgs* hunting houses, and from thence we marched to *Berlin*, where his Majestie was Royally entertained by the Duke, and that his Majestie might thinke he was welcome, after the feast the Castle of *Spandaw* was delivered in his Majestie custodie, where incontinent Colonell *Axellilly*, with foure hundred *Swedes* were left in Garrison, being a strength one of the fastest in *Germanie*, fortifed well with Fossees and Countersharpes of free stone, and an earthen wall above, having one hundred and fiftie pieces of Cannon on it, and Armes for twentie thousand foote and horse, with Amunition answerable; Provided also sufficiently with store of victualls for an Armie of ten thousand men for a long space: and though the Garrison were *Swedes*, they were sworne to obey the Duke; and his Majestie was obliged by his Royall word past to the Duke, to restore it againe when ever the Duke desired to have it, if the Duke of *Saxony* should not joyne with his Majestie against the Emperour.

The third day after the agreement, the whole Armie brake up, and marched to another passe, three miles from *Spandaw*, called *Spotsdamme*, where we lay not intrencht the space of ten dayes, till his Majesties Ambassadours were returned from the Duke of *Saxon*, with an answer, that the Duke would not assist his Majestie for the reliefe of *Madeburg*, neither yet would the Duke grant to his Majestie free passage through his Country, which was the losse of many poore soules within *Madeburg*, being cut off by the crueltie of Generall *Tillies* Armie, having surprized the Towne that was never taken before, sparing neither man, woman nor childe, but putting all alike cruelly to death, and in the end, the Towne was burnt downe, which  was occasioned by the breach of the Dukes promise, in not assisting his Majestie of *Sweden*, being on his march to relieve it.

His Majestie not assured of the Duke of *Brandenburg* behinde him, our Armie turning faces about, we marched backe to *Spandaw*, and lay downe in the Fields in order of Battaile, where we remained certaine dayes, till such time as it behoved his Majestie, for keeping of his Royall word, to restore backe to the Duke the Castle of *Spandaw*, and his Majesties Garrison being brought out, it was manned againe by the Dukes Forces.

The Castle restored, his Majesty was so incensed against the Duke, though his owne brother in law, that he sware to take in *Berlin*, which was the Dukes residence; as also he was resolved to take the Duke prisoner, except he would joyne in confederacy with him, without the Duke of *Saxon*; whereupon our Army did breake up, and marched towards *Berlin* in hostile manner, and lying downe before it, the Duke not able to resist, entred in a Treaty with his Majesty; and to move his Majesty the more, the Dutchesse and her mother with a traine of Great Ladies, came to the fields to entertaine his Majesty, with offering in the Dukes name all due respect to his Majesty, and promising all things should be done by the Duke, what his Majesty would desire.  To which his Majesty answered merrily, that if the Duke would not end with him friendly before night, he would send the Dutchesse and all the Ladies prisoners to *Sweden*, and the Duke should follow. [II-43]

Incontinent the treaty begun; the Duke getting short time to resolve, was forced to end with his Majesty, and to joyne in confederacie with him, offensive and defensive, against the Emperour, and that without the *Saxons* consent: and in the treaty it was concluded, the Duke should give a great supply of men, monies and Artillery to his Majesty, for the advanceing of the warres, besides the ordinary inquartering of his Majesties Army; and the paiments of the monethly contribution, out of the Dukes lands was also agreed upon, and Commissioners were appointed, for the ingathering of the first tearmes contribution: during which collection, his Majesties Army was laid in quarters to refresh them, till his Majesty should retire from *Statin*, being gone thither to give presence to the *Russian* Ambassadour, and his Majesty being returned from *Statin* the twenty ninth of Iune he quartered in my quarters in *Barnow*, where we had orders given us to be in readinesse to march to old *Brandenburg* on the first of Iuly.

*The tenth Observation.*

His Majesty could never be assured of the Princes friendship, till first he had forced their enemies to give ground, being made to leave behind them

*Pomeren Maclenburg*, and the three markes of *Brandenburg*, without any Emperiall Garrison, except one was left in *Gripswald*, but so soone as the Duke of *Brandenburg* did see the enemy retiring, and his Majestie prevailing, he then begun to enter in treaty, and to give his Majestie assurance of his loyall friendship, by subscribing of certaine Articles condescended upon betwixt them, at *Barleene* in Iune 1631.

On this march, though short, we had many variable resolutions and changes, which were caused by the changable accidents happening in the course of this warre, which made his Majesties resolutions to vary, as the time changed, sometimes through feare of his strong enemy, sometimes by suspecting the Princes, who were also affrighted and feared, being astonished in their mindes, they were not able to discerne what was most profitable for them, so that their doubting and feare suffered them not to hazard any notable thing, in assisting his Majesty against their common enemy; but still lingred to joyne with his Majesty, expecting the enemy would prevaile, and then they would joyne with the Master of the fields, as ordinarily is done over all *Dutchland* in all degrees, from the highest to the lowest, they wagge as the bush doth resolving ever to quit their best friends in adversity.

Here we see the inconstancy of the Dukes friendship, that will not be friends as well in adversity, as in prosperity: for when fortune favours us, all the world would seme to laugh on us; but when we are but once kik't in the heele with any malignant chance of misfortune, then our supposed friends fly from us, at a farre distance, while they see us like to be tossed by the Tempest of adversity. But as soone as they see the Tempest over-past, and fortune beginning to smile on us againe, then begin they (as the Princes did) to returne, and to desire to be made partakers of our good fortunes, though they had no minde to taste of the bitter cup of his Majesties adversity; but once seeing the sweete commodity of the peace, which they, their country and subjects did reape by his Majesties valour (with the hazard of his person, and the lives of many Cavaliers who followed him) then their ene- [II-44] mies being farre removed from them, they desire his Majesty for their Admirall, to attend when he makes saile, having seene he did valiantly ride out the storme, promising againe when his sailes were full, to bide by him; and to follow him until death should sunder them. But if they had bin generously minded, they had imbraced the danger, and taken part with his Majesty when honour was to be got, in the middest of greatest danger; since common danger doth conjoyne the coldest friends, to goe together against their common enemies. Likewise here we may see and observe a Royall King most loyall in keeping his Princely Parole and promise to the Duke his brother, in rendring backe *Spandaw*, though to his disadvantage, keeping his covenant, albeit he should lose thereby, teaching, by his owne example, all Cavaliers to keepe their word, though given to their enemies. For his Majesty knew well, that nothing was to be thought more unworthy in a Prince or common-weale, then to breake word or promise; for of all vertues in a Prince truth is the chiefest, which once being lost returnes not againe.

His Majesty taking to heart, that the Duke had so peremptorily sought the restitution of this strength, his Majesty being free of his word, and his Garrison march't forth, he incontinent marched to *Berlin*, and got both the Duke and the City into his power, in interchange of the Castle of *Spandaw*, which then his Majesty knew how to get againe, as he did shortly after. Where we may see, there is no Oratory of such force to gaine both men and women, as a strong well conducted Army, as this was.

Here also we may see, what evill oftimes doth happen by cunctation, or delayes, as doth witnesse the overthrow and ruine of *Madeburg*, the Citizens whereof, in their prosperity, would not suffer a Souldier to enter into their houses, but made them build Huts and Tents along the wall; which wall, for their pride, was alike brought low with the ground, where before their death for their pride they were punished with fire and sword, so that they having disdained Souldiers, they were by the enemies Souldiers justly rewarded, being denied of mercy in their greatest extremity, and the houses, they so much esteemed of, cannot this day be seene, what for houses they were, and his Majesty his wisdome is commendable, who seing *Madeburg* lost, the enemy strong, the Dukes wavering, contrary to his minde and custome, his Majesty retired with his Army backe to *Spandaw*, and from thence to *Berlin*, making himselfe sure of the one, though not of the other, leaping the Dike where he found it weakest, and missing to catch a goose, he thought it sure to catch the goselings, though he was his good brother, he did looke to his owne standing, fearing Generall *Tillie* and the *Saxon* might joyne together, not being farre different in conditions, to make his retreat sure, his Majesty did beset *Spandaw* againe with a *Swedens* Garrison.

At this time a great number of *Hamburgh* marchants, amongst which were some *English*, going by the Army with great packes, were seized upon, and their goods taken from them, whereof his Majesty being made foreseene, orders were given, that the whole packs, under paine of death, should be brought to his Majesty, as they were, our Army being very hungry, and almost brought to discontent, for lacke of monies, his Majesty in a faire way, was content to restore the *Hamburgers* goods, providing the marchants amongst them would advance upon Band and surety, to [II-45] his Majesty two hundred thousand Dolers, to give some contentment to his hungry Army which the Marchants condescended unto & advanced the mony, wherof the *English* advanced no part: Neverthelesse they had favor shewed unto thé, in the restitution of their goods, by the request of the Cavaliers (who interceeded for them to his Majesty) their country-men both *Scots* & *English*.

This kinde of favour showne to Marchants by Souldiers occurres not often: for sometimes the Souldiers (the worst sort of them) measured the packes belonging to the Marchants with the long ell, and if this sort of dealing should but only happen to the churlish Marchant, it were the lesse to be regarded; but honest Souldiers should be ever honest in their dealings towards the rancke Merchants, that have worth and discretion to respect Cavaliers being in neede, and common Souldiers also, as I have knowne by experience some worthy *English* Marchants to have done worthily, in relieving the necessities of the common Souldiers of their country-men, and therefore in my esteeme, of all Nations, for their charity, they doe best merit the name of gentlemen Marchants.

We see also here, that notwithstanding of the termes his Majesty did stand unto with the Duke of *Saxon*, and with *Tillie*, who might have come to have made a visit in *Brandenburg* his lands, where our Army were laid in quarters: Neverthelesse, his Majesty was not afraid to leave his Army, and to returne to *Statin* to give presence to the *Russian* Ambassadour, and to dispatch him; being alike ready to Governe the affaires of the state, as he was to fight against his enemies, he staied not long, but having recollected his forces, that were come from *Sweden*, *Spruce* and *Scotland*; giving them orders to march to old *Brandenburg*, his Majesty getting intelligence *Tillie* was gone from *Hessen*, he then begun to make the best use of the time.

---

### *The eleventh Duty discharged of our March to old* Brandenburg.

The first of July, the *Swedens* of *Axellily* his Regiment, that lay in *Barnoe*, and we did breake up, having got orders to march to old *Brandenburg*, being appointed then for the Generall Randevouz of our Army to come together at. This *Barnoe* is a Towne in the Marke of *Brandenburg*, renowned of old, for brewing of good beere, which during our residence there with the *Swedes*, we did merrily try, till that we had both quarrelling and swaggering amongst our selves, who before our departure againe were made good friends, reserving our enmity, till we saw our common enemy, and so we marched together following our orders towards old *Brandenburg*, taking but easie marches, being without feare of an enemy, and being tied to no particular diet, we tooke quarters, where we found the best entertainment to be, either in Dorpe or Towne.

Notwithstanding our easie march and good quarters, there were some under both the Regiments unworthy the name of good Souldiers, who in [II-46] their march leaving their Colours, and staying behinde did plunder, and oppresse the *Boores*, for remedy whereof, the Souldiers being complained on, accused and convicted, they were made, for punishment to suffer Gatlop, where they were well whip't for their insolency.

Likewise on this march, some of our Souldiers in their rancks, their Colours flying, did beate one another, for which over-sight I did cashiere a Sergeant, after I had cut him over the head, for suffering such abuse to have beene done in his presence, where such insurrection, amongst Souldiers being in their armes, might have brought the whole Regiment into factions, where I alone was too weake, for all my authority, to command them asunder. And therefore such faults ought ever to be suppressed at first, and to be stilled by any Officer, that chanceth to be neerest him, who did give the first evill example.

Having marched three dayes, the fourth we arrived at *Brandenburg*, the Pest raging in extremity of the heate in the City, we were commanded to quarter without in the fields, and presently there was a certain quantity of the workes about the Leaguer appointed for us, within foure dayes to complete and make ready: during which time, *Robert Monro* Furer to Captaine *Hector* his Colours, died of the Pest, and was much regrated, being a youth of good hopes.

Here also did dye of the plague, Segeant *Robert Monro, Cull-crags* sonne, and *Andrew Monro* was executed at *Statin*, for having, contrary to his Majesties Articles and discipline of warre, beaten a Burger in the night within his owne house, for whose life there was much solicitation made by the Dutchesse of *Pomeren*, and sundry noble Ladies, but all in vaine, yet to be lamented; since divers times before he had given proofe of his valour, especially at the siege of *Trailesound* in his Majesties service of *Denmarke*, where he was made lame of the left arme, who being young was well bred by his Parents at home, and abroad in *France*, though it was his misfortune to have suffered an examplary death, for such an over-sight committed through sudden passion, being *Summum jus*, in respect that the party had forgiven the fault, but the Governour, being a churlish *Swede*, would not remit the satisfaction due to his Majesty and justice.

### *The eleventh Observation.*

This Regiment in nine yeeres time, under his Majesty of *Denmarke*, and in *Dutch-land*, had ever good lucke to get good quarters, where they did get much good wine, and great quantity of good beere, beginning first with *Hamburg* beere in *Holsten*, and after that in *Denmarke* they had plenty of *Rustocke* beere, and now at *Barnoe*, and thereafter they tasted the good *Calvinists* beere at *Serbest*, and our march continuing out of low *Germany*, towards the upper *Circles* of the Empire, as in *Franconia, Swabland, Elsas* and the *Paltz*, they were oft merry with the fruits and juice of the best berries that grew in those Circles, for to my knowledge, they never suffered either penury or want, I being the Leader, but oftimes I did complaine and grieve at their plenty, seeing they were better to be commanded, when they dranke water, then when they got too much beere or wine. But my choice of all beeres is *Serbester* beere, being the wholsomest for the body, and cleerest from all filth or barme, as their Re- [II-47] ligion is best for the soule, and cleerest from the dregs of superstition.

Being once at dinner with the Rex Chancellor of *Sweden*, having drunke good *Seebester* beere, he asked me what I thought of that beere; I answered it pleased my taste well, he replied merrily, no wonder it taste well to your palat, being it is the good beere of your ill religion. I asked his Excellence how the good wine on the Rhine would taste at *Mentz*, being the good wine of a worse religion; he answered, he liked the wine and the beere better than both the Religions. But I said, to be his Excellence neighbour, neare *Mentz* in the *Paltz*, at *Crewtsenach*, I would be content to keepe mine owne Religion, and to drinke good Rhinish wine for my life time.

Nothing is more necessary on a march, then to keepe good discipline, without which there is no order, nor feare of God amongst Officers, that will suffer their Souldiers to grinde the faces of the poore by oppression, from whence oftimes doth come the unfortunat, and unhappy events of warlike enterprises and expeditions: for where the feare of God is taken away, there the common-weale must needes decay, and then the ruine of the people doth follow.

Likewise we see here, that all that come to the warres, (as many foolish men doe thinke) are not killed, but some die, through one kinde of death, and some by another, so that we ought ever be prepared and ready, not knowing how, when, or where to die. Happy then is that man, that is prepared to die, as if he should die to morrow; for many have I seene rise well in the morning (the time of these warres) who went not to bed at night. Our care then should be still, to meditate on the end, that it may be good, and then doubtlesse we shall die well.

The infection being great at this time, in *Brandenburg* I contracted a sodaine fit of sicknesse, that was vehement, and therefore did not continue above forty eight houres: It was so vehement, that if I had not suddenly overcome it, doubtlesse it had overcome me, but praised be God, then I banished death by imagination, as I did divers times before, yet at last, I know he will have about with me, but my confidence is, that by the helpe of the Conqueror I will overcome him in th'end, as my Captaine and Leader hath done, who is gone before me, and opened a Dore to me to enter at, where I may sing Triumphing over my enemies, with those that follow the Lambe in the Communion of the Saints blessed for ever.

---

*The twelfth Duty discharged of our March from* Brandenburg *over the* Elve *at* Tangermound *and from thence to* Werben.

In the middest of Iuly our Army did breake up from *Brandenburg*, marched towards *Ratenough*, the Emperialists having left it, being marched towards *Tangermound*, his Majesty advanced with the commanded Musketiers, and a strong party of horse, who having set through the River of the *Elve*, they surprized the enemy at *Werben*, where a Lievetenant [II-48] Colonell was taken prisoner, and then after Colonell *Dowbatle* with his Dragoniers did take in by surprize also *Tangermound*, before his Majesty was come with the party, and being come, immediatly he caused to set over the River a ship-bridge, which was fortified before the entry; over which our foote Army did passe, and our horse with the Cannon, Amunition and baggage, did wade through the River, where never one was seene to passe with Cannon before, so that without impediment our Cannon and baggage for the most part, came safely through, but those waggons that were lightest, being loaden with *Boores* trash, as it came lightly, so it went lightly with the streame. *Et meritò.*

The Emperialists at *Carleben*, hearing we had crossed the *Elve*, tooke them to their flight, to provide betimes for their winter quarters; *Wolmerstat* also was taken by a weake party of our horsemen; having heard our Army had crossed the River of the *Elve*, such a feare came among them, that they never looked behind them, but still fled, directing Poast upon Poast to Generall *Tillie* to retire backe from *During*, being minded unto *Hessen*, who receiving newes of his Majesties crossing the *Elve*, he turning faces about, with his whole Army continued his expedition backward to finde us at *Werben*, before we could be intrenched, as he thought.

But where he did but march with his Army in the day time, we with spades and shovells, wrought our selves night and day in the ground, so that, before his coming, we had put our selves our of danger of his Cannon.

Generall *Bannier*, with the rest of our Army coming after us, tooke in *Hagleberg* in his way, and beset it with a strong Garrison, where Generall Major *Kagg* did command, to whom was conjoyned my cozen *Fowles* his Regiment, after he had taken the Castle of *Bloe* in *Macleburgh* in his march, with his owne Regiment alone, where they made good booty, but their Souldiers got but sleight quarters, as *Bannier* did give at the intaking of this Towne and Castle of *Hagleberg*.

### The twelfth Observation.

At this time I did remarke the great, wonderfull, rare and extraordinary mercy of God towards our Leader the Kings Majesty, and his Royall little Army, which, before our removing from old *Brandenburg*, was much infected with the plague of Pestilence, so that we knew not the sicke from the whole: for of our Regiment alone, there died in one weeke, above thirty Souldiers, and being but removed six dayes, at our downe-lying at *Werben*, we scarce knew there was any infection amongst us, so that in a moneths time, we were miraculously rid of it, and for mine owne part, I neither know, nor can conjecture any reason for it (cheifely being in the dogge dayes, and in a Leaguer) but the Lords mercy towards his Majesty and his Army, being at this time, farre inferiour in strength to our enemies.

Many examples and testimonies of Gods favour towards his Majesty I did observe on this march: for such terror was put in their hearts, by his Majesties victory obtained at *Francford* and *Lansberg*, that they fled, where once they did heare of our coming, being perswaded and informed by their consciences, that, if his Majesty were victorious, they should get no better [II-49] quarters, then were given by them at *Madeburg*, which made them quit strong Garrisons, before they would attend or abide the danger.

Wherefore we may plainly conclude, that they doe not merit the name of Souldiers, nor yet the title of couragious Cómanders, that did succumbe before they saw or felt the dinte of their enemies valour. Fie then on such Commanders! If they were of my friends, I would allow them a Pinne higher on the Gallowes, then is allowed for common offences: for such Cullions that quite places for feare, not seeing their enemies, are unworthy the name of Souldiers; but I thinke they were too rich, and consequently, they grew too feeble.

Lifewise here I did rejoyce, and was glad, when I did observe that it is not, nor was not peculiar to any still to have overcome, or to be victorious: the Emperialists, I know by experience, and so did the Regiment I commanded, had their time of the victory against the King of *Denmarke* (where I did learne to make a retreate) but now being come under another Leader, there Fortune began to change and to retire from us, we learning under the invincible *Gustavus*, to advance orderly, never falling off, but ever keeping faces to our enemy, a brave lesson learned from a brave Commander. So that we see here, victory keepes no constant dwelling, being now here, now there, yet we see, that it is best kept with counsell and vertue, neither can I thinke, but fortune, and chance hath a great hand in it, for it is a greater matter to use victory well, then to overcome, and all victors have an insatiable desire of their prosperous fortune, never appointing an end to their desires; And nothing brings victory more, next unto God, then good Commanders, whereof King *Gustavus* the invincible had many.

Here also at the intaking of *Hagleberg*, Generall *Bannier* did well in giving the Souldiers some liberty of booty: to the end they might prove the more resolute another time, for Souldiers will not refuse to undergoe any hazard, when they see their Officers willing to reward them with honour and profit.

---

### The thirteenth Duty discharged at our Royall Leaguer of Werben *on the* Elve *against Generall* Tillie *his Army.*

About the middest of Iuly 1631 his Majesties forces being come together of Horse and Foote, he did resolve to set downe his Leaguer at *Werben* on the *Elve*, where the River of the *Haggle* enters into it, and spying a parcell of ground, the most commodious that could be had, for situation, and aire, having first the commodity of transportation by water, on the River of the *Haggle* running into the *Elve* at the Leaguer, whereon all provisions could be brought for maintaining of his Army; He had also the whole country on the other side of the *Elve*, behinde him as his friends.

This Leaguer lay along the side of the River on a plaine meadow, being [II-50] guarded by the River on one side, and the foreside was guarded by a long earthen Dike, which of old was made to hold off the River from the Land, which Dike his Majesties made use of, dividing it by Skonces and Redoubts, which defended one another with Flanckering, having Batteries and Cannon set within them, alongst the whole Leaguer: he did also set over the River a Ship-bridge, for his Retreate in neede, as also for bringing commodiously of provision and succours, from the Country, and Garrisons on the other side, as *Hagleberg*, *Rateno*, *Perleberg*, and others.

In like manner his Majestie did fortifie the Towne of *Werben* for his *Magazin*; being close to the Leaguer, with workes about it, which defended the Leaguer, and the Leaguer-workes were made to defend the Towne also, so that they could relieve one another being in most distresse, and both the Towne-wall and Leaguer-wall, were so thicke and firme of old earth, faced up with new, that no Cartow could enter into it. The Bulwarkes on which the Batteries were made for the Cannon, were also very strong and formally built, and they flanckered one another, so that none could finde but folly in pressing to enter by storme;

And betwixt the flanckerens were left voides, for letting Troopes of horse in and out, with slawght Bommes before them, where strong guards were kept for defending the passage.

And on the one side of this Leaguer were planted above one hundred and fiftie pieces of Cannon, great and small, besides those that were planted on the Towne-workes, and our whole Horsemen were quartered within the Leaguer.

The manner we were ordained to watch this Leaguer, every Briggad of foote had such a portion of the Leaguer appointed for them to watch and maintaine by sight, in case of a storme, which part they had fortified themselves, and Briggads of horse were ordained to attend particularly on a foote Briggad, to second them, if that the enemy, at a storme, should beate the foot backe from their Poasts, then the horse Briggad was ready to charge, till the foote might be recollected by the diligence and a valour of their Officers: for besides the watch ordinary on the Poasts, the whole Briggads of foote stood in readinesse at all Alarums behinde the guard, and the horse Briggads did stand in Battaile behinde them. Likewise without the Leaguer, there were squadrons of our horsemen to stand in readinesse at one end, that while as the enemies foote should march on to the storme, our horsemen might charge through to the end of the Leaguer, where they were to be received againe within the Leaguer, being hardly followed, so that the judicious Reader can easily judge, what a difficultie it was to storme such a Leaguer.

Being thus provided to welcome our enemy, his Majestie hearing of his enemies neere approach with a strong Armie, his Majestie did resolve like a wise Generall to try his enemies courage in the Field, before they should come neare to discourage his little Armie. And therefore his Majestie commanded out a strong partie of two thousand Musketiers, and a thousand horse, which partie he did lead himselfe, and finding by his intelligence *Tillies* Armie were advanced so farre, as to *Wolmerstat*, his Majestie *Ame omnia*, called in unto the Leaguer all the Garrisons, which were without on that side of the River, whereon the enemy did march, and getting good intelligence of the enemies fore-Troopes, being foure Regiments of horse, the best of *Tillies* Armie (*viz.*) Colonell *Harmesteans* his Regiment of Curassiers, Mounte *Cuculies* Regiment, *Holks* Regiment of Curassiers, and *Cor-* [II-51] *ramino* his Regiment, which were all about fortie two Cornets of Curassiers, being quartered beside *Tangermonde*, not knowing how neere they were come unto the valiant *Gustavus*, that, though a King, would not stand on a Ceremony, to make the first visit unto such valourous *Cavaliers* of their worths, and to make his Majesties visit the more gracefull (though lesse acceptable well I wot) he did send the *Rhine-grave* and Colonell *Gollenbagh*, with five hundred Dragoniers, and their owne two Regiments of horse, to salute them at their quarter in his Majesties name, honouring them first with a *Salve* of Muskets, lest they should thinke it discourtesie, to have come unto them without sending before, which being mis-taken by the enemy, the skirmish went on, Colonell *Harmestean* was killed, *Holke* and Coronell *Corramino* fled, so that the enemies fore-Troops were driven to confusion, having lost twenty-nine Cornets; the Troopes whereof were defeated and ruined, so that our horsemen did make good bootie, having gotten horses, and a great deale of riches. The enemy in this Conflict did lose above a thousand men, and his Majesties losse was great also, having lost his owne sisters sonne, the young *Rhinegrave*, bing killed on his first exployt, being the seventeenth of *Iuly*; the Cavaliers death was much regrated by his Majestie and the whole Armie, but the exployt ended, his Majestie did retire towards the Leaguer, having left some Officers and Horsemen, that had followed in the flight Generall *Tilly*, and Colonell *Holke*, dogging them to their Quarters, where both hardly escaped untaken. The *Swedens* disappointed of their onslaught, retired after his Majestie to their Leaguer, and having put a terror in the enemies Armie, by this defeat; he did get foure dayes longer continuation, to put all things in good Order against their coming; during which time, the enemy was busied in recollecting of his scattered Troopes, and in putting his Armie in good Order, forgetting of his revenge.

His Majestie as soone as he came backe, did send incontinent Orders to all the chiefe Officers of the Armie, to come instantly to his Tent, where being come, he asked their advice, whether it were best, the enemy being strong, timely to retire over the *Elve*, or that he should bide their coming before the Leaguer, and finding no man to answer him, all turning it over upon himselfe, being wise, knowing that Counsell would be allowed of by a King, but according to event; But his Majestie perceiving their intentions, he resolved to abide the enemies coming, what ever might follow, and instantly he gave all Officers and Commanders of Briggads charge to see their workes accomplished, and finished, for if the enemy would stay but three dayes, he would be no more afraid of him, than if he were in the strongest Island could be imagined, being he was assured, God would fight for him, and with him, and besides, he knew he had as good Commanders and Souldiers of horse and foote, as *Tilly* was able to bring against him, and which was more, he could get his Armie longer and better entertained than *Tilly* could get, seeing he had the Country to enemy, which was his Majesties friend.

This resolution being taken, his Majestie went to visit the Leaguer, being accompanied with the *Marquesse* of *Hamilton*, come then from *Britaine*, with an Armie of six thousand foote, as complete as could be desired to be seene for personages of men, in complete Armes, being well araide, and furnished of Artillery, and of all things fitting for the adorning of an Armie, his Majestie being exceeding glad of such a timely supply, he did most heartily welcome the *Marquesse*, by entertaining him with gracefull counte- [II-52] nance and respect, in giving him such entertainement as the time could affoord, and in the interim, his Majestie went along with his *Excellence*, to let him see the fortifications and preparations he had made against *Tillies* comming, which being so neare, made his Majestie after some considerable discourses had with the *Marquesse* concerning his Armie, wherein his Majestie declared he was sorry the *Marquesse* with his Armie were arrived in such parts of the Country, that was ruined, and not able to entertaine his *Excellence*, and his Armie with bread, much lesse to be furnished with necessaries convenient for them, or with such as his Majestie would willingly bestow on them, if the Country, or his power were able to furnish it.  Other private discourses they had together, concerning the service, that the *Marquesse* with his Armie was to be imployed on: And his *Excellence* having received his Majesties instructions, being both pressed by shortnesse of time, his *Excellence* was graciously dismissed, to returne to his Armie, then being come upon the *Oder*, being then the most ruined part within the Empire, by reason both the Armies had laine there above a yeare before, which caused that Summer both famine and plague, the smart whereof his *Excellence* Armie suffered at their first coming, where they died of the plague above two hundreth a weeke, so that it was impossible for them to subsist long; and the plague was so rife, that his *Excellence* servants and family, were not free.  Neverthelesse, none can say, but for the well and furtherance of the good cause, they did arrive in a good time, having diverted from his Majestie a great part of the enemies forces towards *Silesia*, being more afraid of their coming, than of an Armie twice stronger, and the diversion thus made, was a great furtherance to the joyning of his Majestie with the Duke of *Saxon*, and consequently of his Majesties advancement in *Dutchland*, and of his victory obtained against his enemies at *Leipsigh*; for nothing doth more crosse the designes of a mightie enemy, than to beare a forraigne supply of valiant men to come to his enemy, which no doubt, would force to alter his former Designes, which once altered unadvisedly in haste, might marre the happie event of his former Conclusions.

Likewise, his *Excellence* being dismissed, the *Landgrave* of *Hessen*, the Duke *Barnard* of *Wymar*, did come unto his Majestie, with the offer of their service, (knowing his Majestie had gotten a supply to his Armie out of *Britaine*, which did encourage them, and the most part of the Townes of the foure upper Circles of the Empire, to offer to joyne with his Majestie in confederacy, having seene the appearance of the strong partie his Majestie could make, being assured of the friendship and concurrence of great *Britaine*) they were both graciously accepted of, and so much the more, that they were the first did hazard with a private Convoy to come to his Majestie through their enemies; for which his Majestie did thanke them, who the next day were dispatched to returne, for advanceing of the cause in doing his Majestie good service, by collecting of more forces, as they did soone after.

They being gone, the twenty-two of *Iuly* Generall *Tilly*, with his mightie Armie, did present himselfe before our Leaguer, about two of the clocke in the after-noone, and begun to salute us with thirty-two pieces of great Ordnance of their carriage, discharging through and through our Leaguer, till he made us to draw to our Armes, and stand in Battaile, horse and foote, under the walles, which did shelter us from his Cannon, where we stood till night, looking for his on-falling, requiting and honouring him now and [II-53] then with interchange of Cannon-Bullets, till it begun to grow darke, that he retired his Cannon to the body of his Armie, having lyen all night in Battaile, without being intrencht, though strongly fortified without him, with strong Guards, both of horse and foote, having his Crabbats and Dragoniers without them againe.

His Majestie having commanded out strong Horse-guards to watch without the Leaguer, I was commanded, as least worthy of a thousand, that night to watch without the Leaguer, with five hundred commanded Musketiers, which were ordained to lye in readinesse, betwixt the enemies Armie and the Leaguer, almost a Cannon-shot from our workes, getting orders from his Majestie himselfe, how I should keepe good watch, and how to behave my selfe, in case of the enemies pursute, and being come the length of the ground appointed for me to watch on, having consolidated the body of my Musketiers in the safest ground I could finde for them to stand on, their Armes rested, and in readinesse. First I caused set out my *Perdues* without my other Centries, not trusting the giving of an Alarum altogether to our horse Centries, and then to the end the enemy might not surprize us being sleeping, I ordained the halfe of our Musketiers to stand for two houres in readinesse, till the Centries were relieved, and then I suffered the other halfe to rest them, so long as the other did before; and thus orderly wee past over the nights watch, having had sundry naughtie Alarums in the night without continuance. Our dutie was to be the more strict, having received command of his Majestie, not to quit that ground, except the enemy by greatnesse of strength, would beate me from it, and then I should retire orderly skirmishing with the enemy, our faces to them still, and our Armes, giving fire on them till we came under our walles, so that, by that meanes the Leaguer would get time to be in readinesse to receive them.

By the breake of day, friend to valour and courage, the enemies Horseguards begun to skirmish with ours, who being stronger, made our Horsemen to give ground, the Commander of the Watch sent to me for a supply of fiftie Musketiers, which I accordingly did send, with a Lievetenant, giving him charge how to behave himselfe, who having a little skirmished with the enemies Dragoniers and Horsemen, was made to give ground also, and having commanded out a Captaine with fiftie Musketiers more, he was also repulsed, I wondring at their carriage, advanced to recognosce the bounds they were on, and spying an advantage of ground, I tooke out a hundred Musketiers, giving a Captaine charge to remaine by the remnant of my Musketiers, and putting a hedge betwixt us and the enemy, we advanced till we were in even line with them, and then giving a *Salve* amongst them, incontinent we made the enemy retire, so that our Horsemen did advance to their former stations: His Majestie having heard the service, ordained the Armie should be in readinesse, and coming forth from the Leaguer, accompanied with Generall Lievetenant *Bawtish*, and Baron *Tyvell*, where his Majestie begun to enquire of me, how all passed, which accordingly I related. But though his Majestie was pleased, yet he checked me for leaving of the Reserve to another, when I went on service, which I confesse was more suddenly done than wisely, and ever after, I promised to his Majestie, to avoide the like over-sight, though it succeeded well.

His Majestie incontinent, since they had tryed his guards, he would also try in earnest, what for Officers and Souldiers they did command, and to that [II-54] effect, his Majestie sent Orders to the Leaguer to command out eight hundred Horsemen of *Hagapells*, and a thousand Musketiers, with foure small Field-pieces of Cannon, with the five hundred Musketiers I commanded on the Poste, which all being set in order, his Majestie directed the Colonell of his Leefe

Regiment *Here Tyvell* to leade on the foote towards a Dorpe, that lay neere the enemies Armie, and his Majestie with Generall Lievetenant *Bawtish* commanded the Horse, taking the Cannon along with them, and comming neare the enemies Guards, consisting of a thousand Currassiers, having given fire with the Cannon amongst them, they charged furiously with the Horse in middest of the enemy, and putting them in disorder, they cut them downe from their Horses as they retired at the spurres, being still followed unto the body of their Armie: And our Musketiers falling up alike, discharging amongst them, the enemy at first in great feare was almost put in confusion, the most part of their Horsemen being abroad on Forrage, their Guards did stand to their Armes, till the Armie was drawne in Battaile, and their Horse spanned, or put before their Cannon; during which time our Souldiers continued in giving fire amongst them, till his Majestie did give orders for our Retreate, which we softly made, giving now and then faces about, skirmishing with Cannon and Musket, and then retiring againe orderly, being pressed thereto by their Cannon, giving fire after us, and their Horsemen calling up ours in our Reare, till at last we being retired the length of my Poste, our Cannon being able to reach them, they were made to make a stand, and I was ordained with my Musketiers to remain on our former Poste, his Majestie and the rest of the partie being retired within the Leaguer. Incontinent from our Batteries, our Cannon did play againe within the Leaguer, which continued the whole day, doing great hurt on both sides, where the whole time, I with my partie, did lie on our Poste, as betwixt the Devill and the deepe Sea, for sometimes our owne Cannon would light short, and grase over us, and so did the enemies also, where we had three shot with the Cannon, till I directed an Officer to our owne Batteries, acquainting them with our hurt, and desiring they should stell or plant their Cannon higher. In the morning also we lost on the skirmish, thirteene Souldiers, besides those were hurt. The day thus past, I was relieved at night, and the next morning, before day, Generall *Tilly* made a shew of on-falling on our Leaguer, by making all his Trumpets to sound, and his Drummes to beate, making a great noise, we being prepared to receive them. The morning being darke, with a cloudy mist, so that none could see, the enemy being retired with his Army, having broke up, at night, he marched towards *Tangermonde*, and the day being cleared up, his Majestie with a strong partie went forth to drive up their Reare, with six small pieces of Ordnance, even to the body of their maine Armie, which consisted then of twenty-six thousand men; while as we were not in the Leaguer, and at *Hagleberg*, twelve thousand men, foote and horse, till afterwards that the Feltmarshall *Gustavus Horne* did come from the *Oder* towards *Rateno*, with foure thousand complete Souldiers, and Generall *Tilly* having lyen some few dayes at *Tangermonde*, suffering daily losses by his Majesties parties; at length, through scarcitie of victualls, he was forced to march unto *Hall*, and in the *Saxons* Country, being made weaker by six thousand men than he came downe, having had to doe with the Invincible *Gustavus*, who still did out-shoot him out of his owne Bowe, having had the right hand of the LORD for his assistance. [II-55]

## The thirteenth Observation.

His Majestie wisely made choice of a fit place for his Leaguer, being commodious for transportation of victualls unto his Armie, without being in danger of his enemies. In like manner we see his Majesties wisedome in making his friends sure behinde him (*viz.*) the Duke of *Brandenburg*, the Dukes of *Pomeren* and *Machlenburg*, from whence his victualls and his supplies must needs come, and as his Leaguer was commodious for furnishing the Armie, so it was commodiously situated for defence against the enemy, the one halfe, or backe, being naturally defended by the course of the water running by; and on the other side, it was defended by the Towne, and by the helpe of the old Dike, which easily was fortified.

His Majesties wisedome also was seene, by keeping of his Souldiers still in Action, never suffering them to be idle (as a wise Generall ought to doe) for either they were imployed on marches, or lying still, in working, or in fighting by parties, or in grosse, as occasion offered: For this Generall knew well, that he was but the carrion of a man, and not a man, that did live idle, having in a living body but a dead minde.

Here also I did remarke and observe, *Homo homini quid inter est*: for we finde a great difference betwixt his Majesties welcoming of *Tilly* to *Werben*, and the Felt-marshall *Twifenbacke* his welcome made to his Majestie before *Francford* on the *Oder*; who never did present himselfe in the Fields, though almost as strong as we were: but here we finde the contrary, that notwithstanding of *Tillies* strength, being twenty-six thousand men, *Gustavus* was not afraid to have invaded his fore-Troopes with a weake partie, and did defeate them; shewing unto us the difference betwixt Commanders, by his owne valourous example, incouraging his little Armie before the enemies coming; he would not first meete his enemy with an Army, but having strengthened his Leaguer with *Baniers* Forces, and called in his weake Garrisons from danger, and then taking all victualls out of his enemies way, bringing it within his Leaguer, he then armed with courage and resolution, adventures to Rancounter his enemy with a partie, and having tryed them to their losse, he retired againe with credit, preparing his Leaguer, being strongly beset with men, Amunition and victualls, he was not afraid to be taken unawares, as the *French* were within *Philipsburg*, not being provided to oppose their enemies, for their sloath they were cruelly murthered. Teaching others, by their examples, not to trust too much in securitie, be the place never so strong, if they be left unto themselves, and grow carelesse, they must needs suffer under the Tyranny of their enemies.

Likewise his Majestie, not trusting to his owne wisedome, he did call his chiefe Officers to Counsell, asking them, what was to be done (as wise Commanders ought to doe) and finding them all by silence to relie on his Majesties will, giving Orders for all things that were to be done before their coming, he resolved to stand to it, being truely couragious, as he did not adventure rashly, without asking his Officers advice, knowing once their resolution agreeable to his owne, he was not inconsiderately afraid of his enemies strength, though mightie and strong, neither was he unprovided against their coming. [II-56]

His Majesties dexteritie of Command is seene here, by the order of his discipline, in giving good orders for watching: First he divided the Postes, and appointed what footmen or Briggad should watch on the serverall Posts, as they were severally fortified by themselves, to the end, no man might blame their owne worke, for insufficiency to hold out the enemy. As also he appointed severall Briggads of horse to second the Postes severally, every one knowing where to repaire in time of service: As also he did instruct them of the manner they were to fight, in resisting the enemies entry: As also in case of their entry, he did instruct both foote and horse, how and in what manner they should be repulsed againe, promising, according to his wonted Custome, to be a Companion both of their travells and dangers, and that he should never leave them, till first they should quit him, and that he would promise as he was a Royall King.

A worthy saying of a worthy King and Generall, whose prudence and wisedome in Command, was ever answerable to the dignitie of his majesticke person, that ought and should be endued with infinite vertues, since infinite were those things he had to foresee, and which are needfull for a man of his place. Infinite chances, and altogether divers, every moment were set before him, in so much, that *Argos Eyes* were too few for him, not onely in respect of the weight of his Command, but also in respect of the wit and prudence which was requisit for him.

All other commands belonging to a Souldier are so inferiour to this of a Generall, that almost they are nothing in respect of this, who amongst others his great gifts, he must know severly to command, and softly to beare with others. As also, he must learne patiently to give place to others contumacy, and he must not onely be powerfull to strengthen for his owne affaires, but also he must weaken his enemies, and chiefely, he must make warre by policy, without giving battell, or travell (as this wise Generall did deale twice with old *Tillie*) who was forced after a long march, having but visited him, and seene his orders, to retire againe, with the losse of many men, without any detriment or hurt at all to his Majesties owne litle Army, which he kept ever to the best, by preserving them from their enemies, and by supplying of them, as they became weake, so that their weaknesse could never be truly discerned. Who would not then admire the wisdome and for sight of this Generall, in preserving this little Army, at this time, for a second fitter occasion. Who ever then was so worthy of the honourable title of a Generall as he? For though he had bin no King, he was a brave warriour, and which is more, a good man, magnificent, wise, just, meeke, indued with learning, and the gift of tongues, and as he had strength of body, and a manlike stature; he had also the ornaments of the minde, fitting a brave Commander: he knew how to dally, and weary an Army led by such an old Generall as *Tillie* was: for though he did vaunt, he had beaten two Kings before, in an open field, the third King made him for all his experience and old yeares, to be thought but a child againe, having made him traverse with his Army, before in the winter, from *Rapin* to new *Brandenburg*, and backe againe to *Madeburg*, finding the King did lie in suerty at *Swede*, till he was gone, and then tooke in both *Francford* and *Lanseberg*: and againe, he made him retire from *During* to *Verben*, for a visit, and then forced him to returne againe to *Saxonie*, with the losse of six thousand men, without effecting any thing for his coming, not the least advantage; undo- [II-57] ing himselfe and his Army by the seasons, sometimes with the extremity of cold; in the middest of winter, and at his time, he made him march in the middest of the dogge dayes, for lacke of victualls, and his Majesty having discouraged this old Generall and his Army, he thought then, it was fit time to follow, and to search him out, till he was made to fight.

This resolute King did not sleepe long, in suffering *Tillies* bravade made before *Verben* to be unrepayed, having the next morning hunted, and chased his courrasiers with a few number of *Haggapells*, to the middest of their Army, having with honour retired againe, he thought *Tillie* was ingaged to storme his Leaguer, in reveng, but all could not winde or draw him to it: But was forced through hunger to retire, all provisions being taken out of his way, for his Majesty knew well, when they should be oppressed with hunger at their coming, they could thinke on no generous exploit: for oftimes an Army is lost sooner by hunger then by fighting, and hunger it selfe is crueller a great deale, then the sword; For to hunger, and to fight valiantly, doth not agree with nature, and in an Army hunger is more intolerable then the thundering of Cannon and Musket: Armes doe resist Armes, but to resist hunger, no Fort, no Strength, no Moate or Fossie is able to doe it.

To conclude then this my observation, when God is with us, all things succeede well unto us, as did with this fortunate King *Gustavus*, who I knew did feare God; and I perswade my selfe, by his example, and after him, by the example of another *Gustavus*, Felt-marshall *Horne* (who truly feared God in his calling without pride or ostentation) many others under them following their examples (though Souldiers) did the like. Therefore no wonder, that they and those who followed them, were happy in their enterprises, having had such Leaders: for that is most sure and infallible, where most feare of God is, and true piety, there is most happinesse; and this piety is enought to save Princes. And on the contrary, without her, Armies can doe nothing, Horse or strength of man, gold or money can doe nothing. Let us then following the example of this King, who was Godly, seek to the King of Kings for his Kingdome, & the righteousnesse thereof, & then surely all other things will goe well with us, as it did with our Master and Leader.

---

*The fourteenth Duty discharged of our March from* Wirben
*to our Leaguer at* Wittenberg.

The certainty of General *Tillies* march with the Army unto *Saxonie* being come unto his Majesty, and that he was to joyne at *Leipsigh*, with the forces were come to him from the upper Circles of *Germany*, as also out of *Italy*; which being joyned together, his resolution was to spoile the Dukes country, or to force him to turne *Emperialist*: which being understood by his Majesty, his Majesty very wisely resolved to prevent him in this, as he had done in his former intentions: And there- [II-58] fore with diligence, bringing together the whole strength of his horses, with two thousand Dragoniers, he marched towards *Rattino*, where Felt-marshall *Horne* did lie, with a part of the Army, to whom he gave orders to be in readinesse, on his first advertisment, as also, he appointed Generall *Bannier*, to recollect and bring up such forces as were levied in the Markes of *Brandenburg*, and to be in readinesse at this Majesties appointment for a march.

In like manner his Majesty did leave the care of commanding the Leaguer at *Werben* to Generall Lievetenant *Bautis*, so farre as concerned the command of the *Cavalerie*, and Sr. *Iohn Hepburne* was ordained to command, and to care for the foote, which being done, his Majesty continued his march towards the passe of *Wittenberg*, for to meete Felt-marshall *Arnham*, who was appointed by the Duke of *Saxon* to treate with his Majesty, for confirming of the Aliance and confederacy formerly treated betwixt his Majesty and the Duke, in time of the Treaty, his Majesty being in hopes, of a happy conclusion, he did direct orders to the Felt-marshall *Horne*, and to Generall Lievetenant *Bawtis*, to breake up with both their forces of horse and foote, and to march towards *Wittenberg*. Likewise order was sent to Colonell *Cagge* to breake up from *Haggleberg*, with his Regiment, and with Colonell *Monro* of *Fowles* his Regiment, for to joyne both with the Army, on their march (which continued orderly to the Randezvouz appointed to meete with the Felt-marshall being within foure miles of *Wittenberg*, where we did come together, and immediatly the Felt-marshall did put the Army in good order of Battell, horse foote and Artillery; The baggage also was placed and directed to march a part from the Army.

On Sunday the twenty eight of August 1631. we continue our march towards *Wittenberg*, where a mile from the Towne we rejoyced at the sight of our Master and Leader, *Gustavus* the invincible, who with the party did joyne with us, and immediatly he tooke the paines to bring that Royall Army in order of Battaile, whereon the sudden, his Majesties dexterity in command did appeare to the great contentment of the whole Army, and marching a while in Battell order, having halted neere the part, where our Leaguer was appointed to be, we were commanded to incampe for that night on the field, as we stood in Battell. The next morning the Leaguer being divided in severall quarters, and our Quarter-masters, and Furriers, having made their right designation of every Regiments quarter, and having divided their quarters proportionally amongst the companies, they being ready, every Briggad whose quarters were first design'd, marched unto the Leaguer, possessing themselves with their Quarters, they begun orderly to place their Colours and their watch; then every particular Cameradship did strive, who could best provide themselves of convenient lodgings, where we were to rest for a weeke.

Lievetenant Colonell *Iohn Munro*, being come before his Colonell from *Scotland* with a company, he was made to march from *Statin* to *Werben*, and from thence to *Wittenberg*, being then ordained to march with our Regiment, with whom did come from *Scotland, Robert Munro, Kilternes* sonne, out of love, to see his friends, who contracting a feaver at *Wittenberg*, died there, and was honourably buried. [II-59]

## The fourteenth Observation.

His Majesty, like a wise and prudent Generall, we see would not sturre from his Leaguer at *Werben*, till first he was made certaine by good intelligence, of his enemies designe, counsell and resolution, which being well knowne, his Majesty then resolved, by preventing of them, to make them unprofitable: and truly the discoverer of such, plots and counsells ought to be well rewarded, seeing by the discovery of our enemies designes, we were made to resist his intended evill against us. Happy therefore are those intelligences that come in time, and there ought to be no delay used, in taking that counsell that cannot be praised, till the turne be done, and things once deliberated should be quickly done, and though he be a brave fellow, who doubts in advising, yet in action he ought to be confident, as *Gustavus* was, getting intelligence of the enemies designe with celerity, he tooke his horses and Dragoniers with him, and leaving his foote and Cannon, he advanced to the passe of *Wittenberg*, for to prevent *Tillie*, who was striving to make the Duke turne *Emperialist*, but *Gustavus* wisely taking the ball at the right rebound, he did turne the Duke, by Gods providence, both soule and body good *Swede*. Where cleerely we may see the Lords powerfull hand and providence in this, as in all humane affaires, suffering things sometimes to take delayes. Notwithstanding of mans instant urging, the Lord deferres to his appointed time, that the glory may be given unto himselfe alone, and not to mans wit or policy. For as the Rudder in a ship doth with a little motion governe all the ship: even so, God the director and governour of the world, doth move the whole, himselfe not sturring. And as there is one God in the heavens, that governes all the frame of the earth: so the Lord hath his Substitutes on earth, whom he hath made above their fellowes in judgment, and heroike vertues, yet he himselfe keepes the Prerogative above them all in commanding them, to let us see, that all the event, and conclusions of Kings projects and intentions, be they never so powerfull, availe nothing to the furtherance of their intentions, till they first acknowledge them to come from the fountaine God, that distributes them againe on his servants, when he pleaseth, that they may learne to glorify him, and not their owne wit or policy, which is so much as nothing, till he consent. This God then, the author and doer of all things (and of this union and confederacy) that eternall (I say) and provident Godhead, that governes the motions of the Heavens, the starres variable courses, the Elementary changes, all things above, and beneath the earth, ruling and governing, spreading, where he pleaseth his light beames from his eternity, and with a winke, piercing into the Bowells of heaven, earth and sea, he doth not only goe before them, but in them, seeing and knowing all, and governing them all, his will is so, that he converts our noisomnesse unto health, and our sinnes being ill, he turnes them unto our good: that eternall Governour triumphs in the Chariot of his providence, and if willingly we follow him, then freely, as his Souldiers, if unwillingly, we must follow him, as captives and servants. We see then here by Gods providence, the Duke was contented to joyne his Army with the Kings Majesties Army being come to *Wittenberg*, to goe *Conjunctis viribus* against their common enemy the house of *Austria,* and the Catholique league.

[II-60]

It had beene for *Madeburg* this union had beene sooner concluded, but the Lord would not have it, seeing their punishments, by Generall *Tillies* Army (their scourge) was decreed long before. But now the Duke of *Saxon* terrified by their example, thinkes it better to prevent such another wound, by joyning with his Majesty, being made warie by others fall: for it is better late to thrive then never, and it is better to prevent evill, then to suffer; and it was better for the Duke of *Saxon*, to blush in time, then out of time to grow pale; for now being taken at the rebound, *Tillies* Army being at *Lipsigh*, seing his own house on fire to be relieved, he offers his service to his Majesty, damning himselfe, soule and body, if ever he will forsake his Majesty and his Crowne, if then he would but helpe him to beate the enemy out of his country againe: So that he, which could not be tied with one knot before, is now hard tied by foure great points, which he was made to condescend unto, on his honour and credit, to have bin kept unviolable. And his Majesty getting him once thus bound, the way to make him sure, was to make him fight, that having dipped his hands once in the bould of his enemies, he was not suddenly to be clensed, and this was the manner to tye him harder, then the custome was of old amongst the *Germans,* who were wont (when they entred in confederacy) to draw bloud in a Goblet of both their browes, and drinke of it mutually, for the more strict observance of their fidelities to each others. But shortly after this confederacy was made, much *German* bloud was drawne, and of other strangers bloud, to make the tie so much the harder, and before the tie was broke, his Majesties bloud was shed, to the perpetuall disgrace of him, that after his Majesties death, forgetting his honour and credit, did violate his confederacy made with the crowne, as with the King our Master, of never dying memory.

---

*The fifteenth Dutie discharged of our March over the*
Elve *at* Wittenberg *to* Diben.

The Conjunction agreed upon betwixt his Majestie and the Duke of *Saxon*, all things sealed and subscribed, his Majestie gave Orders to breake up with the Armie, and to crosse the *Elve,* over the bridge at *Wittenberg*, for to joyne with the Dukes Armie; the orders were obeyed with great contentment, and entering into *Saxonie*, we quartered the first night not farre from *Diben*, the place appointed for our Randez-vouz; the next morning we marched thither, and were drawne up in battaile on the Fields, where in the after-noone the Dukes Armie arrived, being drawne up in battaile within Cannon shot of us, the whole Officers of our Armie, were commanded to be in readinesse on horse-backe, to convey his Majestie for to welcome the Duke and his Armie, which for pleasing the eye, was the most complete little Armie, for personages of men, comely statures, well armed, and well arraide, that ever mine eyes did looke on, whose Officers did all looke, as if they were going in their best Apparell and Armes to be painted; where nothing was defective the eye could behold. [II-61]

This shew seene by his Majestie and his Officers; his Majestie returning; the Duke with his followers did convey his Majestie to the sight of our Armie, which being called to their Armes, having lyen over-night on a parcell of plowd ground, they were so dusty, they looked out like Kitchin-servants, with their uncleanely Rags, within which were hidden couragious hearts, being old experimented blades, which for the most part, had overcome by custome the toyle of warres; yet these *Saxons* gentry, in their bravery, did judge of us and ours, according to our out-sides, thinking but little of us; neverthelesse, we thought not the worse of our selves. The ceremony past, we were all remitted to take rest for that night in our former quarters: the next morning, by breake of day, we were called up to march, where both our Armies were ordained to march on severall streets; one Randezvouz being appointed for us at night, within a mile and a halfe of the enemies Armie; where being come to our Randezvouz by foure a clocke in the after-noone, and drawn up in battaile; our guards drawne out to watch, were directed to their Postes, and then we resting by our Armes, as we were in battaile, we slept lying where we stood, that in case of a Alarum, we were not to be found in disorder, being ready to fight where we stood.

Immediately after the Armie was setled in Quarters, newes was come to his Majestie in poste, that the Castle of *Leipsigh* was given over by accord to the enemy: As also that Generall *Tilly* with a mightie and strong Armie, was come a mile from *Leipsigh*, and was preparing for a Fight: which newes did no wayes alter his Majesties countenance, being resolved before for the like, to have sought him to Fight. So that being both willing, and so neare, it was easie bringing them together; our baggage was appointed to goe backe to *Diben*, our horse and foote watches were strengthened, and we were in readinesse, and refreshing first our bodies with victualls, we slept till the next morning.

### The fifteenth Observation.

Nothing earthly is more pleasant to be seene, than to see brethren in Christ conjoyned against Gods enemies, for advancing of the glory of God, in promoting of his Gospell, and for setting at libertie those poore soules (our brethren in Christ) that were kept long under the yoke and tyranny of the house of *Austria*, and the Catholique League their mortall enemies. Who would not then, for their liberties that were banished, (that they might one day retire to their possessions) who would not, I say, be willing, yea more, who would not rejoyce (having such a Leader as *Gustavus* was) to hazard their lives for the weale of their publique, yea more, for the promoting of *Christs Gospell?* Surely for mine owne part, I was most willing and wished long to have seene a day, wherein I might hazard my life in this quarrell, in being one of the number of Fighters, before I did come at it; for many reasons, but especially for the libertie of the daughter of our dread *Soveraigne*, the distressed *Queene* of *Bohemia*, and her Princely Issue; next, for the libertie of our distressed brethen in Christ; and thirdly, for my better instruction, in the profession of Armes, which is my calling; for having before seene many occurrences that did belong to our Calling, I longed to have seene a Battaile fought in the Fields in such a quarrell, being led by such a magnanimous King, of Heroick spirit, that had much more on [II-62] hazard that day than I had, who had onely to hazard but my life and credit; while as he a King was to hazard his life, his Crowne, his reputation, and all for strangers.

Having thus the night before meditated, I found a motion rejoycing my heart, in making mee resolute, to fight in this Cause; being tied in dutie, not onely for my person, but also tied to give Counsaile and direction, as the Lord did enable mee, by giving instruction, good heartning, and good example to others, who were bound to follow mee, as I was bound to follow my Master the King; seeing the Lord by his providence, had brought mee thither, with a number of my friends to follow, and obey him, as they were bound by oath to obey mee. And then I thought with my selfe, after I had awaked from sleepe, going on to march, that my life was much like a tale, and that we should not care how long this life of ours should last, but that wee should bee carefull, how well our life should bee acted: for it is no matter, where wee end, if wee end well; and we should not aske, when, or where, but we ought to bee ever mindfull, how wee are prepared going to fight. Nature did beget us miserable, we live over-burthened with cares, and like a flower, wee vanish soone away, and dye. Our hunting then here, and our care should bee onely for a perpetuall good name to leave behind us, that so being absent wee are present, and being dead, wee live.

---

### *The sixteenth Duty discharged on our Fight at* Leipsigh.

As the Larke begunne to peepe, the seventh of September 1631. having stood all night in battaile a mile from *Tillies* Armie, in the morning, the Trumpets sound to horse, the Drummes calling to March, being at our Armes, and in readinesse, having before meditated in the night, and resolved with our Consciences; we begunne the morning with offering our soules and bodies, as living Sacrifices unto God, with Confession of our sinnes, lifting up our hearts and hands to Heaven, we begged for reconciliation in Christ, by our publique prayers, and secret sighes, and groanes; recommending our selves, the successe, and event of the day unto God, our Father in Christ, which done by us all, we marched forwards in Gods name a little, and then halted againe, till the whole

Armie; both the *Dukes*, and Ours, were put in good Order: our Armie marching
on the right hand, and the Dukes on the left, our commanded Musketeres
marching in the *Van-Guarde*, being in one bodie before the Armie consisting of
three Regiments, whereof two of *Scotts*, and one *Dutch*, *all Musketieres*, led by
three *Scotts Colonels*, *men of valour* and courage, fit for the Commaund
concredited unto them, being made choice of, as men, that could fight
*Exemplarie* to others: (*viz.*) *Sir Iames Ramsey*, called the Blacke, *Sir Iohn
Hamilton*, and *Robert Monro* Baron of *Fowles*; we marched thus, both the
Armies in Battaile, Horse, foote, and Artillerie, till about nine of the Clocke in
the morning, wee halted halfe a mile distant from the *Emperiall* Armie, that were
attending us in Battaile; consisting of fortie foure thousand men, horse, and
foote, our Armie, consisting of thirtie thousand men, whereof, to my judgement,
His Majesties Ar- [II-63] mie; were eight thousand foote, and seven thousand
horse; The *Duke* also, would be eleven thousand foote, and foure thousand
horse; having refreshed ourselves with victuals, leaving our Coaches behind us.
The whole Armie did get greene Branches on their heads; and the word was
given, God with us: a little short speech made by His Majestie, being in order of
Battaile, we marched towards the enemie, who had taken the advantage of the
ground, having placed his Armie on a place called *Gods* Acre; where their
Generall did make choice of the ground most advantagious for his foote,
Artillerie, and horses; he also did beset the *Dorpes,* that invironed the ground,
which was left for us, with Dragoniers and Crabbats: to incomber our wings by
their evill Neighbourhood: yet, notwithstanding of all the advantages hee had of
Ground, Wind, and Sunne; our *magnanimious* King and Leader; under God,
inferiour to no Generall we ever reade of, for wisedome, courage, dexteritie, and
good Conduct, he was not dejected; but with magnanimitie, and Christian
resolution, having recommended himselfe, his Armie, and successe to God, the
Director of men and Angells; able to give victory with few against many; He
ordered his Armie, and directed every supreame Officer of the Field, on their
particular charge and stations committed unto them, for that day: As also he
acquainted them severally, of the forme he was to fight unto, and he appointed
Plottons of Musketiers, by fifties, which were commanded by sufficient Officers
to attend on severall Regiments of horse; and he instructed the Officers how to
behave themselves in discharging their duties on service. Likewise he directed
the Officers belonging to the Artillery, how to carry themselves; which orderly
done, the commanded Musketiers were directed to their stand where to fight; his
Majestie then led up the foure Briggads of foote, which were appointed to be the
Battaile of the Armie, with a distance betwixt every Briggad, that a Regiment of
horse might march out in grosse betwixt the Briggads, all foure being in one
front, having their Ordnance planted before every Briggad, being foure pieces of
great Cannon, and eight small; whereof, foure stood before the Colours, that
were the Battaile of the Briggad, with Amunition and Constables to attend them;
on the right hand Pikes, before the Colours were the other foure pieces of
Cannon, with Amunition and Constables conforme; and on the left wing of Pikes
and Colours were placed the other foure pieces of Cannon, as we said before.

Behinde these foure Briggads were drawne up the three Briggads of Reserve, with their Artillery before them, standing at a proportionable distance behinde the other foure Briggads, with the like distance betwixt them, as was betwixt the Briggads of the Battaile.

The Briggads of horse which had Plottons of Musketiers to attend them, were placed on the right and left wings of the foote, and some were placed betwixt the Battaile of foote and the Reserve, to second the foote as neede were; other Briggads of horse were drawne up behinde the Reserve of the foote Briggads.

The Felt-marshall *Horne,* Generall *Banier,* and Lievetenant Generall *Bawtish* were commanded to over-see the Horsemen, his Majestie, the Baron *Tyvell,* and Grave *Neles,* were to command the Battaile of foote; Sir *Iames Ramsey,* as eldest Colonell, had the command of the fore-Troopes, or commanded Musketiers; and Sir *Iohn Hepburne,* as eldest Colonell, commanded the three Briggads of Reserve: Our Armie thus ordered, the Duke of *Saxon* [II-64] and his Feltmarshall *Arnhem,* having ordered their Armie (whereof I was not particularly inquisitive of the manner) they were ordained to draw up on our left hand, and being both in one front thus ordered, we marched in Battaile a little, and then halted againe, till his Majestie had commanded out some commanded Horsemen, on the wings of the Armie, a large distance from the body, to scoure the fields of the Crabbats; we marched againe in order of Battaile, with Trumpets sounding, Drummes beating, and Colours advanced and flying, till we came within reach of Cannon to our enemies Armie; then the magnifick and magnanimous *Gustavus* the Invincible, leads up the Briggads of horse one after another to their ground, with their Plottons of shot to attend them: As also he led up the Briggads of foote one after another to their ground, during which time we were drawne up according to our former plot, the enemy was thundering amongst us, with the noise, and roaring whisling and flying of Cannon Bullets; where you may imagine the hurt was great; the sound of such musick being scarce worth the hearing, though martiall I confesse, yet, if you can have so much patience, with farre lesse danger, to reade this dutie to an end, you shall finde the musicke well paide; but with such Coyne, that the players would not stay for a world to receive the last of it, being over-joyed in their flying.

By twelve of the Clock on wednesday the seventh of *September,* in despight of the fury of the enemies Cannon, and of his advantages taken, they were drawne up in even front with the enemy, and then our Cannon begun to roare, great and small, paying the enemy with the like coyne, which thundering continued alike on both sides for two houres and an halfe, during which time, our Battailes of horse and foote stood firme like a wall, the Cannon now and then making great breaches amongst us, which was diligently looked unto, on all hands, by the diligence of Officers in filling up the voide parts, and in setting aside of the wounded towards Chirurgians, every Officer standing firme, over-seeing their Commands in their owne stations, succeeding one another as occasion offered.

By halfe three, our Cannon a little ceasing, the Horsemen on both wings charged furiously one another, our Horsemen with a resolution, abiding unloosing a Pistoll, till the enemy had discharged first, and then at a neere distance our Musketiers meeting them with a *Salve*; then our horsemen discharged their Pistolls, and then charged through them with swords; and at their returne the Musketiers were ready againe to give the second *Salve* of Musket amongst them; the enemy thus valiantly resisted by our Horsemen, and cruelly plagued by our Plottons of Musketiers; you may imagine, how soone he would be discouraged after charging twice in this manner, and repulsed.

Our Horsemen of the right wing of Finnes and Haggapells, led by the valourous Feltmarshall *Horne*, finding the enemies Horsemen out of Order, with resolution he charged the enemies left wing, forcing them to retire disorderly on their battailes of foote, which caused disorder among the foote, who were forced then to fall to the right hand; our Horsemen retiring, his Majestie seeing the enemy in disorder, played with Ordnance amongst them, during which time, the force of the enemies Battailes falls on the Duke of *Saxon*, charging with Horse first in the middest of the Battailes, and then the foote giving two *Salves* of Musket amongst them, they were put to the Rout, horse and foote, and the enemy following them cryed *Victoria*, as if the [II-65] day had beene wonne, triumphing before the victory; But our Horsemen charging the remnant of their horse and foote, where their Generall stood, they were made to retire in disorder to the other hand towards *Leipsigh*; our Armie of foote standing firme, not having loosed one Musket; the smoake being great, by the rising of the dust, for a long time we were not able to see about us; but being cleared up, we did see on the left hand of our reserve two great Battailes of foote, which we imagined to have beene *Saxons*, that were forced to give ground; having heard the service, though not seene it, we found they were enemies, being a great deale neerer than the *Saxons* were: His Majestie having sent Baron *Tyvell* to know the certaintie, coming before our Briggad, I certified him they were enemies, and he returning towards his Majestie, was shot dead; his Majestie coming by, gave direction to Colonell *Hepburne*, to cause the Briggads on his right and left wing to wheele, and then to charge the enemy, the Orders given, his Majestie retired, promising to bring succours unto us.

The enemies Battaile standing firme, looking on us at a neere distance, and seeing the other Briggads and ours wheeleing about, making front unto them, they were prepared with a firme resolution to receive us with a salve of Cannon and Muskets; but our small Ordinance being twice discharged amongst them, and before we stirred, we charged them with a salve of muskets, which was repaied, and incontinent our Briggad advancing unto them with push of pike, putting one of their battailes in disorder, fell on the execution, so that they were put to the route.

I having commanded the right wing of our musketiers, being my Lord of *Rhees* and *Lumsdells*, we advanced on the other body of the enemies, which defended their Cannon, and beating them from their Cannon, we were masters of their Cannon, and consequently of the field, but the smoake being great, the dust being raised, we were as in a darke cloude, not seeing the halfe of our actions, much lesse discerning, either the way of our enemies, or yet the rest of our Briggads: whereupon, having a drummer by me, I caused him beate the *Scots* march, till it cleered up, which recollected our friends unto us, and dispersed our enemies being overcome; so that the Briggad coming together, such as were alive missed their dead and hurt Camerades.

Colonell *Lumsdell* was hurt at the first, and Lievetenant Colonell *Musten* also, with divers other Ensignes were hurt and killed, and sundry Colours were missing for that night; which were found the next day; The enemy thus fled, our horsemen were pursuing hard, till it was darke, and the blew Briggad, and the commanded musketiers were sent by his Majesty to helpe us, but before their coming, the victory and the credit of the day, as being last ingaged, was ascribed to our Briggad, being the reserve, were thanked by his Majesty for their service, in publique audience, and in view of the whole Army, we were promised to be rewarded.

The Battaile thus happily wonne, his Majesty did principally under God ascribe the glory of the victory to the *Sweds*, and *Fynnes* horsemen, who were led by the valorous Felt-marshall *Gustavus Horne*; For though the *Dutch* horsemen did behave themselves valorously divers times that day; yet it was not their fortune to have done the charge, which did put the enemy to flight, and though there were brave Briggads of *Sweds* and *Dutch* in the field, yet it was the *Scots* Briggads fortune to have gotten the praise for [II-66] the foote service: and not without cause, having behaved themselves well, being led and conducted by an expert Cavalier and fortunat, the valiant *Hepburne*, being followed by Colonell *Lumsdell*, Lievetenant Colonell *Musten,* Major *Monypenney*, Major *Sinclaire*, and Lievetenant Colonell *Iohn Munro*, with divers others Cavaliers of valour, experience and of conduct, who thereafter were suddainely advanced unto higher charges. The victory being ours, we incamped over night on the place of Battaile, the living merry and rejoycing, though without drinke at the night-wake of their dead Camerades and friends, lying then on the ground in the bed of honour, being glad the Lord had prolonged their dayes for to discharge the last honourable duty, in burying of their Comerades.

Our bone-fiers were made of the enemies Amunition waggons, and Pikes left, for want of good fellowes to use them; and all this night our brave Camerades, the *Saxons* were making use of their heeles in flying, thinking all was lost, they made booty of our waggons and goods, too good a recompence for Cullions that had left their Duke, betrayed their country and the good cause, when as strangers were hazarding their lives for their freedomes.

Our losse this day with the *Saxons*, did not exceede three thousand men, which for the most part were killed by the enemies Cannon: of principall Officers we lost a number, and chiefely our horsemen; as Colonell *Collenbagh*, Colonell *Hall*, and *Addergest*; and of the foote Colonells, the Barron *Tivell*, being all of them brave and valorous gentlemen, we lost also foure Lievetenant Colonells, together with a number of Rutmasters, Captaines, Lievetenants and Ensignes.

Of the *Saxons* were lost five Colonells, three Lievetenant Colonells, with divers Rut-masters and Captaines, and of inferiours Officers many.

To the enemy were lost on the field neere eight thousand, besides Officers of note, such as the Felt-marshall *Fustenberg*: the Duke of *Holsten*, the Count of *Shomeberg*; old Generall *Tillie* hurt and almost taken; a number of other Officers of the Field were killed, and taken prisoners. They lost also thirty two peeces of Cannon, with three score waggons of Amunition, and their Generall, and *Papingham* were chased towards *Hall*, and from thence were forced with a small convoy to take their flight for refuge to *Hamell* on the *Waser*.

### The sixteenth Observation.

First then we see here the goodnesse that followes on that laudable and Christian custome, used by those, that doe first begin the workes of their calling with their true humiliation to God by prayers, in acknowledging their sinnes and unworthinesse, and in renouncing trust or confidence in any thing but in God alone, knowing their owne wisdome, strength and valour to be of no moment, without the speciall aide and assistance of the Almighty and powerfull God; who alone can teach our fingers to fight, giving victory with few as with many.

And therefore it was that this Magnanimous and religious warriour, with his whole Army, publiquely did call on the Lord, praying for his assistance against his enemies, and for a happy event of the day, before he begun to set his Army to worke against their enemies, the enemies of God and the [II-67] true Catholique and Apostolique faith; which they had endeavoured to subvert with the professors of the truth, to hold up and maintaine the man of sinne and his erronious doctrine, by the power of the house of *Austria*, and of the Catholique League. We see then, this duty being religiously and piously discharged by his Majesty and his Army, the fruite was answerable to their desire: having obtained victory over our enemies by the good command of his Majesty, and the ready obedience, dexterity and valour of his Majesties supreme Officers of the field; who in all charges did direct those under them to the ready discharge of their duties, every one of the whole united body of the Army following the example of their head and Leader, the magnifick amd Magnanimous King, for to abate and lay downe the pride of the house of *Austria*; and for to teare and strip naked that old proud and Ambitious Generall *Tillie* of his former glory and honour; for having bragged and vainely gloried, he had conquered two Kings before: here now the Captaine of Kings, and King of Captaines doth victoriously Triumph, having robbed him of glory, and clipped the wings of the Empire with his little Royall Army.

Likewise, next unto God, a second helpe unto this glorious victory, was the great execution made by his Majesties Cannon; and though ever before, *Tillie* did pride himselfe all his life time in the course of the warres, in his dexterity of his great Cannon; here from a Master he was turned againe unto a prentice, being cunningly over shot with Cannon, so that his Cannon, and three score waggons belonging thereto, were taken from him by *Gustavus* the first, and most valiant

Captaine of the world, with the helpe of the nation which was never conquered by any forraine enemy, the invincible *Scots*; whose prayers to God were more effectuall through Christ, then theirs through the intercession of Saints.

The third cause of this glorious victory, was his Majesties good discipline houlden over the Army, horse and foote, not suffering them without great and extraordinay punishment, to oppresse the poore, which made them cry for a blessing to his Majesty and his Army.

The enemy on the contrary provoked the wrath of God against themselves and their Army, for their cruelty used in torturing the poore, and forcing their monies from them did  further their punishment, and his Majesties glorious victory.

The fourth helpe to this victory, was the plottons of Musketiers, his Majesty had very wisely ordained to attend the horsemen, being a great safety for them, and a great prejudice to the enemy, the Musket ball carrying and piercing farther then the Pistolet: As also the great celerity used in charging and discharging of our small cannon brought the enemies battaile in disorder, to the furtherance of this victory: As also the extraordinary care and diligence, that was used by his Majesty, and his Officers, in seeing and foreseeing of the defects and disorders amongst our selves; which being suddenly remedied, was also a helpe to this victory: And last of all, the invincible courage and resolution both of Officers and souldiers in standing firme, Notwithstanding of the fury of their enemies; and which was more, they were no wayes dismayed or discouraged at the flight of the *Saxons*, but thought it their greatest glory to be victorious without them; standing resolutly till they saw the backe of their enemies, the undoubted tokens of their glorious victory. [II-68]

His Majesties Army on this service as at all times, might be called truely valorous, for those are called valorous Captaines, and holden for such; that when their Camerades are flying, they notably with hands, voice and wounds (if wounded) sustaine the fight, doing at once the duty of Souldiers and of Captaines, by those meanes, bringing backe, and restoring the suspected losse unto victory, for their credits.  For as ignorance doth easily precipitate men into danger, even so to a generous heart nothing can seeme difficult or fearefull, being once resolved to fall on, though towards the mouth of the cannon; but before resolution flesh and blood have their owne disturbances, even in the most valorous: and valorous men, as they feare nothing after resolution; so they disdaine nothing entering upon danger.

Here also the resolution of our horsemen on this service was praise worthy, seeing they never loosed a pistoll at the enemy, till first they had discharged theirs: for the enemy being fierce and furious; while ours were stout and slow, the enemy was made weary when ours were fresh, which made the enemy being weary, and charged with a fresh succour, being once set on going, they followed hard their victory, not giving them time to breath, or recollect their forces againe, till they were utterly defeated; that the night and darkenesse was their best safety. For I did observe here, that the duty of valiant Commanders is to know not onely the nature of their enemies, but also their spirit, and wherein they pride them most: we ought to make our best use for to deceive and out-shoote them in those same things wherein they delight and trust most unto. Likewise this day I did observe, that as the inticement to great travell and paines is glory and honour, even so courage and constant valour may be attained unto by exercise in warre, and frequenting of dangers, wherein Souldiers, Companies or Briggads are used with, and made once familiar with that cruell and vehement, horrible and terrible fellow, death, having seene many dead bodies before; and being inured to bloud, such Souldiers will stand to it and desire to fight, when ignorant Novices (as the *Saxons* were) are afraid of death; who seeking their safety in flying, they were miserably cut downe by their enemies.

I did likewise observe this day, that it is not the multitude doth the turne, but under God it is good command, good conduct, art, and skill in handling the weapons of our warfare, and in taking the occasions in time that beget victory.

Therefore he that would labour an Army as *Gustavus* did, he will finde fruite, yea even the best that groweth under the Empire, good Rhenish and Necker wine, not onely for himselfe, but for the meanest Souldier, and that unto excesse, which hath made me sometimes complaine more of the plenty our Souldiers had after this victory, through the abuse of it, then ever I did before for any penury. He is therefore in my opinion farre deceived that thinkes that it is the time or number of yeares that makes a good Souldier; no, no, it is rather the continuall meditation of exercise and practise; for Souldiers should be in running, not in running away, as horsemen ordinarily doe. But on the contrary, that with the greater Force they may be able to invade their enemies, as our Briggad did here, who seeing the enemy in confusion with their Pikes charged ranne fiercely upon them till they were beaten. And surely I doe thinke no man so ignorant, but knowes that more come to be good Souldiers by exercise and frequency of danger and use, then by nature: and he is not a man that will not sweat, nor couragi- [II-69] ous, that eschewes danger, when hee should fight, as our *Camerades* did the painted Souldiers the *Saxons*, with their plumed Officers; which feathers served them I thinke in their flight, for tokens rather to cut them downe by, than for their safeties.

Courage should growe by frequencie of danger, the onely way, in my opinion, to feare nothing, and then he may be called stout, before the maker of a quarrell at home, who once drawing a sworde, when he knowes of twentie Parters, or Redders, is there called stout, but when he comes abroad to the warres, at first, the thundering of the Cannon and Musket roaring in his eares makes him sicke, before he come neere danger, as I have known some: but where vertue and honour doth growe, there labour, exercise and danger is needfull: *Nam ardua & difficilis virtutis est via, tamen, nil tam difficile est, quod non solertia vincat*; And death it selfe is never bitter, when it leaves an immortall, and glorious name behind it; *Vivit enim post funera virtus: & animus moderatis laboribus adjuvatur, immoderatis autem abluitur.*

To conclude then this observation, we see that as courage in warres is much worth, for obtaining of victory: so is the wisedome of a Generall or Leader in warres, as *Gustavus* was, of so much worth, even in the obtaining of this victory, that the spirit of him alone, and skill in direction, was better than thousands of armed men. The enemy being in this Battaile neere twelve thousand men, at least, stronger than we; yet *Gustavus* alone on our side was better, and of more worth to us, then that multitude to our enemies.

Wee see then here, that no greater joy or pleasure can come to mortall man, than to overcome his enemy by Armes: and we see also, that the event of Battaile doth not consist in number of Fighters, but, under God, in the order and courage used in Battaile.

Here also we see, that a good cause and a good quarrell is ever to be had, if thou wouldest have victory over thine enemies; and who would wish a better quarrell then we fought for, this day being for the reliefe of our distressed friends, and for the libertie and promotion of Christs Gospell; or who would not hazard, in such a quarrell; especially against such enemies, that had banished the daughter of our dread Soveraigne, and her royall Issue, from her Kingdome and Dignities?

O would to God I had once such a Leader againe to fight such an other day; in this old quarrell! And though I died standing, I should be perswaded, I died well; and I wish, that as wee have received the light of truth happily, that fought in that quarrell: even so we may happen to restore that light againe pleasantly, that as wee did overcome that day our carnall enemies; even so we may overcome in our last fight our spirituall enemies; that after death we may be crowned with immortall Glorie.

---

### The seventeenth Dutie discharged of our March from the place of Battaile towards Leipsigh.

Having merrily past the night on the place of Battaile, with varietle of pleasant discourses of our severall observations of the day; having hunted a Foxe, that was both old and craftie; though hee had [II-70] escaped with his life, he had a torne skinne, and a brused bodie; and being long chased, in end he got a hole to hide him in: for sure he did thinke, there was no long safetie for him, if oft hee did but meete with such cunning hunters; that had laid all passes for him, to keepe him in: for though, at this time, hee had stripped away his taile, yet his traine (for the most part) were either taken or killed.

Other Discourses wee had of plentie, and of want, being some of us extreamely hungrie, others pined with extraordinary thirst, having no water neere unto us, nor vessels to bring it from a farre, our servants being left farre behind us, who were plundred by those cowards that had fled from us, who also furnished a great part of our nights Discourse, having wondered at their carriage, that had such externall showes, with so few inward giftes of the minde.

The night thus past, the day peeping every one, that missed a loving friend, or a Camerade, went neere to the ground, on which they sundered, making diligent search to finde them, either dead or alive; sundries of both were found, the dead were put under ground, being honourably buried like souldiers, that had given their lives for the weale of the publique, the wounded were convoyed unto *Dorpes*, where Chirurgians were appointed to attend their cure.

By nine of the Clocke, the Armie was drawne up in Battaile, where the difference was great, betwixt our show then, and the fight of the day before; His Majestie having overviewed the Armie, he tooke the most part of the Horsemen with him, and commanded to march towards *Leipsigh* with the rest of the Armie, to be rested there till further Orders; and His Majestie with the Horsemen advanced after the enemie; prosecuting the victorie, in taking Order with those they had left behind, for making their Retreate sure, whereof there were left at *Leipsigh* three thousand men, whom His Majestie in his by-going gave Orders to pursue, and advanced to a Castle called *Morshberg*, where there were a great many of the enemie, who rendered themselves, and tooke service.

Our March continuing to *Leipsigh*, at our comming there, we found a well provided Leaguer for our hungrie stomackes, of all sort of good victuals, where about the Leaguer, there were feeding, Kine, Sheepe, Calves, Geese, Hennes: they left also Corne in abundance, and flower in readinesse; which was the more acceptable, being found at hand, without travelling for it; and to avoide strife and disorder; before we entered the Leaguer, it was divided proportionally amongst the Regiments, as we would part quarters, where no man was suffered to take any thing out of anothers quarter, but it behoved him to be content with his lot, whither good or bad; so that being quartered, they were happie to their meate, having come, as they say, to a peeld egge; where we laie two nights refreshing our selves, till our bagage was come after us from *Diben*: during which time, the *Saxons* were comming together, their feare being past at *Leipsigh*, where *Felt Marshall Harnam* was appointed, with the *Dukes* forces, to take in both the Towne and Castle, which immediatly were given over on accord. [II-71]

## The seventeenth Observation.

Here we found the Proverbe verified, that they never had an evill day, who got a merry night after: and the long expectation of this our happinesse made our joye the more welcome; for wee helped with great labour, toyle, and travell to have brought this dayes worke to a good end: we rejoyced that the labour and danger being vanished, the good of it remained with us: and though our Commons were but short, our mirth was never the lesse; for we ought not to care how laborious or painefull our actions are, if the fruite be honest and good; for though the paines be first tedious, yet betime they will yeeld content. What matter is it then of our toyle, and travell; or what care should we take of trouble or danger, so our joyes may be enlarged? *Job* was not so miserable in his affliction, as he was happy in his patience. Which should teach all men of our Profession to beare their disturbances and troubles patiently; that in the end they may come to their wished for credit and honour. For he is not worthy the sweete, that cannot suffer the sower; neither is he worthy to be made participant of such mirth, as we enjoyed this night, that ranne away in time of danger.

Here also we see, that it is the dutie of the longest livers, to see to the honour and credit of their dead friends, in taking care of their burialls, as the last dutie: as also, to shew their compassion to their hurt Camerades alive, who perhaps received their wounds in rescuing of others, whose skinnes were kept sound, though theirs torne.

Here we also see, that death is fatall unto all, both to feeble and couragious, but a glorious death is onely proper unto the valiant; who oftest doth eschew death, when the fearefull perisheth in an instant; and therefore it is that the valiant man doth choose rather to die honourably, than to live in ignominy, as the feeble doth; but these died here valiantly; the brightnesse of their Actions, done in their life time, remaines firme in the minds of men unto all ages; And to their posterities in writing, never suffering their memories to rotte with the time; whose burialls, though meane, on this place of Battaile, yet they are commemorations of their vertuous lives to posteritie: whose killing was no punishment (say the world what they list) but rather the beginning of their glory: And therefore, how ever a man dies, he dies well that dies in Christ, ending his dayes with honour.

At this dayes service I was rich in friends, that helped to the obtaining of this victory with credit; but soone after we found the fruits of mortalitie, death having sealed more on our kindred, than on any other Family of our Nation, that were employed in this warre; and the unthankfulnesse of those we served hath beene such, that those who suffered most, were least rewarded; as we may justly say, having lost our Master and King, who did see our actions, and had rewarded them, had he lived. And though I will not vaunt, neither of my friends, nor of our travells, none can blame me to say, as the *Puppie* said, wee Dogges kill'd the Hare, since we were with the rest at *Leipsigh*, the center of *Germanie*, which was, and is, and shall be *Sedes Belli*, till the cause be wonne, and those we fought for be restored; and then I would bee content to lay up my sworde, and live a retired life, serving God and the Publique at home, as we did abroade. [II-72]

---

### *The eighteenth Duty discharged of the intaking of* Hall *and of the Castle, and of our March from* Leipsigh *to* Hall.

His Majesty having left Felt-marshall *Harnam* with the Dukes forces, to accord with *Leipsigh* and the Castle, the eleventh of September, we continued our march towards *Hall*; and coming at the appointed Randezvouz, we halted in the fields, where we were to quarter over night; his Majesty accompanied with a great and honourable traine of Cavaliers, lighted from his horse on the head of our Briggad; the Officers whereof coming together about his Majesty in a Ring, his Majesty made a speech of commendation of the Briggad, thanking them for their good service, and exhorting them for the continuance thereof, promising, as he was a Royall King, he would not forget to reward them; and turning him towards the supreme Officers, they in all humility did kisse his Majesties hand, in confirmation of their loyalty in time to come, the whole inferiour Officers and Souldiers cried aloud, they hoped to doe his Majesty better service then ever they had done.

His Majesty taking horse againe with his Royall traine, he directed Generall *Bannier* to goe and distribute the three thousand foote prisoners that were willing to take service, under the *Dutch* Regiments: Whereupon, I approached unto his Majesty, intreating his Majesty to consider the great losse our Regiment had sustained on all the former occasions of service, that seeing we were become weake like to other Regiments; Therefore his Majesty might be gratiously pleased to give order to Generall *Bannier*, that I might have all the *Britaines* and *Irish* that were amongst the prisoners, to strengthen our Regiment, which his Majesty granting, directed a Cavalier with me unto the Generall, commanding I should have them: I was overjoyed, thinking to get a recreut of old Souldiers; and the Cavalier having declared his Majesties will unto the Generall, the Generall said, with all his heart I should have them, and when I had made try all to finde out the number; there were but three *Irish* amongst them all, and being disappointed of a strong Recreut, I did over-see those, to follow their Camerades; and being returned, his Majesty asked me how I sped; I told his Majesty, *Britaines* were so farre addicted to his Majesty and the cause, that few of them served the Emperour, whereupon I intreated his Majesty for some *Dutch*, but his Majesty refusing, promised to put me and the Regiment alone upon an occasion, where I should get not onely the prisoners, but good booty also.

The next morning continuing our march towards *Hall*, the most part of my folkes were commanded for the intaking of the Castle of *Hall*, the party being commanded by the Colonell of the Artillery, Captaine *William Stewart, Clare* his brother, then Captaine under our Regiment, was commanded with the commanded men, the Castle being taken by accord, we did get fifty old Souldiers that tooke service under our Regiment.

His Majesty on the Sabboth day in the morning went to Church, to give thankes to God for his by-past victories, this church being the Bishops [II-73] Cathedrall seate, I did heare there sung the sweetest melodious musicke that could be heard, where I did also see the most beautifull women *Dutchland* could affoord.

The next day the Duke of *Saxon*, with a princely traine, came unto *Hall*, to congratulate his Majesties victory, and was invited to sup with his Majesty, where they made merry, and the next day held counsell how to maintaine the warres, and how they should prosecute their victory, where it was concluded, that his Majesty with his Army should advance towards *Erford*, and, then over *Duringer Valt* unto *Franconia*; and that the Dukes Army should march unto *Silesia*; and towards the *Crantzis*, or Frontiers of *Bohemia*. After this conclusion, his Majesty sent post unto *Spruce* to call the Chancellor of *Sweden* from thence, to be at *Hall* as Legate for his Majesty, to disburden him of the politicke affaires, having burthen enough of the military employment, and of the receiving and dispatching of forraine Ambassadors; and till the Chancellors coming he did leave Colonell *Winckle* with a strong Garrison in *Hall*, having wisely fore-seene both the way, how to prosecute his victory, as also to maintaine his Conquest.

## *The eighteenth Observation.*

This great Army of Generall *Tillies* being defeated, did seperate themselves in great Troopes and bands, especially the foote; who ought ever to stand well, and fight with courage bouldly in field, and not to suffer themselves to be rent; though the horsemen should runne away, and being they cannot runne so fast for their safeties; my counsell then shall be ever to them, to fight well for victory, and though they should lose all hope of victory, I would not have them to disbandon or scatter; but rather to stand together, till at last they might get honourable quarters for themselves, rather then shamefully to be cut off in flying away.

Here we see, that the foote Souldiers suffer ever the greatest losse in extremity, and they have ever least gaines, though most credit: but we see his Majesty with clemency doth follow the example of the ancient *Romans*, who, of all victories, thought that victory best, which least was stained with bloud, having given quarters and service to three thousand Emperiall Souldiers, without drawing one drop of bloud.

Likewise we see here the continuance of his Majesties industry and diligence, as well in prosecuting his victory, as he was valiant in obtaining of it, in the one as in the other vindicating his owne honour, and the honour of his noble friends, shewing, after the fury was past, his clemency and meekenesse towards his enemies; yet who ever was more valiant than he, being ever in all his on-sets a Leader?  And as we see his Majesties valour and diligence, in prosecuting his victory: so we see also his care, in supplying the weakenesse of his Army, as a wise Generall should doe, in not letting his enemies see the weakenesse of his Army, which ought never to be knowne to those, who should rejoyce at the same.

Likewise here I did observe a great thankefulnesse in a King, in acknowledging openly in view of an Army, the good service done by his servants: wherein I did especially see his love to our Nation beyond all others, that did [II-74] serve him, to make other Nations emulous of their glory, in following of their vertues; and though his Majesty used them here, rather like unto friends then to servants, it should not make them the more sawcy, but rather the more humble, as both Officers and Souldiers did verifie, in promising the continuance of their faithfull obedience, and of better service, as the Lord would enable them, on the next occasions.

Likewise wee did see here, how few of our Nation are induced to serve those Catholique Potentates: and for my part, I finde the reason good: for if we have any enemies in *Europe*, it must be those, that would not onely overthrow our estates at home (if they could) but would also force us (if it lay in their powers) to make shipwracke of our consciences, by leading us unto Idolatry.

Moreover we see here, that his Majesty and the Duke of *Saxon* having once beene companions of danger together; they were then entertaining one anothers familiarity, in renewing of their friendship, confirmed againe with the *German* custome, in making their League the firmer, by drinking brother-ship together, where I have entred the *Hall*, and being seene by his Majesty, I was presently kindely embraced by houlding his Arme over my shoulder: wishing I could beare as much drinke, as old Generall Major *Ruthven*, that I might helpe his Majesty to make his Guests merry, and holding me fast by the hand, calling to the Duke of *Saxon*, declared unto him, what service our Nation had done his Father and him, and the best last, at *Leipsigh*: commending in particular to the Duke, Colonell *Hepburne*, and *Lumsdell*, and having called Colonell *Hepburne* unto him, he did reiterate the former discourse, and much more, in commendation of the *Scots.*

In the continuance of this warre in *Germany* (as the sequell of the Story will prove) from the Balticke coast unto the *Alpes* and *Tyroll*; where Colonell *Hepburne* was sent out as Colonell, to command a party, I was sent with him, as his second, being ever much obliged unto him, not onely for his love on those occasions, but also for his good counsell, his being long before me in the *Swedens* service. And as we were oft Camerades of danger together; so being long acquainted, we were Camerades in love: first at *Colledge*, next in our travells in *France*, at *Paris,* and *Poictiers*, Anno 1615. till we met againe in *Spruce* at *Elben* in August 1630. Nothing therefore in my opinion, more worthy to be kept next unto Faith, then this kinde of friendship, growne up with education, confirmed by familiarity, in frequenting the dangers of warre, and who is more worthy to be chosen for a friend, then one who hath showne himselfe both valiant and constant against his enemies, as the worthy *Hepburne* hath done, who is generally so well knowne in Armies, that he needes no testimony of a friend, having credit and reputation enough amongst his enemies.

To conclude then this observation as I begunne it, I cannot but commend his Majesties wisdome and fore-sight, in bringing the Rex-chancellor *Oxensterne* on the *Dutch* bottome, to be second to his Majesty, and to free him of a part of his burthens, by placing him at *Hall* (as Legate) being *Centrum Germania.* [II-75]

---

### The ninteenth Duty discharged of our March from Hall *towards* Erfort *in* During-land.

His Majesty having left Colonell *Winkle* at *Hall* as Governour, with a strong Garrison to command the Towne, he ordained and left the Duke of *Anhalt* as Stat-houlder, not only over the Towne, but also over the whole Stifft of *Madeburg*: having taken leave of the Duke of *Saxon*, after many protestations and promises of mutuall friendship; our march did continue towards *Efort;* and before up-breaking, the Castle of *Leipsigh* was given over by the accord unto the Duke of *Saxon*: and the Dukes Army was also marching towards *Silesia* and *Bohemia*.

The seventeenth of September, our first nights quarter was taken at a Dorpe, two miles from *Hall*; where those of *Erfort* being so displeased at our coming, as unwilling to entertaine such Guests (they being all Catholiques, Iesuits and Monkes) being mightily afraid, they did send their Commissioners before them, to treate with his Majesty, but his Majesty did give them their answers, by Duke *William* of *Wymar*, that they should quit the Catholique faction, and give their oath of fidelity to his Majesty of *Sweden*, and that they should take in his Garrisons within their Towne, and render up to his Majesty the Castle of *Eryackburg*, with the Colleges to come in his Majesties will; who should suffer them to be untroubled in their Religion, paying their contribution to the warres, like the other Burgers and country.

The Commissioners thinking their conditions to be hard, they tooke leave of his Majesty, promising to referre the businesse to the Towne and Clergie: and they being departed, the Duke of *Wymar* with a Regiment of horse was directed after them; having charge to ride as hard as they could, and entering the Portes with a few horse at the first, commanded the Guard to lay downe their Armes, which hardly they could refuse, the rest being so neere; they entred the Towne and marched peaceably unto the market place, which caused an extraordinary feare amongst the Burgers, and yet a greater terrour amongst the Clergy.

The Councell being called to come on the market place, they were commanded to render the Towne keyes unto the Duke; who getting the keyes, the Towne was taken without bloud.

The twenty two of September, his Majesty having quartered the greatest part of the Army without the Towne, he entred the Towne with eight thousand men foote and horse, which were all quartered within the Towne, and Cloisters; having all free entertainment, in abundance; some of the clergy removed themselves, those who pleased to stay, were not troubled but in their meanes, and his Majesty promised unto the Towne and Councell the free enjoyment of their former liberties.

His Majesty having rested the Army some few dayes, Duke *William* of *Wymar* was made Stat-houlder, who had absolute command over three thousand horse and foote, getting also full power to take in the contribution, and to give out Patents, for leavying of horse and foote Regiments for his Majesties service.

[II-76]

My cozen, the Baron of *Fowles*, with his Regiment of foote, being left there in Garrison, tooke afterwards Patent of the Duke of *Wymar* for leavying a Regiment of horse, which he after brought to passe.

His Majesty giving direction for repairing the fortifications of the Towne, there were Orders given to the Armie to be in readinesse, for to march over *Durengerwalt* unto *Franconia*, and the Regiment had orders to provide their Souldiers sufficiently of Pikes and Muskets, being desired to send unto *Erfort* for such as they stood in need of.

### The nineteenth Observation.

His Majestie as he was valourous and diligent in conquering; so hee was carefull to maintaine his Conquest: the one being as necessarie as the other. Likewise wee see his Majesties wisedome, in appointing the *Duke* of *Anhalt* (in respect of his power in those quarters) to be *Stat-holder* at *Hall*, and over the *Stifft* of *Madeburg*, till the Chancellor of *Swedens* comming, where we see, that His Majestie, for his own Aimes, did make no difference betwixt Protestants and *Lutherans*, but made a like use of them both. For though the Duke of *Anhalt* was a Protestant, he being powerfull in those Quarters, to doe his Majestie service (being Father in law to *Duke William* of *Wymar*) this *Commaund* was imposed upon him.

Here also at *Erfort*, being the first part in Dutchland belonging unto the Catholique League, as appertaining to the Bishopricke of *Mentz*, notwithstanding, we see His Majestie clemencie towards the Papists, in using no violence against them, save onely, *Iure Belli*, as those who were conquer'd by the sword; His Majestie did exacte of them contribution to the warres, and their fidelitie in giving their Oathes to be true unto His Majestie, in doing no harme unto his person or Armie; by entertaining correspondence with his enemies, and on those termes, His Majestie was pleased, to let them remaine untroubled in their consciences, and those that were scrupulous to give this Oath, were suffered to depart in peace, and those who were contented to give it, could not say, they were injured.

Here then we see, that *Princes* Charters are no others over their conquered lands, than their sworde, and the Oath of fidelitie.

It is reported of *Peter Count* of *Savoye*, that he coming to give his Oath of fidelitie to the *Emperour Otto* the fourth, he came presenting himselfe before the Emperour, the one halfe of his body clad over with cloth of gold, and his left side clad over with glittering Armour; the one, to testifie the honour and respect he carryed to the Emperour; the other, how ready he was to fight against his enemies, or those that durst speake evill of His Majestie: and being asked for his Charters, which he had of lands given him in time of warres, he drew his sworde, saying; here they are, signifying thereby, that brave warriours, Kings or Princes had no better right than their swordes.

Here also we see, that nothing is more powerfull, to bring our enemies to an accord, than a strong Armie, while as they want strength to oppose them; for the Conquest will render and give such conditions to the Conquerour, as he pleaseth to further, good or bad.

We see all here as formerly, his Majestie in respect of the *Duke* of *Wimar* his power in those Quarters (which in effect is great) appointed him *Stat-houlder*, and supreame Commissioner in His Majesties absence, in gover- [II-77] ning the Countrie, and in strengthening the Armie, by leavying of forces, of horse and foote, being a fit Man for such employment, that part of the Country being the most populous part in *Germanie*, and cheapest to entertaine them, through the fertilitie of ground in those parts, rendering increase beyond any part of lower *Germanie*.

---

*The twentieth Dutie discharged of our March towards*
Wurtzburg *in* Franconia.

The twenty-six of *September*, his Majestie divided the Armie in two Deales or parts, considering the difficultie he had to march over *During-vault* with a strong Armie. And therefore being minded to march unto *Franconia*, to visit the Bishops of *Bamberg* and *Wurtzburg,* he tooke the one halfe of the Armie with himselfe, crossing over the *Vault* towards *Konickhoffen* and *Swinfort*; and directed Lievetenant Generall *Bawtish*, and Sir *Iohn Hepburne*, with the other halfe of the Armie, to march over the *Vault* unto *Franconia*, upon *Smalka* and *Newstat*, the Randezvouz appointed for the Army to meet at was *Wurtzburg* on the *Maine*, being the Bishop his chiefe residence, where there was a great Citie and a strong Citadell or Castle, wherein lay a strong Garrison, and the most part of the riches of the Country, being esteemed by them as impregnable, in respect of the Situation, being seated on a high hill unaccessible, save onely from the Towne, so that it was hard to doe it any hurt by Cannon, being so strong by nature, and fortified with divers out-workes, on the accessible side that lay to the Citie.

The Army thus divided, and marching alike to one centre or Randezvouz, his Majestie was provided to take in the strengths that lay in his way, and *Bawtizen* and *Hepburne* had Orders to bring under Contribution such Cities, as they marched on, as they did.

His Majestie tooke in his way *Konickhoffen* by accord, being strong, and having beset it with a Garrison, he marched from thence to *Swinfort*, and tooke it in also; and having beset it with a Garrison, the Burgers being made to give their Oath of fidelitie, Duke *Ernest* of *Wymar* was appointed Stat-holder over *Franconia.*

In this time we marched over the *Vault* to *Smalka,* and from thence to *Newstat, Milerstad, Gemond,* and *Carlestat* on the *Maine.* The first night we quartered on the side of the *Vault* next unto *Franconia*, in a Citie called *Smalka,* where we were well quartered; and the next morning we marched to *Mainigen,* and from thence to *Mellerstat*, and then to *Newstat* on the *Sale*, from thence to *Hamelburg*, from thence to *Gemond*, and from *Gemond* to *Carlstat*; and these six Cities we tooke in by accord; and having gotten a Composition of moneys of them, they being sworne to give their obedience unto his Majestie, having quartered in them as we past, they were free, paying the moneys they had promised, and the monethly Contribution. In this march, though the Generall Lievetenant commanded in chiefe, and made the Accord most to his owne advantage; having got of these Townes above fiftie thousand Dollers, whereof he made neither accompt to his Majestie, nor yet was he [II-78] any wayes beneficiall to the Colonells, who did the service; but put all in his owne purse; neither yet did he acknowledge Sir *Iohn Hepburne* with the least token of his bountie, whose merit, at this time, was not inferiour to his owne.

His Majesty having taken in *Swinfort,* and beset it, he continued his march to *Wurtzburg,* and coming before the Towne, he summoned them to render, whereupon they did send Father *Ogleby,* Abbot of the *Scots* Cloyster at *Wurtzburg,* to capitulate with his Majestie, in the behalfe of the Burgers, who got granted unto them the like accord, as was made with *Erfort,* in all degrees; the accord subscribed, his Majestie entered the Towne the same day that our forces arrived at *Carlstat,* being within two miles of them that night.

The Citie given over, the Castle refusing to heare of any Treatie, they begunne from the Castle-workes to plague his Majesties Armie with Cannon; where ever they could lie or stand, within or without the Citie, on either side of the *Maine,* they were cruelly tormented by the enemies Cannon; so that at last it went on in earnest on both sides, for his Majestie having had intelligence, that Generall *Tilly* with a strong Armie of fiftie thousand men, being joyned with the Duke of *Loraine,* were coming for the reliefe of the Castle; his Majestie resolved, that taking of time was best, and that it behooved him on the sudden to have it, or not at all.

The Castle being a strong Strength, sequestred on a height from the Towne; and the Souldiers as they retired from the Towne, they did breake off one Arch of the Bridge, to hinder his Majesties passage over the Bridge unto the Castle; being the onely way he could get to it; and the Castle-workes did so command the Bridge, that a single man could not passe over without great danger of life, being the whole Bridge did lie open just under the Castle; where there was one long plancke laid over the broken Arch, being distant in height from the water, neere eight fathom, so that it seemed a hazard or torment to any man, to passe over alongst the plancke; where some valourous Officers and Souldiers would rather adventure to goe before the mouth of the Cannon, than to crosse over the plancke, though there were no danger of the enemies Cannon or Musket, which still played furiously on that passe of the Bridge, to hinder his Majesties Souldiers in setting over; where at first, two valourous Gentlemen of our Nation, being brethren, were killed on the Bridge (*viz.*) Sir *Iames Ramsey* his Major, called *Bothwell* and his brother.

Neverthelesse, before our coming from *Carlstat,* being within two miles; his Majestie had ingaged the rest of our Country-men that were with him, on this piece of service, being the most desperate, and of the greatest importance, that was ever done in *Dutchland,* during the continuance of the warres; And therefore Sir *Iames Ramsey* and Sir *Iohn Hamilton* were made choice of, with their Regiments by his Majestie, who knew both their worth and valour, being perswaded, if they refused it, none would undertake the service after them; the passage being so dangerous, and of such hazard, that without great difficultie, there was no probabilitie to gaine much credit there; and his Majestie resolved, except those *Cavaliers* with their followers, would make way to others, the wished event could not be hoped for at that time, seeing the enemy was within three dayes march to relieve it; and to the end, they might shew good example to others, they were commanded, with their fellowes, being all Musketiers, to crosse the Bridge, and to beate the [II-79] enemy from the water side, and then to force a passage for the rest of the Armie towards the Castle; the orders were as hard, as the passage was difficult, yet *Cavaliers* of courage, being daring men, and once resolved, nothing could seeme difficult unto them, to gaine honour and credit to themselves and Country; especially being made choice of by a King, out of his Armie, to give testimony publikely, in view of the whole Armie, of their valour and resolution exemplary, forcing their enemies to give ground for them and theirs, having had not one foote of ground on that side of the water, till they should gaine it at their landing: for I was none of the actors, nor yet of the spectators, till I had viewed it the next day, being informed particularly by my Camerades of the manner of their on-falling.

The bridge lay over the *Maine*, with six Arches in length, being a very faire and spatious bridge (over which sixtie men could well march in front) lying open unto the Castle batteries and workes; the middle Arch whereof being broke, a plancke was set over, where with difficultie strong-headed Souldiers might crosse one after another, under mercy of Cannon and Musket; and while as they could but file over, the enemy could receive them with full bodies of pikes and muskets, which was a great disadvantage; and the distance, betwixt the water and the plancke, would terrifie any to venter over, for feare of drowning, though he were in no feare of an enemy; so that many, who went with resolution to passe over, returned againe, choosing rather to crosse alongst the water, in small boates; Notwithstanding, the enemy would emptie *Salves* of muskets on them before their landing; Neverthelesse, Sir *Iames Ramsey* and Sir *Iohn Hamilton*, in obedience to his Majesties commands, with a few Souldiers adventured to crosse the River with small Boates; their Souldiers giving fire before their landing, and in their landing, against their enemies, and being happily once landed, and beginning to skirmish, their Souldiers they left behinde them, who before durst not adventure to crosse alongst the plancke, seeing their Officers and Camerades ingaged with the enemy, to helpe them, they ranne over the plancke one after another so fast as they could runne; till at last they past all and made a strong head against the enemy; till, by the valourous Conduct of their Leaders, and their following, they forced the enemy to give ground, retiring unto their workes.

Their Leaders, desirous to gaine further honour and reputation, pursued the enemy so hard, till they had beaten them out of a *Torme,* they had fled unto. At which time, Sir *Iames Ramsey* was shot lame in the left arme, and then his Camerade Sir *Iohn Hamilton* succeeding him both in command and courage; notwithstanding of the enemies strength and great fury used against them, having disputed with long service for the ground; at last it was made good by Sir *Iohn* and his followers; till such time his Majestie had set over after them the most part of the Armie, so that they were blocked up on all quarters, and forced to remaine within their workes; till that against night, the service being ceased, we with the rest of the Armie were come from *Carlstat*, and quarterd that night without the Towne on the other side of the *Maine*.

His Majestie before day, gave Orders to the *Swedes*, and some *Dutch* Regiments, to storme the enemies workes, who having kept slight watch, were unawares surprized by some *Swedes*, that had entered with ladders over the wall, so that a panick feare having possessed them, they retired in dis- [II-80] order from their Poste; and the *Swedes* and *Dutch* followed so hard, that they had not time to draw up their draw-bridge, neither yet to let downe the Portcullis of their inward Ports; being so amazed, our people flocking in after them, cut them downe as they were found, giving no quarters at all, so that they that entred first made the best bootie, though least service. Here fortune favoured his Majestie miraculously at this time, beyond mens expectation, as formerly; having here a great deal of riches; as also many Cannon, and great store of Amunition; and of all sort of victualls abundance. The fury past, his Majestie set a Governour on the Castle, and a Garrison, which was strong, and he gave Orders presently to beginne to repaire the workes, seeing Generall *Tilly*, with his Armie, were drawing neere; and his Majestie having got intelligence, that they were quartered within two miles of *Wurtzburg*, according to his accustomed manner, his Majestie with a partie of Horse and Dragoniers fell upon their neerest quarters in the night, and defeated foure Regiments of their Horse, and retired the next night unto *Wurtzburg* attending when the enemy would seeke for his revenge.

### The twentieth Observation.

His Majestie at this time, as formerly, used great expedition in marching unto *Franconia*, knowing it was one of the Circles of the whole Empire, that was of most importance for the enemy; being a straite and a strong Country, by reason of the strengths within it: And therefore it was, that he divided his Armie in crossing the *Vault*, at divers places; that his Artillery might passe the sooner through. For he knew, who ever was the Master of *Wurtzburg*, he commanded the whole River of the *Maine*, and consequently, whole *Franconia*; which fortunately happened, according to his Majesties deliberation.

Here also we see the evill that comes of greedinesse, in making generall Commanders to be hated by those that follow them; for *Bowtizen* having got a great summe of money of these Townes, by the helpe and service of the foote, it became him, according to right and discretion, to have shared with the Colonells, who commanded the Briggads and Regiments, but seeing his want of discretion in not acknowledging them, they being once joyned againe to his Majesties Army, would never consent to be commanded by him a foot-step afterwards; for ought his Majestie could doe, having dealt so niggardly with *Cavaliers* of their worth, so that his Majestie was forced to direct him to command elsewhere.

This greedinesse is the most pestiferous roote that ever grew in a generall Commander; for on this march, Souldiers were usually commanded to lie in the Fields, and not suffered to quarter in the Townes, which they had taken, for feare to hinder the payment of the moneys imposed on them; so that publique employment is ill bestowed upon a greedy person; and this greedinesse in a man of warre, to gather riches, may lose him all his fortunes; and avarice hath beene the losse of many Armies, and so many Kingdomes also; for no vice is more pestiferous in the extraordinary use, than this, to bring a man to be disdained of others, especially of those would follow him.

Here also we see, that of old, our Nation was much esteemed of abroad, especially the Clergie, who in all Kingdomes, as in *Germanie*, had their [II-81] Cloisters, as here, and at *Erfort*; and he was a *Scots* man, that brought the Christian Religion first into *Franconia*, but was evill rewarded, being there afterwards murthered.

It was the custome observed ordinarily by his Majesty of *Sweden*, to make use of our countrimen on service, wherein he desired they should shew themselves examplary to others, as at this time, he made choice of Sr. *Iames Ramsey* and Sr. *Iohn Hamilton*, to be the first should adventure, of the whole Army, to force the enemy to give way to his Majesty to set his Army over the Maine; where, on that bridge Major *Bodwell* and his brother being killed, were buried in *Wurtzburg* Church, leaving the Trophie of their valour amongst strangers, in honour of the Nation, that was ever glorious abroad.

Sr. *Iohn Hamilton* disdaining the orders his Majesty did give, for storming the Castle, having employed the *Sweds* and *Dutch* on the storme, neglecting him and the *Scots,* who had made the way to the rest, in the extremity of the danger, the Cavalier, I say, therefore disdaining the service, seeing his countrimen neglected, he desired of his Majesty his honourable passe, which his Majesty delayed, promising to give content another time, which he utterly refused, but tooke his passe, seeing he thought the Nation was wronged; for which in my opinion he merits praise: for if many such Cavaliers thus served strangers, that would not care for them nor their service, when once they begin to neglect them, others that were but Cavaliers of Fortune of the Nation, would be the better respected and used. Which should teach all Cavaliers that serve truely abroad to take their time with credit of those they serve, seeing they doe not respect Cavaliers, but when they have most use of them.

Here then we see that no strength, be it never so strong, is able to hould out, when as God doth not watch the Fort, the watch-man watches in vaine, and we see by the submission of *Franconie* after this victory, that the victorious Ensignes are ever followed: for where Fortune doth favour, there the Commons doe follow, and their study also with their favour followes the victorious.

Here also we see Generall *Tillie*, though beaten at *Leipsigh*, in lesse then five weekes time, he drawes together againe a strong Army, with Fifty thousand men, and lies downes within three miles of his Majesties Army, but his Majesty having wisely beset the passes on the Maine, before his comming, winter drawing neere, and the country being a streite country by nature, for woods, hills and water; As also, furrage and provision for horses being taken out of his way, his horsemen in that country were made unprofitable for him to stay there, for lacke of entertainment, which was defective for his foote also, so that it was impossible for him to stay long; so seeing his Majesty had resolved in that country, and for that season to make a defensive warre, having divided his Army, both horse and foote within Townes and strengthes, he suffered *Tillie* to ruine his young Novices with marches in cold weather, who being for the most part *French* and *Italians*, could not endure the cold ayre of that country being hilly: His Majesty having beset all the Garrisons on the *Maine* streame, he suffered *Tillie*, as he did the yeare before, in *Pomeren* and *Madeburg* and the *Markes*, to traverse with his Army in the cold, while as he lay still with his Souldiers with-[II-82] in the warme stove; and when he found the storme over-past, he was ready to neglect no time.

---

## The twenty one Duty discharged at Oxenford on the the Maine in Franconia.

His Majesty having intelligence, that Generall *Tillie* had intention to have fallen on *Oxenford*, to patronize the passe over the *Maine*, where his Majesty had sent but one hundred and fifty musketiers, whom he judged to be too weake for defending of the Towne, and considering with himselfe, the enemy might likewise pursue *Wurtzburg*, having made but a faint at *Oxenford*; and perhaps his intention might be to pursue both alike, his Majesty under night coming alone on horsebacke from the Castle, towards my quarter, being then in the remotest part of the whole Towne, I being at supper, his Majesties foote-man tould me, the King was below, and desired I should come unto him; being come to his Majesty, he commanded me in all haste to bring our Briggad in Armes, and to draw them up on that part against his returne; and to command Sr. *Iohn Hepburne* in his name to meete him there, which immediatly being obeyed accordingly, his Majesty being returned commanded *Hepburne* to leade off the Musketiers of the whole Briggad, being then eight hundred, and to follow his Majesty whether so ever he went, who commanded me to bring up the Reare, leaving our Colours and pike-men behinde us there, till further orders: we marched on in the night halfe a mile without the Towne, before we knew whether we were going, or what the exploite could be that we were going on, having left both our horses and servants behinde us: at last, his Majesty acquainting Colonell *Hepburne* with his designe, he marched towards *Oxenford*, being convoyed with foure score horses alongst the side of the *Maine*, and we followed with our foote, marching in seven houres those foure miles, and before two of the clocke in the morning, we arrived there, without halt or drawing of breath by the way. At our coming we were let in alongst the bridge, unto the market place, where our Souldiers, after this wearisome march, were commanded to stay by their Armes all night in readinesse, and houses were appointed for the Officers to remaine in all night.

The next morning by day light his Majesty did send for Colonell *Hepburne* and me, and tells he was going to visit the walles without, and he commanded to send two hundred musketiers of our Regiment towards the Port before him, which being done, his Majesty accompanied with some Cavaliers walked out: and the night before, at his Majesties coming to Towne he had directed fifty horse to watch halfe a mile without the Towne, betwixt him and the enemy. At his Majesties out-going, we heare the enemies Dragoniers, with some horsemen making service against the watch, who were forced to retire: whereupon his Majesty commanded me to send forth fifty musketiers with a Lievetenant to skirmish with the enemy, till the horsemen might retire; the musketiers being advanced, they skirmished with the enemy in view of his Majesty, houlding up the enemy till the horsemen were [II-83] by: but the enemy being too farre strong, made our musketiers lose ground in retiring; and his Majesty suspecting the enemy was back't with stronger forces, his Majesty commanded me, to command a hundred musketiers more, with a sufficient Officer to march incontinent, for reliefe of their Camerades; and commanded me to goe withall, and to place them in the most advantagious ground, which I did, and incontinently the reliefe begun the service a fresh, forcing the enemy to retire backe over the top of the hill; which his Majesy perceiving was wondrous glad, saying, the *Scots* skirmish well, who had made the enemy quit their ground, which they possest and kept: the other side of the hill being all plaine, his Majesty commanded out a troope of horse, for to recognize the enemies designe, and calling Colonell *Hepburne* unto him he said, he would leave us there, and fearing the enemy might have a designe upon *Wurtzburg*, he would returne thither, being of greatest moment, and so he gave orders to *Hepburne* to defend the Towne so long as he could, and then, in case of necessity, to retire over the bridge, and to breake it off behinde him.

His Majesty being gone, Colonell *Hepburne* begun to put all things in good order, preparing for the enemies coming, casting downe houses and walles, which might serve without the Towne for the enemies advantage, as also, cutting downe trees and hedges, which might serve to shelter the enemy; As also making Scaffolds about the walles, for musketiers to make service from; ordaining the severall postes to be repaired and defended, in case of the enemies pursuite; ordering also the watches, and by watches, to observe the precise houres, making also provision betimes for store of Amunition, and giving diligent and capable men charge over it, and appointing guards for it, with severall other directions befitting an able Commander to give out at such times; being looking for a mighty enemy to pursue a skurvy irregular hole; where no Cavalier could gaine credit without overmuch hazard; yet such a Master would be so served.

All things thus provided, the Curriers went night and day betwixt his Majesty and the Governour, for mutuall intelligence, till the third night before day, the enemies Trumpets and Drummes made such a noise, as though Heaven and earth were going together, continuing as if the enemy were marching to the walles for a generall storme: our horse guards being beaten in under the walles, were refused of entry, and the out-guards of foote also; and then every man within walles did repaire to their posts, expecting a generall storme, and the pitterding of the ports. The Colonell having visited the whole guards, and made the Rounde of the whole Towne, seeing all things were in good order, and the day drawing neere, we found the enemy was retiring from us, having begun his march at midnight towards *Newringburg*, and the upper *Paltz*. The day cleering, our horsemen having come from the other side of the *Maine*, being led and commanded by Duke *Bernard* of *Wymar*, whereof foure hundred were commanded towards the enemies quarters, to take order with those were left behinde, who did get but slight quarters.

The enemies Army being marched, his Majesty was advertized, who sent orders incontinent to Sr. *Iohn Hepburne* to breake up in the night, with five hundred musketiers, and to march by the enemy, in the night towards *Wintzsen*, which (by appearance) was too hazardous. The enemy being too farre before, and in his way also, which made his Majesty to countermand [II-84] his former orders against his custome; and then the Colonell being commanded to beset the garrison, he was recald with the party to returne to *Wurtzberg*. After *Tillies* departure, his Majesty caused publish an Edict over all *Franconia,* that both Clergy and Laikes, none excepted, should come and sweare their fidelity to his Majesty. Whereupon the full liberty of their profession in religion should be granted unto them untroubled. As also they should have his Majesties safeguards for the conservation of their worldly estates; and in this Edict were contained a great part of his Majesties former victories obtained against his enemies, with the causes and motives, which moved him to undertake warre against the Emperour, together with the successe followed his Maiesty in this warre, in having freed *Pomeren, Maclenburg*, the three *Markes* of *Brandenburg*, the *Stift Breame*, the *Stift Madeberg, Saxon* and *Duringer*, already of the enemy; As also *Franconia*, after the in-taking of *Wurtzburg*, in forcing *Tillie* with his Army, that did come for their reliefes, for scarcity to retire unto the upper *Paltz*, from whence shortly he hoped to make him retire to *Bavaria*, towards the *Danow* streame, as he had made him retire before from *Leipsigh* to the *Waser* streame; and at last, he hoped he should bring out of the Emperour and their Catholique League, against all their wills, a good Generall peace, unto all the Evangelists and those of the reformed Religion in *Germanie*; and he hoped to pay them home againe *Iure Talionis*, in using their landes in *Byerland*, as they had done his friends Landes in *Maclenburg* and *Pomeren.*

About this time, *Madeburg* was blocked up by Generall *Banier* and the *Britaines* forces, commanded and led by the Marquesse of *Hamilton*, at which time also his Majesties Ambassadour of great *Britaine*, Sir *Henry Vaine*, arrived at *Wurtzburg*, where his Honour, with his noble traine, had the good attendance and respect due given unto him by the whole Officers, who were there of both Nations, *Scots* and *English*, whom my Lord Ambassadour courteously and kindly did entertaine, with such respect as became his Honour to give unto *Cavaliers*; and those who followed his Honour, did also keepe familiaritie alike with both Nations.

At this time also was Lievetenant Colonell *Huball* sent with a Convoy of Horse, and a thousand Dragoniers towards H*anow*, who tooke it in by surprize, with very little losse, where some hurt Officers that were come from *Leipsigh* were taken prisoners, being under cure there.

The Towne being taken, *Huball* being but before Livetenant Colonell to the blew Regiment, having brought a part of the Countrie under contribution, he gave out Patents, for leavying of horse and foote, in his owne name, having had a sure muster-place, and the helpe of Franckford besides: immediatly he did get a Commission of his Majestie, for leavying three thousand horse and foote, to be in two Regiments under his Command; he was thus suddenly made up by one fortunate exploite, without any great service, or hurt to himselfe, or those he did command.  At this same time, or there abouts was *Prague* in *Bohemia* given over, by accord unto *Arnham* Generall to the *Saxons* Armie.

### The twenty one Observation.

Here His Majestie was put to the triall of his judgement, and dexteritie in Command: after the intaking of *Wurtzburg*, his Armie for the most part being sent from him, under Command of *Gustavus* [II-85] *Horne* towards *Bambridge*, as also having weakened his Armie, by beseting the Garrisons on the *Maine,* not keeping above eight thousand foote and horse by himselfe at *Wurtzburg*, while as Generall *Tillie, Altringer, Feutker,* and the *Duke* of *Loraine* had joyned their forces together, making up fiftie thousand men, of intention to force a passe over the *Maine*, to come at His Majestie; His Majestie being sure, *Tillie* would not harme the Countrie being Papists, he resolved by cunctation, and delaies to wearie him with a defensive warre, keeping the maine strength of his Army, within *Wurtzburg*, being well provided of all furniture for horse and man; he begunne to strengthen the Towne with the spade and the shovell, in making of redoutes and skonces without it, in manner of a Winter Leaguer: he also caused Scaffold the walles round about within the Towne; and fearing his coming on *Oxenford*, he did the like, discharging all duties himselfe; from one place to an other, as became a wise Generall, that did foresee the designes of his enemie, by a timely prevention, according to the accidents, circumstances, and situation of places, seeing his enemies strong; and himselfe weake, he tooke the first advantage.

This charge of a Generall to an Armie is a place of such weight and importance, that few ought to long to intrude themselves in this kinde of Generall command, being subject to infinite chances, and altogether divers, almost every houre set before him.  Truly though this King had a rare judgement, wit and dexteritie, with great experience in his Command: Neverthelesse, to speake truth, all the time I did follow his Majestie on occasions, being neere three yeeres, I did never see His Majestie so much troubled in minde and resolution, as at this time in *Oxenford*, not knowing well himselfe what to resolve, the enemie being behinde him and before him; able to pursue *Wurtzburg*, and *Oxenford* alike; and to my minde if he had, he might have carried both at that time; for our Armie was not only scattered and dispersed; but also we were weake, and, which was worse, we were all of us discontented; being too much toyled with marching, working and watching, without any pay or gaines for honest men.

At this time, his Majestie stood in neede of assistance and good Counsell, having enemies on all hands, and a strong enemy; the Country also unsure, being unfriends and Papists, and he being wise, resolved without giving Battaile, his best was, to presse to overcome them with the season, with hunger and cold, with marches and delayes, keeping himselfe within walles, he knew well twelve Souldiers with a good Officer to direct them, were better, being willing to attend, than a hundred naked and hungry Souldiers without, whereby his enemies Armie were undone, without hurt or detriment of his owne, being well commanded, and well foreseene and provided of all necessaries, having given them besides, as reward of their former services, a little money, knowing well how hungry men could be contented with little, in time of neede: for he resolved, if the enemy pushed him hard within *Wurtzburg*, he could not suffer himselfe to be beleaguered with a strong Armie, in a straite place; and to goe to the Fields with a discontented weake Armie (which it behooved him to doe) was not good. The consideration of this forced him to give some moneys in hand, to content them, and hand-writ, and assignations for more moneys to be payd unto them out of *Newrenberg*, within six moneths afterwards.

As also his Majestie knew well the enemies Armie neere hand, hearing [II-86] there was money given out by his Majestie, that it was the onely way to weaken and dissolve the enemies Armie, in making their Souldiers runne away, and to take service under his Majestie, which in effect accordingly fell out: for it being neere Winter, and their Armie marched away, their stragling Souldiers did strengthen our Garrisons, having taken service under us; having but heard of the brute of money, that was given out amongst us. Where we see, how necessary it was, at this time, in such a dangerous extremitie, for this little Armie to have beene commanded by a wise Generall, that steered his course aright in middest of the greatest tempest, like to a skilfull marriner, where an arrogant fellow, without skill, that had commanded, had made shipwracke of all.

As his Majestie was wise and moderate in his Command; so those who obeyed were faithfull and intire to their Superiour. Here inferiours whom Fortune favoureth, though weakest, were subject in all things to him, who was Fortunes *Minion*, and *Mars* his equall, *Gustavus* the Invincible; that by his wisedome, and foresight, forced old *Tillie* to retire to *Nurenberg*, having gained nothing but losse, which retreate was the presage of his future ruine, at the *Leacke*, where it enters into the *Danow*.

Here also we are instructed, as well by his Majesties politique government, as by his military; He being alike expert in both, discharging the dutie of a King, and a Generall, *Tam Arte, quam Marte*: for the enemy was no sooner gone, but incontinent his Majestie caused serve his publique *Edicts*, for bringing in the Country-men, to give their oaths of fidelitie; moving them thereto partly by compulsion, and partly by promises of dutie and of libertie to their Consciences, two strong Arguments to move those to obedience, who had seene their friends forced to turne backes upon them, from whom, under God, they did expect Reliefe to come.

Moreover we see here, that those who are honoured by God, are also worthy of honour from their equalls: other Kings, Princes, and Confederates sending their Ambassadours unto them, to *congratulate* their good Fortunes and successe; as also to Treate with them in matters belonging to their mutuall States and standing: at this time also, there were Commissioners sent from *Vlme, Strasburg, Nurenberg*, and *Francford*, treating with His Majestie for themselves apart, as free from the bodie of the Empire: And such feathers his Majestie was glad to get out of the Emperours wings, knowing the more he wanted of such feathers, the worse he could flie: and some of them were light, changing as the winde. To conclude then, whom fortune favours, the world laughs on, as may be seene here, by the example of Lievetenant Colonell *Howbalt*, after the intaking of *Hanow* by meere fortune being surprized; which was the occasion, this Cavalier was so suddenly made up, in getting Command over horse and foote, from Livetenent Colonell; who, foure yeeres before, was Sergeant under the blew Regiment. Yet notwithstanding the good he had received under his Majestie and his Crowne, he afterwards quit them and their service; in their greatest extreamitie, which was unthankfully done of him, being more unkindly, then friendly. [II-87]

---

### *The twenty second Duty discharged of our March from* Wurtzburg *to* Francford *on the* Maine.

His Majesty having beset *Wurtzburg* Castle with a strong *Swedens* Garrison, under command of Colonell *Axellille*, preparation being made for the march, the Colonell of the Artillery, *Leonard Richardson* a *Swede*, was directed downe the *Maine*, with the great Cannon, and three hundred commanded musketiers of *Scots*, of Sr. *Iames Ramsey* his Regiment comanded by *Alexander Hanan*, being a discreete Cavalier, of good command and conduct, and valorous also: they had abundance of Cannon, fire-workes, Amunition, and all other furniture belonging to Artillery, with them by water, having got orders to take in all strengths on the *Maine*, which lay in their way, where they and he who commanded them, made good booty, having taken in severall Castles, and *Miltenburg* also, and from thence continued their course downe the water towards *Ashaffenburg*, a City and a Castle on the *Maine* belonging to the Bishop of *Mentz*, where they had orders to remaine till his Majesties coming with the Army.

This march continued for five dayes, where we had nightly good quarters by the way, being in feare of no enemy we kept the whole march, the *Maine* on our right hand, & our horsemen upon the left, having had the Felt-marshall with his Army lying at *Bambridge*, betwixt us and the enemy, so that this march, though in winter, was not so troublesome unto us, as their travelling is to them, who journey in forraine countries, for to see strange faces, where they must needs lay out monies for their entertainment, some of us on this march were well entertained, and did get mony besides to spend at *Francford*.

Likewise when it behoved travellers to hire guides, and sometimes to hire convoies for their safeties, we had *Gustavus* a King under God, our Leader, and a powerfull Army to convoy us, and at night, the sweete, and sociable society of our countrimen and strangers, the one to season the other, which made our march pleasant, alongst the pleasant and fruitfull River of the *Maine*, that runnes through faire *Franconia* into the Rhine at *Mentz*.

Having come with the Army, the length of *Hanow*, leaving *Ashaffenburg* behinde us, we marched to *Steinhem*, which presently we tooke in by accord, where the most part of the Souldiers did take service, which being done, his Majesty did send unto the Lords of *Francford*, desiring them for the well of the professours of the Evangell, to take in a Garrison, with a protestation, if they refused to doe it willingly, it behoved him otherwise to deale with them, which was not his desire.

They having taken the proposition, for two dayes, in advisement, his Majesty the sixteenth of November, did let quarter the Army before their Ports in *Offenback*, *Ober* and *Nider Rode*; the next day they consented, his Majesties Army should march through, leaving six hundred men in Garrison in *Saxenhowsen*, the Lords giving their Oath to secure the Garrison of *Saxenhowsen* of all dangers, and on the seventeenth of November his Maje- [II-88] sty with the whole Army in comely order marched alonst the bridge, from *Saxenhowsen* through the Towne of *Francford* towards *Hechst*, where there lay two miles off the Towne a Garrison of the enemies. In this march through *Francford*, such order was kept without any disorder, as if it were the solemne procession of a King and his nobles in parliament, every one admiring of his Majesties good order and discipline kept over his Army.

The nineteenth of November, *Hechst* was taken in by his Majesty with accord, where the Souldiers for the most part tooke service. The next day the Army lying still in Dorpes, his Majesty returned to *Francford*, and met with the *Landgrave* of *Hessen*, the *Landgrave* of *Darmstat* and with the Earles of the *Vetro*, where it was agreed amongst them, for the defence of the Land, to joyne in one confederacy, where the Castle of *Russelshem* was given unto his Majesty by the *Landgrave* of *Darmstat*, whereon two hundred *Scots* of Colonell *Lodewick Lesly* his Regiment were set, under command of Captaine *Macdowgall*.

The next day being the two and twentith of November, his Majesty returned to *Hechst* againe, and having put forth the Papists, placing his owne Preachers, on *Sunday* his Majesty thanked God, that he had gotten in *Francfort* without bloud or stroake of sword. His Majesty caused to set over a ship-bridge at *Hechst*, and sent ships before *Mentz*, to blocke it by water, till his Majesty with the Army crossed the *Maine*, and marched by *Darmstat* in the *Bergstrasse*, of intention to have gone for *Heidelberg*, but retiring downe neere the *Rhine*, having quartered the Army, his Majesty with a party did visit the Skonce of *Openham*, and thereafter resolved to take it in.

### The twenty second Observation.

This march being profitable as it was pleasant to the eye, we see that Souldiers have not alwayes so hard a life, as the common opinion is; for sometimes as they have abundance, so they have variety of pleasure in marching softly, without feare or danger, through fertill soyles and pleasant countries, their marches being more like to a Kingly progresse, then to warres, being in a fat land, as this was, abounding in all things, except peace: they had plenty of corne, wine, fruite, gold, silver, Iewells, and of all sort of riches could be thought of, on this River of the *Maine*, where the Townes and pleasant Flects lie by the water, not distant, in many places, halfe an *English* mile from one another; being one of the pleasantest parts, and wholesomest for ayre that I did see in all *Germany*, having a great Traffique by water from thence unto the west sea, by the *Rhine* running northward unto *Holland*. This Towne of *Francford* is so pleasant for ayre, situation, buildings, traffique, commerce with all Nations, by water and by land, that it is and may be thought the Garden of *Germany*, and consequently of *Europe*; seeing no continent in *Europe* is comparable unto *Germany*, for fertility, riches, corne, wine, traffique by land, pleasant Cities, faire buildings, rare orchards, woods, and planting, civility, as well in the country as in the cities; their Dorpes and Flects walled about; The Boores inhabitants having their wines in Sellers set in great, rife or plentifull as wa- [II- 89] ter, to entertaine their friends, in a bountifull manner, especially alongst this pleasant River of the *Maine*.

Here at *Francford* is the *Mart*, called the *Francforter Masse*, whether the Marchants resort from all partes of *Europe* for the mutuall interchange of money and wares: Hether also are brought twice in the yeare from all parts of *Europe*, the travells and bookes written by the learned of all sciences, and of all controversies of Religion, to be transported againe from thence, for the use of other Kingdomes.

The inhabitants of *Francford*, we see here are content to take in his Majesties Garrison in *Saxonhousen*, without compulsion or losing of bloud: and this kinde of conquest is the best conquest, when we conquer more by love then by force; where they, by their timely yeelding, preserved their Towne, their buildings, their orchards, their houses of pleasure undestroied, when others through their pride stoode out, till they were punished by the ruine of their Townes, the losing of their moveables, as their gold, their silver, their rich cupboords, their Iewells, their ornaments, their orchards, their gardens, in regard of their pride in time of their plenty.

But his City of *Francford* was made wise, by the ruine of other Cities, whose intemperate troubles made them moderate. Thus concord is the mother of all happinesse in the Common-weale; for she debarres enemies, augments wealth, makes the Cities sure without a guard, and oftimes we see that those who contemne Peace, seeking glory, they lose both peace and glory.

Therefore the Lords of *Francford* did well, in preferring good conditions of peace before an uncertaine warr, especially against such a Heroick King as *Gustavus* was, then the Patriot & Protectour of their faith and Religion, and consequently of their freedome, and their countries freedome, and for their rewards, to my knowledge, they were inriched three yeares together (by the hant of the Army) with the substance of the foure upper Circles of *Germany*; which in th'end they rewarded with unthankefulnesse, and doubtlesse will be punished for it sometime.

Here also we have the power of example; for the Towne of *Francford* having taken his Majesty of *Sweden* for their Protector, following their examples, the two *Landgraves Hessen* and *Darmstat*, with the Earles of the *Veteraw* desire also to be in the confederacy, and were most gladly accepted of. *Vlme*, *Nurenberg* and *Strasburg* ended also their confederacy with his Majesty after the example of *Francford*, promising supply of men, money and victualls for the Army, Amunition and horses for the Artillery, with abundance of Armes for horse and foote, with powder, ball, match, waggons, spades, shovells, Pikes, mattockes, axes and all other things fitting for the advancement of the warres. Here was a greate conquest without stroake of sword, shewing unto us the number of friends we get, when fortune smiles on us: but how soone this Heroicke Person is but once gone, and that fortune beginneth to frowne, then these variable friends quit their confederacy againe; following the strongest, for which one day the sword of their enemies will come amongst them with hunger and pestilence. At this time the Queenes Majesty of *Sweden* was come to *Statin*, and from thence on her journey towards *Francford*. Here also the Kings Majesty of *Bohemia* was come to visit his Majesty of *Sweden*, and was Royally received by his Majesty as likewise by the Lords of *Francford*, and was wonderfully well liked [II-90] of by the whole Communalty of the Cities and Countries, where ever his Majesty did come.

Here also the *Marquesse* of *Hamilton* did come unto his Majesty againe, being followed like a Prince, and well respected by both the Kings. The Ambassadors of *Britaine* and of *France* were there also, and the Rex-chancellor of *Sweden* being come with the Queenes Majesty and Sir *Patricke Ruthvene* come from *Spruce*, were all made welcome to this Court then at *Francford*, which was not inferiour to the Emperours owne Court, in respect of great confluence of people, that came from all parts to congratulate the *Lyon* of the north his victories, and to admire his fortunes, being so increased in two yeares time, that all things succeeded happily unto his Majesty according to his owne hearts desire.

---

*The twenty third Duty discharged of the intaking of the Skonce at* Oppenham, *and his Maiesties crossing the Rhine.*

His Majesty having viewed and well recognosced the Skonce on the Rhine, over against *Oppenham*, the River being interjected betwixt it and the Towne, his Majesty did leade Colonell *Hepburnes* Briggad, and Colonell *Winckles* being the blew, with some cannon, great and small before it, where his Majesty did stay till the *Batteries* were made, and the approaches begun, then leaving the command on Colonell *Hepburne*, with tempestuous cold weather, with hard frosts and snow, we lay downe on the fields, having no shelter, but some bushes by the side of the Rhine.

The Skonce was really fortified with Fossees, that were broad, deepe, and full of water, with a draw-bridge over the Moate, and the Skonce was well beset with a thousand men, and well provided of victualls, fire and Amunition, having free passage at their pleasure without danger, from the Towne unto the Skonce, and backe againe: The Castle and the hill on the other side of the Rhine, being mounted high, their cannon from their batteries did cleanse and scowre the fields about the Skonce, being a razed *Champange*, and plaine without any shelter of their batteries; on the other side they plagued us still with cannon, especially in the night time, while it behooved us to have fire, which was their marke, so that sundry were lost, and one night sitting at supper, a Bullet of thirty two pound weight, shot right out betwixt Colonell *Hepburnes* shoulder and mine, going through the Colonells Coach; the next shot kill'd a Sergeant of mine, by the fire, drinking a pipe of Tobacco. This night the enemy made an out-fall, to try his valour, thinking to beate us from our cannon, but he was bravely repulsed by push of Pike, slightly esteeming of their muskets, and scorning to use ours, with sharpe points of pikes conveied them home to their Graffe. [II-91]

The next day in the morning, knowing his Majesty had crossed the Rhine, they did capitulate with Colonell *Hepburne*, who did give them, being *Italians*, more honourable quarters then in truth their carriage did deserve, having got licence to march out, Bag and Baggage, with full Armes, with a convoy to the next Garrison, they being marched, his Majesty having crossed the Rhine in the night, where the *Spaniard* made some resistance, but in vaine, his Majesty having got over, the next morning he marched towards *Openham* in the *Paltz*, on the one side of the Towne, and we setting over also, we pursued the Towne and the Castle on the other side, but Sr. *Iames Ramsey* his musketiers being led by their Major, finding a privy passage about the Castle, they stormed over the walles, coming betwixt the outward Skonce and the castle, and finding the draw-bridge downe, on a sudden they entered the Castle, and put all to the sword: the rest of the enemy finding the Castle to be in, they runne all to storme the Skonce, on which were nine Companies of *Italians*, with their colours; their Officers finding the castle surprized behinde them, and the storme going on before them, they threw downe their Armes calling for quarters, which was granted: but their colours taken from them, they willing to take service were all disposed by his Majesty to Sr. *Iohn Hepburne*, who was not only a Colonell unto them, but a kinde Patron, putting them in good Quarters till they were armed and clad againe. But their unthankfulnesse was such, that they stayed not, but disbandoned all, in *Bireland*; for having once got the warme ayre of the Summer, they were all gone before Winter.

## The twenty-third Observation.

Here then we see, that it is the dutie of all wise Generals, of intention to beleaguer Citie, Fort, or Strength, first to recognosce, and having once recognosced, then to proceed, as they finde most advantagious for the Beleaguerer, and disadvantagious for the assailed: the pursuer must know, what number of men are requisite for the pursute, as well offensive as defensive.

In this point of recognoscing his Majesties judgement was wonderfull, as in all other practicall duties fitting a great Commander, and as his Majesties judgement was great and good, so he was of that minde, nothing in this kinde could be well done, which he did not himselfe, neither could his Majestie abide, at such times, as he went to recognosce, any other to accompany him in the danger, other reasons doubtlesse His Majestie had, which were onely privie unto himselfe. This point how necessarie it is, for a great Commander to be judicious of, no Souldier will doubt.

Here also we see, His Majestie made no difference of season, or weather, in prosecuting his enemie, whenever he found any advantage. And therefore it was His Majesties wise resolution, to crosse the *Rhine*, while Generall *Tillies* Armie, in the Wintertime, was farthest from him, and making but a faint here before *Oppenham*, his ayme and designe was to crosse the *Rhine* at an other part by shipping, that while the enemie was busied in defence of the Skonce, His Majestie might crosse at another part: for the Armie once crossed, the Skonce was lost, for want of supplie; and His Majestie once over, the whole *Paltz* and *Mentz* were in feare.

Nothing is more powerfull to resist resolution, than resolution: for it is [II-92] said of the Oake, being hard timber, for to cleave it a sunder, there must be wedges made of it selfe, that hardnesse may overcome hardnesse. My advise then to all brave fellowes watching in trenches, or guarding Cannon, while as the enemie would try their valour by out-falling, in assailing them, at such times, let the defender doe as was done here, leaving the use of the Musket, as being more unreadie, let them make use of their pikes, meeting their enemies in the teeth, with a strong firme bodie of Pikes, (after the old *Scots* fashion, used by our Predecessours, that fought pell mell; with two-hand swordes, till one of the parties did quit the field) for though they suffer losse, sure they must winne credit, that repulse their enemie, rather than disgracefully suffer their Cannon to be nayled, or their braines knockt out in trenches, while as they take them to the uncertaintie of the musket. Therefore let resolution be ever present, repulsing force with force; for if thou wouldest be esteemed amongst the number of brave fellowes, thou must resolve to shew thy selfe resolute, couragious, and valiant, going before others in good example, choosing rather to dye with credit standing, serving the publique, than ignominiously to live in shame, disgracing both thy selfe and Countrie. Who would not then at such times choose vertue before vice; glorie, honour, and immortall fame, before an ignominious, shamefull, and detestable life? Let then my deere Camerades of the Brittish Nation, where ever they serve, embrace this my exhortation, and lay it up in the secret corners of their heart and minde, that they may be ever mindefull of their credits, preferring credit to life, for the honour of the invincible Nation, doing ever, as was done here by their Countrie men, in one night thrice, at three severall partes, whereof twice in sight of their King and Master.

His Majestie crossing the *Rhine*, did take with him the *Scots*, which were there, Sir *Iames Ramseys* Regiment, of old *Spense* his Regiment, and of *My Lord Rhees*; being landed, the Spanish horsemen having furiously charged, the *Scots,* with a little advantage of a hedge, stood by His Majestie against the Spanish horsemen, and with a strong body of pikes, and salves of musket, resisted valiantly the horsemen, till the rest were landed, to relieve them. As also the next day, the Musketieres of *Ramseys* Regiment, that on all occasions were wont to shew their valour, were the first stormed the walles, at *Oppenham*; as they were the first, with their Camerades, that accompanied His Majestie, at his landing in the *Paltz*, testifying how willing they were to oppose danger, in sight of their King and Master, revenging themselves on the Spaniard (a cruell enemy to the Daughter of our King, and Sister to our Dread Soveraigne, the Queene of *Bohemia*) whom before they had removed, by force the Armes, from the sweete land of the *Paltz*, where at this time, they were fighting, to invest againe His Majestie of *Bohemia* her Husband, and his Royall issue, being under the Conduct of the Lyon of the *North*, the invincible King of *Sweden*, their Leader; who was carelesse (as he said himselfe that night) to incurre the feude, or the enmity and anger, both of the House of *Austria*, and King of *Spaine*, to doe service to his Deere Sister, the Queene of *Bohemia*. Who would not then, my deere Camerades, Companions, not of want, but of valour and courage, at such a time, being the time we all of us longed to see, who would not (I say) presse to discharge the dutie of valourous Souldiers and Captaines, in sight of their Master and King, having crossed the *Rhine,* fighting for the Queene of Souldiers, being led by the King of Captaines, and Captaine of Kings; who would not then, [II-93] as true valourous *Scots*, with heart and hand sustaine the Fight, discharging at once the dutie of Souldiers, and valourous Captaines, by that meanes so farre as in them lay, restoring the *Paltz*, contemning death, striving to get victory over their enemies, and freedome of Conscience to their distressed brethren long kept in bondage, and under tyranny of their enemies, the space of ten yeares, till the coming of this magnanimous King, and great Captaine; who in six moneths time after, did free the *Paltz* of all *Spanish* Forces, setting them at libertie; having brought the Keyes of all Goales with him, and opened the doores, not onely of all prisons, but also of all houses and Churches in the *Paltz*, that had beene closed ten yeares before, through the banishment of the owners, bringing backe to their houses againe, and having removed the Idolatrous worship of *Papists* out of their Churches, suffered them againe to serve God peaceably in their former true, undoubted and onely pure profession of the Faith of Christs Gospell.

## The twenty-fourth Dutie discharged of our March to
### Mentz, *and of the intaking of it.*

His Majestie having laien here at *Oppenham* some three dayes, till the rest of the Armie were come over at *Oppenham,* and at *Stockstat,* the Armie being come over, the *Spaniards* were afraid to stay in any place, that was not wondrous strong; and their feare being so great, they quit *Stagne* setting it on fire; as also the *Lotterings* Garrison did quit *Wormes,* having first abused the Towne with plundering, and other intolerable damage and hurt, they retired all unto *Frankendall,* being strong by fortification, they made it strong of men, having retired above eight thousand *Spaniards* within it, who being blocked up, had never the resolution or courage once to have falne forth on the *Swedens* Forces, but kept themselves close within walles.

His Majestie taking his march towards *Mentz,* which before was blockt up, on the other side of the *Rhine* next to *Franckford,* with Shippes, and with the Landgrave of *Hessens* Forces, his majestie about the middest of *December,* in cruell tempestuous weather for frost and snow, coming before it on a Sunday in the afternoone, and having himselfe rode about the Towne, on the *Paltz* side, and recognosced both workes and walles, the Armie standing in Battaile, his Majestie having first commanded the Horsemen, some to quarters, and some on dutie: The foote Briggads were commanded towards their severall Postes, where Colonell *Hepburnes* Briggad (according to use) was directed to the most dangerous Poste, next the enemy; and the rest to theirs. The night coming on, we begunne our approaches, and prepared for making readie of our Battailes, where, according to custome, men were ordained to make Cannon Baskets, some to provide materialls, some to watch, some to worke, some to guard the Artillery, and some to guard the work-men, and some to guard the Colours before the Briggad: the day approaching, having made ready the Batteries in the night; as also having wrought in the approaching by day: the service on both sides beginneth with Cannon and Musket, so that our Cannon off the water, and from the other side, did shoot blancke within the Towne, which made great terrour. [II-94] amongst the Inhabitants, the Bishop being removed towards *Cowblance,* he did leave two thousand *Spaniards* within the Towne, who were in doubt of the Burgers fidelitie, neither yet did they expect any reliefe, and the Towne being wide of circumference, more than they were able to beset, they begun betimes to thinke on Accord; yet, they resolved to make it the more honourable, their best was to prolong time.

Colonell *Axallilly,* a *Swede,* being come to visit his Majestie, having had no employment in the beleaguering, being at supper with Colonell *Hepburne* and me, on our Poste, by our Guard-fire, being merrily discoursing, that if a misfortune should happen unto him there, what should be thought of it, having had no charge, he having foretold a mishap unto himselfe, the next day after dinner hard by me, the legge was shot from him with a Cannon Bullet, who after that was carried by my folkes unto his lodging, and being cured, served after with a treene or woodden legge.

At this Siege our Briggad did sustaine more hurt than the rest of the Armie, being most employed on all commands, both in respect of their valour, and of the good conduct and fortune followed them, and their Leaders.

The third day, the Skonce without the Towne being hard pressed, and we having on our quarter approached to the walles, and the Towne, from the water, and from the Landgrave side, having sustained great losse by their Cannon. The enemy finding there was no hope of reliefe, he entered in a Treatie, and gave up the Towne on accord; being suffered to march out without Armes, they were conveyed to *Cowblance*: they being gone, Quarters were made for the whole foote within the Towne, where three dayes before Christmasse we were quartered, and remained there, being lodged in the extremitie of the cold with the *Hopstaffe*, to the fifth of *March* 1632.

### The twenty-fourth Observation.

His Majestie of *Sweden* having crost the *Rhine*, the Prisoners that were long banished, being ten yeares out of the *Paltz*, were then incouraged by their libertie attained unto, through the valour and wisedome of his Majestie of *Sweden*, who did bring the keyes of the prison, and of their houses, and the passe once opened, they begunne to returne home, and the strangers removed, they rejoyced at their home coming, in the entertaining of their friends, that fought for them, and they did perceive the terrour and feare of their enemies, that drew all unto *Franckendale*, as unto the strongest corner of their feeble hearts, where it was evident to see, their removing from all was drawing neere. *Franckendale* being blocked up, and victualls debarred from them, it was impossible for them to subsist long.

I did observe here, at the in-taking of *Mentz*, that toyle, travell, danger and resolution were our best meanes, in getting this Towne in three dayes time; our Cannon having from the *Hessen* side so spoyled the Burgers on the streets, and within their houses, finding their owne hurt, being stronger than the Garrison, forced the Garrison to Accord, by that meanes preventing their owne ruine, and the losse of their goods, if the Towne had beene taken by storme of hand. And therefore, for sparing of their Citie, they promised his Majestie, for keeping good order, threescore thousand Dollers.

Likewise I did observe, by *Axallillies* losse of his legge, that many times [II-95] hurt comes to men in that kinde, as a presage of worldly lucke, in getting, as they say, something to the sore foote; for he, before this, being but meane in estate and employment, was afterwards made rich by governments. Divers others I could instance under our Armie, were advanced to riches, after receiving of meane hurts, and on meane occasions of service, as this was, being but a looker on. But for me, let me have health, and glad povertie with credit, for riches I desire not, if that I may have more of credit than others; and that shall be my prayer, to keepe my minde in an invincible place, that externall things move me not: neither would I suffer fortune to be able with her threatnings to pierce me, having tryed sharper that could not dare. Let us then be content with our lot, and though the meanes we should live on, be detained from us, yet let us wrong no body by oppression, in conquering by unlawfull meanes, and doubtlesse the Lord will conserve our healths, and sustaine our bodies with sufficiency, and so being honest, we neede never be ashamed to be thought poore in mens esteeme, being rich in Christ.

Here also I did observe, that oftentimes those, that durst not lift up their heads in time of danger, doe often better speed and thrive in worldly things, than those that merit the best: as was seene on those Briggads entred first into *Mentz*, that did get both Prisoners and spoyle with the best Quarters, when others, that deserved better, were worse quartered in emptie houses, while as other Colonells and Souldiers, of farre lesse deserving, were making up of estates for their posteritie, in better Quarters, within the *Paltz* and *Franckonie*.

But on the contrary, valourous men their labours and travells ought to be rewarded, with honour and profit, by those they did truely serve. For if great undertakings in this kinde, before Townes, in extremitie of danger, were nobly recompenced with great rewards; that would incourage men againe to refuse nothing to be undertaken, that was honourable: and on the contrary; nothing discontents worthy men more, than to be rewarded like Cowards; and those that stood out the danger, like those that durst not lift head when the storme blew; and when the hope of reward is the comfort of mens labours, than all toyle seemes to be easie: and it is a hard thing, when the diligent and industrious is disappointed of his hyre, and when he is rewarded with injury, who did merit well; this of all evills, is most unsufferable, when he must suffer losse that expected helpe: for on the contrary, it were more just, that notable vertues should be notably rewarded, with badges of honour, to make all others treade in the glorious path of vertue, and well-doing.

---

*The twenty-fifth Dutie discharged of my March*
*with a partie to the* Mosell.

While we lay at *Mentz*, his Majestie having heard that the Spaniard had set over a strong Armie at *Spier*, of intention to fall on the *Rhinegrave* his Regiment of horse, lying in the hinder *Paltz*, betwixt *Bachrach* and the *Mosell*, who having no foote forces with him, his [II-96] Majestie made choice of me, to be sent unto him with a partie of five hundred commanded Musketiers, for to assist him in maintaining the Garrisons in those parts, from the incursion of the *Spaniard,* and his Majestie hearing of the Queenes coming towards *Francford*, leaving orders with Duke *Barnard* of *Wymar* (then Governour of *Mentz*, and commander over the Armie in his Majesties absence) to direct me away with the partie to the *Rhinegrave*, his Majestie being gone, I was sent for by the Duke to receive my Orders, which were, I should receive five hundred commanded Musketiers, with sufficient victualls and Amunition, and then to ship them at *Mentz*, and to goe downe to the *Rhine* towards *Bachrach*, and there to send to the *Rhinegrave* for further orders, but before my departing, I took orders in writ from the Duke, how to carry my selfe in obeying of the *Rhinegrave* his commands, and immediately I went and received the partie, being in readinesse on the market-place, with Proviant and Amunition for the voyage, and being shipt we went downe the *Rhine* towards *Bingen* on the *Noe*, that runs by *Creutznach* through the *Paltz* into the *Rhine* at *Bingen*, where Sir *Iames Ramseys* Regiment did lie in Garrison, out of which there went with me of that Regiment a Captaine with a hundred Musketiers; being shipped, we continued our course towards *Bachrach*, where being landed, I desired from the Governour (being a Captaine under the Red Regiment) Quarters for my Souldiers, till I got orders whether to march, but the Captaine being discourteous, closed the Ports, using us unfriendly, whereupon I desired to be let in to speake with him, which being granted for me alone, I entered, and having spoke with the Captaine, was refused of Quarters, and of Proviant for my Souldiers, whereupon I retired forth, & the Ports being closed againe, I made our Souldiers make good fires of the driest wood without the Towne, whereof there was no scarcitie; and being darke, the Towne lying alongst the River, we getting intelligence there; was a water gate, where there stood a Centry, I tooke a small Boat and two Officers with me, and entering the sallying Port, the Centry suspecting no enemy, we tooke him off, swearing if he cryed, we would kill him, and bringing him to our Guard, left him to their keeping, and immediately I went in at the sallying Port, accompanied with my Officers and some Musketiers, and having set a Guard at the Port, we went to the Captaines quarter, and tooke in his lodging, where we made good cheare, jeering the Captaine, till he was contented to send forth abundance of victuals for the whole party; & to make good quarters for our whole Officers within the Towne, where they did get both meat & money, and beside; I made all the Dorpes that were without the Towne belonging to it, to pay a contribution of money to me & my Officers, for keeping good order, w^{ch} we did to repay the Captaines unthankfulnesse.

The next day leaving the partie to make good cheare, I went to the *Rhinegrave* to receive his Commands, who directed me to march to a Dorpe within two miles of *Coblentz*, and to quarter there until further Orders; I retired to the partie, and forcing the Captaine to send fiftie Musketiers with me; wee followed our Orders, and quartered within two miles of *Coblentz*.

The *Rhinegrave* having gotten intelligence where some of the *Spaniards* did lie in quarters, with his Regiment falling into their quarters, he did defeat two Regiments of them, that were come over the *Mosell* before the Armie.

The next day, he advertised me, he was to advance with his Regiment towards *Spier*, neere the *Mosell*, to attend the enemies coming, and if he were distressed, he would advertise me, whereby I might timely beset the Strengths. [II-97]

The *Spaniard* having set over his Army at *Spier*, being ten thousand strong, getting intelligence of the *Rhinegraves* Quarter, they marched on it, where he lay in open Dorpes, in a manner trusting and reposing too much unto himselfe and his strength, mis-regarding his enemies, being a Cavalier who was both couragious and resolute, who had also resolute and valourous Officers and Souldiers under him, a sudden alarum had no power to fright him or his, being his watch was commanded by Rutmaster *Hume* of *Carrelside*, who was a Cavalier of courage and of good experience, finding by intelligence the enemy was approaching on his Guard, he advertised his Colonell timely to draw out on horse-backe, and to expect his enemy in the field, who did take no notice of the first advertisement, till the Rutmaster rode to him, and advertised him to draw to the fields, he commanded him againe to retire unto his watch, he knew his owne time, the Rutmaster scarce returned, when he with his watch were charged by three Troopes, which charge he received, and charged them againe, and then retired on the Colonels quarter, being so hard followed, that by the Colonell was on horse-backe, he was invironed by three Regiméts of the enemies, whom he bravely charged home, with foure troops of his, and making them to retire, he did caracolle about from the enemy, having suffered losse on the charge. The young Grave of *Nassaw*, then a Rutmaster, being hurt and taken, and divers more inferiours being retired, he commanded Rutmaster *Hume* with the other foure Troopes, to make a stand before the enemy; to hold them off till such time he were retired.

The Rutmaster seeing the enemies strong, coming up in full squadrons one after another, he drew up very wisely his foure troops in the entry of a wood, making a large and broad front, whereby the enemy might judge, he was stronger than he was; as also, that they might thinke he had Musketiers behinde him in Ambuscade for a reserve or hinderhalt, which made the enemy give them the longer time, and the better opportunitie to his Colonell to retire with ease. The Rutmaster finding the enemy to fall off a little, he retired his troope at an easie trot, till he overtooke the Colonell, who thought before their coming they had beene all cut off.

Immediatly the *Rhinegrave* sent to me to beset the Garrisons (as I did) and then he sent Poste unto his Majestie, acquainting his Majestie how all had past, and of the enemies strength; which his Majestie having knowne, he drew his Armie together at *Mentz*, with a resolution to fight with the *Spaniard,* before he were suffered to relieve *Franckendale*, but the enemy hearing of his Majesties preparation, they retired over the *Mosell* againe, and they being retired, I was recall'd with the partie unto *Mentz*, where having left a Captaine and a hundred Musketiers with the *Rhinegrave* to be disposed on, having got orders to that effect from his Majestie, which afterwards were all cut off by the enemy; the rest of the partie dismist, I retired to my Commands.

### The twenty five Observation.

The duty of an Officer leading a party is almost alike to the duty of a Generall leading an Army, in fight, in march, in quartering, in command; and those he commands ought to give the like obedience unto him, though strangers, as if absolutly they were of his owne Regiment; and his care for them should be as for himselfe. He ought also at the undertaking of the command or charge over

them, to foresee to be [II-98] sufficiently provided of all things necessary for such
service, as he is commanded on, of Ammunition, spades, shovels, materials for
his cannon and Pettards, with his guides to convey him from one place to
another, till he come to the end of his intended march, doing all things by wise
and deliberate stedfastnesse, in command without wavering, not altering his
orders, as he must answer to his Generall, to whom he is to give account: and his
best is, to have his orders in writing, that in case of variance betwixt
Commanders, writing will beare him thorough, when orders by mouth may be
denied: neither ought he in his command to be timorous or rash, but either
resolute and remisse, as occasion offers, and on occasions apart when his
command must be relative to anothers direction, that is but subordinat to a
Generall, he must deliberat wisely what to doe, and he must foresee the best and
worst of things; but having once deliberated, let him be as resolute in the
execution as he can.

Likewise here we see in the *Rhinegrave* a rare example, both of remisnesse
and courage in one person. For first being made foreseene of the enemies
coming, he shewed his remisnesse, having refused to give care to the severall
advertisments, till in th'end he was pursued unawares, and then he did testifie his
inward courage and resolution in charging the enemy, being three Regiments,
with foure troopes putting them to a retreat.

Neverthelesse, we see him alike beholden to the Rut-master for his
advertisment, as for his safe retreat, having first and last suffered the dent of the
enemies Armes on him, and houlding it off his Commander. A brave example to
be imitated and followed of all Cavaliers, that would gaine honour and
reputation.

---

*The twenty sixth Duty discharged of the accidents occurred
in our warres during our lying in* Mentz.

This following discourse, being no direct part of the discharge of duty
intended of the Regiment, neverthelesse for lacke of emploiment in my calling,
at that time being idle in Garrison, I remarked, so farre as I could by report, the
actions of others as they occurred then, being out of action my selfe; yet I can
affirme, what I relate will be found true, if not, let me be no more blamed than
those that gave the intelligence.

His Majesty having gone to meete the Queene being come then from
*Leipsigh* to *Hano*, the twenty second of Ianuary 1632. his Majesty conveyed the
Queene to *Francford*, where all the cannons went off, after their entries. At this
time also, the Rex-chancellour *Oxensterne* came from *Spruce*, conveyed by our
countrimen Sr. *Patrick Ruthven*, then eldest Colonell of *Scots* under his Majesty,
being then Governour of *Mariburg*, and Colonell of a *Dutch* Regiment lay there,
with whom did come from *Spruce* Lievetenant Colonell *Hugh Hamilton*, who
was Lievetenant Colonell then to Sr. *George* [II-99] *Cuningham* his Regiment of

*Scots* that lay in *Spruce*, Captaine *Mongomery* came also with them, who soone after was made Lievetenant Colonell to a free Squadron of foote, and after that was killed in combat on horsbacke by the Generall Quarter-master *Bullion*, at first Captaine under me. At this time also came with him Quarter-master *Sandelence*, who afterwards was Captaine Major and Lievetenant Colonell, having ascended by degrees, according to worth and deserving.

The Chancellor being come, his Majesty and he sat ordinarily all day in counsell, treating on weighty matters; At which time, the Cullens Ambassadour was treating apart with his Majesty for neutrality, affirming he had given no assistance to the last League, neither yet was he of the League; As also he affirmed that at the last *Westphalia* convention he refused assistance to the rest of the League: his Majesty replied to the Cullens Ambassadour, how hardly and unchristianly they had dealt with the Evangelists stends, worse then if they had beene *Iewes* or *Turkes*, in taking their Churches from them, and in banishing themselves. Neverthelesse there were some Articles proposed unto them concerning the Neutrality (*viz.*) First of all, molesting the Evangelists, under whatsoever pretence to be abolished and put away. Secondly, the free liberty of the Religion to be granted and suffered, and that the Students of the Religion should be taken aswell in the Colleges as the Papists. Thirdly, in all Cities, the Evangelists to be so free to traffique as the Papists. Fourthly, they should give no assistance unto the Kings Majesties enemies, nor no contribution, nor Bills to answer monies on exchange. Fifthly, to give free passage through their land aswell to his Majesties Army, as to his enemies, nor to hinder them of it, both alike. Sixthly, that his Majestie of *Swedens* servants should have the passes open, when they pleased to passe and repasse. Seaventhly, that his Majesties Agents might lie at *Cullen* to see the Neutrality were justly observed. Eighthly, that his Majesty of *Sweden* his friends and confederats, should have free traffique in their Townes and territories.

The *Cullens* Ambassadour returned from *Francford* with these sleight points to be granted by their Bishop. The *Swedens* were come so neere *Cullen* that the Superiours were reprehended for it by the Clergy out of the Pulpits; for giving such liberty to *Hereticks* to come againe so neere unto their jurisdictions.

By this time the *Landgrave* of *Hessen* with his Army, being neere ten thousand strong of horse and foote, for our assistance did lie on the other side of the Rhine, over against us, and from thence they fell strong on the *Spaniards* which were in *Rinskoe*, making them also quit those parts, and the inhabitants for feare, forsaking their houses, his Majesty promised them his gracious protection to stay and remaine in their houses, paying their weekely contribution they payed before to the Bishop of *Mentz*.

Being here also at *Mentz*, the *French* Ambassadour I did see get audience, the reason of his coming being to shew his Majesty of *Sweden*, that the Kings Majesty of *France* was offended, his Majesty of *Sweden* had crost the Rhine against his paction, and confederacy made with the King of *France*, and therefore desired he should retire againe with his Army. His Majesty answered he did but prosecute his enemy, and if his Majesty of *France* was offended, he could not helpe it, and those that would make him retire over the Rhine againe, it behooved them to doe it with the sword in their hand, for other- [II-100] wise he was not minded to leave it but to a stronger, and if his Majesty of *France* should anger him much, he knew the way to *Paris*, and he had hungry Souldiers would drinke wine, and eate with as good will in *France* as in *Germany*. Therefore he hoped his Majesty would be better advised in sending the next Ambassage in milder termes. This interchange of message went betwixt them, till at last, they were setled on secondary conditions of a new League offensive and defensive.

At this time the Felt-marshall *Gustavus Horne* tooke in *Mergenhem* on the *Sawler streame*, *Hailburne*, on the *Necker*, *Wmpviniphen*, and *Necker Olin*.

Likewise *Kunickstene* in the *Vetro*, was taken in by accord after *Mentz*, as also the *Spaniard* left *Vieitzler*, and *Geylhousen*, leaving them both unto the *Sweden*, without shot of musket or cannon.

His Majesty at this time, caused to publish an Edict, where all Marchants of whatsoever Religion, or Nation they were of, should be free to passe and repasse with their goods to the *Francforder Masse*, and that none of his Majesties Army of whatsoever condition they were, either of horse or foote, should trouble them, under paine of death, where the concealer of the wrong being got notice of should be punished to death, as the Actor.

Likewise the twelfth of Ianuary *Babenhowsen* was taken in by accord, by his Majesties order and direction, and in the end of December, *Manhem* was taken in by Duke *Barnard* of *Wymar*, having surprized their guards, whereabove two hundred and fifty were cut off, of the strangers, and quarters and service given to the *Dutch*; where a Captaine and his Ensigne were taken prisoners, and let loose againe, for the paiment of their Ransome, and being come to *Heidelberg* they were executed by the Governours direction there, for over-seeing their duties, and these of the League, lying at *Heidelberg* were mightily troubled with the neerenesse of the *Swedens* neighbour-hood, having gotten *Manhem*, their passage unto the Rhine was altogether cut off from them.

Likewise the *Spaniard* did quit *Garmarsham*, and retiring to *Franckendale*, they had no more in the *Paltz* but that and *Heidelberg*, his Majestie wonderfully having gotten in *Creutznach*, and the Castle, where Lievetenant Colonell *Tabot* was killed, and the worthy Captaine *Dowglas*, and Sir *Henry Vaines* sonne was shot in the Arme.

Colonell *Alexander Ramsey* was placed Governour of *Creutznach* by his Majestie of *Sweden*, as a beginning of reward for his old service and attendance, who loved nothing better than nobly and kindly to entertaine his friends and strangers, being the common receptacle and refuge of all his Country-men, that liked to honour him with their company: As also he was most willing to entertaine and respect strangers of the best qualitie, and most of all he was peremptory in maintaining his Countries credit, obligeing all *Cavaliers* to his power. But most unwilling to be beholden to others, carrying still a noble minde.

At this time, his Majestie being in *Mentz*, *Bingen*, *Bagherach* on the *Rhine*, and *Shaule*, were taken in by Scalade, with a surprize by the *Scots* of Sir *Iames*

*Ramseys* Regiment, where those within were thrice stronger than those pursued them, but being once entred the Towne, the Inhabitants assisting the *Scots*, they put all to the sword, except the Officers that were taken Prisoners [II-101] by Major *Hanam*, a Gentleman of much worth, valour, and discretion in Command, whose losse was much lamented, he having died soone after of a Consumption, was much regrated of all his acquaintance, and of my selfe in particular, being my olde Camerade.

At this time also the Towne of *Spier* came under his Majesties protection and devotion, and leavied three Companies for his Majesties service; *Landaw* also and *Crowneweisenburg* did become good *Swedens*, *Landstall* was taken in also by storme, by the helpe of the Country Boores; shortly after was *Elwangen*, *Oberwesell*, *Papart*, and *Lovensteene* taken in by accord: Also the Castle of *Erenfells*, and Towle-house over against *Bingen* was taken in by the Landgrave of *Hessens* folke.

By this time was *Damets* in *Maclenburg* given over by Accord, unto Generall Major *Lowhowsen*; as also *Wesmer* on the *Baltick* Coast was taken in by Accord the tenth of *Ianuary* 1632. And the Garrison marched out three thousand strong, being commanded by Colonell *Grame*, who having buried some Cannon, robbed the shippes, and tooke away against Accord a number of Armes. Likewise on his march unto *Silesia*, he killed a *Swedens* Lievtenant; but being followed, the *Swedens* (at the command of Generall *Tott*) Generall Major *Lowhowsen* having overtaken them, five hundred were killed, and two thousand taken prisoners that tooke service; and Colonell *Grame* was sent prisoner to *Gripswale*, to remaine there till further tryall.

By this time also, Generall *Tott* his Armie marched over the *Elve* towards *Luneburg*, being neere foureteene thousand strong of foote and horse, under whom were severall *Scots* Regiments come from *Scotland* the Harvest before (*viz.*) Sir *Iames Lumsdells* Regiment, to whom *Robert Stewart* was Lievetenant Colonell. The Master of *Forbesse* his Regiment, to whom Sir *Arthur Forbesse* was Lievetenant Colonell; Sir *Frederick Hamiltons* Regiment, to whom *Alexander Cunningham* was Lievetenant Colonell; Colonell *Astins English* Regiment, to whom *Vavezer* was Lievetenant Colonell; Colonell *Monro* of *Obstell* his Regiment, to whom *Iohn Monro* was Lievetenant Colonell; and a Squadron of *English*, commanded by Lievetenant Colonell *Mon-Gorge*, being the Remainder of Sir *Thomas Conwayes* Regiment; and Colonell *Robert Lesly*, his old Regiment of *Scots*. Generall *Tott* his Armie being over the *Elve*; Colonell *Ryneaker*, and *Curmago* did gather all the Emperialists, and those of the League out of all other Garrisons, towards *Stoade*; and *Buckstihoode*, to defend themselves; where leaving them to some other penne to write of, I returne to the *Rhine*. His Majestie being making preparation towards the *Danube*, to visit the *Byerforst*, and *Tillie*: where I minde to follow out my march, our idle time being almost spent.

His Majestie did write unto the States of *Holland*, to draw sooner unto the fields, than their custome was, to hinder the *Spaniards* from sending forces unto *Dutchland*, which letters mooved the States to giue out Edicts, that all Regiments and Companies should be complete, under paine of cashiering, to draw to the fields against the first of March. By this time, his Majesty of *France* having a strong Army together on the borders of *Dutchland*, the Catholique League did what they could, to put his Majestie of *France* by the eares with the King of *Sweden*, alleadging his Majesty of *Swedens* intention was fully to roote out the Catholique Religion; and that he had already banished a number of them from their Cloysters, which was an [II-102] untruth; for his Majestie of *Sweden* banished none, but those who through feare did banish themselves. But on the contrary, his Majestie in all places he had taken in, suffered them the free libertie and use of their Religion untroubled, without troubling of any mans Conscience in matters of Religion. But his Majestie of *France*, being better informed, refused any assistance to the Catholique League, against his Majestie of *Sweden*; but wished rather the Catholique League to remaine *neutrall*; and that he would interpose with his Majestie of *Sweden* for obtaining the *Neutralitie*; whereupon instantly they begunne to treate of the *Neutralitie* and Monsieur *Seharnasse* was sent Ambassadour to his Majestie of *Sweden* to that effect, and his Majestie proposed, and set downe the points he desired of them, if he should yeeld unto the *Neutralitie*.

First, they should give his Majestie and his Armie free passage through their Lands, especially over the *Danube*.

Secondly, they should take all their Forces from the *Emperialists*, and be bound hereafter to give them no more helpe.

Thirdly, they should restore the *Palatinate* unto the former estate, and all others they had take beside.

Fourthly, they should contribute to the maintaining of the *Swedens* Armie.

The *French* Ambassadour having promised within fourteene dayes to get the foresaid Articles confirmed, his Majestie granted a fort'nights Stillstand, providing the Ambassadour would make *Papenham* retire his Forces out of *Westphalia*, and *Stifft-madeburg*; As also that those Forces the Duke of *Bavaria* and the League had in *Bohemia*, should also retire; and that such parts as his Majesties Armie had beleaguered or blockered, they should goe on nothwithstanding of the Still-stand, till they came to an Accord, or forced to quit them. The time of this Treatie, the Catholique League found many doubts.

First, that it was hard for them being so much obliged to the house of *Austria*, to forsake them in their greatest neede.

Secondly, the Catholike Religion, in that case, did lacke a strong Protectour; whose like they could not soone finde againe.

Thirdly, the King of *France* had his owne pretentions in this Treatie, to wit, to weaken the house of *Austria*; which his Majestie of *France* could easily doe, by separating the League from the house of *Austria*. It was easie then uuto him to transferre the Empire unto another Family: and the League embracing the *Neutralitie*, the Crown of *France* had wonne their point against the house of *Austria*; and if the *Neutralitie* were not granted or accepted by the League, the Kings Majestie of *France* would not quit the *Swedens* faction; but rather favourize all their enterprizes; whereby, in times comming, he should have the lesse cause to feare the house of *Austria*, but in the end, the seeking of this *Neutralitie* was but for meere policie, to hinder his Majestie of *Swedens* progresse, till such time, as that Generall *Tilly* could make a strong head againe, and to winne time of his Majestie to prepare themselves for warre.

This Treatie turning to nought without any fruit; neither were the *Spaniards* still this time, but having drawne to a strong head, they came over the *Mosell* againe unto the *Paltz*, and were beaten backe with great losse, and the whole *Paltz* made free of them. [II-103]

In which conflict Master *Home* in presence of the Rex-chancellor *Oxensterne*, before the face of the whole Army, with his owne troope, and two other troopes of horse, charged a strong body of the *Spanish* horsmen, & tooke nine Cornets from them, having hunted and chased them, to their great shame, and to the perpetuall credits of the pursuers, especially of the Leader, whose actions are worthy to be recorded to Posterity.

After this victory obtained over the *Spaniard*, his Majesty of *Sweden* did propose certaine propositions and Articles unto the Duke of *Bavier*, and the Catholique Stends that were confederat with him. First, to breake the Emperiall Edict that was published over the Empire. Secondly, both the Evangelists Religion to be let free and untroubled by the Papists. Thirdly, *Bohemia*, *Nerlin* and *Silezia* to be restored in the old manner, and the banished freely to returne to their lands and country. Fourthly, to set his Majesty of *Bohemia* free againe in the *Paltz*. Fifthly, the Dukedome of *Bavier* to be transferred on him againe. Sixthly, the Towne of *Ausburg* to be put in the former estate againe, and the exercise of the Evangelists Religion to be free againe unto it as before. Seventhly, all Iesuits to be put away and banished out of the Empire, as the Pest of the Common-weale. Eighthly, all Evangelists Cloisters to be restored againe, as well as the Catholique Cloisters. Ninthly, all Cloisters in *Wartenburgland*, to be restored againe. Tenthly, to choose his Majesty of *Sweden*, as King of the *Romans*.

About the end of Ianuary *Papinham* gathered the whole Garrisons together that were in *Brunswicke* lands, and *Westfalia*, and relieved *Madeburg*; forcing *Banier* to retire on *Calbe*; alleadging he had a mandat of his Majestie of *Sweden* not to fight; *Papenham*, who having relieved the Towne, and gotten intelligence the Duke of *Luneburg* with a strong Army, was to come on him from *Wolfenbetle*; he having left *Madeburg*, and taken out the Garrison having nailed the cannon, and destroyed all he could, in casting it into the *Elve*, which he could not take with him on waggons; having spoiled their best cannon, leaving the bare walles to the *Swedens*; which they immediatly beset againe with three Companies: *Papenham* marched towards *Wolfenbetle* to meete the Duke of *Luneburg*.

Likewise *Palsgrave Wolfegan William*, did also by his brothers intercession, *Palsgrave Augustus*, hould on with his Majesty of *Sweden* for a Neutrality, but in vaine. The fourteene dayes of still-stand being out, they fell to worke againe, every one for himselfe.

*Bamberg* also taken by *Gustavus Horne* Felt-marshall, and shortly after was *Tillie* come thither with a strong Army from *Nerlin*, unlooked for, set on *Gustavus Hornes* forces, the Towne being almost made fast by the *Swedens*, *Tilly* with his Army falls on: and the Felt-marshall having put his cannon away by water on the *Maine*, retired in haste with losse upon *Harsford*, after a long skirmish had with the Emperialists, and having gotten intelligence of foure Regiments of *Tillies*, that had past by *Halstad*, he did breake up with the Cavalerie, and in their quarter to *Oberbyde*, being but halfe a mile from *Bamberg*, falls on them two houres before day, and defeats two Regiments, to wit, *Planck*, *Hartish* and *Merodish* the youngers Regiment by fire and sword, where he got but two Cornets, the rest being burnt in the fire, with their goods: The Crabbats were forced to swimme the *Maine*, the rest betooke themselves for refuge unto the Dragoniers [II-104] quarters that lay at *Stafflebach*, and retiring to the Church-yard, the Felt-marshall having no musketiers with him, pressed to fire them out, but in vaine, so that he retired againe with his Officers on *Hasford* and *Swineford*. These newes coming unto his Majesty, he prepared for a march unto *Franconia*, bringing the rest of his Majesties forces together, that were with the Felt-marshall; and he did send unto *During*, to the Duke of *Wymar*, and to Generall *Banier* to bring their forces together, to meete betwixt *Nurenberg* and *Donavert*, to search out Generall *Tilly*, and about the middest of March 1632. we brake up from *Mentz*, having left the Rex-chancellor *Oxensterne*, and Duke *Bernard* of *Wymar*, with eight thousand men in the *Paltz*, to attend the *Spaniards* further intentions on the Rhine.

## The twenty-sixth Observation.

The Catholique League, seeing the *Spaniard* terrified in the *Paltz*, and almost beaten away, they begun being members of that head, to quake and tremble for feare of the *Swedens* neighbourhood, and therefore the Bishops of *Mentz*, *Triere*, *Cullen*, *Wurtzburg* and of *Bambrick* presently resolved, out of their policy, to treat for a neutrality, pressing, so farre as lay in them, to bring the King of *France* and his Majesty of *Sweden* to pull at each others beards; alleadging the *Swedens* intentions were only to subvert the Catholique Religion, and the professours of Popery, as he had already (as they alleadged) persecuted and banished the Churchmen out of *Erford*, *Wurtzburg*, *Francford*, *Hickst*, and out of all other parts where they were: whereupon his Majesty of *France* notwithstanding of his confederacy with the King of *Sweden* was commoved at his crossing the Rhine, fearing he might bring the Catholique League on his side, and then turne his Armes against *France*, which suspitions wrought an Ambassage from his Majesty of *France*, towards his Majesty of *Sweden*, for treaty of neutrality betwixt the King of *Sweden* and the Catholique League, which in th'end turned to nothing. Where we see, that all Potentates and great Kings, doe keepe no Confederacy nor League, but only so farre as they are helpfull for their owne aimes and designes; preferring their benefit before the keeping of their covenants; where we see, that Kings hand-writings or seales, in pactions making, tye them no more then as nothing, when they finde them prejudiciall to their owne greatnesse, and cannot be made to keepe their covenants, but with stronger power. Then we see here, his Majesty of *Sweden* was nothing moved with the King of *France* his threatning (except he would retire over the Rhine againe) seeing he knew his owne ability at that time, that being once over the Rhine, he could march unto *France*. The consideration whereof made them agree better on secondary conditions, having past from the first covenant; so that we see there is no dealing with Kings but on equall termes, and then are they most reasonable; but the example of Kings, in this point of their covenants, is not to be imitated by any other inferiours; for in respect of them, though not in respect of God, they are privileged persons; who cannot be punished for their faults but by God alone. And therefore, amongst inferiours, nothing is to be kept more strict next unto faith unviolated, then mens word and promise, especially promises betwixt old friends. But alas! no friendship is permanent, seeing [II-105] many things come betwixt, turning it unto hatred and hostility; for where love doth not grow, the friendship is not durable.

Likewise here we see, his Majesty of *France* made haste to interpose his request for the weale of the Catholique League, shewing himselfe discontented with their usage, to make them the more ready to thinke on him, before they should any wayes leane in their necessity to the King of *Sweden*. As also we see the policy of the League, though in their necessity they seemed to make use of the King of *France* his friendship, yet they would not cast off the house of *Austria*, and King of *Spaine* their ould friends, for the hope they had in their new friend the King of *France*, lest their new friend might disappoint them of their expectations, as he did in th'end, missing his owne aimes.

We see also here the *Frenches* policy, in making haste to intercede for the *Leagueistes*, lest the danger might come on himselfe; for the King of *France* hearing the King of *Sweden* had crossed the Rhine, he did not stay to bring his Army together, till the League should call for his helpe, lest it should be too late, but incontinent brought his Army to the *Mosell*, and then sent his Ambassador to *Mentz* to his Majesty of *Sweden* to treat, having his Army at hand, which was the only sure way then to get the better conditions, knowing the King of *Sweden* had already too many Irons in the fire.

Those we see are the best friends, that in necessity keepe their paction, as the Catholique League did at all times unto the Emperour, who otherwise had bin no Emperour, neither yet had he bin Emperour, had the Evangelists kept together and hazarded their meanes and bloud, in defence of the publique cause, as the Catholiques did in their greatest necessity, once every yeere setting up ever new Armies, as one was beaten unto them: their wisdome and constancy were so great, that presently the next Spring, through their power and diligence, they had ever another new Army afoote, which in th'end made their enemies the Evangelists weary, sparing their meanes, they suffered in a manner the cause and the publique to be neere lost; being since beaten by their owne Armes and meanes, seeing they neglected time, while as they might employ their meanes to the finall overthrow of their enemies: and yet to my knowledge, in *Germany*, if they would conjoyne their strengths together constantly against the Papists, they are powerfull enough to free all *Germany* of Popery, banishing them over the *Alpes*, from whence they came. And I perswade my selfe, none that knowes *Germany*, but in his conscience he must confesse this to be truth. But when our fellowes in friendship faile us, as the Evangelists one after another, for a skurvy losse, quit the Crowne of *Sweden*, the great Duke of *Saxon* having left them first, breaking his oath and promise, in prejudice of the publique peace, excluding the Protestants impiously for his owne aimes, he did prejudice the Gospell, his country, and confederates, and by his evill example: for plaine necessity, while a storme should blow over the townes of the upper Circles of the Empire, as *Strasburg*, *Vlme*, *Nurenberg* & *Francford* did accept of an unsetled peace, contrary to their mindes, in prejudice of the publique, losing themselves and the publique, for the losse of one day, being without their head, which first brought them together.

Here then we see the great difference of friendship in prosperity and in [II-106] adversity: for his Majesty of *Sweden* being at *Francford*, as a victorious King, he had then, in his prosperity, the conflux of friendship, some seeking his protection, others his friendship and confederacy, others for feare of the dint of his Armes, seeking to be Neutrall, who before were enemies; other Kings and Potentats, Republiques and Cities sending their Ambassadours congratulating his successe; yea, and which was more and rare to be seene, his Majesty of *Bohemia* in person came unto him, to offer him assistance Royall, in leavying of an Army for himselfe, and was refused, as unwilling other Armies should be in *Dutchland*, to be participant of his glory, but his owne. Where we see Fortunes Favourit laught on by the world, but how soone againe Fortune begun to frowne on his successour, who having got but one Buffet, all men would kill him, his friends (*nomine tenus*) aswell as his enemies. Where we see cleerely that there is no friend in adversity, except it be a friend in Christ, who will never forsake or leave us. This then is the friendship we should make to league and confederate with, our brethren in Christ, with whom we have unity in Faith; if that we would have our friendship durable and constant: others will change as the winde blowes plenty or penury upon us; being but temporary friends (as many of the *Dutch* are) but our brethren in Christ will never totally leave us, no not in our greatest wants and extremity of Fortune. Which should make us choose such, and to live and dye with such, fighting for them and their liberties, who will never leave us, though death sever us, but after death, they will prove constant friends to our successours (as the *Germans* did not to the Chancellor of *Sweden*) if they succeede unto us in the true and undoubted Faith. And to verifie this, I can beare witnesse, that though the enemy did keepe our brethren in Christ, that were in the *Paltz*, under ten yeares bondage; Neverthelesse that bondage, nor the tyranny used unto them by their enemies, made them never forget their fidelity and love to their King and Prince; neither yet could their tyranny make them forsake or renounce their faith in Christ, but as they continued true to God, so were they faithfull in their love to their King and Master; not only to his Majesty, but also shewed their love and kindnesse unto us, being his Majesties friends, whom they knew to be one in faith with themselves. And therefore they were ever ready and willing to undergoe alike danger with us against our common enemies; as doth witness their assistance given to the *Scots* of Sir *Iames Ramseys* Regiment, having *Conjuctis viribus* beaten their enemies on divers occasions.

The Kings Majesty of *Sweden*, though before this time none of the greatest Kings, yet in this warre, having begun with a little Army of ten thousand strong, in three yeares time he grew so great, that he was carelesse of the threatning of the great King of *France*, having entertained then in readinesse foure Armies at once, his owne which he led himselfe, under which I was still; The Felt-marshall *Gustavus Hornes* Armie, Generall *Totts* Army on the *Wazer*, and the Marquesse of *Hamiltons* Army, with whom *Banier* was joyned on the *Elve*. These foure Armies his Majesty commanded alike, and at one time, having the Emperour, the King of *Spaine*, the Catholique League, and the Duke of *Bavier* his enemies. And though the Duke of *Saxon* had an Army apart, yet his Majestie would not suffer the King of *Bohemia*, the Duke of *Lunenburg* the Landgrave of *Hessen*, nor the Dukes of *Wymar* to lead Armies in *Dutch* [II-107] *land*, but as Subalternes to his Command. And I thinke he had reason: for if his Majestie of *Bohemia* had had an Armie in the fields, it behooved the *Swedens* to have beene subalterne to the *Dutch* and *Scots*, who were then strong in the fields, in commanding strangers, as they did their owne Country-men. Notwithstanding of all these forces led and commanded by his Majestie of *Sweden*, we see that the Empire is like a depth without a bottome, that cannot be sounded. For though they lost severall Battailes, their power was so great, that incontinent they made up Armies againe, one after another, for the space of twentie yeares together; so that, with difficultie, they made the body of the Empire to stand, though the wings were very neere clipped by his Majestie of *Sweden*; who, in three yeares time, subdued the most part of the Empire, and with his owne little Armie, in one Winter, freed the *Paltz* of the *Spanish* Forces (except *Heidelberg* alone) on which occasions those of our Nation that followed his Majestie, shewed both their valour and their love, especially those of my Lord *Spence* his Regiment, seconded well by those of my Lord *Rhees* Regiment, and Sir *Iames Ramseys* worthy Regiment, were well seconded by Colonell *Lodowicke Leslyes* Regiment, which formerly were Sir *Iohn Hamiltons*. These foure Regiments of foote having followed his Majesties owne person in all occasions, were worthy their deeds should be Registred to all posteritie. Other six Regiments of *Scots*, under Generall *Tott*, and two of *English*, being yonger in the service than the former foure, were also shorter of continuance; whose actions I cannot relate, but by Information. Therefore I will be sparing, lest I should derogate from their worth, or oversee my selfe.

At this time also there were a great many worthy Cavaliers of our Nation under his Majestie, who, for their long experience and valour, had attained to the honour, not onely to be trusted before others with Governments, but also were honoured in commanding of strangers, both *Dutch* and *Swedens*, whereof some were employed in *Dutchland*, some in *Sweden*, some in *Liffeland*, and some in

*Spruce*; all alike serving their Master to his minde, where he liked best to make use of them for the weale and advancement of his service.

Sir *Patricke Ruthven*, Generall Major and Governour of *Vlme*, Colonell over *Dutch* to foote and to horse; Sir *Alexander Lesly*, Generall Major and Governour over the whole Cities, alongst the Balticke Coast; Sir *David Drummond*, Generall Major and Governour of *Statin*, over a Regiment of *Swedens*; Sir *Iohn Hepburne*, Colonell over the *Scots* Briggad; Generall Major *King*, Colonell to horse and foote of *Dutch*; Colonell *Carre*, Colonell to foote of *Scots*; Sir *Iohn Ruthven*, Generall Major, Colonell of *Dutch*; Colonell *Robert Monro* of *Fowles*, Colonell to foote and to horse over *Dutch*; The Earle of *Crawford*, Colonell to foote over *Dutch*; Colonell *Baily*, Colonell to foote over *Dutch*; Colonell *Ramsey*, Governour of *Cretesnough*, and Commander of *Dutch*; Colonell *Alexander Hamilton*, Colonell of *Scots*; Sir *Iames Ramsey*, Colonell of foote over *Scots*; Sir *William Ballentine*, Colonell over *English*; Colonell *Dowglas*, Colonell of *Dutch* horsemen; Colonell *Hume*, Colonell of *Dutch* horsemen; Colonell *Alexander Lesly* the younger, Colonell to foote over *Dutch*; Colonell *Iohn Lesly*, Colonell to foote over *Scots*; Colonell *William Gunne*, Colonell to foote over *Dutch*; Colonell *Kinninmond*, Colonell of *Swedens*; Colonell *Hugh Hamilton*, Colonell to foote over *Dutch*; Colonell *Finnes Forbesse*, and his brother, [II-108] both Colonells to foote over strangers; Colonell *Iohn Forbesse*, Colonell to foote over *Dutch*; Colonell *Alexander Forbesse*, called the bald, Colonell to foote over *Dutch*; which all, with the former twelve Regiments, were employed severally, upon the *Dutch* bottome, during his Majesties time; and since, to the great credit of their Nation; as likewise other Cavaliers of them were employed in *Sweden*; such as Colonell *Scot*, Colonell *Seaton*, and Colonell *Thomson*, others also, were employed in his Majesties service in *Spruce*; as Sir *George Fleetwood*, Colonell to foote over *English*; *Francis Ruthven*, Colonell to foote over *Scots*, and *William Kunningham*, Colonell to foote over *Scots*, *Alexander Gordon*, Colonell to foote over *Dutch*; which Officers, with their Regiments, after conclusion of the peace made with the Kings Majestie of *Poile*, were also brought into *Dutchland*, against the *Saxon*, and the Emperour. Thus farre, *en passant*, I was bold to inferre, to satisfie the curious Reader, and his Highnesse, to whom we all vowed faith and obedience, being formerly led by such a Generall, as the *Lyon of the North*, the invincible King of *Sweden*, who did instruct us all, to doe his Highnesse service, in all respects, to the sacrificing of our lives, untill his Highnesse be avenged of his enemies, and most honourably restored to his Country, credit, honours, and former losses. For we know *Germany* so well, that without guides, we can enter their Cities where we know them weakest; having helped to subdue many of them before; as shall be evident, before our expedition come to an end. Where we would with such a Leader as his Highnesse, or one of the race, come of the Iewell of *Europe*, his Royall Mother, for whom and her royall Issue, we are obliged and resolved yet to fight, till her Throne be established in despight of her enemies.

Here also we see God will not suffer those Christians unpunished, that violate their promise, as was seene on Colonell *Grame*, whose fault is too common amongst their faction, that hold for a *maxime*, they are not bound to keepe promise or accord unto us; as was seene on Colonell *Monro* of *Fowles* his Regiment marching out of *Stobing*; the conditions of their accord being broken unto them, the Souldiers were forced to serve, and the Officers were made prisoners. If my fortune were once againe to command the Guards in *Memmungen* in *Bavier* (the Dukes chiefe residence) though I would not breake my word, I would hazard to breake my sword, to be avenged on those who keepe no promise or oath, being enemies to God and to his truth, as they did witnesse by their cruelty used at *Bamberg;* where the Felt-marshall being set on unawares, was forced to retire, having sent away his cannon before him, choosing the least of two inconveniences, having thought better to endanger a few men in skirmish, than by standing to hazard the losse of all, and of his cannon. Where we see that it is hard for a brave Commander to make a good retreat without cannon, where on the contrary having a little time, with some advantage of ground, it is easie retiring from the fiercest enemy, who may lose himselfe and his Army with pressing too farre forwards against cannon.

Likewise there is nothing more able for to make a partie of horsmen fortunate, than a reasonable supply of musketiers ever to attend them, for they are ever best together: Moreover, we have here a laudable custome of a brave Commander, as his Majesty was, being as carefull in maintaining his conquest, as he was fortunat in conquering: for before his Majesty would march from the Rhine towards the *Danow*, he first established the Rex- [II-109] chancellor of *Sweden* at *Mentz*, leaving unto his care the direction of the Army left in the *Palatinat* to attend the *Spaniard*, which Army was to be led by *Palsgrave Christian Brickafield*, being at least eight thousand strong.

---

## The twenty seventh Duty discharged of our March from Mentz *unto* Francony *and to* Shawbach.

His Majesty having got intelligence of the *Ruffle*, Generall *Tilly* had given at *Bamberg* to Felt-marshall *Horne*, and hearing the Felt-marshall was retired on *Swinford*, incontinent his Majesties Army was brought together at *Mentz*, and leaving the Rex-chancellor *Oxensterne* in the *Paltz* at *Mentz*, as director, and to attend on the *Spanish* forces, till the *Paltz* were cleered of the enemie.

The sixth of *March*, his Majesty did breake up from *Francford*, where in the fields before *Aschaffenburg*, the Army made a shew in presence of his Majesty of *Bohemia*, Marquesse of *Hamilton*, and divers others, men of quality, and having passed the bridge, we quartered over night in the fields on the backe side of the hill, and the next day continued our march towards *Lore*, and having sent before to make provision for the Army in all parts, where he resolved to quarter, through *Franconia* being free of our enemies. The next night we quartered at *Erinfield*, and our Briggad passing by *Gemond* we marched on *Carlestat*, where we quartered over night: the next day continuing our march, we joyned at night with the army at *Tettelbach*, where before our upbreaking the next morning, a fire being entred in the Subburbs, as his Majesty was marching out of quarter, those of *Spences* Regiment were blamed for this accident, though innocent: Neverthelesse his Majesties rage continued the whole day, and we being separated, his Majesty marched on *Kitchen*, on the *Maine* to joyne with the Felt-marshall; and we were commanded to march on *Oxenford* on the *Maine*, and from thence to *Vinchen*, where we againe were to joyne with the Army, having ever our cannon and Amunition waggons along with us.

On Sunday in the afternoone, his Majesty againe over-viewed the Army, being set in order of Battaile, the Felt-marshalls forces, and some new forces having joyned with us, being pleasant to behould, where in time of the show, his Majesty of *Bohemia* did come and salute our Briggad, being resaluted with all due respect of the whole body of the Briggad, where his Majesty was pleased to shew us, how glad he was of the good report and commendation, his Majesty of *Sweden* had given of our good service, the continuance whereof he hartily wished.

Our Army this day was above twenty thousand men, horse and foote, besides those did belong to the Artillery, being all in good order, Generall *Tilly* having understood of his Majesties coming, and of the strength of his Army, he thought, as best for the safety of his Army, not to stay our coming, and besetting *Bamberg* and *Forcham* with new levied men, taking the ould Souldiers with him, he marched towards *Newmarke* in the upper [II-110] *Palatinat*, having taken all the best things he could finde within the Bishop-ricke of *Bamberg* with him on waggons: And having sent his Generall Quartermaster before him towards *Loaffe*, he was met by some of the *Swedens* party, and being kill'd, all his letters were brought unto his Majesty, and before his Majesty brake up with the Army, he caused to publish an Edict over all *Franconia*, that all sort of people which had before bin fugitives for feare of Religion, they were all free to returne unto their houses againe, not being molested or troubled in the peaceable labouring of the ground.

Likewise on this march, a strong party of our Army, led by Colonell *Sparereutter*, Rancountring with the enemies party by *Schawbbishhall*, after a long skirmish the Emperialists were made to retire with losse towards the Castle of *Danberg*, where Lievetenant Colonell *Buckoy*, that had the command of the Emperialists, was sore wounded, a Rut-master of the *Crabbats* and a Lievetenant was kill'd; and aboue twenty six Souldiers, besides a hundred and thirty were taken prisoners. The newes came to his Majesty on our march, which we continued from *Winsen* on *Wolmersdorffe*; and from thence, the next day being the twentith of *March* to *Furt*, a passe on the River of *Pegnets*, a mile from *Nurenberg*; where the Army lay but one night, so long as his Majesty did visit *Nurenberg*; and the next day our march continued towards a little Towne called *Schawbach*, where his Majesty rested the Army two dayes, till that the Duke of *Wymars* forces, with Generall *Banier* coming from *During*, were come within one dayes march of us; his Majesties intentions being towards *Donavert* on the *Danube*; where my Cozen *Fowles* with both his Regiments joyned with us. His Majesty of *Sweden* accompanied with the King of *Bohemia* and *Palsgrave Augustus*, and divers Princes more, before their coming to *Nurenberg*, they were met by the Lords of the Towne, with a great convoy on horsbacke, and were most nobly welcomed, where the whole inhabitants were overjoyed at the sight of his Majesty of *Sweden*, but chiefely their affections most abundantly did extend towards his Majesty of *Bohemia*, which is impossible for any tongue to expresse. But well I know, my eyes did see their eyes shedding teares of joy, being overjoyed with the sight of two Kings at once, as they thought, sent by the King of Kings for their reliefes; and to make their welcome the more respected, the whole City, Burgers and Souldiers were in their brightest Armes; and being conveyed unto the City, they were sumptuously banqueted; and in testimony of their love, they gifted unto his Majesty of *Sweden* foure halfe *Cartowes*, with all furniture belonging to them, together with two silver Globes, one *Coelestiall*, the other *Terrestiall*: there were also presented unto him drinking *Credences* many, with some Antiquities that were rare, and with all testifying their affection in way of complement, they assure his Majesty that not only with words but with their whole estate, they were ready to serve the common cause, to, die and live with his Majesty, in the defence of the publique. His Majesty thus taking leave of *Nurenberg*, promises to continue their friend, and shewes them he was to goe with his Army towards the *Danow* streame, to see how to get a passe over the *Danow* for to visit the Duke of *Bavier*, and he hoped he would make *Tilly* with his Army to retire thence. But *Tilly* finding his Majesties Army growing still stronger and stronger, he retired backe unto the upper *Palatinat*, and from thence, he crossed the *Danow* to [II-111] joyne with the Duke of *Bavaria*, to hinder our coming unto *Bavaria*; being then, of his owne forces, neere eighteene thousand men, foote and horse: But many of them were new leavied folkes; and the Duke of *Bavaria* had also a strong Armie together; but for the most part, they were such as could not indure the noise or whisling of the Cannon Bullets.

By this time, Grave *Henry William Fonselins*, being shot in the leg before *Bamberg*, was departed at *Swineford* of a burning feaver, contracted through the paine of the shot; whose death his Majestie of *Sweden* did much lament.

### The twenty-seventh Observation.

The fifth of March, 1632. his Majestie having left sure footing in the *Paltz*, with a bridge over the *Rhine*, and the *Mayne*, where it enters into the *Rhine*; where also was begunne, as the Trophee of his victorie, the foundation of a Citie and strength called *Gustavus-Burg*. Then in the beginning of the Spring, we sprung forth from the *Rhine*, towards the *Danow* streame, being on this march royally accompanyed by his Majestie of *Bohemia*, whom his Majestie esteemed of, as of himselfe, in all quartering ordaining his quarters before his owne; continuing the march, through *Franconia* in suretie, having the yeere before freed that whole circle from the enemie, so that the Inhabitants had given their Oath of fealtie unto His Majestie.

This March was pleasant, through a plentifull Countrie at this time, being a progresse befitting two Kings, with a Royall Armie, and forces from other partes joyning with us; as we drew neere our enemies; we made all sure behinde us, both for our Retreates in case of neede, as also for the safetie of those were to come after us; and thirdly, for the furnishing our Armie in Amunition and victuals, to be brought unto us in case of want.

His Majestie here being of intention to get a passe over the *Danow* (having before made the Towne of *Vlme* sure) for his retreate; for the more abundance, his Majestie resolved to have the passe of *Donavert*, being the right passe betwixt *Nurenberg* and *Ausburg*.

Before *Tillyes* Armie could joyne with the Duke of *Baviere*, his Majestie resolved it was not best to give them time, but with celeritie concluded to march towards them, knowing it was but follie and madnesse, to stay till they were joyned; and the Duke of *Baviere* being assured of his Majesty comming to visit his Countrie, he closed the passes the best he could; both *Donavert*, *Rhine*, and *Ratisbone*. And as he did beset well the frontier Garrisons, before his Majesties comming, he also very circumspectly betimes tooke all victuals out of his Majesties way, towards *Engolstat*, as a wise Commander ought to doe, where he made his Magazin, being the onely part, he was assured of for his retreate; and such a parte, as he knew well, we were not able to get without treason; and then being assured he had time to provide an Armie to oppose his Majesty, himselfe not being taken unawares.

It is the dutie of all good Commanders, at their downe lying and uprising from quarters, to be very carefull to prevent fire; seeing thereby the whole Armie may be endangered by the losse of men, Amunition, Armes and Artillery; and since such losse is irrecoverable, our care should be the greater to avoyde the hurt. And therefore Order should be given to all Guardes, to [II-112] make diligent roundes over the Quarters, to prevent the like accidents, and to give Orders to the Gavilliger and his servants, to oversee all fires, and to see them quencht, at all upbreakings, and dislodging: otherwise, the enemy being neere, great inconvenience might happen, and if any enemy, at such times, trusting to our disorder, should offer to invade us, finding the contrary, it were easie to beate them backe; as also, it were a fit time to try their valour, they being more than halfe afraid. But I will advise all you, that desire to gaine credit, to seeke out your enemy, rather than to stay his comming unto you, and by this meanes, haply you may set up your *Trophees* in his owne Country, to speake to posteritie, as doth *Gustavus-Burg* betwixt the *Maine* and the *Rhine*.

## The twenty-eight Dutie discharged of our March
## to Donavert, for the In-taking of it.

The twenty-fourth of *March*, his Majestie with the Armie continued the march, from *Schwabach* towards *Donavert* upon *Ottengen* & *Pleinfelt*, and went before the Castle of *Mansfield* on the hill, being the strongest of any one in *Dutchland*, and finding he could get nothing done, young *Papenham* being Commandant there, was advertised by his Majestie, if that he would not give over the Castle, his Fathers Earledome thereabouts should be ruind (which he, though unwilling, behooved to suffer) but the Cavalier regardlesse of his Majesties threats, did keepe out the Castle, so that his Majestie, for that time, was forced to leave it.

His Majestie leaving a strong Garrison in the Towne next to it, he continued his march towards *Donavert*, and quartered the Armie on the Hill above the Towne: by this time his Majestie of *Pole* died, as also then Duke *Barnard* of *Wymar* had put a thousand *Finnes* on the other side of the *Rhine*, in *Bissen*, and beset *Spier*, at which time the *Spaniard* againe did set over the *Mosell*, of intention to relieve *Franckendale*, but was sent backe with shame over the *Mosell* by the Dukes Armie then left in the *Paltz*: at which time the Chancellor *Oxensterne* being there in person, and Palsgrave *Christian Birkafield*, his Excellence the Rex-chancellor caused the *Dutch* Regiments marching towards the enemy, to beate the *Scots* march, thinking thereby to affright the enemy; but it fell out contrary; the *Dutch* that marched in the Van with the *Scots* march, being charged by the enemy, made a base retreate, till they were holden up againe by the valour of the *Scots*, that were there (*viz.*) Sir *Iohn Ruthven*, and his Regiment, having had all his Officers of valiant *Scots*, as Lievetenant Colonell *Iohn Lesly*, Major *Lyell*, Captaine *David King*, and divers others, resolute Cavaliers, that stood to it, with the assistance of Colonell *Lodowicke Lesly*, and his Regiment and Officers: being all old beaten Souldiers, formerly called Sir *Iohn Hamiltons* Regiment; by their valour, resisting the enemy, and encouraging their Camerades, who were flying; the victory, that before was doubtfull, is restored againe to the *Swedens*; so that Palsgrave *Christian* did sweare, in audience of the whole Armie, to his Excellence the Rex-chancellor, that had it not beene for the [II-113] valour of the *Scots* Briggad, they had all beene lost and defeated by the *Spaniard*.

Here also was evidently seene, as was formerly mentioned, the valour of Rutmaster *Hume*, in view of his Exellence, in defeating the *Spanish* horsemen, being farre inferiour in number unto them, where the *Dutch Cavalerie*, led by him, repaired the over-sight of their *Infanterie*, that had the Vanguard. To returne to the beleaguering of *Donavert*, wherein did lie *Hertzog Randolph*, *Maximilian* of *Saxonlawenburgh*, with fifteene hundred Souldiers, and five hundred Boores of foote, wherein were also five hundred horsemen, who finding his Majestie was come to visit him, resolved to defend the Towne so long as he could, and to that effect, begunne with Cannon and Musket to play amongst us, who seeing his Majestie had caused to plant some Cannon before the Port, to play alongst the Bridge, he sallied out bravely, and did beate the *Swedens*, that guarded the Cannon, from their Cannon, which they nayled; and a *Scots* Captaine called *Semple*, that commanded the *Swedens*, was blamed, for the *Swedens* fault, that did leave him alone; who unwisely, fearing to be taken prisoner, came off after his fellowes, and we having beaten backe the enemy; the Captaine was put in arrest, till he were heard before a Councell of warres.

Incontinent after that, his Majestie planted Batteries on the hill, for to play with Cannon on a long stone-house, that lay on the other side of the River; wherein were a number of foote and horse, come from *Bavaria*, to strengthen the Garrison, but their entry was hindered by our timely comming; on which our Cannon played so hard, till the house was crevised, so that they were forced to quit it, with the losse of many men, and they being gone, our Cannon then played hard on the Towne-Ports and walles, doing the enemy great hurt.

The night drawing on, his Majestie commanded Colonell *Hepburne*, with his Briggad, to march to a Bridge a mile above *Donavert*, and to crosse over for to beset the other side of the Towne, whereon his Majestie thought the enemy would presse to escape: before mid-night the Colonell arriving there, did place our Musketiers in strong Plottons, by hundreds, in the most advantagious parts, for offending the enemy; our Pikes and Colours were drawne up in three strong bodies, or squadrons, and were commanded to stand by their Armes, to be in readinesse, in case of Alarum: And having placed our Centries, *Perdues*, and others, by breake of day the enemy fell forth eight hundred strong of Musketiers on our Quarter; the service begunne by our Musketiers, we came up with full squadrons of Pikes amongst them, and entred on the execution, till we made them throw downe their Armes, and cry for Quarters; some for safetie retired backe to the Towne, and were followed in by us, and cut off within the Towne; while others made way for his Majesties Forces to enter from the other side; so that the enemy were pittifully cut downe the most part of them in the fury. The Towne also was spolyed and quite plundered: but some of the Souldiers, with the Iesuites and Monkes, that had escaped alongst the Bridge, being sent after were overtaken, and the most part cut off: the rest above three hundred were brought backe prisoners: within the Garrison were found dead above five hundred, and some were drowned in the streame, and a thousand that had gotte their lives, were forced to take service under the Regiments; but being Papists of *Bavaria*, as soone as they [II-114] smelt the smell of their Fathers houses, in lesse than ten dayes they were all gone.

The in-taking of this passe on such a sudden, wrought a terrible feare amongst all the Papists in *Bavaria*; in like manner, his Majestie did send Palgrave *Augustus*, with some Forces to *Hechstat*, a passe on the *Danube*, which he immediatly tooke in, and by this time was Generall *Tilly* with his Armie come on the *Leacke* towards *Rhine* on the River: and having beset it strong, he beset also all other parts betwixt that and *Ausburg*, and the Duke himselfe caused to take their Armes from all the professors of the reformed Religion in *Ausburg*, and having beset it with two thousand Souldiers, he retired himselfe to *Engolstat*.

His Majestie after the in-taking of *Donavert*, commanded Generall *Bannier*, with a partie of foure thousand strong, of horse, foote, and Artillery, towards *Newburg* on the *Danube*; but it was beset before their comming, and they retiring againe to *Donavert*, where our whole Armie being joyned, we marched towards the River of the *Leacke*, of intention to force a passe unto *Bavaria*, being then thirtie two thousand strong, of horse and foote.

### The twenty-eight Observation.

Generall *Tilly* knowing his Majestie was so neere with a strong Armie to be revenged on him, for the Ruffle he had given to *Gustavus Horne* at *Bambricke*: he never rested his Armie, but continually kept them on foote, attending still our comming; and we, to verifie the desire we had to be revenged on him, did neglect no time, till at last, we found him out, where we intended to try Fortune againe, which never smiles always on one, but is ever variable, keeping no constant course, being whiles here, now there; and commonly we see, that those who have beene most fortunate in their time (as this old Generall was) they have an insatiable desire of victory, and prosperous fortune, till neere their end, that they are overcome themselves.

Here we see his Majesties diligence alike, in following of his enemy, as he fled before him; as in his pursute at *Donavert*, being the passe, we were holden up at, which his Majestie with diligence did get in his power, being so hard pursued, that the enemy got no time to relieve it, though the Cavalier that defended it, shewed himselfe resolute in defending of it, as in out-falling on our Guards, which were *Swedens*, who having neglected their dutie, were blame-worthy, as their Captaine that commanded them, who ought to have preferred death before life, ere he had quite his Poste; seeing his standing could have moved others to helpe him, though the *Swedens* left him. But his Majestie having got the victory over the Towne, by the valour of the Captaines Country-men, their intercession then procured his pardon, though not his admission to his former Command.

Likewise here we see that stone houses are vaine defenses against cannon: where the walles once pierc't, those within are in worse case then if they stood on plaine fields. Therefore at such times, it is better to adventure forth unto the fields out of reach, then to be smothered within walles, as were many within this house both of horse and foote. [II-115]

Here also as in the continuance of the Story, we see the valour of *Hepburne* and of his Briggad praise worthy, being first and last instruments of the enemies overthrow in grosse or by parties, being commanded men: where often we were well seconded by *Ramseys* men, seeing those were ever commanded on desperat exploits, being still appointed the fore-troopes of the Army, well led and conducted by Major *Sidserffe*, who was a Cavalier both diligent and valorous, being also trusted on good occasions for his judgment in command.

As his Majesty was diligent in the taking of this passe, so he was carefull to repaire it, by helping of the ruins, and in besetting it againe with a strong

Garrison, establishing good order and discipline, having left Colonell *Worbrane*, an *Osterriker Freher*, as Governour, being a man expert in making of cannon, and in devising of fire-workes; As also he understood well how best to fortifie irregular workes as these were.  And therefore his Majesty most wisely did concredit, according to his gifts, the maintaining of this passe to his care and diligence, which both he did shew in fortifying the Towne, even so farre as Art could be helpefull to nature.

---

### The twenty ninth Duty discharged of his Maiesties forcing the passage over the Leacke, and of the intaking of Ausburg.

*Donavert* being taken, and beset againe with a *Swedens* Garrison, caused a great feare and astonishment to seaze upon all the Papists in *Bavaria*, which made the *Iesuits* and Monkes flie unto *Tilligen, Mynckine, Neuburg*, and *Engolstat*: where above twenty thousand of the Clergy were unwilling to fight with the Duke against his Majesties forces, and seeing *Vindligan*, the Castle of *Oberdorffe*, and divers other places taken in by his Majesty, those of *Neighburg* desired his Majesties safeguardes, in respect the *Swedens* were making great booty over all, where ever they came hanging the Papists by their purse, not sparing to torment their shinnes, as they did in *Pomeren* and in the Markes of *Brandenburg* to the Protestants, in exacting their monies, which they were made to repay againe, *Lege talionis*.

Generall *Tilly* by this time had intrenched his Army about the Rhine, by the side of the *Leacke*, to hinder his Majesties passage unto *Bavaria*, with a strong Army, which lay on the other side of the River, right against *Tillies* Army, where his Majesty did set over a bridge made with boates and planckes, having planted seventy two peeces of cannon, great and small, on the borders of the River, which did play continually into the middest of *Tillies* Army, who were drawne up in Battaile, on the other side, to hinder his Majesties passage, but our messengers were so swift and diligent, that through importunity, they obtained a grant of the passage, where many [II-116] were made to lie dead by our cannon; for those that were not hurt by the Bullets, they were lamed by branches and trees, cut by the cannon, being they stood in a thicke wood, which shooting continued a whole day, being on the fifth of *Aprill* 1632; a day ominous to Generall *Tilly*, who was shot in the knee with a cannon bullet; a cruell blow for an ould man of seventy two yeeres, who, being carried from thence to *Engolstat*, died within three dayes, being cruelly tormented with the smart of his wound.

*Tilly* being gone, the Army discouraged for their great losse sustained; The Duke remarking his Majesty would force the passage, he thought best in time to retire, taking his flight confusedly upon *Engolstat* and *Nuburg*: after that *Altringer*, then a Colonell was shot in the head, and above a thousand did lie dead on the place they stood on.

His Majesty having crost over with the Army, he incontinent commanded certaine Troopes to follow the fugitives, getting orders to cut them off as they were found.

The victory happily attained unto by his Majesty, incontinent the Towne of *Rhine*, being the first frontier Garrison in *Bavaria*, rendered up, and his Majesty having beset *Rhine* with a Garrison, he marched with the Army alongst the *Leacke* side on *Ausburg*; where by the way a Commissary from *Nuburg* came to his Majesty, making their excuse for receiving of *Tillies* forces, and withall they declared, that the enemy had quit their Towne againe; and therefore they interposed with his Majesty for neutrality, which being refused unto them, a Garrison was sent to keepe them in awe, to bring their landes in contribution, and to repaire the bridge which was broken by the Dukes command.

His Majesty having continued his march towards *Ausburg*, the eigth of *Aprill* we lay downe before it, and immediatly we set over a bridge over the *Leacke*, during which time the Commandant spared not his Amunition, but continually Cannonaded amongst us; but our batteries being once ready, they received their interchange, and his Majesty offered the Garrison free passage, and to retire in safety with his folkes, whether he pleased, otherwise there should no quarter be granted unto them, if they pressed to hould out longer, whereupon the Governour resolved to accept of his Majesties offer, and having made his Accord, on the tenth of *Aprill* he marched out, and was conveyed towards *Engolstat*.

Incontinent thereafter, his Majesty did beset the Towne with a strong Garrison, and the next day before his Majesty entred the Towne, all Papists were ordained to assemble and meete at *Leckhousen*, where they were set off the Towne Councell, that were knowne to be Papists, and Protestants were placed; So that the fourteenth of *Aprill* his Majesty entred the Towne, going first unto the Church called St. *Annes* Church, and there in presence of his Majesty of *Bohemia*, *Palsgrave Augustus*, and Duke *William* of *Wymar*, Duke *Hannes* of *Howlsten*, *Markgrave Christopher Fontarlach* and *Bawden*, and other Potentats and Ambassadours, did heare a Sermon, and praised God for the victory obtained against their enemies; The Text being taken out of the twelfth *Psalme* and fifth *verse. For the oppression of the needy, and for the sighes of the poore, I will now up saith the Lord, and will set at liberty him, whom the wicked had snared.*

After Sermon his Majesty went to the market place, where some *Swedens* Regiments were brought, and where the Burgers were also injoyned to [II-117] come to present their service unto his Majesty, and a table being set openly and covered, a present was sent to his Majesty from the new set Protestant Councell, of Corne, Fish and Wine, and the next day being the fifteenth of *Aprill*, his Majesty with the whole Army, was ready to march unto *Bavaria*.

### The twenty ninth Observation.

Generall *Tillie* being neere unto his end, behooved to make a march unto *Bambricke*, to shew the *Swedens* by his retreat the right passe unto *Bavaria*, with his owne death. Wherin we have a notable example of an old expert Generall, who being seventy two yeeres of age, was ready to die in defence of his Religion and Country, and in defence of those whom he served, being then Generall for the Catholique League: which end of his should encourage all brave Cavaliers, following the laudable profession of Armes, to follow his example in life and death, as valorous Souldiers: where we see, that though death be fatall unto all, yet such a death, as happened unto this old Generall, is only proper unto the valiant, who though often contemned death and eschewed death, during the warfare, yet at last he is overtaken by Gods Almighty hand and power, though formerly in his life-time he had escaped, by the same providence, many dangers. And sometimes we see in the very entrance of warres, some suddenly taken away, to teach us alwayes to trust more unto God then unto the arme of man, which is but a vaine strength.

Likewise, though this worthy Generall did fight often, and obtained many notable victories till this time, against Kings, yet at last he is overcome by a King, and a more skilfull Generall then he was, and though before the battaile of *Leipsigh*, he did give no higher title to his Majesty then to a Cavalier: Neverthelesse his Majesty hearing of his death, called him Honourable old *Tilly*, whose Acts were so Heroicke in his life time, that after his death, they were his everlasting monuments, making his memory eternall, suffering his name never to rot with the time. And my wish were, I might prove as valiant in advancing Christs Kingdome (though I should die in the quarrell) as he was forward in hindering of it; my death then should not be bitter unto my friends, I leaving an immortall name behinde me.

Also here we see the great force of Artillery, either in forcing of passes against our enemies, or in maintaining of passes with a little advantage of ground, for seventy two peeces of Ordinance, with such continuance, were of mighty force to make passage to an Army: for this victory was obtained by the force of our Cannon alone, which made the enemy runne away, before we could come at them to fight, and the discouragment given unto them, by the losse of their Leaders caused their disorder, and consequently safety to us in our passage. Where we see, that as victorie is from God, so the helpe, judgment and dexterity of good Commanders is furthersome to the victory, as the lawfull meanes ordained by God.

Moreover we see here, how easie it is for a victorious Armie, that is once master of the Field, to take in Frontier Garrisons, while as they are possessed instantly with a Panicke feare, especially being taken at the Stot or rebound, before they have time to disgest their feare. But had Generall *Tilly* drawne up [II-118] his Army out of reach of his Majesties Cannon, and resolved to suffer his Majesty to have set over his Army, the passe being so narrow, that scarce three men could march in Front, *Tillies* advantage had bin the greater to receive them as they came, who might have cut them off by divisions, which had bin more to his credit: yet we see as the Prophet saies, *Except the Lord watch, the watch-man watcheth in vaine.* And we see, God would have these people punished for their former cruelties; and therefore he tooke away their judgment, and confounded their Counsell, making them erre, till they ranne to their owne ruine.

As his Majesties Iudgment in command was great, so his Example was good and commendable, in giving God thankes in his Church, for his victories and for the preservation of his life from danger; wherein his Majesty chiefely shewed the example of his Piety and religious exercise, for he knew well that Religion and Iustice were the fundaments of all good society, and being much inclined unto both, he would winne the people by his owne example: since of all men it becomes Kings and Princes worst to be irreligious and ungodly: for on earth we have nothing more worthy than Religion to be respected and honoured, it being unto Heaven our guide, on earth the fountaine of our Iustice, whereby we governe our affaires well or ill, expelling and putting away unjustice or unrighteousnesse: for where there is most Religion or piety; there also is most happinesse: and without her no Crowne can be established; and as his Majesty was religious himselfe, so he maintained good lawes and good discipline, grounded on religion and holinesse of life, which made the happy events and fortunate end of his warlike expeditions to follow. Blessed therefore shall they be, who follow his Majesties example in this, as in all other his warlike enterprizes; for I dare affirme on my conscience, never man served this Master truly (whom his Majesty our Master did serve with his heart) without a reward.

---

*The thirtieth Duty discharged of our expedition toward* Engolstat.

The sixteenth of *Aprill* his Majesty did breake up with the Army from *Ausburg*, taking his march towards *Engolstat*, of intention to start the Duke of *Bavier* from thence, having left so many of our Army behinde us as tooke in *Launceberg*, *Mindelhaim*, *Fussen*, *Showngow* and divers other parts in *Schwabland* by accord, where Generall Major *Ruthven* then Governour of *Vlme*, had brought with his Forces that were also behinde us, all the Papists Townes that were betwixt *Vlme* and *Lindaw* under his Majesty of *Swedens* contribution, and most part of *Schwabland* also, for which service his Majesty gifted unto him, under his hand and seale, the *Graveshaft* or Earldome of *Kirkberg*, lying next adjacent to the city of *Vlme*, which belonged to the *Fuckers* of *Ausburg*, that were made Earles by the Emperour, from Marchants having turn'd Souldiers, to serve his Emperiall [II-119] Majestie: which Graveshaft or Earledome could pay yearely, beside Contribution to the warres, ten thousand Rex-Dollers, being a good augmentation of pay for an old servant, who had served long and valourously, without the least blot of discredit, and retired bravely with meanes and credit to his Country, carrying the markes of his valour in his body, being above the waste full of tokens of valour, credibly gotten in his Masters service;

for as he was couragious before his enemy, he was also fortunate in his Conduct, in obtaining victory beyond his fellowes; and being often singled out, man to man, to make his courage the more undoubted, he alwayes gave testimony in this kinde of his valour, answerable to the externall shew and hansome frame of his body, being in personage inferiour to no man, for strength and comely stature.

His Majesty continuing his March towards *Engolstat*, coming within sight of the Towne, he drew his Armie in Battaile, horse, foote, and Artillery, where we stood the whole night at Armes. The next day drawing neerer to the enemies Armie being incamped before us, *Ex opposito*, on the other side of the *Danube*, ready to second the Towne on all occasions, which his Majestie considering, gave order to draw out our Leaguer, and to set men to worke after we were quartered; where, for our welcome, the enemy from the Towne did salute us furiously with Cannon; so that at first, the head was shot from the young Markgrave of *Baden*, and his Majestie recognosceing, the legge was shot from his Horse; divers others were also here lamed by the Cannon.

The night drawing on, his Majestie expecting a strong out-fall from the Towne, their Armie being so neere, our Briggad, according to custome, was commanded to march, and to stand the whole night in Armes, on a razed Champaigne, under mercie of Cannon and musket, being ordained in case of the enemies out-fall, by fighting to hold them up, till our Armie might be in readinesse to relieve us; being in Aprill, though the aire was cold, the service being hot, sundrie were taken away in full rancks with the Cannon, being in no action our selves, but standing ready to maintaine our ground, in case the enemie should pursue us, which to my minde, was the longest night in the yeare, though in Aprill; for at one shot I lost twelve men of my owne Companie, not knowing what became of them, being all taken alike with the Cannon; and he that was not this night, in this stand afraid of a Cannon bullet, might in my opinion, the next night, be made gunpowder of without paine, and who would sweare he was not afrighted for a shot, I would not trust him againe, though he spake truth.

His Majestie, in the beginning of the night, commanded a thousand *Swedens*, being Musketiers, led by sufficient Officers in his Majesties owne presence, to fall on the Skonce, before the bridge, which was beset with fifteene hundred foote, and five hundred horse, lying open on the side, that lay next the Towne, that if the enemie should storme and enter, he might be clensed out againe with Cannon and musket, from the Towne wall; notwithstanding whereof, the *Swedens* bravely and advanced, even to the graffe, being ready to storme they were plagued with the musket, and with fire-workes, that leaving three hundred men killed about the Skonce, they were forced to retire; the enemy continuing a thunder-clap of Muskets for one halfe houre, till they were fully retired. His Majestie finding nothing could be effectuate in this manner; retired with the Musketiers, leaving us and our Briggad in [II-120] the former stand, to attend the enemies out-coming, to make us acquainted with the thundering of Cannon; where no man, were he never so stout, could be blamed to stoope, seeing the Cannon in the night fireing in a right line before him, he that would not shift his body, to eschew the graseing of a Bullet, was not to be pittied, if killed through ostentation.

Here *death*, that cruell fellow, courted all alike, yet none was so enamoured, as willingly to embrace him, though well I know, many brave fellowes were resolved to meet him, for to give him the foyle before he came neere.

This night a souldier though not stout, might passe prentise in our Calling in one night, for resolution; where having stayed till it was day, we retired to the Leaguer, with great losse of men, that were killed and hurt, where they that had escaped the *Malheur*, were glad to discourse at large of their nights watch.

His Majestie finding this Towne strong by nature, situation, and art, lying on the *Danube*, really fortified with a bridge over the River; fortified also before the entry, and the Towne being well provided of all furniture, having a strong Garrison, and in neede an Armie to supply it, which made his Majestie, for that time, rise from it, having gotten intelligence, that the Duke of *Baviers* Forces by sleight had taken in *Rhinsberg*, where the most part of the Armie was sent thither to beset the passe, who immediatly after their entry, disarmed the Citizens, being all Protestants, having quartered above twentie Souldiers in every house, where also the Duke himselfe did march with the rest of his Armie, knowing his Majestie was not able to gaine credit before *Engolstat*, he went away, suffering his Majestie to stay behinde, to try his fortune against the Towne, who also did breake up, and marching away, the enemy with a strong partie of Horsemen, and of Dragoniers, charged our Reare-guard; General *Banier* being commanded to make the retreate, where the enemy having charged, he behaved himselfe well by good Command, charging the enemy with small Troopes, forcing them to retire, while as the body of the Armie was retiring, the Generall commanding still fresh Troopes, one after another, to receive the enemies charge, till at last all were safely retired, and the enemy retired also, not daring to shew himselfe without the passes on the field, being well beaten at an out-fall by the *Swedens* the day before.

The Retreate honourably made, his Majestie continued his march on *Mosburg*, having lyne that night on the Hill at *Gysenfelt*, having in the afternoone before drawne the whole Armie in one Front, Horse, Foote, and Cannon, for doing the funerall Rites of the Markgrave of *Bawden*, whose corps being appointed to be sent away with a Convoy to be buried; before their departure, the whole Cannon was twice discharged, and then the whole Musketiers of the Army from the right hand to the left, did give two salves of Musket, and after them, the whole Armie of horse did give two salves of Pistoll. This day also, old Captaine *David Ramsey* was buried, having died of a consuming Feaver.

The next day our march continuing towards *Mosburg*, where we did lie five dayes, his Majestie having sent Felt-marshall *Horne*, with a strong partie of horse, foote, and Cannon, towards *Landshut*; where *Hepburne* with his Briggad was also employed. The Towne not being strong, the enemy, after a little skirmish made with horse in the Feilds, retired over the water, [II-121] casting off the Bridge behinde them, they escaped, having left a weake Garrison of foote in the Towne and Castle, to make an Accord, for keeping the Towne unplundered, which was suddenly agreed on, so that before night, we were quartered in the Towne, the enemy being retired, where divers of our Briggad made bootie worth their paines.

The next day his Majestie hearing we had taken in the Towne, did breake up with the Armie towards *Memmungen*, leaving Orders for the Felt-marshall to joyne with the Armie at *Freisingen*, having got moneyes for his Majestie, both from *Landshut*, and the Bishopricke of *Freisingen*, for keeping them unplundered.

*Hohnwart*, *Pfafenhowen*, being two walled Townes, with the Abbacie of St. *Morris*, and the Abbacie of St. *George*, were also brought under Contribution; where the Boores on the march cruelly used our Souldiers (that went aside to plunder) in cutting off their noses and eares, hands and feete, pulling out their eyes, with sundry other cruelties which they used, being justly repayed by the Souldiers, in burning of many Dorpes on the march, leaving also the Boores dead, where they were found.

A strong partie of the *Dukes* Souldiers, thinking to have surprized the *Swedens* in their quarters, they fell themselves in the ditch that they prepared for others, so that very few of them escaped with life out of the *Swedens* hands.

By this time also *Weysenburg* not farre from *Nurenberg*, was taken in by the *Dukes* Forces, having got some Cannon from the Castle of *Weiltzburg*: Neverthelesse, the *Swedens* Garrison behaved themselves valourously, in making an honourable Accord, though those Papists unworthily brake their promise, for those that would not willingly serve, were cut downe, and the Towne by condescending was also plundered, their wives and children were abused, and the Burgomasters and Preachers were taken prisoners unto *Engolstat*, and the Ports of the Towne they razed and burnt.

### The thirtieth Observation.

In this Expedition, as in all the former, his Majesties wisedome and diligence, is praise-worthy; for prosecuting his victories so orderly on the hot sent, as the cunning Hunter doth his prey, in giving one sweat after another, till he kill or derne, in putting the Fox in the earth, and then hooke him out, or starve him.

Likewise, His Majestie also very wisely advancing within his enemies Country; First made the passes sure behinde him, in case of Retreate, or of scarcitie of Amunition or victualls, most prudently he left Generall *Ruthven* at *Vlme*, as Governour, being his Magazin-place, and surest retreate; being also made certaine of the Duke of *Wittenbergs* friendship, who in necessitie was able to furnish him with a great supply of men, moneys, victualls, and Amunition for his Armie; being then one of the most powerfull Princes within *Germany*. As also, his Majestie having got *Ausburg* under subjection, he very wisely left a part of his Armie to subdue the adjacent Cities in *Schwabland*, to helpe his

Contribution, as *Memmungen, Pibrach, Brandenburg* on the River *Elve*, as also *Middleham, Kawffbire,* and *Kempten* on the *Leacke,* and *Elve*; and that by the industry and diligence of Generall Major *Ruthven,* with the rest of the young Cavaliers of the *Scots* Nation, that followed [II-122] him; such as Colonell *Hugh Hamilton,* Colonell *Iohn Forbesse*; Lievetenant Colonell *Gunne,* Lievetenant Colonell *Mongomerie,* Major *Ruthven,* Major *Brumfield,* and divers other *Scots* Captaines, such as Captaine *Dumbarre,* that was killed by the Boores neere *Vlme*; who all were obliged to Generall *Ruthven,* not onely for their advancements, but also for their meanes, which they made in short time, beyond their fellowes, who had served longer; by reason their lot was to have fallen in a fat soyle, that abounded in riches, and as their service to his Majestie was faithfull and loyall; so his Majestie was liberall and bountifull, in advancing them to titles of honour; As also in bestowing on them Cadoucks and casualties, to inrich them more than others, whose fortunes were not to be so rewarded, though their deservings were no lesse; so that being rich in credit, they care not for the want of abundance of externall things, being inwardly contented through their vertue.

Here also we see, that as his Majestie was circumspect for his retreate; even so he was fore-seeing for the safetie of his Armie, in not hazarding to ingage it too farre with disadvantage against the Dukes Armie, and the strong Citie of *Engolstat*; being the best Strength for one within the Empire. Neverthelesse, having once recognosced the Citie, he would not leave it, till he had showne his resolution, and left his intrenchment, as the tokens of his worth, in hazarding to beleaguer it, having an Armie to second them; and while as his Majesties horse was shot under him, he said, it did put him in minde, he was but mortall and subject to mischances, as others; and therefore he knew no better remedie, but to resigne himselfe and all his to the providence of the Almightie: and that he was perswaded, that though *God* should call him out of the world, yet the Lord would not abandon his owne Cause, being so just, but he was assured, *God* would stirre up some other worthier than he, to put a period to those warres, for the libertie of *Gods* service in *Dutchland*; and withall, he tooke *God* to witnesse, he had no other intention in prosecuting those warres, but onely to pull downe the tyranny of the house of *Austria*; and to obtaine a solid and a setled peace unto all men, that were interessed in the quarrell.

Where, by this his speech, we see, that as he was a brave and valourous King; so he was wise at this time in preserving himselfe and his Armie from losing them before such a strong Citie. As also we see, that the Conditions of mortall men have their changes common unto them, that oft-times they are crossed by contrary fortunes, as formerly they did prosper; and the Lord doth hide the causes of both from us, to spurre us ever to seeke to his Majestie, in doing good; and those good of themselves, as this just King was, who notwithstanding had need of Gods direction in all his wayes and enterprises: which should make us all earnest in seeking the *Lord,* to direct us in all our wayes; seeing of our selves we are not able to doe any thing that is good; neither ought we to ascribe any thing of our prosperous successe or fortune unto our selves, being but the Lords servants, and instruments he useth, as weake meanes of his glory, and the well-fare of his Church on earth. Our daily delight should be then to learne wisedome out of the actions of others; and like the Bee that makes the honey, to converse amongst good company, that we may favour at least of their goodnesse, following the footsteps of this Heroick and godly King, fructifying ever during our life times, unto all sort of well-doing, till such time as we may end with glory, living after death. [II-123]

Moreover, here we see his Majestie, though on a march, not neglective to discharge that last and honourable dutie to the corps of that noble and worthy Cavalier, the Markgrave of *Turlagh* and *Bawden*, by making the whole Armie to give two *Salves* of Cannon, Musket, and Pistoll in comely order, as the Custome is at such times; where it is to be regrated, how oft-times death doth prevent the expected goodnesse of many a brave fellow, as this young Cavalier was, the worthy sonne of a worthy Father, who carried divers times the title of a Generall.

Here also I would exhort by the way, all worthy Souldiers, who aime at credit, never to give themselves to mouze or plunder aside from the Armie, lest they be punished, in dying ignominiously by the hands of cruell tyrants, as the ignorant Papist-Boores, that have no more knowledge of *God*, than to tell over their Beads, being taught, as their best devotion and knowledge of the mysteries of *God* tending to salvation, to glory in their ignorance, which makes many of them to commit any wickednesse whatsoever, to winne damnation to themselves; being once commanded by a Priest, that can make the poore ignorant beleeve, that to doe wickedly is the way to heaven. Who cannot then see, how detestable this Doctrine is, that gives people libertie to commit all villany, and then to assure them of pardon for it?

The use then we should make of this, who professe another truth, is to abhorre their examples of life, as we doe their doctrine; seeing wee should know, that no crime before God is so abominable, as to glory in sinne; for where sinne groweth, there groweth also the punishment: And he that sinnes openly with an out-stretched necke, as these villaines did in *Wisenburg*, in sight of God and before the Sunne and the world, they offended double, teaching others by their example to sinne.

Happie therefore is the man, who delights not in sinne, but happier is he, that glories not in sinne, yea happiest of all, that continues not in sinne, but repenteth of the evill done, and ceaseth to doe so any more.

---

*The thirty one Duty discharged of our Expedition*
*unto* Munchen, *and of our abode there.*

Being retired from *Landshut*, a pretty little Towne and Castle in *Bavaria*, lying on the *Eiser*, we continued our march after his Majesty, and marched towards *Frising*, where we joyned with his Majesty, and incamped over night in the fields, where his Majesty had intelligence, that *Wallestine* with a strong

Army, was on his march towards the upper *Paltz*, which made his Majesty make the greater haste to visit *Munchen*, the Duke of *Bavaria* his chiefe Towne of residence, having made the Bishop of *Frising* pay fifty thousand Dollers, and promise contribution beside, out of the whole Bishopricke, and continuing our march the sixth of *May*, towards *Munchen*; on our way, the Commissioners from *Munchen* did come and salute his Majesty, offering all kinde of submission, for to spare from plundering of their City, and from ruinating of their houses and policy. [II-124] His Majesty lying over night in the fields, within halfe a mile of the City, his Majesty commanded Colonell *Hepburne* with our Briggad to march away and to make the Circuit of the Towne, & to lie over-night at the bridge that went over the *Eiser*, with his Briggad to guard the bridge, that none should passe or repasse till his Majesties coming to the Towne, which accordingly we obyed, and guarded the bridge till the next morning: his Maiesty encamped the whole Army without the Towne, marching in with our Briggad alone, where Colonell *Hepburnes* Regiment had the watch on the market place, and the guarding of the Ports; his Maiesty of *Sweden* and the King of *Bohemia* being lodged on the Castle, I was commanded with our Regiment, and my Lord *Spences* Regiment, led by Lievetenant Colonell *Musten*, and ordained to lie in the great Courte of the Palace, night and day at our Armes, to guard both the Kings persons, and to set out all Guards about the Palace, where I was commanded with our whole Officers, not to stirre off our watch, having allowance of Table and diet for us and our Officers within his Maiesties house, to the end we might the better looke to our watch: and the command of all directions under stayers was put upon me, being then Commander of the Guards; where I had power over the whole offices belonging to the house, and might have commanded to give out any thing to pleasure Cavaliers; having stayed in this charge three weekes nobly entertained.

Here in *Munchen* the *Boarish-Boares* alleadged the dead were risen, since before his Maiesties coming, by the Dukes command, the great cannon were buried, side by side in the *Magazin* house; whereof his Maiesty being made acquainted, they were digged up out of the ground, and carried away to *Ausburg*, above one hundred and fourty peeces of Cannon great and small, whereof there were twelve Apostles, and other Cannon which formerly were taken from the *Elector Palatine*, and the Duke of *Brunswicke*, with their names and Armes on them, of which one was found, wherein there were thirty thousand Duckets of gold, being a present for a King.

Likewise in this *Magazin* house there were found clothes and Armes ready to cloth an Army of ten thousand foote, which helped our Army much; many other rarieties were gotten in this house worth much mony, which were transported away by both the Kings. As also all the Dukes servants of his whole houshold were there, that bare offices about the house, and the house it selfe was as well replenished and furnished, as any Kings Palace needed to be, of all magnificent furniture, for bed, board and hangings, which were sumptuous and costly.

Here also about this Palace were pleasant gardens, fish-ponds, water-workes, and all things yeelding pleasure in the most splendid grandure, that can be imagined, with a pleasant Tennis-court for recreation, where both the Kings sometimes did recreat themselves.

Moreover this house was so magnificently situated, that for three miles about it there was such pleasant Hare hunting, that sometimes we could see the Hares flocking together in troopes above twenty; As also for the Princes pleasure there could be brought together in prospect of the Palace, heards of Deare, sometimes above five hundred at once, and sometimes for pleasure, a thousand to be brought together.

His Maiesty having remained here above a fort'night, and getting intelli-
[II-125] gence of some turbulent uproares made by the *Papists Boores* in *Schwabland*, his Maiesty leaving Generall *Banier* to command over the Army at *Monchen*; his Maiesty with a strong party of horse, and two Briggads of foote, marched towards *Memmungen* in *Schwabland*, and having presently stilled the uproare, he retired upon *Ausburg*, and from thence to *Munchen* againe, where his Majesty on a sudden taxed the Towne in a hundred thousand Rex Dolours, which the Burgers and Clergy were willing to give his Majesty, to keepe the City unplundered, for which summe there were fifty of the speciall Burgers and Clergy given as pledges unto his Majesty, till paiment were made of the monies against a certaine day; and to that effect, the pledges were sent with a Convoy unto *Ausburg*, to be kept there till the monies were paied.

His Majesty then fearing that *Walestine* lately made *Generalissimus* to the Emperours whole Army, was coming with a strong Army out of *Bohemia*, and his Majesty thinking he was to fall with those Forces into the Duke of *Saxons* country, and seeing the Duke of *Bavier* had his Army ready at *Rhinsberg*, and the passe open, he might joyne with *Walestine* when he pleased, and therefore his Majesty resolved suddenly to breake up with his Army from *Munchen*, giving orders all should be in readinesse against the twenty sixth of *May*, to march towards *Donavert*, and from thence in haste to *Nurenberg*.

### The thirty-one Observation.

Wise Generalls must resolve in time to rule their affaires according to the occurrences happening in the course of warres: for the Duke of *Bavier* finding himselfe, after *Tillies* death and his losse sustained at *Rhine* on the *Leacke*, not bastant to rancounter his Majesties Army in the fields, he very wisely resolved to make a defensive warre, betaking himselfe with his Army within his Strengths and Passes, collecting his Forces together at those two places of *Engolstat* and *Rhinsberg*, which his Majesty perceiving, thought againe, it was not time for him to enter in beleaguering of such strengths being so strongly beset, and so well provided, especially seeing his enemies were drawing strong to the fields from all parts.

The *Spaniard* forcing his troopes on the *Rhine* within the *Palatinat*, Generall Major *Ossa* coming behinde him with an Army in *Schwabland*, the Duke of *Bavier* lying strong with his Army betwixt him and *Nurenburg*, on the passes of *Engolstat* and *Rhinsberg*, *Walestine* also drawing neere to the Duke of

*Saxon*, with a strong Army to fall into his country, betwixt his Majesty and home; and *Papenhaim* then dominiering in the nether *Saxon Creitches*: in consideration whereof, his Majesty very wisely resolved to hang the little Townes, Cloisters and *Abbacies* belonging to the *Papists* in *Bavaria* by the Purse: taking of them on the sudden all the monies they were able to give him, and pledges for the rest, promising unto them, unlesse they would duely pay their promised contribution unto his Commissaries, the next time he would burne their Dorpes and houses, and put all to the sword; whereas then he had used clemency, in hope they would give the like obedience unto him as unto the Duke their Master. For his Majesty did see, the enemy forced him by a diversion; And therefore he used his time [II-126] while he was in *Bavaria*; that they might not forget he had bin there: but rather tooke tokens with him; as men, mony, Armes, rare monuments of antiquity, and rich Iewells, and which was worse (wherein his Majesty had neither hand nor direction) many of their houses, Dorpes and Castles were burnt to the ground by evill and wicked instruments, that repaied burning with burning, using the *Papists* at home, as they used *Protestants* abroade, being neere the *Baltique* coast, they never dreamed that the *Protestants* would come so farre up as to repay them under the foote of the *Alpes*. And had *Gustavus* lived, we had gone neere to warme them within *Rome*, for their by-past cruelties, where we see, that God the righteous judge punisheth sinne with sinne, and man by his owne iniquity.

His Majesty leaving no Garrison in *Bavaria*, to keepe the country the better in awe and obedience, he tooke Hostages and pledges of speciall men from them along with him, to make them the readier to pay the summes they had promised; As also their contribution: and to make them the loather to rise againe in Armes against his Majesties Garrisons, which lay adjacent unto them.

The Duke of *Baviers* forces being retired within their strengths & passes, finding themselves not Bastant to offend his Majesties Army, they fall out on the other side of the *Danube*, towards the upper *Paltz*, making their incursions there, and take in *Wisenburg*, where they used both Burgers and Souldiers more unhumanly, then became Christians to doe.

In like manner we see here the diligence and celerity used by his Majesty, accordng to the occasions that happened, in going so suddenly towards *Ossa*, and in returning againe at the Poast, with a convoy of Dragoniers towards *Munchen*, to breake up with his Army, having left Duke *Barnard* of *Wymar* with Generall Major *Ruthven* to attend on *Ossa* his Army, on the borders of *Tyroll*, towards *Landaw* and the *Boden* sea, till businesse were pacified.

Here then we see, that his Majesties diligence and experience in warlike actions was so great, that his enemies never plotted that enterprize, but how soone it came once to his knowledge, he presently with celerity and quicknesse of judgment could finde out the contrary remedy, ever to make himselfe appeare in effect the most fortunate Commander that ever we read of. For his great experience in warlike actions did confirme his judgment and his courage; for he was not affraid to doe what he did learne and practice before; and like a wise Generall, he did ever watch against all unlooked for stroakes: for nothing could come wrong unto him, because he was alike for all, having had the whole compend of wit in his braines, he could well and wisely governe the Common-wealth, to fight battailes was his delight; in the making of Leaguers he excelled all other Generalls (as *Tilly* did know) Engines to devise, to passe over Rivers or Fossies or walles, was his master-peece (as *Tillies* death can witnesse at the *Leacke*) to plante batteries or to change, therein he was profound; witnesse also his crossing the *Leacke*; if lines or approaches were to be altered, his judgment then behooved to be used; in a word he was the Master of Military discipline, being risen from a prentise, to the great professor of Arts, in this eminent and high calling of a Souldier: where it is requisit, that as a man is valorous and judicious, so he ought to be constant in keeping his word and truth inviolable, as this King did to all his confederats, and to his enemies also.  And therefore as a [II-127] most pretious Iewell, his remarkable example of vertue is to be followed by those, who would prove Heroicke and Magnificent as he was.

And therefore I was serious to prie so deepe into his actions, as that those, whom I wish to succeede him in his vertues, may follow his practices used in the conquest of a great part of *Germany*: for his spirit alone and skill in warres was better then thousands of Armed men.  The like gifts I heartily wish to my Noble Patron his Highnesse, the Prince *Elector Palatine*, whom I wish to succeede him, not only in his vertues but in his conquest also.

Seing then the greatest part of humane happinesse doth consist in vertue, who ever then would be wise, let him fix his eyes and his minde to judge other mens actions, thereby to correct his owne, looking unto all that was and is, to th'end that through their example he may learne to better himselfe; for so long he shall florish, as wisdome and counsell are his guides, which both I wish we may follow.

---

### The thirty-two Duty discharged of our March
### *to* Donavert, *and from thence to* Furt *on the* Peignets.

The first of *Iune* our Army did breake up from *Munchen* in *Bavaria*, towards *Donavert*, having left an Army behinde us in *Schwabland* of eight thousand strong, led by Duke *Barnard* of *Wymar*, and Generall Major *Ruthven* to attend on *Ossa*; having crossed the *Leacke* againe at *Rhine*, we continued our march towards our Randez-vouz at *Donavert*, where we were appointed to joyne with the rest of our Army; and from thence we continued our march upon *Weisenburg*, being the passe betwixt *Donavert* and *Nurenberg*, where on our march we had certainty, that Duke *Barnard* had defeated a Regiment of horse, and taken eight Cornets from *Ossa*, and that *Hanniball* Count of *Hohemems* was immediatly sent prisoner to *Vlme*; and *Banier* was left for a time at *Ausburg*, for to settle the Garrison, where the pledges were left in custody.  His Majesty very wisely before this march confirmed his confederacy with the Duke of *Wirtenberg* being of great force to advance his Majesties affaires and the cause, with men, meate and mony, being the next neighbour to *Vlme*.

His Majesty also at this time did give Patents to *Hugh Hamilton* and to *Iohn Forbesse*, as Colonells to leavie two Regiments of foote on the borders of *Sweetzerland*, at which time his Majesty did write a favourable Letter unto the *Protestant* Cantons in *Sweetzerland*, to give no passe through their country unto the *Spaniard* from *Italy*, and that for weighty reasons; chiefly calling them to memory, that the house of *Austria* and *Spaine* were ever great crossers of the liberties of their Common-wealth, and most of all, of the liberty of their consciences: which Letter was gratiously accepted by the *Sweetzers*, and the passage after that was closed up. [II-128]

Our march continuing to to *Furt*, on our way the Bishopricks of *Aichstat* and *Tilligen* were brought under his Majesties contribution, as also *Papenhaim* Castle was taken in, being the second marshall house belonging to the Empire, not distant above two miles from *Wysenburg*, where before our coming to *Wysenburg*, the Duke of *Bavier* his Forces were retired againe, for their safeties unto *Engolstat*, being led by *Crats*, so that without impediment, our march continued to *Furt* on the *Pegnets*, besides *Nurenburg*: where we incamped againe on the fields, the seventh of *Iune*, and remained there till the Lords of *Nurenburg* invited his Majesty to their City, where his Majesty was Royally entertained, and bountifully offered what in their powers lay, to be given unto his Majesty, either for his Army or his Majesties contentment otherwise: and in this meanetime, the Duke of *Bavaria* his forces were ioyned with *Valestine* his Army at *Egger*; having used all the diligence he could in helping his foote forwards on horse-backe and waggons: and in their by-going the seventh of *Iune*, they tooke in *Schultzbach* in the over *Paltz*, having no Garrison in it but Burgers, who defended themselves till they made an Accord, which was not kept unto them.

### The thirty-two Observation.

Here we see againe his Majesties wonderfull diligence, wherein doth ever consist the best part of warre; for hearing in *Bavaria*, that *Walestine* was marched with a strong Armie out of *Bohemia* towards the over *Paltz*; and knowing the Duke of *Baviere* had the passe of *Rhinesberg* free unto the upper *Paltz*, he was not able to hinder their Conjunction, if *Walestine* his designe were on *Nurenberg*, as it was; his Majestie knew then diligence was to be used for the reliefe of *Nurenberg*; and therefore, though about, he hasted his march thither; for his Majestie knew well, that the taking of time in warres was of much importance, especially, knowing the enemies designe being on *Nurenberg*, which to have, the enemy he knew, would not spare either money or travell; for if they could cut off his Majestie from the helpe and assistance of this Towne, it was the best way to defend *Baviere*, *Schwabland*, and *Ostreigh*.

Likewise, it was the onely meanes to recover againe the Bishopricke of *Wurtzburg*, and the Dukedome of *Franconia*, and by that meanes (if not altogether) yet farre they might, drive backe againe his Majestie of *Sweden* and his Forces, keeping him out of *Bavaria*; as also out of the Emperours hereditarie lands. This was their cunning enterprise on *Nurenberg*, and the reasons of it, which his Majestie of *Sweden*, that Heroicke and magnanimous King tooke betimes unto his consideration; having had a wake-rife or vigilant eye over the safetie and preservation of this Citie; seeing it stood of so much importance unto his Majestie, and unto the whole *Evangelists* Confederates, that the enemy should not be Master of it.   And therefore to prevent the hurt thereof, his Majestie used the greater haste out of *Bavaria*.  For his Majestie knew well, that the opportunitie of time was a swift Eagle, which being at ones foote may be taken, but when once he mounts in the ayre, he laughes at those would catch him, not meaning to returne unto them: which moved his Majestie, not to suffer the Eagle to mount so high, [II-129] as to be laughed at, but imbracing opportunitie, while he had it, he prevented the enemies designe by taking of time, that augments our experience in warfare; which experience gives us confidence in our behaviours, in the greatest extremitie, giving us resolution and courage against our enemies; as also graces our behaviour towards our friends and confederates.

Here then we see the enemies designes prevented by the diligence, labour, and danger of the most valiant, the *Lyon of the North*, the invincible King of *Sweden*; who was so diligent or wake-rife, that his delight was to try the Conclusions of Fortune against his enemies; forcing Fortune to make him her Favourite, and sometimes her Master, as he was on this expedition, in coming betwixt the enemy and the Citie of *Nurenberg*, as a good Shepheard goeth betwixt the Flocke and the Corne.

Moreover, here we see also the great wisedome of his Majestie, in making his league and confederacy sure with the Duke of *Wirtenberg*, before he could perceive the enemies strength that were coming against him, taking a catch of time, which being over-seene, could never have beene had againe; and therefore it was, that his Majestie used the greater celeritie in binding up that confederacy, having then his Armie under the Duke of *Wirtenbergs* nose, to force him to Conditions, if he had not willingly yeelded: where we see, that the power of an Armie, led by a King, much availeth to bring inferiours to Conditions, not being able againe to resist a Kings power with Force.  And as his Majestie was wise in making his confederacy with the Duke, so he was diligent in fore-seeing to write to the *Republique* of *Switzerland*, to get the passage closed on his enemies behinde him; As also we see here his Majesties care to supply his Armie, by giving Patents to our Country-men, whose fortunes were much to be lamented; for having brought their Regiments suddenly together, they were as suddenly scattered: for both the Colonells being taken prisoners, they were kept pittifully in bondage for the space of three yeares, being neglected of their Superiours, till they were forced to ransome themselves, and Colonell *Iohn Forbesse* having afterwards taken service under the King of *France*, being of short continuance, was much regrated, he being a young Cavalier, free and liberall, and of good hope.

To conclude then this observation, it was necessitie, that vehement fellow, did bring his Majestie and his Armie so soone out of *Bavaria*, being the enemy pressed strong against our friends, he was diverted.   Where we see, that necessitie in warres admits of no reason, more than in other things; for seldome it suffers to make choice of times. And therefore it is holden as the best teacher, that teacheth all most diligently, even Kings as well as meane men, and Armies as well as parties, and parties as private men: for it brings ever great celerity and quicknesse with it, as it did on this our march, for the safetie of *Nurenberg.* [II-130]

---

### The thirty-three Dutie discharged of our Expedition
### from Furt *unto the vpper* Palatinate.

The Towne of *Nurenberg* having accommodated and submitted themselves in all things unto his Majesties will, for the furtherance of the good cause, they furnished victualls, Armes, and Amunition, with Artillery for his Majesties Armie; and then his Majestie did breake up with his Armie from *Furt*, and marched by *Nurenberg* towards the upper *Paltz*, of intention to get betwixt the enemy and *Nurenberg*, that where ever the enemy could march, his Majestie might be provided to follow him, or to prevent his Designes.

The first night our Armie lay in the fields at *Lawffe*, and the next day our march continued beyond *Harshbrooke*, where wee incamped over-night, till his Majesties Troopes sent out to *Sultzbach*, were returned with true *Conshaft* or intelligence; which being got, we continued our march towards *Fortmanshowen*, and taking it in by Accord, the enemy retired to *Amberg*.

The Country being destroyed thereabout, having camped two nights in the fields, Colonell *Hepburne* and I were commanded with two thousand Musketiers, to second the Horsemen in case of neede. But his Majestie having got sudden intelligence of *Walestines* marching towards him, he retired betime to *Harshbrooke* againe, and we with the Horsemen retired also, having the Reare-guard, with much rainie weather, which spoyled both our Armes and Cloaths for a whole fortnight together, being incamped at *Harshbrooke*; where his Majestie hearing of the enemies approaching, having had then but a weake and a discontented Armie, according to his accustomed manner, he thought it was then fit time to make a reckoning with the Armie, for their by-past lendings, and to cast some thing in their teeth, being much discontented. To satisfie our hunger a little, we did get of by-past lendings three paid us in hand, and Bills of Exchange given us for one and twentie lendings more, which should have beene payed at *Ausburg*, of the *Munchen* moneys; which we accepted of for payment, but were never paid: and being thus a little content, we retired on *Nurenberg*, making all the haste we could to inclose our selves in a close Leaguer about *Nurenberg*, before the enemies comming.

During this time, *Walenstine* being on his march to us-ward, he did take in *Egra* and *Soultzbatch*, and approaching still with his Armie towards *Nurenberg*, where his Majestie being come before him the sixteenth of *Iune*, we resolved, being but weake, to expect his coming, and in the meanetime, his Majestie directed for Forces from *During*, and *Schwabland*, and the Feltmarshall *Horne* was sent away towards the *Palatinate*, and from thence to *Elsasse*; and his Majestie engaged to defend *Nurenberg*, we wrought hard, till we were in suretie; and by this time, being the twenty-sixth of *Iune*, *Walenstine* being joyned with the Duke of *Baviere* his Armie, they marched towards *Nurenberg*, where they met with Colonell *Dowbattle* his Dragoniers, and with foure Troopes of spare Rutters horsemen, which being defeated, Colonell *Dowbattle* was taken prisoner, who being a valourous Cavalier, of much worth, that had behaved himselfe well on many occasions, as on this last. The re- [II-131] port whereof moved *Walenstine*, out of his clemency, to set him free within three dayes, without ransome; and after that they approaching to *Nurenberg*, divers hot skirmishes past betwixt our horsemen and theirs; where there was good service done of both parties; for their credits, in making their first acquaintance, they interchanged a number of Bullets, welcoming one another unto *Nurenberg*. And on the twenty-eight of *Iune*, they appointed their chiefe Magazine for their Armie, to be at *Fryenstat* in the upper *Paltz*: and on the thirtieth of *Iune*, they came to *Schawbach*, being then fiftie thousand strong, of horse and foote, we not exceeding sixteene thousand; and on the fourth of *Iuly*, they lay downe with their Armie betwixt the River *Pegnets*, and the River *Rednets*; being betwixt our Armie and *Franconia*, from whence our Forces, supply, and victualls were to come; and his Majestie for their welcome, the fifth of *Iuly* did cut off three Troopes of Horse of theirs, having got their three Cornets, as *Bonum omen* unto us.

### The thirty-three Observation.

His Majestie having concluded for to stand to the defence of *Nurenberg* against the strong and mightie Emperiall armie, led by *Walenstine*, and the Duke of *Baviere*; where we have first set before us the reasons of his Majesties Conjunction and Confederacy with *Nurenberg* against their common enemy.

First being both of one religion, their consciences tied them, not to see one anothers hurt or detriment.

Secondly, they saw and considered, that the good arising of the union redounded alike to both their wealls. Thirdly, the feare they had conceived of their owne weakenesse, by reason of the enemies strength, made them joyne the faster together. Fourthly, their hatred they bare to the enemies of the Gospell, who sought nothing more then their overthrow and ruine, made them looke the better unto themselves. Fifthly, his Majesty stood in neede of the *Nurenbergers* assistance, of men, meate and moneyes; and they stood in neede of his Majesties concurrence, to keepe the overplus of their meanes, and the freedome of their consciences to themselves, and their posterity, by keeping the enemies fury off them.

All these considered, they joyned hand in hand, and with one courage they resolved to be enemies to those that were come to be their enemies, finding it was lawfull for them, before God and the whole world, to defend themselves: And therefore they prepared for it, where at first the Towne of *Nurenberg* made up twenty foure strong Companies of foote, that carried in their Colours the twenty foure letters of the Alphabet, which they ordained for a supply for his Majesties Army, that their City might be the better watched, for they resolved, their best remedy against feare was not to feare at all, since they had *Gustavus* and his Fortunes under God for their Leader: And therefore they were assured of deliverance from their enemies, with the losse of a little mony, and the spending of a little provision, which they had long kept in store to sustaine them in their necessities, having had within their walls to sustaine dayly besides the Army, eight hundred thousand soules, being no small burthen to a Land-towne.

Here also we see his Majesties fore-sight in giving a kinde of content unto his Army, according to his custome at such times, the enemy drawing [II-132] neere unto him, to tie the Souldiers and their Officers to the greater obedience unto his Majesties commandements, to undergoe whatsoever he was to command them, and for to grieve the enemies by the rumour of monies, which then was given out to his Majesties Souldiers; the enemies Army might be disbandoned, and monies being so rife amongst them, to forsake their owne Colours and runne away unto his Majesties Army.

It must needs have bin an extraordinary great provision, that sustained so many soules a day within the City, whereunto a great part of the country people, Gentry and Boores had runne together for refuge, being a great number of people besides the Army, which was sustained for three moneths together by the providence of God, the Rector and Governour of the world, and the Fountaine of all goodnesse; this *Omnipotent, Omniscient,* and *Invincible* God governing all and over-seeing all by his providence, at this time did so direct this people in middest of their troubles, that they having recommended themselves, and the event of their affaires to this great God, they concluded that it was better to prevent, then to suffer under the Tyranny of their enemies; And therefore they fell to worke in earnest, for their owne safeties and the safety of his Majesties Army, being under God resolved to protect them.

---

*The thirty-fourth Duty discharged at* Nurenberg, *and of the occurrences there.*

His Majesty having Recognosced the City and situation thereof, finding his Forces weake in respect of the enemies, he resolved to take all the advantage he could in setting downe his Leaguer, for the preservation of his Army, and the safety of the City, and therefore he caused to draw the draught of the Leaguer to goe in a circular *Orbe,* round the whole City, the water running through the middest of it; The Leaguer begun at the East, without the Suburbes called in *Dutch Marke,* were towards the South, to the part called *Lightenhooffe;* where his Majesties quarter was, and from thence towards the west, to the Townes new workes, crossing over the water; This Leaguer being accomplished in ten dayes, and in full defence, with strong Skonces, Redoutes, Fossies, batteries, and being well fortified round with Stakkets, without the Fossie; and at all sorting Ports, being well foreseene with slaught-bomes and triangles; well fastened and close; His Majesty then upon the North side of the City, made the retrenchment goe likewise round the City, being also well fortified with strong Skonces and Fossies, from the East unto the West, beginning at the *Marke Flect Were*, and going round the *Inden boole*, even to St. *Iohn*, and the water closed: Above the water on the hight, was made a great Skonce, and another great Skonce was made in the corner at *Gostenhooffe*, with deepe water graffes, having workes without it againe, and halfe moones: also before *Steeneboole*, over against *Schwennaw* there was another Skonce, fast and strong: Likewise at the backe of the Dorpe *Steene-* [II-133] *boole,* towards the Leaguer, there was another strong Skonce made: likewise towards the wood at the South, on the street called *Rottenbacherstreete* there was made an extraordinary strong Skonce, set about with foure crossed Stakkets, of strong timber, so that there was no meanes to storme it; the like was made on the streete called *Altoffer* streete. These workes, Skonces and Redoutes being accomplished, a great number of Cannon great and small, were brought on the workes; the Batteries all ready, there could be reckoned in the Leaguer about this Towne, without the walls, of Cannon on their Carriages, above three hundred, great and small.

Our Leaguer thus fortifed, the Emperiall Army led by the Duke of *Fridland Walestine* joyned with the Duke of *Bavaria* his Forces, consisting both of fifty thousand men, having the first of *Iuly* taken in *Schawbach*; the second day after they drew towards the Dorpe called *Steyne* over against *Nurenberg*, which doth lie about a *Dutch* mile from the Towne; there they begun to pitch a Leaguer, and from *Steyne* towards the *Fleckt* called *Zerndorfe*, the Leaguer being well fortified, on the seventh of *Iuly*, the Duke of *Fridland* made his Leaguer also towards *Zerndorfe* on the top of the hill called *Altberg*; wherein he tooke, for an advantage, an old ruinous and waste Castle, neere which there lay a hunting house in the wood, on the top of the hill over against the *Fleckt-Fort*, which was called the old strength in *Dutch*, This Fort he caused strongly to pallisade without the workes, with Fossies and Stakkets without the fossie, other great and strong Skonces; he caused to make, and divers other strong Skonces on the old hill, the Fossies and brest workes were all fortified with great and strong Trees, and within the workes, were severall barrells or hogsheads filled with sand and stones for throwing, placed on the Batteries, and by this strong and great Leaguer *Valestine* did cut off from his Majesties Army and the Towne of *Nurenberg* all kinde of victualls or provision, could come unto them by the *Axile*, thinking thereby to blocke up his Majesties Army, forceing him to take another resolution, and then he thought to compell the Kings Majesty to a peace, according to his minde.

These two Armies thus incamped and set downe opposite one against another, they begun all of them, as they went forth in the country about, to steale, to rob, to plunder and to spoile the whole country, for to supply with victualls and other furniture these two great new-founded Cities of short continuance, though it is certaine, many of them did get life-rent-leases of their new built houses.

Thus having set downe the manner of both the Armies incamping, we lay still one against another a long time, neither giving nor offering offence one to another, except it were by meere accident in the country, amongst stragling troopes. Nevertheless though we looked on each others, we had our watches night and day, before one anothers noses, without loosing of one Pistoll, or without one Alarum in two moneths time, as if in effect there were a Stil-stand of Peace.

During this time we were thus looking one to another, the *Spaniard* finding his Majesty with the maine Army farre off, he resolved to take his time in the *Paltz*, and crossing the *Mosel* againe towards *Alzie*; his Excellence the Rex-chancellour *Oxensterne* having intelligence of their coming, he did bring his horsemen over the *Rhine* and suffered the *Spaniard* to draw neere [II-134] *Mentz* and then marched unto them; in the meane time the *Spanish* Generall *Comissary Lookas Cagro* did breake up with twelve Companies of horse, giving orders to the rest to follow him, of intention to fall unlooked for on the *Rhine-graves* quarter; But he did count without his Hoste, the *Rhinegraves* folke being betimes acquainted of their coming, and to their helpe, having got a supply timely sent unto them by his Excellence the Rex-chancellour, the enemy was so welcomed by them, that he was put in confusion, and then chased so hard, that there were a hundred and twenty killed unto him, many taken prisoners, and seven Standards of theirs were taken, as Trophees of the *Rhine-graves* victory over them.

In revenge whereof shortly after, the *Grave fon Ridberg* with a strong party of horse and foote did fall upon that part of the *Paltz*, called *Hundsrucke* betwixt the *Mosell* and the *Noe*, and coming on *Spier*, where the *Swedens* Colonell called *Hornegt* without any resistance gave over *Spier*, notwithstanding of a succourse was sent unto him from *Mentz* that was at hand: whereupon the Colonell was afterwards brought prisoner to *Mentz*, to be adjudged there for his evill carriage.

The *Spaniard* taking out of *Spier* Cannon, Amunition and Armes, with all that could be found, together with a great deale of mony exacted from the Burgers, he had also an intention on *Wormes*, but in vaine, being strongly beset with the *Swedens* forces, so that the *Spaniards* at this time, as many times before, were forced to quit the *Paltz*, and to draw backe againe into *Holland*; and the States Army being come to lie before *Mastricht*, were forced to breake up from *Spier* with their Army, and whole baggage and Cannon: The *Swedens* getting notice of their upbreaking, desirous to convey them, the Rex-chancellor and *Palsgrave Christian* breakes up from *Mentz* towards *Altson*, and the next day they came to *Belchin*, two miles from the part the *Spaniard* had broken up from, and following them hard till they got sight of the *Spanish* Army, which the *Spaniard* perceiving directs his baggage before, and drew up in battaile on a plaine neere a wood, where incontinent they were brought in disorder by the *Swedens*, that they were forced with the losse of three Cornets and some foote, to retire into the wood, and finding the whole *Swedens* Army following up, they resolved with one consent by flying to save themselves were their best, and taking the night to their helpe, they marched so hard as they could. But yet the *Swedens* continued their march after them, till the *Spaniard* coming to a passe in the hills, threw off the bridges behinde them; Neverthelesse the *Swedens* repaired the bridges and followed hard after, and by *Lantericke* came in sight of them againe, that neither day nor night were they suffered to rest, so that the *Spaniard* was forced to burne some of his baggage on his march, and some he left to the *Swedens*, that they might, the lighter they were, come the easier off: in the end a part of them by *Lanterick* was attrapped by the *Rhine-graves* Horsmen, where some were cut downe and their baggage taken. The *Spaniard* thus in great feare, and confounded by the hastinesse of his march, and the *Swedens* wearied with long following, were content at last, the *Spaniards* should goe their way with so little reputation out of the *Paltz*, at their last good night, having lost above two thousand men and their whole Baggage.

By this time also the Boores in *Schwabland* againe began to be tumultuous and unquiet, so that by *Kempten*, they drew together very strong, of full intention to chase the *Swedens* out of their lands. But his uproare continued [II-135] but short; for when the *Swedens* Forces drew out of the Garrisons, they killed the most part, and drove the rest unto woods, to seeke their food with the Swine, in burning a number of their Dorpes, to give them worke to thinke on against the winter, to build new houses, or to dwell in woods: but repenting their Rebellion, they turned their Armes against their owne Masters, that moved them to rise against the *Swedens*: and cutting off a number of them, they possessed their houses, turning good *Swedens* againe, being beaten with the rod of Correction in their bodies and meanes.

By this time Duke *Barnard* of *Wymar*, with his Troopes did cut off above five hundred men of *Leopaldus* folke by *Fussen* on the *Leacke*, where he caused to demolish sundry Skonces made up by the Country-Boores, in time of their uproare, and divers of their skinnes were pierced by Musket and Pistoll, till they were taught to be more sober and quiet, on their owne charges; and after this uproare was setled, the *Leopoldish* Boores againe out of *Tyroll* recollected stronger Forces, and marched towards the *Leacke* againe on *Fussen*, and *Lansberg*, both strong passes, and got them in; yet in the end all turned to a slight conclusion: for Duke *Barnard* of *Wymar* againe, having come upon them with his Forces; First he tooke in *Lansberg* and then on the sixteenth of *Iuly*, he cut off two Companies of *Leopoldish* Dragoniers, and a Troope of Horsemen, by a Towne call *Rosshaupten*, where few or none did escape, and in the end, marching on *Fussen*, having stormed the Towne, they cut off above three hundred of the Garrison, and tooke prisoners eleven hundred with their Officers; and a number of the Country Gentlemen, that were Papists, and sought to save themselves in that strength, were deceived, their Colours being taken from them, and above a thousand of their Souldiers were forced to take service.

By this time also a little Flecke, *Freidberg* in *Schwabland* neere to *Ausburg*, treacherously having called some Crabbats of the enemies to their assistance, they murthered all the *Swedens* safeguards that lay thereabout; whereupon the *Swedens* Forces, to be revenged on them, did fall upon the Flecke, or little Towne, and killed all the male-kinde they could finde, and taking their wives and children out of the Towne to the fields, they set the Towne on fire; so that there is no memory left of this Towne, for their perfidiousnesse to those they got to save them from the injuries of others.

I hope the Reader will excuse this extravagancie of discourse, seeing all this time we lay idle at *Nurenberg*, being sometimes without imployment in our calling, I thought better to collect at this time somewhat of the actions of others, than to be altogether idle. Therefore I crave pardon againe, to tell as yet somewhat that happened about this time in the neather *Saxon Creitzis*, which I set downe in paper, as his Majestie was informed of it, we being then at *Nurenberg* without hostile employment.

By this time the Earle of *Papenhaim*, a worthy brave fellow, though he was our enemy, his valour and resolution I esteemed so much of, that it doth me good to call his vertuous actions somewhat to memory, and the successe he had at this time in warlike and martiall exployts, in the neather *Saxon Creitzis*. First then he had not onely offended the *Hessen* and *Lunenburg*, but also by skirmish he made them feele the dint of the valour, which accompanied him unto his death; and as they felt his skill in the fields by fighting disbanded in skirmish, so also they were made to understand his experience in beleaguering of Townes, having taken in before their noses, their Armie [II-136] being neere unto him, *Eynbeck* and divers places more, and then having recreued his Armie againe out of *Westfalia*, he then marched on *Stoade*, and relieved it before Generall *Tott* his nose, that lay before it, and about it; and all things succeeding still well with him, he not alone relieved the Towne in making the *Swedens* to quit it, but also cut off unto them fifteene hundred men, which were but Novices, being new levied; and he did get divers colours of theirs, as Trophees of his victorie; amongst others he did get three colours of Colonell *Monro* of *Obstell* his Regiment, which were then led by Captaine *Francis Sinclaire*, who after a little skirmish had with the enemie, their powder being spent, and they environed by the horsemen, knowing of no reliefe, tooke quarters for the Souldiers, and the Officers were prisoners, being long kept unrelieved at *Minden*, above a yeare and a halfe; but the Captaine having ransom'd himselfe came loose soone after he was taken; but two Lievetenants *Monro*, and Ensigne *Monro* remained eighteene moneths longer in prison.

*Papenhaim* after relieving of *Stoade*, having gotten intelligence, that Duke *Francis Carolus* of *Saxon Lovanburg* had come to the *Swedens*, with two strong Regiments, of intention to blocke up *Stoade* againe, the *Swedens* growing still stronger and stronger, so that it was thought *Papenhaim* was inclosed as in a snare or grinne, and which was worse, that he was scarce of victuals in the Towne, and the Towne not strong enough to hold out, he then resolved to quit it, taking out with him the Emperiall Garrison that was therein, and taking his march againe towards the *Weser* streame; so that he leaving it, the *Swedens* patronizing the Towne they did beset it againe with a Garrison.

Shortly after this brave fellow rencountring againe with some *Hessen* troopes, he did sore beate them also backe and side. By this time Generall Lievetenant *Bawtishen* had got the Command of the *Swedens* Army, after Generall *Tott* had quit it; who incontinent after followed *Papenhaim* towards the *Weser*; But this brave fellow *Papenhaim* not for feare of *Bawtish* comming, but being called by the *Infanta* for ayde, crossed the *Weser*; and comming on the River of *Rhine*, continued his march towards *Mastricht* to assist the *Spaniard* in their need. This brave Commander, as he was full of action, so he was still employed, and I was sorry he was not of my minde in serving the good cause.

*Papenhaim* gone to *Mastricht*, *Lunenburg*, and Generall *Bawtish* (under whom was my brother Colonell *Monro* of *Obstell*) they returned towards *Duderstat*, which *Papenhaim* had strongly beset before his going away, and they neverthelesse got it in with little paines, by reason the Souldiers, that were therein, being fifteene hundred begunne to mutine, and to give themselves over unto the *Swedens* service; after this they commanded some forces to blockquer *Wolfembittle*, wherein the Duke of *Lunenburg* in person was employed; And Generall Major King, being with some forces employed on a Poste apart, the Duke hearing the enemie was marching strong, for the reliefe of the Towne, he did breake up, and marched away for his owne safetie, without advertizing Generall Major King of the danger he was left unto, by the enemies approaching so strong, till in the end they came so neere to the Generall Majors Poste, having no conshaft of them, till they had strongly invironed him with their horsemen, so that the Generall Major finding no passage open, he being pursued did valourously with a few men defend themselves, till in end being weakest, they were made to yeeld, where [II-137] after divers wounds honourably received, the Generall Major was taken prisoner, and kept long under cure, till that after he ransomed himselfe, and being come loose againe, he levied more Forces of horse and foote for the *Swedens* service, to be the better revenged of his enemies, and after that fortunately and valourously behaved himselfe, with the generall applause as well of strangers as of his Country-men; being also well reported of by his very enemies, so that since his vertures and noble carriage have still advanced his credit, which for my part, I wish to continue, he being now Lievetenant Generall.

Having thus farre spoken of the passages, which occurred by this time in the neather *Saxon Creitzis*, I returne againe to shew the rest of our intelligence at *Nurenberg*, come from the Bishopricke of *Tryer* on the *Rhine*; where also on divers occasions did passe some rare accidents.

This Bishop having concluded a *Neutralitie* with his Majestie of *France*, as also with his Majestie of *Sweden*, but seeing the *Spanish* not to remove, neither yet that the principalls of the Gentry of the Land were willing to embrace the *Neutralitie*: Neverthelesse, the Bishop remained in his former resolution, and the Strength called vulgarly *Hermensteyne*, he gives it to the *French*, so that they being so neere, in neighbour-hood to the *Spaniard* in *Coblentz*, they did agree together as Catts and Ratts: in the end the *French* seeing the *Spanish* Garrison growing weake day by day, the *Swedens* by vertue of their confederacie with the *French*, they came in for their owne hand, as third men, and drawing before *Coblentz*, after a short beleaguering, they make the *Spaniard* quit it, and getting of the Citie a summe of money, they remove, giving the Citie over unto the *French*: the *Spaniard* after losing of *Coblentz*, *Mountebowre*, *Engers*, and other places thereabouts belonging to the Bishopricke of *Tryer*, they goe their wayes.

The Feltmarshall *Gustavus Horne*, being by this time sent by his Majestie from *Nurenberg* towards the *Rhine* streame, to make resistance to the *Emperialists* beginnings there; comming towards *Trarbach* on the *Mosell* with his Forces, being the passe the *Spaniard* was wont to crosse at, to come unto the *Paltz*; after a short beleaguering, he got in the Towne and Castle by Accord, and then retired unto the *Maine* to draw more Forces together, and from thence continued his march towards *Manheime*, of intention to joyne with the Duke of *Wirtenberg*, for to make resistance to *Ossa* and the *Emperialists*, which were recollecting themselves strongly in *Elsas* againe, having understood *Ossa* was joyned with three Regiments of the Catholique League, the Grave *Fon Brunckhurst* his Regiment of horse; as also the free *Here Fon Rollingen* his Regiment, and Colonell *Metternight* his Regiment of foote, which were levied for the defence of *Coblentz*; but shortly after, through the alteration that happened in those quarters, were brought unto *Elsas*; and being joyned to twenty-five Companies of Horse, and some Regiments more of foote, they crossed the *Rhine* unto *Turloch*, and further unto *Brittenie*, where they compell'd the *Swedens* Garrison there, being two hundred, to take service of them, and then plundered out the Towne, burnt the Ports, and demolished a part of the walles, being in *Wirtenberg-land*.

The *Grave Fon Mountecucule* was Generall over these folkes, who perceiving that the Duke of *Wirtenberg* with some new levied Forces had passed over *Kinbis*, he retired upon *Kintlingen*, and scaling the Towne, puts three hundred to the sword, plundered all out, and burnt all the Towne to three houses.

[II-138]

By this time the Garrison of *Heidelberg* coming towards *Wisloch*, wherein did lie a company of Dragoniers, and a Troope of Horse of the Markgrave *Fon Tourlochs* folke beleaguers it, and by casting fire in the Towne sets three houses on fire, whereof the Felt-marshall *Gustavus Horne* being made fore-seene, he with all his Forces did breake up, and marched; the *Heidelbergish* Garrison being acquainted with this advancement of the Felt-marshalls, they incontinent retired in great haste on *Heidelberg*, and having before their up-breaking from *Heidelberg* desired succours from *Ossa* and *Mountecucule*, their Corporall and six Horsemen at their backe coming being taken prisoners by the *Swedens*, the Feltmarshall did finde by their Letters, that on the sixt of *August*, their whole Horsemen had appointed Randezvouz at *Metternigh*, to goe for *Wisloch*, whereupon his *Excellence* did draw neere to their Randezvouz place, and attended their coming, being unlooked for by them, in the meane time the *Emperialists* were advertised, that those of *Heidelberg* had got in *Wisloch*, and were againe blocked up by some *Swedens* Forces, whereupon *Ossa*, *Mountecucule*, the Colonell *Mountelabam*, and *Witzone*, with the fore-Troopes of Horse, being a thousand Horse, march on for the Reliefe, and unlooked for were pursued by the *Swedens*, whereof two hundred, among whom was the Colonell *Mountelaban* and other Officers, were killed, many taken, and the rest all scattered. Whereupon *Ossa* and *Mountecucule*, with the rest of the folke, that were lying at *Oberhawsen* and *Rhinehawsen*, in all haste did set over the *Rhine* at *Philipsburg*. The Feltmarshall followed hard, and finding he could get no more of them, he returned over the *Rhine* againe, and getting the *Strasburg* passe *Rhinebroucke*, he held on his march further unto *Elsas* with the Horsemen, during which time his foote Forces with the *Wirtenbergers* beleaguered the passe *Stolhossen*, and getting it in by Accord, they marched five thousand strong over at *Strasburg* unto upper *Elsas*, whereat the *Emperialists* were mightily afraid, and without night or dayes rest they marched towards *Colmarsohletstad*, *Brisach*, in the upper *Elsas* in all haste, by taking them to those parts for their Retreate, but the *Swedens* following them hot-foote, they tooke in divers places, and made good bootie on their march, and at last, after in-taking of *Offenburg* by Accord, they marched then towards *Bentfield*, the Bishop his chiefe Strength, and beleaguered it.

By this time also, Feltmarshall *Arnheim* leading the *Saxons* Armie, did fall in strong into *Silesia*, taking in *Groseglogaw*, and other parts thereabouts, and all the *Emperialists* marched towards him with a strong and mightie Armie. There were incontinent certaine *Swedish* and *Brandeburgh* forces joyned with *Arnheim*, who did set on the *Emperialists* by *Steinove*, beate them in the fields, and followed them unto *Brisloe*; and then after the *Emperialists* intrenched themselves betwixt *Bresloe* and the *Oder*. Neverthelesse, they were hunted up againe by the *Swedens* and *Saxons*, who followed them from place to place, and did get the *Thumbe* at *Bresloe*, where they did get great bootie from the *Emperialists*, and not contented with this, the *Swedens* and *Saxons* followed them over the River at *Ollawe*, and did set on the *Emperialists* againe, not farre from *Wintsloe*, obtaining a great victory over them againe, where many brave fellowes were taken prisoners, many also were killed, and the rest scattered; so that the *Swedens* and *Saxons* were Masters of the greatest part of *Silesia*, and they made the Towne of *Bresloe* to accommodate themselves in confederacy, on certaine Conditions, with the *Swedens* and *Saxons*, while as [II-139] we at *Nurenberg* for six weekes together used no great hostilitie, but lay secure within our Leaguers, as within walled Townes, but at such times as we were commanded forth, as Convoyes for our Horsemen, that went for forrage, and then sometimes we lighted on one another, striving alwayes for elbowroome, whereof at length the *Emperialists* made us very crimpe or scarce, having but one quarter of our Leaguer free, to bring in our forrage, being onely from the *Southwest*.

### The thirty-fourth Observation.

Wee reade in *Dion*, that after *Cæsar* had wonne the Battaile of *Pharsalia*, amongst the honours the Senate had ordained to be given unto him, they commanded to dresse for him a Triumphing Chariot, which was set opposite to *Iupiter* within the *Capitoll*, and that he should stand on a Globe, representing the world, with the inscription, *Semi-Deus est*: Even so the Lords of *Nurenberg* in consideration of the great respect they carried unto his Majesty of *Sweden*, at the first entering their City, after the Battaile of *Leipsigh*, they presented two Globes unto his Majesty, a *Terrestiall* and a *Coelestiall*, in signe of their love and obedience unto his Majesty, and his Majesty againe by his Royall word, promised, under God to defend and protect them against all mortalls; and being thus engaged unto them, their enemies menacing their ruine, with a mighty and a strong Army, being minded to overcome them with the sword, or to make them starve by hunger, having closed up as they thought all passes, where through succours could come unto them, by planting of a wonderfull strong Leaguer about them, of intention to blocke them, and his Majesties Army both within them, being then but weake within their Trenches and walles.

His Majesty againe like a wise Generall, pondering and considering how weighty his enemies enterprizes were, in seeking to overcome *Nurenberg*, and knowing, if that once they did get *Nurenberg* on their side, the rest of the great Cities would follow, in regard whereof his Majesty resolved, the safest course for him and the Towne both was, to set downe his Leaguer strongly betwixt the Towne and the enemy, aswell to hinder their correspondence, in case of their unconstancy, as for their defence, in case of their loyalty. For his Majesty knew well there was as great vertue in keeping of a conquest, as in getting of it: And therefore at this time, as formerly at *Statin*, *Werben* and at *Wertzburg* against *Tilly*, he resolved to take him to a defensive warre, with the spade and the shovell, putting his Army within workes, having the supply of such a back-friend as *Nurenberg* was, to assist him with men, meate and Amunition, untill such time as he might weary his enemy, as formerly he had done, or that succours might come to him, that he were bastant for them in the fields: and having thus happily resolved, both the Armies strongly intrenched before others, they did bring the eyes of all the Potentates in *Europe* upon their actions, and designes, to see how the end would prove, and who should be thought wisest of both. But you shall see that he that was at this time the terrour of the world, the subduer of *Sweden*, the daunter of *Pole* and *Denmark*, and [II-140] the hope of *Britaine*, *Holland* and *Germany*, was able even unto his death to suppresse the pride and Tyranny of the house of *Austria*, and of his Ministers and Servants, being all but Novices in warres, in comparison to the *Lyon* of the North, the invincible *Gustavus*, who in glory and dignity did farre surpasse all his enemies, as is cleered by his former wisdome, in Governing his victories, and hereby his great care and diligence in preserving his friends from the fury of their enemies, exercising his Army within a close Leaguer, to handle their Armes well, after his owne new discipline, being taught to keepe their faces to their enemies in retiring as in advancing, never turning backs on their enemies as of old.

It is also to be admired the great provision this City was provided with, being no Sea-towne, as of victualls and Amunition, where it was reported that they had oates, which was distributed to the Army, that had bin kept above a hundred yeares, and this City was ever from the beginning renowned for their wisdome and policy in counsell, more then for their force in Armes, from whence did come the *Dutch* Proverbe, that he who had the wit of *Nurenberg*, the money of *Vlme*, the pride of *Ausburg*, with the power of *Venice*, might doe much in this world.

Here then at *Nurenberg*, as at a safe bay, his Majesty like unto a wise Master of a ship perceiving the storme coming on, casts out his best Anckers, riding out the storme till it blowes over, and then finding the Gale to favour him, he lanches forth to looke for his enemies. For his Majesty knew well when it was time to give a blow, as he did know the surest way to ward and hold off a blow: and we see here his Majesties counsell was of much worth to the good of the City, as his power in Armes; so that his very enemies did not only praise his wisdome, but oftimes did admire it, and as the enemy did strive to starve us, his Majesty knew well, that such a strong Army as they were in the dogge-dayes, lying in the Leaguer in time of so great infection, betime would become neere as weake as we were. As also his Majesty knowing the evill that is incident to all Armies through idlenesse, he pressed to keepe us still in handling and exercising our Armes; for he knew well, mans nature was like Iron, that did rust when it was not used, and on the contrary, he knew that well exercised Souldiers, as he had, would desire to fight, when Novices (as his enemies had) would be afraid to stirre out of their Leaguers: for oftimes it is not the multitude doth the turne, but it is Art begets victory.

Having spoken in the discharge of this duty of the actions of some worthy personages, I minde here to observe somewhat in commemoration of the persons worths that did leade them.

First then we see, that the *Spaniard* divers times was forced with little credit to retire out of the *Paltz*, and that in respect he never turned faces about in making use of ground, Cannon, Pike or Musket: which proves his retreates to have bin dishonourable, and the Leaders to have bin no Souldiers. For we presuppose, in foure dayes retreat the defender could once have made choice of ground, where making use of his Cannon, his enemies would be glad they had not advanced so farre; but rather that they had suffered them to passe: but an enemy once feared never fights well, except extremity make him desperate, and then it is not safe to deale with him.

Likewise, we see here, as they were not all *Spaniards*, that fled, so they were not all *Swedens*, that followed: so that we finde there are some good of [II-141] all Nations: but it is certaine that at such times the worth and valour of a Leader is best knowne, not only in fighting examplary to others, but specially in directing others.

We see here, that the turbulent insurrection of the Boores in *Schwabland* is soone stilled, when they want a head to leade them, where we see, the giddy-headed multitude doth ever wagge like the bush: for though sometimes they grow pale for feare, they are so impudent, that they never blush at their faults, though oftimes they are well corrected for their errors.

Here also we see, the valour and policy of Duke *Barnard* much to be commended, as a prudent Commander in all his enterprizes, overcoming more by wit and policy, then by dint of Armes. For though resolution never failes, yet by stratagems he overcomes more, then by killing; and being victorious he did shew his clemency, that another time his enemies might yeeld the sooner unto him, seeing he had used these well, whom formerly he had subdued: and this Cavalier being noble, according to his birth, he knew that the strength of victory consisteth in the using of it well, which made hime ever give the better quarters; for as he was noble, to make him the more noble, he was indued with reason; so that he conjoined Nobility with Vertue, which made his worth much esteemed of, and though he was descended of noble Progenitors, yet his minde raised him above his condition, he being fit to command Armies, and his birth did beget the greatest obedience next unto his Majesty over the whole Army, being resolute, noble, and prudent withall.

In the former discourse had of the acts of that noble and worthy Cavalier, though our enemy *Papenhaim*, his name merits to be inregistred, for his valorous courage, extraordinary diligence in his expeditions, and the fortunate successe, that did accompany his valorous conduct at divers times, even unto his death. This noble Cavalier was so generous, that nothing seemed difficult unto him, fearing nothing, not death itselfe, once resolved, and as he was valiant, so he was most diligent in all his expeditions; for while he lived, those Armies next unto him were never suffered to sleepe sound, which made his Majesty of *Sweden* esteeme more of him alone, then of all the Generalls that served the Emperour, wishing one day he might rancounter with him, to try his valour, whom he honoured so much, though his enemy.

This valorous Captaine after the Battaile of *Leipsigh*, was the first that adventured, with a single Convoy, to passe through his Majesties Armies, unto the neather *Saxon Creitz* to put life in the cause, being come againe betwixt his Majesty of *Sweden* and home, desirous to gaine credit, he delaied no time, but on the contrary used all diligence, till he got an Army of old Souldiers together out of the Garrisons, and then began to take advantage of his enemies, catching them unawares, like a valiant Captaine and Chieftaine, he suffered no grasse to grow where his Army did tread, but traversed from one place to another, adding and augmenting still to his owne credit, but diminishing and subtracting from the reputation of other Generalls, till he obtained the name and fame of the most valiant, and most vigilant Generall that served the Emperour, being in effect more furious sometimes in his conduct then requisit for a Generall, fearing nothing but the indignation of his Superiour, whom he served valianty and truely. This kinde of bouldnesse, though haply it doth prosper for a time, yet sometimes in others, it [II-142] may overwhelme all the good fortune that formerly they attained unto. For nothing is lesse to be allowed of in a Commander, then bouldnesse without reason, though sometimes things happen to succeed well, being pregnable for such daring men, as the King of *Sweden* and *Papenhaim* was, being both truely couragious. Neverthelesse, this daring is not to be made a custome of; so being oftimes the example is as faulty, as the deede in an Army.

This *Papenhaim* in his attempts, so farre as I could learne, was unblameable in his carriage, as a Leader, except at *Mastreicht*, where he was blamed for too much forwardnesse with disadvantage, having lost more men then the attempt proved credible.

As this valiant Cavalier strived to doe notable service unto the Emperour, even so Felt-marshall *Gustavus Horne*, being a valiant Cavalier, without either gall or bitternesse (as they say) but on the contrary he was wise, valiant, sober, modest, vigilant and diligent, striving in all his actions to please God, and his Master the King of *Sweden*.

And as *Papenhaim* was thought bould, and heady in his resolutions; The other *Gustavus Horne* was remisse in advising, but very resolute and couragious in the execution; partes most worthy praise in a Commander, being Subalterne to anothers command, as he was unto his Majesty of *Sweden*, who could never enterprize of himselfe, more then was allowed unto him by his instructions had in writing, so as he attempted nothing rashly, he feared no danger, once being entred, and he was so meeke in his command, that with love he obliged the Cavaliers that followed him, to obedience, more then another could doe by austerity: being the best meanes to conquer with, and the safest way to maintaine reputation and credit; Thus beloved of all men, he was very wise, and silent, keeping *Decorum* in his actions and gestures, being to my judgment powerfull to command himselfe, as he did command others.

Here also we have occasion to praise the wise and valorous conduct of the Felt-marshall *Arnheim* in *Silesia*, where he obtained great victory over his enemies, being indued with a singular gift befitting a great Commander, in giving every man that was under his command, his due meanes allowed to him by his Superiour, a rare quality in a great Commander, being one of the speciall points that is powerfull to oblige the love of Officers, and Souldiers unto their Superiours, making them refuse nothing against their enemies they are commanded unto: in the greatest extremity Souldiers can feare no danger, being well paied by their Superiours.

This vertue *Iustitia Distributiva* includes many other vertues under it, proper to a great Commander, as his actions in *Silesia* doe witnesse, having obtained severall victories there over the *Emperialists*.

As for the vices of men of this quality, making profession of Armes, being my Superiours, duty will not permit me to speake, but reverently of them; And therefore what faults they have (as none lives without some) they shall be better divulged by some other tongue then mine: *Nam quod tibi fieri non vis, alteri ne feceris.* [II-143]

---

### The thirty-fifth Duty discharged of the Accidents that occurred at Nurenberg *before the succourse was come.*

Having lyen long still as in a sleepe, without feare of our enemies, being within a fast Leaguer, in th'end his Majesty begun to stirre first, causing parties to present themselves before *Walestines* Leaguer, as if they went to borrow a Beare, or rather to provoke their enemy to try their valour, but the *Emperialists* having no great desire to fight, but attempted only in the night to fall over the *Pegnets*, giving us Alarums to little purpose, being soone repulsed, finding us alwayes ready on our Guards attending their nightly comming, our outward watches being a mile from us, so farre as *Furt* on the side of the River, having also Perdues a foote without the Leaguer, our Centries on the walles at Batteries, Colours and Corp-du-guards; so that it was hard to surprize us. But the greatest hurt they did us, was by their *Crabbats*, while as our servants and horses went forth to forrage, for in one day for my part I lost three of my servants, and five of my best horses; But in th'end our forrage grew so scarce, that many did quit their horses for want of entertainment; Neverthelesse, twice every weeke strong parties of horse, with strong Convoyes of Musketiers were sent forth to bring in forrage, where it was my fortune to have bin oft commanded with the foote; little skirmishes we had without great hurt, being alwayes in hope of reliefe in neede; Neverthelesse, whatsoever streete we went out on, their Garrisons were still ready to snap some or other amongst us on our wings, and then away they went unto their Strengths; sometimes they came from *Forchem*, sometimes from *Buche*, and sometimes from *Rottenburg*, so that alwayes some Devilish Garrison or other snatched at us aside, though they durst not draw neere our bodies; neither could the enemy know on what quarter we went forth on, and if they knew, sure that quarter we went out on was beset by Ambuscades of our people, to attend them, in case they should fall in betwixt us.

On the twenty-eight of *Iuly*, his Majestie had commanded out Colonell *Dowbattle*, with some Troopes of Horse, and some Dragoniers, towards *Furstat* in the upper *Paltz*, which lay but two miles from *Newmarck*, where the *Emperiall* Army had their Magazin-house for their Victualls, and Amunition; which was beset with five hundred Souldiers; *Dowbattle* the thirtieth of *Iuly* coming before it ere it was day, he divided incontinent his folkes in two Deales, putting the one halfe to the over doore or Port, and the other halfe to the other Port; the over Port made up with a Pittard, the *Swedens* entring, they gave fire; and at their entry they killed the Lievetenant Colonell *Revenheller*, being one of their owne, thinking he was an enemy, being shot in the shoulder he died shortly after at *Nurenberg*. All the Emperiall Garrison was almost cut off; the Proviant waggons were plundered, and the Towne was burnt, having brought foure hundred Oxen, that were both great and fat, unto *Nurenberg*. [II-144]

His Majestie immediatly after Colonell *Dowbattle* was marched, followed with a partie of a thousand Musketiers, and some eight hundred Horse towards *Bergthane* on the Dorpes; thinking, if the enemy got intelligence of *Dowbattles* march, they would set after him; And therefore to make his Retreate good, his Majestie went towards *Bosbowre*. At the same time Generall Major *Sparre*, with eight hundred horse, twenty Cornets of Crabats, and five hundred Musketiers commanded by Lievetenant Colonell *Gordon*, and Major *Lesly*, which partie of the enemy had an enterprise on *Lawffe*, to take it in, for hindring us from Forrage, having no doore open to goe out on, but that onely; and having met with his Majestie in the fields, his Majestie most Heroickly charged them, and killed many with the first charge: Generall Major *Sparre* kept himselfe by *Colleredo* his Horsemen, and the foote were commanded by *Gordon* and *Lesly*, two *Scots* Cavaliers, who then serving the Emperour did behave themselves valiantly for a time, as I did heare his Majestie of *Sweden* give testimony of their valour, alleaging if the Emperours Horsemen had behaved themselves like the foote, his Majestie had not returned victorious; for *Sparre* intending to have broken through his Majesties Horses, the Crabats having runne away, the rest of the *Emperiall* horsemen were overcome, and then most part of their foote were cut downe, Generall Major *Sparre* was taken prisoner, with *Gordon* and *Lesly*, and were brought all three unto *Nurenberg*, with three Cornets.

In obtaining this victory Colonell *Ree* was kill'd, his Majestie after his death being forced to light from his Horse, and command the Musketiers, having skirmished well for an houre on both sides, the praise whereof his Majestie did give to the *Scots* Cavaliers, that commanded the *Emperialists*, to whom he promised before they were taken, within three dayes to let them loose againe Ransome-free. Neverthelesse, they were kept for five weekes with us their Country-men, where we made merry as friends. Here also in this Conflict was killed his Majesties Camerjounker, called *Boyen*; and an other Chamberman, called *Cratzistene*, that attended his Majestie.

About the ninth of *August*, the Emperialists catched a great number of our Horses at forrage, and waited on us so well, that there was no more hopes to bring forrage unto the Leaguer; so that many of our Horsemen, for want of Horses, were put to their feete, till our succours were come unto us.

### The thirty-fift Observation.

Here we have two mightie Armies waiting to take advantages one of another, being resolved for to gaine credit to endure all toyle and misery, and they contemned all hazard and danger, to winne glory to themselves, being armed with courage and military vertue, contemning spoyle and riches, leaning to their vertue they delight in the warre, being taught by discipline heartily to embrace povertie for their Mistresse; and here the Souldier wearied, is content to make the ground his bed to lie on, as also making the first morsell, that chances to his hand, to satisfie his appetite, and in stead of sleeping out the whole night, he is contented with a nod, nothing seeming impossible or impregnable unto his couragious and resolute minde, glorying more in his contented povertie, than others doe in [II-145] their greatest riches; for he thinkes he hath not to doe with gold, being able to command his owne desires: as the bravest Leaders, and most valiant Captaines of Armies have ever made greater esteeme of honour and renowne, than deceivable riches, or of the spoyle of their enemies; reserving glory and honour unto themselves, they allowed the spoyle for the common Souldier, hunting after an immortall name to leave behinde them after death, rather than with the spoyle of others to be thought rich, robbing themselves of a good name, and their soule and conscience of eternall rest.

We see then, that it is much better to contest with honest men for vertue and a good name, than with the avaritious or niggard, that hath come to an estate with the spoyle of his enemies, or perhaps with the spoyle of his friends, or worst of all, by detaining their meanes from them, who did serve valiantly for it, with the losse of their bloud. Such Conquests unlawfully made by some Officers, are rather to be pittied than envied; and I am of the minde, he hath provided well for his wife, children, and friends, that leaves an immortall name behinde him for himselfe and his after death, rather than to leave them rich in the Devills name by unlawfull Conquest.

His Majestie of *Sweden* having had here but a weake Armie (though expert in military vertue) he resolved to weary the enemy having a strong and mightie Armie, to be entertained with all sort of provision, which must needs be brought from a farre, out of *Bavaria*, upon the *Axell* or Waggons, being a labour of infinit paine and toyle, to transport entertainment for fiftie thousand men daily, and Corne for Horses such a farre way; and having appointed their *Magazin-*house in the upper *Paltz*, to weary them the sooner, his Majestie very wisely, as we see, plotted the ruine of it, to be effectuated by Colonell *Dowbattle*, being knowne for a Cavalier of much worth, that formerly had done his Majestie divers notable good services, as at this time, which made his Majestie to be more carefull of his safe retreate, in comming himselfe with a partie betwixt the enemy and him, to be his second; being no small honour, where the first Rancounter Colonell *Ree* was killed, and then a little Captaine of the Leeffe Regiment, throwing off his Doublet did valourously command, supplying the place of the Colonell, till such time as his Majestie tooke notice of his noble carriage, and then lighted from his Horse, taking the Command to himselfe: Neverthelesse, at his Majesties returne to Quarters, he did give his owne Pourtraict, with a gold chaine to the Captaine, and advanced him to a Lievetenant Colonells place, for reward of his vertuous carriage in sight of his Master.

Colonell *Ree* being kill'd, I being the eldest Lievetenant Colonell, under his Majesties Armie of foote, having served three yeares before as Lievetenant Colonell, I sought of his Majestie, as my due, according to the custome then used, that I might be made Colonell to *Rees* Regiment, which his Majestie confessed openly to have been my due; Neverthelesse, on other considerations shewed by his Majestie unto me, I was contented to give way to his Majesties will; whereupon his Majestie urged me to be Colonell to the Regiment I had commanded so long, in absence of my Lord of *Rhees*, seeing his Lordship had advertised his Majestie, he was not to returne to his Charge: As also, he had sent his Warrant under his hand unto me, to deale with his Majestie to get the Regiment being weake to be made up for my selfe; but I being desirous to have commanded strangers, the other Regiment being strong, and ours very weake, my intention was to have joyned [II-146] them both in one, seeing at that time his Majestie would not admit me to recrue the Regiment from *Scotland;* but having given me Patent as Colonell, his Majestie assigned a Muster-place for me in *Schwabland*, from whence I was to receive moneys to strengthen my Regiment (being then but seven Companies) to twelve; and before the next Summer, I made them up to ten Companies, His Majestie having the eighteenth of *August* 1632, placed me Colonell over the Regiment, at which time Major *Iohn Sinclair* was placed my Lievetenant Colonell, and Captaine *William Stewart* was made Major.

---

*The thirty-sixt Dutie discharged of the joyning of our Armie with the Succours,*
*and of our service at* Nurenburg.

The sixteenth of *August* the succours being come from *Saxon, Hessen,* and
*During,* brought up by the Rex-chancellor *Oxensterne,* and Duke *William* of
*Wymar,* being come together at *Ventzhame,* the eighteenth at *Aiorach* and *Prugg,*
and the twenty-one at *Furt,* by foure of the Clocke in the morning they presented
themselves in Battaile before *Furt,* where did lie above a thousand *Emperialists,*
which were presently chased away, taking their Retreate unto *Walestines*
Leaguer; which done, Duke *Barnard* of *Wymar,* and Generall *Banier* continued
the Armies march, being thirtie thousand strong, through the fields towards a
Dorpe called *Grosseroote,* and draws up in Battaile in plaine Champaigne, halfe
a mile from the enemies Leaguer; his Majestie then marching out of his Leaguer
with the Armie from *Swyno* towards *Clyneroote*; incontinent presented himselfe
in Battaile before the enemies Leaguer; but the *Emperialists* unwilling to be
seene in the fields, they kept themselves close within their Leaguer, playing on
us with their Cannon, having done no more hurt, than the killing of one
Constable and a few Souldiers, and we attending their resolution and out-
coming, enterprized nothing all day, but stood ready in Battaile till night, that the
foote Briggads had orders to advance within Cannon reach of their Leaguer,
where our Batteries were ordained to be made all in Front, as our Armie stood,
alongst the face of the enemies Leaguer, where we had cast up a running trench
before the front of our Armie, from the right hand to the left, going from one
Battery to another; on which Batteries were planted seventy-two pieces of
Cannon, great and small, well guarded with strong guards of Musketiers and
Pikemen; the Briggads lying ready at hand to relieve them in time of need, and
our horse-Briggads being appointed without them, to stand in readinesse for to
second the foote.

The day peeping, the *Emperiall* Generalls were saluted with a *salve* of
Cannon, which untimely stirred some from their rest, making them retire unto
their Strengths, not having the courage to shew their faces in the fields. [II-147]

This service of Cannon having continued the whole day, in the night the
*Emperialists* retired their Forces towards their workes on the old hill, being
mighty strong on that quarter, so that there was no possibility to harme them
anymore with Cannon.

His Majestie thinking, if it were possible to get in the hill, he was then able
to beate the enemy out of his Leaguer, and therefore in the night gave Orders to
draw off the Cannon from the Batteries, and having the Armie in readinesse, we
marched in the night through *Furt,* towards the other side of the enemies
Leaguer, of intention to take in the hill, and then to beate them out of their
Leaguer, and his Majestie having got intelligence, the enemy had marched away
and left but a Reare-guard on the Hill, to make his Retreate good, we marched
neere the Hill, and drew up in Battaile alongst the side of it, horse, foote and

Cannon, by seven of the Clocke in the morning, where incontinent, on slight information, his Majestie resolved, in earnest to pursue the Hill.

Duke *William* of *Wymar* the Lievetenant Generall next unto his Majestie had the command of the Armie, Generall *Banier* had the Command of the foote, and Duke *Barnard* of *Wymar* Commanded the Horse, Colonell *Leonard Richardson* had the Command of the Artillery; divers other Cavaliers of note were ordained to attend his Majestie, for giving assistance in Command, to be directed by his Majestie, as occasion offered; such as Grave *Neeles* a *Sweden*, then Generall Major of foote, Generall Major *Boetius* a *Dutch*, Sir *Iohn Hepburne* then having left command of the Briggad, being out of employment he attended his Majestie, Generall Major *Rusteine* being then Stallemaster to his Majestie attended also, Generall Major *Striffe* commanded the Horse next to Duke *Barnard.*

The Armie thus in Battaile, and the whole Officers of the field attending his Majestie, and their severall Charges, the service being but begunne, Generall *Banier* was shot in the Arme, and so retired; Generall Major *Rusteine* being also shot did retire incontinent, his Majestie commanded strong parties of commanded Musketiers out of all Briggads, led by a Colonell, a Lievetenant Colonell, and a competent number of other inferiour Officers, to leade on the partie towards the Hill, to force a passage or entry unto the enemies workes; which being hardly resisted, the service went on cruell hot on both sides, so that the parties were no sooner entered on service, but it behooved the reliefes to be incontinent ready to second them, death being so frequent amongst Officers and Souldiers, that those who were hurt rejoyced, having escaped with their lives, seeing in effect the service desperate on our side, losing still our men without gaining any advantage over our enemies, being alwayes within their close workes, while as we, both Officers and Souldiers, stood bare and naked before them, as markes to shoot at, without any shelter whatsoever, but the shadow of some great trees, being in a wood, so that we lost still our best Officers and Souldiers, while as the basest sort durst not lift head in the storme.

The service continued in this manner the whole day, so that the Hill was nothing els but fire and smoke, like to the thundering Echo of a Thunderclap, with the noise of Cannon and Musket, so that the noise was enough to terrifie Novices; we losing still our best Souldiers, grew so weake in the end, that the Briggads of foote had scarce bodies of Pikemen to Guard their Colours, the Musketiers being almost vanished and spent by the continu- [II-148] ance of hot service, where the service was not alone amongst the foote in pursuing of the hill, but also about the hill without the wood, on the wings, the horse men furiously charged one another, being also well seconded by Dragoniers and Musketiers, that did come on fresh with the reliefes.

By one a clocke in the afternoone, *Duke William* of *Wymar* commanded me (being the first service I was on as Colonell) for my credit, to goe towards the Poste on the hill, where the *Grave fon Torne* was shot, and to command those five hundred Musketiers, I taking leave of my Camerades went to the Poste, and finding the place warme at my coming, divers Officers and Souldiers lying bloudy on the ground, I went first and ordered the Souldiers on the Poste, to my judgment, as most to our advantage for our safeties and the harming of our enemies, and perceiving the enemy sometimes to fall out with small Plottons of Musketiers to give fire on us, and to spie our actions, returning againe, as their powder was spent, to trap them the next time, I advanced a Sergeant with twenty foure Musketiers, to lie in Ambush to attend on their next out-coming, which they perceiving came out no more, but one single man to spie; I retiring againe to my maine reserve to direct others, sometimes standing, sometimes walking, and being taken notice of, as a chiefe Officer, the enemy commanded out a single man, with a long peece, who from a tree aiming at me, shot me right above the Hanch-bone, on the leftside, which lighted fortunatly for me on the Iron clicket of my hanger, which cut close the Iron away, taking the force from the Bullet, which being battered flat with the Iron entred not above two inches in my side, where I found, a little Armes of proofe being well put on most commodious, in preserving my life, by Gods providence for that time.

Notwithstanding of this my hurt, finding my selfe in strength, though I lost much bloud, I remained on my Poste till neere night; my Lievetenant Colonell *Iohn Sinclair* was sent with five hundred Musketiers to relieve me, where I did bring off but the least number of men, having lost neere two hundred, besides those Officers and Souldiers that were hurt, and my Lievetenant Colonell brought off the next morning fewer than I did: for those who were not kill'd or hurt, being in the night, through plaine feare they left him, so that at last he brought not off of his whole number above thirty, Officers and all.

On this occasion a valorous young Gentleman, being one of my Captaines, call *Patrike Ennis*, who having behaved himselfe well the whole time that he was on service, being commanded amongst strangers on another Poste than mine, a reliefe being come to releeve him, he went to shew the Poste he was on to his Camerade, and shewing him where his Centries stoode, then after, out of resolution to shew more courage than was needfull in open view of his enemy, florishing his sword, and crying aloud, *Vive Gustavus*, he was shot through the head, being much regrated by all his Camerades. Likewise with him a young man *Hector Monro Catvalls* Sonne, uncommanded voluntarily having taken a Musket, and gone on service, he was shot alongst the braines, and lived a fortnight after, which shot was wonderfull; for the side of his head that the Bullet lighted on, the skull was whole; nevertheless, through his great torment, the Chirurgian having made incision on the other side of his head, to see if the skull was whole, but being found splent [II-149] on that side, so that his braines could be seene, his wound was uncurable.

Likewise on this dayes service were killed on our side, Generall Major *Boetius*, Lievetenant Colonell *Septer*, Lievetenant Colonell *Macken*, Rutmaster *Morrits*, Lievetenant Colonell *Welsten*, and divers inferiour Officers, and above twelve hundered Souldiers, the *Grave Fon Erbach* was also killed, and divers Officers were hurt, as the *Grave Fon Ebersteene*, the *Grave Fon Torne,* Colonell *Porte*, and of our country-men under *Spence* his Regiment, Captaine *Traile* was shot through the throate; As also Captaine *Vausse*, under Colonell *Munro* of

*Fowles* his Regiment, was shot in the shoulder, and the Colonell of the Artillery, *Leonard Richardson*, with Colonell *Erich Handson*, being both *Swedens* with two Lievetenant Colonells were taken Prisoners.

Likewise on this service there were hurt of our Souldiers above two thousand, which were put under cure in *Nurenburg*.

The Officers killed of the *Emperialists* were, Colonell *Iacob Fugger*, Colonell *Oba'o Brandine*, Colonell *Fon Maria de Caras*, and above forty inferiour Officers, with twelve hundred Souldiers, which they lost.

Likewise *Walestine* his horse, and Duke *Barnard* of *Wymars* were both shot under them. The day thus past, in the night for the most part, they lay quiet, and the day being come, I was commanded notwithstanding of my hurt, by Duke *William* of *Wymar* having attended on him the whole last night, to goe and receive five hundred Musketiers, for to bring off those had bin all night on the Poste, being ordained to come off with them, and to make the retreate good; I being gone to receive the party come together, his Majesty coming by, and knowing I was hurt, commanded me to retire backe with the party, and went himselfe to make the retreate wonderfully; bringing them off from all Poasts without one shot of Musket or Pistoll, till we drew up the Army againe, within reach of Cannon, so that there were killed to me of my owne Company three Souldiers, and having removed a little further off, his Majesty drawing up the whole Army in Battaile, Horse, Foote and Artillery, there was presently order given for drawing out of a new Leaguer, the draught whereof being finished, every Briggads quarter being knowne, we begun to worke againe, in sight of the enemy, till that in spight of him we were closed in ten dayes time within a fast Leaguer againe, which was strongly pallisaded without the Graffe, where we did lie without invasion in quietnesse to the sixt of *September*, that his Majesty perceiving the scarcity of victualls growing great from day to day, and the scarcity of forrage; Therefore his Majesty resolved to take the start of his enemy, in being the first up-breaker, knowing assuredly he was not able to lie long after him.

### *The thirty-sixt Observation.*

Here we see, that nothing is more forcible to suppresse the vanting of an enemy, than a timely succours, as came here unto our Army in despight of the enemy, who, before their coming, did mightily vaunt would cut off our succours, before they could joyne [II-150] with us really; and then they would with hunger, starve both the City and our Leaguer, which hardly they could doe, we being provided of good men to fight, as also of good entertainment to sustaine our number. But the enemy feebly remaining within his workes, though beyond us in number, we thundered on them with Cannon, repaying their cannonading spent before *Verbine*, the yeare before, on the *Elve*. And it is thought, that the invention of Cannon was found first at *Nurenburg*, for the ruine of man, being at first a long time used for battering downe of walles and Cities, and for counter-batteries; till at last they were  used in the fields, to breake the Squadrons and battailes of foote and horse, some carrying peeces called *Spingards*, of f~ure foote and a halfe long, that shot many bullets at once, no greater then Walnuts, which were carried in the fields on little Chariots behinde the troopes, and how soone the Trumpet did found the enemy was thundred on, first with those, as with shoures of haile-stone, so that the enemies were cruelly affrighted with them, men of valour being suddenly taken away, who before were wont to fight valiantly and long with the Sword and Launce, more for the honour of victory, then for any desire of shedding of bloud: but now men are marteryzed and cut downe, at more than a halfe a mile of distance, by those furious and thundring Engines of great Cannon, that sometimes shoote fiery bullets able to burne whole Cities, Castles, houses or bridges, where they chance to light; and if they happen to light within walles, or amongst the Briggad of foote or horse, as they did at *Leipsigh* on the *Grave fon Torne* his Briggad, spoiling a number at once, as doubtlesse his Devilish invention did within *Walestine* his Leaguer at this time.

Likewise here we have set before us the revolution of humane affaires, being ever inconstant, shewing us that good Fortune, Lucke, or chance, as they call it, is never still in one side: for his Majesty that formerly was alike fortunate with few, as with many, here though having a mighty strong Army, he is crossed, being frustrate of his expectation, arising by the neglect of a small point of recognoscing, his Majesty having trusted too much to others wrong relation, that did not satisfie themselves; which made his Majesty contrary to his custome ingage his Army, and once being ingaged upon slight intelligence, the reliefes went on so fast, the service being so hot for a time, that it was long before the losse was perceived, where it is to be pittied, that the errour and fault of another should be made to posterity, as his Majesties over-sight, by those that know no better: for though a King leading an Army had *Argos* eyes, yet it is impossible he should looke unto all things himselfe. The fault of one here we see with the losse of many was irrecoverable, and he that before this day was the terrour of the Empire, by his former successe, being deceived with false intelligence, is thought to have overseene himselfe, the errour of another being imputed unto his Majesty in losing so many brave fellowes; which shou'd teach others to be the more circumspect in recognoscing, before they should ingage men in bringing them upon the shamble-bankes.

Here also we see, that his Majesty was was ever enemy to idlenesse: for he had no sooner brought off his Army from pursuing his enemies, but incontinent he sets them againe to worke, for their owne safeties, and that within reach of his enemies Cannon, to the end it might not be said, but he attended their out-comming, lest his Army might be discouraged at a present [II-151] Retreate, after such a great losse, for if the service had continued, the whole Armie had beene indangered; yet a valourous Captaine, as our Leader was, as he feares nothing entering on service, so he ought to set light by nothing, he sees tending to his prejudice, but ought timely to retire, with as little losse as he may: for it were a grosse errour to despise our enemies through too much confidence in our selves; for some times by despising our enemies (as here) we make them the more valiant, and if they be ambitious, the more respect we give them, the lesse we neede to feare them. And it is necessarie, when an Armie doth get a clappe, as we did here, then incontinent and with all diligence we should presse to trie our enemie againe; wheresoever we can have any advantage, lest our enemy might judge us altogether to have yeelded and given over, which were very dangerous.

The bouldnesse of one bould fellow at first, being a Leader may ingage a whole Armie for want of judgement, as was done here going before this hill of *Nurenberg*, where as many were brought in danger, as did tread in the first Leaders paths, through lacke of judgement, having beene all of them more heady than wise; yet to dare being annexed unto vertue is the beginning of victory: neverthelesse, a hasty man in an Armie, without judgement and discretion, is to be disallowed of, aswell as a coward.

On my Poste under the Hill, after I was shot, a sudden feare came amongst the Souldiers, some thirtie horse having suddenly come through the wood, as if they had beene chased, the most part both Officers and Souldiers ranne away, leaving mee with a few number on the Poste, so that if the enemie had fallen out, I could not have escaped from being kill'd or taken; but as soone as they perceived, that I with the Souldiers remained by me, had unhorsed and taken some of the horsemen, who were found to bee friends, they being ashamed of their miscarriage retired, having accidentally rencountred with *Hepburs* Captaine Lievetenant, who brought them up againe, whom I threatned to shew his Majestie of their behaviours: neverthelesse being loath to incurre the hatred of a brave Nation, for the misbehaviour of some unworthy fellowes, their blemishes I pressed to cover: notwithstanding afterwards some of the Officers amongst themselves came to a publique hearing, having blamed one another, till the question and disgrace was taken away; by shewing their particular courage in fighting one against another, whereof I kept my self free, suffering them to deale amongst them, being Country-men.

This kinde of Panicke feare without cause doth betray many brave men, and divers good enterprizes. And therfore all good Commanders ought most carefully to looke unto it, to avoyde the inconveniences incident unto the like, while as they leade either partie or Armie. Wee once marching through a woode towards *Franckfurt* on the *Oder*, the white Regiment marching in the Van, having a naturall foole, that marched alwayes before them, going within a bush, throwing off his clothes returning naked, and crying, he had seene the enemie, the whole Souldiers of that Briggad throwing downe their Armes, they ranne backe on the next Briggad being *Swedens*, and they running also away, till they were holden up with pikes by our Briggad, being the third, who having stood, and asked the reason of their running away; in end, being found a false, and a foolish Alarum, the poore foole was pittifully cut and carved by the Officers, for the Souldiers phantasticke feare, being a poore revenge for their cowardize, so that we see by example of the third Briggad, that the best remedie against such Panicke feares is not to feare at all; and none should leade Armies, but those that are both wise and stout. [II-152]

*The thirty-seventh Duty discharged of our up-breaking,*
*from* Nurenberg *towards* Newstat.

After this last dayes service, his Majestie having intrenched his Armie before the Emperiall Leaguer, and finding them unwilling to hazard the Combate, as also the scarcitie of victuals growing so great on both sides; his Majestie resolved to beset *Nurenberg* with foure Regiments, *Fowles* his Regiment being one, Generall Major *Kniphowsen* had the Command over the *Swedens,* and Generall Major *Salammers-dorffe* had Command over the *Burgers*; and the *Rex-chancellor Oxesterne* was appointed by his Majestie to have the direction of all.

His Majestie leaving *Nurenberg* in this manner, in the night he sent away his great Cannon with a Convoy towards *Newstat,* and before day the whole Drummes had orders to beate, first afore troope gathering, and then a march, so that we were in readinesse standing in Battaile before the enemies Leaguer by day: where we stood till mid-day, and then the whole Armie was commanded to make a quarter Toure to the right hand, making our front before, to be our left Flancke, whereon our Coulours and small Ordinance did march, and our right wing being our Van, we marched off, in view of the enemie, Duke *Bernard* of *Wymare* with a thousand horse, and five hundred musketiers, commanded by my Lievenant Colonell *Iohn Sinclaire,* who was appointed to march in the Reare, for making our Retreate good, which in a manner was needlesse, seeing our enemie lacked courage to follow us, but suffered us to depart in peace.

At night we drew up in Battaile a mile from the enemies Leaguer, where we incamped setting forth strong watches of horse, and musketiers on the passes betwixt us and the enemie, and our Reare-Guarde betwixt us and them, and our owne Guardes, without our Briggads, so having quietly passed over the night, the next morning we marched to *Newstad,* being the fifteenth of *September,* where we resolved to stay a few dayes, attending what the Emperiall Armie would undertake, having still an eye in our necke-pole.

We got intelligence, that the Duke of *Fridland Walestine,* and the Duke of *Bavere* did breake up with their Armies, taking their march through *Furt,* towards *Boocke,* and then to *Forcham,* burning off all the dorpes, that lay nearest *Nurenberg*; being all the valiant deedes, they had done the whole Summer: and the fourteenth of *September,* being quite gone, divers Burgers and Souldiers of the *Nurenbergers* with the Countrie Boores in all haste ranne unto their Leaguer, where they found a thousand waggons, besides those were burnt, which they transported to *Nurenberg,* together with a great quantitie of Iron, above tenne thousand Centeurs of waight, and a great quantitie of meale, corn and flesh, which all in foureteene dayes was not brought unto the Towne after their going, whereat many did wonder.

The enemie also left behind them many sicke and wonded Souldiers un-cured; amongst whom all that time death was very frequent, aswell of men, as of beasts, for thousands of horse and cattell were lost. Likewise, in the *Swedens*

Leaguer, about the Citie were fallen above foure thousand horse and cattell, and within the Citie were also many dead. [II-153]

As *Walestine* was come to *Forcham*, he directed Generall Major *Galasse* with some horse and foote, unto the *Woigkeland*, who in his march by *Nurenberg*, did deale very slightly with *Lawffe, Griffenberg, Welden*, and *Harchbrook*, which he tooke in; and *Griffenberg* he burnt, and in the rest he caused to cut off divers Burgers and Souldiers, making many poore men with plundering, and cruell exactions of mony, and from thence, in *Woiteland*, towards *Egger*, and further; till he joyned with *Holke*, being both as *Simeon* and *Levi*, continuing their march towards the *Elve*, taking in *Kemnets, Friberg, Meissen*, and divers other partes, exacting great contribution, and borneshets, or compositions, pressing an infinite deale of money out of the Duke of *Saxons* hereditary lands; using great and extraordinary enormities over the whole lands belonging to the *Saxon*, by reason the Dukes Armie lay then farre off in *Silesia*, not being possible for him to releeve his owne Countrey; *Walestine* also, from *Forcham* marched towards *Saxonie*; and the Duke of *Bavaria*, to quench the fire, that was already kindled there by the *Swedens*, marched to *Bavere*.

The Emperiall Armie thus separated, his Majestie laie still in *Newstad*, till such time, as he saw their severall intentions, and then disposing of his Armie accordingly.

First, the Marquesse of *Hamilton* was gratiously dismissed by his Majestie, taking his journey from thence towards *France* unto *Brittaine* and having taken leave of his Majestie at *Newstad*, his Excellence was most honourably conveyed by the whole Officers his Country-men, that served the *Swedens*, who having taken leave of his Excellence, a mile from the Leaguer, they returned, and his Excellence, accompanied with Sir *Iames Hamilton* of *Priestfeild*, Colonell Sir *Iames Ramsey*, called the Faire Colonell, and Sir *Iohn Hepburne* Colonell, having taken good night of all their Noble Camerades they continued their journey unto *Brittaine;* and we returned to prepare ourselves for a march, and a separation; which immediatly the next day did follow; his Maiestie having given orders to call in all Safe-guardes, and the next morning to be in readinesse to march.

### The thirty-seventh Observation.

The separation of these two mightie Armies was wonderfull, without shot of Cannon, Musket, or Pistoll, the like we can hardly finde in any Historie.

We see then here, that when the foundation of mans actions is laid sure by vertue, the building hardly can faile, especially when we lay our chiefe dependance on *God*, and our cause being good, the lawfull meanes used (as was done here by the *Lyon of the North*, the Invincible King of *Sweden*) in defence of *Nurenberg*, the libertie of *Dutch-land*, and freedome of *Christs Gospell*, then I say, the event must needs be answerable to the ground laid, to wit, the freedome of this Citie, and the preservation of his Majesties Armie, both which we see by this separation, where the enemy had not the heart to pursue us; having *Gustavus* and his Fortunes with us; Notwithstanding of their powerfull and mightie Armie; which the *Papists* themselves did set and esteeme to be threescore thousand men, being then of opinion, that that Summer they were able to over-swimme the whole Empire, and [II-154] all their enemies; yet, with all their bragging, they durst never present themselves in the Fields, with one Cornet, Colour, or Regiment before *Gustavus,* being terrified at his presence, which did prove their valour was not correspondent to their power in Armes, otherwise they had given us greater reason to have esteemed better of their Conduct, so that wee see, there is neither wisedome, force, or power of counsell, that can prevaile against that cause the *Lord* defends; and who can thinke those could prosper better, who formerly pressed by their crueltie to have subverted the truth of Religion; by banishing the Gospell, and Ministers of it, forcing Commons against Conscience, either to forsake their Country and possessions, or to renounce the truth they professed, persecuting those that would not conforme themselves to their Devilish Traditions; what wonder then, those Generalls could not prosper against the truth, or against him that tooke the defence, both of truth and people, against the Tyranny of the house of *Austria*, and their cruell Generalls, that were not onely cruell to their enemies, but also to their servants and Souldiers, whom they left bleeding behinde them in their Leaguer, destitute of all comfort; not so much as once to cause to dresse their wounds, that they received honourably for their safeties? Truly I dare be bold to say, the *Lord* will not suffer the negligence and inhumane crueltie of such Commanders to be unpunished, that left unchristianly those poore Souldiers, which were bould to open their brests to receive wounds, for the safetie of those that had no compassion on them in their extremities. O crueltie of all cruelties! when we see a valiant Souldier naked, hungry, or pined, with his wounds bleeding for our sakes, and then to leave them destitute of helpe, to the mercy of their enemies, especially, when we are not compelled to leave them! This fault of all faults in a Commander or Souldier, in my minde, is most unpardonable, which is too common. Therefore, I conclude, such persons to be unworthy Command, that preferre any thing before the health of those, who were willing to give their lives for the safetie of their Commanders.

Sith then we see, that the greatest part of humane happinesse doth consist in vertue, let him that would prove wise, fix his eyes and minde to judge other mens actions, to the end he may grow the more circumspect and prudent, pressing to doe good by continuance of time, if he but observe the varieties of chances incident unto all estates, from the Crowne to the lowest Cottage, in the end, through their examples, he may learne to better himselfe, and become wise in his profession: for a diligent servant to such a Master as *Gustavus* was, might in a few yeares time observe many things belonging to the knowledge of a Commander, though I grant, never attaine unto the perfection of his Calling; for the accidents of warres being infinite, the knowledge of them can never be limited. But we must alwayes be learning of new things, till we become more prudent, though not perfectly wise in our calling, being infinite; and though many thinke a man may be wise, and not couragious, seeing the wise fore-sees all dangers; truely I will thinke, he that is circumspect and wise in this kinde, may be called a stout Commander: for to a wise man, we say, nothing comes wrong; and he that cannot be surprized in this kinde, must needs be both wise and stout.

To conclude then this Observation, out of the separation of the Marquesse and his Country-men, at our leave-takings, and at the parting of the Colonell *Lodowicke Lesly*, and his Regiment from *Spence* his Regiment, going with [II-155] Duke *Barnard* unto *Saxonie* from us; which separation was like to the separation death makes betwixt friends and the soule of man, being sorry that those who had lived so long together in amitie and friendship, as also in mutuall dangers, in weale & in woe, & fearing we should not meet againe; the splendour of our former mirth was obnubilated with a cloud of griefe & sorrow; which vanished and dissolved in mutuall teares of love, severing from others, as our *Saviour* did from his Disciples, in love and amitie; wishing one another the mutuall enterchange of our affections, as Souldiers and not as Complementing Courtiers, in the way of love and courtesie, we wished againe and againe, being loathe to depart from others, the accomplishment of all happinesse here, and of eternall glory else-where.

---

### The thirty-eighth Dutie discharged of our March from Newstade towards Winchene.

Having come unto the fields, the Armie being drawne up and divided, Duke *Barnard* of *Wymar* was directed to march on *Kitchen* on the *Maine*, and the rest of the Armie on *Vinzeine*, and his Majestie with a strong partie marched backe unto *Nurenberg*, to see the enemies Leaguer, and the unhappie Castle on the old hill, where so many brave fellowes were lost. From thence his Majestie returned on *Outzbach*, at which time on the march some new levied men, that were come from *Switzerland*, joyned with the Armie at *Winchene*, where we rested two dayes, I being cruelly tormented with a burning Ague, contracted with neglecting of my wound received at *Nurenberg*.

*Walestine* his Feltmarshall *Holke* at this time with his little Armie did dominier in *Saxonie*, using barbarous crueltie in burning, scalding, and plundering of Townes, Flecks, and Dorpes; murthering and cutting downe the Inhabitants, that it was pittie to heare of such barbaritie in a civill land to be used by one of their owne profession; making no conscience of Religion, he shewed lesse compassion then the *Papists* did: for their villany, whom he led, was so great, that after abusing the women, in satisfying their filthy lusts, they did burne them and their families, their hearts thus hardned, that it was evident, that the judgements of the *Lord* were not farre from them, and those he commanded, having suffered such tyranny to have been used to *Christians*, before a moneth was past, he died raging of the plague, and those who followed him were also rewarded of *God* for their crueltie.

The eighteenth of *August*, *Holke* tooke in *Zincko* by accord, promising unto the Burgers the freedome of their Religion and liberties, providing they would take in a Garrison of two hundred *Emperialists*; then *Gallas* and *Holke* being joyned, soone after *Walestine* himselfe, after the in-taking of *Coburg*, continued his march toward *Leipsigh*; after spoyling the land of *Coburg* and *Culnebush*, he marched through the *Voigland* towards *Owltenberg*; and from thence to *Leipsigh*, which he got in on Accord the twenty-second of *October*, and on the twenty-third he got in the Castle of *Pleisenburg*, putting out the [II-156] Dukes Garrison, and putting in his owne. And after he tooke in *Weysenfelse, Morsburg, Nawmburg*, and divers Townes more in *Saxonie*, spoyling and ruining all that side of the *Elve*: *Hall* also he tooke in, but the Castle of *Morsburg*, being well beset by the *Swedens*, by that time could not be brought to heare of any Accord.

*Papenhaim* now retired from *Mastricht*, having in vaine attempted then the reliefe of it; at his backe-coming he relieved the City of *Patterburne* from the beleaguering, and skirmished with the Lievetenant Generall *Bawtish*, he also dissolved the blockquering of *Volfenbittle*, and did get some Cornets and Colours from the *Brunswicker* forces, and from thence he did come before *Heldishem*; alleaging, he had beaten the Duke of *Lunenbeug* and *Bawtishen*, by which stratagem he did get *Heldishem* in his power, and beset it with a Garrison, as the principall Strength on the *Wezer* streame, appointing the *Grave Fon Gronsfield* to command there, and then he marched towards *Eichfield*, and tooke in *Milhousen*, getting a great composition of money from them, he marched on *Saltz* and plundered it out, wherein he did get much hidden riches, and his Souldiers making rich booty, they did cast in the water, that which they could not carry; he proceeded also in the same manner with *Theanestade*, from whence he carried with him the Burger-masters in pledge of their Cities Ransome, and finding by the way they were not able to pay, what they had promised, he caused to take all three and hang them up, till they were halfe dead, and then caused suddenly to cut them downe: *Cretzburg* also he used little better, from *Erfort* he desired twenty thousand Dollers, and threatned if the monies were not tould downe, he would not faile to doe them all the mischiefe he could, whereupon with much adoe they did get him two thousand Dollers, and hearing his Majesty of *Sweden* was drawing neere, he staied not on the rest; but marched to *Morsburg* at *Hall*.

### *The thirty-eighth Observation.*

Memory and forgetfulnesse are both necessary in friendship. Shall I then forget here to speake of our separation, being so long companions of one danger together? No, this love of Camerades to each others is most worthy remembrance, seeing we were divers times willing to give our lives for one anothers safeties: shall we then be oblivious of this mutuall love and dangers? No, though distance of place separate our bodies, we shall still be conjoyned in minde, and power against our common enemy, that desireth the hurt of us all alike. Let us then though severed, maintaine one anothers credit in absence, ever honouring the worth and vertues of our dear Camerades, for the kindnesse past, let us learne to be ever thankfull to their friends alive, and after their death, let our love increase to their successours; for if there be any *Nectar* in this life, it is in sorrowes we endure for the goodnesse and love of our absent friends, especially of those that were our dearest Camerades; for if we sorrow for them, amending our lives, knowing we must passe shortly through the same passage, they did passe before us, truely one day our sorrow shall turne to joy, and our teares shall turne to smiles, our weeping unto a streame of pleasures, and our [II-157] labour unto eternall rest, that as we followed the *Lyon* of the North, the invincible King of *Sweden*, in fighting the Lords Battailes here, even so we shall follow the Lambe unto the Heavenly *Ierusalem* hereafter.

The cruelty and Tyranny used by the Emperiall Officers in *Saxony*, who neither spared man nor woman, is rather to be pittied by Christians, then any wayes to be imitated, which cruelty did presage their ruine to come; for nothing vehement in that kinde did ever remaine long unpunished, and though for a time the Devills rage, at last they are cast into perpetuall darkenesse.

*Papenhaim* returning from *Mastricht*, we see was immoderate in his victories, and forbearing to shew mercy at all, he domineered in his Tyranny, running so long as he had feete, some he did hang by their purses, and some by their neckes by halfes, for not paying the Ransome of others. Such injustice the God of mercy and goodnesse did not suffer long unpunished: and it is to be pittied, that such exorbitant pride had bin cohabitant in so valorous a Captaine, for it is certaine, when a man of warre groweth too proud of his victories, refusing mercy, then commonly approach punishments woe, for a proud warriour as this was (*viz.*) errour in counsell, and unhappy successe in his best actions; for how soone a man beginneth to grow proud and to be secure, then cometh punishment; and as pride groweth, so vertue decaieth, and though the punishment of pride and cruelty sometimes comes late, yet sure it never comes light, and it is most certaine, there is ever some fatality incident unto those, who are desirous of vaine glory through pride. Our desire then should be, to be humble, that we be not rejected with disdaine, as those proud Cavaliers rejected the poore Supplicants, who though begging mercy, were not heard: whose exorbitant wickednesse should teach us, not to imitate their examples, but rather through grace, presse to eschew their punishment both temporall and eternall.

---

*The thirty-ninth Duty discharged of our March to* Dunkelspill,
*and from thence unto* Bavier.

His Majesty returning from *Rottenburg* with the Queenes Majesty, they marched with the Army towards *Dunkelspill*, where they did lie three dayes; during which time I was glad, looking for no life, to have bin eased by the helpe of good and learned Physitians. There I was left, the Army continuing their march upon *Nerling*, making all the expedition and haste was possible, to relieve

*Rhine* on the *Leacke* being beleagured by the Duke of *Bavier* his forces, and his
Majesty coming to the *Leacke*, he received newes, the Towne was given over,
and the Bridge being cast off, his Majesty was hindered the passage, whereupon
his Majesty directed backe the Queene to *Donavert*, and incontinent begunne to
prepare for the beleaguering of *Rhine* againe, the Bridge being repared, he set
over his Army, the thirtith of *September*, and incontinent begun his aproaches,
the *Empe-* [II-158] *rialists* at first plaied hard with Cannon and Musket till night,
that his Majesties Batteries were ready.

The first of *October* early in the morning the mist was so thicke, that his
Majesty approached very neere the walles, and that orderly the Batteries being
ready, the Cannon planted in the mist, by nine of the clocke his Majesty saluted
the Towne with a *Salve* of Musket and Cannon, where incontinent the feeble,
Bearish Commanders entred in accord, which was granted unto them, so that his
Majesty, by the assistance of God, got this Towne againe in two houres time,
after the Batteries were ready, and that contrary to his Majesties expectation,
who did not expect the getting of it in lesse then six dayes.

The Dukes foote Souldiers were suffered to march out without Armes, and
the horsmen without their horses, and his Majesty being offended with the *Dutch*
Colonell called *Metzfell*, notwithstanding of the recovery of the Towne, he was
brought before a Counsell of warres at *Newburg* on the *Danow*, being accused,
he had given over the Towne without any necessity, making his Accord contrary
to his Officers wills, which they having testified against him, by a sentence of the
Counsell of warre he was beheaded the eighth of *October*, and those Officers of
his Regiment, which subscribed the Accord, were ordained to carry no charge
under his Majesties Army; and the Officers, which withstoode the Accord, were
assoiled from the sentence, as faithfull servants to their Master.

The said day, after the execution, his Majesty returned with the Army,
towards *Rhine* from *Newburg*, where againe his Majesty divided the Army, and
having beset *Ausburg*, *Rhine* and *Donavert* well, he tooke the yellow and blew
Briggad with himselfe, leaving our Briggad after long advisement, and the rest of
the Army under the Command of the *Palsgrave Christian, Fon Brickfeld,* and
Generall Major *Ruthven* to attend on the Dukes forces, and to maintaine
*Schwabland* with the passes, which we had already in *Bavaria*. His Majesty then
taking leave of our Briggad, in view of the whole Army thanked us for our
former service, and in particular he expressed his affection unto me, and to
Lievetenant Colonell *Mustein*: shewing he was greeved to leave us behinde, yet,
in respect of the long march he had unto *Saxony*, and considering the
weakenesse of both our Regiments, that were weakned by the toyle of warre, and
the dint of the enemies Armies, and therefore in consideration of their former
good service, he had ordained Muster-places for us, the best in *Schwabland*, for
to strengthen our Regiments, against his returne, and withall, commanded us to
see it done, as we would expect his favour: and then calling on *Palsgrave
Christian*, to whom he had given command over us and the Army,
recommending us particularly unto him, desired him to give us contentment of

the monies were then resting unto us, and that out of the first money was to be received at *Ausburg.*

Having after that taken leave of the whole Army, his Majesty returned to *Donavert,* where the Queene did attend his coming, being making ready for the march unto *Saxon.* As soone as his Majesty had dined at *Donavert* with the Queene, going to his Coach, I tooke leave of his Majesty and the Queene, in presence of Generall *Banier, Palsgrave Christian,* Sir *Patrike Ruthven* and divers other worthy Cavaliers, being the most dolefull parting I ever suffered, having bin still both I and our Regiment with his Majesty, on all service of importance, since his Majesties upbreaking from *Stetin* in [II-159] *Pomeren,* till this parting at *Donavert* on the *Danube,* the eleventh of *October.* 1632.

His Majesty having that night lien at *Nerlin,* from thence the next day he directed the Queenes Majesty with the foote Briggads to march on *Dunkelspill,* and from thence to *Rottenberg, h*is Majesty then with a party went for *Nurenberg,* and before his coming, *Kniphowsen w*ith some forces was marched to take in *Lawffe* from the enemy, who at first defended themselves well; But in the end they were compelled to come forth and be at his pleasure, and were all made prisoners. By midday his Majesty hearing there were not farre from *Nurenberg* some *Emperialists* seene, so soone as his Majesty had gotten sure intelligence of them, he brake up with seventeene Troopes of horse and some foote, and marched on *Enschbrooke,* whence the *Emperialists* had gone but a little before, his Majesty lying there that night, getting intelligence againe of some *Crabbats* that did ly on the Castle *Richell, s*hewing there were some six hundred *Emperialists* coming to releeve *Lawffe,* hearing of his Majesties being there, they retired towards *Bavaria,* yet his Majesty following them in the night falls on them, and cuts off three hundred, where fifty were prisoners and two Cornets taken from them, with a great deale of booty; his Majesty then turning backe continued his march towards *Saxony,* having left all behinde him in *Franconia* and *Schwabland* in good order, his Majesty in all haste to releeve the Duke of *Saxon* and his country, went from *Nurenberg* to *Swinefort,* and thence over *During Vault,* where he joyned his forces with Duke *Barnard* of *Wymar,* and then continued the march towards *Arnestat,* where they lay still two dayes, to refresh the Army wearied with hard marching; and from *Arnestat* he marched to the generall Randez-vouz, being then appointed at *Erfort,* the Army being then eighteene thousand strong, under whom there was no other *Scots* Regiment, but Colonell *Lodowicke Lesly* his Regiment.

His Majesty having made a speech to the Counsell of *Erfort,* he left the Queenes Majesty there and blessed her, and then marched from thence on *Boodestawde,* from whence *Papenhaim* with the *Leguisticall* Army had but passed a few dayes before, and his Majesty having quartered the Army in the *Ampt Freeburg,* he commanded Duke *Barnard* of *Wymar,* with fifteene hundred horse to fall on the enemies reare or hinder Troopes: But *Papenhaim* having in haste past over the *Sale* towards *Morsburg,* the Duke could have no advantage of him, but retired againe to his Maiesties Army.

His Maiesty understanding the *Emperialists* had sent thirty musketiers towards *Nawmburg*, to get in the rest of the money, they had promised unto *Tilly* the yeere before; His Majesty incontinent commanded some forces with Colonell *Brandesten* to see if they could get in *Nawmburg*, who having come before it, the twenty ninth of *October* before day, desired to make up the Portes in his Majesties name of *Sweden*, those who had the watch at the Port answered it behooved them first to shew their Commanders of it, otherwise they could not answer for it, which they understanding, unwilling to stay so long, taking a short resolution, with axes and hammers they cut downe the Port and entred perforce, finding at another Port a wicket open, they enter also, and incontinent they bring the Towne in subjection, the *Emperialists* then in the Towne were in danger, if the inhabitants had not interceeded for them to spare them, who did get quarters; soone after six hundred *Emperialists* horsmen came before the Towne, led by Colonell *Breda*, who de- [II-160] sired to make quarters in the Towne, but beyond their expectation having perceived the *Swedens* horse-watch before the Ports, altering their resolution, incontinent they retired backe towards *Visenfelts*.

The thirtieth of *October*, betimes in the morning his Majestie sets over the *Sale*, with the Horsemen at the Dorpe *Altenburg*, directing the Infantrie to passe at the Bridge, where before mid-day the whole Armie were come to *Nawmburg*, and marching by on this side of it, they lay that day, and two dayes after that in the fields before *Iacobs* Port, on the streete that goeth to *Leipsigh*.

After this his Majestie being advertised, that *Walestine* with his Armie was marching on *Visenfelts*, shewing himselfe as if he meant to stand and fight; incontinent his Majestie intrenched his Armie about *Nawmburg* with Skonces and Redoubts, and set two Bridges over the *Sale*, where on all occasions he could transport the Infantrie over such a water, and being readie, then he threw off all Bridges from thence over the *Vustront* till *Freeburg*, whereby they should not be helpfull unto the enemy. Whereupon the Duke of *Freedland Walestine* changing resolution, the Towne and Castle of *Visenfelts* being in his power to use them for his advantage, he plundering both Towne and Castle the fourth of *November*, marched with his Armie towards *Leitzen*, two miles from *Leipsigh*, and incamped there.

### The thirty-ninth Observation.

In the discharge of the former dutie we see his Majestie was troubled with a double care; the one for his *Queene*, the other for his Armie; being diligent in bringing both forwards, as also carefull to put them both in assurance; for having left the *Queene* at *Donavert*, he marched on *Rhine* to subdue his enemies. Where we see, that it behooved him first to put his *Impedimenta* in assurance, teaching thereby Cavaliers, that followed him in time of service, to quit their wives, whereby their care might be the better employed in discharging the points of their Calling; which shews us, that such impediments at such times were better away than present: for our nature is ever to grieve much for the losse of things we love. Therefore our care that are Souldiers having wives should be to settle them, where they should not be *Impedimenta* unto us, in discharging of our duties before our Enemy, to the end we might the better be freed of this double care, his Majestie was subject unto at this time, which no question troubled his Majesties resolutions more than any thing else.

The tragicall end of this *Dutch* Colonell *Metzslaffe*, should teach all Cavaliers, to whom Strengths are concredited, not to give over without great necessitie; especially being made fore-seene of a Reliefe to come. And the greatest blame, that was imputed unto him, was too much neglect of the duties of his Calling, being too carefull to entertaine Cameradeship night and day, the fruit whereof in the end was ignominie, with the losse of life and credit. Which should teach all men to avoide such a beastly life, dishonouring the noble profession of Armes.

We see then no law or justice is more strict or more summary, than the Discipline military; where the Articles we are sworne unto, are our lawes [II-161] which being transgressed, we are subject to the punishment: and if our lawes were not strict, and our punishment sharpe, it were impossible to keepe us in obedience. But I am sorry, that for the most part we abstaine more for feare of punishment, than for obedience to *God* and the law. This censure though hard from me, the truth is still the same, though man were silent.

On this march towards *Saxonie*, all things succeeded to his Majesties desire, as presages of his ensuing victorie; seeing Fortune smiled on him, during his life time, being Fortunes fellow, he was still incouraged to the Combat, though weakest: for magnanimitie and the vertue of true humilitie were both cohabitant in him. For as he had courage with a weake Armie to rancounter a stronger; Even so he humbled himselfe before *God*, acknowledging before the people, he was but dust and ashes, like unto other men. And therfore he wished the people they should not trust or repose any thing in him, but to put their trust and confidence in *God*, saying, he was but a servant: and though the *Lord* would be pleased to take him away from amongst them, yet, he doubted not, but the *Lord* would raise up others more powerfull than he, to defend the good Cause he had begunne, till at last it were brought to a good end.

These speeches, and much more to this purpose, his Majestie out of humilitie uttered on this march; and as his Majestie was humble, so his courtesie to all men that loved him, was the gemme of his Crowne, especially honouring and respecting ever His *Queene*, as the glory of her sex, his Royall Majestie being truely indued with such true splendour of noble worth, that he ever seemed like unto the Sunne, that shineth alike on the Paisant in the field, as it doth on the Emperour in his Throne. And when his Majestie departed from us at *Rhine* on the *Leacke*, then our Sunne on the earth went away unto another *Horizon*, leaving us eclipsed, through the want of our Leader; so that in the rest of our warfare we had none to depend on, but on *God* alone, the onely sure Anchor for a troubled soule to rest on.

To conclude then this Observation, having followed the *Lyon of the North* thus farre unto the Battaile of *Leitzen*, though I was not at the Battaile, yet for my love to my Master, and to discharge the dutie I owe unto my Countrie, I will relate the true manner of this Battaile in short, being the end of the second part of my expedition, under his Majestie of *Sweden*, of never dying memory, leaving the third part of the expedition to a fitter opportunitie; except so farre as we marched before we were sworne to the Evangelist Stends, under the Conduct of Palsgrave *Christian Brickerfeild* in *Baviere*, and afterward under the Feltmarshall *Gustavus Horne* in *Schwabland.*

---

### The fortieth Dutie discharged of the
### Battaile of Leitzen.

The Kings Majestie of *Sweden* knowing that the Duke of *Freedland* had quit the Towne and Castle of *Visenfelts*, and had the fourth of *November* marched with his Armie towards *Leitzen*, two miles from *Leipsigh*, his Majestie on the fift of *November*, with the whole Armie, two [II-162] houres before day brake up from *Nawmburg*, setting after the enemy, coming the same day after a noone-tide in sight of them; He presented himselfe with his Armie in order of Battaile, so that incontinently the skirmish went on apace by the Troopes, which were commanded out from both Armies, whereupon the *Swedens* made still good use with their small Cannon, till the night did put them asunder. In which skirmish the *Swedens* had gotten one of the Crabats Standards, whereon was drawne the Fortune, and the Eagle, which on our side was holden for a good beginning.

The *Swedens* Armie this whole night standing in Battaile, his Majestie was of intention to have fallen on the Emperiall Armie two houres before day: but by reason of a thicke mist which had fallen, it behooved his Majestie to attend the rising and clearing up of the day. But the enemy perceiving the *Swedens* coming so neere unto him, it could not goe off without fighting: he did in the meane time see well to his owne advantage, giving out orders they should incontinent make the Graffe or Ditch, they had before their Front, deeper than it was first made, and to lodge Musketiers within it, which they might have before them, equall to any breast-worke or Parapet for their better safeties.

His Majestie then having ended the morning prayers, and that the mist was vanishing away, by the rising of the Sunne, giving out, by all appearance, the tokens of a cleare day. His Majestie then with comfortable exhortation exhorted every man, foote, and horse, to fight bravely, especially directing his speech unto the *Swedens* and *Finnes*: You true and valiant brethen, see that you doe valiantly carry your selves this day, fighting bravely for *Gods* Word, and your *King*; which if you doe, so will you have mercy of *God*, and honour before the world; and I will truely reward you; but if you doe not, I sweare unto you, that your bones shall never come in *Sweden* againe.

The *Dutch* also his Majesty exhorted after this manner: You true and worthy *Dutch* brethren, Officers and common Souldiers, I exhort you all, carry your selves manly, and fight truely with me; runne not away, and I shall hazard my body and bloud with you for your best, if you stand with me, so I hope in *God* to obtaine victory, the profit whereof will redownd to you and your successours: and if otherwise you doe, so are you and your liberties lost. His Majestie having ended this speech saith, now let us to it, and let us cry unto *God* with one voice, *Iesu, Iesu, Iesu* helpe me this day to fight, for the Glory of thy Name: He advanced then in full Battaile fasting, having neither tasted meate not drinke, right forwards towards the Towne of *Leitzen*, where on both sides the Duke of *Freedland* his Horsemen did present themselves, untill such time as their Generall had brought their Infantrie in Battaile, beside the Winde-mill, and then to a side, by the Ditch that was before their Front, they retired backe a little, and set themselves in Battaile, on the right hand of the Towne of *Leitzen*, and then putting the Towne on fire, to the end the *Swedens* on that quarter could doe them no harme.

Notwithstanding whereof, with full resolution of the *Swedens* Armie, in full Battaile marched by the side of the Towne on the ditch, where their Musketiers were lodged, and presented themselves in good order, against the mighty and strong Emperiall Armie, whereupon, the Emperialists great Cannon, that were planted by the winde-mill, began to give fire in the middest of the *Swedens* Armie, and were incontinent repayed and answered with the like [II-163] noyse; so that the Cannon played two long houres on both sides, the fight going bravely on, betwixt nine and tenne of the clocke, that his Majestie himselfe advanced towards the enemie, with the Van-guarde of his Armie, even to their Graffe, where their Musketiers were set much to his Majestie disadvantage, so that sundries of his Majestie forces fell therein; Neverthelesse, they chased the enemie a little out of the ditch, and tooke seven of the Emperialists Cannon, that were planted alongst the Graffe. After this, the other *Swedens* Briggad, or yellow Regiment of the Guard is come after, and not esteeming of the Graffe in their way, or of the three squadrons, or Battailes of the enemies foote, being foure times stronger than they, which they manfully did beate, making them to give ground, till they were ruin'd, and then on the second time, scattering them also even untill the third advancing, and being growne weake, and wearie with so many brave Charges, being resisted by the enemies third Battaile, which were seconded well with two squadrons of horsemen, at last, with the blew Regiments comming up to relieve them, driven backe, and almost so scattered, that they were ruined, and the seven Cannon which formerly they had wonne, were taken from them againe. In the meane time, the *Swedens* small Cannon, that were planted before the Briggads, being righted on the enemies Cannon at the winde-mill, whereon also Duke *Barnards* Cannon, which were before his Briggad, played on the enemies Cannon towards the wind-mill, doing great hurt to the enemie, so that they were forced to retire their Cannon a little behinde the Millars house; in this meane time, his Majestie with some squadrons of horse charged the enemie, that was thrice stronger than they, charging with their right wing, his left wing falling on them with such furie, that their Reare-guard, or reserve were astonished, being so furious, that they went through their enemies, putting them to the flight. But especially his Majestie himselfe having charged too farre with foure Cornets in the midd'st of the enemies troopes being deadly wonded gave up the Ghost, fighting for God and for the defence of the true Religion, he departed valiantly and happily for him, in *Christ* our Saviour.

Neverthelesse two great bodies of *Crabbats* of the enemies left wing stood firme, and falling on the right wing of the *Swedens* horsemen, with such a crie and furie, advanced so farre, that they were Masters of the *Swedens* Amunition waggons, bringing also some of the *Swedens* horsemen in disorder: whereupon incontinent did fall on three squadrons of the *Swedens* horsemen, under whom Lievetenant Colonell *Relingen* was one, that did second the rest bravely, who was shot in the Arme. Neverthelesse the *Crabbats* were beaten backe againe with losse, during which time, Duke *Barnard* of *Wymar* was not idle, with the left wing of the *Swedens* horsemen, but with the commanded musketiers being of *Leslies* Regiment, and with the small Cannon, charged the enemies right wing, making them retire on their Cannon by the wind-mill and Gallowes, and after long fighting, they were made at last to give ground, quitting to the *Swedens* fourteene peeces of great Ordinance.

As the Duke of *Wymar* did charge the enemie, their Amunition waggons tooke fire, which did indammage the enemie much, but thereafter, *Papenhaim* comming from *Hall* with a fresh supplie unlooked for, the service was begunne againe more sharpe and violent, than before, which continued for a while very vehement, he having recollected the scattered Troopes, the Order whereof can scarce bee well set downe, by reason it was so neere night, [II-164] Before *Papenhaims* comming; yet the service continued hot and cruell so long as he lived, till it was past eight a Clocke at night, that in end *Papenhaim* being kill'd, the *Emperialists* losing courage, through the assistance of God, and the manly, and valiant courage of Duke *Barnard* of *Wymar*, the victorie was come on the *Swedens* side, the enemie having quit the field, and burnt off his Leaguer with his whole Baggage, and three peeces of Cannon, which he could not get carryed away with him; hee tooke his retreate againe on *Leipsigh*.

There were killed of the *Emperialists* the Abbot of *Fulda*, the Grave *Fon Papenhaim*, Colonell *Lane*, Colonell *Vestrum*, Lievetenant Colonell *Lorda*, Livetenant Colonell *Taphim*, Lievetenant Colonell *Camerhooffe*, Colonell *Soves* with many other inferiour Officers and Souldiers.

On the *Swedens* side were lost with his Majestie Generall Major *Isler*, Colonell *Gerstorfe*, Generall Major *Grave Neeles* a *Sweden*, Colonell *Vildesten*, and divers more were hurt, and of our Nation was hurt with the Cannon, and musket twice Captaine *Henry Lindesey* brother to *Bainshow* who for a time did lie almost dead in the field, divers Officers of Colonell *Lodowicke Leslie* his Regiment were also hurt, having behaved themselves well, being, for the most part, old, expert Officers, and old beaten blades of Souldiers.

In this Battaile as was thought, were killed nine thousand men, besides, those were hurt, whereof many thereafter dyed of their woundes, such as on the Emperours side *Grave Berherthold, Fon Walestine,* Colonell *Comargo,* Colonell *Browner,* the old Colonell *Viltzleben,* and others. On the *Swedens* side also dyed of his wounds after the Battaile, Generall Major *Grave Neeles.*

After his Majesties death, there was a great and extraordinary griefe and sorrow over the whole Armie; yet they never suffered the same to be seene outwardly, but prosecuted still the enemie more vehemently, and more cruelly than before. For the Duke of *Wymar*, and the rest of the Cavaliers of the Armie understanding the great misfortune of his Majestie death, resolved all alike, it was better to dye on the place with his Majestie, than to retire one foote of ground: which resolution was the cause, that in the end they did crowne the lamentable death of the Kings Majestie with a stately and heroicall Victorie, so that his Majestie in the highest degree of glorie, may be imagined before any King, or Emperour to have dyed, and his life doth eternize alike both his prayse and glorie, being victorious before death, in his death, and after death.

The Duke of *Fridland Walestine*, after the losing of this Battaile, retired with his scattered Armie towards *Leipsigh*, and having had no time to continue there, he was forced to take his retreate further unto the Hill's of *Bohemia*, and thereafter *Leipsigh* was freed from the enemies forces, by the Duke of *Lunenburg*, and the *Saxons*, that were comming with succours unto his Majestie before the Battaile, whose march was too slow, their succours being come but after the stroaks were given.

The Castle of *Leipsigh* called *Plassenburg* having holden out long, was taken againe, together with which all other partes in *Saxon*, that the *Emperialists* had taken, were freed againe, by the *Swedens* the second time, as *Camnits, Fryburg*, &c. For which service the *Swedens* were evill recompensed by the ungratefull *Saxon*, whose unthankfullnesse to the Crowne of *Sweden* will never be forgotten.

In all this time the *Swedens Felt-marshall Gustavus Horne* did prosper very fortunately in *Alsas,* not onely in taking in the strong and fast Episcopall Strength *Bennenfeld*, in spight of the *Emperialists,* who had pressed to relieve it, [II-165] after a long Siege of two moneths time; The Feltmarshall did take it in by Accord. As also the Townes *Schletstad, Colmare, Haggeno, Molshen*, and almost whole upper *Alsas* in a short time he brought under his Contribution and power.

### The fortieth Observation.

His Majestie at this time, though a great deale weaker in strength than the enemy, notwithstanding he was loath to delay time, finding *Walestine* once removing from him, *Papenhaim* being also absent with the Armie of the League, his Majestie resolved as best to embrace the occasion, not giving time to his enemy, either to take more advantage, or yet to recollect the Forces which were scattered from him, thinking it was best to deale with one before another, and he knew it was a kinde of madnesse to stay till his enemies Forces were augmented, seeing occasion taken in warres doth often profit more than courage it selfe. Therefore we see, there was a necessitie laid on his Majestie to fight this Battaile in time, seeing the enemy coming together was twice stronger than he, and then his Majestie had no place of Retreate within ten miles, which would not onely

ruine his Armie, but also discourage his friends and Confederates, for whose
reliefe he did come.

*Walestine* retired from his Majestie of purpose to put off time, till
*Papenhaim* had come to him, or till they might draw his Majesties Army
between them, which his Majestie fore-seeing adventured the Combat, in seeking
first unto *Walestine* before *Papenhaims* coming. It is needlesse to reason more
of his Majesties resolution, since all counsells and advisements are allowed of,
as they happen to succeede; which is most unjust.

Here also we see, what a great charge is laid on him that leads an Armie;
and of all charges the greatest is, to fight a Battaile well with a weake Army
against a strong. Wherein is requisit a wise and a couragious Commander; for
when a Battaile is to be fought, it is dangerous for a King, the Head and the
Heart of an Armie, with the danger of his whole Armie, to hazard himselfe and
his Kingdome to the decision or arbitrement of variable *Fortune*, or to enterprize
difficult matters, setting all his estate in hazard, seeing the safetie of the whole
depends on him alone: for there is nothing more fearfull to a Commander, and
with all diligence to be eschewed, than that he doe not at one time, and one
moment, commit his whole estate and Kingdome unto the decision of Chance,
without great advantage offered. Neither ought a King to fight with all his
Forces at once, except he could perceive a sure overthrow to be seene cleerely
unto himselfe, or to his enemies, and if then he resolve to fight, for eschewing of
factions, let one supreame Commander command, which is ever best; since many
wits in Command doe but breed confusion. Therefore it is most requisit, that
one command and the rest obey, as was done here at *Leitzen*, and the best way of
Command is, to keepe men in awe of dutie, not so much with crueltie (as many
base Generalls doe) as with a moderate severenesse: for alwayes Commanders
ought to doe, as wise Marriners, not to steere their course still one way, but
sometimes to give way to the tempest, which being past, let him follow his
course [II-166] gaine: even so wise Commanders should moderate their Commands
according to the time. For as in a calme sea any fellow may steere, but in a great
tempest, a skilfull and wise Marriner is requisit: even so in Command, when a
Battaile is to be fought, a wise and a stout Commander is requisite; for no man
can command well, who did not learne to obey. Therefore it is the most difficult
thing in the world to command well, either our selves or others: and he that
would command well, must not shew himselfe cruell in words or strokes, but if
possible, he ought to bring men to his minde with intreaty and friendly
exhortations, shewing himselfe grave, majestique and benevolent, gaining of
others his inferiours reverence, feare and munificence, with due obedience; and
this is the only best way to command, and to keepe men in obedience: which
qualities were all plentifull in the *Lyon* of the North, the invincible *Gustavus*,
who after this manner incouraged his owne countrimen and subjects, to fight, as
also in a brotherly manner of love incouraged the *Dutch*, being his sworne
servants. Who would not obey such a Commander to fight well, being assured
under his fortunate conduct after travell and paine, to obtaine Glory and honour

here, and an immortall Crowne after death, for fighting well the Battells of the Lord?

As his Majesty went about his enemies with wisdome and courage: so *Walestine* went about his with craft and policy, casting a ditch before our forces to fall in, which was made the buriall place of his owne Souldiers, being fallen in the ditch they had prepared for others.

I confesse there is nothing more commodious in warre then to deceive an enemy, and oftimes through deceit men obtaine victory: yet the wisdome of *Gustavus* seasoned with infinite courage could not be trapped with a Fowlers grinne, but brake through it with the assistance of God, till he was victorious over his crafty enemies.

This Magnanimous King for his valour might have bin well called the Magnifique King, and holden for such, who while as he once saw appearance of the losse of the day, seeing some forces beaten backe, and some flying, he valorously did charge in the middest of his enemies with hand and voice, though thrice shot, sustained the fight, doing alike, the duty of a Souldier and of a King, till with the losse of his owne life he did restore the victory to his eternall credit, he died standing serving the publique, *Pro Deo et Religione tuenda*; and receiving three Bullets, one in the body, one in the Arme, and the third in the head, he most willingly gave up the Ghost, being all his life time a King that feared God and walked uprightly in his calling; and as he lived Christianly, so he died most happily, in the defence of the truth: and to witnesse all this was true, I could take Heaven and Earth, Sun and Moone, mineralls &c. to witnesse that his Colours ever florished and spred in the name of the Lord, and that his confidence was not set on the Arme of man, though he was a warriour from his youth up, he was the Captaine over *Iraell*, whose fingers the Lord taught to fight, and to leade his people.

He had the heart of a *Lyon*, that by Gods helpe had done such things, that those that had seene and heard it as I did, must needs have said, that it was the Lord that did it and not he, being it was the Lords worke. But our adversaries and their damned crew of Iesuits and Monkes, will say, that it was their power and might, and the goodnesse of their cause, that made his Roy- [II-167] all Maiesty to fall. But we may say with *Salomon* in the twenty-eighth of the *Proverbs* and twenty-one verse. *It was for the sinnes of the Land, and our sinnes, that he was taken from amongst us*, and from those poore Cavaliers, that did follow him, for his Maiesties love, and the love of the cause. He was shot with three Bullets, dead with the last, for our sinnes and the sinnes of the Land. And what he did before his death, for the liberty of *Dutch-land*, and freedome of the Gospell none but knowes it: he left his owne Kingdome, to bring strangers to freedome in theirs, he set light by his owne life for *Dutch-land*, that they might keepe theirs, he waked and cared day and night for them, as a father for his children, that at last he might bring peace for them to sleepe sound; he brought the keyes and opened their Church doores that were closed up by the Antichristian Idolaters, that the Devills doctrine was banished againe out of the

*Paltz*, and Christs Gospell preached, and the Sacraments duely administred, which I saw, and was partaker of, singing thankes unto God for their deliverance.

He it was and none other under God, who helped them to their liberties, He it was and none other releeved *Israell*.  Notwithstanding whereof, the unthankfulnesse of the people was so great, that with my eares, divers times I did heare some of them say, he might as wel have stayed in his own country, till they had sent for him, so great was their unthankfulnesse!  Likewise they said, if he had had much at home, he had not come unto them over seas such a farre Iourney.  Was not this to recompence good with evill?  Was not this right the chiefe Butlers part, that did not remember *Ioseph*, but forgot him?  Was not this *Ioas* his part to *Iehoida*, his Father?  O then this was the poisonable bullet of ingratitude of the people, for which our King and Master was taken away!  Oh would to God the people had never bin so unthankfull, that our King, Captaine and Master had yet lived!

Moreover as these people were unthankfull, so they were Godlesse many of them in the time of their troubles, as I did behould oftimes with mine eyes a carelesse security amongst them, thinking their victories were so frequent, and their owne power so great, they needed not the assistance of the *Swedens* nor of strangers, and their pride was so great, that disesteeming of strangers in their pride, they led a life very insolent and deboist, being given to the workes of the flesh, adultery, fornication, uncleannesse, lasciviousnesse, idolatry &c.  In a word, it was even amongst them, as it was in the dayes before the flood, as if the Lord had forgotten them, or could not see their villany, so it behooved God to have punished them by his Majesties death.  For in their hearts they said there was no God; so that their mischiefe came on them unawares; and this the peoples carriage caused his Majesties untimely death, being shot the second time.  O would to God they had done otherwise, and served God more truely, that we might have had the presence and conduct of our Magnanimous King longer, till the pride of *Austria* had bin more humbled, and the whore of *Babylon* brought unto repentance of her Idolatries!  O would to God I could enough lament his death!  As also lament my owne sinnes, and the wickednesse of the people, that was the cause of his untimely death, through their sinnes!  And his Majesties selfe also being a sinner, as he himselfe oftimes confessed, wishing that God would not lay to his charge the greate respect and reverence the best sort of the people did give unto him, being but a sinfull man, as they were; for which he feared the Lord was angry with him; shewing by his cõfession he [II-168] did glory in nothing but in the Lord, ascribing over all his victories unto God, and nothing presuming of himselfe.  For I dare be bould to say he was a man according to Gods minde, if there was one on earth.  Such was our Master, Captaine and King.  As was *Abraham* the Father of many, so was our Master, Captaine and King.  Was *Noah* in his time unreproveable?  So was our Master, Captaine and King.  Was *Iob* in his sufferings patient?  So was our Master, Captaine and King.  Was *Ionathan* true and upright in keeping his word?  So was our Master, Captaine and King.  Was *Iehosaphat* in his warres penitent, and busie craving the helpe of the Lord?  So was our Master, Captaine and King.  Was *Simeon* good and full of the spirit? So was our Master, Captaine and King. Was young *Tobias* mindfull all his days of the Lord, in his heart, and his will not set to sinne? So was our Master, Captaine, and King, like unto a stone most precious, even like a *Iasper*, cleere as *Christall* ever and ever. And truely if *Apelles* with his skill in painting, and *Cicero* with his tongue in speaking, were both alive, and pressed to adde any thing to the perfection of our Master, Captaine and King; truely the ones best Colours, and the others best Words were not able to adde one shaddow to the brightnesse of his Royall Minde and Spirit; So that while the world stands, our King, Captaine and Master cannot be enough praised. Alas then! it was our sinnes, and the sinnes of the Army, and the Land, was the cause of our punishment in losing of him, with that unhappy last bullet of the three shot through his head, who was the head of us all under God our Father in Christ, that did undoe us, it was we, I say, that sinned against the Lord and his Anointed. It was our misdeedes did thus grow over our heads that made us lose our Head and Leader. Woe, woe then to us that left the Lord, till we made the Lord take him from us, that was our guard and comforter under God in all our troubles! What then ought we to doe that one day we may raigne with him in glory? While it is to day we must cast off the workes of darknesse, and embrace the light in newnesse of life, repenting of the evill, and turning away from our wickednesse by repentance, not like unto *Cain*, not like unto *Saul*, not like unto *Achitophell*, not like to *Iudas Iscariot*, who all doubted; but like those of *Nineve* in dust and ashes, to fast and pray beleeving in the Lord; and with *David* to say, *We have sinned against thee, and against the Heavens*, be mercifull unto us o Lord: like unto *Peter*, let us, ô Lord, *Weepe bitterly*; let us then repent, and beleeve the Gospell, beleeve, yea and turne to the Lord with all our hearts, with fasting and praying, and mourning with *Saul*, that said, *Thou art more righteous then I, in shewing me good for evill:* much more ought we lift up our voices, and with teares of repentance mourne for the losse of our Master, Captaine and King, through our sinnes and unthankfulnesse. Therefore to day while we have time, let us acknowledge our sinnes before the Lord, and repent, *lest a worse come unto us*, and that then we be cast into prison, *till that we pay the last farthing*; for if the Lord spared not his owne Sonne who was blamelesse and without sinne, while he tooke on him our sinnes, what shall then become of us? No otherwise, but except we turne from our sinnes, we must also die the death. Let us not then close our eares, as at *Meriba* and at *Massa* in the wildernesse; but with the forlorne Child cry, *Father we have sinned against thee, and against heaven, and are not more worthy to be called thy Sonnes*. Lord therefore be mercifull unto us, and enter not into judgment with us. Then let us all weare mourning, and lament the death of the valiant [II-169] King *Gustavus Adolphus,* while we breath. Yet what helpe? *Res est irrevocabilis, et quod factum est infectum fieri nequit,* what is done cannot be recalled, and should we mourne like unto those who have no hope? Farre be it from us, seing it cannot helpe us in this life, or in the life to come. Let us then say with *Micha*, let it be with us as it pleaseth God, and let us say with *David, It is good for us o Lord, that thou hast chastened us with thy Rod;* thou canst also helpe us, and bring us to an happy end of all our miseries, the Lord will not suffer us nor our seede to lacke bread, and the Lord our God did ever give unto the people of *Israell* at all times Rulers, Iudges and Kings, and *Iael*, though a woman despised, was strong enough to drive a naile in the right cause. Shall not then the Lord on our repentance, sturre up one, yet to take his cause in hand, who are also *Israels*, and the Lords people and inheritance, being also christened in the Lords name? And as a Mother doth not forget her Child, so will not the Lord forget us, but in place of our Master, Captaine and King, will yet give unto us a valiant Leader, come, I hope, of the valiant *Bruce*, & of the first King of the *Stewarts*, of the Issue of the *Elizabeth* the Queene of *Bohemia*, and Iewell of her sex, the most splendid in brightnesse of minde, for a woman, that the Earth doth affoord. From her I wish the Leader to come into the field, to fight with good lucke & victory, with strength & power, with wisdome and understanding &c. against her enemies and our enemies, alwayes well furnished and prepared, the Lord will give him an Horne of Iron and feete of Brasse to beate his enemies in peeces, the Lord will lift up his hand upon his adversaries, and cut off all his enemies; and to conclude, he will make them treade the Devill under his feete. The Lord of this infinite mercy grant unto us such a Leader in place of our valiant Master, Captaine and King of never dying memory, the *Lyon* of the North, the invincible King of *Sweden*! so shall we not neede in any manner of way to doubt of a wished happy end, both to the warre and to our selves, being victorious over all our enemies temporall and spirituall. *Amen.*

---

### The fourty-one Duty discharged at the intaking of Landsberg *on the* Leake, *and the reliefe of* Rhine.

*Palsgrave Christian* being left by his Majesty to command the Army in *Bavier*, having left *Rhine* with foure Companies of *Swedens* commanded by Colonell *Worbran* his Major, he brake up with the Army towards *Aichstade* in *Bavier*, and having taken it by Accord he continued his march towards *Landsberg* on the *Leake*. Where having arrived within halfe a mile of the Towne, we quartered for a night, till preparation were made of victualls and furniture convenient for the beleaguering, which being made, the next day we marched towards the Towne in Battaile, drawing up within reach of Cannon to the walles in the safest part: they thundering with cannon amongst us, our foote Army was divided in Briggads, and directed to severall Posts, our horsemen were also divided. Some were com- [II-170] manded out to scoure the fields on that side the enemy was to come, others were appointed to remaine beside the Infantry, to second us against the out-falling: or otherwise to second us against the reliefe, that might come to the Towne. The rest of our Horsemen were directed to Quarters, having left Ordonance Rutters to bring them intelligence.

The Towne being beleaguered on all Quarters, a Bridge was made over the River, where a strong Guard of horse and foote were sent to hinder both their supply and escape on that side. Likewise the approaches were begun, and orders were given in haste for making the Batteries. And the Guards being set both to the Cannon, and to those that wrought in the Trenches, the Colonells were Recognosceing about the walls before their severall Postes. Where at the first, Colonell *Fowle* was shot through the thigh with a Musket, who immediatly was sent to *Ausburg* to be cured.

Before night a second partie of Horse were sent forth for Intelligence, lest any mis-fortune might befall the first partie; whereby we might not be surprized by the Enemy being strong together at *Minchen*. *Spence* his Regiment and mine were appointed to attend to the Generall at his Quarter, my Lievetenant Colonell commanded the Guards on the Battery and the Trenches on our Quarter. And the Generall Major *Ruthven* his Briggad being on the other Quarter next the water, there grew a contestation of vertue betwixt the Officers of both Briggads, who should first with their approaches come to the wall; but those of *Ruthvens* Briggad were forced, notwithstanding of their diligence, to yeeld the precedency unto us being older blades than themselves: for in effect we were their Schoolemasters in Discipline, as they could not but acknowledge. So being they were trained up by us from Souldiers to be inferiour Officers, and then for their preferments and advancement they went from us with our favours towards the Generall Major, such as Captaine *Gunne*, Lievetenant *Brumfield*, Lievetenant *Dumbarre*, Lievetenant *Macboy,* Lievetenant *Southerland,* Ensigne *Denune*, and divers more, which were preferred under *Ruthvens* Regiment, till in the end they did strive in vertue to goe beyond their former Leaders. Neverthelesse we kept ever that due correspondence together, that where ever we did meet we were but one, not without the envie of others.

This strife amongst us furthered so the victory, that before the next morning, from our Battery, where *Sinclaire* did command, there was a breach shot in the Skonce without the Towne, as also from the Generall Major his Quarter, there were two Officers of the enemies killed on the wall, their Cannon dismounted, and a great breach made in the wall. So that the enemy perceiving he had two breaches to defend, he tuck't a Drumme, desiring to parlé. Which being granted; the Accord went on, and they were suffered to march out with their Armes, seeing the Generall had intelligence their Armie was comming to releeve them, he was glad to grant them any Conditions, before he were forced to rise from the Towne by the Enemy, being so neare for reliefe of it.

The enemy being marched out and convoyed away, the Generall directed Generall Major *Ruthven* into the Towne with a strong partie of foote to beset all the Posts, and then to take notice of all provision and goods that were in the Towne; such as Corne, Wine, Artillery, Amunition, Horses, and all other goods or cadducks in generall, to be used at their pleasure. Which being done, the foote Armie were directed to their former Quarters, to rest [II-171] till further Orders. The Horsemen were directed also to Quarters, and then there were Quarters made in the Towne for the Generall and the *Hoofstaffe,* as also for Colonells of horse and foote, during the Generall his further pleasure.

Diverse of our foote Souldiers were hurt on the Batteries and Trenches, which got Quarters in the Towne, being allowed to have Chirurgians to cure them. And the Towne was incontinent beset againe with foure Companies of Colonell *Hugh Hamilton* his Regiment, being new levied men out of *Switzerland*, and his Major being an *Irish*-man, commanded the men. But another *Dutch* Major called *Mountague* was left to Command the Garrison. Where those that entred first the Towne, did make good bootie of horses and other goods. But the most part was seazed upon by the Generall *Persons*, taking the benefit unto themselves, though not the paine. Where we did first finde missing of our former Leader the invincible *Gustavus*, who not onely respected Cavaliers of merit, at such times, but also was ready to reward them by his bountie, allowing *Cadducks* unto them, as he did unto Lievetenant Colonell *Gunne*.

The next day a partie of a thousand Horse, with eight hundred Musketiers, were commanded out toward *Minchen*, to get intelligence of the Enemies designes, getting Orders to fall into their Quarters, if conveniently they could. But beside their expectation the Enemy being together and in readinesse in a Wood, unawares our partie was ingaged amongst them, so that with difficultie having lost prisoners, they were forced to retire, and the Enemy getting intelligence that the Towne was given over, to prevent us they continued their march towards *Rhine* on the *Leacke*, to take it in, in compensation of the losse of *Lansberg*.

The partie being retired, and the Generall understanding the Dukes Army had marched on *Rhine*, he brake up with our Armie, and marched on the other side of the *Leacke* towards *Ausburg*. And fearing the Skonce at *Rhine* and the bridge might be taken by the Enemy, he did direct Captaine *Iames Lyell* with two hundred Musketiers as a supply to the Skonce, being ordained at his comming thither to take the Command of the Skonce on him. Who being come, finding Colonell *Wornbran* there, shewing his Orders, he was made welcome by the Colonell, being hard pressed by the Enemy, and mightily afraid: so that the Captaine had no difficultie in getting the command, which he gladly accepted, being more ambitious of credit than of gaines, directly opposit to the Colonels humour.

The Armie having come in time for the reliefe, our Horsemen were left on the side of the River next to *Donavert*, except my Cosen *Fowles* his Regiment, which marched over the Bridge with the Infantry, being ordained the first nights watch to second the foot. And immediatly after our over-going there were five hundred Musketiers of supply sent unto the Towne, in despite of the Dukes Armie. And then we begun to make up our Batteries, and to run our lines of approach towards the Towne, advancing our Redoubts and Batteries, as our approaches were advanced.

The second night our Batteries being readie, there were mutuall interchanges of Cannonading amongst us, where Ensigne *Murray* was shot dead with the Cannon, his thigh bone being broken, who was much lamented, being a daintie Souldier and expert, full of courage to his very end.

On Sunday in the afternoone the Enemy having heard certaintie of his [II-172] Maiesties death, they drew up their whole Armie, Horse, Foote and Cannon before the Towne; and rejoycing at the Newes, they gave three *salves* of Cannon, Musket, and Pistoll. Which we not understanding, made us admire the more. Neverthelesse, the Generall resolved to get some prisoners of them, to cause to make an out-fall the next morning: and to that effect, five hundred Commanded Musketiers were sent under the Command of Lievetenant Colonell *Lesly*, who had Orders to fall out before day upon the Enemy. Which he did; and beating them from their Posts, there were above three-score killed, and thirtie taken prisoners; which revealed the reason of their *salve*. As also by them it was found, the Armie had been broken up at midnight, and crossed the *Danube*, having made over a Ship-bridge, thinking with expedition to haste unto *Saxonie*, to supply the *Imperialists,* that were retiring after their defeat at *Leitzen* unto *Boheme.*

Notwithstanding of the advantages we had to prosecute the Enemy, being divided by the River, our Generall would not suffer to pursue them, though Generall Major *Ruthven* with the whole Officers offered to doe good service. The Generall fearing they might be brought to fight through despaire, he would not permit to follow them, but choosed rather to lose a golden opportunitie.

Within three dayes afterwards, we marched towards *Ausburg*, where we lay two moneths in open Feilds, in the extremitie of cold, without houses or buildings, which undid the Army being idle without hostile imployment, our Generalls giving time to our Enemies to gather strength to beat us againe out of the Country, which formerly we had subdued by his Majesties valour and good Conduct.

During this time I remained on my Muster place at *Webling* Cloister, giving out patents to my Officers, and money to recrue and strengthen their Companies. But the enemy having taken-in the Passe and Towne of *Landsberg*, which was given over upon accord by Colonell *Hugh Hamilton*, who was prisoner, and kept almost three yeares; so the enemie getting the Passe unto *Schwabland*, they marched towards *Menning*, and from thence to *Brandenburg* on the *Eler*, and chased mee over the *Danube*. Being forced to quit a good Muster place, we retired unto *Ausburg*, having set the *Danube* betwixt us and the enemie; where, on our march unfortunately my horse fell on my leg, and being six weekes under cure I continued still with the Armie, on all occasions commanding on horse-backe, being unable to travell a foote.

The next day after our comming to *Ausburg*, Generall *Bannier* did breake up with the Armie to march towards *Vlme* on the *Danube*, there to joyne with the Felt-marshall *Gustavus Horne*, who was to come with a strong partie of horse, foot, and Artillerie from *Elsas*, with whom was come Major *Sidserfe*, and the whole Musketiers of Sir *Iames Ramsey* his Regiment; who being valourous and expert old Soldiers, they were commanded on all exploits of importance, being conducted and led by a discret Cavalier their Major.

The enemie, before our joyning with the Felt-marshall, had taken in *Landsberg, Kaufbeyre, Kempten* and *Menning* where their Armie did lie, while as we joyned with the Felt-marshall at *Vlme*. *Palsgrave Christian* being directed to command the Armie on the *Rhine*, Generall *Bawtishen* having left them voluntarily to goe for his wedding unto *Denmark*.

Generall *Bannier* being also sickly, not yet fully cured of his hurt, that he did get at *Nurenberg*, he was directed to the *Steifft Madeburg* to collect new [II-173] Forces there to joyne with the Duke of *Lunenburg* and the *Saxon*, who all this time, after his Majesties death, were pursuing hard the *Imperialists conjunctis viribus*, assisting the Duke of *Wymar* and the *Swedens* Armie. At which time the Rex-chancellour *Oxestern* made offer, after his Majesties death, to the Duke of *Saxon*, to be made and chosen Directour of the Armies; who was neither willing to accept it himselfe, nor yet willingly would condescend to be directed by any other; so that their division did by time fully ruine the Armie, and almost lost the good cause, few or none looking to the weale of the publique, but all pleasing their owne fancies, suffering the enemie to take advantage, every one looking to their particular commodities, which did occasion the meeting of *Hailbrun*.

### The fourty-one Observation.

After his Majesties departure unto *Saxony*, our Briggad, which formerly on all occasions followed his Majestie, being often the Guard of his person, as at his crossing the *Rhine* and at *Miniken*, were left behind; which then we thought very hard, as if thereby we had beene lost, which may be was the meanes of our safetie; for as some flying from danger meet with death, others doe finde protection in the very jawes of mischiefe, and some others in their sleepe are cast into fortunes lap, while as others, for all their industrie, cannot purchase one smile from her. Wee see then, that man is but meerely the ball of time, being tost too and fro is governed by a power that must be obeyed: and we know there is a providence ordering all things, as it pleaseth him, for which no man is able to finde or give a reason: we must therefore beleeve S$^t$ *Ierome*, saying, *Providentiâ Dei omnia gubernantur, & quae putatur poena, medicina est.*

In vaine then we murmur at the things that must be, and in vaine we mourne for what we cannot remedie. Therefore let this be our chiefe comfort, that we are alwayes in the hands of a Royall Protectour: what ever then befalls us, we must be contented, not strugling against power.

We see also there is nothing more dangerous for Commanders in warres, then to be thought once by their fellowes, Officers and Souldiers to be greedy of the evill of gaine: which opinion once received by inferiours, may mightily crosse the fortunes of their Leaders: for when Officers and Souldiers conceive an evill opinion of their Leaders, no eloquence is able to make them thinke well of them thereafter; for, a supreme Officer being once remarked to keepe the meanes of those that served them, they are without doubt thereafter despised by their followers. And therefore he is never worthy the name of a glorious Commander, that doth not preferre the vertue of liberalitie before the love of perishing gold; otherwise in his teeth he will be aswell despised by the common Soldiers, as by his betters; for a brave Commander ought never to make an Idol of the moneys which should satisfie Souldiers, but he should rather looke unto that which may follow, to wit, his overthrow, or at least his contempt. Therefore I would advise Cavaliers, that command and leade others, to entertaine the affection of those that have served bravely and truly, lest being unjustly disdained, they might turne their Armes the contrary way.

Wee see also the emulation of vertue betwixt friends commendable, in striving who should force the enemy first unto a parlé; where the diligence and valour of Major *Sinclaire* is praise-worthy, who feared nothing but discredit; [II-174] where we see, that the enticement to great travell and paines is glory and honour. And we see, all Arts and sciences are attained unto with diligent exercise; So that it is not time, or number of yeares that makes a brave Souldier, but the continuall meditation of exercise and practise; For Souldiers should be frequented in running, not to runne away, as some doe, but on the contrary, that with the greatest celerity that may prosecute their enemies, taking time in overtaking their flying enemies, and that they may the better releeve their friends, for more come to be good Souldiers by use then by nature. Here also I did see our Generall following *Guischardin* his counsell, that wished to make a silver bridge to let passe our enemies, but if the enemy on his retreat would grow carelesse and amuse himselfe once on booty, then it were a fit time to medle with him being loaden with booty.

After his Majesties death we see the alteration of time did give greater advantage unto our enemies; for while as our Army lay idle the whole winter in *Ausburg*, the enemy was gathering his forces, and we losing time neglected our duty, having lost our Head and Leader, when we ought rather to have followed our enemies with fire, sword, spoile and slaughter, till we had subdued them, than to have suffered the enemy before our noses to have taken from us that, which we by his Majesties good conduct had conquered before, So that we see it is vicissitude that maintaines the world: and as one scale is not alwayes in depression, nor the other lifted ever higher; even so, like unto the alternate wave of the Beame, we were at this time with both our Armies kept ever in the play of motion.

---

*The fourty-two Duty of our March through* Schwabland
*under the* Alpes *to our Leaguer at* Donavert, *being the*
*end of my Expedition with theRegiment.*

Having joyned with the Felt-marshall at *Vlme*, we crossed the *Danube*, and quartered over-night in the Earldome of *Kirkberg*, being Generall Major *Ruthven* his lands, disposed unto him by his Majesty for good service; and hearing the enemies Army were at *Memming* within six miles of us, we advanced the next morning towards them, with a resolution to beate them backe unto *Bavier*, being almost equall with them in Strength, we continued our march with extreme cold, till the second night that we quartered in a great Dorpe, a mile from the enemy, so that in the night fire entring in our quarter, with difficulty we saved our Amunition and Artillery, having lost many Horses, and the most part of the Armies Baggage. Notwithstanding whereof, we marched the next day towards *Memming*, and before our coming the enemy having strongly beset the Towne, he marched away two miles from the Towne, thinking to ingage us with the Towne, that he might returne againe with advantage to releeve it, seeing we had not time to intrench our selves, he being then so neere. [II-175]

But we finde at our coming the enemy was gone, we drew up in battaile within reach of Cannon to the Towne, where they saluted us with Cannon till it drew neere night, and then leaving strong watches before the Towne, for feare of out-falling, laying our watches to keepe them in, we quartred over-night in Dorps, attending the up coming of our Baggage, being scarce of victualls and without forrage, but such as we brought with us. The next morning our baggage being come, and hearing the enemy was within two miles of us, leaving a strong hinder-halt to keepe in the Garrison, we marched with the rest of the Army after the enemy, where before night our fore-troopes did skirmish together, and we having the best of it, the enemey was forced to leave a strong Reare-guard of Horse and Dragoniers, making the rest of his Army to march away unto a passe beside *Kempten*, being a strong streight Passe, the country being streight and hilly, full of woods, very commodious for Ambuscadoes, so that we could not march to them, but in order of Battaile; our fore-troopes of horse and Dragoniers advancing softly on the enemy, being forced to recognize still before them, till at last they charged their horse-watches, which being beaten by ours, we did get three Cornets from them, where incontinent Major *Sidserffe* with *Ramseys* Musketiers fell on their Dragoniers and skirmished with them, till they were forced to retire, and being darke, our Army having set out their horse and foote watches before them, they stoode the whole night in battaile, till it was day, and the enemy being gone in the night, the way thwart and deepe, some of his Cannon being left behinde, were buried, burning their Carriages with their waggons as they did breake, making them unprofitable for us.

We continued our march in the morning, minding to attrap them, so that by midday they having turned their Cannon on the Passe towards us, they forced our Army to stand without reach of their Cannon, trying on both hands of the Passe to win through, but in vaine, seeing there was no passage neere hand, but at that one place, where we did cannonade one against another for two dayes, till the enemy retired their Cannon within *Kempten*, and the rest of their Army unto *Bavier*, having crost both the *Leake* and the *Eler* againe.

The enemy being gone, we retired for want of victualls and forrage, the country being spoyled, we were forced to over-see the beleaguering of *Memming*, for that time passing by it towards *Mendelheim*, where we rested two dayes, and then marched on *Kauffbier*, where in two dayes we forced the Garrison to a composition, being content to march away without Armes, getting a Convoy to *Landsberg* on the *Leake*.

The weather being extremely cold under the snowy *Alpes*, we refreshed our Army three dayes at *Kauffbier*, and the fourth day marched towards the *Eler*, where the water being small, we made a bridge of our small Cannon with their Carriage, being placed two and two alongst the River at an equall distance of eight foote asunder, where we layd over Deales betwixt the Cannon, passing over our whole Infantry alongst the bridge; which being past and the Deales taken off, the horses spanned before the Cannon, led them away after the Army. And quartering that night in the fields, the next morning we beleaguered *Kempten*; Having battered hard for three dayes together with Cannon, at last the breach being made and the Towne almost brought to an Accord, having lost divers Souldiers and Officers before it, [II-176] hearing the Duke of *Bavier* his Army was crost the *Leake* againe at *Landsberg,* having gotten a strong supply, and being made certaine, they were to march unto the Duke of *Vertenbergs* Land, the Felt-marshall, after great paines taken, was forced to quit *Kempten*, and to march with the Army to be before them in *Vertenberg.*

The Dukes Army on their march by the way, tooke in a Castle besides *Koffbier*, where Captaine *Bruntfield* and Quarter-master *Sandelens* were taken Prisoners, and were sent to be kept at *Lindaw*. As also in their by-going, they tooke in *Koffbier*, and continued their march alongst the *Eler*, till they crossed with their Army at *Brandenburg*, we lying that night with our Army within a mile of them; The next day we strived who might passe the *Danube* first for going to *Vertenberg*, where it was our Fortune to get betwixt them and the passe, having line at *Monderkine*, while as they had crossed a mile below us on the River. Which when we understood by our intelligence of their being so neere, incontinent the Felt-marshall caused our Artillery and foote to march over in the night, so that before day our Army advanced towards the Passe, leaving the Dragoniers behinde us, to burne and to cast off the Bridge; But the Bridge was no sooner set on fire, but the enemies fore-troopes did drive our Dragoniers after us, they coming up full Squadrons of horse and foote, consisting of three Regiments of horse, Colonell *Daggenfield,* Colonell *Cratzstein* and Colonell *Monro* of *Fowles,* being three valorous Barons, who resolved amongst themselves, *Daggenfield* should charge the enemy first, which he manfully did, and then retired, who immediatly was rescued by Colonell *Monro,* having charged the enemy, retired, being shot through the right foote with a Musket Bullet, and Colonell *Cratzstein* rescuing him againe, charged the enemy the last time, keeping them up till the rest were safely retired, and then retiring himselfe at the Spurres, being last, was pittifully cut over the head with a *Poles-shable,* the enemy following them still, till they were repulsed by our Dragoniers. Neverthelesse they did get the most part of our baggage, and a great number of the horsmens led horses, servants and Coaches.

The Passe being narrow, and we having the advantage of them, being able to receive with our whole army, horse and foote, while as they could not advance unto us but by divisions, at most thirty in Front against a steepe hill, where our Army was standing ready in battaile, to receive them horse, foote and Artillery. Which they considering the great disadvantage they had to pursue us, drawing their Army also in battaile, they planted their ordinance against us, where once begun, we continued the whole day Cannonading one against another, where neither foote nor horse could joyne to skirmish. But the night comming on, the Felt-marshall directed his great Cannon away before, and leaving a strong Reare-guard of Horse and Dragoniers at the Passe, getting orders to remaine there till midnight, wee retired the rest of our Army unto *Vertenberg* land, having five miles to march, before day, our retreate being in the night, though safe, was confusedly made.

The Enemy finding at mid-night that we were gone, followed up our Rere-guard, skirmishing a little, in the end retired. And the whole Armie crossed the *Danube* againe, of intention to ruine all our Muster-places in [II-177] *Schwabland:* and in their way they tooke a *French* Marquesse prisoner on his Muster-place, and Colonell *Iohn Forbesse*, being both carelesse they were surprized in their Quarters, and were kept prisoners for three yeares.

The Army quartered themselves in *Schwabland* and *Tyroll* alongst the *Boden* Sea, setting Garrisons in Townes, as in *Costance, Pybrach, Vberling*, and divers more. During this time our Armie was well entertained and refreshed in good quarters in *Vertenbergland*, having secured them for that time from their Enemies, we attended the *Rhinegrave* his comming with a supply from *Elsas*: as also we did get a strong supply of Country Souldiers from the Duke of *Vertenberg*, with a great deale of Amunition, and a supply of Horse and Cannon. The *Rhinegrave* being come, finding our selves strong againe, we resolved to search the Enemy, for to make him retire unto *Baviere* againe, which we effectuated within ten dayes. After our up-breaking having crossed the *Danube* againe, the Enemy being retired, our Armie did settle themselves in a close Leaguer at *Donavert* for three moneths together, attending the conclusion of the meeting at *Hailbron*, resolving to enterprise no exployt or hostility against the Enemy, till such time as they should know, who should content them for their by-past service, as also whom they should serve in times coming.

During which time I went to *Hailbron* to solicite my Regiments affaires with the *Rex-chancellor*, and being there my Cosen Colonell *Monro* of *Fowles* dyed of his wounds at *Vlme*, where he was buried, and there after my brother was killed by the insolency of some *Dutch* Souldiers, which were of another Regiment, not his owne, who was also buried at *Bachrach* on the *Rhine*, and his Lievetenant Colonell *Iohn Monro* discharging himselfe of the Regiment, they were reduced at *Heidelberg* on the *Neckar* to two Companies under Captaine *Adam Gordon*, and Captaine *Nicholas Rosse*: which two Companies by the Chancellor his Orders I tooke from Palsgrave *Christian* his Armie, and marched with them to *Donavert*, where in *Iuly* 1633. I joyned them to my Regiment, of whom I tooke leave, leaving them under Command of my Lievetenant Colonell *Iohn Sinclaire*, who immediatly afterward was killed at *Newmark* in the upper *Palatinate*, and was transported to be buried at *Donavert*. My Major *William Stewart* succeeded to the Lievetenant Colonell's place, I being gone for a Recreut to my Regiment unto *Britaine*. From that time to the Battaile of *Nerling*, being a yeare, they were led by Lievetenant Colonell *Stewart*, brother to *Claire*.

And since I did not see the service, I continue to speake of the last yeares Expedition, till I be informed of those who did see the service, as I did the rest.

### The forty-two Observation; being the last.

In warres wisedome is of such worth, that the spirit and skill of one Commander is sometimes better than thousands of armed men. And nothing encourages an Enemy more than the foolishnesse and ignorance of their Enemies in warlike businesse: But on the contrary, he sleepes not sound that hath a wise enemy. For a wise Leader doth all things wisely, and it becomes not a Leader to use himselfe to vanitie, or to intemperate appetites, for, how [II-178] can he command others, that never pressed to command his owne inordinate desires? and brave Leaders of Armies and valourous Captaines should ever looke to their honour and renowne, more than unto riches or pleasure, spoyle or gaine, quitting the spoyle of their Enemies to their Souldiers, they ought to reserve the honour and fame for themselves: for, he wants not meanes but inriches his family, that hath wonne credit, and leaves it to his posteritie. Our contestation then should be for honour and credit, and not for unlawfull spoyle or gaine, esteeming more of magnanimitie, where ever it is found, than of riches attained unto; it may be, through feeblenesse and cowardice, lying in a Garrison, having never seen an enemy, or a man killed in the Fields; when other Cavaliers did shew their valour before their enemies, gaining more credit, though lesse wealth, which is of shortest continuance. For we are not worthy the name of Souldiers, if we glory (as many doe) more in gathering riches (that perish faster than they come) than we doe to get an immortall good name: for we must thinke still, that true honour doth consist onely in vertuous actions, which should make us more ambitious of credit, than of unlawfull gaine attained unto by avarice.

Here also we see great difference betwixt Leaders; For after we had gotten Feltmarshall *Horne* to leade us, we began by his valourous good Conduct to recover againe, what others had suffered the Enemy to possesse: and before he advanced, he made his friends sure behind him, as *Vlme*, and the Duke of *Vertenberg*, that alwayes in necessitie he might make a safe retreate, as a wise Generall ought to doe, looking what might happen. So then we see, that as Resolution is needfull, Counsell is not to be despised coming from a stedfast minde; for it is better to save our selves and others, than to be the Instruments to lose both. But when we have no time to resolve long in matters deplorable, then resolution should have place before long advisement.

Here also I did observe, that Generalls are forced to be ruled according to the occurrences in warre. For the Feltmarshall thinking to get advantage of the enemies Armie, he left the Garrison of *Memming* behinde him; For he knew well, if once he did beate or remove the enemies Armie, he could deale the easier with the Garrison in subduing of it. Moreover, we see here, how necessary Cannon are to a Generall to make a safe Retreate, getting any advantage of ground.

Likewise we see here the goodnesse of Intelligence, which is ever most necessary to an Armie, without which no good can be done or effectuated. Which made the Feltmarshall quit the gaining of *Kempten*, to save the Country of *Vertenberg* by his diligence and celeritie, in marching to gaine the passe before the *Imperialists*.

On the other part, sloath and neglective watch is to be condemned, while as through securitie Cavaliers suffer themselves be surprised, as became of the *French* Marquesse and Colonell *Iohn Forbesse*, being both taken in their beds, who ought rather, through good Intelligence, to have been on Horsebacke in the Fields before the Enemies comming.

Also the valour of those Cavaliers that made the Retreate good, is worthy praise, they having carried the tokens of their valour in their bodies, for the safetie of their Camerades. [II-179]

My Cosen *Fowles* being shot in the foot, retired to *Vlme* to be cured, who through the smart of his wound fell into a languishing Feaver: and as the wound was painfull to the body, so the sinfull body was painfull to the soule, the body being endangered except the wound were cured, and the soule was not found till the bodies sinne were healed, and both for six weekes did much smart the patient, while as his wounds were dressed. But though his bodily wound was incurable, yet his soule was cured by the punishment of his body. For, all the time, he like to a good Christian, made himselfe night and day familiar by prayers unto *God*, till he found reconciliation through Christ. So that his end was glorious, having long smarted under correction, though his life was painfull.

O happie wounds that killed the body, being they were the meanes to save the soule by bringing him to repentance! Let no friend then bedew their eyes for him that lived honourable as a Souldier, and dyed so happie as a good Christian. My brother Colonell *Monro* of *Obstell* being untimely and innocently taken out of this life, being a true Christain and a right Traveller. His life was his walke, Christ his way, and Heaven his home. And though during his life time his pilgrimage was painfull, yet the world knowes, his way did lead to perfection: for he leaned still on Christ, in whom he was made perfect. And therefore let no man doubt, that though his end was sudden, but his home was pleasing, being by his brethren after death made welcome to Heaven: and though he travelled hard, yet I perswade my selfe he walked right, and therefore was rewarded and made welcome through *Christ* his Redeemer.

Shortly after him, my dear Cosen and Lievetenant Colonell *Iohn Sinclaire* being killed at *Newmark*, he did leave me and all his acquaintance sorrowfull, especially those brave Heroicks (Duke *Barnard* of *Wymar* and Feltmarshall *Horne*) whom he truely followed and valourously obeyed till his last houre, having much worth he was much lamented, as being without gall or bitternesse.

Likewise at this time Lievetenant *Hector Monro*, being also a stout and a valorous Gentleman, died of a languishing Ague in *Vertenberg*, being much lamented by his Camerades and friends.

We reade in the *Roman* Story; That the memory of the dead was ever honourable and precious, so that the *Romans* wore mourning for their dead friends above a yeare. And the *Athenians* had an Order amongst them, that all those who dyed bravely in warres, their names should be inregistred and set in Chronicle: as also frequent mention was ordained to be made of their names, and of the exploits done by them, in the publique meetings. Moreover, it was ordained by them to celebrate dayes in their remembrance, wherein the youth should be exercised in divers exercises of body, called *Sepulchres*, whereby the people might be incouraged to follow Armes, for to gaine honour to themselves, to the end that disdaining death they might be encouraged to fight for the weale of the publique. And *Polemarche* the Leader for those youths, in time of their Exercise, was wont to sing Verses and Songs made in praise of those that dyed valourously serving the publique, and to incite others to the like magnanimitie. The youths did sing them also before the people. [II-180]

To conclude then this Observation; since God hath made me poore by the want of my Friends, I finde no other remedie, but to inrich my selfe in being content with his will; being perswaded, as they have gone the way before me, I must needs follow, and then others by my example must learne to be contented to want me: And though I leave them poore, they can be rich in God being content; For, we are neither rich nor poore by what we possesse, but by what we desire. [II-181] [II-182]

# AN
# ABRIDGEMENT
# OF EXERCISE FOR THE
# Younger Souldier his better Instruction.

Wherein first we shew a complete Company,
and then we make twelve Companies
to complete a Briggad.

To make a complete Company of marching men under Armes, there must be one hundred twenty six men in Armes, being reckoned to twenty-one Rots, each Rot being six men, of which two are esteemed as Leaders, being a Corporall a Rot-master or Leader, and an under Rot-master, being the last man of the six in field, which also is sometimes a Leader when on occasion his Leader is made to be under Rot-master; then in a Company you have twenty-one Leaders being six of them Corporalls, and fifteene Rot-masters, which to close the fields have allowed twenty-one men, called under Rot-masters: a Company thus consisting of twenty-one Rots, is divided in six Corporall-ships, whereof three being Pikemen, and three Rot, being eighteen men, makes a Corporall-ship of Pikes. Also there must be to complete this Company, three Corporall-ships of Musketiers, each Corporall-ship being counted twenty-foure men, being foure Rots, so that to make up the Company complete, there must be nine Rots of Pikemen, which have the Right hand, and twelve Rots of Musketiers on the left hand, being drawne in one Front, they make a complete body of a Company without Officers.

This Company hath allowed them for Officers, a Captaine, a Lievetenant, an Ensigne, two Sergeants, foure under-Beefeeles, being a Captaine of Armes, a furer of Colours, a furrier, and a Muster-schriver; as also to serve the Company, three Drummers are allowed, and fourteen passe-volants, with foure muster-youngs, are allowed to the Captaine, as free men unmustered, to make up the complete number of one hundred and fiftie, besides the Officers.

The Company being drawne up complete, the Pikes on the Right hand, and the Musketiers on the left hand, then the Ensigne or his furer with a [II-183] Drummer and three Rots of Pikes goes to bring out the Colours to be placed in Front of the Company, before they march; As also the Colours are to be conveyed againe, in this manner, at all lodging and dislodging.

The Company marching to Parad or watch, with complete Officers, the Captaine leads off six Rots of Musketiers, his Drumme beating betwixt the second and the third Ranke, then followes up after that division the oldest Sergeant, leading up the first five Rots of Pikemen, the Ensigne leading up the other Division of Pikes, his Furer furing his Colours after him, and the second Drummer beating betwixt the two Divisions, then the Lievetenant leads up the last Division of Musketiers, being six Rots also, and coming in equall Front with the rest, the Captaine making a signe for the Drumme beating, they order their Armes, the Captaine standing in Front on the Right hand, the Ensigne on his left, and the Lievetenant on the left hand of both, with a Sergeant on each Flancke, and the under-Beifells with halfe Pikes stand in the Reare of the Company.

Twelve Companies thus complete would make up three Squadrons, every Squadron of Pikes and Muskets being drawne up severall apart, after the former example of the lesse body, Pikes and Colours on the right hand, and the Musketiers on the left, which three Squadrons thus drawne up and complete would make a complete Briggad of Foote, to be divided as followes (*viz.*) eight Corporall-ships of Musketiers, being thirty-two Rots divided in foure Plottons, every Plotton being eight in front, led off by a Captaine, and every Division after him led up by a sufficient Officer, till at a haulte all were drawne in even front, after this Division should follow the thirty-six Rots of Pikes, being twelve Corporall-ships with their Colours, a Captaine leading off the first five Rots before the foure Colours should stirre, where betwixt the second and third Ranke of the first Division of Pikes, the Drummer should beate, then the Ensignes should leade off the other Division, their Furers with their Colours following them, till they drew up in even Front with the first Division of Pikes, which ought to be in one Front with the thirty-two Rots of Musketiers, that make the right wing of the Briggad, keeping their Armes orderly shouldered, till they were commanded otherwise, and their Sergeants ought to looke unto the Flanks, till such time that the whole Squadron of Pikes being thirty-six Rots were drawne up in even Front with the Musketiers, after this manner, the other Squadron of Pikes being thirty-six Rots also, which should make the Battaile of the Briggad, ought to march by Divisions, being led up in all respects and order, after the manner of the former Squadron of Pikes, till they were in even Front with the rest, then the other thirty-two Rots of Musketiers belonging to that Squadron, which are appointed to be the Battaile of the Briggad, ought to be led up as the first Division of Musketiers were in all points, which ought to draw up at a reasonable distance behinde their owne Squadron of Pikes, appointed for the Battaile of the Briggad: where their Sergeants on the Flancks ought to looke to their order, and not to suffer them to stirre their Armes, till they were commanded. And after them should march up the last Squadron of Pikes in all respects observing the order of the former Squadrons in their marching, till they were led up in equall Front with the other Pikes, and then march up the last thirty-two Rots of Musketiers in foure Divisions, observing the order of the former Divisions, till they were in equall Front with the whole Pikes, and then they making up the left wing [II-184] of the Briggad, the Colonel of the Briggad ordaines, the battell of Pikes being the middle Squadron of Pikes to advance in one body before the rest, till they are free of the Musketiers and Pikes, which makes the wings of the Briggad, and then the battaile of Pikes standing firme, the thirty-two Rot of Musketiers which were drawne up behinde them, march up, till they fill up the voide betwixt the Squadrons of pikes standing right behinde their owne pikes, that is the battaile of the Briggad, and then the Colonell making a signe to the Drummers, they beate all alike, till the Briggad in one instant doth order their Armes, all Officers of the Briggad standing on their stations, according as they were directed, then the superplus of the three Squadrons of musketiers being fourty-eight Rot, are drawne up, behinde the Briggad, having also Officers to command them, they attend orders, which they are to obey, being commanded out as pleaseth their Officers, either to guard Cannon or Baggage, or to be Convoyes to bring Amunition or victualls to the rest.

---

## A direction to Traine single Souldiers apart.

Having thus formed a Company, and showne the manner to draw up a complete Briggad, for the younger Officer his better understanding, being a Novice to this Discipline, I will set downe briefely the best way, suddenly to bring a young Company to be exercised, which in my opinion would be thus. First, since every Rot of the twenty-one, whereof the Company doth consist, hath allowed a Corporall or a Rot-master as the Leader of the other five, which Leader is supposed to be more expert in handling of Pike or Musket, then the other five, who make up the Rot, and the under Rot-master is supposed to be more expert in handling his Armes than the other foure, so that he is appointed as a second to the Leader, being sometimes a Leader himselfe, then after the company is made up, for the first weeke I would have every Corporall of the six, and the fifteene Rot-masters, being Leaders, with the helpe of their under Rot-masters, in a weekes time, to make the other foure as expert in handling of Pike and Musket, as themselves, or to be punished with Irons in case of their neglect, which the Sergeants should see done, as they should answer to the Lievetenant, the Lievetenant to the Captaine, and the Captaine to the Major, the Major to the Lievetenant Colonell, and they all to the Colonell, which they ought to practise in the fields apart, till the Rot were acquainted, every one with his Leader, from the first to the last: and while as the under Rot-master should turne Leader, then all the followers before, were then Leaders also, and then the Rot being apart, the middle man of the Rot should be taught to double to the Front, till their deepe were three, that was six before, and in falling off againe, the middle man should turne to the contrary side or hand he came up upon, carrying their Armes handsomly free from others [II-185] without making noise in their retiring to their former station, and orders.

Likewise I would have the Corporall, Rot-master or Leader, being a Musketier, having his Rot once expert, in handling severally the Musket well, then to discharge their Muskets in winning ground, advancing to an enemy, the Leader having discharged his musket, standing still to blow his panne and prime againe, having cast off his loose powder, then to cast about his Musket to his left side, drawing backe with his Musket his left foote and hand, till the mouth of the musket come right to his hand, to charge againe in the same place, standing firme till his follower marched by him on his right hand, standing at the same distance before him, that he stood behinde, and then to give fire, blowing his pan, priming, casting off and retiring his musket with his left hand and foote, and to charge againe, as is said, and so forth, one after another, discharging at a like distance, till at last the Rot-master should be under-rot, and the under-rot Leader, and then his follower marching up by him, while as he is charging, giving fire on the enemy, and having discharged, standing still also charging, till in th'end, the Rot-master come to be Leader againe, and so forth, still advancing *per vices*, till the enemy turne backe, or that they come to push of Pike, and Buts of Muskets. Thus having exercised the Rots apart for a weeke or two, doubtlesse they will become expert Souldiers in using their Armes, when they are joyned in a strong body, lesse or more. The Pike men would be exercised also by Rots apart, in the severall Postures thereof, till they were acquainted also with their Leaders, and were made expert in using their Pikes aright, till thereafter the whole body of Pikes might be exercised apart, with great ease to their Officers; The Musketiers being drawne in a body, being sixteene or thirty-two men in Front, being but six Rancks deep, the first Rancke discharging at once, casting about their muskets and charging all alike, the second Rancke marches through every follower, going by on the right hand of his Leader, standing before him at the distance they were behinde, and then being firme, they give fire all alike on their enemies, blowing, priming, casting about and charging all alike where they stand, till *per vices* the whole Ranckes have discharged, and so forth *ut antea*, successively advancing and giving fire, till the enemy turne backe, or that they come to push of Pike, and being thus well exercised in advancing to the enemy, and winning ground, if through necessity they be forced to retire from an enemy, losing ground, they must also keepe their faces to their enemies, the Reare being still in fire, and the last Rancke having given fire, they march through the Rancks till they were last are first comming off and so *per vices*, till they have made a safe retreate, the Reare which is ever the Front, coming from an enemy is in fire. [II-186]

## The manner to exercise a body of Musketiers.

To exercise a Squadron of Musketiers, how strong soever they be, the number of Rancks being no deeper than six, the files being even may be so many as your voice can extend to, ever observing that your Command be given in the Front, otherwise may breede disorder, and before you begin to command, you would enter first with a Prologue, as good Orators commonly doe, to reconciliat their hearers attendance: even so you ought with an exhortation of attendance entreate, but by way of command, your Souldiers not to be gazing in time of their exercise, but with stedfastnesse to settle their mindes on their exercise, that they may the better observe and obey the words of command; and above all things, you are to command them to keepe silence, not babling one to another, neither in their motions, to suffer their Armes to rattle one against another, always to take heede to their Leaders, that goe before them, and to follow them orderly without disturbance, keeping and observing their due distance either of Ranckes or Files: which may be easily done, if they but duely follow their Leaders, and have an eye on their right and left fellow Camerades, for keeping their Ranckes even in a like Front. Likewise they are to observe when they are commanded to turne any where, whether it be by Rancks or Files, that their faces may by turned to the hand they are commanded to, before they sturre to march, and then to march alike, and when ever they double Rancks or Files, or counter-march, they must ever observe to retire to the contrary hand, they were commanded to double on, if they doubled to the right, when they fall off they retire turning to the left hand, *et contra*, for avoiding of disorder or hinderance, that their Armes would make, if they retired to the same hand they were commanded to double or march to; In their counter-marches it is also requisit in time of exercise, that neither Officer nor Souldier doe presume to command, direct, or finde fault with the errour, but he that commands in chiefe, whether he be superiour or inferiour Officer for the time, since it is said, when many speake few heare; Therefore he must command alone, suffering no rivall, for avoiding of disorder. Order therefore of distance being a chiefe point observed in exercising is threefold, to wit, Open order of Rancks or Files is six foote of distance, being betwixt Rancks and Files both alike, only requisit to be observed in mustering, or while as they stand in danger of Cannon, not being in battaile, where in battaile order the distance to be observed betwixt Rancks or Files should be three foote, where Elbow to Elbow of the side Camerades may joyne, where in the open order aforesaid, hand to hand can but joyne. But in close order used most in conversion, or wheeling is shoulder to shoulder, and foote to foote, firme keeping themselves together, for feare to be put asunder by the force of their enemies, and then to disorder, which is ever to be looked unto, chiefely before an enemy. Your speech thus ended, for your generall directions, you begin againe to command silence, and to take heed what is commanded to be done, saying. Height [II-187] your Musketiers, dress your Rancks and files, to your open order of six foote, and take heede.

> *To the right hand turne,*
>         *as you were.*
> *To the left hand turne,*
>         *as you were.*
> *To the right hand about turne,*
>         *as you were.*
> *To the left hand about turne,*
>         *as you were.*
> *To the right hand double your Rancks,*
>         *as you were.*
> *To the left hand double your Rancks,*
>         *as you were.*

The even Rancks or Files double ever unto the odde, and the fourth Rancke is the middle Rancke of six.

> *To the right hand double your Files,*
>         *as you were.*
> *To the left hand double your Files,*
>         *as you were.*
> *Middle-men or fourth Rancke to the right hand double your Front,*
>         *To the left hand retire as you were.*
> *Middle-men to the left hand double your Front,*
>         *To the right hand as you were.*

*Nota.* The sixth Rancke is called bringers up or reare, or under Rotmasters.

> *Bringers up to the right hand double your Front,*
>         *To the left hand as you were.*
> *Bringers up to the left hand double your Front,*
>         *To the right hand as you were.*

All that doubled, turne first about, and then they retire falling behinde those were their Leaders, before in the same place or distance. This doubling of the bringers up or of middle-men, is very requisit in giving a generall *salve* of Musket, and as it is to be observed in rancks, that the best men are placed in front, reare and middle, even so in files, every Corporal-ship being foure files of Musketiers, the likeliest are put ever in the right and left files of the foure, being also of best experience.

The doubling of rancks being done, and all remitted in good order, and to their first distance of open order, you are to command, and exercise Souldiers in three severall wayes of counter-marching, requisit in some respects, but in my opinion to be used but seldome, except it be in necessity in such parts, as the ground will not permit otherwise, therefore to avoide disorder, Souldiers ought not to be ignorant of any of the three sorts of counter-marching. [II-188]

First having commanded the Souldiers to dress their rancks and files, and to carry their Muskets handsomly keeping silence, say.

> *To the right hand the counter-march without noise or losing of ground.*
> *To the left hand retire againe to the former ground.*

Then command againe to dresse rancks and files, and to right their Armes keeping silence, taking heede to what is to be commanded, and say.

> *To the right hand turne.*

Then the Flancke before being now the Front command,

> *To the right hand counter-march and lose no ground.*
> *To the left hand as you were.*

This is used ordinarily to change one wing of Battaile in place of the other then that the Front may be as it was first before they Countermarcht.

> *To the left hand turne, dresse your Rankes and Files, and be silent.*

Another sort of Countermarch is the *Slavonian* countermarch, where you lose ground, the Front being changed also: then you command the first Ranke to turne about to the right hand, then you say to the rest,

> *Countermarch, and through to your former distance after your*
> *Leaders.*

Then say, *Leaders as you were*; and to the rest:

> *To the left hand countermarch as you were to your first ground.*

The third sort of countermarch I esteeme most of to be practised, being rather a conversion very requisit to be well knowne to all Souldiers in all Armies, chiefly to be used before an enemy: for as it is most sudden; so in my opinion, it breeds least disorder and disturbance, the Souldiers once used to it of themselves they will willingly doe it on any occasion, the body being before in open order or Battaile order, say. Close the Ranks and Files to your closse order, without encumbering one of another, every man following right his owne Leader, keeping closse to his side man, then say. To the right hand the quarter turne halfe or whole, as the occasion and the ground doth permit, and then say. Dresse your Armes, and follow your Leaders, and open againe to your Battaile order.

Lastly, the body of your Musketiers exercised perfectly after this manner, for the better bringing of them in exercise and breath, that in case any disorder may happen amongst them, they may the better afterward be acquainted one with another, say to your open order of six foote distances. Open both Rankes and Files, and set downe your Armes handsomely where you stand, then command your Sargeant to goe an hundred paces from the [II-189] body of your Musketiers, and sticke in his Holbert in the ground, and then admonish your Souldiers, that at the tucke of your Drumme they runne from their Armes about the Holbert, and to stay there till the Drumme recall them againe to their Armes, which being done, it makes the Souldiers able in breath to know one anothers place, in case they should be brought at any time in disorder, to recover themselves the better. Thus much for the training of Souldiers in changing of place, as you will have them, without giving of fire.

When you have gotten your Souldiers thus experimented in their motions, then are you to acquaint them with shot in giving of fire, to make them fix against their enemies, which is easily done, having once apart and singularly used their Muskets, after the order of the severall postures, belonging thereto, as was commanded their inferiour Officers and Leaders to teach them before they were exercised. Therefore before you come to the particular formes of giving fire, you shall first give some generall directious to be observed by all, for avoiding the hurting of themselves, or of their Camerades as also how they can best offend their enemies; and to this effect, you shall admonish in love all brave Musketiers, first to have their Muskets cleere and hansome, and above all fix in the worke, especially every Souldier would be well knowne with his owne Musket and cocke, to cocke aright, then to hold the mouth or Cannon of his Musket ever high up, either being on his shoulder, or in priming or guarding of his panne, but in giving fire, never higher or lower than levell with the enemies middle; then your Musketiers being in readinesse, your Muskets charged, they may be commanded to give fire in skirmish, disbandoned as their Officers doe direct them to advance or retire, as the occasion offers; also to give fire by Ranckes, Files, Divisions, or in *Salves*, as the Officer pleaseth to command, to the effect that they may be fixed *Omni mode*, though in my opinion, one way is the best, yet there are severall wayes of giving fire in advancing to an enemy as retiring from an enemy, or in standing firme before an enemy, either by Rancks, or by Files made to Rancks.

Advancing to an enemy not being disbandoned, but in one bodie they give fire by Rancks to Rancks, having made readie alike, they advance ten paces before the bodie, being led up by an Officer that stands in even Front with them, the Cannon or mouth of their Muskets of both Rancks being past his bodie. The second Rancke being close to the backe of the foremost both gives fire alike, priming and casting about their Muskets they charge againe where they stand, till the other two Rancks advance before them and give fire after the same manner, till the whole Troope hath discharged and so to beginne againe as before, after the order of the through-countermarch; ever advancing to an enemie, never turning backe without death or victorie. And this is the forme that I esteeme to be the best: as for the rest, they are not to be much used; but this order can be used winning ground, advancing and losing ground in a Retreate. When you would command the body of your Musketiers to give fire in a *Salve*, as is ordinarie in Battell, before an enemy joyne, or against Horsemen; then you command the bringers up or Reare to double the Front to the right hand, and to make readie, having the match cocked and their pannes well guarded, having closed the three Rancks, though not the Files, the Officers standing in equall Front with the foremost Rancke, betwixt two Divisions, he commands [II-190] to give fire, one *Salve*, two or three, and having charged againe, and shouldered their Armes, they retire to the left hand againe, every man falling behinde his owne Leader.

Being on retiring from the enemie, the whole bodie having made readie, as they march off in order, a qualified Officer being in the *Reare*, and qualified Officers in the *Van* to order them that fall up, the last two Rancks in the *Reare* turne faces about, and the whole body with them, and the two Rancks having given fire, they march through the body to the *Van*, and order themselves as they were before, and so successively the whole bodie gives fire ever by two Rancks, and falls off till such time as they have made their Retreate sure. Thus much of fire-giving by Rancks on two or three, as you please, at once and no more.

Now a little for the exercising of the Squadron of Pikes in generall; for the generall motion certaine directions are to be observed concerning Pikes, that the Souldiers keepe their Pikes cleane and cleere, and never to be suffered to cut off the lengths of their Pikes, as often is seene upon marches, being very uncomely to see a Squadron of Pikes not of one length; likewise in all motions with the Pike, the hand and foote ought to goe alike, and the Souldier would be expert in giving the right pousse with the Pike backwards and forwards. Your Squadron of Pikes as they ought to march with the Drumme; so they ought to obey the Drumme beating a Troope, a Charge, a Call, a Retreate. As also to traile their Pikes, to make reverence with the Pike being shouldred: and your Squadron of Pikes being but six deepe in Rancke, your Files may be so many, as can well heare your voyce in Command, providing there be no odde File; and thus well ordered at their open order of six foote distance, command to mount their Pikes, then calling for a Drumme beside you, let him beate a march, then they are to shoulder their Pikes, flat or slaunt carried, and then to march a little, let your Drumme againe beate a Troope, then they mount their Pikes and troope away fast or slow, as your passe leades them stopping, or advancing as you doe, then let your Drumme beate a Charge, then they charge their Pikes and advance fast or slow, as you lead them, and retire also backwards, their Pikes charged as you will have them, then troope againe, and they mount their Pikes, march and shoulder; and haulting, let the Drumme beate againe, and they order their Pikes on the ground as first, being at their distance, and trooping againe they mount their Pikes, so that you can command them to Battell order or closse order, for Wheeling or Counter-marching at your owne pleasure.

In repayring to their Colours, or comming from watch, they should ever walke with their Pikes mounted, as also they may use this posture on Centrie; and your Pikes mounted and at your open order, you can use all doublings that your Musketiers used, as also to present, to Front, Reare, right or left hand, the curiositie of the turnes to the right or the left hand in *Van* or *Reare*, the Pike being shouldred, you can also teach them, as you will, though not much to be used in exercise: and the Pikes thus well exercised having seene frequent danger, can doe good service against Horsemen and against foote to foote, either in battell entering a Towne or breach, or retiring, or advancing to choake an enemie, on walls within [II-191] Townes or Forts they are very commodious for service, providing they resolve to fight well and to abide by their Officers, and, in my opinion, being well led they may beate Musketiers accidently off the Feild, and being well lined with shot they are a safeguard against Horsemen, having the least advantage of ground. Thus much in briefe for the use of the Pike, the most honourable of all weapons, and my choice in day of battell, and leaping a storme or entering a breach with a light brest-plate and a good head-piece, being seconded with good fellowes, I would choose a good half-Pike to enter with. [II-192]

# Certaine
# Observations
# Worthy the Yovnger
# Officer his consideration, being short and

practicall for his Highnesse
speciall use.

## I.

This life is a Comedy or a Play, wherein ever one doth his part, we should presse to passe it over with moderate affections, that the end be not cruell or dolefull, as in Tragedies, but full of mirth like a Comedy.

## II.

Vnto the Victor the life is sweete and happy, but to those that are overcome, nothing is more bitter, then to put their hopes in their Enemies mercy.

## III.

As unto Champions of old lots gave fellowes, and not election, with whom they should fight: so every one of us hath destines in our times, where with to strive.

## IIII.

As he who goeth a journy doth reckon the miles: so he that hath entred the way of this life, shall not determine of his yeares. For as from the spring flow the Rivers, from the roote the branch: so from the first education cometh the rest of mans life: And if thou wouldst live truely, thou must presse to profit thy country, to defend the Common-wealth, and to live well without liberty: thou must preferre death before ignominious shame, [II-193] or slavery. For as this life is Rosie, so it hath flowers mixed with thornes, the one to be plucked up, the other to be eschewed so farre as we may.

## V.

It is a part of victory to trouble the enemy before we fight, and as it is laudable to overcome an enemy, it is no lesse praise worthy to have pitty on the miserable. For as courage doth merit infinite glory, so the love of all, and the good will of all merits mercy and meekenesse.

## VI.

The feeble and the weake minded man is ever pridfull in prosperity: for he thinkes his vertues are such, as can maintaine the Fortunes which he hath gotten, and thinks still he is able to attaine and acquire more and more: but when the tempest of adversity doth arise, then is he so farre afraid, that he becomes voide of all hopes; and this oftentimes is the cause of the suddaine change of his fortunes.

## VII.

Nothing doth diminish more the publishing of praise, then when one continually casteth up his owne successe in actions of warre, and oftimes striving to get abundance of honour; men show their riches, of swelling pride; for disdaining his former friends, he misknowes his acquaintance, pressing to goe before, he is greevous or displeasing to all his familiars. Our care then should be, to want this arrogancy, ostentation or pride, and pray for humility, being more acceptable unto God then detestable pride, which is an unprofitable evill, a secret poyson, a hidden pest, the ingenier of deceipt, the mother of hypocrisie, the parent of envy, the beginner of vice, the moth of holinesse, the blinder of hearts, breeding sicknesse out of remedies, and begetting langour out of medicine.

## VIII.

There is ever some fatality incident unto those that desire vaine-glory or ostentation: and those that are proud rejecting the prayers of the humble with disdaine, they often incurre the indignation of God, and fall oft into calamity, except they take heede unto themselves.

## IX.

These spirits are bentest on ambition that are of great and sharpe wits, and of high minds, being ready to thinke on great matters, and to undertake them: but Heroicke spirits on the contrary, considering the worthy acts of others, are stirr'd up unto vertue, while as others with glory of succession becoming more insolent and negligent, make Tragicall ends, being oppressed with small things, they die unworthily. [II-194]

## X.

The duty of a good man, is to reserve himselfe for the well and use of his country and friends, being wary lest he should be lost rashly (as my deere and only Brother was) who did not neglect his duty, neither in word nor deede, but to his death served God in his calling, though his death was sudden, being the condition of mortall men, that are still subject unto such changes, that oftimes in their greatest prosperity comes adversity, and from their adversity their prosperity againe, God hiding the cause of both from us. It were better then to prevent a wound, then out of time to seeke remedy: for in the middest of evill is not the time to be merry, and those hurts are most, which we receive unlooked for. Therefore it were much better to prevent, then to suffer, and it were much better to enter in danger being guarded, then out of time to grow pale. Vaine then are the counsells of mortall men, when we see no humane happinesse to be permanent, since the Roots are taken up before they come to maturity, except they be confirmed by the divine providence; And chiefely in warres, as being most uncertaine, as we see by the untimely death spoken of; but no man can forbid Gods decree. Neverthelesse men that through age, and long experience have obtained wisdome, before they enter in a businesse, they should looke unto the event, and unto that, which by all expectation may happen: for it is ever the greatest wisdome to use the present time best; we ought then on all occasions we are employed on, to strengthen our minds with vertue, that we may be safe overcoming all incumbrances, that once we have condemned in the judgment seate of wisdome, which alwayes is accompanied with praise and glory, when we not only equall our selves with those that excelled in vertue, but also presse to goe before them.

## XI.

Wisdome goeth before all other things in esteeme, as the most pretious Iewell we can possesse, being spread she is gathered, given away shee returneth, being published groweth greater; by her the Noble treasure of conscience is spread unto the secrets of the minde, the fruit of inward joy by her is attained unto: this is the Sunne wherewith the light of the minde doth shew it selfe and appeare in darknesse, being the eye of the heart, the delightfull Paradise of the soule, the Heaven upon Earth immortall, changing man into God, through knowledge, deifying him, this fellow is invincible against all strokes, he stirres not a foote for poverty, griefe, ignominy, paine, he is afraid of nothing, and is ever full of joy, merry, pleasant and untouched, living like a God. Who desireth then to be wise and partake of this goodnesse that is so excellent, they must not use themselves to vanity, but they must thinke on that which is most profitable for them, being not forbidden to use bodily exercise moderatly: they may become wise, first by thinking what is past, and in whose time of their Predecessours things were best governed. Secondly, he must diligently observe the good to come, what can be profitable for him and what not, that he may eschew the evill to come, and embrace the good. Thirdly, he should observe the good customes and lawes past, being provident, mindfull, and understand- [II-195] ing, reasonable, diligent, tractable, expert and cunning; and he must consider foure good things; What is his aime; The way and manner he aimes at; The person aiming; And those he governes.

## XII.

A Souldier without letters is like a ship without a Rudder, or like a bird without feathers; but having letters, he findes wherewith he can be made wiser, finding out by letters, courage, and many other great helpes to governe and direct those aright, whom he commands: neither is that fortune in the world to be had, where out of letters his knowledge may not be bettered, if he be but painfull, for being lettered he can strictly keepe under the cruell, and defend lawes without terrour, temperating them to his minde, the meeke also he can civilly admonish, and the deceitfull he can wisely goe about, and the simple he can handle with lenity, shewing his prudency in all his actions, foreseeing all dangers which may happen. Therefore we see, that science to a man of warre is a brave Mistresse, teaching him to doe all things as they did in old times.

## XIII.

It is a hard matter when the diligent, and industrious Souldier is disappointed of his hire, and that he is rewarded with injury who did merit better. This of all evills is most insufferable, that he, who deserveth a reward, should be frustrate of his hopes: for reward is due unto valiant Captaines and Souldiers that were instruments in chiefe of victory, glory and honour: as Sir *Iames Ramsey* and Sir *Iohn Hamilton* were, in forcing the passage to the Castle of *Vertzberg*, who neverthelesse were frustrate of reward, and therefore I cannot but allow of the resolution of Sir *Iohn Hamilton* being no Souldier of Fortune, that tooke his Passe of the *Sweden* for being frustrate of the reward of his vertue, seeing those disdained that did merit best. Where we see that a gentle heart, being crossed contrary to reason, doth presently resent his wrongs, pointing out to the world, that he is not the man that can suffer or swallow a seene injury done to him and his Nation.

## XIIII.

It is better to feare evill, preparing our selves for danger, then through too much security, and contempt of the enemy to suffer our selves to be overcome; for it is dangerous to have to doe with a desperate body, seeing necessity maketh those that are fearefull to become stout, and those who feare no dangers are easily lost, as witnesseth the death of the Invincible King of *Sweden*: and those dangers ought to be eschewed, from whence ariseth greatest evill; and experience hath taught us, that nothing is more dangerous in warres, then to fight great battailes on unequall termes, as witnesseth the dolefull battaile fought at *Nerling* in *August* 1634. After which losse those, that should have fought for their country, their wives and children, did prove feeble cowards (*viz.*) the *German* Princes, *Saxon, Brandeburg, Lunenburg*, with the rest of the Gentrie, giving occasion to others; that came to helpe them, for to leave them. It is no wonder then, they be plagued them- [II-196] selves wishing helpe another time, when justly they cannot have it, having rewarded their helpers so ill as they have done, and through their covetousnesse and niggardly sparing bin the cause and instruments of their owne overthrowes, and of the losse of the cause, being I feare the fore-runners of their Successours punishment, which I wish may not happen.

## XV.

Before the fall of Kingdomes arise dissensions, that overthrow the confederates more than their enemies, as it happened here in our late warres of *Germanie*, after the death of his Majestie of *Sweden*, the *Dutch* Princes, especially *Saxon*, slighting his Excellencie the Rex-chancellour of *Sweden* and his *Directorium* as Supreame, calling him disdainfully a Pedant, or a Penman. So that wee see that dissension, or discord amongst the Superiours was the first cause of the suddaine losse of *Nerling*. Next wee see that the Countrie was destroyed, not onely for their sinnes, but also for not punishing of sinne. For after his Majesties death, what punishment was to be seene in our Armie? none at all: when our owne horsemen plundered their friends, not being punished, they began to intercept Letters, and to robbe the common Poste, and to hinder the Countries correspondencie, and common traffique: which being overseene, and winked at by our Generalls, they begun then to plunder the Chancelours owne waggons, abusing his servants, and taking his baggage: thereafter the strongest amongst themselves set the weakest party to foote, taking away their horses, till at last the whole Armie refused to obey the *Director* and his *Concilium formatum*, lying idle for three moneths in *Donavert* Leaguer, suffering the enemie to over-runne the Countrie, and all because that the Officers alleadg'd after his Majesties death, that the Scriveners who followed the Chancelour, were in better esteeme, than the Cavaliers, that had done notable good service unto his Majestie: so that, through this jealousie, the Armie came in disorder, being the first change, and the rest, piece and piece did follow, till at last the whole Armie was lost, through the number of wrongs that went before, in the end custome and use of wrongs infected the nature it selfe, and the lacke, or want of punishment, and the libertie and freedome, which was given to offend, at last the ruine of families, that were famous did follow, for not punishing of sinne. We see then, when a potent King, and Heroique, as *Gustavus* was in the time hee did live, all things florished in a good order, but he once gone, the Comon-wealth was punished for their former sinnes committed in time of their plentie, and peace; when they had their heaven upon earth, as other Nations have now, who ought to looke unto themselves in time, lest that the Lord raise not up an other Heroique to make them to be punished, as other Nations have bin, to the eversion of great Cities, as *Magdeburg*, and divers others: for when the publique burthens doe grow, then Governements doe change, as was seene here; for lawes being cast away, and discipline put in fetters; then suddenly did follow change, and great ruine, after the Kings death of worthy memorie. [II-197]

### XVI.

Nothing loses more, as we see, the common cause, than the want of authoritie in one person, as was formerly said of the *Saxons* jealousie over the Rex-chancelors Governement. Also the same fault was seene in the Armie under Commanders: as at *Nerling*, betwixt Supreme Officers, as also betwixt their inferiours: who for want of one Supreme Commander, as *Gustavus* was, they could not agree among themselves. Likewise the dissension and jealousie betwixt Duke *Barnard*, and the *Rhinegrave* helpes nothing to the futherance of the good cause, being both brave Commanders: though seldome seene command in one place, and it is to be pitied, how the *Rhinegrave* after the losse of *Nerling*, not being bastant against the enemie, was forced to swimme the *Rhine* on horse-backe, and dyed soone thereafter; who was a renowned, valourous Cavalier, as ever I was acquainted with of the *Dutch* Nation, serving in those warres; all these mischiefes were caused through the want of one Supreme Leader to conduct them, as the enemie had. Which should teach all men to submit themselves to authoritie, lest by doing otherwise they procure their owne ruine.

### XVII.

To repent a thing, when it is done, is most foolish, which might have beene prevented with counsell: for none that doe repent counsell can be esteemed wise. Therefore a Counsellour should bee very faithfull, never counselling his friend for his owne ayme, lest he that is counselled perceive not his drift, and then be deceived. But counsell is taken from necessitie, and follow'd. And a good Commander deserves prayse as well for his wisedome, as for his valour: But evill counsell is a plague or judgement from the Lord; yet those counsells are ever safest, that come from him that will be partaker both of the danger, and of the counsell. Therefore it is not good rashly to use the counsell of a Traitor, nor of an enemie: but wee should rather examine, and shift counsells, and not trust easily, and bee deceived. Counsell then we see is the chiefe ground to governe matters well, being secret, true and free, without flatterie, or respect of persons, just and holy, casting aside all private gaines, and utilitie, foreseing the publique weale; and if thou wouldest be truly counselled, thou must take heed to those Caveats: first that the speech be wholesome, and unreproveable; his counsell profitable, his life honest, his sentence pleasant, not wavering like a childe, or unconstant, neither ought you aske many what you would doe, but shew it to a few and trustie friends, which are rare to be found: and when thy neere friends cannot resolve thee, flee to those for their counsells, whose daily experience is approved for their wisedome in their owne affaires, and then you shall doe well.

## XVIII.

Militarie discipline is lost, when the crueltie and avarice of Officers is extended in detaining of Souldiers meanes; and Supreme Officers neglecting to content Cavaliers, make the whole Armie turne rebellious, as at *Donavert*, The *Concilium formatum* and their Treasurer, having not given the Armie one [II-198] moneths meanes complet of the whole contribution they had collected the yeere after his Majesties death, but payed themselves, and their Secretaries dulie, which raised great envie against them, the Armie having mutined for want of pay: which made them afterward want both the contribution and the Country, through misgovernement of their *Consilium*.

## XIX.

It is in vaine for a Cavalier to feare any thing but God, and the offence of his Supreme Officer; for being honest, modesty hindering his flight makes him victorious in middest of danger, and of his enemies: as chanced me and my Collegues at *Rugenwoulde* in *Pomeren*, having escaped danger by Sea, were come to Land in danger of our enemies, but the Lord and the dutie we ought our Maister, made us abide the danger of our enemies, which the Lord turned to our best, giving us victorie and freedome. Shall I then distrust this God, having had this time, and divers times before, great experience of his mercies? God forbid. No, I will still trust in him, doe to mee what he will; for I know his mercies goe beyond all his workes, and they endure for ever.

## XX.

A man unjustly hurt, as many were, that served the *Sweden*, once escaped, their Commanders are now their greatest enemies; for the memorie of injuries received, is ever more recent in the Actor, than in the patient: and is also more difficult to be reconciled: as oft times experience doth prove. Therefore I would advise my friend not to suffer injurie if he can, & if injurie be done him, not to passe it over for flatterie, lest in accepting of a slight satisfaction, he should injure himselfe more, than the other did. But by the contrary, I would advise him timely to repaire himselfe, that he may preserve the former dignity. Likewise the greater our injuries received are, & the greater they commove us, the more ought our wit to moderate our revenge; seeing to moderate our selves, and to overcome our desires, is the greatest prayse wee can have, being revenged. Yet injuries doe ever sticke neerer unto us, then the remembrance of benefits received: for in remembring of benefits, wee ascribe the good to our owne merits, flattering our selves; but on the contrary, remembring our injuries received, we call them to minde a great deale more cruelly, than they were done without moderation. I must then advise my friend, that he not only prevent the deede of his enemy, but also his counsells, lest they bring detriment upon him: for he ought to be alike with the offer of an injury being a Cavalier, and with the intention, as if the deede had followed. The offering then of a stroke may be repaired with a sword, the giving of a lie is repaired with a blow, words not tending to disgrace are repaired with words againe, the losse of goods is restored by restitution, with circumstances convenient, and to quarrell for a light occasion is want of understanding, especially with thy betters in esteeme. For there should be had respect of persons, of times, and of circumstances observed, before a man should quarrell; and having once quarrelled, I would advise my friend not to be put backe without honourable satisfaction, or at least great hazard, not coming unto the fields for the first bout, or bloud, and then to returne with [II-199] disgrace unthought of by thy selfe, though much by others, as I have knowne Cavaliers doe.

## XXI.

In Battaile fighting with the enemy, at the first be very slow against a fierce enemie, that the enemy being weary your strength fresh and a little succours joyned unto you, the enemy is soone beaten, and having once begun warre, follow it with sword, fire, spoile, slaughter, till the streets be full; a Rover should never be a Rewer, so long as his hands are unto it, and you should never give time to the enemy to joyne forces, but pursue them ever as they come, never neglecting an enemy, though he be weake, but still keepe a good reserve by your selfe, and pursue by parties supplying your owne, as they neede, and timely, and without doubt you shall gaine honour and credit.

## XXII.

Trust never thy selfe rashly to a reconciled enemy, without pledges first had, for keeping good peace; and being desirous to possesse any thing belonging to thy enemy, thou hast neede to use rather dilgence, then delay, that thou mayest catch them unawares, as *Gustavus* did *Frankfurt* on the *Oder*. And nothing is more to be suspected, then a neere enemy, which *Lansberg* did finde after the taking of *Franckfurt*, and nothing is more cruell then a Barbarous enemy, as was found by our Regiment at *New-brandenburg*, and thereafter by our Camerades at *Magdeburg*.

## XXIII.

Warres may be taken on by the counsell of sluggards, but they must be sustained with the labour, and danger of the most valiant, as was well seene after *Gustavus* the invincibles death: It was not the Princes confederats, or their *Consilium*, was able to doe the turne, whose reward to Cavaliers was but paper. As their reward was naught, so their *Consilium* turned to nothing, and which was worse, to contempt, except the Director alone, who as yet hath kept life in the cause, though without their means or assistance: and which is more honourable for him, he maintaines the warre against them, who unworthily have broken their oathes and fidelity, having turned their Armes against those who formerly had releeved them, to their perpetuall disgrace, shame and ignominy, having scorned men, that had merited well in offering to reward them with paper, their punishment is that for their infamy, their names shall rot in oblivion. *Nam ubi orta est culpa, ibi poena consistit.*

## XXIIII.

All things here being but humane, are unstable and unconstant, so that there is nothing sure, except true piety; and we see our lives bring many things forth contrary to our expectation, so that the condition of our humane life containes the first, and the last day. For it is much to be look't un [II-200] to, with what lucke we did begin, and with what we ended. We judge him then happy, who did receive the light happily, and happened to restore it againe pleasantly, which that we may doe, I humbly crave of God Almighty.

---

*A short observation of Intelligence, necessary for a Commander.*

Conshaft or Intelligence in an Army is so necessary, that without it no direction can be given with assurance, without it we cannot discerne betwixt our friends and our enemies, who are with us, or against us, which is the first point a Commander hath to know; comming in an enemies country: Next he ought to know the strength of his enemies Army, foote and horse, that he may the better dispose of his owne: he ought also to know how his enemy is quartred in Garrison, Leaguer, Field or Dorpe, and what watch they keepe in all those parts: And how farre their horsemen doe lie from their foote, and how guarded. To have certainty of all his he must have some secret friend with the enemy, for giving him secret intelligence, and that he should not trust too much in one, he must have a subtill Boore, now and then frequenting without suspision amongst them, as ordinarily his Majesty of worthy memory had: likewise it were needfull that they deboished some Secretary on their side, for getting the Lists of their Strengths, Officers and Souldiers, as also for their qualities, that he might the better dispose himselfe against them, in directing private parties on the wayes they travell to get prisoners, and failing thereof to fall on their watch or within their quarters.

He ought also on all marches to have a knowne Boore with him, to acquaint him with all passes or straights, on which the enemy can repare to him, or from him, conferring his land mappe with the Boores intelligence, which betime would enable him in knowing all the Passes.

Likewise he ought to have intelligence out of the enemies Leaguer, how they were provided in victualls, Amunition or forrage, and of their healths, if there were any infections amongst them, or what sport or recreation they used without their quarters, and what streetes they goe on, and how they are conveyed, striving still to get prisoners, for the better intelligence how their Amunition is kept, and with what Guards, that if it were possible, accidentall fire might be set to it, and for getting this good of intelligence, the chiefe Officers would be liberall to those whom they put in trust, seeing without it little good service can be effected, and the getting of it is the safety of many Cavaliers and their credits.

Therefore whether he be defender or pursuer, intelligence gives him a kinde of assurance in all his actions, and the losse, or neglect of it hath robbed many a brave Commander of their fame and credit, being surprized through over-sight, as *Gustavus Horne* was at *Bambricke*: It was also the losse of *Hano*, and *Philipsburg*: Intelligence then being of such moment, it [II-201] should make Generalls, and all Commanders under them, according to their qualities and charge, to be open handed; otherwise it is impossible to subsist long not being surprised.

---

## Of Recognoscing.

Having intelligence of our enemies strength, how he lies, whether in Quarter, Garrison, Field, or Leaguer, then having an exployt to goe on, we must recognosce on horse or foote, according to the exployt we have before us. As if we were to blocke up a Towne with a part of an Armie, we must first being accompanied with a few Horsemen recognosce the bounds, riding the Circuit short or long from it, fore-seeing how to divide our number on the Passes & Avenues from or towards the Towne, to stop out-fallings, or in-commings, in ordering such Workes and Skonces to be made on the passages, as may put us in safetie, as well against out-fallings, as against their pretended Reliefes to come: and our watches one from another, must keepe due correspondence by their Centries, that none can passe betwixt them without advertising one anothers guard.

Next being to beleaguer a Towne neere hand, we ought to recognosce also neerer, having first placed our Armie foote and horse Battell without reach of their Cannon, though in their view: having first directed our parties of horse to batter the streets without us, then the Commander is to ride the circuit of the

Towne within shot, as neere as he can, having another riding at a distance behinde him, and having a Boore beside him, resolving him of all Questions concerning their Ports, their Graffes, their Bulworkes, where weakest, and where the Graffe is shallowest; which being knowne, he disposeth the Armie on severall Posts, where againe the Commanders are to recognosce neerer the walls, where they can best lodge their greatest bodie in most safetie, where to place their Guard before them, and where their Centries; as also where to place their Batteries, and where to beginne their Approaches: which being done, they are thought the best fellowes, that shew most diligence, and least losse to come to the walles; the same circumstances are to be observed by any Commander, who leads a partie before a Strength or Castle to blocke it, or beleaguer it, having Cannon, Pittards, and fireworkes, with sufficient men and furniture belonging to the Artillerie, that can discharge their duties, as they are directed by the Commander of the partie, who must see to all things himselfe, that it be well done, as in speciall to the placing of his Batteries, and in ordering all things to be brought to the Batteries that are needfull, by the Souldiers commanded out to attend the workes, beside the guard of the Cannon, and of the workemen, he must also be very vigilant in visiting the Approaches, Batteries, and Guards, admonishing them to be carefull against out-falls on the Trenches, Batteries, or Guards, giving orders to the Captaine of the Watches to receive the enemie falling out with a strong bodie of Pikes and Muskets closse together to beate them backe, being received with Pikes charged, bravely flancked and lined with shot, [II-202] which being done, to advance their workes againe night and day, till the enemy be forced to Accord.

In the night also a sufficient Sergeant being seconded by another stout fellow, should creepe to the Graffe, with two halfe-Pikes, for to wade through, to know the shallowest parts, being helpt thereto by some knowne Boore, who might give certaintie of the enemies strength within, and of their defects they have of victualls, Amunition, fire or water. As also to know their private sorting-Ports, to watch their out-commings; he ought also to learne what draw-bridges are within, and what Portcullis, and what store of victualls, or Amunition is to be had within, is case the Strength be pregnable, that he may the better make his Accord. Also he ought to learne what Artillery or Armes are within, and what Caducks, or what number of Horses pertaining to the enemie, and what other riches they have, and where kept; or if otherwise the Towne be not taken by Accord, or strength of hand, we must strive to force it to yeeld by hunger, or by lacke of fire or water, or otherwise by throwing Artificiall fire amongst them with Cannon, or with other fiery Engins, fiering their houses, or spoyling their Watches on their Posts or Guards; as also we must deale by fraud to convey private Letters unto them, for deboysing the Inhabitants, to resist the Garrison in making either Port or Post good, while as the pursuer intends to fall on, on storme or breach.

Likewise the pursuer had neede to dispose well of his owne watches without, that he be not surprized, his hooffe-watch, particular watches, reserves, or by-watches, are to be still in readinesse to attend the enemies out-falling, lest he may cut off his Guards, or spoyle his Cannon by nayling of them, or by burning their Carriages, or Amunition, being disgracefull in the highest manner, as oft-times hath hapned to unprovident and sluggish Commanders, who have unwisely despised their enemies.

An enemy being in the Field, either with a strong partie or Armie, a sufficient Commander must be carefull in recognoscing the Field about him, for taking his advantage of the ground, in advancing to an enemie, as also in spying his advantage in case he be put to a Retreat, that he may the better retire in order, not being put to rout, as our Armie was at *Nerling*, which never hapned unto them before during the time I served the *Sweden*. As also being in the Field he ought to observe where most conveniently he can plant his Ordnance, as Generall *Tillie* did at *Leipsigh*, and as the *Emperialists* did on the Hill at *Nurenberg*; as also at *Nerling*. For Ordnance being planted with advantage is oft-times the winning of the Field, and the losse of Artillery is ever reputed and holden for a defeate, although both foote and horse be preserved. There is also advantage of ground very requisit to be taken by foote against foote, as the advantage of hights, passages, woods, hedges, ditches, as also the advantage of Sunne and Winde with you, and against your enemie; which his Majestie of worthy memory did strive to get at *Leipsigh* against the *Emperialists*.

Likewise it is a great advantage of ground, when one of both the Armies is brought to that inconvenience, that they cannot come to fight, but the one Armie may be forced to come up but by Divisions, while as the other by advantage of the ground may receive them with full Battailes of horse and foote, the one to second the other; and this advantage *Gustavus Horne* did get of the *Emperialists*, while as he retired before them unto *Vertenberg-land* [II-203] in March 1633. the enemy not being able to pursue our Armie but with great disadvantage, which freed us of them for that time, he being stronger than we, and afterward the *Rhinegraves* Forces come from *Alsas* being joyned with us, we made the *Emperialists* againe retire over the *Danube* unto *Schwaland* at the passe of *Munderken*, where we came within Cannon-shot; yet they getting the passe, retired in safetie; as they did another time from us, out of *Schwabland* unto *Bierland*, having got the passe before us at *Kempten*, and afterward over the *Eler* in *Schwabland*, having (I say) got the passe before us, they were safe, and we frustrate. So that the advantage of ground is of great importance in warres, as I have often knowne by experience, especially before the Hill at *Nurenberg*.

Likewise a wise Commander being defender must observe all Circumstances, as he did in pursuing for his owne safetie; he must also being defender beset well all passes, and frontier Garrisons, whereupon the enemie must passe to come unto him, having timely recognosced the same, that it may either be beset by him, or otherwise being found more advantagious for the enemie, it would then be timely demolished.

As also your enemies Armie, or strong partie being drawne up in the field, you are to recognosce both his strength and order, by the sight of your eye, before you intend to pursue him, where you are to consider, how he can advance to you, or you to him without disorder, but doe you never pursue, except with advantage; though you shall be deemed by others to be remisse, but rather suffer him to be gone, than to take the disadvantage of pursute, since time will alter any thing, and he that preserves an Armie will doubtlesse finde a convenient time to fight. And it had beene good for the *Evangelists* in *Dutchland*, that this point had beene more wisely lookt unto at *Nerling* than it was, for they might have saved their Armie and Countrey both, had they not presumed with disadvantage in their owne strength and courage, where GOD the disposer of hearts made their pride a great fall.

---

### A short Observation to be observed in Garrison.

Entering the place before all things you are to visit the Posts, and being duely recognosced, the round or circuit should be measured, and then the Posts to be dealt proportionably, according to the severall strengths, that no man have just cause to complaine.

The posts then orderly and well beset, there should be orders given for by-watch, or reserve, where to stand in readinesse, whether on the Market-place, or some other convenient part, having sufficient Officers ever to command them, who must be kept to strictnesse of dutie, lest they should be to seeke when honour were to be maintained, while as on Alarum they were to repaire to poste, street, or wall, to resist the enemie, and to succourse the weaknesse of any accident might befall by pursute or fire, or to resist enemies [II-204] within or without, being as well on continuall Guard against the Inhabitants, in case of uproares, or treacherie, as against their outward enemies: since no enemy is so dangerous, as the inward enemy being least suspected.

Likewise the Governour or Commandant ought to observe and keepe a due proportion in all commandements given either for workes, service, watches, or parties, that no man might justly complaine, that there is more dutie layd on him than on his neighbour, but according to proportion of strength.

The keyes of the Ports, and of all sorting doores and prisons, are to be brought in and out by the Captaine of the maine Watch to the Governour, and the Captaine of the Watch is to appoint Guards, to stand at the drawbridges, Portcullis, and sorting Ports, and he is obliged to bring all intelligence himselfe unto the Governour, and never to open a doore night or day without a sufficient Guard by him with the Limits past, for feare he might be surprised, and the whole Garrison in danger.

Also the Governour is to give Orders at night, whether every man must resort with their Armes in case of Alarum, and the Towne being divided, both Burgers and Souldiers should know their Posts they are to repaire to, from the Alarum place.

And to supply the defects of the fortifications, the Towne shou'd be divided into equall deales, to worke their day about, with all materialls needfull for repayring the defects, that there be nothing to mend when they ought to fight;

and to that effect, Officers should be appointed by the Governour to over-see the workes, that things may be the better done, and the Governour must often visit all himselfe, taking reckoning what is done every day, till all be put in good order. The Governour ought to have a Register of all inquartering, that he may the better be made acquainted by the Burgers of every mans behaviour for keeping good order. He ought also to have account of all victualls in their store-houses, both of Corne and all other furniture, and of all Caducks within the Garrison; and the out-setting of all safeguards belongs unto him as his due. He ought to suffer no man to make commoditie without his knowledge, but all to put in to him, that he may the better maintaine his state, and entertaine strangers seeing he ought to be a good fellow, and a common receipt for commers and goers, otherwise he will faile to be thought of; and he must give orders to the Captaine of the watch, that no man come or goe without his knowledge, under paine of punishment, and the Captaine of the watch should direct those that enter the Citie, having seene their passes, with a Convoy and an Officer by night or by day, unto the Governour to be inquired of at his pleasure.

The Governour as he ought to give out the word, so he ought to see all Parads at the ordinary time they goe to watch, where comming off againe, they ought to repaire to the Parad-place, and draw up orderly, before they lodge their Colours, and the Governour is obliged to visit the Posts, and to goe the round himselfe, and to make the rest goe the rounds orderly after him.

Likewise it is his due to command out all parties, being first drawne up on the Parad-place, seeing them to be provided of Amunition, and of all necessaries, before their parting, giving strict orders that at their returnes all bootie be brought orderly before him, and nothing to be put out of the way or a- [II-205] side, on the paine of punishing the Officer that commanded the partie, and the goods being knowne, they are to be confiscated to the Governour, seeing all bootie ought to be distributed at his discretion: and in dividing the Quarters, the Governour ought to have allowed him some free houses, to contribute to his Kitchen, as also some houses kept free to lodge strangers, which ought to acknowledge the Governour so long as they have no other burthen, and if the Garrison be such a place as yeelds other commodities by traffique, by water or land, the Governour, besides the ordinary custome or toale, ought to be acknowledged by those who transport goods or Cattell, by or through his Garrison, if they come under the compasse of his watch. As also he may take of adjacent lands belonging to the enemy, as high a contribution as he can rack them to, providing he prove not dishonest to his Master in taking moneys, for being friend to his Masters enemies.

---

## For making of Accord, an Observation.

His Majestie of worthy memory, I being with him at *Damaine,* *Brandenburg, Lantsberg, Verben, Erfort, Mentz, Ausburg, Rhine* and *Munchen* in *Baviere*, did never trust the making of the Treatie to any other than himselfe: for how soone either Trumpeter or Drummer were conveyed (blind-folded by the Officer of the Watch) unto him, then being discovered, having delivered their message and receiving an answer, the same or another being directed backe, then pledges were delivered to be kept on both sides, till such time as the accord were condescended to or left off, in case of variance; being continued to a second resolution, and then the pledges were to be retired *Hinc inde*. Those pledges at such times ought to be modest, sober and discreet in their discourses, lest some things might slip them, tending to prejudice of either parties: and if the pledges be wise, they may save some Commodities for a friend. When the defender makes a slight Accord, the heads whereof are set downe in writing, and afterward advised, but once granted cannot be recall'd; the guard once changed, a Commander doth goe to possesse withall, according to the Accord, where incontinent the pursuer makes preparation for the enemies out-comming, that there be no disorder committed in breaking the Accord by either of the parties; for it is a grosse errour for a Christian to violate their word once given: but they doe strive before ending, for honourable Conditions on both sides, the particulars accorded on are not necessary to be inserted here, since they doe varie according to the occasions; where sometimes the defender makes Conditions for the Citie, their Liberties, Traffique and Religion, as the place is of importance; and if the defender looke for succours seeing his advantage, he shifts in making the Accord, prolonging time till in the end, as sometimes, the Treatie dissolves; as was done at *Traylesound* 1628. against the *Emperialists*. And the partie beleaguerer finding himselfe weake without, he continues their out-marching till his weaknesse be supplied; as his Majestie of worthy memory [II-206] did before *Lansberg*, where the enemy was to march out three thousand stronger then we were without, which delayed his out-coming, till supply was come to us from *Francfurt*.

When treaties are ended, the Conquerour of the place, after making his accord, having made his best advantage of all provisions found in such parts, as of Cannon, Armes, Clothes, Amunition, Libraries, Monuments, being all transported, and put in assurance, then the Towne being in the Conquerours power, he may beset it with a Garrison, or demolish it by rasing of the walles, and it had bin good the *Swedens* had done so in *Bavier* with *Donavert*, *Rhine*, *Ausburg*, *Aychstat*, *Landsout* and *Munchen*; if they had beene rased at first, we had not bin troubled by taking them in twice thereafter, and it had bin better to have plundred them first, then to have compounded with them for monies, having after the losing of *Nerling* battaile lost our monies, the pledges, the country and City, which had bin better to have raced them to the ground (as Trophees of our victories) at our being there, then to have taken pledges for money, and lose all againe.

It is also to be observed in making of all accords, that such prisoners as are within the place, may be let free, that doe belong to the beleaguerer, and such Souldiers as were run away from the pursuer, may be restored againe to be punished or pardoned, as pleaseth their Officers. But no man belonging to the enemy may be detained contrary to their wills.

As also no Cannon taken of the pursuer before, can be taken out of the Strength, nowithstanding that Cannon be allowed unto him, by his accord, he must transport none that belonged formerly to another.

Likewise no more horses can be allowed to be transported by Officers, then are mentioned in their accord, and that proportionally according to their degrees they serve in, and no more: and if it be found, that the defender fraudulently beyond his accord, hath either stolne away, destroyed, or hid any goods, Armes, Cannon or Amunition, being knowne or revealed, *ipso facto* the pursuer or Conquerour is not obliged to keepe their paction, but they may use them as the *Swedens* did Colonell *Gramme*, after his marching out of *Wesmer*, having broken treacherously his accord.

---

### Of the taking of Prisoners an observation.

His Majesty having taken in *Frankfurt* on the *Oder*, I did grant quarters to two young Cavaliers, who had begged my protection, to save them from the fury, and having once protected them, though with difficulty, I had a care no man should wrong them: as all Cavaliers ought to doe in extremity to those that stand in neede of mercy, not [II-207] plundring men to their skinnes, as some unworthy doe; But on the contrary having once granted quarter, men ought to be carefull, not only in guarding their lives from others, but also they ought to foresee for entertainment civilly, at least for their money, being Cavaliers of charge, which may be presupposed able to entertaine themselves, or if otherwise they cannot doe it, our charity and compassion should move us to provide bread for them, who cannot provide for themselves, otherwise our over-sight in suffering them to starve for want of bread, deserves a greater punishment, then if we suffered others to have killed them at first being enemies, so that I wish no man so uncivill as to dominier over a reconciled enemy being in bonds.

Likewise Prisoners being civilly entertained according to their degrees, neverthelesse they ought to be look't unto as Prisoners; if they be common Souldiers, they should be commited to the Generall Gavilliger, to be attended there, with a guard to watch them, being in Irons, and according to their behaviours, to be kept closer, or at more liberty, and being on marches, they ought not to be suffered to come so neere the Army as to be spies over others, and especially being Officers concredited to a Gavilliger, they ought to be so kept as they could not remarke, either the strength or the discipline of the Army; and being come to quarters, they ought to be visited as Cavaliers, but in discourse men ought to be sparing with them, as with prisoners: neither must you injure them or suffer others to doe it, seeing Prisoners can doe no reason to Cavaliers, and giving once their *Parole*, they may have some freedome to walke without suspition within shot of Cannon.

But when either Trumpeter or Drummer is sent with letters, or message to prisoners, he ought before he come neere the Guards, sound his Trumpet or beate his Drumme, giving advertisment to the Guards before he enter within their outward Centries, otherwise he is lyable to the highest punishment, but having lawfully aduertised the Guard, an Officer by command of the Captaine of the watch with a Convoy of Musketiers ought to meete him, and having enquired for his commission and passe, and seene his open letters, having search't him for private letters, and finding none, then he ought to sile or blinde him up, and convay him blinded unto the chiefe Commander, who receives his letters, reades, and delivers them, and then after he being siled up againe, he is convaied unto the Gavilliger, where he is kept till he be ready, and suffered to depart againe with open Letters, being convayed out as he came in: and no Prisoner ought to deliver any letters, though open, to any man, till first he acquaint his Guard, who ought to impart it to the Commander of the place, and it is ordinary to Governours or Commanders, to whom Trumpeters or Drummers doe come, having received their answer, being brought siled from the Gavilligers unto their lodging, first to talke merrily with them, and then to cause attenders drinke to them till they be merry, and then being siled againe, they are convayed without the whole Centries, having their passe, they are free to returne.

Prisoners having agreed for their Ransomes, or being exchanged out for others, they ought not be suffered to depart, without getting first the Generalls passe, and then he may goe with a Trumpeter or without one, to the next friendly Garrison. [II-208]

---

## For quartering an Army in field upon March, Dorpe, Towne, or Leaguer, An Observation.

A Commander ought not be ignorant of the circumstances belonging to the quartering of an Army, therefore for the better Information of the younger sort, who have not seene such Marches as I have bin at, with his Majesty of worthy memory, who quartered his Army Summer or Winter, according as the occasion or neerenesse of his enemy did offer, where many times the whole winters night, the Army, horse, foote and Artillery, being without fire, did stand in battaile order by their Armes in the fields, having placed their Artillery apart, with a guard to attend them, their baggage also being behinde them apart, and well guarded, and a maine guard being commanded out apart before the Army, of horse and foote; And the Armies being neere one another, all Officers were commanded to abide on their severall charges, as they were commanded on the March, to leade Briggads, Troopes or Divisions; The commanded men being also apart next unto the enemy, with their Officers by them, which all being orderly quartered in this first manner, they entertained one another with such dainties as the time afforded, passing the night with variety of merry jests and discourses till day, that either Drumme or Trumpet did invite them unto earnest.

The second forme of our quartering was in the fields not being neere an enemy, where we quartered a little more commodiously for our ease, being commonly drawne up by foure or five of the clocke in the afternoone, neere some Towne or village, in some faire meadow by water, if it could be had in the Summer, and in the Winter being quartered, we drew neere the side of some wood, both for fire, and for build or shelter; The Army drew up in battaile by Briggads, as they marched, where behinde the place the Briggads drew up unto, at a reasonable distance, their quarters were marked out severally according as they stood in battaile, and before the Briggads removed from their Armes, their guards were first commanded out, every Briggads guard being placed at a distance of foure-score paces from their Colours, where they were appointed to watch, and the watch being set, Centries were put to the Colours, and then the Pike-men were ordained to fix their Pikes fast in the ground as they stood in battaile, the Musketiers also were ordained in dry wether to set up their Muskets in order in even front, with their Colours, but when it rained, they were commanded to keepe them carefully dry by themselves, which all orderly done they were suffered part and part to goe, and provide themselves of straw and fire, providing also many times well for their Officers Kitchins beside.

The Artillery and Amunition waggons being also drawne up a part, and well guarded, their horses were sent to grasse for good quarters, then the Baggage and wagons as they came up did draw up orderly behinde their owne [II-209] Regiments, and their horses being sent to grasse, the Officers Tents were set up orderly at a distance before their Colours, and then cookes went to dresse meate and all being returned to quarters before supper, the whole Drummes of the Army did beate before their severall briggads, inviting all to publique prayers, which were never forgotten; And after prayer the Majors of the Regiments did give out orders for the night to the Sergeants, and for up-breaking the next morning, and then all went to meate first, and next to rest, and the whole horsemen were drawne up in this fashion, and parties were sent out of their quarters to batter the streets, two or three mile off, the whole night, lest we should be surprised by an enemy without intelligence.

The next morning Drummes having called all to Armes, the Briggad, that had the Van, marched out first in a new ground, and drew up, the Briggad, that had the Van the day before, marched out, drawing up on their left hand having fallen backe one degree from the Van, and then the rest of the Briggads drew out orderly, one after another, till the left hand of the foote Army were closed up, and then they went to prayers, and the prayers ended, they marched, the Baggage marching after, being drawne up in order, as the Briggads or Regiments did march, so did they. The Artillery marched with the Briggads, in part, and the rest marched before the Army with their Convoyes, and guard of Musketiers, which were changed every two dayes, being commanded men out of all Regiments proportionally, having Officers, commanded them accordingly. Thus much of quartering in the fields.

The third manner of quartering, and enemy being a farre off, and we neere Townes, only in cold weather, quarterings were given for the *Hoffestaffe* (being the King or Generall and their followers) and the principall Officers of the Army, including his Majesties houshold, whose quarters were first appointed by the generall quarter-master in the Townes, and next to the *Hoffe-staffe* the Colonells, that commanded Briggads, were quartered, and next to them, the Colonells of Regiments, their Officers and Souldiers: a great part, and the best of the quarters ordained for the Officers belonging to the Artillery, their horses and servants. The Artillery and baggage standing without the Towne, those who quartered within the Towne, had allowance of free meate and drinke, and no more; sometimes without Townes we had quarters given to Briggads apart in Dorps, Randez-vouz being appointed for us, the next morning to draw upon for to joyne with the Army, and while as we quartered in Dorps being drawne up without the Dorpe, first we sighted the passes, and the guards placed in the fields on the *Avenues*, lest the enemy unawares might enter the quarters, the Centries duely set, our Colours were conveyed with a Troope to their lodging or quarter, their furriers shuts leading them aright till the Colours were quartered and guarded, then the rest showne unto their quarter, men were appointed to goe meete the Baggage to leade them to their quarters. Orders given, every man entertained another, as they had best reason, and all being setled, parties of horse were sent forth to scoure the fields for intelligence, and lest they might be trapped by the enemy, a second party was sent out after them, both getting orders, how farre to ride, and upon what streets, being commanded where to hault, and forrage, as also being admonished to have still a party on horsbacke to advertise the rest from being surprized, which [II-210] done, Ordnance-Rutters of every Briggad were left to waite on the Generall, at his Quarter, for Orders; the generall Randez-vouz for the Horse being appointed, where to meete when ever they got Orders.

The fourth manner of quartering an Armie is in a fast Leaguer, as at *Statin*, *Swede*, *Brandenburg*, *Verben*, *Donavert*, *Ausburg*, *Engolstat*, *Nurenberg*, which manner of quartering is most troublesome both for Officers and Souldiers, who having builded Receptacles for themselves, their charges and travels bestowed in vaine, many times they leave their houses to their enemies, yet the forme is commendable, being under an Armie that is well payd, where all things may be had for money, and then the Leaguer being kept cleane, and in good order, it represents a Common-weale or a Citie defensible against all incumbrances which may occurre; except it please the *Lord* to wagge his hand, and then no counsell or strength can availe against Him who is the God of Hostes. The use Cavaliers, or Commanders have to make of this sort of quartering is, that in case they happen to have Command themselves, they may learne through this practise to command others, as also through fore-sight they may timely take themselves to this kinde of defensive warre, till they be able to come into the Fields, as his Majesty of worthy memory did, being forced to retire by the power of his enemies to the former Leaguers, wherein there was discipline and good practice to be observed by Cavaliers, where the Kings Majestie was made to dwell as the meanest Souldier, being alike subject to the inconvenience as others, which might happen, of ayre, sicknesse, infection, or of watching. Thus farre then for the quartering of an Armie.

---

## Of Artillerie an Observation.

Artillery being the third part of an Armie, without which no Armie can be gloriously led; it is requisit then somewhat briefly to speake of the advantages we have by Artillerie, being well foreseene and commanded, as it was by the Captaine of Kings and King of Captaines, *Gustavus* the Invincible, who with as little Charge did as much as any King or Captaine could (in doing of so great exploits as he did) with his Artillery. But lest I should be thought to neglect a part of my dutie in this point concerning Cannon, I will set downe here when his Majestie made most use of Cannon, to my knowledge; which being rightly considered, will be thought strange, seeing in the whole course of his Majesties warres during his time, I never saw or did learne he shot a breach in any place, except at *Garts*, though otherwise I knew well his Majestie made good use of his Artillerie, as at *Leipsigh*, the *Leacke*, and at *Leitzen*, where in all three he shewed him selfe Master of that Art. But against either Towne, or Fort, I did never see in his Majesties time one breach shot or entred, his fortune being such, and his diligence so great, that his enemies did ever Parlé before they would abide the furie of his Cannon; as at *Brandenburg, Damaine, Francfurt, Mentz, Donavert, Ausburg*, and divers more; and in my opinion, the terrour the Cannon breeds [II-211] is as much to be feared as the execution that followes, though it be great; and Artillery in all Armies and things belonging thereto, are of infinit moment on all occasions. So that they may be called *Sine quo nihil*; but supreame Officers of the Field, are no more troubled with them, but so farre as they direct others to doe the service, their owne Officers being appointed to attend them, as the Generall to the Artillerie, his Colonells, Lievetenant-Colonells, Majors, Captaines, Lievetenants, Constables, and all other inferiour Officers needfull to attend, who know and keepe their owne Turnes and Reliefes, as other Officers doe theirs; their furniture is great and their charges also in buying Horses to draw their Cannon and Amunition, Waggons with Powder, Ball, Match, Materials, Fire-Engins, Petards, storming Ladders, Artificiall Bridges carried on Waggons to passe over Rivers or Graffes.

In all quartering they are quartered next after the Hoffestaffe before any Briggad, and the furniture and charges needfull to maintaine this third part of the Armie is extraordinary great, there being alwayes something to be repaired, while as the Armie doth rest; and oft-times they must be provided of a great deale of new furniture, and they lose yearely an extraordinary number of Horses of great price. But his Majestie during his time was very fortunate in this, as in other things; for I never knew his Majestie lose any Ordnance but I have seene him get supply of Amunition and Cannon from his enemies, as first, at *Garts* and *Grefenhaugne, Damaine, Francford, Lansburg, Glogo, Leipsigh, Vertsburg,*

*Mentz*, and *Munchen*, besides the supply his Majestie did get for his Artillerie from *Nurenberg, Francfurt, Ausburg, Strasburg* and *Vlme*; and to discourse largely of this subject alone, would take a volume of paper. But when every Cavalier is commanded apart with a partie where he must make use of Cannon, he would be (before his departure with his partie) very carefull to receive his Cannon with the furniture belonging unto it timely together, with sufficient Officers for discharging that part of the dutie, on his march he must command his partie as if it were a little Armie, being ever well provided of Guides, and of carefull, wittie, and painefull Intelligencers, that he may leade and quarter his partie with assurance, directing alwayes his Intelligencer before him, being ever carefull to beset the passes and avenues well. As also sufficiently to guard his Cannon, Baggage, and Amunition, since many times great hurt doth come thorow the neglect of guarding the Cannon and Amunition: which over-sights once committed are irrecoverable; in regard whereof I must entreate the gentle Reader to pardon me a little here out of Historie (for the younger Souldier his better instruction) to discourse a little of the hurt and inconvenience hath happened many times by Cannon and powder; as also of the manner they were first invented, being found out by *Gods* permission for the ruine of man punished for sinne; experience doth teach daily that the strength of it is not to be resisted.

*Estiene Forcatell* in his fourth booke of the Empire and of the Philosophy of the *Gaulles*, doth attribute the invention of powder and Cannon to the *Germanes*, saying that a peece by the helpe of some kindled powder did spue a ball, the noise whereof was like to thunder, and killed. The maker of it an Abbot, the childe of the Devill, assisted by his Father found out this cruell invention, which serves alike for the pursuer of Townes as for the defender, till it ruine both. It is said of *Archidamus*, Sonne of the King *Agesilaus*, wondering at a new invention of Cannon brought from *Sicilie*, complained the [II- 212] valour of men was beaten downe and trod under foote, seeing there was no more fighting without monstrous hardnesse and Armour. And it is thought that a blacke fellow called *Berthold Schuvart* an Abbot invented it. Reade *Polydore Virgil*, in his second booke and sixt Chapter *de invent.* and *Sabellicus* in his *Ennead. lib.* 9. a fellow having some beaten Brimstone for Physicke closed in a pot covered with a stone, he striking with a file on a stone to give fire, a sparke lighted in the pot, and incontinent the flame came forth, heaving the stone in the ayre; and chewing his Cud thereon, he made a Cannon of Iron, closing powder within it, till that peece and peece he found out the invention. And we reade that in the Kingdome of *China*, in the *East Indies*, both Printing and Artillerie were knowne and practised there, long before they were found out in *Europe*, and that there, there be many Cannons, which I will rather beleeve than go to see.

*Virgil* also in the sixt booke of his *Æneids* doth speake of the like in his description of *Salmoneus*; and *Iosephus*, in his third booke and ninth Chapter of the *Iewes* warres, makes mention of an Instrument they used against the Towne of *Iotapat* in *Galilee*, and saith, the stones shot by Engines did breake the walles and Towers, and there was no Troope of men so well ordered, but was scattered by it, and beaten to the ground. The same Author speaking of the Batteries made against the walles of *Ierusalem*, affirmes that the stones shot by the Engines were as heavie as a man: And neverthelesse they were carried above six hundred paces by the Engine, killing many men.

*Plinius* writes in his thirty-one booke and tenth Chapter, in his voyage unto *Babylon*, that powder was in use of old, and reporteth he did see powder-milles on the River *Euphrates*, though of another sort than our powder.

Of this invention also you may reade *Cornel de Campe*, in his storie of *Frise*, in his second booke and twentieth Chapter. Also *Simoscus* King of *Frise*, *Beresne* Lord of *Holland*, and *Olympia* Daughter to the Earle of *Holland*, where it is said, that *Simoscus* killed with one shot of Pistoll the Earle and his two sonnes; and that afterward he would have killed *Rowland* Earle of *Flanders*, but the Pistoll mis-giving, *Rowland* did kill him with his sword, and did throw the Pistoll in the Sea. But we reade that *Barbadigue* Admirall of *Venice* was the first that carried them on his Gallies and Shippes, wherewith he did terrifie the *Genoweys*, being at hunting by their noise: and *Paul Iove*, in his third booke of illustrious persons, writes that *Barthelem Cokone* Generall to the *Venetians* for the space of twentie yeares and more, was the first that used Cannon in the Fields, while as the banished people of *Florence* made warres against the familie *De Medices*, being first used to make breaches in walles, and to defend walles: but afterward they came in use to breake the Battailes of horse and foote; for if the warres of old, and their inventions were compared to now adayes, it were a sport to laugh at, rather than warres.

Now of late the invention is found out of burning Bullets, full of fire, shot out of Cannon, to fire houses within Strengths, and to fire Pallesads and Gabeons set before Batteries on walles or in Fields, whereof his Majestie of *Polle Estien Bathon* made good use in his warres of *Musco*, within a few yeares.

This invention is thought to have been invented by the King of *Pole* himselfe in his civill warres of *Hungarie*, finding other Cannon made greater noise than hurt. [II-213]

The manner a piece is charged with a hot Bullet, is, the piece is charged with powder convenient, then it is covered with sand in a little quantitie above the powder, then with a little greene grasse presently pluct, being a little dampish or moist, then the hot Bullet being put in must be presently discharged, otherwise the Invention is very dangerous for the Constables; for oft-times minding to ruine others, they are ruined themselves.

*Albert Gantz* writes, that *Christophel* King of *Denmarke* was killed by a shot of Cannon in the yeare 1280. Also we have a deplorable storie written by *Gyrrard de Rooe* and *Conrade Decius*, of the Battaile betwixt the Emperour *Albert* and the *Poles* in *Bohemia*. Amongst their Cannons there was one Cannon greater than the rest, which for her execution was most used, shee killed so many of the *Poles*, that they were so affraid, that they ranne all away, leaving their tents: and it is reported, that at one shot shee killed fourescore men, the Divell (as I said before) was (by the permission of God) the inventor of such a Monster, being offended with mankinde in this last old age of the world, those thunder-claps putting us in minde that this whole round Globe shall be shaken and perish.

We reade also in the thirty-fourth booke of *Paul Iove* his story, the answer of a *Turke* reprehended of his cowardize, having runne away at the noise of a Cannon, being besieged by the Emperour within *Goullet*.

*Adrian Barbarossa* reproaching *Sinas* for losing courage, he answered so long as we have to doe to fight against Armed men, you and my enemies doe know I served ever with reputation and credit, but to fight against the Devill and the fury of Hell-fire, having against us such terrible Monsters, be not you astonished that I sought to eschew death, to th'end I might remaine whole to doe you service.

We reade also in the bloudy battaile of *Ravenne* fought on *Easter day*, 1512. betwixt the *French* and *Dutch*, and the *Spaniard*, that one shot of a double Cannon did kill (as *Michaell de Chochen*) forty Horsmen. We reade also that in the Sea-fight betwixt the *French* and the *Emperialists*, on the River of *Melphe*, neere the straight of *Salerne*, in the yeare 1628, shot out of the *Gally* of Captaine *Philip Dore*, a Cannon Bullet that killed above thirty *Spaniards*, and hurt many others, as reporteth *Paulus Euterus*, in his story of the warres of *Italy*: and *Paul Iove* writing of the same Battaile more largely and curiously, being eye-witnesse himselfe, or at least, within hearing of the Cannon on the Isle of *Ænary*, where he did see the smoke of the Cannon, saith, *Philip Dore* diligent to make good execution with Cannon, and not in vaine spending pouder and shot on the *Spaniard*, his great piece called the *Basiliske*, the ball being monstrous great, broke through the whole ship, even to her keele, and killing thirty, wounded severall Captaines and Gentlemen, that were mutilated or dismembred; So that the *Marquesse* of *Guat* was all spoiled with the bloud and entralls of the dead.

*Guicciardin* reported that at the siege of *Calis*, in the yeare 1558. by the Duke of *Guise*, in the name of the King of *France*, on the three Kings day, in the morning, with thirty three double Cannon from one battery, made such a noyse, that the sound was heard five houres going beyond *Calis*, being twenty *English* miles. And lest the judicious Reader will thinke this is an untruth, I would warrant it from my owne deede, for he that pleaseth, may reade the story written by the Author *Guicciardin*. But those peeces of Cannon that are farthest hard, are called pot-peeces or *Mortiers*, such as *Mounts* [II-214] on the Castle of *Edenburrough*, being so wide, that it is reported, that a man did get a Child within, which I also warrant from my owne deede, but the truth is, it is a huge great peece, from whence did come our old *Scots* Proverbe, the Devill shoote *Mounts* in your arse. Gentle Reader excuse my homelinesse, since I was not the Inventor of this Proverbe.

These kinde of Peeces are very large, and carry stones for bullets. The *Mortiers* of *Soliman* at the Siege of *Rhodes*, in the yeare 1522. their bullets wayed some of them two hundred weight, the least one hundred and fifty pounds of great weight, when they light on a house, they goe through from top to ground; and *Paulus Iovius* reports of a Mine made by *Peter Valler*, which made entrance for the *Spaniard* within the new Castle of *Naples*, kept by the *French*, the *French* were so astonished with the surprize of the Mine, that they retired unto the last and furthest Court, so that the guards had not time to draw up their

Draw-bridges, and the *French* letting downe the *Portcullies* to hinder the *Spaniards* entry, coming with a furious presse, the *French* bring a peece of Cannon to terrifie the *Spaniards*, that had entred one Gate, or the first Court, and shoote amongst them, where by chance the Iron bullet tooke hould of the thicke of the Port, where it remaines to this day showne for a Monument unto strangers, that have got the credit to goe within this Castle to see it. Many such Stories we could inferre, but let these suffise in this place for this time. [II-215] [II-216]

# THE
# CHRISTIAN
# SOVLDIER GOING
# ON SERVICE HIS
# Meditations.

## I.

When thou seest thy Camerade going to Muster with a faire shew outwardly, deckt with brave clothes, and delighting in his Plumes, thinke with thy selfe, such an outward shew is nothing, without the inward gifts of the minde: for if thou desirest to be a Souldier of Christ, thou must be adorned with all vertues; that inwardly thou mayest be such, as outwardly thou doest appeare unto the world. Thou must then learne to mortifie those vices to which thou art most subject, taking accompt of thy selfe, how thou hast resisted vice, and what good thou hast done, and say then, when thou findest thou hast done nothing that is good, Lord make us every day to renounce sinne, and resist vice, that our love and zeale to thee may be inflamed to well-doing, even in the greatest extremity of adversity.

## II.

When thou seest the Kings Majesty thy Master, or his Generall coming to looke on the battaile, when all Front towards the King, with due respect and reverence, thinke then againe with thy selfe, and say, as for me it is good to draw neere unto thee, O Lord, for thou art my King and my God, thee alone will I worship and love; make me happy in thy love, and for thy sake, I will despise all things: for thou art the strength of my head, and my portion for ever; for through hope, we attaine unto thee by Faith. [II-217]

### III.

When thou seest thy Camerads knitting all things about them handsome and fast, before they march, say thou then, knit mine heart unto thee, O Lord, that I may feare thy name, for he that loveth not thee, must quake and feare, and it is a fearefull thing to fall into thy hands; for thy coming unto Iudgment is terrible, thy roaring is like a *Lyon*, and thy Sword a consuming fire, no place can hide man from thy presence, thou seest the heart and the Reines, no secret is hid from thee, and who can escape thy vengeance? None, except they repent. Lord therefore save me from that bitter death, and give me grace to repent, that I may bewaile my misery, before I depart.

### IIII.

When thou art entred in the troublesome way of thy march, and sufferest toyle, travell, heate, cold, hunger, thirst, nakednesse, perill, being called to labour, and to suffer, and not to live in pleasure and idlenesse, say then; my sorrow O Lord is ever before me, for in me dwelleth no good, I offend day by day; and which is worse, I cannot repent; sinne increaseth, and the Fountaine of grace is stopped, and I finde no comfort. Say then againe, O Lord spurre me and whip me with thy Rod, before I perish, and reserve not thy punishment, lest at last I shall be made to pay the uttermost farthing. Lord therefore create a new heart within me, that I may prepare a habitation for thee to rest in, a cleere conscience. O Lord for thy Sonne Christs sake, suffer me not to goe away empty, for with thee is mercy, and great redemption, therefore I will be comforted whilst thou givest me time to amend my life.

### V.

When thou seest thy Camerads for love of credit, and the favour of their Officers, making no difference betwixt faire and foule way, but with patience induring all toile, to come to the end of their march, thinke then with thy selfe, that after this manner of old, the servants of Christ, for the favour and love of God, and of his glory, did serve the Lord in hunger and thirst, in cold, in nakednesse, in watching and fasting, in prayers, in meditations, in manifould persecutions and troubles, contemning all pleasurs for Christ; they sought the glory of God, more than their owne fame. Lord therefore make us contemne and slight all things, for the love of Christ; altering from vice to vertue, mortifying our lusts, that we may become Souldiers of Christ, loving nothing so much as God and the salvation of our soule.

## VI.

When thou seest thy Camerade fix in his Armes, and well exercised with Pike, Musket and Sword; then thinke with thy selfe, that thy duty is, to trust in the Lord, and to doe good, that thou mayest dwell in the [II-218] land, and be fed assuredly, thy delight must be in the law of the Lord, and thou must be exercised therein day and night, that thou mayest be full of hope and strength, remembring thy end, ever redeeming the time, takeing heede of small sinnes, that by time thou maist avoide the greatest, and if thou shalt behave thy selfe godly in the day, thou mayst be assured to be merry at night.

## VII.

When thou hearest the Alarum given, going to thine Armes, thinke then with thy selfe, that it is more then time to abandon the universall world, and to imbrace God: and say, as for me, it is good to draw neere to God, and to put my trust in him, that I may declare all his Workes, *For whom have I in heaven but him, and on earth I desire none but him, he will guide me by his counsell, and afterwards receive me unto glory.*

## VIII.

When thou seest thy Camerade making ready, and fix against his enemies, girding his loynes, that he may fight the more valiantly, then thinke with thy selfe, that it is thy duty, to put on the spirituall Armour, and to gird thy loynes against Satan, the world and the flesh, that thou mayst fight the spirituall combat, bridling thy riotous appetite, bringing under the flesh, despising the worlds glory, be at no time altogther idle, but ever doing somewhat for the publique welfare, discharging the duties of thy calling, beseeching God for Christ thy Captaines sake, to pronounce thee happy, in the day of thy appearance.

## IX.

When thou seest thy Camerade appointed to watch over himselfe and others, lest he be circumvented by his enemies, lost and utterly ruin'd, then thinke with thy selfe, that thy duty is, to watch over thy selfe diligently: lest the wrath of thine enemies seaze upon thee, by Gods permission, for thy punishment, crushing thee to peeces: and consider with thy selfe, that as it is fearefull to fall into the hands of thine enemies; so it is more fearefull to fall into the hands of the living Lord. Stand then in awe to offend him, that infinitely loves thee, let thy chiefest care be then to please God, and to forsake unrighteousnesse, that leadeth unto death, and then surely thou mayst rejoyce, though in trembling, being merry in the Lord.

### X.

When thou seest thy Camerades invironed with enemies, and preparing themselves for Battaile, then thinke with thy selfe, that it is thy dutie also to arme thy selfe against thy spirituall enemies, craving God his assistance, that he leave thee not, nor suffer thee to be tempted above thy strength; and if thou fightest valiantly unto the end, thou art happie, being promised for thy reward, the Ioyes of Heaven: *For the Spirit saith to him that overcommeth, I will give to eate of the tree of life.* [II-219]

### XI.

When thou seest thy Camerades give eare to the words of Command, hearkning unto their Captaines instructions, obeying the tucke of Drumme, or sound of Trumpet, then thinke with thy selfe, that it is thy dutie to hearken unto *Gods* Word, receiving comfort from the mouth of his servants; for blessed are the eares that heare when the *Lord* whispereth, and blessed are those who prepare themselves for the knowledge of God his heavenly mysteries: *Speake therefore, O Lord, for thy servant heareth*; since without mans helpe thou canst instruct, and though man teach the letter, thy Spirit openeth the meaning, they shew the way, and thou givest strength to walke: man deales outwardly, but it is thou that enlightnest the minde; *Paul plants, Thou givest the increase*: speake therefore O Lord againe, which art the ever-living truth, to the comfort of our soules, to the amendment of our lives, and to the advancement of thine everlasting Glory.

### XII.

When thou seest thy Camerade trusting and leaning unto his own strength, and not depending upon God that gives victory; then thinke with thy selfe, that it is thy dutie, not to thinke with thine owne wings to flie unto heaven, but with *Gods* feathers, for it is not in the power of man, to dispose his affaires at his owne pleasure; But it is *God* that giveth victorie, and comforteth whom he will, and when he will, and what he willeth must be: for of our selves we are full of infirmities, except the favour of God shine upon us, and then are we strong enough to overcome all our enemies, by his power that leads us, preserving us from dangers, and delivering us from infinit evils, for he is our Salvation, our Strength and our Shield in the day of Battaile.

### XIII.

When thou seest againe thy Camerade like a valiant Souldier going forwards in well-doing, not fearing any thing to winne credit; then thinke with thy selfe, that it is thy dutie to strive to goe forwards, notwithstanding the wickednesse of thy minde, though Sathan should presse to hinder thee in the course of idlenesse; and to withdraw thee from all religious dutie and exercise, and from thy godly remembrance of Christs paines and wounds, and from thy care of salvation, and from thy Christian resolution to goe forwards in well-doing, making thee abhorre prayer, and the reading and hearing of the Word incorruptible, beleeve him not, and care not for him, but turning his snares on his owne pate, say unto him, avoide Sathan, thou uncleane spirit, blush thou cursed wretch, avoide I say, thou wouldest carry me from my God, but thou shalt not. *Iesus* will assist me, and thou shalt get but a shamefull soyle: I had rather die, than consent unto thee; Therefore be quiet, and hold thy peace, for I will not heare, though thou shouldest trouble me never so much: *The Lord is my light, and my salvation, whom should I feare? the Lord is the strength of my life, of whom should I be afraid*; the *Lord* protecting me, and delivering me? Therefore as a good Souldier strive couragiously, but beware of pride and arrogancie, which hath led many unto errour, and almost unto [II-220] uncurable blindnesse. Therefore pray unto God, that their fall may make thee wise.

## XIV.

When thou seest thy Camerades impatient, and given to pleasure and delectation, unwilling to beare their crosses; then thinke with thy selfe, that it is thy dutie, as the Souldier of *Iesus Christ*, to walke in his wayes without wearying, and to beare thy crosse and miserie patiently. *For Christ suffered, and so entered into his glorie*: Therefore if thou wilt be a Souldier of his, thou must needs walke in this Kingly high way, not quitting thy Ranke for feare, or for persecution, but must resolve to suffer adversitie; for the more the flesh is troubled and weakned by calamitie, the more the Spirit is confirmed by the comfort of the minde; and he that is stedfast in the faith, needs not feare the malice of the Devill.

## XV.

When thou seest thy Camerade loose in behaviour, not fearing *God*, neglecting his dutie to his Commanders, carelesse of life, and unprepared for death; then thinke with thy selfe, that thy dutie is, to prepare thy selfe by unfained repentance, thinking more often of death than of long life, call to minde *Gods* judgements, and the paines of Hell, let thy behaviour be so, as if thou wert presently to die, so cleering thy conscience, thou canst not greatly feare death, being found such as thou wouldest appeare; having lamented and truely repented thee of thy sinnes, thou shalt winne the Field, and mortalitie being swallowed up of life, thou shalt live for ever.

## XVI.

When thou seest thy Camerade rash, headie, or obstinate in his owne opinion, or yet readie to beleeve every man his words, and suddenly rehearsing what hath been told him, then thinke with thy selfe, that, as a Souldier of *Christ*, it is thy dutie, to be wise and setled in thy opinion, not wavering with every winde of doctrine, but constant in the true faith thou professest, that though thou frequentest, and seest men of divers Religions, thou maiest ever prove constant in the truth thou professest: for the Souldiers of *Christ*, as they are constant, so they must be fervent, and godly zealous.

### XVII.

When thou seest thy Camerade arrogant, thinking himselfe better than his fellowes, then thinke with thy selfe, that it is thy dutie, to be humble, familiar, and sociable, rather silent than babling, not hastie & arrogant, as he, lest *God* should condemne thee utterly; thou must not suffer thy selfe to be drawne away with vanitie, stirring with indignation against any, but be meeke and wise, watch and pray, and spend not thy time in idlenesse, but depend on *God*; let thy conversation be honest, living soberly and righteously in his sight, not judging others, blinded with private affection, giving partiall sentence. [II-221]

### XVIII.

When thou seest thy Camerade loving the world better than *God* (oppressing the poore) as a Citizen of *Babylon*, and not as a Souldier of *Christ*, thinke then with thy selfe, that he having made the wrong choice, thy best is to have the true love and feare of *God*, in doing no body wrong, but contented with thy wages, strive to be made a Citizen of *Ierusalem*, and a Souldier of *Christ*; indeavour to be holy, and unblameable before him, in love and charitie, the vertues belonging to the Christian Souldier, that as thou bearest the name, thou be not found voide of the vertues belonging to those that fight *Christs* Battailes, *viz.* love, courage, respect and obedience: for he that loves any thing better than those vertues, is not worthy the name of a Souldier. And he that loveth *Christ* doth not walke in darknesse, but hath the light of life, caring more for a good life, then for a long, hunting after righteousnesse, that all other things may be cast unto him.

### XIX.

When thou seest thy Camerade not faithfull unto his Master, and with love unfained, not advertising him of all he knowes prejudiciall unto him, then thinke with thy selfe, that thou, as a Souldier of *Christ*, oughtst to be faithfull with love unfained towards thy Master, fighting to death for him, till thou overcomest vice, and conquerest thy selfe (of all Combats the best) that thou maiest be esteemed of, as the valiant Souldier of *Christ*, that as thou art vertuous, so thou maiest grow famous in glory, having abandoned thy selfe and thy owne will, to doe the will of God. *Lord* make us doe this, then are we sure to be honourable in thy sight.

## XX.

When thou seest thy Camerade contraried in many things by his betters, and also perhaps scandalized, then thinke with thy selfe, and resolve if thou wouldest be counted as a Souldier of *Christ*, that would reigne with him, thou must also resolve to suffer with him, and not care a rush for the reproaches of men, but thou must take all scandalls in good part, for *Christ* thy Captaine was despised in this world, and at extremitie, his very friends forsooke him. Thinke then, O Souldier, that thou art in respect of him but dust; and forsake this world, if thou wouldest have rest unto thy soule, *for the Kingdome of God is righteousnesse and peace and joy in the holy Ghost*; put then confidence in God, and he will handle thy cause right well, care thou to have a good Conscience in all thy doings, then thou art sure none can hurt thee, for the *Lord* will defend and deliver thee.

## XXI.

When thou seest thy Camerade vaunting or bragging of his owne deeds, without modestie or discretion, and seeking his owne prayse (as many vaine men doe) then thinke with thy selfe, that thy dutie is to contemne worldly praise as vaine, coming from man: for true and eternall glory contemneth worldly [II-222] praise, and as man judgeth of the deed, God regards the intent and minde; presse therefore to doe well, but thinke little of thy selfe, being the surest token of a modest minde; for he that praiseth himselfe is not allowed, but he whom the *Lord* praiseth. Wee ought not therefore to wax proud, but wee ought to watch continually, for *Sathan* sleepeth not, and the flesh is not yet dead.

## XXII.

When thou seest thy Camerade dissolute, vaine, proud, phantasticke, arrogant, windie, railing, back-biting, vaunting of all sinne and mischiefe, then thinke with thy selfe, that these are the notes proper unto the wicked, and if thou wouldest prove a Souldier of *Christ*, thou must oppose thy selfe contrary to them all, being thy dutie, to be lovely, strong, patient, faithfull, wise, meeke, prudent, circumspect, modest, just, not daintie, not light, not given to vanities; but sober, chaste, constant, quiet and temperate in all senses: even with paine living in vertue, for without paine none can love *God*: for if thou wouldest love *God*, thou must be painfull in seeking of him, never leaving him, till he be found of thee, and love thee, bringing thee through his love unto perfection in *Christ*. For he that loves him, will indure all things for his sake, as valiant Souldiers fainting at nothing may happen; yea thou must despise the inticements of Sathan, and of thy fleshly enemies, and that is the valiant exploit, wherewith best thou canst please God.

## XXIII.

When thou seest thy Camerade stand in awe to commit wickednesse, both for feare of punishment, and his love to his Commanders, then thinke with thy selfe, that thy dutie to thy heavenly Father obliges thee to love and to feare him with a filiall feare, standing awe to sinne against him; for cursed is he that heareth the word of the *Lord*, and despiseth it. Blush thou therefore, that takest more pleasure in vanitie, than in the truth, in time call thy sinnes to remembrance, and that with sorrow, let thy Religion be in thy heart, not in thy mouth, wish for heavenly things, and contemne the world, seeke to be made strong in the love of the *Lord*, and constant to continue: for nothing in heaven above, or in the earth beneath, is comparable to this love of God in Christ; he that hath this love, hath all in all. Say then O my God, and my love, as thou art mine make me wholy thine.

### XXIIII, *And last Meditation going before thine Enemie.*

When thou seest thy Camerade for the love of honour and worldly credit not fearing to die, but readie to open his breast like a valiant Souldier to receive wounds for his Masters sake, then thinke with thy selfe, that it is thy dutie, as the spirituall Souldier of *Christ*, not to feare to die, but rather looking unto the glasse of life, the rule of righteousnesse, the light of the Soule, the joy of the Conscience, like a valourous Souldier for his love, rather let all things seeme sweet unto thee for his sake, who is and should be the end of all [II-223] our thoughts, of all our actions, of all our speeches, of our reading, praying and meditating; for through him we attaine unto salvation, and everlasting life; for his love, we will not feare to die, nor refuse to live. Say then, O *Iesu*, how can I praise thee as I ought, or thinke of thee as I am bound, for thy infinite mercies? Thee will I praise, I will be readie to suffer for thee, being assisted by thy grace, I will magnifie and glorifie thee, I humbly desire thy favour, vouchsafe therefore to doe good unto me, write my name in thy booke, and let me never be blotted out; but let me be accounted amongst the least of thine Elect; I presume nothing of my selfe, let all my comfort be in thy pretious bloud shed for me a sinner, wherein I onely repose; my desire is to be with thee in the land of the living, in the Kingdome of heaven. In the meane time, I will behold thee in this life with the eyes of faith, placing my joy in thee, in this my pilgrimage; and though I should be tossed too and fro, yet will I retaine thee fast in my minde; for thou art my brother, that hast taken my flesh and bones on thee, thanks be unto thee, sweet *Iesu*, that hast united thy humane nature unto the Divine, unite me unto thee, sweet *Iesu*, and leave not my soule in the grave, for thou art my Saviour and Redeemer for ever.

A M E N. [II-224]

# THE
# TABLE OF
# THE SECOND
# PART.

## A.

[Table II-1]

## B.

## C.

### D.

### E.

## F.

                                                                **[Table II-9]**

## K.

## L.

## M.

## N.

## O.

## Q.

## R.

Rich *he is in God and not poore who ever is content with his Fortune.*  *181*

S.

## T.

## V.

## VV.

## Y.

Licence is granted for the printing of this Booke.
*Hampton Court, Decemb.* 8. 1636

*John Coke*

[Table II-18]

# Glossary of Place Names

The place names appearing in *Expedition* are, for the most part, phonetic spellings of German and Danish sites. It is significant that most spellings permit easy location on a modern map, as most still exist and Monro's spellings are similar to modern spellings. By following Monro's narrative and logs, place names can generally be located easily; unusual place names can usually be found between two known places. With the inclusion of only one egregious error— Monro placed Tryer on the Rhine [*Expedition*, II–138] and not on the Mosel—it may be concluded that Monro was quite accurate in his route descriptions. This also indicates that Monro either had access to a daily journal, such as a *Tagebuch*, or a personal diary, or to another source of information, such as *The Swedish Intelligencer*.

It is significant that a text spelling (Parts I and II) is almost always different from a "Log" spelling, indicating that the material was probably dictated, most likely to two or more amanuenses. Variations in spelling, often occurring on the same page, lead also to this conclusion. It is interesting that Monro's rendition of place names is more than a simplistic conversion from German to English, whereby *w* has a "Vee" sound, although this does occur (as when *Wertheim* becomes *Vertzheim*). Monro's German is clearly affected by the non– standardized, non–Hochdeutsch pronunciations of the early modern era. *Cullen*, for example, is a phonetic rendition of the Rheinische pronunciation of *Köln* ("*Kerl–luhn*"), while *Pibrach* would similarly be a phonetic Schwäbische pronunciation of *Biberach* ("*Pee–brach*").

This glossary provides spelling variations of specific sites that Monro either passed while on military service or that were of significance to the regiment. The first column provides the spellings as they appear within the various parts of *Expedition*. The center column provides the modern spelling, with additional German, Danish, or Polish spellings for ease in locating specific sites on a modern map. The third column lists the first time the various spellings appeared in a specific part of *Expedition*, that is, Part I or II, Logs, or elsewhere. The first spelling listed in the first column is that of its first occurrence in *Expedition*; variations are then listed. These variations are cited in the following manner: if there is but one spelling with two citations, the spelling was consistent in both parts; if a comma separates two or more spellings, then those spellings occur within the same part of *Expedition*; if a variation is merely an added letter, it is included parenthetically and is referenced parenthetically; if a semicolon separates the spellings, the spelling appears in a separate section of *Expedition* and the citation follows a semicolon.

This glossary should not be construed as all inclusive or as an index of all occurrences and/or all spellings. Errors regarding the location of the first appearance are the sole responsibility of the editor. For a complete listing of place names and their locations within this edition, see the Index. Maps which provide excellent detail may be found in Michael Roberts, *Gustavus Adolphus, A History of Sweden: 1611–1632*, vol. 2 (London: Longmans, Green, 1958), 432, and C. R. L. Fletcher, *Gustavus Adolphus and the Struggle of Protestantism for Existence* (New York: G. P. Putnam's Sons, 1895), 316.

| | | |
|---|---|---|
| Aichstad; Aichstade, Aychstat | Aichach | Log II–4; II–170, II–207 |
| Aickilfourd, Aickleford; | | |
|     Aikel–ford | Ekernförde | I–50, I–55; Log I–2 |
| Alzenburgh | Helsingborg | I–82 |
| Alzenheure, Alshenure; Alzenheur | Elsinore/ | |
| |   Helsingør | I–61, I–62; I–85, Log I–2 |
| Amberg | Amberg | Log II–4, II–131 |
| Ancklam; Anclam | Anklam | II–23; Log II–2 |
| Angle (Isle of) | Angeln (Holsten) | I–85 (Log I–2) |
| Ashaffenburg, Aschaffenburg; | | |
|     Asschaiffenbourg | Aschaffenburg | II–88, II–110; Log II–3 |
| Assens | Assens | I–26; Log I–1 |
| Ausburg | Augsburg | Log II–4, II–103 |
| Babenhowsen | Babenhausen | II–101 |
| Bachrach, Bagherach | Bacharach | II–96, II–101 |
| Baltick(e) Sea/Coast; Baltique | Baltic | I–6 (II–75); Log I–1, |
| | |   II–127 |
| Bamberg | Bamberg | II–78 |
| Barno; Barnow, Barnoe | Bernau | Log II–2; II–44, II–46 |
| Bavier(e), Bavaria | Bavaria/Bayern | II–104 (II–112, Log II–4); |
| | |   II–85 |
| Bawden, Baden | Baden | II–117, II–120 |
| Belt, Palt [generic—sea channel] | Angelandsbælt | I–41; Log I–2 |
| Berlein; Berlin, Barleene | Berlin | Log II–2; II–42, II–44 |

| | | |
|---|---|---|
| Bingen on the Noe | Bingen on the Nahe | II–97 |
| Blanckeneas; Blanckenesse | Blakenese | I–8; Log I–1 |
| Boden Sea | Lake Constance/ Bodensee | II–127 |
| Bohemia, Bomeme | Bohemia | Intro–3; II–173 |
| Botsaw | Bernau | II–42 |
| Brandenburg | Brandenburg | Log I–2, II–13 |
| Bredenberg, Castle of | Breddenburg | I–12 |
| Bremen | Bremen | Log I–1 |
| Brounesberry in Spruce; Brownesbery | Braunsberg | Log II–2; II–1 |
| Buckstehood; Bucstihoode | Buxtehude | I–8; Log I–1 |
| Burnehollem Road | Bornholmsgatted | II–3 |
| Byerland, Bireland [see also Bavier] | Bavaria/Bayern | II–85, II–92 |
| Bysenbourg; B(e)ysenburgh; Beysenburg | Boizenburg | I–7; I–8 (I–10); I–38, Log I–1 |
| Carlstot; Carl(e)stat on Maine | Karlstadt | Log II–3; II–78 (II–78) |
| Colberg(e) | Kolberg/ Kolobrzeg | Log II–1, II–7 (II–5) |
| Colnoe | Gollnow/ Goleniów | II–11 |
| Copemanhagen; Copmanhagen | Copenhagen/ København | I–61; I–75, Log I–2 |
| Costance | Konstanz | II–178 |
| Cowblance, Coblentz at Mosell | Koblenz | II–95, II–97 |
| Crempe | Krampe | I–1 |
| Crewtsenach; Creutznach; Cretesnough | Bad Kreuznach | II–48; II–97; II–108 |
| Cromartie | Cromarty [Scotland] | Log I–1 |
| Cullen | Cologne/Köln | II–100 |
| Damaine, Dameine | Demmin | Log II–1, II–19; II–15 |
| Dantsick(e) | Danzig/Gdansk | II–4 (II–6) |
| Danube; Danow | Danube/ Donau River | Intro–5, I–6, II–102; II–85 |
| Darmstat; Darmestot | Darmstadt | II–89; Log II–3 |
| Denmark(e) | Denmark | Intro–1, I–6, II–13 (Intro–3, I–1, Log I–1, II–1) |
| Dieben, Diben | Bad Düben | Log II–2; II–61 |
| Donavert | Donauwörth | Log II–3, II–105 |
| Dunkelspeill; Dunkelspill | Dinkelsbühl | Log II–4; II–158 |

| Durengerwalt; During–vault; Vault | Thüringer Forest/Wald | II–77; II–78; II–78 |
| During(land) | Thuringia | II–9 (Log II–2) |
| Dutchland [see also Germany(ie)] | Deutschland/ Germany | I–1, II–1 |
| Eiser River by Munchen | Isar River | II–124 |
| Eittho | Itzehoe | I–4 |
| Eler River by Kempten | Iller River | II–173 |
| Elsas(se) | Alsace/Elsass | II–47 (II–131) |
| Elve | Elbe River | I–1, Log I–1, II–11 |
| Engolstat | Ingolstadt | Log II–4; II–112 |
| Erford; Ertfurt | Erfurt | II–74; Log II–2 |
| Eryackburg in During–land [Castle] | (by Erfurt) | II–76 |
| Eslengan | Esslingen | Log II–5 |
| Feamor; Feamer, Isle of | Fehmarn [Island] | I–27; I–45, Log I–2 |
| Finland, Funland; Funeland | Fyn | I–30, I–33; I–61, Log I–1 |
| Flinesborrie; Flensborre | Flensburg | I–28; Log I–1 |
| Forcham | Forchheim | II–110 |
| Fortmanshowen | (by Amberg) | II–131 |
| Francfurt, Francford | Frankfurt am [on Main] | Log II–3, II–152; II–87 |
| Franckeford; Francford; Franckfurt on the Oder | Frankfurt ob der [on the] Oder | I–67; II–24; Log II–2, II–207 |
| Franconia | Franconia | Log II–2, II–74 |
| Frankendall; Franckendale | Frankenthal | II–94; II–98 |
| Freddesborree, Palace of | Fredensborg | I–86 |
| Freisin; Freisingen; Frising | Freising | Log II–4; II–122, II–124 |
| Fridland; Freedland | Friedland | Log II–2, II–67; II–19 |
| Fuister | Falster [Island] | Log I–2 |
| Furt on the Pegnitz | Fürth | Log II–3, II–111 |
| Fussen | Füssen | II–119 |
| Gaisenfels; Gysenfelt | Gaisenfeld | Log II–4; II–121 |
| Gamund; Gemond | Gemünden | Log II–3; II–78 |
| Gart(t)s | Gartz | II–13 (II–8) |
| Germany(ie) [see also Dutchland] | Germany/ Deutschland | Intro–3, I–11, II–47 (I–2, II–43) |
| Gods–acre | [Breitenfeld] | Log II–2, II–64 |
| Griffenberg; Griffinberg | Greifenberg/ Gryice | Log II–1; II–9 |
| Griffenhawgen on Oder, Griffen–hagen; Grefenhaugne | Greifenhagen/ Gryfino | II–8, II–13, II–212 |

| | | |
|---|---|---|
| (Gros)Glogo(e) | Glogow | (T–II–7) II–42 (II–34) |
| Grottenbro(d)de | Grossenbrode | I–58; Log I–2 |
| Gustavus–Burg, where | | |
|     Mayne enters the Rhine | Main/Rhine | II–112 |
| Haggel(l) | Havel River | II–48 (I–10) |
| Hag(g)leberge | Havelberg | II–48 (II–59) |
| Hailburne, Hailbrun, Hailbron | Heilbronn | II–101, I–174, I–178 |
| Hall | Halle | Log II–2, II–55 |
| Hamburgh; Hamburg | Hamburg | I–7, II–45; List–3, II–47 |
| Hamell on the Weser | Hameln | II–67 |
| Ham(m)elburg | Hammelburg | II–78 (Log II–3) |
| Hano | Hanau | II–99 |
| Harsburg; Harshbrooke | Hersbruck | Log II–4; II–131 |
| Hechstat on Danube | Höchstädt | II–115 |
| Heghst; Hechst, Hickst | Höchst | Log II–3; II–89, II–105 |
| Heidelberg | Heidelberg | II–89 |
| Heligenhoven | Heiligenhafen | I–17, Log I–1 |
| Hensberrie [see Flensborrie] | | |
| Hinder Pomerne | Pomerania/Hinter | |
| |     Pommern | Log II–1, II–5 |
| Holsten; Holstein; Howlsten | Holstein | I–1, Log–1; II–11, |
| | |     Log I–1;II–117 |
| Kauffebeyren; Kauffbier, Koffbier | Kaufbeuren | Log II–4; II–176, II–177 |
| Ke(e)le, Keel; Kyel | Kiel | I–53 (I–58); T–I–3; |
| | |     Log I–2 |
| Kempten | Kempten | Log II–4, II–122 |
| Kitchen | Kitzingen | II–110 |
| Konickhoffen | Bad Königshofen | II–78 |
| Landaw, Lindaw | Lindau | II–102, II–119 |
| Landsberg; Lan(t)sberg on Wart; | | |
|     Laudsberg/Wert | Landsberg/Gorzów/ | |
| |     on Warthe | II–14; II–30 (Log II–2); |
| | |     II–8 |
| Landshude; Landshut, Landsout | Landshut | Log II–4; II–121; II–207 |
| Langland | Langeland | I–41 |
| Lantericke | Lauterecken | II–135 |
| Lantsberg | Landsberg on | |
| |     Lech | Log II–4; II–206 |
| Lasknets, Lecknetts | Löcknitz | II–14, II–25 |
| Lauffe; Loaffe, Lawffe | Lauf | Log II–4; II–111, II–131 |
| Lawenburg, Lovenburgh | Lauenburg | I–4, I–8 |
| Leacke | Lech River | Log II–4, II–115 |
| Lecknetts [see Lasknets] | | |
| Leipsigh | Leipzig | Log II–2, II–64 |
| Leitzen | Lützen | II–161 |

| | | |
|---|---|---|
| Letz; Letts | Loitz | Log II–1; II–15 |
| London in Skoneland | Lund | I–82 |
| Lor(e) | Lohr | Log II–3 (II–110) |
| Loughstad; Lukstad; Luckstad; Lugstad | Glückstadt | I–1; I–12; I–33, II–11; I–38, Log I–1 |
| Lowland | Lolland | I–41, Log I–2 |
| Lubeck | Lübeck | I–83 |
| Luniburgh | Lüneburg | I–8 |
| Ma(g)deburg | Magdeburg | II–43 (I–67, II–23) |
| Maine; Mayne | Main River | I–31, Log II–3, II–77; II–112 |
| Mainigane; Mainigen | Meiningen | Log II–3; II–78 |
| Malchen(e) in Macklenburg | Malchin | Log II–2 (II–19) |
| Malemce, Malmee | Malmö | I–88; Log I–2 |
| Malline in Skoneland | (by Malmö) | I–82 |
| Manhem | Mannheim | II–101 |
| Marbo | Maribo | I–42, Log I–2 |
| Meclinburgh, Mechlenburg, Macklenburg | Mecklenburg | I–12; Log I–1; Log II–2 |
| Memming; Memmungen; Menning | Memmingen | Log II–4, II–175; II–109; II–173 |
| Mentz on the Rhine | Mainz | I–31, Log II–3, II–48 |
| Millarstot; Milerstad, Mellerstat | Mellrichstadt | Log II–3; II–77, II–77 |
| Miltenburg | Miltenberg | Log II–3, II–88 |
| Middelhem; Mindelhaim | Mindelheim | Log II–4; II–119 |
| Morsburg; Mosburg | Moosburg | Log II–4, II–157; II–121 |
| Mosell | Moselle/ Mosel River | II–96 |
| Munchen; Monchen; Minchen | Munich/ München | Log II–4, II–124; II–126; II–171 |
| Munderkin; Monderkine | Munderkingen | Log II–4; II–177 |
| Necoppine, Nicoppen | Nykøbing | I–42; Log I–2 |
| Nerlin(g) | Nördlingen | Intro–2, II–104 (Intro–1, List–3, Log II–3, II–158) |
| Neuburg, Neighburg; Nuburg on the Danube | Neuburg | II–116; II–117 |
| New Brandenburg | Neubrandenburg | Log II–1; II–13 |
| Nistot on the Sale Newstat, Newstad; | Bad Neustadt | Log II–3; II–78, II-153 |
| Noe | Nahe River | II–97 |

| | | |
|---|---|---|
| Nurenburg; Nurenberg; Newringburg; Newrenberg | Nuremberg/ Nürnberg | II–126; Log II–3, II–87; II–84; II–86 |
| Oberwesell | Oberwesel | II–102 |
| Offenbach | Offenbach | Log II–3 |
| Old Brandenburg | Brandenburg | Log II–2; II–44 |
| old land on the Elve side; Oldland | (by Hamburg) | I–8; Log I–1 |
| Olme; Vlme | Ulm | II–24; Log II–4, II–87 |
| Openham; Oppenhem in the Paltz | Oppenheim | Log II–3; II–89 |
| Ostreigh | Austria/ Österreich | II–129 |
| Ottengen | Oettingen | II–113 |
| Ouldenburg(h); Oldenburg(h), Owldenburg(h) | Oldenburg in Holstein | I–6 (I–20); Log I–1 (I–17); I–26 (I–20) |
| Oxenford on the Maine | Ochsenfurt | Log II–3, II–83 |
| Palt [see Belt] | | |
| Paltz | Palatinate/Pfalz | II–47 |
| Panco | Pankow | II–43 |
| Papart | Boppard | II–102 |
| Pegnets | Pegnitz River | Log II–3, II–111 |
| Perlesberg | Perleberg | I–15 |
| Pibrach; Pybrach | Biberach | Log II–4; II–122; II–178 |
| Pillo in Spruce, the | Pillau | Log II–1, II–1 |
| Pomeren; Pomerne | Pomerania | I–80, Log I–2, II–17; II–6 |
| Pooswell, Posewall | Pasewalk | II–19, II–23 |
| Poule; Poole Isle of | Poel [Island] | I–16, T–1–6; Log I–1 |
| Primhausen; Prymhaussen near Stargard; | Priemhausen/ Poland | Log II–1; II–11 |
| Procelden | (by Werthiem) | Log II–3 |
| Rapine; Rapin | [Neu/Alt] Ruppin | I–15, II–23; Log I–1 |
| Ratisbone | Regensburg | II–112 |
| Rattino; Ratenough, Rawtenaw | Rathenow | Log II–2; II–48, II–58 |
| Raynesberge | Rendsburg | I–2 |
| Retlingam | Reutlingen | Log II–5 |
| Rhine | Rhine River | Intro–2, I–6, Log II–3, II–48 |
| Rhine on the Leacke | Rain | Log II–4, II–112 |
| Rottenburg | Rotenburg | I–7, II–144 |
| Rougenvald(e) | Rügenwalde | Log II–1 (II–3) |
| Rubee; Rubie | Rødby | I–42; I–45, Log I–2 |
| Rustocke | Rostock | II–47 |
| Sale | Frankische Saale River | Log II–4, II–78 |

| Saxonie; Saxon | Saxony | II–57; I–31, Log 11–2, II–30 |
|---|---|---|
| Schawbbishhall | Schwäbisch Hall | II–111 |
| Schwabach | Schwabach | Log II–3, II–113 |
| Schwab(e)land; Swa(u)bland; | Swabia/ Schwaben | Log II–5, II–6 (II–24); II–47 (I–6) |
| Serbest | Zerbst | II–47 |
| Shivel–beane; Shevelbean(e) | Schivelbein/ Gryfice | II–7; II–8 (Log II–1, II–8) |
| Showngow | Schongau | II–119 |
| Silesia | Silesia | I–8, II–40 |
| Skonland | Malmöhus | Log I–2, II–1 |
| Smalka | Schmalkalden | Log II–2, II–78 |
| Spando; Spandaw | Spandau | Log II–2; II–43 |
| Spier | Hochspeyer | II–96 |
| Spotsdam(me) | Potsdam | Log II–2 (II–43) |
| Spruce | East Prussia/ Ost Preussen | I–6, Log II–1, II–1 |
| Stargard | Stargard/ Szcecinski | II–10 |
| Statin(e) | Stettin/Szczecin | Log II–1, II–9 (II–5) |
| Steinhem | (by Offenbach) | Log II–3, II–88 |
| Steyne | Stein | II–134 |
| Stoade | Stade | I–4, II–102 |
| Stockholme | Stockholm | II–1 |
| Stockstat | (by Mainz) | II–94 |
| Sultzbach | (by Frankfurt am Main) | Log II–3, II–131 |
| Swede on the Oder | Scwedt | Log II–2, II–23 |
| Sweetzerland, Switzerland | Switzerland | II–128, II–130 |
| Swinfort | Schweinfurt | II–78 |
| Tangermond(e); Tannermonde, Tangermound; | Tangermünde | Log II–2 (II–52); II–41, II–48; |
| Tettelbach | Dettelbach | Log II–3, II–110 |
| Trailesound; Trailsound | Stralsund | I–59, II–47; I–69; Log I–2 |
| Trepto; Triptowe | Altentreptow | Log II–1, II–15; II–19 |
| Tryer on the Rhine | Trier on the Mosel | II–138 |
| upper Paltz | Upper Palatinate | II–84 |
| Vault [see Durengerwalt] | | |
| Vberling | Überlingen | II–178 |
| Verben; Verbum, Werben | Werben | Log II–2, II–57; II–41, II–48 |

| | | |
|---|---|---|
| Vertenberg([s]land) | Württemberg | II–177 ([II–177] Log II–5) II–104 |
| Vertzburg [see Wurtzburg] | | |
| Vertzhem | Wertheim | Log II–3 |
| Veysenburg [see Weisenburg] | | |
| Vintzin; Vinchen, Winsen, Winchene | Windsheim | Log II–3; II–110, II–111, II–156 |
| Vittenberg [see Wittenberg] | | |
| Vlme [see Olme] | | |
| Volgast [see Wolgast] | | |
| Volmarsdorffe; Wolmersdorffe | (by Fürth) | Log II–3; II–111 |
| Vrbowe | Örebro | II–2 |
| Wart; Wert | Warthe River | Log II–2, II-2; II–38 |
| Wartenburgland [see Vertenberg] | | |
| Waser streame; Weser; Wazer | Weser River | I–4, II-85; Log I–1, II-137; II–107 |
| Werben [see Verbum] | | |
| Wesmar, Wismer(e), Wismar | Wismar | I–6; I–17 (I–15), I–85 |
| Weysenburg; Veysenburg; Weisenburg | Weissenburg | Log II–3, II–122; Log II–4; II–128 |
| Winsen [see Vinchen] | | |
| Wittenberg; Vyttenberg on the Elve, Vittenberg | Wittenberg | II–41; Log II–2, Log II–2 |
| Wolgast in Pomeren; Volgast | Wolgast | I–37, Log I–1, II–3; T–I–6 |
| Wolmersdorffe, see Volmarsdorffe | | |
| Wolmerstat | Wolmirstedt | II–49 |
| Wormes | Worms | Intro–1, II–94 |
| Wurtzburg; Vertzburg; Vertzberg | Würzburg | II–78; Log II–3; II–196 |
| Wymar(e) | Weimar | I–12, II–53 (II–153) |
| Yewtland | Jutland | I–28 |
| Zeland; Zealand | Sjælland | I–61; Log I–2 |
| Zerndorfe | Zirndorf | II–134 |

# Glossary of Persons

Names often appear in *Expedition* without clarification and without consistency in spelling. This glossary provides names and titles of some of the important general officers and secular rulers who appear in the text, the location of their first appearance in a given section of *Expedition*, and a brief identification of an individual, including the generally accepted title and name. The Glossary is not a list of all persons mentioned in *Expedition*, only those of relevance to the regiment's activities. Also included are other Scottish officers who were of significance to Monro.


Arn(e)hem; Harnam (Felt–marshall)  I–86, II–65 (I–67); II–71
  Arnim, Johann Georg von (1581–1641). Swedish commander (1613).
  Imperial army, rising to rank of Field Marshal (1625–1631), and Saxon
  General (1631–1635).

Bannier(e); Banier (Generall)  II–18 (II–13); II–18
  Banèr, Johan (1596–1641). Swedish officer (1613–1641), rising to
  rank of Field Marshal.

Bavier (Duke of)  II–104
  Maximilian I of Bavaria (1573–1651). Duke (1597), then Elector
  (1523) of Bavaria. Organized and led Catholic League.

Bawtee, Bautis, Bawtish (Generall)  II–8, II–59, II–64
  Baudissin, Wolf Heinrich von (1597–1646). Began service with
  Denmark, then Sweden, rising to rank of Major General (1629–1635).
  Commanded Saxon forces (1635).

Bohemia (King of)                              II–90
    Frederick V of the Palatinate (1596–1632). Elector Palatine (1610).
    Calvinist leader and Director of Protestant Union (1608). Elected King
    of Bohemia (1619–1621), in exile after Battle of White Mountain
    (1620). Married Elizabeth Stuart [see Bohemia, Queene of] (1613).

Bohemia (Queene of)                            Intro–3, I–6, II–93
    Elizabeth Stuart (1596–1662). Daughter of James VI of Scotland (I of
    England), married to Frederick of the Palatine.

Brandenburg (Elector/Duke)                     II–30
    George William (1595–1640). Elector of Brandenburg (1619) and
    irresolute Calvinist ruler of Lutherans. Brother–in–law of Gustavus
    Adolphus. Forced to accept a Swedish alliance (1631), switched
    support to Emperor (1635), lands devastated by Swedes thereafter.

Christian (Palsgrave)                          II–110
    Christian (1581–1655). Margrave of Brandenburg–Kulmbach and
    Swedish general.

Denmarke (King/Majestie)                       Intro–1, I–6, II–1
    Christian IV (1577–1648). King of Denmark and Norway (1588).
    Intervened in Thirty Years' War (1625–1629) until Peace of Lübeck
    ended participation.

Emperour of Austria                            Intro–1, I–6, II–11
    Ferdinand II (1578–1637). Habsburg Archduke of Inner Austria, King
    of Bohemia (1617), Holy Roman Emperor (1619). Thirty Years' War
    began when Bohemian nobles revolted, replacing him as King with
    Frederick of the Palatinate. Roman Catholic champion, determined to
    restore Catholicism throughout Empire and to assert his authority as
    Emperor.

Gallas                                         II–156
    Gallas, Matthias, Count (1584–1645). Served in Spanish and Bavarian
    armies (to 1629), Imperial General (to 1634), Commander of Imperial
    army (1634–1644).

Gustavus the Invincible [see Sweden]

Hamilton, Marquesse of                         II–52
    Hamilton, James, Marquis of (1606–1649). General and Commander
    of the Scottish army in Germany (1630–1632). Executed during
    English Civil War by Parliament.

Hepburn, Sir Iohn (Colonell)            II–5
> Hepburn, Sir John (1598–1636). Swedish service (1625–1632), rising to rank of Colonel. French service (1632–1636), rising to rank of Maréchal du France. Killed at Saverne.

Holke (Colonell)                         I–64; II–52
> Hol(c)k, Henrik, Count (1599–1633). Danish Commander (to 1629), Imperial service (1629–1633).

Horne, Gustavus (Felt–marshall)          II–9
> Horn, Gustav (1592–1657). Swedish service (1612–1634), rising to rank of Field Marshall. Captured at Nördlingen and held captive (1634–1642). Administrator until death.

King (Generall Major)                    II–108
> King, Sir James, Baron Eythin (1589–1652). Swedish service, rising to rank of Major General by 1632. Returned to Scotland in 1640, Lieutenant General of Scottish forces during English Civil War. Died in Sweden.

Kniphowsen (Generall Major)              II–7
> Knyphausen, Dodo, Reichsfreiherr zu Innhausen und (1583–1636). Began career in 1613, later in Danish service (to 1629). Swedish service as Major General (1630–1634). French service as army commander until killed (1635–1636).

Lesly (Governour of Trailsound)          I–75, II–12
> Leslie, Sir Alexander, Earl of Leven (c. 1580–1661). In Swedish service for thirty years, rising to rank of Field Marshal. Returned to Scotland in 1637 to command Covenanter army, served as Commander of Scottish forces during English Civil War. Prisoner of Parliament (1651–1654).

Mac–key (Colonell), Lord Rhees           Intro–1, I–3, II–17
> Mackay, Sir Donald, Lord Reay (1591–1651). Colonel of Scottish Regiment (1627–1631). Interested primarily in recruiting. Financed printing of *Expedition*. Fought on side of Charles I in English Civil War. Retired to Denmark (1648).

Monro (Colonel)
> Monro, Robert (c. 1590–1680). Anti–Imperial service (1627–1633), rising to rank of Colonel. Author of *Expedition*. Commanded Scots army in Ulster (1642–1649), captured at Carrickfergus (1648), imprisoned in Tower of London (to 1654). Retired to Ulster.

Monro of Fowles; Foules (Barron/Colonell) I–1, II–1; Intro–15, II–195

> Monro, Robert, Black Laird of Foulis (d. 1633). Anti–Imperial service (1627–32), rising to rank of Colonel. Died of battle wounds suffered at Ulm. Cousin of Robert Monro and head of the family of Monro. The author's eulogy to him appears at Intro–14, a translation of which is: "To the illustrious and generous Lord, Sir Robert Munro, Military Tribune, Epitaph. The famous Robert Munro with great power, who was Baron of Foulis, head of the Munro [clan], to whom twice [was given] the legion of infantry and cavalry to serve, to which he joined love of Country and Religion, After he fought energetically on the borders of Leipzig, and all over gave martial injuries to the Austrians, at last thrown down by a great hostile wound, greatly wounded by the enemy he left his fallen body in the soil of Ulm. His spirit with great power surmounting death in Heaven received rewards worthy of Heroes. Learn, Germans, and study with grateful mind, how many brave men have fallen for you! How many Heroes have died for your freedom–Sons of the Caledonian race and of the Munro [clan]!"

Monro of Obstell (Colonell)                           I–19, II–12

> Monro, John of Obsdale (d. 1633). Elder brother of Robert Monro. Anti-Imperial service (1627–1632), rising to rank of Colonel. Killed during altercation with German troops in Swedish service. The author's eulogy to him appears at Intro–15, a translation of which is: "To the illustrious and generous Lord, Sir John Munro, Military Tribune, Epitaph. In this tomb lies the Tribune of the Scottish race, John who was the most famous Munro in the world. The Barons of Foulis are said to have born him, to whom the Eagle and roaring Lion give their signs. Whose glory and pedigree has been thriving under the name Munro for three hundred and twice thirty years. Here grave with piety, and serviceable to the just, virtuous, and waging war with fearless breast, while he restrains with his voice the rage of an unbridled soldier, he dies, touched by the thunderbolt of one ungrateful [person]. The Swedes mourn him; the German earth is in mourning because of the shameful murder of the faithful Hero. Especially his offspring, which he begat with one single mother (indeed nine sons, four daughters) weep. He has loved well for forty-four years, an unexpected death allowed him to live better. City lying on the Rhine, Temple of Bacchus, honored by this good [deed], give rest to his body. His spirit ascends into the ethereal reaches of Heroes, and leaves grief in his world.

Mounte DeCucule; Mountecuculie         II–34; II–138

> Montecuccoli, Raimondo (1609–1680). Imperial service from 1625, rising to rank of Field Marshal. Following Thirty Years' War served Habsburgs in wars with France and the Turks.

Oxensterne, Directour General/Chancellor    Intro–1, II–75
    Oxenstierna, Axel (1583–1654). Swedish Chancellor from 1612, and
    directed foreign policy for Gustavus Adolphus and his daughter
    Christina (b. 1626; Queen, 1632).

Palatine of Rhine, Prince Elector            Intro–3, I–37, II–128
    Charles Louis, Count Palatine of Rhine (1617-1680). In exile until
    1648 and restored as Elector Palatine at Peace of Westphalia.
    *Expedition* dedicated to him. Younger brother was Rupert, third son of
    the King and Queen of Bohemia (1619–1682). General and Admiral of
    Royalist forces throughout English Civil War. Returned to England
    1660 and served in military capacities, including First Lord of the
    Admiralty (to 1679).

Papingham; Papenha(i)m            II–67; II–103 (II–126)
    Pappenheim, Gottfried Heinrich von, Count (1594–1632). Catholic
    convert from Lutheranism. Served Bavarian and Imperial forces
    (1619—1632), rising to rank of General. Killed at Lützen.

Ramsey, Sir Iames (Colonell)            II–63
    Ramsey, Sir James (1589–1639). Anti–Imperial service, 1627–1639,
    rising to rank of Major General in Swedish service. Killed at Hanover.

Rhee, Lord of [see Mac–Key]

Rhinegrave                          I–21, II–31
    Otto Ludwig, Count Palatine (d. 1634). Served as cavalry regiment
    commander in Danish army. Commanded cavalry regiment in army of
    Gustavus Adolphus. Fought at Nördlingen and died shortly thereafter.

Ruthven (Generall Major)            I–82, II–24
    Ruthven, Sir Patrick, Earl of Forth and Brentford (1583–1651). Served
    Sweden (1612–1638), rising to rank of Field Marshall. Returned to
    Scotland (1638) and commanded Scottish forces against Charles I.
    Commanded Royalist forces in English Civil War and was declared
    traitor by the Scottish Parliament.

Saxon, Duke of                          II–30
    John George (1585–1656). Lutheran Elector of Saxony who preferred
    neutrality. Forced to ally with Sweden (1631–1635). Vacillation led
    to repeated devastations of his lands by both sides.

Slamersdorffe(dorph) Generall Major        I–12 (I–34)
    Schlammersdorf, Balthazar Jacob von. General in the service of
    Saxony.

Sweden (Invincible King; Lyon of North; Maiesty)     (Intro–1; I–5; Intro–2)
      Gustavus Adolphus (1594–1632).   King of Sweden (1611).   Began
      Continental wars with attack on Poland (1621).   Entered Thirty Years'
      War as Protestant savior (1630).   Killed at Lützen.

Tillie; Tilley; Tylly; Tilly, Generall          I–12, II–23; I–39; II–18; II–23
      Tilly, Jean 't Serclaes, Count (1559–1632).   Imperial service in Army
      of Flanders (1585–1600), commanded army of the Catholic League
      army (1610–1632),  and killed at Rain on the Lech River.

Tuffenback; Tiffenbacke (Felt–marshall)     II–30; II–34
      Tiefenbach Rudolph von (1582–1653).   Imperial Field Marshal who
      retired in 1631, becoming a diplomat.

Walestein; Wal(l)estine; Valestine          T–1–7; I–69, II–116 (II–124);
                                            II–128
      Wallenstein, Albrecht W. E. von, Duke of Friedland (1583–1634).
      Lutheran convert to Catholicism, commanded Imperial army (1625–
      1630, 1632–1634).   Assassinated after being charged with treason by
      Emperor (1634).

Wymar(e), Duke Barnard of, Generall       I–12, II–53 (II–153)
      Bernard, Duke of Saxe–Weimar (1604–1639).   Anti–Imperial service in
      Low Countries and Germany, rising to rank of General (1621–1630).
      Swedish service (1630–1635); French service (1635–1639).

# Glossary of Terms

Many terms, military and otherwise, that appear in Expedition are either archaic or not explained; and this glossary provides brief definitions for the reader. The list should not be construed as a comprehensive catalogue of unfamiliar terms nor should the definitions be considered complete; it is provided merely for ready reference. Many of the definitions are derived from *The Oxford English Dictionary* (*OED*), 2nd Edition, 20 vols. (Oxford: Clarendon Press, 1989). When *Expedition* examples are cited as part of an *OED* definition, it is so noted. Other definitions or clarifications were gleaned from various military history works, all of which may be found in the bibliography. Citations of appearance in *Expedition* are only for the first usage of a word within a section.

Accord                            I–15, II–15
> Accord: a formal agreement for the surrender of a military position.

Alarum(mes)                   I–6 (I–4)
> Alarm: a call to arms by guards on duty because of impending danger or immediate threat from the enemy.

Armes, Profession of           Intro–1, I–36, II–13
> Profession of Armes: a euphemism for being a mercenary, which, in the seventeenth century, was an acceptable occupation, especially by a Cavalier.

Articles of War, Order of Discipline     I–2/3; II–3
> Articles of War/Order of Discipline/Articles of Military Discipline: terms describing a proscribed code of military conduct for all members of a military unit. It included lists of infractions, a description of the military court, the punishments, and the oath of acceptance that all members of the unit were to swear.

Assisers                                                 I–44

    Assizes: the military court before which charged soldiers were brought when in violation of the Articles of War.

Bandeliers                                               I–23

    Bandolier: a sling that went over the shoulder and across the chest and from which cartridges for the mustket were hung in readiness for use in battle.

Ban(c)ke of the Drummer                    I–4 (I–33, II–34)

    Banke: a drumbeat pattern for a specific military command. Drums were important because they could be heard over the noise of battle. Banke commands were used on marches, to align formations while "drawing into Battaile," and to command specific battlefield maneuvers. Specific drum commands listed by Monro include troope, charge, call, retreat, and march (II–191). According to Monro, the "Scots March" (II–66) was particularly famous and easily recognized.

Barleene Articles                                  II–44

    Berlin Agreement: military alliance between Gustavus Adolphus and George William, Duke of Brandenburg, June 22, 1631.

Bastant                                                  I–80

    Bastant: able to or capable of (*Expedition* cited in *OED*).

Battaile; Battell (drawing into)              I–8; II–8

    Drawing into battle was the maneuvering of a body of troops into battle formation. It required much training and practice, and utilized specific commands and drum bankes. Monro provides a distillation of the techniques in "Abridgement of Exercises for Younger Soldiers" (II: 183–192).

Boores                                                  I–4

    Boors: peasants/farmers or rustics. From Middle German *gebûr* and Low seventeenth century German *buur*, the modern form is German *Bauern* or Dutch *Boer*.

Breast–worke                                        II–8

    Breastwork: a field fortification, usually quickly constructed as protection for infantry and artillery. It consisted of a ditch with a wall behind it, which was made from the dirt from the ditch.

Brickle                                                  II–16

    Brickle: adjective used to describe that which is fragile or brittle.

Briggad(e)                                             List–1, II–14 (II–31)

    Brigade: a subdivision of an army consisting of three to five regiments. Gustavus Adolphus created these units for better battlefield mobility and flexibility. Four Scottish regiments, including Mackay's Regiment, were combined in 1631 to make the Scots Brigade (II–25). As a regiment of full strength contained 1,500 pikemen, musketeers, and officers, a brigade could have had as many as 6,000 men. Battle and disease swiftly reduced units in size, as may be seen in the size of the Scots Brigade in September 1631, when it numbered only about 2,225.

Bucler                                      I–84

    Buckler: a small arm shield fastened by a strap to the arm and used to parry blows.

Bulwarkes                                   II–52

    Bulwark: a more substantial and permanent wall fortification for a military position.

Burgars; Burgers                            I–76; II–9

    Burgers/burghers: town citizens; the term was also used in Britain.

Cadoucks and casualties                     II–123

    Cadoucks and casualties: a Scottish phrase referring to a windfall or unexpected largesse from someone (*Expedition* cited in *OED*).

Camerade(s)                                 Intro–3, I–7, II–14

    Comrades: associates in arms or close companions with whom one had shared the military life. Monro often refers to his comrades as a major reason for writing *Expedition*, as he wanted to perpetuate their memory.

Cannonbaskets                               II–17

    Cannonbaskets/gabions: cylindrical baskets filled with earth/stones and sited in breastworks to protect artillery gunners. They could also be used for immediate protection while breastworks were being dug.

Carracole                                   II–23

    Caracole: a wheeling maneuver by cavalry whereby an enemy position was approached, fire was given, and the unit "wheeled," or turned, to the right or left and reversed direction.

Cartowes                                    I–53; II–51

    Cartowe: a kind of cannon that fired a twenty–five–pound ball (also called a quarter cannon because it fired a ball weighing one–quarter of a one–hundred–pound projectile).

Catholique League, Stends                   II–61, 106

    Catholic League: formed under the leadership of Maximilian of Bavaria (1603). Initially an informal alliance, it was formally created in 1609 and was codirected by the emperor and Maximilian. The Bohemian crisis (1618) allowed Maximilian to demand sole directorship of the Catholic League, in return for his military support against Frederick of the Palatinate and the Protestant Union. Tilly commanded the League's army, which was the only army Ferdinand had available until General Wallenstein created an Imperial army. Stends refers to *Stände*, German for estates (nobles).

Cavalier                                    Intro–1

    Cavalier: a gentleman trained to engage in the "Noble Profession of Armes," which required a social status of knight or better.

Centry                                      I–6

    Sentry: a person or unit posted outside a military camp (Leaguer) to guard against a surprise attack from the enemy as well as to protect the unit from looting by civilians or by other soldiers.

Champagne; *Champange*, Champaigne      I–18; II–91, II–120
> Champaign: a level, or leveled, field whereon military operations were carried out, such as a field of battle. It was also a cleared area surrounding a fortification which provided a clear field of fire for muskets and artillery.

Chirurgians                                              I–33
> Chirurgeon: a surgeon or physician.

Circles; Creitch                                    II–47; II–136
> Imperial Circles (*Reichskreise*): ten "circles" were created in 1512 (Diet of Köln) in an effort to organize the Holy Roman Empire and to maintain peace (*Landfriedenkreise*). It was also an effort to control the power of the emperor. Although the circles existed as administrative units, they had little real power.

Colours                                              I–2, II–12
> Colours: the standard, flag, or banner of a unit. Colours served as a focal point for a unit in battle and as a rallying point after a battle. Losing a unit's colours was considered to be one of the worst military acts possible.

Combate; *Monomachia*                         I–82; I–84
> Combat: duel between two persons to settle a dispute or matter of honor.

Commissaries                                         I–33
> Commissaries: military representatives responsible for performing quartermaster duties, that is the finding of supplies and lodging for troops as well as the distribution of food, ammunition, and supplies to troops when needed.

Commission                                           II–1
> Commission: military authorization to perform a specific service. For the military entrepreneur, a commission granted the recipient a specific rank and authority to raise a specified number of troops. Granted by the person who needed the mercenaries for an army, it was similar to a patent.

Conjunction betwixt his Majestie and the Duke of Saxon      II–61
> Swedish/Saxon alliance: caught between Tilly and Gustavus Adolphus, John George of Saxony chose to ally himself with the Swedes when invaded by Tilly. The alliance, in early September 1631, was immediately followed by the Battle of Breitenfeld (on Gods Acre).

Conshaft                                           II-131, II-201
> Conshaft, or Intelligence. The acquisition of information about the disposition of the enemy was requisite for success.

Contribution                                         I–12, II–5
> Contribution: a euphemism for a forced tax levied by an invading force upon a town or region to support the military needs of the invader. A threat of destruction, if the contribution not paid, usually accompanied the demand(s). The *Kontributionssystem* (German for the systematic

collections of contributions and used to describe the practice) became an integral part of sustaining all military units throughout the Thirty Years' War.

Cornet (of Horse)                                    II–35

Cornet: the standard/flag of a troop of cavalry; the word also became the generic name for a unit of cavalry.

Crabbats                                             II–9

Croats: originally a specific light cavalry unit in Imperial service. Comprised initially of Magyars and/or Croats, the term became a generic reference to Imperial light cavalry forces which were used for reconnaissance and foraging.

Creitches [see Circles]

Cullen Agreement                                     II–100

Bishopric of Köln Agreement: terms offered by Gustavus Adolphus to the Catholic Bishop of Cologne for him to leave their domain alone. It called for religious toleration for Evangelists, free access to their territory by him, and neutrality by the bishop regarding the war. It was accepted January 21, 1632.

Cunctation                                           II–86

Cunctation: a military strategy that employs delaying tactics. Also referred to as Fabian tactics, from Fabius Cunctator, the Roman opponent of Hannibal.

Curassiers                                           II–34

Cuirassiers: heavy cavalry featuring larger horses and thicker body armor for cavalryman.

Danes Crosse                                         I–3

Danish Cross or Danish flag: flag used by Christian IV, under which his soldiers, Scots included, were to fight. Not a national flag at the time, but later become one.

Deales                                               II–205

Deal: to divide into equal parts, portions, or amounts, as is dividing a town into parts, to which units of the army would be assigned.

Deboysing                                            II–202

Deboise: to corrupt, or to render a group less able to resist. Debase might be a later version of the word. A débouché is also an opening in a city or town wall through which troops could exit or withdraw (debouch).

Dor (Franckendore)                                   I–62

Dore or Door: a major door or gate to a town. This becomes the German *Tor*, meaning Gate.

Dorpes                                               I–4, II–11

Dorp: a village, from the German *Dorf*, meaning peasant community or village of Boores.

Dragoniers                                                    I–58, II–5

Dragoons: originally introduced as a special infantry unit provided with mounted transportation. Dragoons usually rode to a place of action, dismounted, and performed as infantry.

Drawbridge                                                    I–7

Drawbridge: a hinged bridge that can be drawn up and let down to allow or refuse entrance to a fortification.

Edict over all Franconia                                       II–85

Edict by Gustavus Adolphus: proclamation by Gustavus Adolphus (October 1631) wherein he declared himself to be the protector of the oppressed Protestants of the states of central Germany. It was also an ultimatum to Catholic bishops for the toleration of Protestants.

Emperialists                                                   I–5

Imperialist: generic term used by anti–Imperial forces to denote Habsburg forces and their allies during the Thirty Years' War. It refers to the supporters of Ferdinand II, in particular, and to the Habsburgs, both Spanish and Austrian, in general.

Entertainment                                                 I–1, II–28

Entertainment: provisions and shelter for the military. It was provided by the Commissaries or through Contribution.

Evangelist Stends                                             II–100

Protestant Union: formed in 1608, it was a defensive alliance between Lutheran and Calvinist princes within the Holy Roman Empire and was directed by Frederick of the Palatinate. Religious differences between the two Protestant sects restricted any coordinated action, a problem for anti–Imperial action throughout the Thirty Years' War. When Frederick accepted the Bohemian crown (1619), most members refused to support him. Stends (from German for *Stände*, or estates) was used by Monro to mean Protestant princes as well as Protestants in general.

Evangelists/Reformed Religion                                 II–85

Evangelical Church: the Lutheran Church, its name in English–speaking areas. In German speaking areas, *Evangelisch* refers to those who belong to the *Evangelische Kirche*.

Field–pieces                                                  II–55

Fieldpieces: light artillery for use on the battlefield. References in *Expedition* are possibly to the leather guns developed by Gustavus Adolphus which were significantly lighter than other artillery pieces of the time and therefore provided his army with greater firepower on the battlefield.

Fire–lock                                                     I–6

Firelock: a musket that used sparks to ignite powder in a pan, which in turn ignited the powder in the musket barrel via a firehole. The wheel–lock was an early version, and was later replaced by the flintlock; both were improvements over the harquebus.

**Fix in his Arms**                                    II–218

Fix: to set oneself in a defensive posture or to arrange in order. This probably refers to a formation in full military garb in dressed (properly aligned) lines.

**Flake**                                              II–33

Flake: antipersonnel grenade or mine–like device which, when exploded, threw off flakes of metal. It was perhaps similar to (a very early version of) a Claymore–like mine.

**Fore–loofe; forloffes**                              I–34; II–25

Furlough: from Scottish forloff, a period of leave for military personnel.

**Fossie; Fossey**                                     I–14; I–28

Fosse: a ditch, usually at or near a fortification, serving as a barrier to an advancing enemy force. It was also called a moat if filled with water.

**Furniture**                                          II–23

Furniture: military accouterments (equipment, weapons of war, and munitions).

**Furriers; Furer; Furiers**                           I–33, II–59; II–18; II–47

Furrier: advance scout sent to secure and arrange for accommodations (*Expedition* cited in *OED*). Another definition was that of a specific officer rank within a company, perhaps from German *Führer*, or leader.

**Gabeons [see Cannonbaskets]**                        II–213

**Gavileger; Gavilliger**                              I–34; I–45, II–114, II–208

Provost or Proforce: officer detailed to arrest and detain those who violated the Articles of War and to carry out punishment on those found guilty.

**German mile**                                        Logs

German mile: equal to about six English miles or about 9.6 kilometers. When compared to actual distances, Monro's numbers, as cited in his Logs, seem to fluctuate between four and six miles. This may be due more to march routes and poor roads of the seventeenth century than to inaccuracy or bad guesses. Monro also cites sea distances as German miles, but the sea distances listed are probably leagues, which would be about three miles.

**Goales**                                             II–94

Gaol: jail.

**Gods Acre**                                          II–64

Breitenfeld, Battle of: fought on September 17, 1631, near Leipzig. Monro also refers to the battle as the Battle of Leipsigh.

**Graffe**                                             I–29, II–11

Graff: a trench or ditch for defense, and either dry or wet. Also called fosse or moat (*Expedition* cited in *OED*).

Hagapells                                                II–55
> *Hakkapelites*: Swedish light cavalry, originally comprised primarily of
> Finnish horsemen.

Hagbuts of Crocke                                        II–15
> Hackbust or Hackbut: from *harquebus*, or hook gun, an early musket
> used with a portable rest. Also called *harquebus á croc* (arquebus with
> hook), which is the term referred to by Monro.

Hailbron, meeting at                                     II–178
> Heilbronn Confederation (April 23, 1633): the death of Gustavus
> Adolphus at Lützen left a leadership vacuum in the Protestant alliance.
> Swedish Chancellor Oxenstierna organized the four south German
> circles into an alliance under Swedish leadership.

Halbert                                                  I–65
> Halbert: combination spear and battle ax with a five to seven foot haft.

Half–moon                                                I–68
> Demi–lune: an outwork fortification in the shape of an arc, or half–
> moon, with the rounded edge facing the enemy.

Half(e)–pike; Jacdart–staffe            II–93 (I–74); I–84
> Half pike, Jacdart, spontoon: a type of halberd or shorter pike carried
> by infantry officers.

Hoffestaffe                                              II–210
> Command staff: closest military advisors of a general or leader.
> Perhaps from *Hof* (German for inner circle) and *Staffel* (echelon).
> Monro states that it was "the King or Generall and their followers."

Incontinent                                              I–11, II–16
> Incontinent: at once or immediately.

Intelligencer                                            II–212
> Intelligence provider: a spy or informant.

Jacdart–staffe [see Half–pike]

Leag(u)er                               I–15, II–35 (Log I–1, II–47)
> Leager: a military camp, especially one built either to besiege or to
> withstand an attack. It can range from the simplest fort to a more
> complex fortification with skonces, stackets, fosses, and so forth.

Lines of Approach                                        II–38
> Lines of Approach: trenches zig–zagging toward a fortification under
> siege, thus protecting the attacking forces from the fire of the defenders.

Lübeck, Peace of                                         I–86
> Treaty of Lübeck (July 7, 1629): agreement between Christian IV of
> Denmark and the Holy Roman Empire which ended the Danish phase of
> the Thirty Years' War. Land taken by imperial forces was restored to
> Christian IV, and he agreed not to interfere in Imperial matters. The
> dukes of Mecklenburg were placed under imperial ban, and Wallenstein
> was invested with their lands.

Magazin                                      I–87, II–51
>    Magazine or armory:  building wherein is stored arms, weapons, and
>    other military stores.  It also referred to the powder magazine.  It was
>    also used to refer to the military stores themselves.

Markes                                       I–6, II–40
>    Mark:  borderlands, or frontier lands, of the Holy Roman Empire.
>    Examples of princes and lords of these areas are the Marks of
>    Mecklenburg and Brandenburg.  Dane Mark was Land of the Danes.

Market(-)place                               I–51, II–97
>    Market place:  a large open area, or square, usually next to the parish
>    church or cathedral in a town or city where market was held.  Usually in
>    the center of a town, hence perfect for soldier formations and for
>    parades.  Although also an English word, a German *Marktplatz* has
>    specific location and social connotations.

Marrish                                      I–7, II–31
>    Marsh:  low–lying wetlands or bog utilized as a military obstacle.

Moate; mote                                  I–7, II–58; II–5
>    Moat:  wide, usually deep ditch filled with water surrounding a
>    fortification.

*Monomachia* [see Combate]

Morgan sterne                                I–65
>    Morgenstern:  hand weapon consisting of a spiked ball attached to a
>    short–handled shaft (a mace).  From the German for "morning star."

Musketiers                                   I–9, II–4
>    Musketeers:  infantry armed with muskets [see Hagbut or Fire–lock]
>    and used in conjunction with pikemen.

Old beaten blades of Soldiers                II–165
>    Old beaten blades:  making steel before the modern era consisted of
>    heating, beating out, reheating, and beating out the metal, again and
>    again, until the impurities in the iron were oxidized out.  Similarly, old
>    beaten blades were soldiers who had been through the fiery furnace of
>    battle and were hardened, combat veterans.

Order of Discipline [see Articles of War]

Pallessad(e)s                                I–53 (I–74)
>    Palisade:  means surround or enclose, but the military usage is more
>    specific, referring to sharpened stakes pointing outward to defend a
>    position from enemy infantry assault.

Parapet                                      II–8
>    Parapet:  wall for protection of infantry, usually atop a bulwark,
>    rampart, or other fieldwork.  Shielded by the parapet, infantry could fire
>    more accurately at an advancing enemy while being protected from
>    enemy fire.

Parle, Parlé; parlee                    I–13, II–19; I–40, II–15; I–13,
                                        II–15

Parley:  discussion between opposing forces regarding terms of
agreement, specifically, terms under which a town, fortification, or
military command would be surrendered.  The final agreement was
called the accord.

Parters or Redders                      II–70

Parter, or Redder:  one who tried to separate feuding persons and to
make peace (*Expedition* cited in *OED*).  The latter term was Scottish.

Partizan                                I–18, II–34

Partisan, partizan:  long–handled spear used by infantry.  Its distinctive
feature was one or more cutting edges projecting from the metal tip.

Passe; Passages                         I–3, II–5; I–71, II–5

Pass:  generally a way through a place or area, but militarily it refers to
a strategic point where the path is more difficult to attack.  River fords,
narrow paths protected by natural defenses, or bridges were considered
choke points, that is, points where movement was restricted (or
constricted) and control was essential.

Patent                                  I–1, II–2

Patent:  an official document that permitted a specific activity.  For the
military entrepreneur, it was a license for recruiting.  Similar to the
commission.

Peace of God                            I–40

God's Peace:  religious requirement for peace and order.  In medieval
times, it referred to restrictions and limitations placed on the petty wars
of the nobility by the universal Church.

Peece and peece                         II–213

Perhaps French *pis-en-pis*:  worse to worse, or bad to worse.  Monro's
describes cannon as the devil's instrument and its invention as making
war more deadly.

Perdue                                  I–68, II–54

Perdu, perdue:  sentry placed in an exposed (hence vulnerable and
dangerous) position.  If used in reference to all sentries as a group, it
refers to all of those on watch.

Pike                                    I–11, 18

Pike:  long shaft (14–16 feet) with a metal pointed tip.  It was the
primary weapon of infantry from the 14th century until the 17th century
until muskets and the bayonet made it obsolete.

Pittards; Pettards                      II–8; II–99

Petard:  fused explosive device, usually encased in a box, used to blow
in a door or gate.

Plotton                                 I–18; II–31, II–183

Platoon:  small body of foot soldiers acting as a unit, either as
musketeers or as pikemen (*Expedition* cited in *OED*).

Porte                              II–8
> Port: the gate or gateway of a walled city. Usually protected by a *turm* (round tower), drawbridge, and/or a portcullis (a heavy grate that slid up and down to block the opening quickly if there were not time to close or bar the *Dor* or gate.

Proforce [see Gavileger]

Proviant                           I–7
> Proviant: provisions for an army (*Expedition* cited in *OED*).

Quarter(s)                         I–39 (II–4)
> Quarter: mercy granted by victor over vanquished in battle, if the latter surrendered in a timely fashion (see Parle and Accord). If not, no quarter, and hence no mercy, was granted; this often led to a massacre.

Quarters                           I–1, II–5
> Quarter: lodging for soldiers, usually provided compulsorily.

Rancounter                         I–8, II–35
> Rencounter: to meet, or encounter, the enemy and give battle.

Randezvouz                         I–4, II–59
> Rendezvous: an appointed meeting place where military units were to assemble at a specific date and time.

Ravelin(e)                         I–68 (I–68)
> Ravelin or triangle: outwork beyond the main fosse or moat, which was constructed in front of the plain wall of a fortified place.

Recognosce(d)                      I–46, II–5 (II–303)
> Recognosce: Scottish for recognize and used in the sense of reconnoiter or reconnaissance, that is, to glean information regarding enemy positions and strength (*Expedition* cited in *OED*).

Recreut(e); Recrew                 I–81 (I–33); I–41, II–137
> Recrew or recruit: to reinforce or bring up to strength, to raise reinforcements or replacements for an army. Recruiting required a commission or patent to be legal (*Expedition* cited in *OED*).

Redoubts, redout                   I–15, II–5
> Redoubt: a smaller work within a ravelin or behind a breastwork into which defenders could retire if the main line were breached.

Roade                              I–37, II–3
> Road: nautical term for a sheltered water area near shore wherein ships might safely anchor or navigate with relative ease.

Rot                                II–183
> Row: a file or row of soldiers.

Running line/trench                I–50
> Running line: a trench connecting outlying fortifications, such as skonces or ravelins, with the Dor or gate of the town. It was usually covered to protect those using it.

Rut–master                         I–37, II–67
> Rittmaster: captain of a troop of cavalry.

Salve(e)                                            I–53 (I–51), II–33

Salvo: volley of weapons fire, be it massed musket fire on command or simultaneous fire by artillery. Gustavus Adolphus pioneered the use of the salvo against advancing enemy units.

Salyed                                                 I–65

Sally: a sudden attack upon the enemy, usually from within a fortification against an attacking force, hence a sallyport is a passage through which troops may exit (and to which they are to return) when making a sally.

Scalade                                             II–101

Scalade: a ladder, hence an attack upon a walled fortification by using ladders.

Sile                                                 II–208

Sile: to deceive another. Means literally to cover the eyes of another.

Skonce                                             I–15, II–5

Skonce, skonce: a small, detached defensive fortification outside the main defensive works and built to defend a pass or dore. It also was built as a counter to enemy fortifications.

Slaught; Slawght bom(m)es                          I–7, II–133; II–51

Slaught–boom: a wooden beam used as a barrier (*Expedition* cited in *OED*).

Slime the ways                                         I–76

Slime the ways: to make a path easier (that is, to grease the skids). From nautical description of moving a ship into drydock or returning it to the water.

Soldateska                                             I–33

Soldatesque: the military or pertaining to soldiers.

Souldier of Fortune                                 II–196

Mercenary: a soldier who serves a military master for money or for base reasons. Monro is careful to distinguish between a soldier of fortune and a soldier who practices the "noble profession of arms" and is "vertuous" in his actions and demeanor [see Cavalier].

Spoyle his Cannon by nayling of them                II–203

Nailing, or spiking a cannon: after capturing a cannon of the enemy, and its recapture is imminent, a nail is driven into the powder hole and broken off, rendering the cannon useless for the moment.

Stack(k)et                                         I–51, II–8 (II–133)

Stacket: a palisade, or to build a palisade (*Expedition* cited twice in *OED*).

Stends [see Catholique League or Evangelist Stends]

Stifft                                                 II–76

*Stift*: a German bishopric (*Expedition* cited in *OED*).

Still–stand                                             I–76

Stillstand: a truce or armistice, from German *Waffenstillstand* (*Expedition* cited in *OED*).

Storme                                              I–11, II–15
    Storm: to attack a town or fortification by a rush of troops.
Stot                                                II–118
    Stot: to rebound or bounce off of (*Expedition* cited in *OED*).
Stout                                               I–10
    Stout: refers to the desired character of a soldier—brave, resolute,
    hardy, vigorous, and brave.
Taking the snuff in his nose                        II–13
    Snuff: one who took snuff inhaled it through the nose, hence this
    aphorism refers to a look of disdain, which approximated the
    appearance of one who had just taken snuff.
Torme                                               II–80
    *Turm*: German for a round tower at the city or castle gate.
Travell                                             I–14, II–6
    Travail: labor, toil, that which must be endured. Also used to mean
    travel (I–43) that was laborious and difficult.
Traverses                                           II–8
    Traverse: trenches or parapets that intersected or crossed main trenches
    or ramparts to prevent enfilading fire from the enemy should a position
    be breached.
Treen or woodden Mare                               I–45
    Treen: a wooden device used for punishment of soldiers. Similar to a
    large carpenter's bench, the soldier was required to sit astride the
    device for a specified period of time.
Treene                                              I–17
    Treen: a device or object made of wood, such as an artificial leg.
Tunne                                               I–57, II–43
    Tun: a large cask for liquids such as wine or beer.
Vertue                                              Intro–7, I–3, II–7
    Virtue: used in the same sense as Stout with the addition of morally
    upright behavior. High moral character had to be the result of voluntary
    restraint from improper acts and not the result of rigid adherence to
    rules or regulations.
Wake–rife                                           II–129
    Wakerife: keeping a vigilant eye open, diligent attention to particulars,
    especially on sentry duty.
Weathergall                                         I–52
    Weather–gall: a natural sky phenomenon, such as a rainbow, that
    appeared unexpectedly. It was believed to presage a storm or other
    disaster.

# Bibliography

## BIBLIOGRAPHICAL SOURCES, CALENDARS, AND COMPENDIA

*Calendar of State Papers of England, 1611–1649* [*CSPD*]. Domestic Series. Various editors. 25 vols. London: H. M. Stationery Office, 1858–1898.

*Calendar of the State Papers Relating to Ireland, of the Reign of Charles I, 1633–1647* [*CSPI*]. Ed. by R. P. Mahaffy. London: H. M. Stationery Office, 1901.

Cockle, Maurice J. D. *A Bibliography of English Military Books to 1642 and of Contemporary Foreign Works.* London: Simpkin, Marshall, 1900.

*Calendar of State Papers Relating to Scotland* [*CSPS*]. Various editors. 13 vols. Edinburgh: H. M. Stationery Office, 1881–1970.

Lee, Sir Sydney, ed. *The Concise Dictionary of National Biography.* Part 1. *From the Beginnings to 1900.* London: Oxford University Press, 1965.

*Register of the Privy Council of Scotland.* [*RPCS*]. 3 series. 1569–1707. Various editors. 37 vols. Edinburgh: H. M. General Register House, 1890–1970.

Stephen, Leslie, and Lee, Sidney, eds. *The Dictionary of National Biography* [*DNB*]. 22 vols. London: Oxford University Press, 1921–1922.

## PRIMARY SOURCES

*Articles of Militarie Discipline.* Edinburgh, 1639. Reprinted as part of *The English Experience: Its Record in Early Printed Books*, vol. 77. New York: Da Capo, 1969.

Circular Letter, January 1639, Public Record Office MSS. Domestic series, *Letters and Papers of Charles I*, Vol. 410, no. 167.

Fleetwood, George. "Letter to his Father, giving an account of the Battle of Lützen and the Death of Gustavus Adolphus" (1633) and reprinted in *Camden Miscellany*, ed. Sir P. G. Malpas–Egerton, vol. 1. London: Camden Society, 1847.

Françisque, Michel. *Les Ecossais en France, les Français en Ecosse.* 2 vols. London: n. p., 1862.

*German Broadsheets.* British Library. 1618–1648.

Gheyn, Jacob de. *The exercise of Armes For Calivres, Mvskettes, and Pikes After the ordre of his Excellence Maurits Prince of Orange . . .* London: n. p., 1607.

"The Great and Famous Battle of Lützen . . . faithfully translated out of the French copy" (1633) and reprinted in *The Harleian Miscellany*, 3rd ed., vol. 4 (London: British Museum, 1809): 197–210.

Grimmelshausen, Hans Jakob Christoffel von. *Der Abenteuerliche Simplicius Simplicissimus.* 1669. Reprint. München: W. Goldman, 1961.

Kellie, Sir Thomas. *Pallas Armata or Militarie Instructions.* Edinburgh, 1627. Reprinted as part of *The English Experience: Its Record in Early Printed Books.* vol. 331. New York: Da Capo, 1969.

Leslie, Alexander, Earl of Leven. *Articles and Ordinances of Warre.* Edinburgh: n. p., 1640.

"A Letter concerning Colonel Monks surprising the Town and Castle of Carrickfergus and Belfast, in Ireland; and his taking General Major Monro prisoner." London: n. p., 1648.

Machiavelli, Niccolò. *The Art of War.* 1521. 1st English ed., 1560. Revised edition of the Ellis Farneworth. Translation by Neal Wood. Indianapolis: Bobbs–Merrill Educational Publishing, 1965.

———. *The Prince.* 1513. 1st English ed. 1602. Edited and translated by David Wootton. Indianapolis: Hackett Publishing, 1995.

Monro, Robert. "Generall Major Monroe his Letter to Generall Lesley" (May 13, 1642). In *A True Relation of the proceedings of the Scottish Armie now in Ireland by three Letters.* London: John Bartlet, 1642.

———. *Monro His Expedition with the Worthy Scots Regiment called Mac–Keys Regiment levied in August 1626 by Sir Donald Mac–Key Lord Rhees, Colonell for his Majesties service of Denmark, and reduced after the Battaile of Nerling, to one Company in September 1634 at Wormes in the Paltz. Discharged in severall Duties and Observations of service first under the magnanimous King of Denmark, during his warres against the Emperour; afterward, under the Invincible King of Sweden, during his Majesties life time; and since, under the Director Generall; the Rex–chancellor Oxensterne and his Generalls. Collected and gathered together at Spare–houres, by Colonell Robert Monro, at first Lievetenant under the said Regiment, to the Noble and worthy Captaine, Thomas Mac–Kenyee, of Kildon, Brother to the noble Lord, the Lord Earle of Seafort; for the use of all worthie Cavaliers favouring the laudable profession of Armes. To which is annexed the Abridgement of Exercise, and divers practicall Observations, for the younger Officer his Consideration; ending with Souldiers Meditations going on service.* London: W. Jones, 1637.

———. "Robert Monro to the Marquis of Argyll" (June 11, 1646). In *The Lord Marques of Argyle's speech to a grand committee of both Houses of parliament the 25th of this instant June, 1646: together with some papers. . . and a letter from General Major Monro concerning the state of affairs in Ireland.* London: Printed for Lawrence Chapman, June 27, 1646.

Montgomery, William, compiler. *The Montgomery Manuscripts (1603–1707).* Edited and annotated by George Hill. Belfast: Archer and Sons, 1869.

Spalding, John. *Memorialls of the Trubles in Scotland and in England, 1624–1645.* Aberdeen: Spalding Club, 1850.

*The Swedish Intelligencer*. London: Printed for Nathaniel Butter and Nicholas Bourne, 1633–1634.

Steuart, A. Francis, ed. *Papers Relating to the Scots in Poland, 1576–1793*. Edinburgh: The Scottish Historical Society, 1915.

Taylor, John. *Taylor, his travels, from the City of London in England to the City of Prague in Bohemia...with many relations worthy of note*. London: N. Okes, 1620.

Terry, C. S., ed. *Papers Relating to the Army of the Solemn League and Covenant, 1643–1647*. 2 vols. Scottish Historical Society. 2nd series, vols. 16 and 17. Edinburgh: T. and A. Constable, 1917.

Turner, James. *Memoirs of his own Life and Times 1632–1670*. Edited by T. Thomson. Bannatyne Club, vol. 28. London: n. p., 1829.

_____. *Pallas Armata*. London: M. W. at the Rose and Crown in St. Paul's Churchyard, 1683.

Vincent, Philip. *The Lamentations of Germany*. London: Printed by E. G. for J. Rothwell, 1638.

## SECONDARY SOURCES

Ailes, Mary Elizabeth. "From British Mercenaries to Swedish Nobles: The Immigration of British Soldiers to Sweden during the Seventeenth Century." Ph.D. dissertation, University of Minnesota, 1997.

Aston, Trevor, ed. *Crisis in Europe, 1560–1660*. London: Routledge and Kegan Paul, 1965.

Bartlett, Thomas and Jeffrey, Keith, eds. *A Military History of Ireland*. Cambridge: Cambridge University Press, 1996.

Barudio, Gunter *Der Teutsche Krieg, 1618–1648*. Frankfurt a. Main: S. Fischer Verlag, 1985.

Baynes, John with Laffin, John. *Soldiers of Scotland*. London: Brassey's Defence Publishers, 1988.

Beller, Elmer A. *Propaganda in Germany during the Thirty Years War*. Princeton: Princeton University Press, 1940.

Berg, Janas and Lagercrantz, Bo. *Scots in Sweden*. Translated by P. A. Hart. Stockholm: Stellan Stal Boktryckeri AB, 1962.

Brockington, William S., Jr. "The Usage of Scottish Mercenaries by the Anti–Imperial Forces in the Thirty Years' War." Master's thesis, University of South Carolina, 1968.

Brown, K. M. *Bloodfeud in Scotland, 1573–1625: Violence, Justice and Politics in an Early Modern Society*. Edinburgh: John Donald, 1986.

Brzezinski, Richard. *The Army of Gustavus Adolphus*: vol. 2, *Infantry*. vol. 262 of Osprey Military Men–at–Arms Series. London: Osprey, 1992.

Brzezinski, Richard and Hook, Richard. *The Army of Gustavus Adolphus*: vol. 1, *Infantry*. vol. 35 of Osprey Military Men–at–Arms Series. London: Osprey, 1991.

Burton, J. H. *The Scot Abroad*. New ed. Edinburgh: W. Blackwood and Sons, 1864.

Clausewitz, Carl von. *On War*. 3 vols. Translated by J. J. Graham and annotated by F. N. Maude. London: Routledge and Kegan Paul, 1966.

Corvisier, Andre. *Armies and Societies in Europe, 1494–1789*. Translated by Abagail T. Siddall. Bloomington: Indiana University Press, 1978.

Coupe, William A. *The German Illustrated Broadsheet in the Seventeenth Century*. 2 vols. Baden–Baden: Verlag Librarie Heitz, 1967.

Creveld, Martin Van. *Supplying War.* London: Cambridge University Press, 1977.

Crichton, A., ed. *Memoirs of Reverend John Blackadder.* Edinburgh: n. p., 1823.

Cronne, H. A., Moody, T. W., and Quinn, D. B. eds. *Essays in British and Irish History in Honour of James Eadie Todd.* London: Frederick Muller, 1949.

Cullen, L. M. and Smout, T. C. *Comparative Aspects of Scottish and Irish Economic and Social History, 1600–1900.* Edinburgh: John Donald, 1976.

Dickenson, W. Croft. *Scotland from the Earliest Times to 1603.* Edited by Archibald A. M. Duncan. 3rd ed. Oxford: Clarendon, 1977.

Donaldson, Gordon, ed. *The Edinburgh History of Scotland.* 4 vols. London: David and Charles, 1965–1977.

Dow, James. *Ruthven's Army in Sweden and Esthonia.* Historiskt Arkiv 13. Stockholm: Kungl. Vitterhets Historie Och Antikvitets Akedemien, 1965.

Dupuy, R. E. and Dupuy, T. N. *The Encyclopedia of Military History from 3500 B.C. to the Present.* 2nd rev. ed. New York: Harper and Row, 1986.

Durant, Will. *The Renaissance: A History of Civilization in Italy from 1304–1576 A.D.* Part 5. *The Story of Civilization.* New York: Simon and Schuster, 1953.

Fallon, James A. "Scottish Mercenaries in the Service of Denmark and Sweden, 1626–1632." Ph.D. dissertation, University of Glasgow, 1972.

*Field Manual 100–5, Operations.* Washington, D.C.: Department of the Army, 1993.

Fischer, Thomas A. [pseud. Ernst Ludwig]. *The Scots in Eastern and Western Prussia.* Edinburgh: Otto Schulze, 1903.

————. *The Scots in Germany, Being a Contribution towards the History of the Scots Abroad.* Edinburgh: Otto Schulze, 1902.

————. *The Scots in Sweden.* Edinburgh: Otto Schulze, 1907.

Fletcher, C. R. L. *Gustavus Adolphus and the Struggle of Protestantism for Existence.* New York: G. P. Putnam's Sons, 1895.

Flinn, Michael *Scottish Population History from the 17th Century to the 1930s.* Cambridge: Cambridge University Press, 1977.

Franklin, T. B. *A History of Scottish Farming.* London: Thomas Nelson and Sons, 1952.

Fraser, Sir William, ed. *The Melvilles, Earls of Melville, and the Leslies, Earls of Leven.* 2 vols. Edinburgh: privately printed, 1890.

Furgol, Edward M. *A Regimental History of the Covenanting Armies, 1639–1651.* Edinburgh: John Donald, 1990.

Gillespie, Raymond. *Colonial Ulster: The Settlement of East Ulster, 1600–1641.* Cork: Cork University Press, 1985.

Grant, James. *Cavaliers of Fortune.* London: Routledge, Warnes, and Routledge, 1859.

————. *Memoirs and Adventures of Sir John Hepburn, Commander of the Scots Brigade under Gustavus Adolphus.* Edinburgh: William Blackwood and Sons, 1851.

————. *The Scottish Soldiers of Fortune.* London: George Routledge and Sons, 1889.

Grimble, Ian. *Chief of Mackay.* London: Routledge and Kegan Paul, 1965.

Houston, R. A. and Whyte, I. D., eds. *Scottish Society, 1500–1800.* Cambridge: Cambridge University Press, 1989.

Langer, Herbert. *The Thirty Years' War.* Dorset: Blandford, 1980.

Lee, Stephen J. *The Thirty Years' War.* London: Routledge, 1992.

Levy, Jack S. *War in the Modern Great Power System, 1495–1975.* Lexington: Kentucky University Press, 1983.

Limm, Peter. *The Thirty Years' War.* Seminar Studies in History. New York: Longman Group, 1984.

Lythe, S. G. E. *The Economy of Scotland in its European Setting, 1550–1625.* London: Oliver and Boyd, 1969.

MacDougall, Norman, ed. *Scotland and War: AD 79–1918*. New York: Barnes and Noble, 1991.

Mackay, John. *An Old Scots Brigade*. Edinburgh: W. Blackwood and Sons, 1885.

Mackenzie, Alexander. *History of the Munros of Fowlis*. Inverness: "Scottish Highlander" Office for A. and W. Mackenzie, 1898.

Maland, David. *Europe at War, 1600–1650*. London: Macmillan Press, 1980.

Moody T. W., Martin, F. X., and Byrne, F. J., eds. *A New History of Ireland*, vol. 3, *Early Modern Ireland, 1534–1691*. Oxford: Clarendon, 1976.

Ohlmeyer, Jane H., ed. *Ireland from Independence to Occupation, 1641–1660*. Cambridge: Cambridge University Press, 1995.

*Oxford English Dictionary, The*. 2nd Edition, 20 vols. Oxford: Clarendon Press, 1989.

Paas, John Roger. *The German Political Broadsheet*, 1600–1700. Vols. 4–5. Wiesbaden: O. Harrassowitz, 1985.

Parker, Geoffrey. *The Military Revolution: Military Innovation and the Rise of the West, 1500–1800*. 2nd ed. Cambridge: Cambridge University Press, 1996.

————. *The Thirty Years' War*. Rev. ed. London: Routledge and Kegan Paul, 1987.

Perceval–Maxwell, Michael. *The Scottish Migration to Ulster in the Reign of James I*. London: Routledge and Kegan Paul, 1973.

Rabb, Theodore K., ed. *The Thirty Years' War*. 2nd ed. New York: University Press of America, 1981.

Redlich, Fritz. *De Praeda Militari: Looting and Booty, 1500–1815*. Vol. 39. *Vierteljahrschrift für Sozial– und Wirtschaftsgeschichte*. Wiesbaden: Franz Steiner, 1956.

————. *The German Military Enterpriser and his Work Force*. Vols. 47, 48. *Vierteljahrschrift für Sozial– und Wirtschaftsgeschichte*. Weisbaden: Franz Steiner, 1964–1965.

Reid, Stuart. *Scots Armies of the Civil War, 1639–1651*. Leigh–on–Sea, U.K.: Partizan Press, 1982.

Roberts, Michael. *Gustavus Adolphus, A History of Sweden: 1611–1632*. 2 vols. London: Longmans, Green, 1953–1958.

————. *The Military Revolution, 1560–1660*. Belfast: Marjory Boyd, 1956.

Robinson, P. S. *The Plantation of Ulster: British Settlement in an Irish Landscape, 1600–1670*. New York: St. Martin's, 1984.

Rogers, Clifford J., ed. *The Military Revolution Debate: Readings on the Military Transformation of Early Modern Europe*. Boulder, Colo.: Westview, 1995.

Sadler, John. *Scottish Battles from Mons Graupius to Culloden*. Edinburgh: Canongate, 1996.

Simpson, G. G., ed. *Scotland and Scandinavia, 800–1800*. Edinburgh: John Donald, 1990.

Smout, T. C, ed. *Scotland and Europe, 1200–1850*. Edinburgh: John Donald, 1986.

Steinberg, S. H. *The Thirty Years' War and the Conflict for European Hegemony, 1600–1660*. Foundations of Modern History series, ed. by A. Goodwin. New York: W. W. Norton, 1966.

Stevenson, David. *Scottish Covenanters and Irish Confederates: Scottish–Irish Relations in the Mid–seventeenth Century*. Belfast: Ulster Historical Foundation, 1981.

————. *The Scottish Revolution, 1637–1644*. New York: St. Martin's, 1973.

Sun Tzu. *The Art of War*. 500 *b.c.e.* Translated and annotated by Samuel B. Griffith. New York: Oxford University Press, 1963.

Terry, Sanford. *The Life and Campaigns of Alexander Leslie*. London: Longmans, Green, 1899.

Turnock, David. *The Historical Geography of Scotland Since 1707.* Cambridge: Cambridge University Press, 1982.

Wedgewood, C. V. *The Thirty Years War.* London: Lowe and Brydone, 1938.

Whittington, G. and Whyte, I. D. *An Historical Geography of Scotland.* New York: Academic Press, 1983.

Wood, Stephen. *The Scottish Soldier.* Manchester: Archive Publications, 1987.


## ARTICLES

Aberg, Alf. "Scottish Soldiers in the Swedish Armies in the Sixteenth and Seventeenth Centuries." In *Scotland and Scandinavia, 800–1800,* ed. by Grant G. Simpson. Edinburgh: John Donald, 1990.

Bartlett, I. R. "Scottish Mercenaries in Europe, 1570–1640: A Study in Attitudes and Policies." *Scottish Tradition,* 13 (1986): 15–24.

Bengtsson, Frans G. "Robert Monro." In *Scots in Sweden,* by Jonas Berg and Bo Lagercrantz. Translated by P. A. Hart. Stockholm: Swedish Institute, 1962.

Brockington, William S., Jr. "Expanding Professions in the Seventeenth Century: Scottish Military Entrepreneurs in the Early Modern Era." Paper presented at the Carolinas Symposium on British Studies, Birmingham, Ala., October 1991.

———. "Scottish Military Emigrants in the Early Modern Era: An Analysis of Demographic Movement in an Emergent Society, 1570–1660." Paper presented at the Southern Conference on British Studies, Fort Worth, Tex. November 1991.

Brzezinski, Richard. "British Mercenaries in the Baltic, 1560–1683 (1)." *Military Illustrated Past and Present,* vol. 4 (December 1986/January 1987): 7–23.

———. "British Mercenaries in the Baltic, 1560–1683 (2)" *Military Illustrated Past and Present,* vol. 6 (April/May 1987): 29–35.

Burschel, Peter. "Krieg als Lebensform: Über ein Tagebuch," a review of *Ein Söldnerleben im Dreissigjährigen Krieg. Eine quelle zur Sozialgeschichte,* ed. Jan Peters. Berlin: Akademie–Verlag, 1993. In *Göttingschen Gelehrten Anzeiger* 246 (1994): 263–272.

Canny, Nicholas. "What Really Happened in Ireland in 1641?" In *Ireland from Independence to Occupation, 1641–1660,* ed. by Jane H. Ohlmeyer. Cambridge: Cambridge University Press, 1995.

Corish, P. J. "The Rising of 1641 and the Confederacy, 1641–45" In *A New History of Ireland,* vol. 3, *Early Modern Ireland, 1534–1691,* ed. by T. W. Moody, F. X. Martin, and F. J. Byrne. Oxford: Clarendon, 1976.

Devine, T. M. "Social Responses to Agrarian 'Improvement': The Highland and Lowland Clearances in Scotland." In *Scottish Society, 1500–1800,* ed. by R. A. Houston and I. D. Whyte. Cambridge: Cambridge University Press, 1989.

Devine, T. M., and Lythe, S. G. E. "The Economy of Scotland under James VI: A Revision Article." *Scottish Historical Review* 50 (October 1971): 91–106.

Dodgson, R. A. "'Pretense of Blude' and 'Place of Thair Dwelling': The Nature of the Highland Clans, 1500–1745." In *Scottish Society, 1500–1800,* ed. by R. A. Houston and I. D. Whyte. Cambridge: Cambridge University Press, 1989.

Dukes, Paul. "The Leslie Family in the Swedish Period (1630–5) of the Thirty Years' War." *European Studies Review* 12 (1982): 401–424.

Gillespie, Raymond. "An Army Sent from God: Scots at War in Ireland, 1642–49." In *Scotland and War, a.d. 79–1918,* ed. by Norman MacDougall. New York: Barnes and Noble, 1991.

Hazlett, Hugh. "The Recruitment and Organisation of the Scottish Army in Ulster, 1642–49." In *Essays in British and Irish History in Honour of James Eadie Todd*, ed. by H. A. Cronne, T. W. Moody, and D. B. Quinn. London: Frederick Muller, 1949.

Kiernan, V. G. "Foreign Mercenaries and Absolute Monarchy." *Past and Present* 11 (1957): 66–86. Reprinted in *Crisis in Europe, 1560–1660*, ed. by Trevor Aston. London: Routledge and Kegan Paul, 1965.

Loeber, Rolf and Parker, Geoffrey. "The Military Revolution in Seventeenth–Century Ireland." In *Ireland from Independence to Occupation, 1641–1660*, ed. by Jane H. Ohlmeyer. Cambridge: Cambridge University Press, 1995.

Lynch, Michael. "National Identity in Ireland and Scotland, 1500–1640." In *Nations, Nationalism and Patriotism in the European Past*, ed. by Claus Bjørn, Alexander Grant and Keith J. Stinger. Copenhagen: Academic Press, 1994.

Mackay, John. "Mackay's Regiment, 1626–1634." *Transactions of the Gaelic Society of Inverness*, 8 (1876/1879): 128–189.

Mackenzie, Alexander. "General Robert Munro—A Cadet of Obsdale." In *History of the Munros of Fowlis*. Inverness: "Scottish Highlander" Office for A. Mackenzie and W. Mackenzie, 1898.

McNeill, William H. "Keeping Together in Time." In *Military History Quarterly*, vol. 7, nr. 2 (1994): 100–109.

"Monro or Munro, Robert." *The Dictionary of National Biography*, ed. by Leslie Stephen and Sidney Lee, vol. 13. London: Oxford University Press, 1921.

Ohlmeyer, Jane H. "The Wars of Religion, 1603–1660." In *A Military History of Ireland*, ed. by Thomas Bartlett and Keith Jeffrey. Cambridge: Cambridge University Press, 1996.

Smout, T. C. "Famine and Famine–relief in Scotland." In *Comparative Aspects of Scottish and Irish Economic and Social History, 1600–1900*, ed. by L. M. Cullen and T. C. Smount. Edinburgh: John Donald, 1976.

Smout, T. C., and Fenton, Alexander. "Scottish Agriculture before the Improvers—An Exploration." *The Agricultural History Review*, vol. 13, part 2 (1965): 73–93.

Whyte, I. D. "Population Mobility in Early Modern Scotland." In *Scottish Society, 1500–1800*, ed. by R. A. Houston and I. D. Whyte. Cambridge: Cambridge University Press, 1989.

# Index

The following index is provided to assist the reader in finding persons, places, and events within this edition; page references are to the pagination of this edition. This index utilizes currently accepted spellings and does not include the myriad of spellings within the original text. Reference to the various glossaries for spelling variations appearing in the original is useful; the last number in the index entry, if bracketed, is the page number where a glossary entry is located. Monro provided his own version of an index—which he labeled as Tables—and these appear on pages 105–112 (Danish service) and 357–375 (Swedish service).

**About the Editor**

WILLIAM S. BROCKINGTON, JR. is Professor of History at the University of South Carolina, Aiken. His major areas of interest have been British and military history, as well as Southern history and culture. His primary focus has been the emigration patterns of Scottish military entrepreneurs in the early modern era, with a secondary emphasis on Scottish emigration patterns to Europe and to the American South.

ISBN 0-275-96267-9

9 780275 962678

HARDCOVER BAR CODE